PERSPECTIVES
CASE STUDIES FOR
READERS AND WRITERS

Delores Zumwalt

PERSPECTIVES
CASE STUDIES FOR
READERS AND WRITERS

JOANNA GIBSON

Texas A&M University

Longman

New York San Francisco Boston
London Toronto Sydney Tokyo Singapore Madrid
Mexico City Munich Paris Cape Town Hong Kong Montreal

Senior Vice President and Publisher: Joseph Opiela
Acquisitions Editor: Susan Kunchandy
Executive Marketing Manager: Carlise Paulson
Supplements Editor: Donna Campion
Production Manager: Ellen MacElree
Project Coordination, Text Design, and Electronic Page Makeup: Electronic Publishing
    Services Inc. NYC
Cover Image: "Girl Before a Mirror," 1932, Pablo Picasso (1881–1973/Spanish), oil on
    canvas, Museum of Modern Art, New York City/Superstock.
Senior Manufacturing Buyer: Dennis J. Para
Printer and Binder: The Maple Vail Book Manufacturing Group
Cover Printer: Phoenix Color Corp.

Gibson, Joanna.
  Perspectives: case studies for readers and writers/Joanna Gibson.—1st ed.
    p. cm.
Includes index.
  ISBN 0-321-01258-5
  1. English language—Rhetoric—Study and teaching—Case studies. 2. Academic writ-
ing—Study and teaching—Case studies. I. Title.
  PE1404 .G57 2002
  808′.042′0711—dc21

2001029483

Please visit our website at http://www.ablongman.com

ISBN 0-321-01258-5

1 2 3 4 5 6 7 8 9 10—MA—04 03 02 01

Contents

v

Chapter 2   Understanding Writing as Process   59

Chapter 3   Developing Skills for Academic Writing 111

Chapter 4   Evaluating Writing   143

Chapter 5   Analyzing Argument   181

Chapter 6   Writing Research Papers   219

Chapter 11   Creating a Context   425

Case Study 3: "Letter From Birmingham Jail"   430

Chapter 12   Reconciling Different Perspectives   471

Case Study 4: Xenotransplantation   476

Chapter 13   Developing an Argument   531

Case Study 5: Politics and Art   542

Preface

Perspectives: Case Studies for Readers and Writers is a cross disciplinary, multicultural rhetorical reader and guide to writing that emphasizes the connection between reading, writing, and critical thinking skills. It introduces students to skills they are most likely to use in academic writing: analyzing and evaluating discourse—the works of others and their own—and summarizing, paraphrasing, and incorporating the words and ideas of other writers. It recognizes the benefits of collaboration and self-reflection at various stages of the writing process. It acknowledges the role of technology in research and in writing. And, most importantly, it encourages students to consider how rhetorical situations shape their reading assignments, and it offers different kinds of rhetorical situations in writing assignments. While there are many reasons to use this textbook, the most compelling is that students will read it. The case studies center on real people—Iva Toguri (also known as Tokyo Rose), "jungle doctor" and late–1950's celebrity Dr. Thomas Anthony Dooley, Dr. Martin Luther King, Jr., AIDS activist Jeff Getty, and Mexican artist Diego Rivera. Their stories are commanding and their experiences are pertinent and relevant to issues students see in today's headlines: the role of the media in shaping our impressions of public figures; privacy issues; civil rights; science and ethics; and censorship. Their stories give students a narrowed focus they don't usually find in textbooks, and illustrate the very nature of research—that is, that sources are often contradictory, biased, and repetitive, and that information in print is not immune from inconsistent or outright erroneous information. These cases, for which there is no right or wrong interpretation, help students understand how information about a person, issue, or event develops in various discourse communities. In addition, the cases provide focus and context for writing assignments.

THE CASE STUDY METHOD—
A FLEXIBLE AND UNIQUE APPROACH

The case study method, a problem—hypothetical or real—presented in narrative form, offers a unique approach to reading and writing instruction. The current proliferation of case studies in literature illustrates the demand and, one might speculate, the success of the case study approach with fiction. For several reasons, case studies are appropriate as well for writing courses that focus on non-fiction prose. In addition to being flexible and adaptable to a variety of teaching styles and pedagogies, case studies

- illustrate a variety of rhetorical situations on the same topic,
- serve as models of sufficiently narrowed topics,
- stress the connection between reading and writing skills,
- provide units of research for a variety of writing assignments, and
- offer the instructor ready access to students' sources.

By focusing on specific issues and relating them to broad concerns (the role of the media, censorship, ethics and science, privacy, and consumerism and education) *Perspectives* takes an inductive approach. Similar to thematic units of reading, a standard approach in any number of composition textbooks, case studies take focus and connection to another level. Students encounter a collection of sources on an event or issue that constitutes a conversation with focal points—that is, with writers responding to each other or to central issues. As I developed the book, one of my goals was to narrow the focus of readings and broaden the scope of rhetorical situations students encountered in their readings. This approach models the kind of research students need to do for college-level research assignments, and provides a focused conversation for students to examine, analyze, evaluate, and synthesize in their own papers. The case studies include a variety of sources: readings are from academic journals; chapters or excerpts from books published by popular and university presses; popular magazines and scholarly journals; newspapers; pamphlets published by special interest groups; government records; and other sources. Offering a variety of perspectives, these multi-layered sources challenge students to re-think or reexamine the stance other writers have taken as well as their own stances on an issue.

OPTIONS

As you will see, the case study approach has unlimited potential for effective and exciting instruction in writing skills. Students can work on the case studies as a class activity, as a collaborative project with a small group, or as individual projects. For the instructor, having access to a writer's sources and, as well, having a clear context for the subject, provide an advantage for determining how effectively students synthesize sources. For the student, knowing that the instructor will be familiar with sources provides an incentive for using those sources fairly.

The instructor's manual provides suggestions for using *Perspectives* in a fifteen-week semester, in the quarter system, and because each case has links to literature, also in a two-semester sequence that moves from an introduction to reading and writing skills to writing about literature. The combined guide to writing and case studies offer options for instructors whether their classes meet in computer classrooms, regular classrooms, or in non-traditional settings. For example, if students do not have access or if they have limited access to library resources, the case studies supply ready-made units of research for writing assignments. *Perspectives* was intended, however, to give students experience in identifying and retrieving print and electronic sources. If students have access to libraries, instructors may want to assign outside research for two or three cases and use one or two as stand alone units for group or individual study.

ORGANIZATION

Perspectives is divided into two parts prefaced by an Introduction that discusses critical thinking skills. Part One covers reading and writing skills, and Part II offers a practice case study followed by five cases each requiring students to work on specific writing skills.

Features—Part One

Part One, a comprehensive guide to writing, includes seven chapters that discuss critical reading skills, writing as process, skills for academic writing, evaluating sources, analyzing argument, writing research papers, and documenting sources. This section includes several special features that make it easy for instructors and students to use.

- Emphasis on Student Writing and Student Voices
  Interspersed throughout these chapters are examples of student writing and exercises that ask students to reflect on their reading. Chapter 2 features an interview with three student writers. Chapter 3 discusses the "voice" of the student writer.

- Emphasis on the Connections between Reading and Writing
  Exercises in each chapter ask students to apply critical reading skills and specific writing skills—summarizing, paraphrasing, and synthesizing—to short writing assignments. "For Practice" exercises in Chapters 1, 3, and 5 ask students to read and write about the *Titanic,* road rage, and rock music, respectively.

- Emphasis on Writing as Process
  Discussion of writing skills includes invention exercises, drafting and revising, instructions for discovery drafts, and lists of questions to ask in peer review and in independent review of a paper. With examples of writing generated by one student in response to a writing assignment, Chapter 2 highlights the importance of multiple drafts, revision, and peer review.

- Emphasis on Writing from Sources
  Part I offers instruction in summarizing, paraphrasing, incorporating quotations, acknowledging other writers' ideas, and documenting sources.

Students practice these skills and apply them to the writing assignments in Part Two.

- Emphasis on Developing Effective Research Skills
- *Perspectives* encourages students to explore both library and electronic resources as they work on developing and narrowing topics and identifying sources to use in writing assignments.

Features—Part Two

Part Two begins with a practice case study. It acquaints students with the format followed throughout this section and the apparatus that emphasizes reading, reflecting, and writing: an introduction previews each case study, discusses a specific writing task, and concludes by asking students to complete a freewriting exercise that draws on their knowledge of a central issue in the case study. The case study follows. Each one moves from narrowed topics to related issues. Readings follow a chronological order and conclude with a selection that offers contemporary perspectives. Writing assignments interspersed with readings include freewriting, writing from sources included in the case study, and writing based on the case study and additional library research. Assignments give students experience in writing for a variety of rhetorical situations. A series of exercises, "Analyzing and Evaluating the Case Study," "Writing About the Case Study," and "Writing About Related Issues," conclude each case study and ask students to practice skills covered in Part One.

- Emphasis on Diversity
  Students examine different perspectives on issues of race, gender, and culture in the experiences of Iva Toguri, Dr. Martin Luther King, Jr., Dr. Tom Dooley, Jeff Getty, and Diego Rivera.

- Emphasis on Issues in the Humanities, Social Science, and Science
  Case studies introduce students to reading across the curriculum—that is, to reading different kinds of texts and to understanding the various concerns and conventions that are important in each discipline.

- Emphasis on Considering Relationships between Writer, Subject, and Readers
  "Reading and Responding" exercises ask students to analyze rhetorical situations. A wide range of readings and rhetorical situations provides extensive practice. Writing assignments include specific rhetorical situations or reminders to identify and analyze the rhetorical situations students select.

- Emphasis on Writing to Understand a Topic
  Writing assignments take students through a series of steps that allows them to discover their own thoughts and reactions to a topic and to collaborate or work individually on short assignments that call for writing to explain some aspect of the case study or writing to persuade. These assignments culminate in a documented paper written from sources.

- Emphasis on Collaborative Activities
  The text encourages students to see writing as a social activity and emphasizes the importance of discussing ideas for writing and the writing process with others. Exercises for collaboration are included throughout the case studies.

SUPPLEMENTS

The Instructor's Manual will assist instructors in teaching with the parent text. The Manual includes not only Exercise Answers and Reading and Chapter Summaries but also Plan Ahead Activities, Computer Classroom Activities, Optional Writing Assignments, and Links to Literature and Film.

A comprehensive website (www.ablongman.com/gibson) contains chapter-specific overviews, online readings, online activities, activities for writing practice, and samples of student writing.

ACKNOWLEDGMENTS

Perspectives began several years ago as a course packet for the first-year composition courses I taught. It developed out of collaboration with editors at Longman Publishing, text reviewers, colleagues at Texas A&M, and students enrolled in sections that class tested the case studies. Their questions, suggestions, and constructive criticism are greatly appreciated. They gave the book shape, form, and direction.

I owe a big "thank you" to my reviewers: Scott Allen, Townson University; Michelle Bellavia, NE Louisiana University; Virginia Crank, Rock Valley College; Mary L. De Nys, George Mason University; Ray Duda, University of Michigan, Dearbon; Kirk Glaser, Santa Clara University; Sophie Glazer, IUPUI Fort Wayne; Kay Halasek, Ohio State University; Pau-san Haruta, Marist College; Ben W. McClelland, University of Mississippi; Lisa J. McClure, Southern Illinois University Carbondale; Roxanne Mountford, Rochester Institute of Technology; Nedra Reynolds, University of Rhode Island; Cynthia Stretch, Southern Connecticut State U; Randy Woodland, University of Michigan, Dearborn. Particularly helpful were their ideas for reworking, adding, and omitting material—especially writing assignments—and their comments on how they could envision using chapters in the guide to writing and the case studies in their own courses. Particularly helpful were their ideas for omitting, reworking, and adding material—especially writing assignments—and their comments on how they could envision using Perspectives with their students. Their suggestions improved *Perspectives* and kept me ever mindful of the dual audience—student and instructor—I wanted to reach.

Most sincere thanks also to everyone at Longman Publishing—from the editorial staff to marketing to production—who contributed to this project. Working with the Longman team has been an enjoyable experience. Anne Smith, Acquisitions Editor at Longman when this project started, accepted and supported my proposal, and Susan Kunchandy, currently Acquisitions Editor at Longman, has seen *Perspectives* through to the end and been an unwavering source of patience, good humor, sound advice and understanding this last year. Karen Helfrich played an important role in coordinating the first round of reviews and trimming down a manuscript that originally included ten case studies. Lynn Huddon was another source of good advice at a crucial point in developing the apparatus for Part II and the practice case study. Other individuals who deserve recognition for their assistance include Rebecca Gilpin, Nancy Garcia, Denise May, Robert Ruggiero, and Ellen MacElree. I'm also grateful to Longman for making Randee Falk available for editing, for using Todd Tedesco to see this project through production, and for selecting Dene Grigar, Texas Woman's University, to be the content provider of the companion website for *Perspectives*.

Several of my colleagues in the Department of English at Texas A&M University deserve acknowledgment. I've had wonderful support throughout this project from J. Lawrence Mitchell, Department Head; my former Directors, Jimmie Killingsworth and Valerie Balester, my current Associate Director Jackie Palmer; and our staff assistant in the Writing Programs Office, Kelli Perry; and many of our graduate assistant teachers: Jim Baker, James Cornish, Nicole and Anton DuPlessis, Jonathan Himes, Susan Murphy, Matt Sherwood, Shane Trayers, and Everett Villarreal.

I was most fortunate to have volunteers class test the case studies in Part II. Very special thanks and Chris Morrow and Dr. Huihui Li, Texas A&M University; Diana Ashe, University of North Carolina, Wilmington; Linda Bow, Blinn College; Samuel L. Gladden, University of Northern Iowa, and William Hooten, Duquesne University. The undergraduate students who allowed me to use their writing in Part I made a major contribution to Perspectives. They include Meghan Fleming, Scott Long, Meredith Fleming, Steffany Fitzpatrick, Amy Pohlmier, Ronny Jimenez, Eric Dickens, Stacy Crane, Whitney Lowrance, Olivia Yang, Tyne Evans, Marcus Fryer, Candice Davis, , Cristina Gargour, Kristin Shaner, Heather Davey, Andrew Robertson, Kelli Shaner, Brent Baker, Camille Ortiz, Kelly Hunt, and Kristal Zimmers.

Other individuals who helped me find information or develop ideas include Wendi Arant-Kasper, Humanities Librarian and Associate Professor, Sterling C. Evans Library, Texas A&M University; Avon Criswell, University of Indiana; William McNitt, Archivist, Gerald R. Ford Library; Vicki Ward, Copy Corner, College Station; and Susan Williams, Graduate Assistant, University of Arkansas.

Finally, I want to express most sincere thanks to my friends and family for their encouragement, support, and confidence in me. I thank my parents, Merle and James Barnett, for showing me the importance at a very early age of being a reader and a writer and for backing me throughout my education. Most of all, I thank my husband, Claude Gibson, for his patience and sense of humor, his willingness to let me bounce ideas around as needed, and his excellent advice throughout this project.

Joanna Gibson

PERSPECTIVES
CASE STUDIES FOR
READERS AND WRITERS

Introduction

Dreaming of apples on a wall,
And dreaming often, dear
I dreamed that, if I counted all—
How many would appear?
　　　　—from *Lewis Carroll's* Games and Puzzles

FOCUS ON CRITICAL THINKING SKILLS

The simple rhyme and rhythm of verse-riddles make them easy to remember and recite, and entertaining to children—of all ages. You may remember some verse-riddles from your childhood. Typically the answers are simple and obvious but children have difficulty determining them. They may not think the riddle through carefully. They may not consider the obvious. If you haven't determined the answer to the verse-riddle above, read it again, this time looking *at* the words. The answer is a word in the riddle. Lewis Carroll, best known for writing *Alice's Adventures in Wonderland,* was fascinated with word play. To solve his riddle, you have to be able to reanalyze one of the words to see it in a new way.

While we think of verse-riddles as "child's play," they are, in fact, a critical thinking activity—that is, a course of thought or mental process requiring intellect, logic, common sense, judgment, or discernment. Notice that the *critical* in *critical thinking* does not mean *looking for fault or error.* Instead, in this use, *critical thinking* means *involving thoughtful evaluation and judgment.* Your thought processes are precise and deliberate, guided by logic. When you think critically, you examine, reflect, analyze, and evaluate. You use critical thinking skills everyday. For example, when you plan your day, you prioritize activities, scheduling things you want to do around obligations—work, classes, family, standing appointments, and

1

social or civic activities. You use critical thinking skills when you figure out how household appliances, office machines, or gadgets work—or why they don't work. You also use critical thinking skills for resolving problems with family or friends when you examine a situation that makes you uneasy or uncomfortable, analyze the situation and possible solutions, and determine the best strategy to follow. While intuition and gut reaction may play a role in how you think through everyday problem-solving activities, we can say that you think critically when judgment, common sense, and logic play a primary role in your decision making.

Certainly, one aspect of thinking critically is seeing things in a new way—thinking outside of the usual boundaries or approaching a situation or problem in a unique, out-of-the-ordinary manner. For example, in 1997, Colin Rizzio, a high school senior from New Hampshire, discovered an ambiguity in the Scholastic Aptitude Test (SAT) I Reasoning Test administered by Educational Testing Services (ETS). He claimed a math problem would result in different answers because the exam didn't specify whether the unknown number "a" was positive or negative and didn't note how the numbers were sequenced. After months of review, ETS admitted that the question was flawed, and Colin and other students who took the exam had their scores raised. According to newspaper reports, this was the first time in 14 years that a SAT question had been challenged and found to be ambiguous. Colin Rizzio made headlines because he worked through a math problem, looking at it from a perspective different than that of the experts who approved the problem for the exam. His discovery was unique. The SAT undergoes extensive review and scrutiny. Imagine how grateful his fellow test-takers were when their scores went up after one of their own applied his critical thinking skills and identified a problem everyone else had overlooked.

Between the nationally administered exams you take for college admission and the college degree you hope to see framed and hanging on the wall someday, you'll encounter a variety of activities that require critical thinking skills. These activities include quizzes, exams, laboratory experiments, and research papers, as well as other activities like lectures, collaborative projects with your peers, and oral presentations. You may not think about the spectrum of skills these activities require. For example, a journalism course requires you to create a media kit—a portfolio on some aspect of a national political campaign. The portfolio includes a letter identifying the issue you selected. You also provide an overview of the issue, a news release for your local newspaper, feature article, fact sheet, and public service announcement. As you work on these assignments you rank the tasks, creating a schedule for research and writing; formulate questions to consider in your research; make assumptions about your topic; analyze information from a variety of sources; categorize and analyze information; and draw inferences and conclusions from your research. Other courses require you to apply these same critical thinking skills to different kinds of assignments. You're capable of applying critical thinking skills to different kinds of tasks if you have the ability to use reason and logic.

The mind is complex and capable of doing various things at one time, so you may be using several critical thinking skills simultaneously. Cartoonists often indicate that a character is thinking by showing a single light bulb above a character's head, but actually when we exercise critical thinking skills, ideas occur recursively—that is, our thought processes are like a circle of blinking holiday lights. For example, consider the mental activities that take place the first time you look at an exam. As you scan the questions, you look for the different kinds of tasks each one requires: multiple choice, short answer, essay, true-false. You evaluate each question reflecting on the degree of difficulty; you recall information you have studied: data, examples, definitions. Finally, you formulate questions to ask before you begin. While you're involved in one activity, the others are going on simultaneously. These mental activities, applications of critical thinking skills, take place in a very short period of time.

While you use critical thinking skills everyday in a variety of ways, the two activities that are most intimately tied to critical thinking skills are reading and writing. And, of course, reading and writing are themselves closely connected in college-level work. Usually, you read in order to generate ideas for writing assignments. And when you write, you read your writing—to generate ideas, to revise passages, and to evaluate your own work.

THE RELATIONSHIP BETWEEN CRITICAL THINKING AND READING

Reading is an activity you engage in so often that you may not realize how adept you are as a reader and how you use critical thinking skills when you read different kinds of texts: newspapers, traffic signs, menus, graffiti, announcements and advertisements posted on bulletin boards, e-mail, regular mail, lab manuals, library books, textbooks. For all of these examples, your mind processes information as you read, but you have different purposes for reading. How you engage with each text will be slightly different. For example, when you check your e-mail and find 10 to 15 new messages, you read the list of senders' names and prioritize as you determine an order for reading your messages. When you read the morning paper, you evaluate the importance of each section and determine which articles you will read and an order for reading them. You scan some articles; you read others carefully, paying close attention to details. You read traffic signs with a quick glance to decide if you should yield, stop, turn, or detour. In a similar manner, you look at announcements posted on a bulletin board in the student union to find information about club activities, job openings, or study groups. As you peruse the bulletin board, you mentally categorize announcements, scanning the least interesting and focusing on those that interest you. You may also read for enjoyment. The point is you have skills you rely on all the time to read different kinds of texts.

When you read in college, you'll need to be a *critical reader,* that is, a reader who uses critical thinking skills. Critical readers have developed the ability to read for more than content alone: They have developed the ability to analyze a piece of writing and to recognize how a writer fails or succeeds in fulfilling his or her purpose in writing and to see how a writer's style helps shape meaning. Most importantly, a critical reader knows to bring a healthy skepticism to the text. A critical reader asks questions, recognizes unsubstantiated claims and generalizations, differentiates between fact and opinion, and recognizes faulty logic, bias, or prejudice. A critical reader understands content well enough to summarize or paraphrase it. And finally, a critical reader is a flexible reader who has developed strategies for reading the different kinds of texts he or she encounters in everyday life and in the academic disciplines, taking each one seriously, and expecting to be challenged.

THE RELATIONSHIP BETWEEN CRITICAL THINKING AND WRITING

In everyday life, we write for any number of reasons. As a college student, the kinds of writing tasks you perform daily may include notes you write to yourself or to others, entries in journals, e-mail to friends and family, applications for jobs or scholarships, and notes from lectures and reading. You may also write papers and answer essay questions on exams. Even when you write to yourself, you probably apply critical thinking skills—for example, you think critically when you determine the best way to record and organize ideas or to express ideas. You use asterisks in a list to note especially important items, or you underline passages in a note you write to yourself as a reminder, emphasizing particularly important ideas. When you write for others, thinking critically about your own writing makes a difference in whether your writing is effective or ineffective, whether your readers read what you've written or stop half way through, and whether you communicate ideas clearly or succeed only in confusing or frustrating your readers.

When writers think critically about their writing, they consider their purpose in writing and their intended readers. In college courses, ultimately the writer's purpose is to answer a question, solve a problem, or lead to a recommendation. Writers have to have a good grasp of their topic to meet these purposes. They have to process information and sort out the relevant points from the irrelevant, the important details from the insignificant, the unusual and interesting items from the obvious and mundane. They have to consider multiple perspectives, alternate answers to questions, and the feasibility of recommendations. They also have to understand that writing isn't done in a vacuum—that writers build relationships with readers when the writer establishes goodwill in a text, shows respect for opposing positions, and demonstrates a thorough understanding of a topic. They work on development of ideas, making their writing interesting and accessible. They revise and edit in order to refine their ideas and improve the manner in which they express ideas. They understand that to write effectively, they have to develop strategies for generating and organizing ideas and for evaluating their own writing with a critical eye.

You link reading and writing skills when you develop the ability for self-assessment—reflecting on your own work and evaluating it. If you can read your own drafts and determine how to revise and improve them, you know that being your own best critic isn't always easy. Your concerns have to move beyond counting words or the number of pages you produced and congratulating yourself because you met the length requirement for a paper, or running a paper through spell check and grammar check and being satisfied with making whatever changes these programs indicated. Meeting requirements for word count and checking for surface errors are important, but they shouldn't be your primary concern when you evaluate your own writing. Critical thinking plays no role in these activities if a word processor does them for you. Critical thinking about your own writing involves reading your drafts to assess the overall effectiveness of your writing, identifying passages to save as they are and passages that don't express ideas fully, clearly, or precisely. Thinking about what you've written, listening to the sound of your own sentences, and discussing your writing with others are ways of reflecting on and evaluating your writing. When you think critically about your own writing, you recognize problems you've encountered in writing a paper and you work on strategies for solving them.

You should expect your written assignments to be diverse in their intended audiences, style, format, and purpose. Your critical thinking skills help you determine an appropriate manner for accomplishing your purpose. They play a role in your ability to produce a written text that offers a suitable style and pertinent, well-organized content for your intended readers, as well as an interesting introduction and a conclusion that sums up the main ideas and offers readers a sense of closure.

READING CRITICALLY TO WRITE EFFECTIVELY

Examples of student writing demonstrate how critical thinking skills help us accomplish our goals as readers and writers.

In a research paper written for an academic audience of college-level students and their professors, a student argued that individuals concerned about animal rights have a moral obligation to prevent animals from being used in scientific experimentation. In the following paragraph, the student drew on a *New Yorker* article, "Adventures in Experimentation," for examples of experiments performed on animals:

> With the ever-growing population, scientific research
> is an important aspect of every human being's life.
> Research scientists provide vaccines and treatments to
> cure certain diseases with hopes of someday finding a
> cure for the fatal virus AIDS. However, why do
> experiments need to be performed on animals? Larry
> Doyle, a scientist who performs adventuresome
> experiments, explains that "grafting the hand of a

capuchin monkey onto a Labrador retriever, I created a
dog that can not only throw a tennis ball sixty yards
while playing fetch with itself, but also scratch the
back of its master" (116). In experiment 235F, Doyle
claims "by sewing white mice directly onto the heads of
male American Bald eagles, I hope to cosmetically
augment their thinning pates and thus increase the
breeding success of this species" (116). Many of the
experiments performed have "no relevance or benefit to
humans." Gail Vines states, "one in five experiments on
primates had 'no justification' and should not be
allowed" (15). The Home Office's Animal Procedures
Committee is currently investigating why these projects
were allowed to be performed and published.

Notice just how unusual the two experiments cited are. *The New Yorker* article is, as you probably guessed, satirical—not to be taken literally. Other experiments cited in the article include transplanting "fifty hummingbirds into a sixty-year-old man suffering from congestive heart failure" and splicing genetic material from Dow Scrubbing Bubbles into a feline zygote and producing a Siamese with the claws that "extrude rug-and-furniture shampoo."

EXERCISE: READING AND RESPONDING

Review the excerpt from the student paper and be prepared to point out passages that suggest that *The New Yorker* article was satirical.

Finding the article listed in the library data base under the subject heading *animal experimentation,* the student took the article at face value. Although the examples seemed unusual, *The New Yorker,* he assumed, would be an accurate and dependable source. If he had been more familiar with the publication, he would have known that the "Shouts and Murmurs" section in which the articles appeared feature humorous pieces intended to entertain, often devoted to satire and irony.

As writers from Jonathan Swift[1] to media star Joe Bob Briggs[2] have learned, satire can be powerful if the reader understands the writer's purpose. However, if

---

[1]Author of "A Modest Proposal," a pamphlet published in 1726. Swift's satirical proposal was to make poor Irish children beneficial to their families and less of a burden to the country. He suggested marketing them as food for rich Englishmen.

[2]Joe Bob Briggs is the redneck persona created by John Bloom. He is currently host of *Monster Vision,* a program broadcast on the Turner Network. In 1985, Briggs was a columnist for the *Dallas Times Herald.* He was dismissed when he wrote a satirical version of a popular recording, "We Are the World; We Are the Children." Many readers failed to see the humor in Briggs' version, "We Are the Stupid."

readers are too literal, they misunderstand the writer's purpose and, for them at least, the satire fails. We can only speculate on why the student misread Doyle's article. We may conclude, though, that while the student's writing skills at the sentence level appear to be competent, his critical thinking skills were not fully employed when he read the article and decided to use it in his paper.

While the student paper may seem like an extreme example, critical thinking skills fall by the wayside every now and then for a variety of reasons—stress, fatigue, or inattentiveness, for example. Reader's expectations can also play a role in the breakdown of critical thinking skills: the reader expected *The New Yorker* to be an acceptable source, so he didn't pay close attention to the article's content—didn't question what it said. When critical thinking skills break down, it sometimes becomes painfully or embarrassingly apparent that something is amiss. The writer's intentions may have been the very best and the writer may have spent hours researching the topic and writing. The result, though, is still an unsuccessful paper that doesn't meet requirements or readers' expectations.

In short, reading and writing are connected. The reading/writing connection is the application of critical thinking skills to reading and to the writing that develops as a result of reading. This textbook recognizes the reading/writing connection as instrumental to academic success. When we read or write ideas that are expressed effectively, the process of reading, applying critical thinking skills, and writing may go unnoticed or be taken for granted. For example, in a research paper entitled "The Roswell Incident," an examination of flying saucer reports in Roswell, New Mexico, a student writer concludes:

```
Because the stories of what happened in Roswell in
July of 1947 vary from source to source, it is
impossible to say what actually occurred. But most
would agree that details have been hidden from the
public, which leaves two questions: What has been
deleted and why? Perhaps the government did not want
to scare the public with news of an extraterrestrial
spacecraft. More logically, perhaps officials were
trying to hide military air technology that the
public would disapprove of. Regardless, the Roswell
incident has left many questions unanswered. But
these answers may lie somewhere within government
confidence, and they are being kept from civilians
for unknown reasons. Hopefully, further investigation
of Roswell will lead to the release of this
information because the public has a right to know of
its government's actions.
```

You can tell that the writer, Alison, evaluates the reliability of her sources, draws conclusions, and offers a stance on the government's actions; however, as you read the paragraph, you probably didn't think about the reading/writing connections she employed—for example, the number of sources she read in order to understand the different perspectives on her topic and the multiple drafts she wrote as she refined the paper. And you probably didn't think about the critical thinking skills she used to determine her topic, find sources, and synthesize those sources into a paper appropriate for her intended readers.

At the heart of critical thinking is seeing more than the obvious, using new innovative approaches to problem solving, and rethinking issues to determine fresh and unique perspectives. Critical thinking is a tall order, but necessary for success in *academic writing*. Very simply defined, this term covers writing that takes place within the scholarly community. You'll read more about academic writing in Part I. The answer to Lewis Carroll's riddle, by the way, is *ten*. You find it in the word *often—dreaming of ten.*

LOOKING AHEAD

This textbook is designed to give you practice in critical thinking skills, in writing for a variety of audiences, and in writing academic papers. In Part I, you'll look at the reading/writing connection. Readings cover a variety of issues: science and technology, the *Titanic* disaster, road rage, and rock music. Assignments will give you practice in reading and *writing as process* (emphasis on multiple drafts and revision) and introduce you to discourse communities, analyzing rhetorical situations, analyzing arguments, and writing research papers. Assignments ask you to think critically about different elements of reading and writing: reading and annotating, planning and drafting a paper, synthesizing sources, considering intended readers, constructing effective arguments, and attributing other writers' ideas fairly. They require working on your own and working with your peers, as well, to evaluate your writing and your responses and reflections on readings. You'll find working together as a community of writers, sharing and responding to each other's works, a good way to become a confident, effective writer. Several examples of student writing are included in Part I—examples of how inexperienced writers approach reading and writing assignments and think critically about their writing.

Part II offers six case studies—focused units that ask you to apply the skills discussed in Part I. A practice case study on education and consumerism introduces you to the case study method, a kind of problem-solving activity that doesn't have a right or wrong answer. Each case study focuses on a specific individual or situation, but asks you to think about related issues. You'll meet Dr. Thomas Anthony Dooley, a doctor who became famous for his humanitarian work in Southeast Asia; Iva Toguri, who allegedly made broadcasts under the name of Tokyo Rose; civil rights leader Dr. Martin Luther King, Jr.; AIDS activists Jeff Getty; and two of the most unlikely partners ever to enter a business deal, Mexican muralist Diego Rivera and Nelson Rockefeller, son of American oil-baron John D. Rockefeller. Their stories are complex and multifaceted, giving you the opportunity to explore multiple perspectives, different cultures, and a variety of discourse communities. Each case study begins with a discussion of a task that is common in academic writing: listening to writers' voices, discovering a topic, providing context for a historical event, reconciling different perspectives, and developing an argument. Reading and writing assignments will help you work on these tasks.

One of the goals of this textbook is to introduce you to effective methods of research and ideas for writing assignments that are narrowed and focused, like the six case studies. Part II features brainstorming sessions, lists of topics to consider for writing assignments, and boxed sections that focus on topics related to issues discussed in the individual case studies. These features are intended to help you develop ideas for writing assignments you complete outside of class. Feel free to add to these lists and develop topics for academic writing that are timely, relevant, and—most of all—interesting.

One last reminder: The philosophy behind this textbook is that writing—academic writing or any other kind of writing—requires practice on a daily basis. You should expect to produce more writing for this course than you do for others. You'll reflect on your own ideas, on your reading, and on your own writing. You can expect to read and write in class and outside of class everyday. The daily assignments combined with formal papers written outside of class may make your composition course appear to be more demanding than courses that center on lectures and three or four exams over the lectures. Remember, though, that you're learning, practicing, and refining reading and writing skills. As you look ahead to a new semester, make a commitment to working on critical thinking skills and developing effective writing skills. *Perspectives: Case Studies for Readers and Writers* is intended to help you meet these goals.

PART ONE
Guide to Writing

Chapter 1

Developing Critical Reading Skills

Read, read, read.... Concentrate on opening your mind. If you're 55 and straight, read *Rolling Stone*. If you're 25 and hip, *Reader's Digest*. If you're liberal, read the *National Review*; conservative, read *New Republic*. You should be reading at least one good book a week—history, anthropology, sociology, politics, urban problems. If you were a fine arts major, read about economics. If you were a business major, find out about ballet. I'm not joking about any of this. You have got to stretch your mind, further and further. The alternative is letting it congeal, harden, and contract.... One of the happy effects of doing a lot of reading is that it will improve your writing, which needs it.

—Advice to journalism majors from Molly Ivins,
The Perils and Pitfalls of Reporting in the Lone Star State

READING TO LEARN

Molly Ivins' advice to journalism majors is appropriate for any college student, regardless of his or her major. Your reading material should be diverse. Read to discover new ideas; read to understand a subject in all its complexity; read for enjoyment; read to understand different perspectives; read to learn how something works; read to challenge what others have written. As a college student, you'll be *required* to do many hours of reading outside of class. Instructors will expect you to read assignments for comprehension and retention—to understand and remember information well enough to ask questions and contribute to class discussion. And they will expect you to read in order to write papers. To prepare for the kinds of reading assignments you will be expected to complete, you want to develop reading skills that facilitate and increase your understanding of ideas. In other words, you want to become a *critical* reader—that is, a reader who has developed skills for understanding the intricacies of a piece of writing. Critical readers read closely, react to another writer's ideas, reflect on them, and evaluate those ideas in view of what they have read or experienced. They connect what they read to their understanding of what other writers have said and identify points on which the writer waffles, generalizes, or offers erroneous or misleading information.

In a world where the amount of information on any topic increases dramatically every year, being a critical reader is crucial. A critical reader can distinguish between a serious article and a satire, spot faulty logic, and recognize weak or insubstantial evidence offered in defense of a position. Critical reading skills are a line of defense against inaccurate, insufficient, trivial, or misleading publications as well as illogical and faulty arguments. But reading with a critical eye isn't just about reading for mistakes and errors. Living in the information age, you need to be a critical reader to understand how things work and how people solve problems. You need to be a critical reader in order to analyze the rationale for a recommendation or the logic behind an argument. And if you follow Molly Ivins' advice, you need to be a critical reader in order to be an effective writer. That's not bad advice, at all.

Academic Discourse

If you're thinking *But I know how to read,* remember that reading assignments required in college-level courses differ in complexity and diversity from the reading assigned in high school classes. You're part of the academic community now, and you'll be expected to understand *academic discourse,* oral or written communication within the intellectual community. Academic discourse published in scholarly journals or in books published by university presses undergoes close scrutiny by review boards prior to publication; therefore, you can assume that these publications have been deemed noteworthy by other scholars. Information published by experts in any field is pertinent to the intellectual community (government documents, for example), too. As you might guess, academic discourse is a broad term. It can include lectures and class discussions; papers students write to meet course requirements; publications in highly specialized journals aimed at well-educated readers; publications scholars write for other scholars to read, discuss, and use in their lectures or research: for example, a book examining the rhetoric of environmental policies in the United States, a biography of Walt Whitman, a collection of essays from a conference on bovine respiratory disease, an article on computer analysis of bingo probabilities, a study of the Texas revolutionary experience, or an article explaining how snakes became limbless. While these publications share the common goal of intellectual inquiry, they differ within each discipline in format, documentation, and, most importantly, vocabulary, content, and concepts.

Discourse Communities

As a student, you'll be part of different discourse communities, groups who share common interests, goals, and values, and use a specialized vocabulary to discuss their interests. For example, computer experts make up a discourse community. If you listened to them discuss their work, you might be puzzled by some of the terms they use and the concepts they discuss. To computer specialists, the language and the concepts are shared knowledge that is meaningful. College students and professors can be seen as members of the academic or scholarly discourse community. This is a very broad, vague community, however. Academia is itself made up of communities whose main concern is intellectual inquiry into their particular subject areas. Thus, it is more useful to think in terms of these subject areas or the three major groups into which they fall. The humanities study issues of human concern and matters of human achievement. Studies in the humanities may range from papers on environmental ethics, to examination of past events and their significance, to analysis of poetry, and other artistic creations. The hard sciences look at the natural world around us, the intricate workings of our bodies, or the delicate balance of the ecosystem. The social scientists focus on human behavior—that is, why people do what they do, and how they engage with each other in family, social, and professional relationships. Studies in the hard sciences and social sciences typically discuss other research and other experiments and draw conclusions from the data collected.

Becoming Part of the Academic Discourse Community

How do you become a part of the diverse academic discourse community? Listening to your professors' lectures and completing daily reading assignments are two good ways to start. Both activities will introduce you to vocabulary in specialized fields of study and to the very different ways in which the humanities, social sciences, and sciences create knowledge about a topic. Another strategy for becoming part of a discourse community is to think about what a topic means to you and what points of reference you might have for understanding it. Such personal points of reference can also help motivate you to enter the conversation that goes on in a discourse community. To take an extreme case, if a family member experiences a life-threatening illness, a person can very quickly make the transition from knowing very little about medical terminology to being able to discuss the illness in detail with members of the medical community.

Becoming part of a discourse community can be difficult when sources use highly technical vocabulary or present ideas that are complex and unfamiliar. In such cases, you'll need to learn new concepts and theoretical or philosophical approaches that are new to you, and more generally, understand subjects that are new and unfamiliar. This may sound like a tall order, but you have already experienced mastering new material, and this textbook will offer strategies to help you bridge the gap that exists between a college student and, say, a scientist arguing for a revised taxonomy of snails.

Skills for Reading Academic Discourse

To meet the challenge of participating in the various discourse communities in academia, you'll find that being a critical reader is crucial. Eventually, you'll specialize and focus on courses in your major. But first, you have to demonstrate diversity as a reader. To paraphrase Molly Ivins, if you're an English major, you have to learn to read and understand articles in the sciences; if you're a biology major, you have to be prepared to read and understand articles in the humanities. This chapter asks you to think about how you read, whether you are an active or passive reader, and how understanding relationships between writers and their subjects and intended readers helps you understand a text.

EXAMINING YOUR OWN READING PROCESS

The reading process, how our minds process written texts, is complex, to say the very least. We know that readers scan, read slowly for understanding, highlight passages, write questions or remarks beside a passage, and review, and reread passages or even an entire text. Formal studies of this process examine the intricacies of cognition for readers—what happens in our minds as we read. Although these studies readily admit that there's still a lot to be learned about reading as a process, it's clear that it is individualized, earmarked by individual preferences for times and places and accessories—for example, listening to background music or working in silence, sitting in a comfortable chair or at a desk.

Try to become aware of which factors facilitate the process for you. Do you prefer reading in the library, at a desk in your room, or stretched out on the couch? How much noise can you tolerate when you're trying to read? What kind of lighting and accessories do you need? How frequently do you need to take breaks? If your goal is to improve your reading skills, these are important questions to consider. With an understanding of your own reading process and the skills you need to work on to be a critical reader, you'll be prepared to plan where you should work on reading assignments and how much time you need to block out to complete them.

EXERCISE: READING AND RESPONDING

In one or two paragraphs, describe the steps you take to complete a reading assignment of approximately 20 to 30 pages for a course other than your composition course (designate a course in your response).

Your response should specify where and when you read, what makes you comfortable when you read, and whether you

- examine an assignment carefully before you read it,
- start at the beginning and read in a linear manner until you reach the end or, alternately,
- skip around,
- underline,

- highlight,
- take notes, or
- discuss a reading assignment with someone else.

Finally, estimate how much time you would need to devote to this type of reading assignment, and speculate on whether you would set aside time in your daily schedule for reading or work it in as best as you could.

As you read this chapter, think about the strategies it outlines and the process you have described. Identify elements of your own process that make it either efficient or inefficient. And consider changes you want to make in your reading process to make yourself a more efficient and effective reader.

You may find the process of reading outlined in this chapter—previewing, reading, annotating, and rereading—time-consuming. But once you work on becoming a critical reader and begin to see results in your ability to read and understand information that is new and challenging, you should be willing to plan ahead and set aside the blocks of time the process requires. It's normal to look for shortcuts. All of us wish we had been blessed with a photographic memory; few of us have, though. Start now to understand that developing effective critical reading skills, like developing any skill, requires pacing, planning, and plenty of time.

BECOMING AN ACTIVE READER

Critical readers have to be active readers. They

- ask questions about the text they are reading, as if the writer were present,
- make mental connections between the text they are reading and other texts they have read,
- vary the pace of their reading according to the difficulty, complexity, or familiarity of the text, and
- focus on the text, blocking potential distractions.

In the academic setting, being an active reader is particularly important because active reading helps you adjust to the needs of different texts and tasks. Regardless of the subject, your assignments will cover a variety of reading tasks—for example, you will read to follow directions (in a course syllabus, handouts, or a textbook), to respond either in writing or orally to questions (quizzes or questions for class discussion), and to analyze and evaluate different kinds of texts—scholarly articles, government reports, textbook discussions, and lab manuals, for example.

Perhaps at one time or another, you've had the experience of reading several pages of a textbook, looking up from the book, and realizing that, although your eyes followed every line on the page, your mind did not absorb the material. In other words, while your eyes followed the routine of reading an assignment, your mind drifted. This type of experience is an extreme example of *passive* reading. Because passive readers are to some extent just going through the motions, the passive reader typically reads the textbook in the same manner he or she reads a novel. Passive reading may give you the right to *claim* that you read an assignment, but reading is useless if you don't remember what you read. Of course, total recall isn't a realistic or, for that matter, worthwhile goal. You want to do more than memorize what you read.

Your goal as a reader should be to understand a text, a reading assignment, or a source for a paper, so that you can discuss it or write about it. Your goal should also be to analyze a text so that you can assess its content and can determine whether it is or is not effective writing. You can't do this if you are a passive reader, as passive reading entails submissively agreeing with the text.

Sometimes, you may be a passive reader because you are *not* part of a writer's intended audience. For example, suppose your reading assignment for a biology course is a paper published in the *Journal of the American Medical Association*, a paper written by an expert for an audience of experts. The terminology may be highly specialized and the content complex. Your knowledge and experience may not provide sufficient context for you to understand the reading. If you are a passive reader, your comments about the paper may be limited to *I didn't understand it* or *It was boring*. Even though it's natural to become a passive reader when content is difficult, you need to make yourself an active reader. Your instructor will expect you to read the paper, and to be responsible for understanding the information in it.

If you tend to be a passive reader, start now to become an active reader—a reader who engages the text. Active reading, always important, becomes all the more so with difficult material. An active reader, when faced with a difficult reading assignment, such as the one previously described, will read, reread, and analyze the article, identifying key words or phrases that appear to be important, defining any of the key words and phrases that are unfamiliar, and marking passages that prompt questions. Activities that will help you become an active reader and that will help you understand a source include previewing, annotating, and discussing your reading with others. As you can probably guess, these activities rule out a quick read with highlighting here and there. Highlighting has its merits. It takes the eyes to specific passages, but it doesn't provide evidence of interaction with a reading assignment.

Previewing

Usually, when you're reading for pleasure, you check out certain features of a book before you purchase it or borrow it from the library. You read the front, take note of any pictures on the cover, note the length, and read blurbs on the back cover or any information about the author. You might even glance through a chapter or two to get a sense of the writer's style. In other words, you give yourself a preview of the book before you invest money or reading time in it.

Previewing is as important for required reading as it is when you get to select a book on your own. Think of it as a scouting expedition, an exploration of a text. You preview to become acquainted with the reading, to establish a first impression, to formulate questions about the topic, and to understand how to read it. Previewing involves scanning the text and noting such matters as the title and any information about the author; date of publication and publisher; format, font size, length; length of chapters and paragraphs; use of white space; pictures, figures, and graphs; headings; documentation; content, its complexity, familiarity, and—of course—interest. Before you preview a source, think about your purpose for reading it. How will you use the information you are going to read? class discussion? final exam? possible source for a documented, argumentative paper? With a definite purpose in mind, scan the text and then read the introduction. This preview should give you some idea of what the text is about, who wrote it, and what its main purpose seems to be, as well as how much time you need to devote to an initial reading, and if necessary, to subsequent readings.

We often make quick judgment calls when we preview a text, which can be borne out—or refuted—by close reading. For example, before Meghan read "Mummy was a fetus: motherhood and fetal ovarian transplant," (an excerpt follows) she previewed the article and quickly concluded that it appeared to be very technical. It wasn't anything she would read on her own; it was required reading. She didn't look forward to reading it, but once she got into it, she found the writer's argument interesting and thought-provoking. Her preview made her realize the article would require multiple readings, so she set aside time for reading and rereading. She considered the article to be challenging, but by being an active reader and using the strategies discussed in this chapter, she felt comfortable discussing it in class. In addition, Meghan was surprised at how much she learned from the article. She said it made her want to read more about this topic.

Annotating

Think of annotating as creating a one-sided conversation with a text. When you annotate, you make brief notes in the margins

- identifying the main ideas the writer is trying to develop;
- reacting to ideas you agree or disagree with;
- marking passages that helped you understand a concept or idea;
- circling key words or terms that are new to you;
- posing questions you had while reading; and
- marking any points that are confusing, unclear, or unsubstantiated.

Think of annotations as quick reference markers—notations to remind you of your first impressions of a text or of questions you had about a text. When Meghan read and reread "Mummy was a fetus, " she annotated the text. In Figure 1.1, you see her annotations.

FOCUS ON STUDENT WRITING: Meghan's Annotations

Review the article Meghan annotated and be prepared to discuss whether or not her annotations would be helpful to you.

MUMMY WAS A FETUS: MOTHERHOOD AND FETAL OVARIAN TRANSPLANTATION

JONATHAN M. BERKOWITZ
Mount Sinai Medical Center, New York, USA

Abstract

Infertility affects 15 per cent of the world's couples. Research at Edinburgh University has been directed at transplanting fetal ovarian tissue into infertile women, thus enabling them to bear children. Fetal ovary transplantation (FOT) has generated substantial controversy; in fact, one ethicist deemed the procedure 'so grotesque as to be unbelievable' (1).

Some have suggested that fetal eggs may harbour unknown chromosomal abnormalities; however, there is no evidence that these eggs possess a higher incidence of genetic anomaly than ova found in a healthy adult female. There is also concern that fetal egg children will be psychologically harmed by the knowledge of their special conceptual status. It will be demonstrated that special conceptual status in and of itself does not determine developmental success. Rather, psychological well-being is dependent upon how the family and child cope with the unique challenges inherent in FOT. Lastly, though considering FOT a legitimate method of family building, given the global population crisis the wisdom of procreational rights will be challenged. Inherent to this challenge is a re-evaluation of the treatment of infertility as a significant disease necessitating remedy.

Handwritten margin notes:

Problems:
1. fetal eggs may harbor unknown chromosomal abnormalities
2. fetal egg children will be psychologically harmed.
3. the wisdom of procreational rights will be challenged.

'Who ran to help me when I fell,
And would some pretty story tell,
Or kiss the place to make it well?
My mother'

Ann Taylor, 'My Mother' (2)

FIGURE 1.1 Annotated Article

Introduction

For most of us the word 'mother' is special. She is the person who gave birth to you, raised you, fed you, loved you, fought with you, and in the final analysis, did her best to be a good mother. For millions of years children, regardless of who raised them, could be certain they had a mother who was once a living person. However, the concept of motherhood has been challenged by research from Edinburgh University aimed at transplanting the ovaries of an aborted fetus into an infertile woman. Fetal ovary transplantation (FOT) will produce for the first time, a child who will inherit the genes of a woman who herself never lived. For many these circumstances are most unsettling (3); a person whose genetic mother was never born contradicts the way people have been born for millions of years.

FOT-produce for the 1st time a child who will inherit the genes of a woman who herself never lived.

But is this really a problem—

Three important issues are raised by the advent of FOT. First, there is concern that by using fetal eggs which have not been subject to environmental pressure we may be introducing additional genetic anomalies into the population. It will be maintained in this paper that fetal eggs are not inferior and do not have a higher incidence of chromosomal abnormality than eggs found in a healthy adult female. Furthermore, it will be asserted that it may be preferable to harvest fetal eggs as they have had less exposure to environmental toxins, which are known to cause to cause chromosomal aberrations.

3 important issues:
1. We may be introducing additional genetic anomalies into pop.
2. concerns about how child will react knowing his mom was an aborted fetus.
3. introducing more children into world not in our best interest.

Second, there are concerns about how a child might react to the knowledge that his mother was an aborted fetus. To this objection will be demonstrated that anxiety over potential emotional damage is unwarranted in light of the significant analogous history of children adopted in infancy and children produced via medically assisted conception (MAC). And lastly, it will be maintained that while FOT is a legitimate method of family building, the development of procedures to introduce additional children into an already over-populated world may not be in society's best interest.

Genetic objections

Concern exists over using fetal eggs which 'have not been subjected to the pressures which govern survival

(continued)

Major concerns
fetal eggs which have not been subjected to pressures that govern survival & normal development to adulthood

and normal development to adulthood' (4): in that it is possible fetal eggs may harbour genetic anomalies not eliminated through natural selection. However, both our current knowledge of oogenesis (5), and studies on human and non-human subjects contradict much of this concern. In fact, this lack of environmental exposure may be preferable, given the established association between advanced material age and increased risk of congenital malformation (6).

what is this?

By the fifth month of gestation the average female fetus will have approximately 7,000,000 eggs, 400,000 of which will remain at puberty with less than 500 of these being ovulated (7). Some may argue that we should avoid using fetal eggs since we are selecting eggs which nave not been 'subject to pressures' which allow specific eggs to survive to ovulation. The actual mechanisms behind why some eggs survive to menarche are not known (8); however, there is no evidence to suggest that a particular egg survives because it is superior to other eggs. This also applies to ovulation where up to 15 follicles (9) mature simultaneously yet only one will ultimately ovulate (10). This process is controlled by subtle temporal hormonal interactions and once again there is no evidence to suggest that the eggs are subject to selective pressure (11).

evidence that indicates major concern is not a concern at all.

Experiments

Besides the lack of evidence that fetal eggs are genetically inferior, the contention that fetal eggs are not subject to environmental pressure is not entirely true. For fetal eggs to mature they must be stimulated by the recipient's maternal hormones. What distinguishes fetal eggs is the temporality of exposure. Fetal tissue grafted into a post-pubescent woman has minimal exposure to a pre-pubescent hormonal environment and significantly less exposure to the post-pubescent hormonal environment. There is no evidence that genetic defect results from a temporal reduction of maternal hormonal exposure. In fact, experiments on both human and non-human subjects indicate ovarian tissue transfer is both a viable and safe procedure. In 1945 embryonic mouse ovarian tissue was grafted into mature mice which suc-

experiments done prove ovarian tissue transfer is a viable & safe procedure.

7 "healthy babies" born using this procedure

cessfully produced young (12). Human births have already been reported using immature eggs harvested from one patient and fertilized via in vitro fertilization (IVF) in another patient who 'delivered healthy triplet girls' (13). Four additional children have been born using this procedure and to this date, they are all 'very healthy' with 'no linked genetic anomaly' (14).

Contrary to concerns over the lack of environmental pressure on transplanted fetal eggs, it may be preferable that fetal eggs have minimal environmental exposure. It is postulated that the association between advanced material age and an increased incidence of birth defects (15) is that; in addition to 'genetic factors' (16), the eggs, having existed longer, suffer more environmental insults (17). While only 10 percent of congenital defects can be directly attributed to 'environmental factors,' the aetiology of approximately 65 percent of all congenital defects is not clear and may represent a combination of both genetic and environmental insults (18). Though teratogenesis concerns post-conceptive insults, it is conceivable that environment similarly affects the unfertilzied, pre-conceptive egg (19). In fact, there are a number of congenital defects, including Down's Syndrome (20), which results from pre-conceptive non-disjunction (21). What role environment plays in these pre-conceptive anomalies remains to be determined; however, 'it has been known for a long time that the likelihood of non-disjunction occurring increases with advancing maternal age' (22). Given this association between advanced maternal age and non-disjunction, one can argue that fetal eggs may harbour fewer genetic anomalies, because they have had less potentially damaging environmental exposure.

Another argument advanced against FOT is that we are skipping a generation of evolution and thus 'breaking a natural law of biology' (4). This is a weak argument as it fails to take into consideration the molecular bias of evolution. Evolution occurs when re-combined or mutated genetic material is passed from one generation to the next at conception (24). The genetic material in a fetal egg has already undergone re-combination and is arrested in an early stage of cell division till ovulation (24). At ovulation, which for some eggs may not occur for forty years, the ovum completes nuclear division and it is not till conception that a unique genome (25) is created. It is important

May be preferable that fetal eggs have minimal environmental exposure.

the likelihood of non-disjunction occurring increases with advancing maternal age

FOT is considered breaking a law of biology. Argued that we are skipping a generation. Weak argument

I disagree

(continued)

to remember that evolution can only occur if genetic material is passed on to progeny. If a fetus is aborted, it can never contribute to our evolutionary heritage as its unique genes are lost forever unless, of course, fetal ova are harvested and grafted into a live reproducing woman. Therefore, concerns about 'skipping a generation' are totally unfounded as abortion (ie, the death of the organism prior to procreation), represents an evolutionary dead end.

Source: Jonathan M. Berkowitz, "Mummy Was a Fetus: Motherhood and Fetal Ovarian Transplantation." *Journal of Medical Ethics* (1995): 298–304.

Notice that Meghan used a combination of underlining and brief notes. Because they are specific remarks, these annotations should be more useful to her than highlighting or underlining alone. This is not to dismiss highlighting or underlining. When you develop your own system of creating a conversation with a text, you will probably include one or the other—or possibly both. The important point is that you use annotations as well. Even if content in a reading assignment is clear and easy to comprehend, include notes that record your initial reactions, questions, and impressions. If a reading assignment is dense and difficult and requires multiple readings, you may even find yourself annotating your annotations as you read and reach a better understanding of a text. Readers can be very creative with their annotations. You can use one color of ink or pencil for annotations in an initial reading and other colors for subsequent readings. Devise a system that works for you. You'll see that annotations are excellent for refreshing your memory even when it's been days since you read the assignment. If you are reading a source with the intention of using it in a writing assignment, annotations are a starting point for analysis.

If you have never annotated reading assignments, you may find that annotations slow you down at first. With practice, though, you should be able to pick up the pace, and you'll discover how helpful annotations are for review. A word of caution: If you are working with library sources, make photocopies of the chapter or the passages you will need and annotate the photocopies.

EXERCISES: READING AND RESPONDING

1. Preview the following article and record your responses to the questions that follow. Your purpose in reading is to discuss the article in class and to write about it in writing assignments that appear in Chapter 3.

   - What expectations do titles of the article or journal raise about content? about the writer's purpose? about the writer's perspective?
   - Which features suggest that the article will be challenging? complex? technical? easy? interesting? uninteresting? relevant? timely?
   - What kind of context do you have for an article on this topic?
   - How much time should you expect to devote to reading and annotating the article?

2. Read and annotate the following article.

IF WE HAVE IT, DO WE USE IT?

NANCY GIBBS

We've seen these visions glinting in the distance for some time— the prospect that one day parents will be able to browse through gene catalogs to special-order a hazel-eyed, redheaded extrovert with perfect pitch. Leave aside for the moment whether scientists actually found an "IQ gene" last week or the argument over what really constitutes intelligence. Every new discovery gives shape and bracing focus to a debate we have barely begun. Even skeptics admit it's only a matter of time before these issues become real. If you could make your kids smarter, would you? If everyone else did, would it be fair not to?

It's an ethical quandary and an economic one, about fairness and fate, about vanity and values. Which side effects would we tolerate? What if making kids smarter also made them meaner? What if only the rich could afford the advantage? Does God give us both the power to re-create ourselves and the moral muscles to resist? "The time to talk about it in schools and churches and magazines and debate societies is now," says bioethicist Arthur Caplan of the University of Pennsylvania. "If you wait, five years from now the gene doctor will be hanging out the MAKE A SMARTER BABY sign down the street."

What makes the conversation tricky is that we're already on the slippery slope. Doctors can screen fetuses for genetic diseases like cystic fibrosis and Duchenne muscular dystrophy; one day they may be able to treat them in utero. But correcting is one thing, perfecting is another. If doctors can someday tinker with a gene to help children with autism, what's to prevent them from tinkering with other genes to make "normal" children smarter? Technology always adapts to demand; prenatal sex-selection tests designed to weed out inherited diseases that strike one gender or the other—hemophilia, for instance—are being used to help families have the son or daughter they always wanted. Human-growth hormone was intended for children with a proven severe deficiency, but it came to be used on self-conscious short kids—if their parents could afford as much as $30,000 for a year's injections.

Self-improvement has forever been an American religion, but the norms about what is normal keep changing. Many parents don't think twice about straightening their kids' crooked teeth but stop short of fixing a crooked nose, and yet, in just the past seven years, plastic surgery performed on teens has doubled. As for intellectual advantages, parents soak their babies in Mozart with dubious effect, put a toy computer in the crib, elbow their way into the best preschools to speed them on their path to Harvard. Infertile couples advertise for an egg donor in the Yale Daily News, while entrepreneurs sold the sperm of Nobel laureates.

"What, if anything, is the difference between getting one's child a better school and getting one's child a better gene?" asks Erik Parens of the Hastings Center, a bioethics think tank. "I think the answer has to do with the difference between cultivating and purchasing capacities." Buying a Harvard education may enhance a child's natural gifts, he argues, but it's not the same as buying the gifts.

Every novel, every movie that updates Frankenstein provides a cautionary tale: these experiments may not turn out as we expect. Genetic engineering is more permanent than a pill or a summer-school class. Parents would be making decisions over which their children had no control and whose long-term impact would be uncertain. "Human organisms are not things you hang ornaments on like a Christmas tree," says Thomas Murray, Hastings' director. "If you make a change in one area, it may cause very subtle changes in some other area. Will there be an imbalance that the scientists are not looking for, not testing for, and might not even show up in mice?"

What if it turned out that by enhancing intellectual ability, some other personality trait changed as well? "Everything comes at a price," argues UCLA neurobiologist Alcino Silva. "Very often when there's a genetic change where we improve something, something else gets hit by it, so it's never a clean thing." The alarmists, like longtime biotech critic

Jeremy Rifkin, go further. "How do you know you're not going to create a mental monster?" he asks. "We may be on the road to programming our own extinction."

The broader concern is one of fairness. Will such enhancement be available to everyone or only to those who can afford it? "Every parent in the world is going to want this," says Rifkin. "But who will have access to it? It will create a new form of discrimination. How will we look at those who are not enhanced, the child with the low IQ?" Who would have the right to know whether your smarts were natural or turbo-charged? How would it affect whom we choose to marry—those with altered genes or those without? If, as a parent, you haven't mortgaged the house to enhance your children, what sort of parent does that make you? Will a child one day be able to sue her parents for failing to do everything they could for her?

But just for the sake of argument, suppose raising IQ didn't require any permanent, expensive genetic engineering at all. Scientists are studying brain-boosting compounds. Suppose they found something as cheap and easy as aspirin; one pill and you wake up the next morning a little bit brighter. Who could argue with that?

Some people are worried about the trend toward making people more alike—taller, thinner, smarter. Maybe it's best for society as a whole to include those with a range of needs and talents and predispositions, warts and all. "As someone who morally values diversity," says ethicist Elizabeth Bounds of Emory University's Candler School of Theology, "I find this frightening. We run the risk of shaping a much more homogeneous community around certain dominant values, a far more engineered community." What sort of lottery would decide who is to leap ahead, who is to be held back for an overall balance? At the moment, nature orchestrates our diversity. But human nature resists leaving so much to chance, if there is actually a choice.

The debate raises an even more basic question: Why would we want to enhance memory in the first place? We may imagine that it would make us happier, except that we all know smart, sad people; or richer, except that there are wildly successful people who can't remember their phone number. Perhaps it would help us get better grades, land a better job, but it might also take us down a road we'd prefer not to travel. "You might say yes, it would be wonderful if we could all have better memories," muses Stanford University neuropsychiatrist Dr. Robert Malenka. "But there's a great adaptive value to being able to forget things. If your memory improves too much, you might not be a happier person. I'm thinking of rape victims and soldiers coming back from war. There's a reason the brain has evolved to forget certain things."

In the end it is the scientists who both offer the vision and raise the alarms. People with exceptional, photographic memories, they note, sometimes complain of mental overload. "Such people," says University of Iowa neurologist Dr. Antonio Damasio, "have enormous difficulty making decisions, because every time they can think of 20 different options to choose from." There is luxury and peace in forgetting, sometimes; it literally clears the mind, allows us to focus on the general rather than the specific and immediate evidence in front of us. Maybe it even makes room for reflection on questions like when better is not necessarily good.

—Reported by David Bjerklie and Emily Mitchell/New York, J. Madeleine Nash/Chicago and Dick Thompson/Washington

EXERCISES: COLLABORATING WITH YOUR PEERS

Work in pairs or in groups to complete the following exercises:

1. Share your responses to the preview questions. Then explain whether the article met your initial expectations.
2. Share your answers to the following questions:
   - What is the writer's purpose?
   - As you read the article, what kinds of connections came to mind?

- What did you learn from reading the article?
- What are the main points in the article?
- Explain why you agree or disagree with the main points of the article.

3. Exchange books and examine your classmates' annotations. Identify annotations you would consider helpful to the reader.

4. What did you learn from reading this article?

5. Explain whether it made you rethink or examine any preconceived ideas you had about the topic.

Discussing Your Reading

You've probably noticed that class discussion of a reading assignment can help you develop a much better understanding of the text and become more engaged with it. This isn't surprising, especially since each person has a different background and hence a somewhat different perspective on a reading. By putting your ideas into words and listening to other readers' ideas, you learn a lot.

It is often a good idea to discuss your reading with someone else—even with someone who hasn't read it. Finding someone to listen shouldn't be difficult. Let your roommate, a close friend, or someone in your family know it is important for you to verbalize your reactions to a reading assignment. Explain your purpose for reading, summarize what you read, describe your initial reactions to the reading ("I liked it because _____" or "I didn't like it because _____"); explore any connections the reading brings to mind ("For some reason, this made me think about _____"); and answer any questions your listener poses. If you can't find someone to listen to you and ask questions, try working with a tape recorder to create a verbal record of yours thoughts and ideas about what you have read.

By articulating what you know and understand about your reading, you may discover new ideas on your own, or your listener may pose questions or offer comments that advance new ideas. The important point is that reading should be an activity that engages you with the writer's ideas or arguments and that prepares you to engage other people—listeners or readers—with your ideas. Finally, when you discuss what you have read with someone else, you may find yourself explaining why you react to a reading assignment. As you articulate why a piece of writing has a certain effect on you, you begin analysis of the reading. Remember, critical reading is reading to find out what a writer has to say about a topic and, most importantly, what *you* think about what the writer says.

This chapter began by recommending that you develop critical reading skills to facilitate your comprehension of ideas. Active reading is the basis of critical reading. Previewing, annotating, and discussing are essentially strategies for active reading used before, during, and after you read. They are the relevant basics of active reading.

UNDERSTANDING RELATIONSHIPS IN THE COMMUNICATION TRIANGLE: WRITER, SUBJECT, AND READER

One of the most important critical thinking skills you will develop in your academic career—as a reader and a writer—is the ability to analyze discourse in order to understand the relationships of the writer to the reader and subject. The writer, the subject, and the reader form the communication triangle (see Figure 1.2). Their relationships tell you a lot about discourse, written or spoken. For example, writers direct the focus of their discourse to themselves, to discussion of the topic, or to the audience. The focus in the writer-subject-reader relationship also tells you about the aim of the discourse:

- emphasis on the writer results in expressive discourse (writer reveals personal experiences, innermost thoughts)
- emphasis on subject results in expository, or informative, discourse (writer informs readers about the subject)
- emphasis on the reader results in persuasive discourse (writer attempts to convince the reader to accept the writer's perspective)

The study of the writer-subject-reader relationship goes back to the ancient Greeks' study of *rhetoric*—the art of using language to persuade an audience. (The term *rhetoric* comes from the Greek word for speaker, *rhetor*.) Today, *rhetoric* is no longer limited to the art of persuasion. The term is much broader in meaning, and can be defined as written or spoken discourse crafted by a speaker or writer for a specific occasion and a specific audience. Thus, *rhetorical situation* refers to the

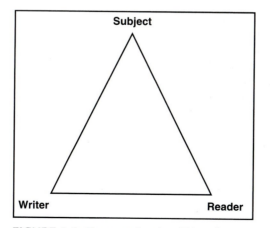

FIGURE 1.2 Communication Triangle

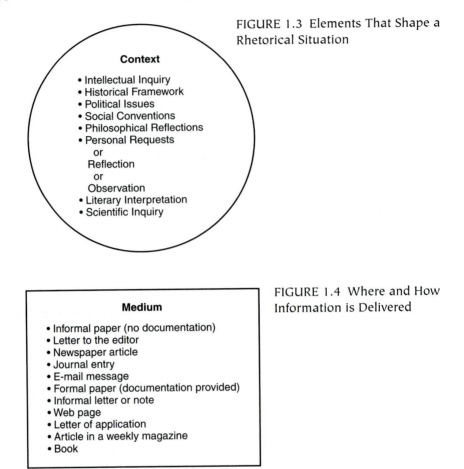

FIGURE 1.3 Elements That Shape a Rhetorical Situation

Context

- Intellectual Inquiry
- Historical Framework
- Political Issues
- Social Conventions
- Philosophical Reflections
- Personal Requests
  or
  Reflection
  or
  Observation
- Literary Interpretation
- Scientific Inquiry

FIGURE 1.4 Where and How Information is Delivered

Medium

- Informal paper (no documentation)
- Letter to the editor
- Newspaper article
- Journal entry
- E-mail message
- Formal paper (documentation provided)
- Informal letter or note
- Web page
- Letter of application
- Article in a weekly magazine
- Book

relationships within the communication triangle, together with features related to the occasion—the context and medium (see Figures 1.3 and 1.4).

In written discourse, the rhetorical situation is created by the following factors:

- the persona or role the writer assumes (for example, writing as an expert, a friend, a layperson, a professional, a concerned citizen, an exasperated consumer)
- the relationship of the writer to the subject (the attitude the writer has toward the subject and the extent and kind of knowledge the writer has about the subject)
- the relationship of the writer to the intended reader (scholar or expert to other scholars or experts, scholar to students, student to students)
- the context (factors that may shape what the writer says and how the writer may envision the intended audience: social, political, intellectual, philosophical, personal)

- the medium of the message: where and how information is delivered (for example—scholarly journal, letter to the editor, congressional report, newspaper editorial, book)

EXAMINING RHETORICAL SITUATIONS
Identifying the Medium

Of the five factors that make up a rhetorical situation, the medium may be the easiest to identify. It's the method of delivery, and it imposes constraints on writing, for example, constraints on length and form. An essay in the *Journal of Medical Ethics* on fetal tissue transplantation, for example, is one medium; a web page devoted to the same topic is another; and a book on the same topic is yet another. The medium allows for differences, sometimes ever so slight, in the way a piece of writing appears to readers. In a scholarly book or journal article, for example, readers find a list of works cited at the end, directing them to studies that support the writer's thesis. If the same information appeared on the Web, readers would probably find hyperlinks within the text and the list of works cited to information that supports or elaborates on the writer's thesis. In weekly newsmagazines you'll find more pictures than you'll find in newspaper articles of headline news. And in business correspondence, you see differences in format in letters, memos, and reports.

Identifying the Context

Writing always has a context: the circumstances in which it occurs. Dates provide one clue to context. An essay or a book written in the United States during the late 1960s, for example, might well reflect the social, political, and intellectual influences of years marked by social unrest, war, and political upheaval. Another way to determine context is to consider the circumstances that prompted the writer to write. Is a piece of writing an intellectual inquiry, a political treatise, a philosophical reflection, a personal reflection or observation, a literary interpretation, or a scientific inquiry? Determining context is essentially categorizing a piece of writing, in part by understanding the writer's subject and the intended discourse community. For example, the title *The Texas Revolutionary Experience* suggests that the author, Dr. Paul Lack, examines revolution, within a specific historical context. This book is an intellectual inquiry as well, written by a historian for other history scholars.

Identifying the Writer's Persona

In your role as a reader, part of examining a rhetorical situation is identifying the persona the writer assumes. As writers, we play different roles or put on different faces for our intended readers. Your professors, for example, assume the role of teacher and scholar when they write your course syllabus or an article for a scholarly journal, and the role of colleague and, possibly, administrator when they write interdepartmental memos. If you read their informal correspondence with old college friends, a reasonable assumption would be that the teacher, scholar, or colleague personas are replaced by the persona of old friends, a persona quite different from roles professors assume in the academic setting. As these examples illustrate, the medium and the context of a piece of writing can help you speculate on the persona you expect a writer to assume.

Identifying the Writer's Relationship to the Subject

Another important point to consider is how much a writer knows about his or her subject. Quite often, publications identify a writer's professional affiliation, credentials, or firsthand experience. This kind of information should help you determine whether the writer is an expert or layperson. Within these two categories, there are varying degrees of expertise. For example, a doctor and the science editor of a major newspaper or weekly magazine are both experts; however, a doctor writing about medical ethics provides a perspective that won't be found in an article on the same topic written by the science editor of *The New York Times*. If a source includes no information about the writer, use the text to make the determination about the writer's level of expertise. Consider the words the writer uses. Does the writer sound like a scholar or layperson? How dense or complex is the information? Does it include unfamiliar terminology that you don't understand?

Regardless of their purpose in writing, all writers have opinions about their subjects. We call the writer's attitude toward his or her subject the writer's *stance*. It's revealed by tone and content in a variety of ways ranging from outright statement (*The Confederate flag is offensive and should not be flown for any reason*) to subtle nuance (*We should value human feeling more than a piece of cloth flying in the wind*). If a writer is indirect in revealing his or her attitude toward a subject, you rely on such matters as word choice, sources the writer quotes, and the amount of space the writer devotes to one side of an issue or another. By paying attention to a writer's tone (sympathetic, sarcastic, earnest, indifferent, skeptical, or enthusiastic, for example) and content, you can determine a writer's stance on a subject.

Identifying the Writer's Relationship to Intended Readers

The writer's words may also reveal something about his or her relationship to intended readers. Does he or she use terms with or without definition? If writers

> ## GUIDELINES FOR ANALYZING
> ## RHETORICAL SITUATIONS
>
> Think of analyzing a rhetorical situation as a reading skill. With close read-ing—in some instances through *multiple* readings—you can create a sce-nario to help you understand writers' choices about content, style, and format. And you can identify elements in a piece of writing that help you understand whether or not a writer has succeeded in his or her purpose. Ana-lyzing a rhetorical situation enables you to see why a piece of writing is effec-tive, even if you didn't find it interesting or enjoyable, or why it is ineffective, even if you liked it. It's important to read for content, but it's even more important to read with an understanding of the five components that make up a rhetorical situation. Answers to the following questions will help you identify these components:
>
> Who is the writer?
>
> What is the writer's attitude toward the subject?
>
> What is the writer's level of knowledge about the subject?
>
> Who is the intended audience?
>
> What is their level of knowledge about the subject?
>
> In what medium did the source appear?
>
> What is the context (social, political, intellectual) that shapes what the writer says and how the writer envisions the intended audience?

define terms and explain concepts, they are assuming that at least some of their intended readers don't know as much about the subject as they do. If, on the other hand, writers use terms without definition and refer to concepts without provid-ing any kind of context, they assume the audience has sufficient knowledge of the subject and does not require definition or background explanation. You'll also find that writers deliberately distance themselves or make themselves intimate with readers.

Two Examples

To illustrate how a writer establishes different relationships with readers, let's look at passages from two articles. The subject of both articles is *Cerion* VIII, a land snail found in the Bahamas. Steven J. Gould, professor of biology, geology, and the his-tory of science at Harvard, is author of the first passage, the introductory paragraph in an article that first appeared in *Natural History* (a publication of the American Museum of Natural History).

OPUS 100*

STEPHEN JAY GOULD

Throughout a long decade of essays I have never, and for definite reasons, written about the biological subject closest to me. Yet for this, my hundredth effort, I ask your indulgence and foist upon you the Bahamian land snail Cerion, mainstay of my own personal research and fieldwork. I love Cerion with all my heart and intellect but have consciously avoided it in this forum because the line between general interest and personal passion cannot be drawn from a perspective of total immersion—the image of doting parents driving friends and neighbors to somnolent distraction with family movies comes too easily to mind. These essays must follow two unbreakable rules: I never lie to you, and I strive mightily not to bore you. But, for this one time in a hundred, I will risk the second for personal pleasure alone.

Cerion is the most prominent land snail of West Indian islands. It ranges from the Florida Keys to the small islands of Aruba, Bonaire, and Curaçao, just off the Venezuelan coast, but the vast majority of species inhabit two principal centers—Cuba and the Bahamas. Cerion's life includes little excitement by our standards. Most species inhabit rocks and sparse vegetation abutting the seashore. They may live for five to ten years, but they spend most of this time in the warm weather equivalent of hibernation (called estivation), hanging upside down from vegetation or affixed to rocks. After a rain or sometimes in the relative cool and damp of night, they descend from their twigs and stones, nibble at the fungi on decaying vegetation, and perhaps even copulate. We have marked and mapped the movement of individual snails and many can be found on the same few square yards of turf, year after year.

Source: Stephen J. Gould, "Opus 100," *The Flamingo's Smile: Reflections in Natural History,* (New York: Norton, 1985).

Notice Gould's use of first person and direct address of the audience in this paragraph. He establishes a kind of intimacy—"I ask your indulgence," "I never lie to you"—by sharing his *"personal* research and fieldwork." And he assures readers that until this article he has avoided "foist[ing]" his "personal passion" upon them. Gould maintains the air of the charming intellectual through word choice—*foist, perspective of total immersion, somnolent distraction.* And notice his reminder, "throughout a long decade of essays I have never, and for definite reasons, written about the biological subject closest to me." He's been at the job for a long time—and he knows he's good at it, confident *finally* to write about the topic that fascinates him the most, taking the "risk" of possibly boring the reader "for personal pleasure alone." While the writer's relationship to the audience is close, the playing field isn't completely even. Gould is an expert addressing a well-educated audience, and, we might reasonably assume, an audience receptive to and interested in whatever Gould has to say. The focus in this paragraph is actually on the writer. As the article progresses, focus shifts to the subject.

Gould and a coauthor, David S. Woodruff, wrote the second passage, the first two paragraphs in a documented scientific article, "Natural History of *Cerion VIII*: Little Bahama Bank—a Revision Based on Genetics, Morphometrics, and Geographic Distribution." The article appeared in a journal associated with Harvard University's Museum of Natural History. The writers' vocabulary is a clear signal that the article is aimed at a highly specialized audience that studies shells. Key terms include *taxonomy*, a system of classification in specific categories; *conchological*, having to do with the study of shells; *monographers*, individuals who have written scholarly books, articles, or pamphlets on a narrowed topic; and *taxa,* organisms making up one of the categories in a taxonomy; for example, a phylum, order, or family.

NATURAL HISTORY OF *CERION VIII*: LITTLE BAHAMA BANK—A REVISION BASED ON GENETICS, MORPHOMETRICS, AND GEOGRAPHIC DISTRIBUTION

STEPHEN J. GOULD AND DAVID S. WOODRUFF

I. Introduction

The current taxonomy of the Little Bahama Bank cerions is a microcosm of the problems that beset this entire fascinating genus, with its 600-odd named taxa (Clench, 1957; Mayr and Rosen, 1956). Little Bahama Bank was spared from visits by the most exuberant conchological splitters, but even its conservative monographers (Clench, 1938, for example) followed the hallowed tradition of naming every distinctive allopatric morphology. Seven species are now recognized for the islands of Little Bahama Bank.

A taxonomic scheme is not merely a neutral description of diversity; it is, as Mayr (1976) has emphasized, a theory of resemblances. And, like all theory, it channels thought along prescribed lines. In *Cerion*, the geographic mapping of described taxa yields a "crazy-quilt" (Mayr and Rosen, 1956) of disordered distribution. Published reports and museum specimens show this pattern for the seven taxa of the Little Bahama Bank. All leading students of *Cerion* have invoked the vagaries of hurricane transport as an explanation for this incoherence (Maynard, 1919; Bartsch, 1920, p. 53; Clench, 1957; Mayr and Rosen, 1956). Yet if the taxonomy is incorrect—if these "species" are only local demes of persistent and widespread biological species—then this biogeographic postulate falls.

The few scientists who approached *Cerion* with the integrative goals of modern evolutionary biology have realized that something in the state of its systematics must be very rotten (Clench, 1957; Mayr, 1963; see also Plate, 1906 and 1907 for similar insights from a non-Darwinian evolutionary perspective). As a primary though generally unrecorded fact, no unambiguous case of sympatry has ever been reported among *Cerion's* 600-odd taxa. The two most probable cases are both in doubt. Mayr (1963, p. 398) reported two species from one of his Cuban localities, but his specimens (S. J. Gould, personal observations) include a few clear intermediates. Bartsch (1920) reported no hybridization between two "species" from Andros Island transplanted to the same locality in the Florida Keys. But he later came to question his own observation (Bartsch, 1931, p. 373). In our own field work, extending over five years and as many major islands, morphotypes ("species" of previous authors) hybridize freely at their zones of contact, no matter how distinct their morphologies—and some of the zones on Long Island mark the smooth mixture of the most distinctly different morphologies within the genus (e.g., smooth, squat "C. *malonei,*" with a long, triangular member of the peculiar subgenus C. (*Umbonis*); see Gould, Woodruff, and Martin 1974, Fig. 1, upper row, specimens 3 and 4). Moreover, we have detected very little genetic difference among animals of divergent shell morphology (Gould, et al., 1974, Woodruff, 1975 a,b). *Cerion* seems to possess a remarkable capacity (among animals) for developing localized, highly distinct morphologies without attendant reproductive isolation from other demes.

Source: Stephen J. Gould, and David S. Woodruff, "Natural History of *Cerion VIII*: Little Bahama Bank—A Revision Based on Genetics, Morphometrics, and Geographic Distribution," *Bulletin of the Museum of Comparative Zoology* 148 (Sept. 1978): 371.

You should notice a distinct difference between this passage and the first one. Gould doesn't confide in readers, use first person, or personalize his remarks. You don't sense the same persona behind the writing in these two paragraphs. You hear the voice of the scientists, Gould and Woodruff, presenting their ideas in technical terms their readers will understand. Gould has a coauthor here, but the addition of that partner doesn't account for the marked difference in tone. If each article were included in its entirety, you would see differences in format, too. It's the audience, context, and medium that mandate the differences. Scholars publish articles in academic journals to inform other scholars of their research—their theories and the evidence that supports them; their experiments or surveys and the conclusions suggested by the data obtained; their discoveries and the significance of these discoveries to the scholarly community. The intended readers for the Gould/Woodruff article would not expect the writers to interject their personalities into the article. The focus throughout is on the subject. Also, intended readers wouldn't have difficulty with content or terminology. While some of these terms may be unfamiliar to you, you can probably get a sense of the writers' aim: Evidence suggests that the "taxonomy [of the Little Bahama Bank *Cerion*] is incorrect," and Gould and Woodruff's purpose is to argue for a revised taxonomy, a new method of classifying Bahamian land snails.

EXERCISES: THINKING CRITICALLY

1. To practice analyzing rhetorical situations, imagine that three index cards are postcards with a picture of your college or university on the front. Your assignment is to write a brief "postcard" to three different audiences. Each note should discuss the same topic: the first weekend of the first term at your college or university. Write the first postcard to your best friend at another institution. Write the second postcard to your grandparents or to an aunt, uncle, or family friend other than your parents. Write the third postcard to a brother, sister, cousin, or family friend who is still in elementary school.

   Now, review your postcards and compare them for content, word choice, sentence length, and tone. Are they different? If they are different—and most students report a radical difference, especially between the note to a friend at another institution and the note to the grandparents—it is the writer's persona, the relationship of the writer to the audience, and social conventions that make the difference. While the topic is the same, you are one person to one audience and another person to another audience. Different social conventions govern these different relationships. As a result, style, tone, and content differ from one note to another.

2. Analyze the rhetorical situation of Nancy Gibbs' article "If We Have It, Do We Use It?" by answering questions in the box on page 33. Be prepared to share your answers with your classmates.

3. For a topic that is currently featured in the news, find two or three sources that discuss the topic. Consult different kinds of sources as you look for information: your campus or local newspaper, newsmagazines, or the World Wide Web. Analyze the rhetorical situation in each text by answering the questions listed in the box on page 33.

EXERCISE: COLLABORATING WITH YOUR PEERS

Cover up the salutation and share your postcards with two or three of your classmates. Ask them to identify the intended audience for each postcard. Ask them to cite specific words or phrases that helped them identify the intended audience and to explain how these words and phrases helped them identity relationships between the writer and intended readers.

In all likelihood, you did not stop and consciously analyze each audience as you wrote the three postcards. You knew your readers and you knew what you wanted to tell them, what they would want to know, what they might not want to know, and what kind of language would be appropriate for each.

EXERCISES: FOCUS ON WRITING

1. Make a list of the kinds of writing you have done recently. Have you written letters or postcards to friends or family? scholarship essays? letters of application to your college admission office? essay exams? minutes from a meeting? e-mail to someone on the Internet whom you have never met personally? e-mail to friends? response to an Internet discussion group? letter to the editor of your local or campus newspaper? job application? letter returning merchandise? letter of complaint? a paper for another class? text for a web page?

    Which medium is most familiar to you? least familiar? Select the medium in which you feel most proficient and explain how you developed proficiency.

2. To practice writing with a specific rhetorical situation in mind, write a review of a movie that impressed you as being innovative—notable for its handling of special effects, costumes, makeup, stunts, lighting, character development, or plot twists and, as a result, unique to its genre (romance, western, action/adventure, coming of age, sports, horror). Select the medium and audience for your review.

3. Using for reference the sources you identified in number 3 of the Thinking Critically exercises on p. 37, draft a news feature for a supermarket tabloid. Be prepared to explain how your news feature would differ in format from the other sources you identified. Bring your sources to class and be prepared to explain how your sources are different or similar in content, format, and style.

READINGS FOR PRACTICE—
READING ABOUT *TITANIC*

The readings that follow will give you practice in previewing, annotating, and discussing your reading as well as analyzing rhetorical situations. The readings illustrate how different academic discourse communities look at a topic. You'll see how the focus changes as writers in the humanities, sciences, and social sciences focus on different aspects of the *Titanic*. For each selection, answer the questions listed under "Guidelines for Analyzing Rhetorical Situations" on page 33 as well as the questions that follow each selection.

If you have seen James Cameron's 1998 film *Titanic*, or for that matter any of the television specials that proliferated during several months of *Titanic*-mania coinciding with the film's release and extended theatrical run, you have a historical context for these sources. If you aren't familiar with the film or the history of the famous ship, a brief summary should suffice: On April 14, 1912, on its maiden voyage from Southampton to New York, the supposedly unsinkable ocean liner *Titanic* struck an iceberg and sank in less than three hours. Out of approximately 2,210 on board, 1,500 people died. The company that owned the ship had not provided enough lifeboats for all the passengers. Until 1985, when Robert Ballard discovered the *Titanic*, the broken ship lay undisturbed on the ocean floor, a watery graveyard for the men, women, and children who lost their lives in the cold Atlantic.

THREE PERSPECTIVES

As you read these selections, notice that the writers include basic facts about the sinking, information about how or why the *Titanic* sank; but that provision of such factual information—the kind of information you would read in a newspaper—is not the primary purpose of the selections. Their assumption is that readers have some context for the topic; it isn't entirely new to them.

The Humanities

Our focus on the *Titanic* begins with Jose Arroyo's review of James Cameron's movie, *Titanic*. While Arroyo acknowledges that Cameron's movie is a major hit with American audiences, he offers a lengthy analysis of the film that leads to his evaluation. Notice that Arroyo refers to popular culture, history, and film history in this review. Before you read this source, preview the text. What are your expectations? What does the title suggest? Can you describe the audience the writer probably had in mind? What cues does the text provide to help you determine the audience?

MASSIVE ATTACK

JOSE ARROYO

"James Cameron's 'Titanic', Currently the Most Expensive Movie Ever, Relies on Old Hollywood Methods as Much as Special Effects, Argues José Arroyo

The sinking of the S.S. *Titanic* on the night of 14 April 1912 is one of the best-known disasters of the twentieth century: even people who don't know much history have heard of it. Movies have been made of it ever since 1912's remarkably instant German reconstruction *In Nacht und Eis* (Mime Misu): the all-star (Barbara Stanwyck, Clifton Webb, Brian Aherne) 1953 *Titanic* directed by Jean Negulesco still crops up on television occasionally, as does the British *A Night to Remember* (Roy Ward Baker, 1958), highly regarded for the way it builds a quiet power through a collage of vignettes. The sinking has also been a minor plot point in countless other films, including musicals: in *The Unsinkable Molly Brown* (Charles Walters, 1964), Debbie Reynolds plays the same Molly that Kathy Bates plays in James Cameron's new *Titanic*. The event has been interpreted as an allegory for capitalism, as divine punishment of human arrogance, as a symbol of the destruction of a privileged way of life and as a portent of the changes World War One was to bring.

It is understandable why Cameron would be attracted to the subject: a historical event loaded with significance, it offers a huge canvas, with potential for great action. And his film does try to bring in these traditional interpretations of the event: we do see class warfare erupting when the icebergs hit, with the lower classes getting locked up in the lower decks. We see the cosmopolitanism of the times, the radical breakthroughs in the arts and the incipient feminism that were to transform the Twentieth Century; the bloody dialectic of enlightenment in which science and progress lead to destruction is illustrated for the umpteenth time. One can hardly blame Cameron for wanting to tackle so weighty a subject—but one can't help noting that he wrung more meaning, significance, seriousness *and* fun from his science-fiction work than he does here, from History.

And it would be surprising if audiences cared much about the meaning of *Titanic*. This is a film that would probably be just as popular (if twice as bad) at half the length, provided the last of its three-and-a-quarter hours, the one with all the action and the special effects, remained as it is here. For what we all want to see is how the ship sinks—and what we get to see here is not simply visually awesome but also great film-making. Indeed, there are amazing shots throughout the film. For example, one shot near the start moves from Leonardo DiCaprio as hero Jack Dawson standing on the banister of the ship's prow, arms outstretched—revelling in the air, the speed of the boat and the freedom of the ocean—through the whole length of the ship and beyond as we see people walking on deck and every detail. The shot is show-offy in its expensiveness and skill, and a sheer pleasure.

Wisely, most of the best is left for the latter part of the film, which thus seems to build and build. It gains speed from the moment Billy Zane as Cal Hockley hears Rose (Kate Win-slet) and Jack declaring their love for one another, and it doesn't stop moving until Jack dies. We see the massive ship break, thousands of extras sliding to their death, and gushing water destroying everything in its path. The way this is filmed turns these scenes into something more than merely spectacle: they are rendered so immediate that the destruction takes on a life of its own. Only with death imminent does everything come to life. Characters shake loose, scenes finally begin to play and drama to happen as the chaos commences. It's as if the icebergs that sink the boat had unshackled Kate and Leo from their keylight and Cameron from his yen for portentous significance. It is in movement that the actors become moving and funny. And it is in and through action that Cameron finally communicates anything worth saying. Cal frantically grabbing a loose baby in order to qualify for a lifeboat says more about his character, his class and the contrasted cultures of that time and ours than does the entire necklace subplot.

In the tradition of High Concept cinema, the plot is easily reducible to stars, title and ad-line: 'Leonardo DiCaprio—Kate Winslet—*Titanic*— Nothing on Earth Could Come between Them' pretty much tells us the story. Jack Dawson, an artist, talented but poor, who won his fare at cards, meets upperclass Rose DeWitt Bukater when he charms her away from jumping overboard (reasons: boyfriend trouble plus general sexual-cultural oppression), saving her life. By the end, when both are in the icy waters, he's still trying to charm her into living even as he's dying. It's true love, you see. Befitting her more practical nature, she pushes his frozen corpse into the Atlantic at the very moment she promises never to let him go, remaining true to her word because (don't gag), she "will always carry him deep in [her] heart." For this is after all one of those romances where a lady with three names falls in love with an artist used to sketching one-legged prostitutes in Paris. And true to type, Everything on Earth *tries* to come between them: her selfish mother (Frances Fisher) is eager to imprison Rose in a loveless marriage, to maintain social status and increase her own standard of living (the father is dead; the family in debt); the intended husband is the sadistic Cal, who beats Rose for being belligerent—and even in more tender moments he treats her merely as an expensive object and is willing to kill her rather than allow her into the arms of another man. The icebergs don't help. Nature fosters Rose's and Jack's union only to demand an earthly separation which simultaneously guarantees the transcendental status of their love. Yes,

Titanic is as trashy as it sounds, and so sometimes it's impossible to keep a straight face, but it is also a lot of fun.

'*Romeo and Juliet* aboard the *Titanic*' is not the most promising pitch for a film—nor is it improved by the decision to let Rose live to be a hundred years old, in order to tell us the story. For the story actually begins in the present, with Brock Lovett (a ruddy Bill Paxton) leading an expedition down to the wreck to find a necklace with a rare blue diamond, 'The Heart of the Ocean'. The safe where the necklace supposedly resides is located and opened—but all Lovett finds is a drawing of a young and topless Rose wearing it. The elderly Rose (Gloria Stuart) sees this picture on television, recognises herself, contacts Lovett and gets helicoptered onto his ship in order to tell him her story. The exploration of the wreck of the *Titanic* and the interaction between Lovett and old Rose takes up a fair amount of running time at beginning and end of the film, and as a narrative device is not without its uses: the audience can be given contextual information on the history of the ship and its passengers, moving between past and present, while several questions can be set in motion. What happened to the necklace? What happened to Rose?

But such benefits do not make up for the device's shortcomings. The good things one remembers in the framing-device sections are few: an abstract shot of submarines resembling spaceships descending towards the final frontier; a cute robot manoeuvring its way through the silt-covered remains of the wreck; computer graphics vividly illustrating what happened to the ship when it hit the iceberg. This section is still not worth the screen-time that it occupies. More story-telling imagination could have structured the central narrative so as to accommodate exposition and set the central quests in motion.

Moreover, the director should have trusted the audience to make the link between the past and the present. That he doesn't is clearly exemplified in the two instances when the film cuts to the present. Each present-day section is intro-duced by Rose's voice-over. Each time there's a cut to the faces of Lovett and his crew listening to her. In other words they are the narrative's stand-ins for the audience. The crew is as visibly moved as the audience of the film is expected to be. But in effect what Cameron has done—probably the worst directing in his career—is to pre-empt and dictate audience response. So hackneyed is this shameless bit of manipulation that it's all too easy to resist.

Clearly the *Titanic* is ideal sub-ject-matter for a disaster movie, for an intimate epic and for a commen-tary on a mythic historical event and long-gone way of life. And Cameron essays all three, with varying degrees of success. The film doesn't quite fit into the disaster genre as we recall it from its 70s peak. Such films as *The Poseidon Adventure* (1972), *Earth-quake* (1974), and *The Towering Inferno* (1974) began (like *Titanic*) by telling us of a situation that couldn't possibly happen, and introducing us to those it couldn't happen to. Then—on as wide a screen as possi-ble and preferably in sensurround— they showed it happening: the eruption of a disaster and how different people coped. Unlike *Titanic*, however, the classic disaster movie introduced a wide array of characters, requiring star casting in order to facilitate characterisation. And always part of the fun was anticipating which stars would live and how the others met their grisly fates (doing Shelley Winters in *The Poseidon Adventure* is still a popular party piece). We need to care—or rather, to judge how well or badly these stars be-haved in the crisis—in order that affect be generated.

Titanic doesn't quite work this way. First, DiCaprio and Bates are the closest the movie gets to stars. Second, we simply never know enough about the many characters to mind about their fate. The unsinkable Bates, Fisher and David Warner are all memorable, but their roles have no character arc—while the evil Zane is all but pure cartoon. Fabrizio (Danny Nucci) is Jack's closest friend in the story, but when the ship's funnel falls on him, we're much more taken up in the aesthet-ics of the shot than the fate of the man.

By focusing on a single relation-ship, in the context of some earth-shattering event, it's clear that Cameron and crew strove to make this movie an intimate epic, not unlike his *Terminator* films or *Aliens*. The rela-tionship is the one between Jack and Rose, with Rose the protagonist (and Cal as the third point of the triangle). Rose—who narrates—begins the film so enslaved by her class and her loveless relationship with Cal that she's contemplating suicide and ends the film as a strong independent woman renouncing her class and willing to fight both for love and life. Jack, sensitive, handsome, charming and in love with her, remains this way throughout the film.

But if the film doesn't quite succeed as intimate epic, it's because it tries to work as myth. Rose not only carries the burden of character but also a significant part of the action. Jack may save her life emotionally (with his charm and encouragement), but she saves his physically (by socking people in the jaw and bringing out the axe). This is familiar Cameron territory. Rose is an intelligent action woman similar to Sarah Connor and Ripley, two of the most powerful feminist icons in contemporary cinema. In Rose, Cameron is obviously striving for an equally mythic character—but this is seemingly easier when dealing with the future than the past. And it is the past that defeats the director's efforts.

Kate Winslet gives a lovely performance. She's given an old-fashioned movie-star entrance at the beginning—as she gets out of her carriage we see her legs and her hat before her face is finally revealed. She's elegantly dressed, perfectly made up and looks beautiful. As the story develops and her character loosens up, she becomes more and more dishevelled and looks more and more ordinary, albeit attractively so. Yet neither presence nor skill can protect her—nor Leo for that matter—from Cameron's choices with

regard to how their characters are written or filmed. Unfortunately most of these choices seem to be informed by old movies.

How Jack looks and acts in the gambling scene immediately recalls one of the Dead End Kids in a typical Warner Brothers movie such as *Angels With Dirty Faces*, where a young kid might grow up to be James Cagney and end up on the wrong side of the law. Cal is strikingly similar to Ballin in *Gilda*: both treat their women as expensive things to be spoilt, abused and controlled. The dialogue is straight out of a pretentious 40s melodrama: a certain painting is apparently by one, "Picasso. He won't amount to much." "Freud?" someone asks: "Who is he? A passenger?" And when Rose tells Jack his drawings are "rather good; very good actually," the line could just as easily (and perhaps more acceptably) have been something Joan Crawford said to John Garfield though even in the 40s such a line was already stilted and phoney: 'movie' dialogue).

The film also looks to have been filmed in accordance with old studio practices, particularly MGM's. The first two hours look gorgeously glamorous—as if everything were lit so as elegantly to gash a precipitous cheekbone with the shadow of an eyelash. This brings out the liner's sumptuousness, and the finery of its passengers—table-settings shine, fireplaces glow, *art-nouveau* hairclips glitter—which also serves a narrative function: for 'richness' is an important story element. But applying the same approach to people becomes stultifying.

Leo and Kate try to bring some sass and energy to their performances, but the director seems to be paying more attention to the actors stepping on their mark so that their hair is haloed in proper movie-star manner than to bringing life (in rhythm or timing) to the acting.

One assumes the type of dialogue and the mode of filming have been chosen deliberately. In its portentousness and historical allusion, this type of dialogue—which was already mythologised in the movies it originally appeared in—is also an attempt at mythmaking. And the filming is the kind that means to turn people into icons. It's almost as if the film-makers had sought an approach significant and grandiose enough to match the sinking of the *Titanic*. But these diverse efforts at mythmaking, operating on so many levels, combine with an already mythic subject matter to ossify everything: the film ends up with an 'importance' and 'significance' it really doesn't need.

The verdict on the film is in, at least from America: a smash. We know the answer to the question the entertainment press has recently been speculating on so insistently: whether or not it makes a vast profit, the most expensive US film to date is at least not sinking ruinously into a sea of red ink.

But is it any good? It is hard to judge whether the budget is on the screen—who's seen a $200 million movie before? But it looks First Class

and its luxurious expensiveness is a pleasure to watch. Its daunting length is painless. Unlike so many contemporary spectacles, it does not resort to a cheap frenzy of visual jolts: it dares to linger on objects, faces and events and to trust plot, pacing and production values to retain audience attention.

Cameron has succeeded in making a disaster movie in which people and relationships are as important as the excellent effects, if not always as successfully realised. Arguably one of the best big-budget films of the past year, *Titanic* is certainly enjoyable. But it's impressive and depressing in about equal measure: it's of a quality Irwin Allen always aspired to and fell short of, for example, yet to be praising one of Hollywood's most imaginative and proficient film-makers for having made a film better than *The Poseidon Adventure* or *The Towering Inferno* is to have lowered expectations into the realm of the tawdry and the absurd. In this sense *Titanic* is emblematic of the state of contemporary Hollywood film-making. This is particularly apparent in scenes *Titanic* shares with *A Night to Remember*, such as the encounters with the ship's guilt-ridden designer, who waits resigned to his fate, or the attempts by crowds to swamp the remaining life boats as the end nears. Cameron's film tries for the same sense of stark terror as the older film, an internalised, gradual awareness of imminent doom, but its scale is too great for such an intimate effect, built on restraint, and subtle turns from character actors sit ill beside the flamboyant ravings of Billy Zane in full cry.

In the twentieth century, speed, movement and action are synonymous with America itself: certainly they were what people all over the world loved US movies for. But US cinema was never just about action: it also had people whose freedom and energy were internationally emulated and stories that enchanted the world. Contemporary US film-making no longer runs to this. Character and stories are now most often the domain of lower-budget films, whatever their quality. Generally (and only generally) the only thing big-budget Hollywood currently does well is action and effects—that is, only through action and effects does big-budget Hollywood have anything to say. It is because of its lack of story-telling skills and its execrable character delineation that *Titanic* is emblematic of contemporary Hollywood action/spectacle—it is also because of this that it is not a good film. But it is because Cameron is so peerless a director of action/spectacle that Titanic is among the best big-budget films of the past year. If the film's lacks seem to be those of contemporary Hollywood in general, its attributes are uniquely its own.

Source: Jose Arroyo, "Massive Attack," *Sight and Sound* (Feb. 1998): 16–19.

EXERCISES: READING AND RESPONDING

1. Identify features of the article that suggest *Sight and Sound* reaches a different audience than a popular movie magazine.
2. Characterize Arroyo's attitude toward the historical event.
3. Characterize Arroyo's attitude toward the movie.
4. Explain why you agree or disagree with Arroyo's evaluation of the movie.
5. How do you interpret the title?

The Social Sciences

In "Black American Perception of the *Titanic* Disaster," Robert G. Weisbord examines the sinking of the *Titanic* from a cultural perspective, explaining how people reacted to the loss of the ocean liner and the people who went down with it. Before you read this source, preview the text. What are your expectations? What information does the article offer about the writer? Can you describe the audience the writer probably had in mind? What cues does the text provide to help you determine the audience?

BLACK AMERICAN PERCEPTION OF THE *TITANIC* DISASTER

ROBERT G. WEISBORD

At first glance it would appear unlikely that any connection could exist between the *Titanic* catastrophe and Black American history. None of that ill-fated vessel's 1,320 passengers was of African descent and it is improbable (though not impossible) that any of the crew of 915 was "colored," to use a term then in vogue in both Britain and the United States. Survivors of the tragedy have no recollection of Black staff.[1] Despite their physical absence, Afro-Americans reacted strongly, albeit in sharply divergent ways to the sinking of the *Titanic* on its maiden voyage.

To comprehend Black reactions, it is imperative to recall their plight in the pre-World War I era. Racism was reaching its zenith in the United States. Conversely, Black fortunes were plummeting. Blacks were citizens in name only. Despite the 15th Amendment to the Constitution, they were systematically disfranchised and the number of Black elected officials had sharply declined since the end of Reconstruction. In the wake of the Supreme Court's Plessy v. Ferguson decision in 1896 permitting separate but equal facilities, Jim Crowism or racial segregation was proliferating so that it touched every facet of American race relations. Violence against persons of color had become commonplace. Race riots which were essentially white assaults on Black communities occurred in the North as well as the South as disillusioned Blacks migrated to urban areas in search of a better life. Lynching became a national pastime. From 1904 to 1913 almost 700 Blacks were put to death by white mobs. Sixty-one were victims of vigilante justice in 1912, the year the *Titanic* went down (*Thirty Years* 29). White supremacy was an article of faith. For the sons and daughters of Africa the future looked bleak in what was trumpeted to be a "white man's country."

Because of white oppression, Blacks were in the slough of despond when the *Titanic* sank. Nevertheless, on the whole, middle-class, educated Blacks, responded to the sinking with concern, sensitivity, and respect. Author Wyn Craig Wade is quite wrong in asserting in his otherwise excellent book on the *Titanic* that the Black intelligentsia ignored the most publicized tragedy of the time (434–35).

Within a week of the maritime catastrophe, Booker T. Washington, the founder of Tuskegee Institute and one of the best-known Blacks of the era, contacted President William Howard Taft to express condolences. On behalf of the faculty and students at the Institute and in the name of participants at an International Conference on the Negro at which many foreign countries and some 36 missionary organizations were represented, Washington, whose racial philosophy was best summarized as "accommodationism" or submission to white dominance, offered his "deep and sincere sympathy" to the loved ones of those who were lost in the "terrible calamity" (Harlan and Smock 522–23).

Editorial comment in the Black press ran along the same altruistic lines. *The Pittsburgh Courier,* among the leading Black newspapers of the day, noted that the human loss had stirred the whole world to grief. "The mind can not picture the distress ... and dispair [sic] which must have been overcoming in the extreme when the two thousand doomed passengers stood face to face with a certain death." Their agony could only be imagined (20 April 1912).

A Black periodical in Philadelphia observed that no members of the "colored race" had forfeited their lives when the *Titanic* sank due to "conditions over which we have no control." Still, at a time of catastrophe, all the world's population are kin and sympathy was expressed for the bereaved families and friends of the poor souls who perished so unexpectedly (*Solid Rock Herald*).[2]

"Nothing but profound sorrow should energize the hearts of mankind the world over in view of the awful calamity," wrote the weekly *Baltimore Afro-American Ledger* which, for a couple of months, devoted considerable space to the *Titanic* saga (20 April 1912).[3]

Also attempting to bridge the racial chasm was a resolution adopted by the fifty-ninth annual session of the Baltimore African Methodist Episcopal Church held in April 1912. It voiced sympathy for the families of the approximately 1,500 *Titanic* victims. A brief, silent prayer followed adoption of the resolution.

Resolutions, sermons, and editorials often pointed out that their material riches notwithstanding, the passengers were at the mercy of God. For *The Crisis*, the organ of the fledgling, bi-racial civil rights organization, the N.A.A.C.P. (National Association for the Advancement of Colored People), the brotherhood of man was the overriding lesson taught by the *Titanic*. Beneficiaries of privilege often indifferent to the lower classes ought to exercise imagination and approach the less fortunate with a sense of democracy and responsibility (June 1912: 71–72). Although Blacks were not explicity cited, the editor of the monthly journal, W.E.B. DuBois, a tireless campaigner for racial justice, surely had his downtrodden brothers and sisters in mind in publishing the editorial.

Given the climate of bigotry and the widespread persecution of Black Americans, the foregoing expressions of concern and compassion are remarkable, but they are not the whole story. In the South where Black families struggled to eke out a living and in the urban ghettos then burgeoning because of the influx of rural migrants, unbeknownst to whites, Blacks, overwhelmingly poor, reacted quite differently to the *Titanic*. They did so verbally—with the toast, a type of oral narrative. In the African motherland and in antebellum slavery when many states forbade teaching bondsmen to read and write, oral tradition was of great cultural significance. Verbal dexterity was highly esteemed.

The toast is sometimes recited. Often it is sung. One of the two most popular works in this genre is the *Titanic* toast which developed in the months and years following the calamity. In its many renditions, it was heard in front of general stores, on neighbors' porches, at social functions, in taverns and pool halls, in barber shops, and, of course, on street corners. Eager to display their verbal skills and to vent their animosity toward the white society which held them in contempt, Black men told and retold their versions of the iceberg and the *Titanic*, typically in mocking, bawdy rhyme.

Many of those accounts featured a fictional Black, ironically named "Shine."[4] In a Harlem version of the toast told to the Black poet Langston Hughes, Shine, a dark-hued Negro, worked aboard the *Titanic* as a stoker (91–92). When the ocean liner began to sink, Shine, portrayed as an articulate trickster, escaped the watery grave of so many whites because of his athletic skills. He ran so fast that he broke down an iron door and abandoned ship. In several versions he swam to safety, ignoring the captain's daughter or wife who offered him sexual favors. Little is left to the imagination and obscene language abounds. Depending on the version, either the captain or an elderly millionaire proffered money to Shine to save them. They too were ignored. Thus, the Black hero resists the sexual and financial blandishments of the white man. Before long, Shine is in Harlem or Los Angeles or even Liverpool safe and sound. He has bested his enemies despite the odds.

In the aftermath of the tragedy, the deaths of the super-rich, e.g., John Jacob Astor, Benjamin Guggenheim, and Mr. and Mrs. Isador Straus, received disproportionate attention. This was the case in the Black American community as well as in the society at large. Fatalities in steerage where most of the passengers were European immigrants were often overlooked. Denied the fruits of America's industrial success, Blacks tended to focus on the tycoons whose enormous wealth could not save them from death in the cold Atlantic. In one epic poem recorded as late as 1964 in Jefferson City, Missouri, four thousand millionaires watched Shine swim away from the foundering *Titanic* (Jackson 218). From the perspective of indigent Blacks, whiteness was synonymous with wealth. In the toasts Jay Gould, "the most hated man in America," is mistakenly listed among the dead and there is reference to a fictional plutocrat, one "Jacob Nash" (Courlander 403).

Fidelity to historical detail is not one of the characteristics of these Black ballads. More often than not they place the disaster in the "merry month of May" rather than April, because May offers more rhyming opportunities (Abrahams 126).[5]

It is the moral of the *Titanic*, a moral drawn from contemporary race relations, that determined the content of the narratives. For example, sidewalk gossip in the Black world long insisted that Jack Johnson, the celebrated Black fighter, the first recognized heavyweight champion of his race, had been refused passage on the *Titanic*. The legendary Black folk artist and balladeer, Huddie Ledbetter or Leadbelly as he was popularly known, performed a toast which held that Johnson wanted to get on board but the *Titanic* skipper, Captain E.J. Smith, hollered that he "ain't hauling no coal" (Asch and Lomax 26, Lomax and Lomax 183).[6]

Idolized by Blacks, Johnson was a villain and a menace to whites. Right after Johnson successfully defended his crown against Jim Jeffries, the "great white hope," in Reno in 1910, race riots rooted in Negrophobia, broke out in many cities across the country. The champion was detested by Causasian America not only because of his pugilistic prowess, but because of his flamboyant life-style and "uppity" manner. Worst of all, he flouted sexual etiquette by marrying three white women in succession and romancing several others.

While Johnson seemed inde-structible in the ring, the government resolved to destroy him in the courts. He was charged with violat-ing the recently enacted Mann Act which prohibited transporting women across state boundaries for immoral purposes. After his conviction, John-son fled the United States in June 1913 rather than serve prison time (Gilmore 133). However, there is no evidence that Johnson attempted to sail on the *Titanic* or that he was snubbed for racial or other reasons by the White Star Line. In fact, he was in the United States, not England, when the *Titanic* sailed from Southampton in April 1912.

Leadbelly, who spent many years in prison, himself rejoiced. "Black men oughta shout for joy," he sang. After all they had lost neither a girl or a boy (Lomax and Lomax 183). In other words, Johnson had ironic-ally survived because of white rac-ism. The belief, erroneous in this instance, that one of their heroes had been rejected by white society, rankled nonetheless.

America's belief in God's omnipotence, in technology as a panacea and in the inevitability of progress were all undermined by the *Titanic* catastrophe. For many, it was the end of a dream. Wyn Craig Wade has written that Americans would turn to the "federal government and politicians for things that they had once sought from the church and its clergy" (Wade 106). Afro-Americans, however, had no reason whatsoever to expect the government to redress their grievances. Knowledge that the white man had gotten his comeup-pance in the *Titanic* episode offered only cold comfort. For Blacks it was not the end of a dream, but the con-tinuation of a nightmare.

Notes

[1]Eva Hart and Marjorie Newell Robb, personal inerviews with the author, 11 April 1987, Wilmington, Delaware.

[2]The comment was quoted in the *Pittsburgh Courier,* 4 May 1912. Other Black newspa-pers commenting on the *Titanic* were the *Richmond Planet* and the *Detroit Informer.*

[3]The *Ledger* of 27 April 1912 carried stories by the Titanic's survivors and a book about the disaster was advertised in several issues.

[4]"Shine" was a derogatory term for Blacks.

[5]Abrahams heard one variant which ran as follows:

> The eight of May was a hell of a day
> When the *Titanic* was sinking away

[6]In 1938, the second bout between Joe Louis, the "Brown Bomber," and Max Schmeling, the German boxer who was seen, quite unfairly, as the embodiment of Nazi racism, conjured up the *Titanic* image. Blacks rejoiced, "Scmeling went down like the *Titanic* when Joe gave him one hard right..." (Levine 437).

Works Cited

Abrahams, Roger D. *Deep Down in the Jungle ...—Negro Narrative Folklore from the Streets of Philadelphia*. Chicago: Aldine, 1970.

Asch, Moses, and Alan Lomax, eds. *The Leadbelly Songbook*. New York: Oak, 1971.

Baltimore Afro-American Ledger 20, 27 Apr. 1912.

Courlander, Harold. *A Treasury of Afro-American Folklore*. New York: Crown, 1976.

The Crisis 4.2 (June 1912).

Gilmore, Al-Tony. *Bad Nigger! The National Impact of Jack Johnson*. Port Washington, NY: Kennikat, 1975.

Harlan, Louis and Raymond W. Smock, eds. *The Booker T. Washington Papers*. Vol 2. 1911–12. Urbana: U of Illinois P, 1981.

Hughes, Langston. *The Book of Negro Humor*. New York: Dodd, Mead and Company, 1966.

Jackson, Bruck. "The Titanic Toast." *Veins of Humor*. Ed. Harry Levin. Cambridge: Harvard UP, 1972. 205–23.

Levine, Lawrence W. *Black Culture and Black Consciousness: Afro-American Folk Thought from Slavery to Freedom*. Oxford: Oxford UP, 1978.

Lomax, John A., and Alan Lomax, eds. *Negro Folk Songs as Sung by Lead Belly*. New York: Macmillan, 1936.

Pittsburgh Courier 4 May 1912.

Pittsburgh Courier 20 Apr. 1912.

Solid Rock Herald n.d.

Thirty Years of Lynching in the United States 1889–1918. New York: National Association for the Advancement of Colored People, 1919.

Wade, Wyn Craig. *The Titanic—End of a Dream*. New York: Penguin, 1985.

Robert G. Welsbord, Department of History, University of Rhode Island, Kingston, RI.

Source: , Robert G. Weisbord, "Black American Perception of the *Titanic* Disaster," *Journal of Popular Culture* 28 (Winter 1994): 245–250.

EXERCISES: READING AND RESPONDING

1. What information does the article include about Weisbord?

2. What does Weisbord's purpose seem to be? How does he achieve his purpose?

3. What assumptions do you think Weisbord made about readers' familiarity with the sinking of the *Titanic*? Cite specific passages that illustrate your answer.

4. Does the text suggest other assumptions that Weisbord might have about readers' knowledge of history? of Black Americans' reactions to the sinking of the *Titanic*?

5. With whom does Weisbord take issue?

6. What do you learn from reading this article?

7. What passages are concerned primarily with cultural matters?

8. How does the writer make this topic interesting and relevant to his intended audience?

9. What purpose do the "Notes" at the end of the article serve?

10. What does the list of "Works Cited" suggest about the writer's research? About what readers might value as sufficient evidence to support the writer's points?

EXERCISE: COLLABORATING WITH YOUR PEERS

Compare your annotations of Source #5 with two or three of your peers. Did you mark the same passages? ask the same questions? Whose annotations appear to be the most thorough and useful?

The Sciences

The article "Priceless Legacy of the *Titanic*" asks you to consider issues about the recovery of artifacts from the *Titanic*. While this isn't a documented article, it is aimed at a specialized reading audience. *New Scientist*, published in England, frequently examines the social consequences of scientific discovery. As you read and annotate, mark terms that are new to you. Also, think about how the scientist's perspective differs from that of the historian or a film critic. What issues are important to the scientist? What kind of questions does the scientist ask? What kind of evidence does the scientist value?

PRICELESS LEGACY OF THE *TITANIC*

MICK HAMER

In an old tannery by a stream in the depths of Burgundy is a laboratory that specialises in conserving objects from shipwrecks. Red and grey plastic containers filled with liquid line the back room. There is a whiff of ammonia in the air. Each of the containers contains a slice of life as it was in 1912. For here in the French countryside are stored the last remains of the *Titanic*.

The great ocean liner was said to be unsinkable. Its hull was divided into compartments, and the water-tight doors connecting them could be shut to contain flooding if the ship was holed. After setting sail from Southampton on 10 April 1912, it called at Cherbourg and the next day at Queenstown in Ireland before set-ting course for New York. At 11.40 pm on 14 April it struck an iceberg in mid-Atlantic. Just 2 hours 40 min-utes later the "unsinkable" liner foundered, claiming the lives of more than 1500 people. There were just over 900 survivors.

For over 70 years the two halves of the *Titanic* rested on the bottom of the Atlantic, four kilometres beneath the waves. Inside the stricken vessel were the ship's instruments, luxury fittings and the passengers' personal effects—items that are now being salvaged and, where possible, restored to their former glory at the laboratory in Burgundy. The results of this restoration effort will be put on public display in London this month, at the National Maritime Museum in Greenwich.

Metal Detector

Since the wreck site was found in 1985, it has been explored by a titanium-hulled submarine owned by IFREMER, the French oceanographic institute. In 1987 the first 1800 relics from the wreck were brought to the surface. Their conservation was undertaken by researchers at Elec-tricité de France, the state-owned electricity company (Technology, 9 January 1993).

In 1993 a second expedition brought up a further 800 artefacts. In the meantime Stephane Pennec, who had been working on the *Titanic* relics at EDF, joined with three part-ners to set up LP3, the company that now runs the Burgundy laboratory. The legal owner of the wreck, a New York company called RMS Titanic, entrusted the conservation of the 1993 finds to Pennec, who will also take charge of objects retrieved dur-ing a further exploration of the wreck this year.

The restoration of artefacts from the *Titanic* has more than just curiosity value. "It is the first conser-vation treatment of the remains from a modern vessel," and that makes it particularly important, says Ian MacLeod, head of materials conser-vation at the Western Australian Mar-itime Museum in Fremantle and a consultant to the project.

The wreck of the Titanic con-tains recognisably modern tech-nologies, including electroplated nickel-silver (EPNS), and communi-cations equipment such as the ship's telegraph and the internal tele-phones. There are manufactured goods from factory production lines, including a packet of cigarettes, pen-cils, a leather wallet, and a large quantity of paper, including post-cards, books, sheet music and letters. There are even gilded chandeliers. Techniques for conserving many of these finds have been developed by the researchers at EDF and LP3.

Some of the relics strike an ironic note. A portion of an electrical control panel made of slate survives, complete with four of the bone labels that identified its switches, fuses and warning lights. "Water-tight door bells" is the legend on one of them. "We shall never know whether they worked or not," MacLeod observes.

Some objects are sublime, such as the perfectly preserved silver table lamp from a first-class cabin, the remains of a bulb still in the bayonet fitting. Others are full of pathos, such as the cheap china souvenir watering can inscribed "A present from Folkestone".

All these objects have spent more than 70 years subjected to pressures of 400 atmospheres while under attack by bacteria and the chloride and sulphate salts in the ice-cold seawater. Never before has material been salvaged from more than 3000 metres beneath the sea. MacLeod says that the finds give "a remarkable insight into the changes which chemical and physical processes give at this depth". "Shipwrecks are the only really valid corrosion experiment," says MacLeod. He believes this may make some of the findings from laboratories such as LP3 useful for industry. Several companies who want to dump toxic waste at sea, for example, propose sealing it in nickel containers, because the metal appears so resistant to attack by seawater. But a dip into one of the tubs at LP3 reveals a pair of nickel cooking pots from the Titanic's galley, and both are corroded. The bottom of one pot has been eaten away by bacteria. The dynamics of the processes that take place at the bottom of the ocean, where the by-products of one corrosion reaction can feed another, cannot be reproduced in a laboratory, he argues.

Paper presents Pennec with one of his biggest challenges. The National Maritime Museum cannot recall another shipwreck from which paper with legible text has been salvaged, so the techniques for conserving the paper and reading what is on it remain highly experimental. "You don't have a second chance," says Pennec. Wet paper is weak and Pennec says that manipulating it takes time. While it is wet the paper has to be supported to stop it falling apart. In some cases the paper can be conserved just by freeze-drying and fumigation. Among the finds that will be on display in October is a typed letter on the headed notepaper of the New York firm of Rosenshine Brothers, manufacturers of ostrich feathers and boas. In it A. Rosenshine tells his brother George that he expects the fashion for wearing ostrich feathers to decline. George Rosenshine perished in the wreck, and the writer of the letter submitted a claim to the *Titanic's* owner, the White Star Line, as compensation for his brother's death.

When the Rosenshine letter was found it was completely unreadable, part of an amorphous brown mass. Chemical analysis established that the paper was heavily contaminated with iron sulphides. "A metal wire had been in contact and so you had iron and sulphur going into the paper," says Pennec. The researchers used a two-stage chemical process to reveal its contents. The first was to oxidise the iron sulphides with a dilute (1.5 per cent) solution of hydrogen peroxide made alkaline with ammonia. The oxidation converted the sulphides into rust—a mixture of iron oxides and hydroxides. The second stage was to dissolve away the rust with oxalic acid in a solution with a sodium citrate buffer. The citrate buffer has the happy knack of not only controlling the pH of the solution but also helping to dissolve the rust. Pennec says that it took two days to develop the letters to the point where they were legible. Finally the paper was freeze-dried. The developing process did not damage the text because the typewriting—carbon particles deposited from the typewriter's ribbon—was relatively inert. But inks are not always resistant to chemical treatment.

The researchers normally try out their techniques on a small part of the material before risking it on the entire artefact. MacLeod says that they also play safe by taking a series of photographs as the treatment progresses, just in case some feature is only revealed for a short while during the process.

Wood and metal parts are common finds in shipwrecks, so the techniques for conserving these materials are better established. The expansion caused by the hydration of the salts as they penetrate into metal hastens the corrosion process. At the bottom of the sea, electrochemical reactions can also make the surrounding water strongly acidic, accelerating the corrosion of metal. Pennec says that the electrochemical corrosion of iron can push the pH down to 2.5 in the surrounding water. The remedy is to put the parts in an alkali. Sodium compounds are used to help extract chloride ions, and copper parts are treated with a mixture of sodium bicarbonate and sodium carbonate—baking soda and washing soda.

The French conservators are treating some iron parts from the *Titanic's* engines in a tank of dilute caustic soda—sodium hydroxide. They monitor the concentration of chloride ions to determine when the solution is exhausted. It usually takes about two weeks for the concentration of chloride ions in the solution to stop rising, which means it is time to replace the solution with fresh caustic soda. Conservation is a process that requires considerable patience. "Some parts can take up to four years to be treated," Pennec says.

Wood is vulnerable to attack by bacteria which degrade the cellulose. The lignins in the wood remain, so wooden parts may look deceptively sturdy when they first come out of the water. But drying them would be fatal: with the cellulose gone, they would shrink catastrophically, or even fall apart. So the conservators replace the missing cellulose in the wood by impregnating it with a 5 per cent solution of polyethylene glycol. The liquid diffuses into the wood, restoring much of its structural strength. "Once you have a reasonable amount of impregnation you can dry it," say MacLeod.

Some objects have survived more or less intact. Others are so severely corroded that only parts remain. MacLeod says that a lot depends on the microenvironment in which the object has spent its time at the bottom of the sea—whether it is partially immersed in mud, and how close it is to other corroding objects.

What is destroyed and what survives is sometimes a matter of luck. In general, wooden remains have not survived as well as metal ones. But there are exceptions. One of these is a Gladstone bag that had contained some carpentry tools, including a hammer. Only the hammer's wooden handle remains; the metal head has completely vanished.

Silver Lining

There is a pair of EPNS side dishes at LP3's laboratory, both stamped underneath with the distinctive mark of the White Star Line. When they were new they were doubtless virtually identical, and one is still in its pristine state. But the other is heavily corroded, and the silver has almost vanished. Corroded cooper is all that remains. It is difficult to believe that they ever looked alike.

Modern composite materials such as EPNS are particularly prone to electrochemical corrosion, because once they are in the seawater the metal parts can create an electric cell. Copper alloys cause the most trouble, says Pennec. "Sometimes the plate silver is the only thing that keeps the object together."

Scientific interest apart, the *Titanic* has yielded a wealth of fascinating ephemera. Among the objects found in the wreck is a Southampton newspaper, published the day before the *Titanic* sailed. Like local newspapers to this day, it has its share of court reports. One concerns John Dixon of no fixed abode, who was charged with stealing a handbag. Dixon had come over from Belfast as a fireman's assistant on the *Titanic*, and the court appearance meant that he missed the chance of sailing to America. As the magistrate sentenced him to 14 days' hard labour, he couldn't have known what a lucky break it was.

Source: Mick Hamer, "Priceless Legacy of the *Titanic*," *New Scientist* 1 (October 1994): 23–25.

EXERCISES: READING AND RESPONDING

1. What is Hamer's purpose in writing this article?
2. How can you tell that Hamer assumes readers will be familiar with the sinking of the *Titanic*? What other assumptions do you think Hamer might have about readers' knowledge of restoration of artifacts?
3. How does Hamer make his topic interesting and relevant to readers?
4. How does Hamer occasionally help his readers understand a term or a difficult concept? Cite an example.
5. At various points in his article, Hamer focuses on passengers' personal effects or their personal stories. He reminds readers that some objects are "full of pathos," or feelings of emotion and sympathy. Why do you think Hamer includes this focus on people in an article that examines a shipwreck as a "valid corrosion experiment"?
6. Who does Hamer cite as an authority on restoration of artifacts?

7. Hamer gives readers some idea of the difficulty of restoring artifacts recovered from a shipwreck. What are the main challenges scientists face recovering wood, paper, and metal?

8. Hamer's article does not mention an important issue: the ethics of reclaiming artifacts from a shipwreck that survives as a grave or memorial to the individuals who lost their lives on the *Titanic*. Should these artifacts be made available for public display? Would this issue be of interest primarily to scholars in the sciences? social scientists? humanities? Explain your response.

LEARNING ABOUT DIFFERENT DISCOURSE COMMUNITIES

One way to learn about various discourse communities is to "listen" to their conversations. The following exercise asks you to listen to scholars and professionals discuss their areas of expertise. To complete this exercise, you'll need an e-mail address.

EXERCISES: READING AND RESPONDING

1. To complete either one of the following two assignments, you should begin at least three weeks before it is due.

   - Subscribe to one of the scholarly and professional electronic conferences that discusses a research project you will complete this term.
   - Subscribe to a scholarly or professional conference that discusses a topic that pertains to the major you intend to pursue.

   HOW TO SUBSCRIBE: Using one of the search engines on the World Wide Web, find the *Directory of Scholarly and Professional E-Conferences*. Follow directions on the page to read the "Subject/Category Listing," a subject-based list of scholarly and professional e-conferences. Click on a heading—for example, *Linguistics and Textual Analysis* or *Literature*. The next page will list abbreviations for conferences. These conferences are discourse communities. Some of their abbreviations will be obvious (for example, ISHMAIL-L discusses the character in *Moby Dick*); some will be clever (HOUNDS-L discusses Sherlock Holmes); and some will be a mystery until you check them out (ACL-L is a discussion list for autograph collectors). Click on the abbreviations to find an explanation of the purpose of the conference. After you have found a conference that interests you, jot down the subscription address. Go back to the first page and look for directions for subscribing to the conference.

   After you have subscribed, you will receive e-mail from the discussion group or listserv participants. There is no way to predict the amount of e-mail you will receive. After two or three days, if discussion is minimal or nonexistent, you may want to try another conference.

After you subscribe and begin receiving e-mail, lurk—that is, read the postings on the list and take notes for a week. You do not have to participate in the discussion, unless you want to do so. And you do not have to print out copies of daily postings.

2. In a letter or memo to your instructor, identify the conference you have selected and explain why you have selected it. Identify any topics you expect the conference to discuss.

   After you have subscribed for at least a week, you should be familiar enough with the conference to analyze the discussion. Answer the following questions. You will use your answers in the second writing assignment.

   a. Who participates in the conference? students? college professors? people who regard the subject of the conference as a special interest? people who consider the subject of the conference related to their profession? (The discussion and signature lines will help you determine who is participating.)

   b. Summarize the major topics of discussion you listened to.

   c. How formal or informal are postings?

   d. If participants used terms that are new to you, provide a few examples. How did you determine the definition of these terms?

   e. Do participants refer frequently to books, journals, or newspapers? If so, what are some of the titles mentioned?

   f. If the discussion led you to web pages, explain how the web pages helped you to understand the discourse community you selected.

   g. What have you learned from the e-mail conference about the project you are working on or the major you plan on pursuing?

   h. Explain why you would or would not recommend this conference to other students with interests similar to yours.

EXERCISE: THINKING CRITCALLY

Submit a report to your instructor that explains the purpose of the conference you subscribed to, provides a profile of the people participating in the conference, and summarizes threads of discussion you listened to. Evaluate the conference you joined:

1. Was it worth the time you devoted to reading e-mail from participants? Why or why not?

2. What kind of information should one expect from this group? Was this what you got?

3. Were there threads of conversation that you found inappropriate or frivolous? Did participants drift off the topic?

4. Did you learn anything from subscribing to this conference?

Chapter 2

Understanding Writing as Process

"… most learning is not linear."
— *Mary Catherine Bateson*. Peripheral Vision.

WRITING—A RECURSIVE ACTIVITY

Imagine a relay race that never stops. The last runner carries the baton across the finish line only to pass it off again to the person who runs the first leg of the relay. The sequence of one runner handing the baton to another occurs over and over. The runners aren't concerned with outrunning other teams or beating the clock. For this relay team, the goal is to practice connecting with each other. Style and technique are important in those split seconds when one runner passes the baton to another. The handoff is a continuous activity repeated over and over. This kind of practice helps the team work as one, connecting smoothly and quickly with one another as they run around the track. Eventually, our imaginary relay team would be in excellent condition and in sync with one another— ready for a real race.

Now, imagine that you have a writing assignment and two weeks to complete it. Do you start at the last minute—the night before—and work until the paper is due? Or do you start early and take the paper through a sequence of steps that allows you to draft and revise, develop and refine ideas? If you start at the last minute, you're following a process that's similar to the relay race that has runners moving as quickly as possible from the starting block to the finish line. If you start early and take a paper through multiple drafts, you're following a process similar to our imaginary relay team. Your recursive activities—drafting and revising, developing ideas and refining how you express them—are a kind of practice that allows you to prepare a draft to hand in for evaluation. You go through a variety of stages, passing a kind of mental baton to yourself over and over as you develop a topic, organize your ideas, and draft different versions, revising and editing as you work. Your ultimate goal is to have a good paper to hand in; however, you understand that you don't do your best writing when your primary concern is to write a paper as quickly as possible. You understand that you have a better chance of doing your best writing if you allow time for reflection and self-evaluation. You understand writing as process. Your experience as a writer has taught you that writing is a recursive activity, a series of thought processes that are repeated a number of times, but not always sequentially: brainstorming, drafting, developing and organizing ideas, adjusting content and form to a specific audience's needs and expectations, revising, and editing.

Mary Catherine Bateson, professor of anthropology and English, theorizes that while we often present learning as linear in the classroom, learning is like a spiral or a recycling of perceptions, memories, and new information. The writing process is similar: It is not linear. We often present it as linear: prewriting activities—rough drafts—final copies, but we know that writing is a circular activity. As we write, we return to ideas to expand them, revise them, or delete them. This process is a kind of mental recycling. In general we can say that the writing process involves the following activities:

- Developing a topic or an idea (generating ideas for something to write about)
- Investigating a topic (reading, thinking, or talking about a subject)
- Shaping and organizing information (formulating a thesis, developing paragraphs, organizing a paper)
- Reflecting and rethinking
- Revising and editing information (reconsidering, changing, and correcting what you have written)

When you write, you move from one activity to another. For example, as you write a sentence, you also revise and edit it. You work with several versions of the sentence before you're satisfied with it. Or as you generate ideas for a paragraph, you think of a related idea you want to include. Your new idea calls for reorganizing your paper and for changes in the way you conclude the paper.

Experienced writers understand that writing is a highly complex activity. It's not an efficient process. It takes blocks of time—how much usually varies from one individual to another. It's not a process that you can shut on and off easily. You can be completely stumped, at a loss for ideas or words one minute, and writing frantically the next, trying to record ideas that flow quickly through your mind. As you read in Chapter 1, writing involves reading skills—reading other writers' ideas and writing about them as well as reading your own writing with a critical eye—and critical thinking skills. Experienced writers know that writing need not be a solitary process. It requires internalizing ideas and finding a voice to express them in an appropriate manner. At various stages a writer needs to work alone, but the entire writing process doesn't have to be a solitary activity done in a vacuum. You'll find that you get good results when you view writing as a social activity, a conversation between a writer and an intended group of readers. Usually your writing is enriched by those occasions that allow you to bounce ideas off of peers or to discuss writing and how to improve it with your instructor.

The title of Ringo Starr's 1971 post-Beatles hit describes the writing process for most of us: "It Don't Come Easy." With practice and an understanding of your own writing process, writing doesn't have to be an insurmountable task.

DEVELOPING IDEAS

Sitting idly and waiting for the Muse to visit and inspire is an approach to writing you want to avoid. As a rule, the Muse won't visit. When you have a writing assignment, take the active approach: Write to discover and develop ideas.

Topic Development

If you've experienced the complete absence of ideas when you start a writing assignment—commonly called *writer's block*—you probably wished for some kind of apparatus that could get the writing process started—like a set of jumper cables that fire up a car battery. Finding a topic to write about can be just as frustrating as being told that you have to write about a specific topic. Given free rein, writers usually want to write about topics they find interesting or that they think their readers will find interesting. Topic development can range from a Eureka moment—*Aha! I know exactly what I want to write about!*—to considering and rejecting any number of topics before you find something that suits you. You can develop topics out of your personal experience, interests, and activities, starting with issues that are important to you. For example, if you're interested in music, collecting, sports, film, theatre, or other hobbies or areas of special interest, you can go to the library or get on the Internet and do research for topic development. Either way, free choice or mandated topic, you need strategies for developing ideas. Your first consideration should be your purpose in writing. What does your assignment ask you to do? Will you write to express your ideas? inform your readers? persuade your readers? Your second consideration should be drafting—getting words on paper (or the computer screen).

Brainstorming

If a writing assignment leaves topic development up to you, try brainstorming, making a list of topics you find interesting and appropriate for the assignment. Storms are systems that generate a good deal of atmospheric activity. Your *brainstorms* should generate a list of a minimum of 5 to 10 topics. Write down whatever comes to mind. For an assignment that asks you to write an argumentative paper about an ethical issue, a brainstorming session yields the following:

Ethical issues

1. Subliminal messages in advertising
2. Politicians accepting campaign contributions from lobbyists
3. Animal experimentation
4. Late-term abortions
5. School vouchers

You can brainstorm on your own or with a friend or a group of writers. Working with other writers, you'll find brainstorming a highly productive collaborative activity because one person's suggestions trigger ideas from someone else. The case studies in Part Two include "Brainstorming" exercises. They begin with a list of topics and ask you to add your own ideas.

EXERCISE: COLLABORATING WITH YOUR PEERS

Expand the list of ethical issues to include ten possible topics. For further practice, brainstorm on local issues of interest to you and your classmates.

Narrowing a Topic

The list generated by the brainstorming session on ethical issues is a place to start, but the topics are too general. Inexperienced writers often begin writing assignments with topics that are so broad or general that they need to be narrowed in scope. There's nothing wrong with starting out with a general topic, but you don't want to stay with a general topic too long. Typically, the broader the topic, the more general a paper will be. With a narrowed topic, you have focus and direction as a writer and you are more likely to select sources that will help you develop specific ideas. Too often the process of narrowing a topic is presented as linear. For example, a broad topic, *education*, is narrowed to *computers in education* and finally narrowed further to *computers in elementary school math classes*. The example is orderly, clear, and neat. It illustrates, to some extent, what happens when a writer narrows a topic; however, the example doesn't illustrate the thought process the writer experienced in arriving at a narrowed topic. You don't see versions of the topic the writer revised or choices the writer rejected. And you have no idea of the internal dialogue that went on in the writer's mind as he or she shaped and narrowed the topic.

Think of narrowing a topic as both exploration of a topic and a kind of mental whittling—going from general to specific and developing a focused topic. Censorship, for example, is a broad topic. Think of it as an umbrella. There are several narrowed topics under the umbrella of censorship—censorship of music, literature, television programming, movies, textbooks, radio broadcasts, or government documents. With broad or general topics, two strategies will help you narrow a topic so that it will be manageable.

Asking Questions

Suppose you knew you wanted to write about censorship. Try asking and answering questions that come to mind. In this way, you can explore a topic, identify a specific example or issue related to censorship, and, at the same time, develop your perspective on the topic. Asking *who, what, where, when,* and *why* questions is another strategy:

Who advocates censorship?

Who opposes censorship?

What are some common forms of censorship?

What are my perspectives on censorship?

What kinds of censorship concern me?

What kinds of censorship have been discussed in the news most recently?

What kinds of censorship have I witnessed firsthand?

Where has censorship occurred?

When has censorship occurred?

Why do people believe we need censorship? Why do people oppose censorship?

The idea is to brainstorm and explore what you know. Work on questions and answers on your own, jotting down whatever comes to mind or ask a friend to help you brainstorm. If you don't know much about your potential topic, you might need to do a little reading before you formulate questions and answers. Yes/no answers will help you determine your stance on a topic. But try to elaborate. As you explore different aspects of a topic, you're more likely to narrow its scope.

Clustering

Another way to explore and narrow a topic is clustering. Figure 2.1 (see page 64) illustrates how Amy used clustering to develop a topic for an argumentative paper on a topic of her choice. A nutrition major, Amy consulted sources in newspapers and popular magazines. Then she brainstormed before she started reading about her topic in scholarly and specialized publications. She started with the topic in the middle, obesity. The clusters she drew on paper helped her determine the subtopics in this general topic. By exploring a topic in this manner, Amy began to see ways to focus on one particular aspect of obesity. After reading about the topic, she started drafting a tentative thesis.

EXERCISE: COLLABORATING WITH YOUR PEERS

Working in pairs or in groups, identify a local topic that will be familiar to your classmates. Complete a clustering exercise for this topic. Be prepared to identify a narrowed topic when you finish this exercise.

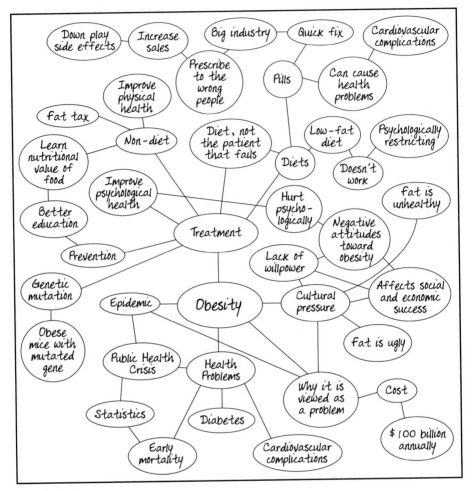

FIGURE 2.1

Drafting and Revising

At the heart of writing as process is drafting and revising. Multiple drafts provide opportunities for writers to refine, rethink, and reorder ideas; to work on word choice and sentence variety; to improve introductions and conclusions; and to make sure the paper meets the needs of the intended readers and the requirements of an assignment. When you revise a draft, you find new ways to present ideas: You add information, delete passages that don't say what you want to say, and revamp the paper any way you can. Don't make the mistake of thinking that drafting and revising is busy work. It's the only way for writers to practice.

If you hear classmates boast of writing one draft, turning it in, and receiving a premium grade on a paper, ignore the claim. The person who makes this claim either overstates the truth a bit or fails to admit being a much more accomplished writer than anyone realizes. The one-draft only paper is not the best route to follow—mainly because it's usually a discovery draft. You want to progress from the discovery stage to drafts that organize and shape ideas. The more time you devote to preliminary drafts and writing that allows you to work out what you know about a topic, the more likely you are to write a paper that—at some point in the drafting process—makes that important leap from being egocentric to conscious of other readers. Early drafts give you a foundation to build on—to discover what you know, where there are gaps in development of ideas, where logic gives way to skewed reasoning or logical fallacies, where formulaic writing becomes apparent, where style is effective or ineffective, and—most important—where you succeed or fall short in audience awareness. Experienced writers will attest to the importance of revising after they have been away from the draft for a few days. Distance gives you a perspective on your own writing you may not have when you are pushing to meet a deadline and having a finished product is foremost in your mind.

If you're resistant to the idea of taking a paper through multiple drafts, think about trying to play a musical instrument—violin, for example. The novice violinist occasionally creates sounds that make your hair stand on end. It's difficult to hit all the right notes and to keep the bow from screeching across the strings. With practice, the sour notes diminish and the music is consistently harmonious. But it's a long road from playing the instrument for the first time to playing first chair in the symphony. Practice is to the musician as drafting is to the writer.

Freewriting

Freewriting is writing for a set period of time—15 to 20 minutes, let's say—without interruption. You write without interruption and without pausing to reflect, revise, or correct what you've written. Your aim is to get as many ideas down on paper as possible without concern for how your ideas are expressed, spelling, or punctuation. You can freewrite to develop a topic or to explore ideas once you've selected a topic.

Freewriting is a way to get started—a good strategy for working out what you know and feel about a topic or for gaining an understanding of your stance on an issue. It allows you to generate ideas in their rawest form. For example, if you're required to write on how the media influenced the 2000 national elections, you devote 15 to 20 minutes to a freewriting exercise. You write whatever comes to mind—examples you're familiar with, questions you have about the topic, your stance on the topic. Anything goes as long as you keep writing. Your goal is to generate ideas. Your freewriting exercise can take the form of a letter to yourself or a friend if you wish, a journal entry, or it can be without any form at all—a record of your ideas that starts at the top of one page and ends on another. You are the audience for a freewriting exercise. Your instructor may see it, but it won't be graded for content, organization, and style.

Freewriting is a valuable option for writers because it provides a place for ideas to germinate. If writer's block sets in, try freewriting. Or use it as a warm-up activity, a way to ease into sitting down and drafting any part of a paper.

Discovery Drafts

After you've completed a freewriting exercise, a discovery draft takes you to the next level. It's the first swing at writing a paper that looks like a paper, complete with introduction, body, and conclusion. It's also a transition from writing without constraints, as you did in the freewriting exercise, to writing with concern for organizational matters and coherent content. While secondary readers may examine your freewriting or discovery drafts, they won't expect the polish of a draft that's been through multiple revisions.

In a discovery draft, you should feel free to rely on first person pronouns, clichés, generalizations, and unsubstantiated assertions. You don't want to rely on these devices in subsequent drafts, but in what is essentially the very first draft, when your aim is to get ideas down on paper, relying on these devices is understandable. To some extent you are the primary intended reader for this draft. One of your goals in subsequent drafts will be to identify and revise the clichés, generalizations, and unsubstantiated claims and to start thinking about your intended readers. But in this early stage, you shouldn't expect your draft to be as specific and well-thought out as it will be after drafting and revising several times.

Writers frequently find a tentative thesis at the end of a discovery draft. In other words, they start out with a generic statement, a fill-in-the-blank sentence: For example, *The 2000 presidential election was a significant event* (_____ was a significant event). You could use any number of events in the sentence. The discovery draft gives you a chance to articulate reasons why the event was significant. It should give you ideas for adding a *because* clause to your generic statement. If your discovery draft focuses on the lawsuits filed as both sides protested the election, expand your generic statement to indicate why these events were noteworthy: *The 2000 presidential election was a significant event because of the Supreme Court's involvement.* If your draft focuses on other reasons as well, look for the strongest points in the draft—the ideas you develop more than others.

If you have a thesis in mind when you start a writing project, use your discovery draft to determine what kind of support you have for it. Did you have difficulty developing any paragraphs? Are underdeveloped paragraphs clearly related to your thesis? Do they develop relevant material? Do they develop interesting information that isn't essential for your purpose in writing? In Chapter 3, you'll read more about developing a thesis and organizing ideas. The discovery draft gives you a strategy for generating ideas that will help you find your stance on a topic.

Organizing and Shaping Ideas

In a coherent well-organized paper, ideas flow smoothly and logically. The pattern of organization—general-to-specific or specific-to-general, least-important-to-most-important or most-important-to-least-important—helps the writer explain ideas or advance an argument. Effective organization is like invisible glue. While content and style may initially grab readers' attention, when they analyze how a writer accomplished his or her purpose effectively, they find that effective organizational patterns bring the ideas together in a manner that makes the writing interesting and accessible. When a writer's ideas are haphazard and rambling, readers tend to give up or finish a paper, questioning the writer's credibility.

One of your primary considerations as you draft your paper will be deciding how your paper will be organized. Try to avoid formulaic writing—writing that follows predictable patterns of organization. You're probably familiar with prescribed approaches to writing an essay—the old formula that dictates where you place your thesis, how many body paragraphs a paper should have, and even how many sentences make up a paragraph. Prescribed formulas help inexperienced writers learn how to organize ideas. At the college level, writers are expected to move beyond this approach.

Patterns of Organization

When you work on organization, think about your readers. As you revise and draft a paper, you become immersed in your topic. You shouldn't expect your intended readers to have the same understanding. You have to present your ideas in a manner that makes ideas easy to follow. The patterns of organization writers most frequently employ in academic writing include the following:

- *Spatial order*: Presenting information in a manner that allows the reader to visualize it—for example, describing your dorm room or a place you enjoy on campus. Details help readers see the place as you see it. Use spatial order if your purpose in writing is to describe a place to your readers.

- *Logical order*: Presenting information in patterns—for example, citing examples, comparing and contrasting, classifying, defining, looking at cause and effect, or offering a narrative. When you write to inform or to persuade, these patterns will help your readers follow unfamiliar ideas and concepts.

- *Chronological order*: Presenting information in a manner that describes a sequence of events—for example, explaining the series of events that took place in England in 1605 that led to celebrating November 5 as Guy Fawkes Day. Chronological order helps readers understand what happened.

As you work on organization, use the informal outline, a numbered or bulleted list, as a place to brainstorm. It allows you to practice ordering information any number of ways and acts as a blueprint if you have to stop mid-draft and return to drafting several hours or days later. Usually the informal outline is cryptic—helpful to the writer, but not to another reader. The informal outline in the next section is an example.

Outlines

As a rule, writers don't like to develop the formal outline. If you're required to develop one, you'll probably do it after you've written your paper. This kind of outline can be most helpful, though. It gives you a way to see how you developed ideas.

Roman and arabic numerals indicate new but related ideas and, within each idea, levels of generalization:

I. Early impostors in Texas
    A. The one who got away: The Great Impostor, Ferdinand Demara
    B. Impostors Revealed
        1. The circus impostor
        2. The bridegroom
II. Recent impostors
    A. In law enforcement
    B. In sports

A formal outline can help you determine whether your development of ideas is extensive or superficial. Use it to examine levels of generalization—the detail and examples you provide to support main ideas. The outline won't tell you if a paper is rhetorically effective, but it will serve as a check on how general or specific the paper is.

Reflecting on Your Writing

If you've looked around a classroom during a timed writing exercise, you'll notice that writers pause periodically and then return to writing. During those pauses, writers often reflect on what they've written, reviewing their ideas and evaluating them at the same time. When you reflect on your writing, you describe and evaluate it. Describing may be as simple as saying, "I've written three drafts and I have an introduction which includes a thesis and five paragraphs, each with topic sentences, to support the thesis. I have a working title, but no idea what to do for a conclusion. My paper cites specific examples." Or your description may indicate that you've drafted an introductory paragraph and two body paragraphs, but you haven't decided where to place the thesis. Review of your progress helps you think about the status of a writing project—what you've done and what still needs to be done. If you've set aside blocks of time to work on writing assignments, spaced out over a two-week period, reflecting on what you've done is a good way to start your work, to get your mind on writing if you've been working on other subjects. Your reflection can also take the form of a memo or e-mail to your instructor describing your progress on a paper. Sometimes instructors make these updates mandatory. Your instructor will appreciate receiving specific information. He or she will appreciate your evaluation of your progress, too.

You'll read about evaluating your own writing in Chapter 4. Most writers agree that being your own best critic is a skill you have to develop, just like reading skills and effective writing skills. In the simplest terms, evaluating your own writing calls for you to read and recognize the strengths and weaknesses of a paper.

Collaborating with Others

This chapter starts out encouraging you to work with your peers whenever the opportunity presents itself. Most writers find the exchange of ideas at various points in the writing process helpful and cathartic. Collaboration gives you the chance to bounce ideas around with other people—your roommate, a close friend, your instructor, or a writing center consultant, for example. Most importantly, collaboration places you in the position of articulating your ideas about your writing. Your instructor can probably cite examples of students coming to the office for a conference and on their own working out whatever problem they seemed to be experiencing in their writing just by talking about it. Collaboration calls for you to take an active role. You have to be prepared to talk about your writing, to share a sample of it, and to make decisions about suggestions and recommendations of your collaborators. Quite simply, you're free to accept or reject them.

Peer Review

As a general rule, collaboration is beneficial at any stage of the writing process. Peer review—sharing drafts of your papers with two or three of your classmates—is a widely practiced collaborative activity in composition classes. You're probably familiar with it already. Chapter 4 provides tips on how to best evaluate the work of your peers. The number one requirement is to take peer review seriously and provide each other with as much constructive criticism as possible.

To help your peers review your paper, try including brief notes in the margins. To provide room for your notes and feedback from your peers, you'll need to allow for wider margins than you usually use—at least an inch and $^1/_4$ on each side. The text will look strange and you'll use more paper than you will in the final draft, but with the wide margins, you and your peers have room to work. When you include notes, you annotate your own text. Your remarks can be as simple as *I need ideas for a transition here* to a longer observation that points out a problem with developing ideas or a note commenting on a passage that establishes audience awareness. The main point here is to make peer review a conversation about writing from the beginning—on paper and in writing groups.

Writing Groups

Writing groups are usually made up of three or four students who work together throughout the semester. Sometimes instructors allot a certain amount of time at each class meeting for writing groups to touch base with each other and brainstorm or talk about research, audience analysis, drafting, revising, or anything else associated with their writing. If all group members have e-mail addresses, the group can hold virtual meetings, too. If you've participated in a writing group, you're familiar with the helpful ideas and general support it provides. If you aren't familiar with this kind of group work, discussing your writing and reviewing drafts, you'll find it a valuable resource. If your instructor doesn't make arrangements for writing groups, try organizing one on your own.

Writing Portfolios

One way to demonstrate your understanding of writing as process is to develop a writing portfolio, a collection of the papers you've completed during the semester accompanied by the drafts, outlines, notes, and copies of any sources you've consulted. Typically, portfolio assignments ask writers to select two or three papers to be graded out of a total of five or six. The papers that aren't graded are an important part of the portfolio, though. Usually, a cover memo explains the writer's choices—why selected papers illustrate effective writing skills and why certain papers weren't chosen for evaluation, for example. The writing portfolio includes additional writing about writing. For example, memos in which the writer discusses some aspect of the writing process accompany each paper. These memos will address any number of topics—for example, why the writer selected a topic, difficulties in writing the paper, audience analysis, or strengths and weaknesses of the paper. The writer could also explain how a paper meets an assignment or how the paper takes a familiar topic but presents it in a unique way. Composition programs in colleges and universities have embraced writing portfolios because they provide evidence of writers developing and improving writing skills over the course of the semester. They also give writers a way to showcase their work.

You have to consider presentation when you submit a portfolio. Three-ring notebooks or accordion files with individual folders for each writing assignment are two common ways of organizing a portfolio. You can even have your work spiral bound. Whatever format you choose, you'll need a cover page, a table of contents, and a cover memo explaining why you've selected certain assignments for evaluation and why you decided not to have other assignments evaluated. You'll also have to decide how you want to organize the portfolio. Here is another project that calls for audience analysis. How will someone read your portfolio? You'll have to decide if you want to start with the final draft of a paper and include preliminary drafts in the order they were written or if you'll use the preliminary drafts to preface the final draft. This chapter ends with a paper that was part of a student's course portfolio. The paper, worksheets, drafts, and peer review evaluations illustrate the kinds of documents writers usually include in a portfolio.

THINKING ABOUT YOUR WRITING PROCESS

Understanding your own writing process is one of the first steps in developing effective writing skills. On those occasions when writing is by necessity a solitary activity with time constraints (for example, timed writing or essay exams), our experiences with writing as process provide us with strategies for drafting, revising, and self-critique. Because you've been writing since you were in elementary school, you probably take how you write for granted, giving it little thought because it's just something you do—like riding a bicycle or skating. When you understand your writing process, you develop a sense of the amount of time you require to take a paper written outside of class through multiple drafts. Drafting and revising, most experienced writers will tell you, are the ways to improve your writing. Both take time, but, of course, developing any skill takes time.

Scheduling Time for Writing

Our discussion of writing as a recursive activity didn't touch on meeting due dates. Try as we may to depart from presenting writing as linear, due dates enter the conversation and force us to impose linear constraints. You receive a writing assignment on Monday and it's due in three weeks. How do you pace yourself? If you have no idea how long it will take to get started, how do you block out your time? The answer is simple: You plan ahead.

Working with a daily planner, an electronic calendar, or a sheet of paper with grids drawn to indicate seven days in a week and a time frame of roughly 8:00 A.M. to midnight, sit down and plan a writing schedule. Start with at least four two-hour blocks during the first week and make a commitment to devote these blocks of time to your writing assignment. Plan the second and third week as well, again designating three two-hour blocks for writing. Include in your schedule dates when you have peer review or some other assignment connected to your paper due—for example, an exercise on developing your thesis or an informal outline. Then set goals for yourself. Record a date for completing a discovery draft and dates for arranging a conference with your instructor or visiting a writing center, if your college or university has one. This kind of organization is the first step in a disciplined approach to writing. Take your schedule as seriously as you would a commitment to other activities you have on a daily or weekly basis.

Writing and Technology

Academic work usually calls for assignments written in class. Unless you're in a computer classroom, you'll complete them the old-fashioned way—with pen or pencil and paper. When you write outside of class, you'll have the choice of writing in longhand or using a computer. You've probably developed a preference for one or the other. Both have advantages and drawbacks. For example, computer programs offer writers time-saving conveniences, especially the ability to cut and paste in the drafting stage. They also offer spell check and grammar check programs that help you edit as you write and programs that help with word choice, much like a thesaurus, offering a list of synonyms for a word you've hightlighted. You don't want to rely on these programs blindly. For example, a spell-check program will help you edit your work, but it won't catch word confusion (*their/there*; *it's/its*; *seam/seem*). And grammar check often marks a sentence as *long sentence* without indicating whether there's a specific error in the sentence or whether it's simply beyond a set word count. Whether you write in longhand or on a computer, you'll need to develop an eye for editing your own work.

At the same time that computers simplify our lives, they can complicate them, too. The old excuse for a late paper used to be *The dog ate my homework*. The new excuse is *My computer ate my paper*—or any number of variations: *My printer ran out of paper/toner* or *My computer crashed, I forgot to make a back-up copy*. When you draft papers on a computer, you'll need to save your work periodically in order to have copies that show how your paper developed. Back up your files. Develop the habit of keeping copies of your work on disk to back up whatever you have on your hard drive.

A good argument for planning ahead and trying to complete a paper in advance of a due date is to allow time for computer glitches or printer problems. If you're cutting it close, invariably whatever can go wrong will go wrong. As you think about your own writing process, consider the role technology plays in it and how well prepared you are to provide your own technological support.

Creating a Writing Environment

You'll need a comfortable place to write—stocked with the supplies writers use: pen, pencil, notepads (small and large), computer disks, reference books (dictionary, thesaurus, handbook), and good lighting. Your preferences may include music, snacks, and a comfortable chair. If your college or university makes computer labs available to students, pack the things that create your ideal writing environment in your backpack or book bag. Include change for a snack or coffee break. And if you have to share space with other writers, be considerate of their needs.

INTERVIEW WITH THREE WRITERS

For each individual, the writing process is as individualized as a fingerprint or a signature. What works for one—physical surroundings, time of day, drafting in longhand, drafting on the computer—doesn't necessarily work for another.

THINKING CRITICALLY ABOUT YOUR WRITING PROCESS

Start now to think about your individual writing process. Your writing process is similar to your reading process in being earmarked by individual preferences for times and places and accessories. As you complete assignments in this chapter, try to become aware of the factors that facilitate your writing process when you write from sources. Think about

1. where and when you write,

2. whether you draft in long hand or on a word processor,

3. what makes you comfortable when you write,

4. how you organize your ideas,

5. how many drafts you would expect to write,

6. whether you revise alone or ask other people to read your paper and make suggestions for revision, and

7. how much time you would need to devote to this assignment.

Interviews with three student writers illustrate this point. Meredith is a senior in high school; Scott is enrolled in a midsize private university; and Meghan attends a large public university. Scott is a junior business major, and Meghan is a senior majoring in public relations. As you will see, all three students are aware of writing as process and their own strengths and weaknesses as writers. Read their responses and be prepared to share your answers to the interview questions.

1. *Do you enjoy writing?*

    MEREDITH: Not really.

    SCOTT: Yes, more in a creative way than for assignments.

    MEGHAN: I enjoy writing if the subject interests me. There are assignments that seem to drag out that are not interesting and, therefore, are difficult to write. In general, I do enjoy writing. I prefer creative writing. As far as media writing is concerned, since that is what I've been studying for three years, I enjoy writing feature stories more than press releases. There is an aspect of creative writing that has to be implemented into feature stories that allows more freedom when you write.

2. *Do you consider yourself a confident writer?*

    MEREDITH: No. Because I don't like to write very much. I'm always concerned that it isn't good enough or that I could word it a different way.

    SCOTT: To a degree. I'm more confident after I've had other people look at my writing.

    MEGHAN: Yes, I consider myself a confident writer. One reason is that I have made excellent grades in writing all through school, including college. I enjoy writing on subjects that interest me. I tend to do better work than I do if I have to write on a boring subject.

3. *Would you rather write with pencil/pen and paper or on a computer? Explain why you favor one over the other.*

    MEREDITH: I prefer to write on a word processor because I tend to type faster than I write. It also means that anything I write is not set in stone and can be changed by the click of a button. I also like to have the automatic spell check.

    SCOTT: I prefer writing on a computer. I rarely make a very rough outline on paper before I begin to type on the computer. I favor the computer because it is easier to look through, rework, and make necessary corrections than it is with pen and paper. The computer points out mistakes and offers suggestions, along with an easily accessible thesaurus as well. I start by getting the general idea typed out and then work back through and add body to it. With this process, a computer is more convenient for me.

    MEGHAN: I would prefer a word processor for things such as rough drafts and final drafts for papers. This way I can get something down, save it, and be able to go back and change any errors or ideas that I have. Pencil/pen and paper causes hand cramps and restricts you from being able to thoroughly examine what you have already written. You begin writing on paper in very legible handwriting, and then as the paper increases in length, it becomes more difficult to decipher what has been written because your hand is tired.

4. *How important are physical surroundings or the time of day to you as a writer? Describe the kinds of supplies you prefer having at hand and your optimum writing environment.*

MEREDITH: For me, physical surroundings and the time of day are very important. Plenty of paper (if a computer is not available) and a pencil are really all the supplies I need unless it is research I'm writing about. I also like to have plenty of food and drink available. I have to have something to keep my mind fresh and my eyes open.

SCOTT: Physical surroundings are somewhat important for me. The setting is much more important than the time of day. I am more likely to work at night, but that is due to convenience and time rather than preference. I like to type in my room, on my computer at my desk, because I can control the rest of my work environment. I will occasionally listen to music, but more often I like it to be quiet, so I can think more clearly. I like to have a notebook to write in, just in case any spur-of-the-moment ideas come to mind while I am typing, and other than that, research material rounds out all of the supplies I like to have on hand.

MEGHAN: The best time for me to write is at night. All I need are my notes and my computer. I like to procrastinate during the day, but I think better at night. As far as the importance of my physical surroundings are concerned, they are not that important to me. I can write during the day if absolutely necessary, but I can also find 150 things I would prefer to do during the day.

5. *Textbooks usually describe the writing process in linear terms: prewriting, writing, and revising. For a mid-length (5–8 pages typed) research assignment for any of the classes you're currently taking, describe what you would do in the prewriting stage. Assume that your intended readers are a group of college students and their instructors.*

MEREDITH: In the prewriting stage for a research paper, I would start by just simply taking notes on notebook paper, paraphrasing and documenting as I went. Then I would arrange the notes in the appropriate order and begin my first draft. Next, I would proofread it myself and make a few changes and then print out a second draft. I would have someone else read and proof the second draft. Finally, I would make the last changes and print out my final copy to turn in.

SCOTT: For the prewriting stage, I would start by looking for and collecting data and research information on the Internet. After finding plenty of sources, I begin to read through and label any relevant information with a "label" to help determine where it will fit into my paper. For instance, I would put everything that I title "general info" in the same paragraph. After this process, I begin to outline on the computer or on paper the overall organization of the research paper. After the layout is finished, I begin writing.

MEGHAN: I research my topic (including library visits, interviews, and the like) and then I sit in front of my computer and I write. I maintain that sitting in front of a computer and getting it done is the best route to take.

6. *Describe what kind of audience analysis you would do as you worked on writing assignments and explain how frequently you would consider your intended readers as you wrote.*

MEREDITH: Most of the writing that I do is for class and therefore is directed to the teacher. I haven't had much experience in writing for a particular audience.

SCOTT: Since most of my writing is done in the Business School, it is intended for a professional audience; therefore, I assume a formal format for my paper. In Freshman Composition, I would consider the audience when I first began to write and make sure that throughout the paper I kept the same format and formality.

MEGHAN: Being a PR (Public Relations) major, I would have to study the demographics of my audience in order to see what appeals to them. I have to consider my audience every time I write a speech, news release, feature story, or newsletter. I have to make sure not to use jargon that my audience wouldn't understand. I also have to be aware of things such as their interests, education, and general lifestyles. This sounds like a lot of things to consider, but audience analysis determines the path my writing takes.

7. *How do you develop a thesis statement? At what stage of the writing process do you develop it?*

MEREDITH: I usually won't have a complete thesis developed until closer to the end of my paper.

SCOTT: I generally try to develop my thesis statement in the prewriting stage of the writing process because it helps control and confine the direction of my paper. Usually in the revision stage of my paper I make sure that the paper is cohesive; if it isn't, I may fine-tune my thesis statement at this stage.

MEGHAN: I do not develop or even think about a thesis statement until the paper is written. In my limited experience, I have discovered that regardless if you have written a thesis or not, a paper can take on a life of its own. Therefore, the thesis is the last thing I do. (I wish I had learned that in school though. English teachers do not teach it that way.)

8. *Do you recommend annotating sources or making note cards? Explain why.*

MEREDITH: Annotating notes because note cards can be complicated if you forget to write a slug [bibliographical citation] or get them out of order. You spend more time trying to fix them than taking the notes.

SCOTT: I recommend annotating sources because that is the way all of the professors I have had in college have wanted me to do it. I also think that through annotation, you can keep the paper more organized, and it makes the writing process flow much easier. I personally do not use note cards very often for writing or studying, so annotation fits best with my writing preferences.

MEGHAN: I have never done note cards. I have somewhat of a photographic memory. Therefore, I rarely annotate unless something in my reading jumps out and grabs my attention. Then I see a reason to maybe summarize it in the margin. But, all things considered, I rely on highlighting and reading.

9. *For the assignment previously described, explain how you would organize your ideas.*

MEREDITH: I would probably just use bold headings and leave room to add things from other sources.

SCOTT: I would start by getting a general concept of what I want my introduction to say and portray. At the same time I would try to organize a thesis statement. Then I would follow by working on each paragraph in the body, getting the basic information in each paragraph. After working back through the body paragraphs, adding quotes and paraphrases, I would revise my paper and check the layout and organization. I like to write the conclusion last so I can include any information I run across in my revising process.

MEGHAN: I sit at my computer, brainstorm a little, jot down ideas on a blank sheet of paper as they come to me, and write down where the idea should be placed in the paper. One of the most common things PR practitioners do is write press releases. When you write a press release, organization is essential. This type of organizing calls for getting all the information needed to create an effective release and placing the facts in order from most important to least important. I have to go through the information and determine which facts will become summary lead statements (or the statement that tells the *who, what, where, when*, and *why*) and then the facts that will apply to the secondary details, and so on.

10. *At what point would you revise your paper?*

MEREDITH: After I complete the rough draft and before I have someone else edit it.

SCOTT: I revise my paper two or three times during the writing stage, first to see if the paper is organized the way I feel is most effective. I will revise it again later to see where information needs to be added or pulled from the paper. Towards the end of the writing process, I will revise it once more. After I have revised my paper, I take my paper to the Writing Center on campus or to someone I can trust to help me revise my paper and add any final suggestions.

MEGHAN: During the drafting and after it is written. I revise as I write. If something has been written three paragraphs ago and I get a brainstorm, I go back and work through it again.

11. *How do you differentiate revising from editing?*

MEREDITH: Revising is the process that I as the writer complete, making sure the paragraphs are in the right sequence and make sense and that my paper stays on track and relates to the thesis. Editing, on the other hand, is grammar: *Did I spell this word right? Is there supposed to be a comma there?*

SCOTT: I feel like revising is done over and over and helps you discern whether or not your paper is organized and flows well. Revising can be done after each stage of the writing process, whereas editing is done towards the end to correct grammatical and structural errors.

MEGHAN: I don't separate the two. I believe they are one in the same.

12. *What's the best advice about writing you've received? What's the best advice you would like to give to other college-level writers?*

MEREDITH: I guess the best advice I have received about writing is to keep an open mind about your topic. If you get boggled down, you can always take a different approach.

SCOTT: I think the best advise about writing I have received would be to stay focused on the main idea of the paper by working within the boundaries of the thesis statement. Therefore, I would tell students my age that a good thesis statement is the key to a good paper. The thesis needs to be short and to the point, but at the same time, it needs to encompass all the ideas expressed in the paper.

MEGHAN: The best advice I ever received on writing was, "Just get something down on paper, so then you can go back and revise as things come to you" and "Write your thesis after you write your body paragraphs." I would give other students the same advice. Actually, I do give my friends the same advice. It is not taught in school and I believe it in some ways hinders students not to know these simple tricks of the trade.

BECOMING AN ACTIVE WRITER

FOCUS ON STUDENT WRITING: Steffany's Writing Project

An example of student writing illustrates how one student used several of the strategies discussed in this chapter to draft and revise a paper. Steffany Fitzpatrick, a first-year composition student, developed a paper on the Firestone tire controversy in response to the following assignment. Steffany's reflections on the process of writing this paper are also included.

ASSIGNMENT: PAPER #1

OVERVIEW

Historically, rhetoric is a process of seeking the best "means of persuasion" to fit an audience and/or opponent. In modern times, rhetoric is often used to describe political propaganda and advertising pitches. This is appropriate, but limiting. Rhetoric has the larger purpose of using emotion, reason, and character to convince an audience of your perspective. During the course of the semester, you will accumulate skills and knowledge to help you write an argumentative research paper on a topic of your choosing. This first paper begins that process by asking you to research a current event or issue of your choice and write an essay that:

1. summarizes the event or issue
2. quotes the reactions and evaluations of popular and academic sources, and
3. states your response to all of the above.

Your aim is to inform your readers; however, your paper may have a persuasive edge if your summary and response encourage readers to rethink or reconsider their understanding of the event or issue you've discussed.

RHETORICAL SITUATION

Because it is necessary to learn the conventions of academic writing, your intended audience must be well-educated. Imagine that you are writing to a professor in an area related to your topic or that you're writing for publication in a scholarly journal.

INSTRUCTIONS

Select a topic. Be sure you have your instructor's approval. Find appropriate sources on your topic by doing research in the library and on the Web.

Read and annotate sources.

Complete assignments in and out of class that help you develop a draft for peer review.

Bring a draft to peer review and get comments from at least two of your peers.

Revise and edit your paper (local and global revision) and
  submit a draft to be graded.

Submit the paper and all supporting materials.

—Prompt developed by Jim Baker and Susan Murphy

This paper was the first of six papers Steffany wrote during the semester. She had three weeks to write this paper. The examples show the process Steffany followed to select a topic, determine what she wanted to say about it, analyze an audience, and revise her paper. The examples include exercises, drafts, copies of sources, and suggestions from peers. As you read these documents, think about the difference in the "one draft only" approach to writing and the multiple drafts and revision you see in Steffany's paper.

Developing a Topic

To begin this assignment, Steffany worked on a clustering exercise on another topic—student life, thinking she might write about students' rights, freedom of speech, or vandalism on campus. But after completing a freewriting exercise, she wasn't happy with these topics. By discussing her writing assignment with friends, she found a current topic she liked.

I sat down with my roommate and told her I needed a topic
for my first paper. Later, I was on the phone with my
boyfriend and I told him I was trying to come up with a
topic and he mentioned the tire recall that was making the
news. I knew the topic was too broad. I had to pick a side.
To me it wasn't right that Ford was being blamed. I talked
to my instructor and she helped me narrow the topic.

To develop ideas for her new topic, Steffany made up a list of five questions about her topic:

1. What exactly is wrong with the tires?
2. Why do they malfunction?
3. Why are only 15-inch tires being recalled?
4. What caused this particular set of tires to malfunction?
5. What is the process of the recall (refund, exchange)?

She also reflected on her reasons for selecting the topic:

I selected this topic because it involves people's safety.
These people could be my friends or family. I also want to
know how something like this could happen. It's important
to me because I'm tired of paying more for less.

Synthesizing Sources

Two of Steffany's sources are included here so that you can see how she annotated them and what kinds of choices she made as she synthesized sources in her paper. (See Figure 2.2 for example of on-line research)

```
I used one of the on-line search engines to investigate
the topic, and then I went to the library and the librar-
ians helped me do a search. They helped me use micro-
fiche. A few days later, I read an article in the campus
newspaper, and I decided to use it. I had trouble finding
academic sources because my topic was so recent. My
instructor suggested finding another similar situation. I
decided to compare the tire recall to the Tylenol recall.
I think this helped my paper.
```

After reading about her topic, Steffany thought about the different kinds of claims she might make in her paper:

```
1. Sixteen-inch tires should also be recalled because
   they were produced poorly just as the 15-inch
   tires were.

2. Firestone should compensate those people who own
   the tires and those who have damage as a result of
   the tires.

3. Sixteen-inch tires should not be recalled because the
   accidents and malfunctions reported are lower for the
   16-inch tires and higher for the 15-inch tires.
```

Drafting a Thesis

Steffany completed an exercise that helped her draft a tentative thesis. First, she wrote three versions of the thesis statement:

1. The fact that Firestone has recalled certain types of their tires does not ease the minds of the public.
2. The public is playing it safe by switching from Firestone tires to other brands, due to the recall.
3. Firestone's recall has the public worried about the safety of their current tires.

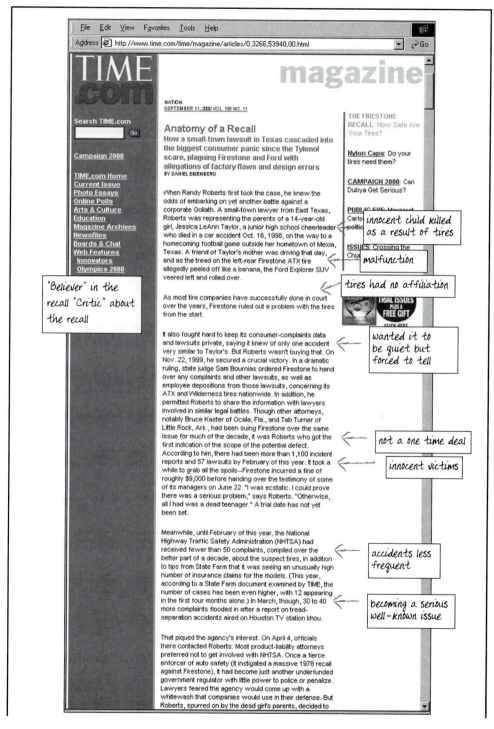

FIGURE 2.2 (continued)

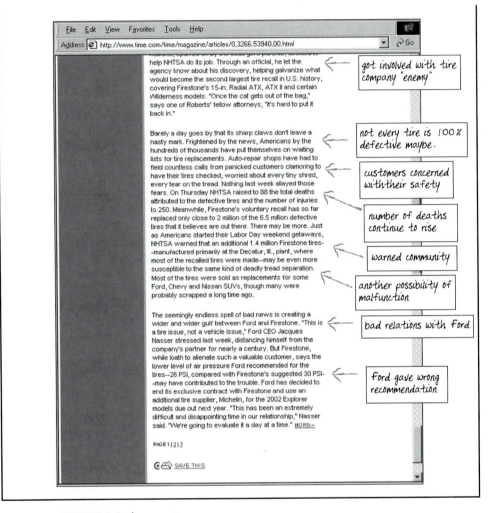

FIGURE 2.2 (*continued*)

Then after sharing her work with her peer review group, she selected the last version of the thesis as her tentative thesis.

```
I chose this sentence because it isn't too specific but
catches the general idea of what my paper will be about.
I liked the thesis exercise because I had to compose
several different versions. It helped me think about ways
to develop my paper.
```

A BURKEAN ANALYSIS OF

THE 1982 AND 1986 TYLENOL POISONING TRAGEDIES

———————————

A DISSERTATION

PRESENTED TO

THE FACULTY OF THE GRADUATE SCHOOL

UNIVERSITY OF MISSOURI-COLUMBIA

———————————

IN PARTIAL FULFILLMENT

OF THE REQUIREMENTS FOR THE DEGREE

DOCTOR OF PHILOSOPHY

———————————

ALAN D. WINEGARDEN

DR. WILLIAM L. BENOIT   DISSERTATION SUPERVISOR

MAY, 1989

Benoit and Lindsay (1987) directly analyzed public persuasive strategies implemented by Johnson & Johnson during the 1982 Tylenol crisis. Prior to the poisonings, Tylenol had based much of its appeal on being safer than aspirin. The vast amount of publicity surrounding the poisonings became "a particularly detrimental development for a product which employs safety as a major selling point" (p. 137). The problem facing Johnson & Johnson, then, was to regain consumer loyalty and market share.

Benoit and Lindsey examined Johnson & Johnson's use of the four strategies of self-defense in the apologetic genre: denial, bolstering, differentiation, and transcendence. They found that Johnson & Johnson's arguments "functioned to deny responsibility for the deaths," "functioned to bolster Tylenol's image of safety," and differentiated Tylenol capsules from other Tylenol products (p. 140). Transcendence as an argumentative strategy was not used in this campaign.

Benoit and Lindsey pointed out that early arguments focused on denial, while bolstering was later used to reestablish Tylenol as a safe product and rebuild market share. One differentiation argument was also used to establish Tylenol's safety. Market share results and the lack of any other compelling explanation indicated the success of Johnson & Johnson's advertising and marketing campaign.

They concluded that Johnson & Johnson conducted an effective campaign to rebuild the Tylenol brand and that the apologetic genre can be applied to different forms or rhetoric which may call for different applications of the apologetic principles and strategies. Argumentative strategies may shift over time depending upon the circumstances. The 1986 Tylenol poisoning recovery campaign was briefly examined, and the authors found that different arguments were used for a very similar situation. They concluded that apologetic discourse in successful campaigns may differ as to argumentative strategies as well as arguments over time and situations.

Mandziuk (1988) examined product recovery and corporate responsibility during the Tylenol tragedies. While the greater share of her analysis dealt with the 1982 tragedy, she did make some comparisons with the handling of the 1986 tragedy. Consumer perceptions were at the core of her analysis, especially perceptions of "responsibility." The mutual assignment of responsibility is a complex interaction which "is best conceptualized as a process of negotiation whereby corporate responsibility is determined through three stages: assessment, response, and transference" (p. 59). In the assessment stage the expectations of the audience are defined based on past experiences. During the response stage the audience evaluates the corporation

for its actions during the event. In the transference
stage, the corporation defines, for the audience, what
are appropriate responses to the corporate actions. If
the corporation has met the expectations of the audience
in the first two stages, it is in a position to set
expectations for the audience.

In the 1982 Tylenol tragedy, audience expectations
were molded by two factors. Media attention to the
poisonings clearly linked Tylenol with death. "The
common sentiment expressed at the time was that the
brand name could not survive due to the "negative
publicity" it had received from its association with
danger-laden terms in headlines and news coverage" (p.
62). The second factor was consumer expectations of
what happens to products when they are associated with
danger. Consumers came to expect the corporation to
assume responsibility for the problems with the
product. Johnson & Johnson met these expectations with
product removal and halting production.

Once Johnson & Johnson had met the audience's
expectation of responsibility in the first stage, this
set of negative expectations had to be overcome. The
link between Tylenol and death had to be overcome by
demonstrating the corporation's integrity, concern, and
interest in the consumer. Two strategies were used.
First, Johnson & Johnson stressed the uniqueness of
this situation. The corporation had not made a mistake.
A murderer was sought. Johnson & Johnson was never
officially blamed for the poisonings and even was
officially cleared of blame. Johnson & Johnson
portrayed Tylenol as a victim, not the cause of the
harm. In this way, "the causality was shifted away from
the company. The responsibility for the deaths instead
was rested upon society" (p. 64). With this shift in
place, the company could move on to demonstrating its

```
concern and integrity through several "responsible"
actions including assistance in the investigation, the
offering of a reward, and developing safer packaging.
Since packaging was perceived as the real danger now,
safer packaging could deal with that perception and
make the product be perceived as safe again.
```

Organizing Ideas

After reading about her topic and deciding on a tentative thesis, Steffany drafted a brief outline:

I. The problem or defect in the tires
II. The specific types of tires recalled
   A. Size
   B. Brands or types/models (ATX, AFXII, Wilderness)
III. The tires by Firestone should be recalled no matter the size
   A. Could be defects in other models or types?
   B. Are there certain plants they come from?
IV. The public's concern
   A. The public is switching brands.
   B. Affects the Ford company.
      1. Contract agreement will end.
      2. Ford Explorer has no correlation.

Writing a Discovery Draft

To fulfill the requirement for topic approval, Steffany wrote a memorandum to her instructor (Figure 2.3) followed by a discovery draft exploring her ideas about the topic (Figure 2.4).

```
TOPIC: THE EFFECT THAT THE FIRESTONE RECALL HAD ON
       THE FORD MOTOR COMPANY.
Name: Steffany D. Fitzpatrick
Composition 104-519
Thesis Statement:
Audience: Academic/Scholarly Audience
List at least 2 sources: CNN, TIME

    I have found articles that link Ford to accidents
where Firestone tires were present. This is because the
```

Ford SUV's come with Firestone tires. As a result of the recall of the tires, Ford is now interrogated about whether or not they knew about the safety hazard. This recall has led people to question other Ford recalls and whether or not they held the safety inspections from the public. I believe this topic is important because Ford was a customer of Firestone and a victim as are the other consumers. If people continue to question Ford about the situation then they are not focusing on getting the tires off the street and the possible safety hazards. Instead, the focus moves to Ford and whether or not their vehicles are safe and acceptable.

FIGURE 2.3

REVERSING A REPUTATION DISCOVERY DRAFT

STEFFANY D. FITZPATRICK

Steffany D. Fitzpatrick
English 104-519
Shane Trayers
September 11, 2000

DISCOVERY DRAFT

Firestone recently recalled two million of six and a half million tires due to a defect in the tires they produced. The recall included the fifteen inch Radial ATX, ATXII and some of the Wilderness models. Ford had a contract with Firestone to provide tires for certain Ford trucks and SUVs, which links Ford to the recall. The Ford Company insists that the recall has nothing to do with their vehicles. On the other hand, Firestone claims that the suggested air pressure levels from both companies differed which supposedly contributed to the accidents and malfunctions (Eisenberg).

FIGURE 2.4 *(continued)*

As a result of Firestone's tire recall, the Ford Motor Company's reputation has become questionable. Both companies are being accused of "hiding" their knowledge of the selling of the unsafe tires. Ford is continuously being investigated and interrogated. Despite the investigators and evidence they are trying to handle the media and court hearings in a way that will give them an appearance of sincerity (Reaves).

Ford can not be held responsible for the Firestone recall yet, the company continues to be impacted and accused as a result. Ford did not make the tires and any other motor company could have been in the contract with Firestone. Ford is trying to distance themselves from Firestone. Ford is a victim of Firestone's recall as well as the consumers. Ford is a consumer of Firestone as the people are consumers of Ford (Eisenberg).

By distancing themselves from Firestone, Ford is trying to gain their reputation back and working to appear loyal to their consumers. Because of Firestone's defective tires, Ford has also been victim of the media, investigators, and lawyers. This could have been avoided if Firestone would accept entire responsibility. Since they are trying to blame Ford for recommending a different air pressure, Ford is being watched carefully. Not only the tires they use but other potential hazards are expanding and becoming major concerns (Eisenberg).

FIGURE 2.4

Here are Steffany's comments about writing a discovery draft.

I liked the discovery draft because it didn't have to be like a rough draft that had to be organized. I knew I would be able to go back and add ideas.

Collaborating with the Instructor

Steffany's instructor invited students to submit a rough draft if they had any questions she could help them answer. Steffany e-mailed her draft and included a note with it. Her instructor answered her questions and offered suggestions for revising the draft (Figure 2.5).

Ms. Trayers

      Sorry about the format but my computer didn't double space or keep my format when I copied it. It won't let me send it as an attachment for some reason. Thanks for help today on all my question BUT, I have one more. My internet source from CNN doesn't have an author but at the bottom of the page there is "Associated Press." I didn't know how to cite this in the particular way i used it so for now i just have Associated Press hold the place. If you could please suggest the correct way to write that i would appreciate it. If there's not a correct way then i will change the structure somehow. Thanks so much.

Show it to me. (Also, if there is no author, skip that info.)   Steffany (519)

Steffany D. Fitzpatrick

Ms. Trayers

English 104.519

22 Sept. 2000

Reversing a Reputation ⟶

      On August 9, 2000, Firestone recalled six and a half million tires due to a defect in the tires they produced. This

write out #. recall was voluntary after officials learned that 88 deaths may have been a result of the defective tires (Metcalf

FIGURE 2.5 *(continued)*

1A). The tires are defective because the tread separates from the rest of the tire. Eisenberg states that a former employee of Firestone recalled a new policy that went into effect around 1993. This policy reduced the time that the tires were bonded together by ten minutes (www).

Need more transition here.

Firestone is responsible for the detrimental reputation of the Ford Motor Company. The Firestone recall included the fifteen-inch Radial ATX, ATXII and Wilderness AT models. Many of these tires were found on Ford vehicles. Ford had a contract with Firestone to provide the tires for certain Ford trucks and Sport Utility Vehicles. The Ford Company insists that the recall had nothing to do with the quality of their vehicles, only the tires on them. Firestone claims that the conflicting suggestions for air pressure levels may have contributed to the malfunctioning of the tires. The recommended air pressures from both companies differed by four-PSI (Eisenberg).

I'm having trouble finding your thesis statement

According to Eisenberg, "Ford has decided to end its exclusive contract with Firestone and use an additional tire supplier, Michelin, for the 2002 Explorer models due out next year (www). This is just one of the steps that Ford is taking in order to regain the confidence of their customers. The Ford Motor Company is also "shutting down production of a number of vehicles to produce a ready

source of replacement tires" (Metcalf
10A). Ford dealers are trying to replace
the tires with ones they already have
even if it means losing money by trading
the customer their bad tires for a high
quality and more expensive tire from Ford
(Metcalf 10A).

Transition

In 1982, Tylenol lost respect from
their customers and lost their reputation
for being a safe and effective product
(Winegarden 14). Capsules of Tylenol had
been poisoned and been placed on the
shelves. Tylenol was not directly
responsible for the poisoning, but it was
their product, and they had to do
something about the poisoning. Johnson &

That's an understatement!

Johnson effectively regained the public's
trust and respect by handling the
situation very responsibly. They took
several steps to attain their old
reputation. Winegarden illustrates these
steps as "assuming responsibility for
problems with the product,"
"demonstrating the corporation's
integrity, concern, and interest in the
consumer," and "portray[ing] Tylenol as a
victim, not the cause of the harm" (17).
Tylenol took the responsibility, showed
their customers that they cared and
shifted the blame on society instead of
on themselves. The strategy worked and as
a result Johnson & Johnson is one of the
world's leading companies with Tylenol as
one of the most prominent sources of
medicine (Winegarden 17).

FIGURE 2.5 *(continued)*

These strategies would help Ford if they applied them to their situation. This is a solution that could restart their old sales numbers and repair their reputation. They should begin by accepting responsibility for the fact that the tires were, in fact, on their vehicles. They would then demonstrate that they are willing to take care of their customers by trading them tires, switching companies, and getting rid of the defective tires in new models. This would show that they cared and that they accept responsibility for the tires being on their vehicles.

They should then also portray themselves as the victim also. The public is a victim of the tire recall because the public buys the tires from Firestone as a customer. Ford is a customer as well. The ~~Associated Press~~ at CNN relates Ford Motor Company as a customer of Firestone (www). By showing that they are willing to help, that they care, and that they are also a victim, they could regain the trust of their customers. These strategies need to be done in a quick effective manner on a large scale so that their reputation will be improved.

Ford Motor Company has a reputation of being scandalous and dishonest as a result of the Firestone recall. Firestone is responsible for this detrimental reputation because of their defective tires. Ford can reverse this reputation if they take the right steps and distance

themselves from Firestone's tire
problems.

Steffany

Ok, you got well-developed paragraphs here, but you want to be clear from the beginning about you thesis. Also, try to transition from one idea to another so the reader can easily follow your train of thought. This is a good start. Keep revising and editing.

FIGURE 2.5

Reflecting

Before participating in peer review, Steffany completed a worksheet identifying her audience, her qualifications to write about the topic, and her tentative thesis (Figure 2.6). She submitted copies of the worksheet to her reviewers. Her comments provide a preview, giving reviewers a context for her paper.

ESSAY WORKSHEET

In a word or phrase, describe your topic: *Firestone Recall*

In a word or phrase, give your working title: *Reversing a Reputation*

Audience Analysis

In two to four sentences, describe your target audience indicated on your assignment prompt as specifically as you can (i.e.; what is the average reading level of your audience? What do they know about your topic?)

My audience is academic, specifically those who are concerned with safety. The audience knows about my topic from the papers and news and in some cases, first hand experience.

In one sentence tell what value your essay holds for its readers. How will they use it or benefit from it?

They will understand why Firestone is responsible and why Ford is just a victim.

In one to two sentences, state (a) the purpose that you want to achieve in writing this essay for this specific audience and (b) the response you expect from this audience.

A) I want the audience to know why Firestone is to blame and what they are doing about it.

FIGURE 2.6 *(continued)*

B)*I expect the audience to understand why Firestone is to blame instead of Ford.*

What actions/beliefs/decisions do you envision from your readers as a result of having read your essay? How will your essay help them to do so?

I believe they will choose the person that they see at fault. My essay will explain how I see or view the situation and help them make theirs.

Author

In a sentence tell why you are an insider on this subject. In other words, what role are you assuming as the author?

I am assuming the role as a defender of the Ford Motor Company.

In a word or phrase, identify the role you are playing as the author of this essay (that is, the persona you are assuming as the author.)

Defender

What are some clichés, stereotypes, or truisms about your topic—that is, standard ways of thinking that your fellow students are likely to associate with your subject matter?

Maybe as someone trying to take the easy way out and blame others.

What do you know about your topic that the majority of the class is not likely to know?

The reasoning that could possibly be the cause of the recall.

List some ways of interpreting or presenting your information that will stimulate your readers to look at the topic in a new way?

- *Portray Ford as the victim*
- *Portray Firestone as the responsible one*

Thesis

In a complete sentence, state your thesis.

Firestone is responsible for the detrimental reputation of the Ford Motor Company.

Write a short topic outline of your paper based on your thesis statement in the space provided below:

Thesis

I. steps taken to regain confidence
  A. ending contract
  B. shutting down production
  C. trading tires out
II. Tylenol Incident
  A. assume responsibility
  B. demonstrate integrity
  C. portraying as victim

III. Solution
  A. assuming responsibility
  B. demonstrating integrity
  C. portrays as victim

FIGURE 2.6

—Work sheet developed by Jim Baker.

Collaborating with Peers

Stephany's peer review draft is annotated. Notice that she poses questions for her reviewers to answer. Kelly responded to her questions and made suggestions for revising and improving the paper (Figure 2.7). On a separate peer workshop response sheet, Kelly commented that Steffany's paper had "very strong evidence" and that the "thesis was bold and clear." Kelly noted that this draft didn't use topic sentences or clear transitions. She also raised questions about how the paragraph on Tylenol fit in with the rest of the paper.

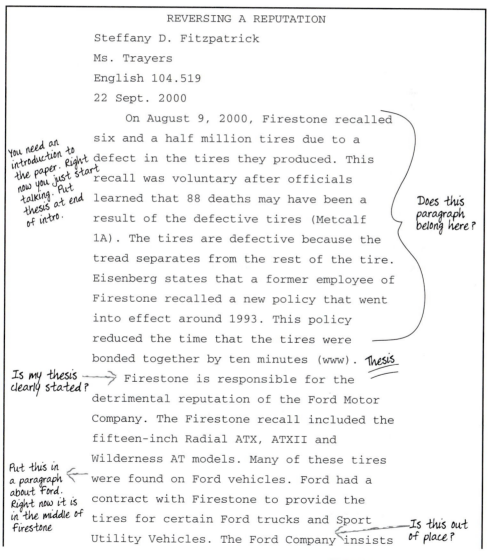

REVERSING A REPUTATION

Steffany D. Fitzpatrick

Ms. Trayers

English 104.519

22 Sept. 2000

On August 9, 2000, Firestone recalled six and a half million tires due to a defect in the tires they produced. This recall was voluntary after officials learned that 88 deaths may have been a result of the defective tires (Metcalf 1A). The tires are defective because the tread separates from the rest of the tire. Eisenberg states that a former employee of Firestone recalled a new policy that went into effect around 1993. This policy reduced the time that the tires were bonded together by ten minutes (www). Firestone is responsible for the detrimental reputation of the Ford Motor Company. The Firestone recall included the fifteen-inch Radial ATX, ATXII and Wilderness AT models. Many of these tires were found on Ford vehicles. Ford had a contract with Firestone to provide the tires for certain Ford trucks and Sport Utility Vehicles. The Ford Company insists

You need an introduction to the paper. Right now you just start talking. Put thesis at end of intro.

Does this paragraph belong here?

Is my thesis clearly stated?

Thesis

Put this in a paragraph about Ford. Right now it is in the middle of Firestone

Is this out of place?

FIGURE 2.7 (continued)

that the recall had nothing to do with the
quality of their vehicles, only the tires
on them. Firestone claims that the
conflicting suggestions for air pressure
levels may have contributed to the

probably after this ¶ on Firestone at the beginning of

malfunctioning of the tires. The
recommended air pressures from both
companies differed by four-PSI
(Eisenberg).   *need more?*

According to Eisenberg, "Ford has
decided to end its exclusive contract
with Firestone and use an additional tire
supplier, Michelin, for the 2002 Explorer
models due out next year (www). This is
just one of the steps that Ford is taking

word choice (sounds fine)

in order to regain the confidence of
their customers. The Ford Motor Company
is also "shutting down production of a
number of vehicles to produce a ready   *OK bc it's a quote*
source of replacement tires" (Metcalf
10A). Ford dealers are trying to replace

on already owned vehicles   *new safe tires*

the tires with ones they already have
even if it means losing money by trading

Does it make sense? Not really the 1st part is unclear

the customer their bad tires for a high*er?*
quality and more expensive tire from Ford
(Metcalf 10A).   *Needs transition*

In 1982, Tylenol lost respect from
their customers and lost their reputation
for being a safe and effective product
(Winegarden 14). Capsules of Tylenol had
been poisoned and been placed on the
shelves. Tylenol was not directly
responsible for the poisoning but it was
their product and they had to do something
about the poisoning. Johnson & Johnson
effectively regained the public's trust

and respect by handling the situation very responsibly. They took several steps to attain their old reputation. Winegarden illustrates these steps as "assuming responsibility for problems with the product," "demonstrating the corporation's integrity, concern, and interest in the consumer," and "portray[ing] Tylenol as a victim, not the cause of the harm" (17). Tylenol took the responsibility, showed their customers that they cared and shifted the blame on society instead of on themselves. The strategy worked and as a result Johnson & Johnson is one of the world's leading companies with Tylenol as one of the most prominent sources of medicine (Winegarden 17).

Quotation marks??? If it is from the same place take out the middle quotes " " & add ....

does this sentence make "good" sense? yes

These strategies would help Ford if they applied them to their situation. This is a solution that could restart their old sales numbers and repair their reputation. They should begin by accepting responsibility for the fact that the tires were, in fact, on their vehicles. They would then demonstrate that they are willing to take care of their customers by trading them tires, switching companies, and getting rid of the defective tires in new models. This would show that they cared and that they accept responsibility for the tires being on their vehicles. Ford They should then also portray themselves as the victim also. The public is a victim of the tire recall because the public buys the tires from Firestone as a customer. Ford is a customer as well. The Associated

You have now contradicted your thesis. You start by saying firestone is responsible, but now act as if ford is.

word choice former

Needs a sentence like...Although ford is not responsible, they need to show the customers that because the tires were on their car it matters to them to make sure their customers are safe.

new paragraph?

FIGURE 2.7 *(continued)*

Press at CNN relates Ford Motor Company as
a customer of Firestone (www). By showing
that they are willing to help, that they
care and that they are also a victim, they
could regain the trust of their customers.
These strategies need to be done in a
quick effective manner on a large scale so   *Contradictory to thesis*
that their reputation will be improved.

Ford Motor Company has a reputation of
being scandalous and dishonest as a result
of the Firestone recall. Firestone is
responsible for ~~this~~ *the* detrimental reputation
of Ford
because of ^their defective tires. Ford can
reverse this reputation if they take the
right steps and distance themselves from
Firestone's tire problems.

Does this conclude this paper well? Sentences out of place, other than that things are fine for a conclusion.

Is there missing information? NO

Is this argumentative? Yes

Do people care?

FIGURE 2.7

Reflecting on the Final Draft

Steffany's graded paper is included here along with a cover memo she wrote to her
instructor in class the day papers were due (Figures 2.8 and 2.9).

To: Miss Trayers

From: Steffany D. Fitzpatrick (SDF)

RE: A good topic gone somewhat bad.

For this writing project I chose the topic of the Firestone recall. My
audience was supposed to be academic but I am not sure it is purely
academic. My thesis argued that Firestone is responsible for the detrimental
reputation at the Ford Motor Company.

When choosing a topic I wanted something that the people would be interested in and a topic that I might be able to explain some things about. When I came up with the topic I thought it was perfect. As I further researched and argued the topic wasn't so perfect anymore.

The topic is one of my weaknesses I believe. It is not the easiest to argue or state claims about. My other weaknesses include how my paper flows and the transitions. I feel that moving paragraph to paragraph can seem a bit "choppy."

My strengths include the evidence and sources that back up my thesis. I think I provided quotes and examples that help explain why Firestone is responsible for Ford's reputation.

I revised the paper using the notes my peers and professor left on my rough draft. I tried to make the paper flow better and transitions seem smoother. When editing my final copy I added a extremely small story about the ten year old boy. I hoped this help grab the readers attention.

I used the critiques that my peers gave and that you pronged. I also used my own critical reading skills.

Overall, I believe my paper is well documented and meets all the requirements. It flows better now that it is the final draft and its well organized. This was definitely a learning process and I will pick a better topic for my next paper, I am sure.

FIGURE 2.8

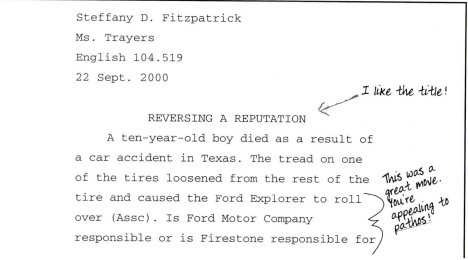

Steffany D. Fitzpatrick
Ms. Trayers
English 104.519
22 Sept. 2000

I like the title!

REVERSING A REPUTATION

A ten-year-old boy died as a result of a car accident in Texas. The tread on one of the tires loosened from the rest of the tire and caused the Ford Explorer to roll over (Assc). Is Ford Motor Company responsible or is Firestone responsible for

This was a great move. You're appealing to pathos!

FIGURE 2.9 (continued)

the defect in the tire? Firestone is

Need more of a transition between ideas.

responsible for the detrimental reputation of the Ford Motor Company.

The tires that separated were recalled on August 9, 2000. Firestone recalled six and a half million tires due to a defect in the tires they produced. This recall was voluntary after officials learned that eighty-eight deaths may have been a result of the defective tires (Metcalf 1A). The tires are defective because the tread separates from the rest of the tire. Eisenberg states that a former employee of Firestone recalled a new policy that went into effect around 1993. This policy reduced the time that the tires were bonded together by ten minutes *author or title* ~~(www)~~.

The Firestone recall included the fifteen-inch Radial ATX, ATXII and Wilderness AT models. These particular tires were found on Ford vehicles. Ford had a contract with Firestone to provide the tires for certain Ford trucks and Sport Utility Vehicles. The Ford Company Insists that the recall had nothing to do with the quality of their vehicles, only the tires on them. Firestone claims that the conflicting suggestions for air pressure levels may have contributed to the malfunctioning of the tires. The recommended air pressures from both

Make air pressure separate

companies differed by four-PSI (Eisenberg).

Put this earlier in the paragraph before.

According to Eisenberg, "Ford has decided to end its exclusive contract with

Firestone and use an additional tire supplier, Michelin, for the 2002 Explorer models due out next year" ~~(www)~~. This is just one of the steps that Ford is taking in order to regain the confidence of their customers. The Ford Motor Company is also "shutting down production of a number of vehicles to produce a ready source of replacement tires" ~~(Metcalf 10A)~~. Ford dealers are trying to replace the customer's tires with ones they have at their dealerships even if it results in profit loss for the Ford dealerships (Metcalf 10A). Ford is defending itself as well as increasing the distance between their relationship with Firestone.

Cite at end of paraphrase, even if after a couple of sentences.

¶ Eighteen years ago a similar situation occurred. Johnson & Johnson had to recall Tylenol off the shelves due to a random poisoning by an unknown person. Johnson & Johnson took several steps to rebuild their reputation. These steps could be applied to the Ford and Firestone tire misfortune.

Put this idea at beginning of paragraph.

I might put this earlier closer to thesis

In 1982, Tylenol lost respect from their customers and lost their reputation for being a safe and effective product (Winegarden 14). Capsules of Tylenol had been poisoned and been placed on the shelves. Tylenol was not directly responsible for the poisoning, but it was their product and they had to resolve the problem immediately. Johnson & Johnson effectively regained the public's trust and respect by handling the situation very responsibly.

FIGURE 2.9 *(continued)*

They took several steps to attain their previous reputation. Winegarden illustrates these steps as "assuming responsibility for problems with the product …, demonstrating the corporation's integrity, concern, and interest in the consumer …, and portray[ing] Tylenol as a victim, not the cause of the harm" (17). Tylenol took the responsibility of handling the situation, they showed their customers that they cared, and they shifted the blame on society instead of on themselves. The strategy worked and as a result Johnson & Johnson is one of the world's leading companies with Tylenol as one of the most prominent sources of medicine (Winegarden 17).

These strategies would benefit Ford, if they applied them to their situation. This is a solution that could restart their former sales numbers and repair their reputation. Ford should begin by accepting responsibility for the fact that the tires were, in fact, on their vehicles, even though they are not at fault for the tread separation. They would then demonstrate that they are willing to take care of their customers by trading them tires, switching companies, and discarding the defective tires in new models. This would show that they were concerned for the safety of their customers and that they accept responsibility for the tires that are on their vehicles. They should then portray themselves as a victim, just as public is a victim of the defective tires. ~~The public~~

~~is a victim of the tire recall because the~~
~~public buys the tires from Firestone as a~~
~~customer.~~ Ford is a customer as well. ~~The~~
~~Associated Press at CNN relates Ford Motor~~
~~Company as a customer of Firestone (www).~~
By showing that they are willing to help,
that they care, and that they are also a
victim, they could regain the trust of
their customers. These strategies need to
be done in a quick effective manner on a
large scale so that their reputation will
be improved.

cut—unnecessary

   Ford Motor Company has a reputation
of being scandalous and dishonest as a
result of the Firestone recall. Firestone
is responsible for this detrimental
reputation because of their defective
tires. Ford can reverse this reputation if
they take the right steps and distance
themselves from Firestone's tire problems.

I'd cut the whole last paragraph—redundant.

WORKS CITED

Eisenburg, Daniel. "Anatomy of a Recall." TIME
    Magazine. Vol. 156. No. 11. 11 Sept. 2000. TIME.COM.
    14 Sept. 2000 http://www.time.com/time/magazine/
    articles/03266,53940,00.html.

"Explorer Tire Tread Separated in Fatal Texas Crash."
    CNN.COM. 4 Sept. 2000. CNN. 7 Sept. 2000
    http://www.cnn.com/US/09/04/firestone.accident.01/in
    dex.html.

Metcalf, Stephen. "Firestone Tire Recall Affects B-CS
    Business." Battalion 11 Sept. 2000: 1B, 10A.

Winegarden, Alan D. A Burkean Analysis of the 1982 and
    1986 Tylenol Poisoning Tragedies. Diss. U. of
    Missouri, Columbia, 1989.

FIGURE 2.9

For audience analysis, I pictured a paper I would have to stand up and read in front of students and professors.

Revising Globally

When Steffany submitted her paper for evaluation, she read it to her class and asked for suggestions. She intended to use the paper for a global revision assignment at the end of the semester. Her peers offered written evaluations focusing primarily on global revision but mentioning local revision as well. Read the suggestions Steffany's classmates made. (Figures 2.10-2.18).

CRITIQUE ON STEPHANIE'S PAPER

Kristin Shaner

English 104

11/20/00

I think that the paper is written well, but that there is more than one idea to each paragraph. I also think that she needs to tell what happened at the end to the boy and his case, did they win or lose? I thought that the tylenol story was a good comparison, but it needs to be used differently in the paper, maybe by showing the results of the cases and not going into that much detail about tylenol because that takes the focus of the main topic. There were only a few punctuation errors that I saw. There needs to be more emphasis on the case itself and say what happened at the end, if the problem was resolved.

FIGURE 2.10

REVERSING A REPUTATION

Heather Davey

Ms. Trayers

11/17/00

I like the way the paper compared the Firestone and Ford issue with that of Tylenol and Johnson and Johnson. It gave the reader a more vivid picture of the problem and injustice that is being done to the Ford company. The audience that I would probably use is that of people who buy or own a Ford. Perhaps you might want to target people who are not aware of what is going on with the Firestone problem. It is easier to persuade those people who do not have an opinion than those that do. This paper takes the direction of a Resemblance argument or somewhat of a causal argument. Both would have to be elaborated further on.

The paper was a good paper, however it needs a little bit of an adjustment. You might want to add some transition words or topic sentences in order to make the paper flow better. I had a hard time following your thoughts. Also, the introduction and the conclusion are very weak. You want to grab the readers attention and keep it so that they will not want to put your paper down. The conclusion should end the paper not leave the reader wondering "is this the end". You night want to try to add something about what the reader can actually do to help the situation too.

FIGURE 2.11

CRITIQUE: STEPHANIE FITZPATRICK

Andrew Robertson

Comp. 104.519   *The proposal argument presented is*

What to Keep: *effective. The pathos used is also effective.*

Your argument is sound. It is made evident that an injustice has occurred upon the Ford Motor Company and the essay clearly suggests the means for repairing their reputation. The grounds that this situation has occurred before in a situation with Johnson and Johnson Company reveal a strong resemblance argument.

What to Change:

Numerous times in your essay the reader would benefit from an explanation of certain terms and phrases. For example, the reference to the PSI of a tire is unclear as well as the statement of the "tread separate[ing] from the rest of the tire". Also, more

FIGURE 2.12 *(continued)*

commentary in the introduction paragraph would help establish a clearer picture of what the essay is trying to accomplish. The grounds that are used reflect the thesis statement; however, a larger number of grounds would make the argument stronger.

FIGURE 2.12

Kelli Shaner

Eng 104

11/19/00

    The paper was pretty good. I think the tylenol part was not important. It side tracked me. I know that you were trying to tie it into the ford incident but I don't think it had the effect you wanted. I would either cut it out or change the wording and tie the two subjects together better. Also their were some short sentences that could either be left out or made into longer ones. I found your thesis easily, but I couldn't tell what the main point of you paper was (paper 1 or 2). If you were supposed to stick to a side I think you need to change some things. I think the topic is very interesting and made for a good choice to write about. I really liked the introduction paragraph. It caught my attention and made me want to read on. Another thing to change is your conclusion. I think you need to make it longer and come to a definite ending. Other tan that the paper was good.

FIGURE 2.13

CRITIQUE

Cristina Gargour

Engl. 104-519

November 20, 2000

    The introduction to the paper is not lengthy enough for the material described. The sentences should be expanded and more information should be provided to make the intro flow better. The thesis is not effective

here in the form of a question, it should be reworded
to fit the paper or the paper should adjust which is
going to be the key aspect to a more successful paper.
Many abbreviations and terms are used in the paper that
the average person that is not familiar with automotive
repair would know about. These all need to be defined
and explained. The paragraph changes are very abrupt.
Place topic sentences in the paragraph to make the
paragraphs connect. The Johnson & Johnson comparison is
not very effective for this short of a paper and should
be omitted. I see where the author is going with the
comparison but is not useful unless the thesis is
altered. I only found one true paragraph that
correlated to the thesis, the paper would be much
stronger if it did not deviate. Their should have just
been more information provided and more support to a
thesis. The audience should be aimed at consumers to
warn them of the dangers of these companies and their
products. Possibly you could change the paper into a
causal argument taking a new angle that if Ford would
do this then the consequences would happen for
consumers and Firestone.

FIGURE 2.14

```
                       CRITIQUE
Brent Baker
Shane Trayers
English 104.519
11/17/00

    The thesis was clearly stated. The evidence in the
paper was substantial. The documentation seemed to be
right in most places and there was plenty of evidence
to back up your claims. The analogy of Tylenol and
Johnson & Johnson was great. It was helpful in
understanding the problem with the Firestone tires. I
thought the paper was very interesting because it is a
```

FIGURE 2.15 *(continued)*

recent issue that I did not know too much about but have heard in the news. The conclusion did a great job of summing up the paper, but it wouldn't hurt to try and make it a little longer. I had no question as to where the paper ended.

The introduction for the paper on Firestone is a tad weak and could use some work. The question in the introductory paragraph is not needed to get the point across. Many of the sentences were choppy and could be combined to make the paper flow a little bit better. I am not sure if the separate paragraph on Tylenol is necessary, but adding some of that to the previous paragraph might work. More information needs to be given on the actual tires that were recalled so we could understand why they were defective (such as the actual making of the tire, what its made of, what part didn't work, etc.).

FIGURE 2.15

CRITIQUE FOR STEFFANY

Camille Ortiz

English 104

11/20/00

Overall, I think you have a great topic to write about. Since this is a pretty recent incident, you have your facts up to date. The thing is, your thesis talks about whether Ford Motor Company is responsible for the defects in the Firestone tire or not, and you don't really talk about it in your paper. What you do talk about, or what comes off to me is that you are talking about whether the Ford Motor Company is a victim or not of the mishap with the tires. You go into specific detail about the steps that Ford should take to make them look like the victim and gain the publics trust again, but not whether Ford is responsible or not. You have very good factual information and I like the way you tied in the incident with Tylenol to be more effective.

One thing you need to work on is explaining yourself little more. You will make claims such as, "This policy reduced the time that the tires were bonded together by 10 min" You do not explain what the normal time is and the purpose for that. This happens a number of times, which I marked for you to go back and look at. Also, be sure that you are talking about only one thing in each paragraph. If not, make a new paragraph.

I also think that you need to change your introduction. My suggestion would be to cite a real life case with names, the place and what exactly happened to provoke pathos and to make your audience side with you. Your conclusion also needs work as well. Go back to your claim and either restate it, or do whatever you need to do.

FIGURE 2.16

CRITIQUE

Kelly Hunt #1

The paper does not have many grammatical errors. It is also organized in a very logical way, which makes it easy for the reader to follow. You should keep the same audience you have now, the educated public.

The introduction and conclusion need to be more powerful to prove to the reader that you are right without a doubt. Some of the paragraphs are also a little confusing because you start to talk about something, but end without a real explanation of what you are talking about or added commentary, especially the first main body paragraph. It makes the reader a little unsure of what you are trying to say. You are off to a good start, just add a little more information and strength to some paragraphs and your paper will be excellent!

FIGURE 2.17

CRITIQUE—STEFFANY'S PAPER

Kristal Zimmers
Section 5 | 9

I would keep the basic ideas of the intro, but expand on them to make your thesis clearer and catch the reader's attention more. Good introductory story. The second paragraph needs some organization. The "defect" (specifics) should be listed after you mention it in the second sentence. The third paragraph sounds slightly repetitious with the words "Ford" and "firestone." I realize you may not be able to change this, but it is worth a try. You could expand on this paragraph, it is confusing. At the end of the fourth paragraph is a statement about the Tylenol company needs to be added to paragraph fire. Paragraph six is also confusing (slightly); some organization would help. The conclusion is very short, you could easily expand it to give the reader a feeling of closure.

Basically, I feel you could cut and redo any of the unorganized, confusing paragraphs I mentioned. Several paragraphs need transitions. I do not want to sound pessimistic; you have done a great job with this paper and only need to do a little work.

I believe the audience is scholarly/academic, but I am unsure.

FIGURE 2.18

EXERCISES: THINKING CRITICALLY ABOUT PEER REVIEW

1. Several of these evaluations are contradictory. One person recommends doing away with the Tylenol analogy; another person likes it. Steffany receives conflicting recommendations on other matters as well—whether she has sufficient evidence, for example, to support her claim. Which evaluations would you find most valuable? Explain why.

2. What steps did Steffany take to write this paper that are normally part of your writing process? What steps did she take that you don't normally take?

3. Compare the draft Steffany e-mailed to her instructor to the draft she submitted for grading. Identify revision in the thesis statement, in supporting ideas, and in the organization of the paper.

Chapter 3

Developing Skills for Academic Writing

Writing, when properly managed (as you may be sure I think mine is),
is but a different name for conversation.

—*Laurence Sterne,* Tristram Shandy.

WRITING IN THE ACADEMY

Academic writing is a term that casts a broad net over writing about any subject studied in colleges and universities: mathematics, biology, business, engineering, history, psychology, film studies, education, kinesiology, poultry science, modern and classical languages, archaeology, horticulture, geography—to name a few. Academic writing takes different forms, such as books, journal articles, proposals, formal reports, and pamphlets; employs specialized vocabulary unique to each subject area; and uses different styles of documentation. With all its diversity, academic writing conforms on several significant points: It is discourse written by college or university students and faculty for other college or university students and faculty; its purpose is to inform, instruct, enlighten, and to persuade; it relies on studies and works published by other scholars; and it undergoes review before it is published. Books and journals published by university presses have editorial boards that serve as referees. They review submissions to make sure that their publications meet high standards and advance scholarship in their area of expertise.

As a college student, you have to learn how to read academic discourse. You also have to learn how to follow the conventions of academic writing: synthesizing sources, following a specific style of documentation, presenting your ideas logically, and offering your intended readers new or fresh ideas and perspectives. This last item may seem like a tall order, but it isn't impossible. You'll find an example of published student writing in the case study in Chapter 12, Rebecca Malouin's "Surgeon's Quest for Life: The History and Future of Xenotransplantation." Malouin

111

combines reading, writing, and research skills. When you read her paper, you have the sense that the writer is serious about her subject and knows it well. She uses language effectively to express her ideas, and she synthesizes sources effectively. The published paper looks professional. It's valid to assume that Rebecca's paper went through multiple drafts and that Rebecca followed the process of writing discussed in Chapter 2. The extended list of works cited indicate that Rebecca also devoted a great deal of time to researching her topic and determining how to use sources in her paper.

The writing process is even more complicated when you write from sources. When you write about yourself or about your personal knowledge of a subject, you work with a personal inventory of knowledge you call on as you draft and revise a paper. You use critical thinking skills—for example, forming opinions, establishing a frame of reference, and making assumptions about your topic and your intended readers' attitude toward the topic. Writing from sources requires activities that are not included when you write about personal experiences or personal opinion. It is generally more time-consuming because of the library work. You locate information, read and react to sources, select passages to cite in a paper, and incorporate sources in a manner that makes ideas clear and meaningful to intended readers. While you use the same critical thinking skills you employ when you write about personal experience, you use other skills as well. For example, you typically evaluate and analyze data, evidence, or experience; ask questions about sources; draw inferences and conclusions from your reading; and summarize, paraphrase, and synthesize information.

PLANNING AND DRAFTING

Effective academic writing, you will learn, requires a set of skills that are applied in the process of writing. To be an effective writer in college-level courses, you will use your reading and writing skills together. Typically, writing assignments will ask you to cite ideas, theories, arguments, propositions, hypotheses, or explanations of published writers in documented papers. The skills you will use most frequently in academic writing include

- understanding your purpose and intended readers;
- formulating a thesis (stating in one sentence the purpose of a paper);
- organizing ideas (to support the thesis);
- paraphrasing (reporting in your own words another writer's ideas);
- summarizing (condensing something you have read, reporting in your own words the main ideas of the original);
- avoiding plagiarism; and
- creating a voice of your own.

Understanding Purpose and Audience

When you begin a writing assignment, think about the communication triangle—that is, your subject, purpose in writing, and audience. What do you want readers to know or to do as a result of reading a paper? As a result of reading your paper, will your intended readers be entertained? informed? persuaded? moved to action? moved to reconsider their opinions? Usually, an assignment will help you determine your purpose in writing. For example, an assignment requires you to

- argue for or against a topic of your choice;
- take a position on a controversial issue and defend that position;
- provide an overview of an event;
- compare and contrast two theories; or
- analyze a work of art, speech, or literary selection.

Notice how key words in these assignments help writers' understand their purpose in writing: *argue, defend a position, provide an overview, compare and contrast, analyze*. After you have reviewed an assignment, talk to your instructor if you have questions about your purpose in writing. When you have a definite purpose in mind, you are ready to consider your intended readers, your audience.

The concept of audience is complex, but nevertheless crucial for success in writing. When you know your intended reader or readers, you have a specific person or group in mind that you address. When you aren't familiar with your intended reader or readers, you have to envision your audience. To illustrate the difference, think about writing a letter or sending e-mail to a friend and writing a letter or sending e-mail to someone you don't know or don't know well. Knowing or not knowing your reader usually makes a difference in what you say and how you say it. Analyzing readers' perspectives on a topic or their attitudes toward a topic is generally easier when you know your readers, but even then, your analysis is, to some degree, speculation. Readers bring their own expectations and perspectives to a text and create meaning on their own.

Throughout the writing process, effective writers analyze their audiences and consider their audiences' expectations and needs. You might say that effective writers have cultivated the ability to envision an audience and to create a sense of that audience in their writing so that their intended audience and the audience implied in the text are one and the same. To envision an intended audience, play the role of the intended reader—that is, an individual who agrees and disagrees with you and raises objections or counterarguments to your ideas just as a friend or classmate would in an informal situation. Inexperienced writers frequently make the mistake of assuming that intended readers will share their perspective on a topic. The kind of writing that results can be described as egocentric. Your experience with everyday audience analysis should tell you that total agreement is the exception rather than the norm. Draw on this sort of analysis—you'll find it relevant. Perhaps you have anticipated objections from parents in discussion of career goals, stifled an angry outburst at a friend when you saw anxiety in your friend's face, or resisted the temptation to laugh at an awkward social situation because you realized that laughter might hurt someone's feelings. These are examples of assessing a situation and responding and reacting to others—not the same kind of analysis required in writing, but a form of audience analysis nonetheless.

To establish a clear rhetorical situation at the outset of a writing assignment, you should analyze your audience by asking the following questions:

Questions for Analyzing an Audience

- What is my relationship to my intended readers?
- What do I share in common with readers? (Consider age, gender, race, education, sexual orientation, politics, religion, priorities, socioeconomic class, and occupation)
- Are readers familiar with or interested in my topic?
- What kinds of perspectives will readers have about the topic?
- What would readers value in a discussion of the topic?

Frequently, writers address a secondary audience as well as a primary audience. For example, if you wrote a letter to the editor of your local or campus newspaper agreeing or disagreeing with a recently published editorial, the primary audience would be the person who wrote the editorial, and the secondary audience would be the people who read the newspaper. To some extent, you have a primary and secondary audience in writing assignments that designate a specific group of readers as your intended audience. That is, the designated readers are the primary audience and the instructor is the secondary audience. Your paper has to meet your intended readers' needs and expectations and, at the same time, has to fit your instructor's assignment in other ways. The important point is that you want to start now to develop a sense of writing for actual readers instead of "writing for the teacher." Try to give your instructor the role of secondary audience.

EXERCISES: FOCUS ON WRITING

1. Draft a letter welcoming visitors who are coming to your campus for an academic conference. Assume that the visitors are college professors from all over the United States. Unfamiliar with your campus, they need to know how to reach the campus, and they will be interested in special features of interest on campus and in your community. Your letter should be no longer than one page.

Draft the same letter for high school students who will visit your campus. Assume that your letter will be used for recruitment purposes. Be sure you mention special features and activities on campus. These students also need to know how to reach the campus. This letter should be no longer than one page.

2. Review letters to the editor in your local or campus newspaper and identify a topic that has generated response from readers. Draft a letter in which you take a stance you know many readers will oppose. Try to establish goodwill and common ground with your readers.

3. Share with your classmates a writing experience in which you didn't know your intended readers, but developed a sense of who they were and what would interest them. Describe any circumstances that helped you envision your audience and address their needs. Also, explain how having a sense of who your audience was resulted in an effective piece of writing.

EXERCISES: COLLABORATING WITH YOUR PEERS

1. Share with your classmates the letters you wrote for number 1 of the Focus on Writing exercises. Discuss whether the information you included seems appropriate, accurate, or helpful for each audience. Discuss ways to revise and improve your letters.

2. Share with your classmates the letter you wrote for number 2 of the Focus on Writing exercises. Explain how you established goodwill and common ground with your readers and how you make your purpose in writing clear to readers. Ask your peers for suggestions for revision.

Formulating a Thesis

The title of a paper usually gives readers their first hint of a paper's subject. The thesis is a statement of the main idea the writer wants to develop. It also gives readers a sense of the writer's aim. For this reason, in a mid-length paper, the thesis statement is typically located in the first or second paragraph of a paper. In a short paper, it may even be the first sentence. The thesis shouldn't be delayed too long because it acts as a road map, pointing the reader in a specific direction. Readers need to know if a writer's purpose is to argue a point, to inform readers, or to reveal something about a personal experience or feelings. And they'll want to know the focus and scope of the paper, as well. In the process of formulating a thesis, you may start out with a general idea and revise and refine in a number of ways. The goal is to have a sentence that, isolated from the rest of the paper, tells the reader what your paper is about. The following is an example from a student's argumentative paper, "Should Public Schools Implement Uniforms?"

Although educators argue that uniforms would reduce gang violence, save money, and improve attendance, there is little evidence to support these claims; therefore, public schools should not require students to wear uniforms to class.

You don't find vague generalities in this sentence. It offers specific information and mentions two perspectives. Notice how the writer provides cues to readers. The writer begins with claims that uniforms solve several problems, but she subordinates this perspective with the word *although*. After she states that "there is little evidence to support these claims," she introduces with the word *therefore* the line of argument the paper will support. The writer's argument is clearly stated.

You should begin to formulate a thesis as soon as you understand your purpose in writing and identify your intended readers. In early drafts, your thesis will be a *tentative* thesis—a thesis sentence that needs revising and refining. You should feel comfortable beginning with something simple and general, knowing that you will improve it as you read about the topic, develop an understanding of the relevant issues, and draft the paper. Suppose, for example, that a student decides to write an argumentative paper about some aspect of corporal punishment in schools. Before doing any reading on the topic, the student might start with a research question that can be developed into a thesis:

> Is corporal punishment in schools good or bad?

Even if the writer has a definite opinion on this issue, the *yes/no* question is a good place to start. It allows you to go beyond your own perspective and find out what experts have to say. What do studies by educators and psychologists suggest about the effectiveness of corporal punishment? The writer reads and annotates sources. He understands that there are good arguments in favor of corporal punishment, but he decides that the most convincing arguments are against it. His tentative thesis becomes *Studies show that corporal punishment in schools is a bad idea.*

There are a number of reasons why the writer doesn't want to use this statement for anything other than an early *tentative* thesis. Notice that it is very general. A reader might ask, why? in all schools? who says it's a bad idea? what do you mean exactly when you call it *a bad idea*? After answering these questions and reading additional sources on the topic, the writer revises the thesis, and it becomes

> While many educators favor corporal punishment, it is a bad idea because it doen't really cure the problem.

While the writer is making progress and trying to indicate why corporal punishment is wrong, the tentative thesis is still vague and too informal for an academic paper: The phrase "bad idea" is a generalization, and saying that corporal punishment "doesn't really cure the problem" doesn't specify what the problem is. Readers receive very little—if any—specific information in this sentence. At this stage, the thesis has meaning to the writer, but it would not be meaningful to readers. The writer needs to revise and improve his thesis, keeping his intended readers in mind and finding words that will make the thesis specific and clear.

Eventually, after reading, developing an understanding of the different perspectives on the topic, and developing an informal outline of issues to discuss in his paper, the writer revises this *tentative* thesis so that it is a sentence that will clearly convey the subject and purpose of the paper:

Many educators claim that corporal punishment in elementary schools is an effective discipline tool; however, recent studies suggest that this form of discipline is ineffective because it causes development of aggressive behavior, withdrawal, and prolonged psychological effects.

STRATEGIES FOR DRAFTING THESIS STATEMENTS

- Start with a question. In early drafts, don't hesitate to make your thesis a question especially if you're uncertain about the perspective you will support. Regardless of your purpose in writing, in the tentative thesis stage, a question will suffice. For example, a writer uses the following questions for a tentative thesis:

    Should cities enforce curfews for teenagers? [Writer's purpose is to develop an argument.]

    Why do cities have curfews for teenagers? [Writer's purpose is to develop an informative paper.]

    If cities don't enforce curfews for teenagers, what can they do to curb juvenile crime? [Writer's purpose is to develop a proposal.]

- Turn the question into a statement. At some stage in drafting the paper, you should revise the question, making it a statement. No one can tell you exactly when this shift from question to statement should take place; however, it's reasonable to assume that your thesis will develop as your paper develops. For example, as you work on freewriting or in a discovery draft, you should expect to articulate answers to use in your tentative thesis. And as you read what others have to say about your topic, you'll find perspectives that will help you answer the question you've posed and qualify the answers:

    Cities should enforce curfews for teenagers because _____.
    studies show curfews cut down on juvenile crime. [Writer's purpose is to develop an argument.]

    The reasons cities have curfews for teenagers include _____.
    cutting down on crime and traffic accidents. [Writer's purpose is to develop an informative paper.]

    If cities don't enforce curfews for teenagers, they should consider

    _____.
    increasing police patrol and encouraging community activities for juveniles. [Writer's purpose is to develop a proposal.]

- Consider focus and scope. In the sample sentences that focus on cities and curfews for teenagers, a writer has to determine how narrow or broad the scope will be. For example, when the writer says *Cities should enforce curfews for teenagers*, is this recommendation for all cities regardless of size? Does the writer want to suggest that a curfew for teenagers would be as effective in Chicago or San Francisco as it would be for Cedar Falls, Iowa?

The writer provides readers with a scope for the topic: corporal punishment in elementary schools, rather than corporal punishment in general. Also, notice that the writer lists specific reasons for the ineffectiveness of corporal punishment: "it causes development of aggressive behavior, withdrawal, and prolonged psychological effects." While this version offers two perspectives on corporal punishment, the order of the sentence and the word that links the two perspectives, *however*, indicates that the writer will argue that "recent studies" prove corporal punishment ineffective.

The Implied Thesis

Sometimes writers use an implied thesis—that is, a thesis that is not stated directly, but rather suggested by the ideas in several sentences. In academic discourse, the stated thesis is usually preferable. In the social sciences and sciences, the thesis very often begins, "The purpose of this paper is to …" and the writer states the purpose. In the humanities, thesis statements usually are not this obvious. If you have questions about whether you should have an implied thesis or a stated thesis, ask your instructor for advice. Even if an implied thesis is acceptable, you will give yourself direction with a stated thesis in mind.

In Chapter 13, you'll read more about formulating argumentative thesis statements. Tips include taking a position on an issue and formulating a thesis statement and avoiding the fill-in-the-blank thesis—a general statement that can be applied to any number of issues. As you work on writing assignments, remember to isolate your thesis sentence periodically. Read and ask yourself if you think readers could identify your topic and your purpose by looking at the sentence. Revise as needed until you have an effective thesis.

EXERCISES: THINKING CRITICALLY

1. The following sentences are taken from argumentative papers. Review each one and determine whether or not it needs revision to make it an effective thesis statement. Consider how much specific information the sentence provides and whether the sentence announces a topic and gives readers a sense of the writer's aim. Revise any sentence that relies on empty words or phrases or that uses vague or general terms.

   a. Although it has been debated for years, the question remains: Was JFK a victim of the CIA?

   b. While the movement supporting laws governing the censoring of the Internet has gained attention and support, regulation of the net is a serious mistake and would ultimately deprive citizens of their first amendment rights.

   c. In today's society, drugs are right around the corner no matter where you live, causing possible death or dependency, so something has to be done to stop the problem, even if it involves teen curfews that a lot of people don't want or stricter rules in public schools.

    d. There are two sides to every story and this is definitely true about the sinking of the battleship Maine during the Spanish-American War.

    e. Capital punishment should be abolished.

    f. Advertising in television programs aimed at children should be limited to products that promote education and good health.

    g. The media play a stronger role in national elections than most people understand and, as a result, elections are easily bought by the candidate with the most money.

    h. If the number of crimes committed on college campuses were reported in full, students might take better precautions about personal safety and security of belongings.

    i. Animal research has yielded many important discoveries; nevertheless, it should be allowed only in medical research and banned in psychological research.

    j. If salmon are to survive in the North Western United States, two dams on the Snake River must be torn down

2. Review the front page and editorial page of your local or campus newspaper. Develop a research question for an argumentative essay and turn that question into a tentative thesis statement.

Organizing Ideas

When you have drafted a tentative thesis, think about how you will support it. Will you offer examples? compare and contrast? use analogies? define terms and concepts? Does your topic require providing context for the reader? Will you begin with your strongest point of support or your weakest point of support? If you are developing an argument, at what point will you discuss weaknesses of counterarguments?

Because your thesis and the ideas that support it will develop as you read about your topic, use a tentative or informal outline to plan your paper. Take this outline through several drafts. As you read about your topic and discover what experts have to say about it, use the tentative outline to block out what you want to say. By blocking, you formulate a plan for paragraph development in the paper. In the following informal outline, Amy organized her argument by blocking ideas and noting in parenthesis sources to use as she drafted the paper. You'll see a draft of Amy's paper in chapter 4.

FOCUS ON STUDENT WRITING: Amy's Outline

Introduction

- Attention getter: grocery store scene
- Qualifications: I'm a nutrition major; I'm citing quotations throughout the paper from experts in the field of nutrition.

- Common ground: Body image is important to all of us because we are all faced with cultural pressure and the social discrimination that comes with being obese.
- Fairness: I'll discuss the other arguments and their strong points. (This is pointed out in the thesis.)

Thesis

- Although medical experts have claimed dieting is the best way to combat obesity, a non-diet technique that combines balanced diet and health education is the safest, least expensive way to treat obese women.

Background

- Statistics (Nemeth)

     Increasing occurrence of obesity
     Unhealthy lifestyle leads to health risks
     Personal experience—my own constant dieting

Lines of argument (order of importance, readers' best interest)

- Increased self-esteem (Cazjka-Narins)
- Exercise (Grunwald)
- Public health education (Kassirer)
- Is there a need to lose weight? (Kassirer, Wickedgren)
- Behavior and diet balance (National Task)

Alternative arguments

- Diet pills (Abbasi, Canedy, National Task Force)
- Expensive, dangerous, regain the weight, addictive
- Changing the environment (Czajka-Narins, Grunwald, Hill, Taubes)

     Technology logically can't be reversed
     Industries want to make money; capitalistic
     Fat tax (Brownell) same as
     Restricting diet
- Genetics (Grunwald, Hill)
- Restricted dieting (Grunwald, Polivy)

Conclusion

If you are required to submit outlines of your paper at various stages of a writing project, remember that for a paper taken through multiple drafts, a tentative or informal outline will change. The best time to make a formal outline of your paper is at the end. Before you submit a paper to your instructor, review paragraphs in the body of the paper, checking to be sure that you have a topic sentence in each paragraph and that each topic sentence supports the thesis.

USING SOURCES

You demonstrate effective critical thinking skills when you select passages from sources that support major points in a paper. As you draft a paper, you must decide when to paraphrase another writer's ideas, when to summarize information, and when to use quotations. Each method requires critical reading skills—recognizing a source's major points and supporting ideas—and critical thinking skills—determining when a source should be presented directly or indirectly. Summaries and paraphrases allow you to present a source indirectly because you use your own words to report another writer's ideas. When you use quotations, you present a source directly, using another writer's words. It's important to understand how to summarize, paraphrase, and incorporate quotations. These are skills you will use throughout your academic career.

Summarizing

A summary is a condensed version of another writer's work, written in your own words. In papers, you summarize when you want to identify the main point a writer makes without including details. When you write a summary, your task involves reporting the main point accurately without oversimplifying or distorting the original. An important part of your task is attributing the ideas you summarize to the original work.

Read "A Skeptic on Dolly Miracle" (Figure 3.1) and the two summaries by student writers that follow. The source was annotated by Olivia, one of the student writers. These annotations helped identify the article's thesis and main points.

A SKEPTIC ON DOLLY MIRACLE

JOHN MORROW

Most scientists are leery when the mainstream press reports breakthroughs set for publication in upcoming academic journals. The media report the findings in breathless terms, giving the research and researchers big play and exciting the public's imagination about the mysteries of the universe. *[common citizens not those in the scientific field]*

Scientific epiphanies make for big headlines and good copy. Unfortunately, the copy is not always accurate or, for that matter, true, and therein lies the problem. *[emphasis of whole is put into this one paragraph]*

In this most recent breakthrough, Scottish researchers report having cloned a sheep. Cloning is something scientists around the world have been struggling with and *[something that's been talked about for years]*

FIGURE 3.1 *(continued)*

---

failing at for years. If accounts are accurate, the ability to make identical sheep from one source of DNA means we're not far from having the wherewithal to make hundreds of Claudia Schiffers or, depending upon your taste, dozens of Roseannes.

cloning people? doubtful but scary—

—very scary

The cloning research is published in the British science journal *Nature*, which is getting a lot of free publicity and no doubt an increase in its subscriber base for landing such a coup.

makes you think it is a stunt

uses negative tone

We should all be skeptical, however. As a scientist, I need to look at the hard evidence, and then delve into the methodology used to reach the conclusions. In other words, I need to prove it to myself. I've seen too many of my colleagues who, in their rush to make significant contributions to their fields, allowed their overeagerness to bend their judgments only to be embarrassed later on.

He is an expert scientist

In the past, there have been other stories of successful cloning. In the 1980s, a German researcher reported cloning mice. While the press went hysterical with visions of the *Boys From Brazil,* a careful examination of the work found that the data were wrong. But what got the bigger headlines?

People don't notice when it's found wrong

- Remember cold fusion? In 1989, researchers at the University of Utah reported—again in *Nature*—that they had created energy using water and nuclear fusion at room temperature. The implications of the supposed findings were extraordinary. Cold fusion as a power source would restructure the economies of the world. Within months, the research was discredited.

- How about electromagnetic fields—power lines—causing cancer? Reported as fact; found to be false.

- Cancer and Vitamin C? Two-time Nobel Prize-winner Linus Pauling, in his declining years, heavily promoted Vitamin C as a cancer-fighting agent. Again a serious examination of the claim found it baseless.

ends all examples w/ a sentence that is trying to prove his point

- Environmental estrogens? A research paper claimed synthetic hormones constituted a major health hazard, including increased breast cancer rates and lower sperm counts. The paper was published to much fanfare but no one has been able to duplicate the report results.

Notice a common theme here? All the widely disseminated reports about startling scientific breakthroughs have to do with hot button issues. Cancer causes and cancer cures. A source of unlimited energy. The ability to duplicate ourselves. They're sexy and simple to grasp. That means they're ripe for mass consumption.

appealing to those who are not experts by making them simple & understandable.

And editors at the for-profit scientific journals, which exist to make money for their owners, know this. That's why reports about cold fusion were published before that study received exacting scrutiny. Sexy stories sell magazines and increase circulation, even among the highbrow science journals. Try and get those same editors to publish research on a topic of little public interest. That's when the editor's pen comes and every word is called into question. It's a remarkable double standard.

publicity stunt

When an isolated finding such as successful cloning of a single sheep is announced, and it goes against the grain of generally accepted science, it should be viewed suspiciously. That doesn't mean the findings are wrong. It means only that before being made public, such a claim should receive the same rigid examination given the most mundane scientific reports.

we should all be more careful

By keeping the standards for publication constant, there will be less chance that overeager scientists will rush their findings into print. If a study has flaws, a thorough review will uncover them before the information reaches the public. Such reviews will spare the reputations of the researchers, retain the credibility of the science journals and keep the mass media from having to figure out how to report an embarrassing retraction and then burying it next to the dog food ads.

same as "But what got the bigger headlines"

So let's take a hard look at this latest research before reaching farfetched conclusions about cloning. If the research can be verified, this is an astounding scientific tour de force. But let's hold off any bizarre ideas about where such a claim leads until the claim has been examined at length and the findings can be duplicated.

And while we should encourage scientists to come forward with their remarkable research, it's important that they be held to the highest standards. It's up to the academic journals to be unbiased gatekeepers. If those journals aren't up to the job, that makes them no more believable than tabloid reports of aliens among us.

comparison of uncredibility

Morrow is a biochemist and professor of cell biology at Texas Tech University in Lubbock.

Source: John Morrow, "A Skeptic on Dolly Miracle," *Houston Chronicle* 2 Mar. 1997: C1 + .

FIGURE 3.1

FOCUS ON STUDENT WRITING: Two Summaries

Olivia's Summary

According to John Morrow, oftentimes the public's excitement gets so wrapped up with new and hot issues that we overlook the possibility of it being incredible. In a recent breakthrough, the media has gone into a frenzy reporting a sheep has been cloned through a piece of DNA. However, with this being so recent, not enough research and evidence has been examined to make it completely foolproof. Many instances have happened in the past where late-breaking news has caught the eye of the media's audience, but then later was falsified. Readers need to be more careful about what they read as fact, while the media needs to remember to print what has been completely looked over.

Tyne's Summary

John Morrow, a biochemist and professor of cell biology at Texas Tech, critiques the standards of scientific journals in his article "A Skeptic on Dolly Miracle," which appeared in the *Houston Chronicle* on March 2, 1997. This article presents examples of scientific findings that have been published in academic journals, later to be found false. He makes a connection between the findings and the glamorizing of the findings by the media.

You'll probably notice a difference in these two summaries. Tyne's summary describes what the article does. It tells the reader that Morrow "makes a connection between the findings and the glamorizing of the findings by the media"; however, this summary doesn't reveal anything about the findings. A reader might ask *why is this connection important*? The last sentence in this summary needs revising and expanding in order to avoid oversimplification. Olivia's summary presents readers with a better overview of the article than Tyne's.

Strategies for Writing Summaries

We often think of the summary as a simple exercise perhaps because a summary requires reporting the main ideas. Fair and accurate summaries, though, can be difficult. To write a summary that is helpful and informative, you must understand the text you are reading. If you do not have a thorough understanding of the text, the summary you write may be misleading or even inaccurate.

If you are summarizing several sentences or a paragraph, read the material several times. Annotate as you read. Try to summarize main ideas periodically in your annotations. Then, without looking at the passage, write your summary. You may refer to your annotations, though. If you are summarizing a longer passage or an entire article or chapter, mark the main points as you read and annotate. An additional step that you might find useful, especially if you find the information you are trying to summarize difficult to understand, is to outline the main points. What is the writer's thesis? What are the topic sentences, the main ideas, offered in paragraphs that support the thesis? After reviewing your annotations or your outline, write your summary.

Be sure to review your summary by comparing it to the original source. Make sure that it is accurate, and make sure you've used your own words. If you discover that you have relied on phrases that appear in the original, place quotation marks around those phrases. If there are several phrases that appear in the original source, rewrite the summary so that you use your words to express the ideas.

Another important issue to consider is whether your summary will be clear to your audience. The summary may be clear to you after you have reviewed the information repeatedly in order to understand it and to express the main ideas. You don't want to forget your readers, though. Make sure the summary will be meaningful to them.

EXERCISES: THINKING CRITICALLY

1. Read the following summaries and be prepared to explain why you think they are or are not informative as well as fair and accurate summaries of Mick Hamer's "Priceless Legacy of the *Titanic*," included in Chapter 1. If you find a summary unsatisfactory, rewrite it to include the main points Hamer makes in the article.

Summary 1

Mick Hamer's article introduces the reader to the concept of the *Titanic* as an ongoing experiment in corrosion. Hamer offers several examples of how wood and lead react to seawater. He includes the human element, too, reminding the reader that people actually died on this indestructible ship.

Summary 2

In "Priceless Legacy of the *Titanic*," Mick Hamer turns from passengers' stories to explanations of how inanimate objects on board have weathered the ocean's depths. Restoration techniques have been applied to paper and parts of the engines. Ultimately, the study of the *Titanic's* remains will help the scientific community understand how materials decompose in the sea. Hamer reminds readers of the loss of human life that was a part of this fascinating, ongoing study in shipwrecks.

Summary 3

Hamer's article focuses on the restoration project that is underway in Burgandy. Scientists have recovered and restored all kinds of objects from the *Titanic* and they will be on display very soon in London.

2. Review the three articles on the *Titanic* in Chapter 1. In each article, note passages that summarize the historical event and note at what point the writer summarizes the event. Compare the length and detail of each summary. What does each summary suggest about intended readers' knowledge of the sinking of the *Titanic*? Identify any summary that seems too detailed or oversimplified and revise it.

3. Review passages in Jose Arroyo's "Massive Attack" (Chapter 1) that summarize the movie *Titanic*. In your opinion, is this a fair and accurate summary? Identify any details that could be omitted and any passages that, in your opinion, oversimplify the movie's plot.

EXERCISES: COLLABORATING WITH YOUR PEERS

1. Working in pairs or in groups, draft summaries of each of the *Titanic* readings in Chapter 1. Be prepared to share your summaries with the class.

2. Compare two of your summaries with your peers. Working in pairs or in groups, identify effective summaries that report the main ideas of these passages. Share them with your classmates by reading each one aloud. If any summaries seem inaccurate or oversimplified, direct the writer to passages that need revision.

EXERCISES: FOCUS ON WRITING

1. Summarize Robert Weisbord's "Black American Perceptions of the *Titanic* Disaster" (Chapter 1). For additional practice, summarize paragraphs 1, 2, and 3.

2. Summarize Nancy Gibbs' article "If We Have It, Do We Use It?" (Chapter 1). For additional practice, summarize paragraphs 1 and 3.

Paraphrasing

When you put another writer's ideas in your own words, giving the supporting details as well as the main points, you have written a paraphrase. You paraphrase when another writer's ideas will help you support or develop an idea but the exact words do not merit inclusion as a quotation. Think of paraphrasing as a strategy for using your own voice. You rely on another writer's ideas, but you select the words.

An important point to remember when you are paraphrasing passages is the necessity of using your own words. Don't assume that transposing or substituting words creates a paraphrase. When you just transpose words, you still rely on another writer's words, phrases, and sentence structure. When you paraphrase, you demonstrate your understanding of another writer's ideas by expressing them in your own words. Sometimes writers use a mixture of paraphrase and quotation—for example, if a source described a public figure you were writing about as "down at the heels" and you believed that that description was better than anything you could express in your own words you would use the phrase and acknowledge that it was someone else's words by putting quotation marks around it. Remember that one of the purposes of paraphrasing is to let intended readers hear your voice. It's best to avoid frequent use of quoted passages in a paraphrase.

Strategies for Writing Paraphrases

When you are paraphrasing, read the material several times and annotate as you read. Don't start your paraphrase until you understand the material and identify the main points and supporting details. Use annotations to put these ideas in your own words. Then, without looking at the passage, write your paraphrase. Your annotations may serve as helpful reminders of the order of information in the original passage. If you are summarizing a long passage, mark the main points and supporting ideas as you read and annotate, and outline the main points and supporting details. After reviewing your outline, write your paraphrase. Keep your intended readers in mind and define terms as needed. When you have drafted your paraphrase, compare it to the original, making sure that you have used your own words and that you have included supporting details. Finally, be sure you haven't changed the meaning of the passage. For example, in the following paraphrase of the last paragraph in "Black American Perceptions of the *Titanic* Disaster," notice how the writer changes the meaning of the original paragraph:

Original passage

America's belief in God's omnipotence, in technology as a panacea, and in the inevitability of progress were all undermined by the *Titanic* catastrophe. For many, it was the end of a dream. Wyn Craig Wade has written that Americans would turn to the "federal government and politicians for things that they had once sought from the church and its clergy" (Wade 106). Afro-Americans, however, had no reason whatsoever to expect the government to redress their grievances. Knowledge that the white man had gotten his comeuppance in the *Titanic* episode offered only cold comfort. For Blacks it was not the end of a dream, but the continuation of a nightmare.

Paraphrase

The sinking of the *Titanic* eroded American's faith in God, in technology, and in progress. The sinking of the great ship signaled the end of the American dream. For most African-American people, the comfort they received from the sinking of the *Titanic* was insignificant because they would continue living in abad dream.

EXERCISE: THINKING CRITICALLY

Read the following examples and determine if the writer has accurately paraphrased the main ideas and supporting details in the original passage. If a writer uses quotations, determine if the quotations should be paraphrased.

Original passage (paragraph 1 "A Skeptic on Dolly Miracle")

Most scientists are leery when the mainstream press reports breakthroughs set for publication in upcoming academic journals. The media report the findings in breathless terms, giving the research and researchers big play and exciting the public's imagination.

Paraphrase

The scientific community is often suspicious when journalists report discoveries set to be announced to the scientific community in scholarly publications. The press frequently plays up this kind of article in order to generate their readers' interest.

Original passage (paragraph 2, Source 4, "Massive Attack")

It is understandable why Cameron would be attracted to the subject: A historical event loaded with significance, it offers a huge canvas, with potential for great action. And his film does try to bring in these traditional interpretations of the event: We see class warfare erupting when the icebergs hit, with the lower classes getting locked up in the lower decks. We see the cosmopolitanism of the times, the radical breakthroughs in the arts and the incipient feminism that were to transform the Twentieth Century: The bloody dialect of enlightenment in which science and progress lead to destruction is illustrated for the umpteenth time.

Paraphrase

Why Cameron became enamored of the *Titanic* story is understandable: It was one of the most noteworthy historical events of the century, a backdrop to intense drama, suspense, and action. The director attempts to portray the events that unfolded that night, especially the clash between first class and steerage passengers after the collision of the iceberg. He allows viewers to witness the opulence of the times, and he introduces social and philosophical issues that cause an old way of life to give way to the new. Most specifically he focuses on science and progress and they improve and, at the same time, complicate our lives.

Like summarizing, paraphrasing tests your reading and writing skills: You must understand a passage to paraphrase it and you must rely on skills such as audience analysis to write an effective paraphrase. For example, if a writer uses a term or concept your readers won't understand, you need to define the term or explain the concept, making the information accessible to your intended readers.

EXERCISES: FOCUS ON WRITING

1. Paraphrase the following passages in "If We Have It, Do We Use It?" (Chapter 1):

   - The first sentence in the first paragraph
   - The third paragraph
   - The ninth paragraph

2. Paraphrase the following material in "Black American Perceptions of the *Titanic* Disaster" (in Chapter 1):

- The last sentence in the first paragraph
- The second paragraph
- The last paragraph

3. Paraphrase the following material in Jose Arroyo's "Massive Attack" (in Chapter 1):

- The first sentence
- Paragraph 3
- Paragraph 7
- The next to last paragraphs

EXERCISE: COLLABORATING WITH YOUR PEERS

Share one of your paraphrases with your classmates. Ask them to evaluate your version for accuracy and fairness (attributing indebtedness). Do you rely too heavily on original phrasing? Do you capture the content of the original passage effectively in your own words? Do you make reference to the author of the original passage?

Incorporating Quotations

Your readers will expect you to use quotations, another writer's original wording, in papers written from sources. Quotations add variety to a paper and allow you to bring in other perspectives and voices. Used effectively, quotations can lend authority and credibility to a paper. In addition to adding a variety of voices to the discussion you present to the reader, they can underscore the seriousness of your topic, the urgency of your call to action, the flaws in an argument you oppose, and so on. Your aim should be to include quotations that intended readers will find meaningful, thought provoking, or powerful.

You don't want to use direct quotations to increase the word count of a paper. The temptation to use direct quotations excessively is understandable. After all, you might think, the original source is clear, precise, eloquent, and maybe difficult to paraphrase or summarize—*why not just use it as it is*? The paper that allows direct quotations to dominate illustrates the writer's failure to use quotations selectively to bolster an argument, explain a difficult concept, or illustrate a point.

Tag Phrases

Quotations should be incorporated into the text with a tag phrase that identifies either the writer's name or, if the writer can't be identified, the name of the source in which the quotation appeared. For example, a short phrase such as *According to*

Mick Hamer, who writes for New Scientist gives readers a context for a quotation from Hamer's article. Without this kind of information, you have a dropped quotation, a complete phrase or sentence that appears in the text with quotation marks and documentation but without any kind of introduction or transition into the quotation. While you fulfill your obligations to documentation with a dropped quotation, you usually leave your readers guessing. The dropped quotation "gets the job done." The writer is "off the hook" on the issue of fair and appropriate attribution, but ultimately negligent of good audience analysis. The tag phrase functions as both a transition into the quotation and a source of information for the reader.

Dropped Quotation:

Ron Weaver, the roster impostor, operated on his own and never received help from university officials. "The deception was born out of a whim and carried out rather clumsily. There were no doctored transcripts, no conspiracy on the part of coaches or schools, and hardly any thought of where this might lead" (Hoffer 27).

Tagged Quotation:

In *Sports Illustrated* Richard Hoffer reported that the roster impostor Ron Weaver operated on his own. Giving Weaver the title, The Great Impostor, Hoffer wrote, "The deception was born out of a whim and carried out rather clumsily. There were no doctored transcripts, no conspiracy on the part of coaches or schools, and hardly any thought of where this might lead (27)."

Strategies for Selecting Quotations

You should use a direct quotation when material does one or more of the following:

- Presents important statistics.
- Is so vivid and striking that to paraphrase it would be to diminish its effectiveness.
- Is from a document that is central to your discussion (for example, text of a speech or a government document).
- Provides strong support for a major point you are developing

Even if it is as little as a phrase, indicate your indebtedness by using quotation marks and appropriate documentation. Chapter 6 discusses some of the common problems writers experience in incorporating quotations.

EXERCISES: THINKING CRITICALLY

1. Review "If We Have It, Do We Use It?" and "Black American Perception of the *Titanic* Disaster." Identify quotations and any paraphrased passages. Speculate on why you think the writer opted for paraphrasing. Explain why you think each writer has or has not incorporated quotations effectively.

2. Assume that you are using "If We Have It, Do We Use It?" (in Chapter 1) in a paper about science and ethics. Review the article and identify pas-

sages you would use as quotations, passages you would paraphrase, and passages you would summarize. Be prepared to explain the rationale for each selection.

3. Review the sources for Steffany's drafts in Chapter 2. Identify passages that summarize information. What kind of information does she summarize? Identify passages that paraphrase information. What kind of information does she paraphrase? Finally, identify passages that quote sources. What kind of information does she quote? How does she introduce quotations into her paper?

Avoiding Plagiarism

Plagiarism, claiming the ideas or words of another writer as your own, is a serious offense. You undermine the idea of scholarly research if you present another writer's ideas as your own. By the same token, academic integrity requires you to make a distinction in ideas you present in your own words and in quotations that present another writer's exact wording. Because plagiarism is a form of scholastic dishonesty, there are severe penalties if you plagiarize that may include a failing grade in a course or suspension from your college or university. Remember, if your name appears in the heading or on a cover sheet, a reader (your instructor included) will expect the work—the ideas and the words—to be yours. It is your responsibility to understand exactly what constitutes plagiarism.

The type of plagiarism you are probably most familiar with is that of a student submitting to an instructor a paper that was actually written in whole or in part by someone else. As discussed earlier in this chapter, failure to attribute sources correctly—that is, to acknowledge with quotation marks and parenthetical documentation indebtedness to another writer—is also a common form of plagiarism. Although this type of plagiarism may not be deliberate, it is plagiarism nevertheless.

EXERCISE: THINKING CRITICALLY

In the following paragraphs, writers summarize a passage from an article in *Time* magazine. Read the passage and the three paragraphs, and decide if the paragraphs are examples of appropriate attribution of sources or plagiarism.

Biologists like to blame Peter Benchley's best-selling 1974 novel *Jaws* and the Steven Spielberg movie that followed for the shark's fearsome reputation as a mindless, relentless, consummate predator. The truth is that people have always been terrified by sharks, probably since humans first ventured into the sea. Who can blame them? As any survivor or witness well knows, a shark attack, especially by one of the larger species considered man-eaters—great whites, bull sharks, tiger sharks—is mind numbing in its speed, violence, gore, and devastation.

What most people don't realize is that it almost never happens. In a particularly bad year, as many as 100 people may be attacked by sharks.

Of those attacks, a small minority—15% at most—prove fatal. Far more people are killed by bees, poisonous snakes and elephants, as well as bathtub falls, and lightning strikes. It's much more dangerous to drive to the beach than to venture into the water once you get there.

Source: Michael O. Lemonick, "Under Attack," *Time* 11 Aug. 1997: 59–64

Paragraph 1

Most people don't realize that their chances of being attacked by a shark are far less than their chances of getting bitten by a poisonous snake, trampled by an elephant, falling in a bathtub, or being struck by lightning. Shark attacks don't happen very often and only about 15% prove fatal. Biologists believe that the movie *Jaws* earned sharks a terrible reputation. Most people think sharks are mindless, relentless, consummate predators (*Time* 59–60).

Paragraph 2

People think of sharks as one of the most dangerous predators they could ever encounter. Biologists theorize that the shark's bad reputation is probably the result of the novel *Jaws*, which was made into a popular movie. While the movie may have convinced the public that the shark was the "consummate predator," shark attacks are actually rare, and no more than 15% are fatal (*Time* 59–60).

Paragraph 3

Fatal shark attacks are unusual: It's actually more dangerous to drive down the highway to the beach than to venture into the water when you arrive. Far more people are killed by bees, poisonous snakes and elephants than by shark attacks. In all likelihood, this concept of the shark as the consummate predator can be traced back to the 1970s, specifically to Stephen Spielberg's movie, *Jaws*.

With careful planning in the rough draft stage, you should be able to avoid using sources haphazardly, carelessly, or inappropriately. Here are some tips on avoiding plagiarism.

- The best way to avoid plagiarism is to have a thorough understanding of what constitutes plagiarism. Pay attention to your instructor's or your textbooks' discussion of plagiarism, paraphrasing, summarizing, and using quotations. Ask questions about appropriate and inappropriate use of sources. If you're unsure about your use of sources, before you submit a paper make an appointment with your instructor to discuss any questions you have.

- You will probably do most of your writing on a computer. Keep in mind, though, that any handwritten preliminary notes or drafts should be in your handwriting. Also, suggestions for revising or correcting a typed draft should be in your handwriting. If during peer review or consultation with writing center or writing lab consultants, other people mark or write on a draft, be sure they are not rewriting your paper. Make notations on drafts other people will mark, for example "Peer Review Draft" or "Writing Center" draft.

- If you take notes on note cards, make a notation—"Quotation"—at the top of every card that is a quotation. Make notations as well for cards that summarize—"Summary"—or paraphrase—"Paraphrase"—passages from a source. Always include the page number and the source on the card. If you keep your notes in computer files, include these same notations to avoid confusing another writer's words for your own.

- When you annotate photocopies, make a notation in the margin of the source, "Quotation," when you select a passage to use as direct quotation. Do the same thing for summaries and paraphrases. Use a pencil or a different color pen than the color you used to annotate. Your notations will help you see how frequently you are quoting, paraphrasing, and summarizing.

- As you draft a paper using a typewriter or word processor, use brackets in the first draft to note when you use a quotation: [Quotation]. In subsequent drafts, do away with the brackets and be sure you provide parenthetical documentation and use quotation marks around another writer's words.

Creating an Authentic Voice

As the excerpts from the Stephen J. Gould articles in Chapter 1 illustrate, writers create different voices for different occasions and different audiences. When you write about your own experiences, you create a persona, a personality that develops in a piece of writing. Because the focus is on you in this kind of writing assignment, readers expect to find a sense of your personality in your words. In academic writing, your papers will focus on a subject or on intended readers. It's important for you to create a voice that discusses a topic seriously and that shows respect for the topic and your intended readers. In your papers, readers should hear the voice of a student.

You'll hear the voice of the scholar in books and journals. The scholarly voice often uses terms that may not be familiar, discusses a topic in a manner that suggests extensive reading and study, and typically explores complex ideas. Don't try to mimic the scholarly voice by using inflated language or terms you don't understand. You probably sense the absence of an authentic voice when a student writer sounds like a physician writing in the *Journal of the American Medical Association*. Mimicking the voice of the scholar or expert can be tempting, but avoid it.

The voice of the student is the voice of a well-educated person who has an interest in a topic or who has read about a topic and understands it enough to write about it, informing or persuading intended readers. To create an authentic voice, it's important to understand your purpose in writing and to reach a level of identification with your topic that allows you to discuss it in your own words and to incorporate sources as they are needed to support your thesis.

Taking a paper through multiple drafts and revising as you draft is a good strategy for creating an authentic voice. As you draft and revise, you will develop an understanding of your topic. Also, as you draft and revise, you should explore ways to present your ideas in order to accomplish whatever purpose you have in writing.

READINGS FOR PRACTICE: READING AND WRITING ABOUT ROAD RAGE

In the readings that follow, you will investigate *road rage*, a term used to describe aggressive driving and hair-trigger tempers that have resulted in uncalled-for violence on the highways. Preview each article, read, and annotate. Be prepared to complete writing assignments that require summarizing, paraphrasing, and incorporating direct quotations. Take each assignment through multiple drafts as you plan, shape, and revise your ideas.

BIGGER AND BETTER HERE: ROAD RAGE

ANDREW STEPHEN

I was driving on a major road about 150 miles south of Washington last week when I suddenly found myself the victim of a phenomenon I thought had been invented by the British tabloid press: road rage. I was driving steadily at the new speed limit in the area of 65mph (well, let's say 69mph) when I suddenly saw a huge "tractor-trailer" (as Americans call articulated lorries) bearing down behind me at around 85mph. I immediately thought of that early Steven Spielberg film Duel, when a driver is pursued and terrorised by a menacing truck with inexplicable, Kafkaesque relentlessness.

Listening to news of cruise missiles raining down on Yugoslavia and suddenly seeing this maniac come close to crashing into me at high speed and then speeding along less than a foot from my car, I soon realised not only that the world is becoming more promiscuously violent but also that road rage is now very real for all of us.

There was heavy traffic on the inside lane and I could not move over for about 30 seconds; as soon as I could, I moved over to let him pass. But then, instead of staying in his lane, he tried to run me off the road by swerving violently across my path; the back of the truck, surreally carrying live chickens, swung precariously as I swerved at high speed into the shoulder and grass to avoid it—which, by the grace of God, I did.

Half a mile ahead, the driver who had seemed in such a hurry stopped on the shoulder—to exchange addresses, I naively presumed, in case my car had been damaged.

Instead, he jumped down from his cab swinging a red baseball bat and then, from about ten yards away, grasped it with both hands and proceeded to take a running swing at my windscreen. For the briefest of moments, I thought the only way of avoiding serious injury—if not worse—to at least one of our four occupants (including two terrified children) was to run him down; but I managed instead to step on the accelerator and swerve away into the oncoming traffic to avoid his blow, and other cars, by inches.

The cops got their man—but we'll return to him later. I discovered on returning to Washington that "road rage" did indeed originate as a UK tabloid term in the late eighties and later made its appearance in the OED in 1997 as "a violent anger caused by the stress and frustration of traffic". But, as with everything American compared with British, the phenomenon has come to be far more lethal here.

There are 187 million drivers in the US and 250,000 have been killed in road accidents since 1990—with road rage cases, according to the American AA, having risen by 51 per cent since then. The Department of Transportation estimates that two-thirds of traffic accidents are now caused by aggressive driving.

And here's the rub. The overwhelming majority of British drivers, however violent, do not carry weapons; but large numbers of Americans (particularly in redneck territory, where I was last week) do. In 37 per cent of the road rage cases enumerated by the AAA, guns were used. In 28 per cent, some other weapon—such as a baseball bat—was deployed, and in 35 per cent of the cases the vehicles themselves were driven as weapons. So if Britons think road rage is bad, they ain't seen nothing compared with this altogether more violent society.

Various states, in fact, now consider road rage to be more serious than drunk driving. Maryland has been running a campaign called "the End of the Road for Aggressive Drivers", and in Michigan two bills are pending for what one senator there calls "attack driving".

The AAA says the typical profile of such a driver is "relatively young, poorly educated males who have criminal records, histories of violence and drug or alcohol problems". This being America, books on the subject now proliferate: you can buy Behind the Wheel: a driving psychology book or Steering Clear of Highway Madness. Which is, literally, what I just managed to do.

The consensus among the psychologists now homing in on the subject is that the everyday stresses of life in 1999 with emphasis on speed—combined with increasingly crowded roads—creates in some individuals

FIGURE 3.2   (continued)

an obsessional priority to get to their destiny in the fastest possible time; anything or anybody who thwarts that goal then becomes the target for what they see as legitimate, intense anger.

I can only speculate what demons possessed the chicken man that day last week. Police identified him as a 32-year-old man working for a farm produce company deep in rural Virginia and gave me his full name, address, social security number and date of birth. Then came my disappointment. Instead of being charged with something sufficiently grave— I thought attempted murder might not be entirely far-fetched—the cops said he would probably be charged with "reckless driving" (never mind the baseball bat assault which came when he was not even at the wheel).

And, added the police, charges could proceed only if we were willing to go to court as witnesses at some unspecified date. We spent the weekend thinking long and hard and then decided to extricate ourselves from what was a nasty and frightening episode: besides the inconvenience of the future court date away from home, I did not want a clearly violent and unstable man knowing our identities and perhaps visiting us at home with more baseball bats or perhaps worse.

But the memories remain vividly with us, and I will never again scoff at the term "road rage" just because it was one dreamt up by the tabloids.

Source: Andrew Stephen, "Bigger and Better Here: Road Rage," *New Statesman* 24 Apr. 1999: 24.

FIGURE 3.2   *(continued)*

'ROAD RAGE' TIED TO MORE TRAFFIC DEATHS

FAYE FIORE

Reversing a long decline, traffic deaths on the nation's roadways have now increased four years in a row, and federal highway officials Thursday attributed much of the carnage to **"road rage."**

Testifying before a House transportation subcommittee, National Highway Traffic Safety Administration officials estimated that two-thirds of the 42,000 highway deaths last year were related to aggressive driving, which appears to have joined drunk driving as a perilous trait of American culture.

Researchers define aggressive driving by certain types of behavior, such as speeding, illegal lane changes and running red lights. **"Road rage"** involves that sort of aggressive driving taken to an extreme.

A study by the AAA Foundation for Traffic Safety that sought to quantify **road rage** looked at 10,000 aggressive driving accidents reported around the nation since 1990. The study indicated that in 35% of the cases, a vehicle was used directly as a weapon. Men between the ages of 18 and 26 were the drivers most likely to be involved in aggressive driving accidents, the study indicated.

About 10% of overall traffic deaths occurred in car-dependent California, which has a higher population and more vehicles on the **road** than any other state. Even so, the state had fewer deaths per mile driven than the national average, a record the highway safety administration attributed to safety programs and the highest rate of seat belt use in the nation—85%.

"California has a lot to be proud of when it comes to traffic safety," said Ricardo Martinez, the highway safety agency's administrator. On the other hand, he noted—in an observation that will come as no surprise to the state's drivers—California "has some real problems regarding congestion and the fact that you can make cars faster than you can make roads."

Researchers have difficulty specifically tracking aggressive driving because it can be displayed in countless ways. But two different studies— one by the highway safety administration surveying police reports from around the nation and the other by the AAA foundation both portray aggressive driving as a growing problem.

"It is a quality of life issue. It frightens people, it makes driving unpleasant, it feels unsafe," said Stephanie Faul, spokeswoman for the AAA foundation. Experts cannot be sure exactly how many crashes aggressive driving causes, she said, but "it's a problem, and we think it's on the increase."

The highway safety administration report went further in quantifying the overall aggressive driving problem. According to the federal researchers, two-thirds of traffic fatalities last year involved behavior related to aggressive driving.

The highway fatality rate has been increasing by small increments for four years—enough to establish a clear trend, researchers say. Overall, the death rate is still relatively low, even while travel is at an all-time high, the highway safety agency reported. But the cause of crashes seems to be shifting to aggression. Overall, federal officials said, traffic accidents cost the nation $150 billion a year.

Researchers have yet to agree on the cause of the apparent increase in driver aggression. Some point to a highly stressed population, others to societal problems that carry over to the roadways. Somewhere along the way, they agree, the nation's drivers have lost civility, giving rise to a rash of tailgating, hand waving, honking, screaming, weaving, dueling and cursing that helped contribute to 12 million crashes last year.

FIGURE 3.3 *(continued)*

Freeway shootings and other highly publicized incidents of aggression once made Los Angeles the talk of the nation. The AAA report to Congress, for example, cited a case in which actor Jack Nicholson allegedly left his car at a red light and, with a golf club, whacked the windshield of a Mercedes he thought had cut him off.

But **road** violence is actually more prevalent in Eastern states, officials said. The attention of Congress was captured by a couple of recent tragedies in the Washington area, including one in which a driver forced an off-duty Washington police officer to the side of the **road,** smashed her car window and tried to strangle her because he thought she had cut him off.

Driver anger is clearly aggravated by increased traffic congestion, creating millions of tightly wound commuters whose lives are speeding up while the roads are slowing down, officials said.

Since 1987, the number of miles of roadway in the United States has increased just 1% while the number of vehicles competing for space on those roads has exploded by 35%, highway safety administration officials reported.

"When driver expectations are unmet, anger and aggression can be unleashed," Martinez told the committee. "If a driver expects a trip to take 10 minutes and it takes more than 30 minutes, frustration grows. Many drivers respond by acting and driving aggressively, sometimes even after the gridlock ends."

There are few drivers among us who have not acted out once in a while, the experts said, suggesting that the driving public needs to be educated about the dangers of blowing off steam while operating more than a ton of steel. Federal highway officials have taken their campaign to television, appearing on shows from "Oprah" to "Real Stories of the Highway Patrol."

A nationwide cellular phone number is being established for motorists to use to report aggressive drivers. Tips on how to avoid **road** wars will be included in the bills sent to 20 million cellular phone subscribers.

Federal officials also have suggested a graduated licensing program that would restrict driving privileges of young drivers until they master basic skills, then upgrade the privileges as they learn more about safety.

California lawmakers have been debating a proposal this year to adopt a graduated licensing program for younger drivers.

Copyright (c) 1997 The Times Mirror Company; Los Angeles Times
Record Number: 000760D1CDA286773AE20
Home Edition, Main News, Washington

Source: Faye Fiore, "'Road Rage' Tied to More Traffic Deaths," *Los Angeles Times* 18 Jul. 1997: A1.

FIGURE 3.3

DEBUNKING A 'TREND'

PAUL OVERBERG

Like others, USA Today had reported the "road rage" story with anecdotes and experts' claims. The premise, that this trend was growing, seemed to ring true—early project meetings ran long as we traded personal horror stories. When we tried to verify and quantify the trend, however, the reporting turned complicated.

We knew there was no real definition of road rage, and we quickly found that there weren't even good measures of its level, let alone whether it was on the rise. It was, we reasoned, the tip of a dangerous iceberg called aggressive driving: acts like running stoplights and stop signs, speeding, and recklessness.

While my colleague, Scott Bowles, started talking to police, traffic, and safety experts, I started trying to find some answers with numbers. Direct measurement seemed impossible. Aggressive driving is fleeting and elusive. I thought about counting red-light runners, for example, but scrapped the idea because it would be too hard to do nationwide.

So I fell back on indirect measures. States keep computer files on tickets and accidents, but the contents and standards vary widely. The insurance industry maintains the best crash databases, but they're private. The National Highway Traffic Safety Administration keeps detailed data on fatal crashes, but they make up just 0.5 percent of crashes reported to police.

Then I found out about NHTSA's lesser-known General Estimates System. Because of the way its approximately 50,000 crashes are chosen each year, they make up a nationally representative sample of police-reported crashes. For each, the agency logs almost 100 items about the circumstances, vehicles, drivers, and passengers.

It took a couple weeks to get the data from NHTSA, import twenty-seven files to database software and fix problems due to bad documentation. As I do with any new human source, I asked the data lots of questions. Over a couple weeks, I ran several hundred queries to see what they knew, check it against other sources, and make sure that I understood what they were telling me.

We checked with experts, debated, and finally worked out a definition of aggressive driving that the data could shed light on: any crash with injuries where at least one driver was cited for running a stop sign or stoplight; or speeding; or failing to yield; or reckless driving. This closely matched working definitions used by AAA (formerly the Automobile Association of America) and NHTSA.

FIGURE 3.4 *(continued)*

Finally, I applied our definition to the data for 1996 and 1988, the newest and oldest available. The results were startling: aggressive driving crashes made up about 20 percent of the total in both years.

What, no trend?

I checked intervening years. Again, no trend. I tweaked the definition, running hundreds of queries to look at all the crashes in the sample, then just at higher-speed crashes, crashes with only severe or fatal injuries, crashes involving just speeding citations, hit-and-run crashes, and crashes just at traffic signals.

But the 20 percent figure remained, suggesting that our definition was solid, and that the widely reported increase in road rage was a mirage. Meanwhile, we could peg the level of aggressive driving and tally its toll, something no one else had published. The work also let us paint a portrait of aggressive driving. That led to more surprises. All else being equal, aggressive drivers were:

Women as often as men.

As likely to drive cars or minivans as pickups or sport-utility vehicles.

Most prevalent in the West and South, least prevalent in the Northeast.

Disproportionately under twenty-five, yet well-represented among the middle-aged.

The annual toll extrapolated from the sample: 1,800 deaths, 800,000 injuries, $24 billion in direct and indirect costs.

I wrote a cautious analysis for Scott and his editor, Lee Ann Ruibal. They were somewhat surprised, but Scott said it clicked with his reporting. No one could cite contrary data. Experts had begun to hedge on what could be interpreted from a key survey and a poll that had often been cited in media accounts about a road rage "epidemic." Best of all, Scott found traffic consultants who explained why our portrait made sense.

So we turned the project around completely. Instead of documenting a trend, we debunked it. But we also focused on the toll, including a page of victims' stories. We painted a detailed portrait with the data and quotes from experts and drivers. As we worked, NHTSA released the 1997 data. They didn't show a trend, either.

The project reminded me what a great tool database journalism is for challenging conventional wisdom, and for moving beyond impressions and anecdotes to get solid answers.

ADDED MATERIAL

Paul Overberg, above; Scott Bowles

Source: Paul Overberg, "Debunking a 'Trend,'" *Columbia Journalism Review* (Mar./Apr. 1999): 28.

FIGURE 3.4

EXERCISES: FOCUS ON WRITING

1. Write a summary of each article.

2. Identify each writer's thesis and paraphrase it.

3. Write a letter to the editor of each publication agreeing or disagreeing with each article.

4. Write a paper that summarizes the two different perspectives on road rage. Your paper should refer to the road rage articles. You should summarize, paraphrase, and incorporate direct quotations in your paper. Assume that your paper will be published in *Car and Driver*, a specialized magazine.

5. Write an opinion paper speculating on why one published source would confirm road rage and why another would debunk it. Which source's analysis of road rage seems accurate to you? Explain why. Draw on the previous articles, personal experience, or library research to defend your thesis.

6. Write an opinion paper that explains your perspective on road rage. Is it a trend? Explain why or why not. Your paper will appear as a "My Turn" feature, a weekly opinion piece, a forum where readers of *Newsweek* can air their concerns.

Chapter 4

Evaluating Writing

Nothing strikes more fear into the average college student's heart than writing a paper. Exams are bad, but they can be fooled. If one knows how to play ball, tests don't necessarily have to be representative of the amount of information actually learned.

Papers, on the other hand, stand as a declaration of one's intelligence and knowledge of the world. They're like stripping naked in a room full of critical doctors and saying, "Here I am. What's wrong with me?"

—*Bryan Goodwin, "Students Don't Learn to Write Right"*

EVALUATING AND ANALYZING

Bryan Goodwin's comparison of a student writer to a naked patient being examined by critical doctors is a striking one. Goodwin was an English major and columnist for *The Battalion*, the student newspaper at Texas A&M University, when he wrote "Students Don't Learn to Write Right," so it is reasonable to assume that he experienced evaluation of his writing weekly, if not daily. Even if his comparison seems grossly exaggerated, certainly there's an inkling of truth in it. Writing is something people evaluate—some more formally, more prescriptively than others.

When you evaluate something, you decide if it's effective, ineffective, mediocre, weak, unsatisfactory, etc. Typically, you base initial evaluation on your personal response to something you read, see, or hear. For example, when you read a book, see a movie, or listen to a new recording, you recommend it to your friends or caution them not to waste their time and money. If it doesn't strike you as particularly good or bad, you may not offer any opinion. But if someone asks why you like, dislike, or feel ambiguous about it, that person is asking you to offer a rationale for your opinion. If you can't support your recommendation with specific reasons, you haven't explored the basis for your evaluation. You support your recommendation by analyzing the work. When you analyze specific characteristics of the work that make it good, bad, or mediocre, you advance beyond personal response. Good friends may value personal response alone; once you move outside of that circle, however, the basis for a recommendation takes on added importance. The more public the evaluation will be, the more concerned the writer must be about the tools of evaluation.

This chapter asks you to practice evaluating your own writing, your peers' writing, and published works. Your critical reading skills and your aptitude for playing the role of intended reader play an important part in your ability to be an effective evaluator of your own work and the works of others. When you provide a written evaluation of the work of your peers or of published works, we call this kind of writing a *critique*. An informal critique often consists of brief comments to the writer, usually with suggestions for improvement. Your instructor's comments on a graded paper, for example, provide a critique. A formal critique or critical review includes a brief summary, evaluation, analysis that supports the evaluation, and usually some kind of recommendation.

EVALUATING YOUR OWN WRITING

You evaluate your own writing to find ways to improve it. You read with a critical eye, asking yourself questions—what works? what doesn't work?—about each sentence and about the paper as a whole. In self-evaluation, you need to play the role of the intended reader—that is, to guess how your intended readers would react to your paper. You also anticipate questions intended readers would ask that are unanswered and objections they might raise to issues you support. You consider how readers will react to your word choice and the way you express ideas. You think about the clarity of content and identify terms that need definition. You consider the dissatisfaction your readers will feel if development of ideas is limited or predictable.

Like some writers, you may find self-evaluation difficult because you haven't developed the skills to ask and answer questions that will help you evaluate your writing. With practice, though, you can learn to evaluate your own writing and to be your own best critic. Even if you know that you will collaborate with others in peer review, it's important to develop the ability to evaluate your own writing. When your peers provide suggestions for revision, you want to make informed decisions when you accept or reject their suggestions.

Revising

Chapter 2 discussed writing as a recursive activity in which revision takes place as a writer is writing. It's important to think about revision as part of the process of generating ideas. When you draft a sentence or a paragraph, you read it with a critical eye, trying to determine if it is effective. If it isn't, you look for ways to refine and improve it. When you have a complete draft of a paper, you go through a similar process of reading and evaluating your work, this time considering how the parts of the paper work together to create a coherent piece of writing.

We call the two different levels of revision global and local. Both levels are a necessary part of evaluating your writing. For global revision, you consider how the parts of a paper work as a coherent whole to fulfill your purpose in writing. For local or sentence-level revision, you concentrate on word choice, specificity of ideas, and sentence structure. At both levels of revision, you consider your intended readers and their reactions to your ideas and the way you express them. You need good critical reading skills for both kinds of revision.

Notice that we haven't mentioned grammar, spelling, and punctuation. When you focus on these elements, you edit your work. As you will see, there's a big difference in editing and revising. As you draft a paper, you will probably revise and edit as you write. When you have a complete draft of a paper, you should work on local and global revision.

EXERCISE: FOCUS ON WRITING

Revise the paper you wrote on road rage or another paper you are working on as you read this chapter. Make global and local revisions as needed to improve the paper, following suggestions for evaluating, revising, and editing your writing.

Global Revision

Global revision is, simply put, considering the paper as a whole and making necessary changes that improve and refine the paper. It isn't a simple task, though. Global revision requires you to consider such matters as audience awareness, organization and content, and style. Because your goal is to evaluate how effectively parts of the paper work together, you should consider the introduction and conclusion, the body paragraphs, and the transitions within and between these paragraphs. You want to determine if all parts of the paper work together to meet your purpose in writing. Global revision may involve deleting passages (painful as that may be), expanding on ideas, or adding new information. It may even call for a complete reworking of ideas—following a new organizational pattern, for example, or reversing your stance on a topic.

Your understanding of rhetorical situations and your critical thinking skills play a role in global revision. It's important to read and evaluate with your intended readers in mind. Try to envision them and their reactions to your paper as you read and revise your work. As you draft a paper, you try to consider your audience, but typically, in early drafts you think as a writer, concentrating primarily on generating ideas and finding the best way to express your ideas. Global revision requires reviewing your paper and analyzing and evaluating your words and ideas. You have to play the role of the reader. You have to read with a critical eye, analyze and evaluate your work, and determine which passages need to be revised and how to revise them.

As you revise on your own, answer the following questions:

✔ **CHECKLIST**
GLOBAL REVISION

Audience Awareness

✔ Do I make the introduction relevant to the reader?

✔ Do I make my subject clear in the thesis?

CHECKLIST *(continued on next page)*

(continued) from page 145

✔ Do I convey my purpose in writing in the thesis?

✔ Do I make my stance on the subject clear in the thesis?

✔ Do I define terms as needed?

✔ Do I consider my intended readers—what they know and don't know—throughout the paper?

✔ Do I give the reader a sense of closure?

Organization

✔ Do I state my thesis early or late in the paper? If it's stated late, what is my reason for delaying it?

✔ Do I use topic sentences in body paragraphs?

✔ Do I support the thesis with each body paragraph?

✔ Do I use smooth transitions between paragraphs?

✔ Do I offer body paragraphs in an order that makes ideas clear and logical?

✔ Do I restate the thesis in the conclusion?

✔ Do I rely on a formulaic plan of organization?

Content

✔ Do I develop ideas adequately using information that will be meaningful to intended readers?

✔ Do I develop paragraphs fully?

✔ Do I incorporate sources effectively by summarizing, paraphrasing, and introducing direct quotations?

✔ Do I provide clear and appropriate explanation of new terms or concepts?

✔ Do I offer readers too much old information about the topic?

✔ Do I offer readers sufficient new information about the topic?

✔ Do I make content interesting and relevant to readers?

Style

✔ Do I use a tone that is formal or informal?

✔ Do I rely primarily on choppy sentences?

✔ Do I need to vary beginnings of sentences?

✔ Do I use active and passive voice effectively?

✔ Do I rely on clichés or generalizations?

Audience Awareness

In general, academic audiences have specific expectations of writers—first and foremost to learn something new or to feel significantly informed by the writer. After doing research on a topic, you are in a good position to help your intended readers learn something or look at a new perspective on a topic. Keep your audience in mind as you draft your paper, and consider such matters as whether they need definitions of terms, explanation of ideas that are complex or unfamiliar, historical background, or some other kind of context for understanding the topic. One way to analyze your readers' needs is to think back to your understanding of your topic before you researched it. What did the topic mean to you? What point of reference did you have for understanding it? What kinds of questions did you have? Were there terms you didn't understand that you understand now? What were they? Were there concepts that were unfamiliar to you? Did you have a historical, political, or social context for the topic?

Writers sometimes make the mistake of assuming that readers will agree with their ideas wholeheartedly. Their writing becomes egocentric—that is, aimed more at the writer than at readers who agree on some points the writer makes and disagree with others. Try to second-guess what your readers know and how they will react to your topic. Will they agree or disagree with the idea you advance in your thesis? How can you motivate readers to consider perspectives they may oppose? Have you said anything that might alienate readers?

Organization and Content

Introductions and conclusions.   Beginnings and endings are key positions for capturing readers' interest or losing readers altogether. When you review your introductory and concluding paragraphs, be aware that these are two places where writers often rely on formulas or predictable statements. These two paragraphs should frame your paper in a manner that is appropriate for the subject and that makes your main points interesting, relevant, and thought-provoking to your intended readers.

Experienced writers frequently write papers from the inside out. They draft the body of the paper and then compose the introduction and conclusion. There are two advantages to this approach. One is that it gives you a thorough understanding of the topic. With the body of the paper drafted, you review your paper and consider ways to introduce and conclude your remarks. The other advantage is that you get words down on paper. If you are writing about a topic that is relatively new to you, your reading and research should prepare you to write about it. Think of drafting the body of the paper first as a confidence builder. You're not looking at a blank page any more; you have a draft. Now you can review what you have said, and you can think about a beginning that will make your readers want to read the paper and an ending that will provide a sense of closure.

Introductions

Engaging the reader.   After you have read and researched your topic, you should have fresh ideas for ways to make your topic relevant and interesting to readers. Try to avoid formulaic introductions such as by beginning with the dictionary definition of a term, "According to *Webster's Dictionary*, xenotransplantation is...." or, in a paper discussing the achievements of Queen Elizabeth, introducing the topic by saying:

> England has seen some remarkable monarchs. Some are more memorable, however, than others. This is especially true of one of the most outstanding, Queen Elizabeth I, who reigned from 1533 to 1603. Intrigue, expansion, and treachery marked her reign.

This isn't to say that you should never use a dictionary definition or start with a general opening that narrows to the thesis. The important point is to avoid the predictable and to offer your intended readers something that will make them want to read the rest of the paper. You may also want to establish common ground with your readers in the introduction.

If you feel helpless starting a draft without an introduction, the formulaic or predictable beginning will be sufficient in an early draft, as long as you revise it at some point. Ask yourself if your purpose in writing would be better served by an introductory paragraph that included a quotation, an anecdote, a brief review of the issue, or a question.

Getting to the main point.   Think of the introduction as a contract you make with the reader. It should designate the topic, make the topic relevant to the reader, indicate your purpose in writing, and state the thesis. In academic writing, readers will expect you to announce your topic and purpose for writing early in the paper—usually, in mid-length papers (800–1,000 words), no later than in the first or second paragraph.

FOCUS ON STUDENT WRITING: Amy's Introduction
Read the introduction to Amy's paper, "Nondiet: The Most Effective Answer to America's Obesity Problem," and be prepared to discuss why it seems effective or ineffective.

```
    A woman enters an Albertson's grocery store. She
glances at the racks of fashion magazines where models
such as 105-pound Kate Moss grace the covers and
headlines boast of new ways to lose weight quickly or
shape one's body for the beach in less than a month.
She passes by the shelves of Snackwell's Fat-Free
Cookies and WOW! Fat-Free Potato Chips. She comes to
the frozen-food section and catches a glimpse of her 5-
foot 4-inch, 190-pound frame in the reflection of the
stainless steel trim. She reaches for a pint of vanilla
```

ice cream and puts it in her cart as a thinner woman grabs the same item and places it in her basket. "Maybe you should try the yogurt," the second woman disapprovingly comments as she walks away.

Americans, especially American women, are constantly faced with cultural pressure to be thin. "Fat is the last type of safe discrimination," comments Carole Boteilho to <u>Life</u> magazine (Grunwald 74). Boteilho and other women who have battled against excess weight know firsthand how obese people are viewed by the majority of American society. Americans are often guilty of measuring a person's character and work ethic in pounds. Research conducted by the <u>New England Journal of Medicine</u> claims the probability of an overweight woman being married is 20 percent less than that of her thinner counterpart. Even more startling is the statistic showing that regardless of her level of education or location, a heavier woman's average household income is over eight thousand dollars lower than that of an averaged-sized woman's earnings (Nemeth 46). Because weight seems to be such a determining factor in a woman's social and economic success, size often determines her feelings of self-worth. This preoccupation with weight combined with statistics, like those in the <u>Journal of the American Medical Association</u> that show that one in every three adults is overweight have caused many American women to demand an answer to the obesity problem (<u>Pharmacotherapy</u> 1907). Although medical experts are considering and have had some success with different approaches for controlling obesity—diet pills, change of environment, food restriction diets, and genetic alterations—a nondiet technique that combines health awareness with improved physical and psychological health is currently the safest, cheapest, and most effective long-term method available.

✔ CHECKLIST
REVISION: INTRODUCTORY PARAGRAPHS

- ✔ What kinds of expectations does the introduction raise?
- ✔ How do I motivate readers to read my paper?
- ✔ Does the introduction seem formulaic or canned?
- ✔ Does the introduction rely on clichés?
- ✔ Have I included a thesis—stated or implied? (If the answer is no, what are my reasons for delaying the thesis?)
- ✔ How do I give readers a sense of my purpose?

EXERCISE: THINKING CRITICALLY

Review the introductory paragraph in the paper you wrote on road rage or in another paper you are currently writing. Considering the suggestions in this chapter and the checklist above, how would you revise the introductory paragraph?

Conclusions

Repeating important points.   Conclusions are sometimes difficult to write because you want to repeat the main ideas of your paper, but you don't want the repetition to be too obvious. In other words, you want to paraphrase your thesis and summarize the main ideas that support it. Readers will invariably notice the wholesale use of a sentence that appears earlier in the paper, so paraphrasing and summarizing skills are important. Think of the conclusion as your last chance to leave the reader with something to consider. In addition to restating the thesis and summarizing the main points of the paper, the conclusion could also offer a plan of action, emphasize the importance of the issue, call for further study of the issue, or discuss or analyze a quotation that is relevant to the issue

Providing closure.   Speakers at high school and college graduation ceremonies frequently make the mistake of signaling the end of their speeches by saying, "In conclusion …" Audiences, concerned primarily with the awarding of diplomas, have been known to applaud as soon as they hear that phrase. While you want readers to recognize the last paragraph as the conclusion, you want to avoid being too obvious. For the speaker and the writer, "In conclusion" signals closure, a way of announcing, "The End." The concluding paragraph should provide readers with the impression that the writer has brought the discussion to an end. You want to do this without being overly dramatic or verbose.

Try to end with your own words. Endings of sentences, paragraphs, and papers are key positions for emphasizing ideas, so it's best to cast those ideas in *your* words. If you use a quotation in the conclusion, comment on the quotation. How does it relate to the topic you discuss in the paper?

FOCUS ON STUDENT WRITING: Amy's Conclusion

Read the concluding paragraph in Amy's paper and be prepared to discuss why it seems effective or ineffective:

> Until the cause of obesity can be discovered and sufficient data can back the claim, we must find some way to improve the health of American society. The least expensive, safest, and most effective way currently known is to implement the nondiet technique. The goal of Americans no matter what they weigh should be to live a healthy lifestyle that includes exercising, a balanced diet, and a positive self-image. When America finally realizes that heaviness is not necessarily a sign of being unhealthy, we will be able to accept each other no matter what we buy at the grocery story or what the scale says. There is no scale for the size of someone's heart.

✔ CHECKLIST
REVISION: CONCLUDING PARAGRAPHS

✔ Do I restate the thesis effectively?

✔ Do I "parrot" the thesis and topic sentences?

✔ Are my restatements of the thesis and topic sentences effective paraphrases?

✔ Do I introduce any new topics in the conclusion that aren't discussed in the paper?

✔ Do I provide readers with a sense of closure?

✔ Do I end with my own words?

EXERCISE: THINKING CRITICALLY

Review the concluding paragraph in the paper you wrote on road rage or in another paper you are currently writing. Considering the suggestions in this chapter and the checklist above, how would you revise the conclusion?

Paragraphs That Support the Thesis

Paragraphs.   The purpose of the paragraph is to focus on one idea and to develop that idea thoroughly. Paragraphs in the body of the paper should support the thesis statement. No one can tell you how long a paragraph should be. You have to consider your intended readers' needs: what they know about the topic, what they don't know, how to make a point vivid and relevant, and how to hold readers' interest. Important questions to ask are *what is the purpose of the paragraph?* and *how can I accomplish this purpose?* Is your purpose to illustrate a point? share an anecdote? compare and contrast something? define a term? break something down into parts? classify items? examine cause and effect? tell a story? answer a question?

As you review your draft, consider how you have used sources to develop paragraphs. Do you have a good synthesis of sources that includes summary, paraphrase, and direct quotations? Do you draw inferences or conclusions from sources? The end of the paragraph is a power position. It's a good place to reiterate a point or, if the paragraph is long, to restate the topic sentence. Try to end each paragraph with your comments about the topic you are developing.

One strategy for determining whether paragraphs form logical, coherent support for the thesis is to develop an outline from the draft. That is, copy your thesis and list topic sentences beneath it. Ask yourself if each paragraph clearly supports the thesis. Also, consider the order of information. Does your paper start with the most important point and end with the least important? Does it start with the least important point and end with the most important? Does it begin with general ideas supported by specific examples? Does it begin with specific examples and end with a generalization drawn from those examples? Does the paper follow a chronological order? How does one block of information build on another? There are a variety of ways to organize ideas. The plan you select should help you support your thesis and help the reader follow your ideas.

Transitions.   Ideally, a paper should be seamless—that is, one idea should flow into another clearly and eloquently. Transitions, words or phrases that create coherence, indicate relationships between ideas, and provide readers with signals that direct the movement of ideas, can create this seamlesssness by connecting ideas within paragraphs and providing a bridge from one paragraph to another. Transitional devices may include repeating words or using transitional expressions. Examples of transitional expressions include *however, for example, moreover, in addition, finally, indeed, therefore, after all, even though, furthermore, on the other hand, and first ... second ... third*—and many more.

Used too frequently, transitions can be distracting. If transitions are used too sparingly, or not at all, your paper will sound choppy and lack the kind of conversational flow readers will expect.

EXERCISE: THINKING CRITICALLY

Review the body paragraphs in the paper you wrote on road rage or in another paper you are currently writing. Add transitions if they are missing. Revise transitions that are too obvious or awkward.

Topic Sentences

Organizing ideas.   Your intended readers will expect a topic sentence, a sentence that states the main point, in every paragraph. And they will expect you to stick to that topic. Each sentence in a paragraph should relate clearly to the topic sentence.

Like the thesis statement, topic sentences can be implied; however, in academic writing, you want ideas to be clear and specific. If your aim is to inform or persuade, the stated topic sentence is usually preferable. Implied topic sentences call on your intended readers to "read between the lines," and readers may not want to do this. Also, if your topic is unfamiliar, readers may not have sufficient understanding to determine the implied topic sentence.

The placement of the topic sentence is your choice. Place it at the beginning if you want to state the idea you'll develop; place it in the middle if you're discussing two closely related ideas; and delay the topic sentence until the end if you want to lead up the main idea. If you postpone the topic sentence, you should have a reason for doing so. In paragraphs that use specific examples that lead to a generalization, the topic sentence can be effective at the end.

EXERCISE: THINKING CRITICALLY

Review the topic sentences in the paper you wrote on road rage or in another paper you are currently writing. Considering the suggestions above, how would could you revise and improve the topic sentences?

Style

In Chapter 1, you read two selections by Stephen J. Gould—both on the same topic, but each with a different style. As a writer, you will have a repertoire of styles to use for different audiences and purposes in writing. If you completed the postcard exercise in Chapter 1, you probably addressed three different audiences in styles ranging in formality. As you assess your style, consider the level of formality you use and ask yourself if it is appropriate for your intended readers.

You make stylistic choices when you determine whether

- Active or passive voice is appropriate
- Clichés are permissible or overused
- Direct address of your audience is appropriate and effective
- Word choice and phrasing are specific, fresh, and vivid
- Long sentences would be more accessible to readers if broken into short sentences
- Variation in sentence structure makes a passage flow
- An idea should be presented as a statement, a question, an exclamation, or a command
- The main point in a sentence should occur at the beginning or the end

The content of a paper can be enhanced or diminished by your style. When you evaluate how various parts of your paper work together, think about how you convey to your intended readers a sense of authority. Your style—how you put words and phrases together—should be one element of the paper that convinces readers that you write as someone who has a thorough understanding of the topic.

In Chapter 1, you read that a writer reveals his or her stance through style and tone. This concept should be clear if you remember at some point in your adolescence saying something that caused an adult to warn, *Don't use that tone of voice with me*. Translation: Do away with the attitude. You might not be reprimanded for the content of your remarks, but the tone might be out of line or offensive. One of the effects of stylistic choices—diction, sentence structure, and imagery— is the tone a writer creates—reverence, sarcasm, seriousness, confidence, judiciousness, compassion, anger. When we write, we create voices with different tones and registers of formality and informality. In Chapter 10, you'll read about listening to writers' voices. You want to develop the ability to hear the tone of your own voice, too.

EXERCISE: THINKING CRITICALLY

Use the checklists included in this chapter to revise your paper on road rage or another paper you are writing.

Local Revision

Sentence-Level Revision

One strategy for sentence-level revision is to read your paper aloud and listen to your own prose. Your ear often detects problem sentences that appear to be okay when you read them to yourself. For example, as you listen to a paragraph read aloud, you realize that your sentences sound too much alike, choppy, or stilted. You hear repetition of words or phrases, or you hear sentences that seem lifeless and dull or awkward. At the same time, you recognize passages that flow skillfully from one idea to another, and you hear phrasing that is fresh and original, a departure from the way other writers express ideas. After you have taken a paper through multiple drafts, you are familiar with your own prose, so listening to it is a way of getting another perspective on the paper, and a good way to reexamine your writing.

Revising for Specific Ideas

In early drafts, your aim is to get ideas down on paper. Vague generalities and clichés—trite, familiar phrases you read and hear frequently—are permissible crutches to a point; however, as you progress through multiple drafts of a paper, consider the level of specific information you provide for intended readers. For example, in an early draft of a paper on the crash of the German dirigible *Hindenburg*, you describe the airship as so big it was awesome. And you state that the crash of the *Hindenburg* was a big event. Because you have researched this event, the words *awesome* and *big* have meaning for you. Your intended reader, however, understandably asks *how big? what exactly does the writer mean by awesome?* or *could the writer provide a basis of comparison?* If you write that the *Hindenburg* was 803.8 feet long and compare it to just short of three football fields, you provide readers with a specific, vivid image. And if you explain that the crash was reported worldwide on radio and received as much coverage in the newspaper as the bombing of the federal building in Oklahoma City, readers have specific points of comparison that are much more meaningful to them than the descriptions *awesome* and *a big event*.

Inexperienced writers often consider clichés to be acceptable ways of expressing ideas. Readers will understand the gist, you might argue. But consider how refreshing your prose is when you avoid the predictable. A well-turned phrase provides the difference between mundane prose and effective prose that invites a second reading. Consider, for example, Carlos Fuentes' description of the Disney Corporation's acquisition of the ABC network as "a grinning death ... a smiling death acted out by smiling robots"—or Bryan Goodwin's comparison of the writer to a naked patient being examined by critical doctors. Both create vivid imagery.

Clichés can be used for effect; however, it's best to avoid them. If you must use them, acknowledge your reliance on a cliché by putting it in quotation marks. If you're unsure about what a cliché is or what effect the use of clichés has on your writing, read the following excerpt from "We've heard it all someplace else" by Glenn Dromgoole.

WE'VE HEARD IT ALL SOMEPLACE ELSE

GLENN DROMGOOLE

Abilene—In the best of all possible worlds, writers should avoid cliches like the plague. But beggars can't be choosers. With all due respect, a bird in the hand is worth two in the bush. Between you and me and the gatepost, a columnist had better be safe than sorry. Our actions speak louder than words.

On the other hand, it goes without saying that, for better or worse, sometimes we can't see the forest for the trees. Sometimes the left hand doesn't know what the right hand is doing. Now that's a horse of a different color, when we can't have our cake and eat it, too.

In other words, we have to fish or cut bait. One has to have both feet firmly planted on the ground to see the handwriting on the wall and proclaim, "Do as I say, not as I do."

That's the way the cookie crumbles, I suppose. We have to take the bitter with the sweet.

Not to beat a dead horse, but sometimes we bite off more than we can chew. We find that we can't be all things to all men, and we have to go back to the drawing board and try to makes heads or tails out of it.

If worse comes to worst, we can always take it like a man and hope we come up smelling like a rose.

But that is putting the cart before the horse. In the long run, if we burn the candle at both ends, seize the bull by the horns, call a spade a spade, and dot the I's and cross the T's, there is not a ghost of a chance that our stories will be dull as dishwater.

However, if we get up on the wrong side of the bed and become satisfied that half a loaf is better than none, we are in danger of jumping out of the frying pan into the fire and turning out copy that isn't worth a hill of beans.

Instead, we need to go whole hog and fall head over heels in love with the Mother Tongue. My English teacher would turn over in her grave, if she had bitten the dust, at the way good writing is dead as a doornail these days.

Source: Glen Dromgoole, "We've Heard It All Someplace Else," *Abilene Reporter-News* 17 Feb. 1996: A11.

Remember that writers usually have several options for making ideas vivid, specific, and memorable. Because words can have the same general meanings, but different connotations or associations, writers often use word choice for great effect. For example, the terms *miser, cheapskate, penny-pincher*, and *fiscal-conservative* all mean a person who watches money carefully, but have very different connotations. Which term would you use to describe a politician who votes against excessive government spending? Which term would you use to describe a wealthy, eccentric neighbor who refuses to lend financial support to community projects? Why do you think Bryan Goodwin used the term *naked* instead of *nude, unclothed,* or *undressed?*

EXERCISE: THINKING CRITICALLY

Read the following paragraphs and underline passages that are vague or general or that rely on clichés. Suggest revisions for these passages:

```
The lure of the impostor is a sure thing. Today's
society is fascinated with things that are not real. A
place called Great Impostors, for example, which
happens to have a store in an upscale area of Austin,
offers copies of every kind of designer jewelry
imaginable. People love this place. It is a well-known
fact that impostors—jewelry or people—are really more
fascinating than the real thing.
```

Impostors are not unique to Texas, though. The ones
we claim as our very own offer evidence of a vim and
vigor that refuses to bow to demands of society. When
the shoe is on the other foot, the impostors who fool
us take advantage of the good people of the Lone Star
State. Their existence is evidence of the good and bad
in human nature, as well as a combination of southern
and frontier hospitality. Every now and then, their
presence is evidence of both a mean streak in human
nature and a fertile imagination in an individual in
pursuit of good times and fast money.

EDITING YOUR WRITING

As you work through multiple drafts of a paper, take time periodically to edit or
proofread your work. Because you get used to looking at your own mistakes, editing can be difficult. You have to identify surface-level errors: comma splices, sub-
ject-verb agreement, pronoun-antecedent agreement, words omitted, words
misspelled, and so on.

Experienced writers are usually aware of the kinds of surface-level problems
that occur frequently in their writing. One strategy for developing skills for editing your own work is to keep a list in a notebook or in a file in your word processor of surface-level errors you find in drafts of your papers and notes on how to
correct them.

A dictionary, handbook, and thesaurus are helpful resources to have on hand
when you edit a paper. If you are working on a word processor, use spell-check and
grammar-check programs. Neither one will catch all errors, but one or the other
may help you identify something you have overlooked.

The following guidelines for editing list other matters to consider as you edit
and clean up a draft. Remember, execution of ideas is important. You don't want to
give readers any reason to discredit your ideas. Unfortunately, a paper riddled with
surface errors may create the impression in readers' minds that you either don't
care about making a good impression or you don't know how to establish your own
credibility by offering a corrected draft free of surface errors.

EXERCISE: THINKING CRITICALLY

Use the checklist that follows to edit your paper on road rage or another paper
you are writing.

GUIDELINES FOR EDITING

- Check for spelling, punctuation, and grammar errors.
- Check for word confusion. Examples of commonly confused words include *its/it's*; *to/too/two*; *their/there/they're*; *affect/effect*.
- Be sure the words *this, that*, and *which* refer clearly to a person, place, or thing.
- Determine whether contractions are appropriate.
- Be sure the paper follows a specific format if one is required (for example, MLA or APA). Check guidelines for the title page, pagination, and, if required, parenthetical documentation and works cited.
- Be sure that works cited at the end of the paper are cited in the text.
- Check for consistency in spelling authors' names and words in the titles of their works.
- If you use parenthetical documentation primarily at the end of each paragraph, provide the reader with cues throughout the paragraph that indicate very clearly that information is from the source cited at the end of the paragraph.
- Read the paper backwards to identify typographical errors.

EVALUATING THE WORK
OF YOUR PEERS

Peer review is a familiar activity in the composition classroom. Working in pairs or in groups, you share copies of your papers and provide one another with an evaluation or critique that points out strengths and weaknesses in the paper and offers suggestions for revision. During peer review, you are obligated to stay on target, be a critical reader, and make your response to a draft helpful to the writer. You will expect the same thing. You should expect constructive criticism in peer review. Hearing about weaknesses in your paper may be painful, but it is important. If you hesitate to point out weaknesses in a paper because you fear hurting someone's feelings, try to understand how *constructive* criticism is better in the long run for the writer. You aren't evaluating the person, you are evaluating the writing.

Peer review is a good place to practice audience analysis and critical reading skills. When you discuss a paper's weaknesses, think of how you would appreciate hearing weaknesses discussed. Try to avoid offering evaluation without analysis. For example, if you tell another writer, "I understand your purpose in this paragraph, but it doesn't really work," you haven't explained why you think the paragraph doesn't work. A helpful response would be to explain that the writer hasn't included sufficient examples; point out that the paragraph rambles, developing more than one idea; or give some other specific reason that paragraph doesn't really work.

When you share drafts of your paper with other readers, ask them to consider global matters. It's good to hear that spelling is correct and all the commas are in the right places, but you want to move beyond sentence-level considerations in peer review. Using the questions in the box with tips for global revision, and substituting *Does the writer* for *Do I,* you and your reviewers can address issues of audience awareness, organization and content, and style.

Writers have the right to accept or reject suggestions for revision, so when peer review is complete, you have decisions to make: Do you make the changes your reviewers suggested? Do their suggestions for revision trigger ideas of your own for revision? Do you reject your peers' suggestions for revision? Don't make changes in your draft blindly. Think about the suggestions your reviewers make and be sure you agree with the changes they suggest.

EXERCISE: THINKING CRITICALLY

Review the responses to the introduction and conclusion of Amy's paper, which are included in this chapter. Do you agree or disagree with the reviewers? Explain why.

✔ CHECKLIST
PEER EVALUATION

✔ Provide each member of your peer review group with a photocopy of your paper.

✔ Ask each member of the group to read his or her paper aloud.

✔ Follow drafts as each person reads.

✔ Mark passages that are vivid and memorable, vague or general, confusing or difficult to follow.

✔ Allow five to ten minutes to provide a short note to the writer. Suggest ways to improve the paper.

✔ Ask each member of the group to discuss the paper's strengths and weaknesses.

✔ Consider content, organization, style, and audience awareness.

✔ Collect photocopies from your group.

✔ Consider your peers' suggestions as you revise your paper.

Evaluation of the Introduction: Great opening paragraph! It made me want to read the paper. I think this anecdote will make everyone read the paper. You really have a two-paragraph introduction—the narrative about the grocery store and the paragraph that follows. I think this is ok. The thesis statement (last sentence in the first paragraph) is really long, but also specific. Should it be streamlined?

Evaluation of the Conclusion: The conclusion summarizes the paper, but seems fairly routine. Perhaps I'm comparing it to the first paragraph. I like the way you come full circle with the subtle reference to the grocery story. This is a nice link to the introduction.

CONSIDERING COHERENCE

For further understanding of why a paper is easily accessible or dense and difficult, consider the different parts of the paper that create a coherent whole.

When you consider coherence (overall coherence in an essay, or coherence at the paragraph level), you are examining the elements that hold the essay together, make it flow, and give it the feeling of not having any rough seams. Whether you are aware of it or not, as a reader you depend on elements that create coherence because these elements help you follow a writer's ideas. If you have difficulty understanding a paper for which you are clearly part of the intended audience, examine elements that undermine coherence in the text:

- A delayed thesis, or no stated or implied thesis
- Few if any transitional devices, or overuse of transitional devices within and between paragraphs
- No topic sentences
- Shifts in verb tense or point of view
- Paragraphs that develop more than one main idea
- Passages that discuss new information (information not previously mentioned in the paper or information that is unfamiliar to the reader) and that do not provide a clear context or a clear concept of the relationship of the new information to old information (information previously discussed in the paper or information familiar to the reader)
- Passages that confuse the reader because methods of development are not used in a satisfactory or clear manner (analogies are not clea+r, terms are not defined, order of events is unclear or puzzling, cause and effect is not clear, description is minimal)
- Passages that confuse or distract the reader because of garbled or convoluted syntax
- Passages that rely primarily on cohesion (repetition of words and phrases) with no discernible connection or relationship of one idea to another

FOCUS ON STUDENT WRITING: Reviewing Ronnie's Draft

To practice reviewing the work of another student writer, read Ronny's draft, "A Moment in Time: The 1968 Olympic Games." Ronny wrote the paper after working on Case Study #3, "Letter From Birmingham Jail" (Chapter 11). Before you read and discuss the paper, review the assignment and Ronny's reflections on his writing that follow.

Ronny's Assignment: Select an event that occurred between 1900 and 1970 —an event

- that the academic community has examined, analyzing its historical, ethical, or intellectual significance;
- that took twenty-four hours or less; and
- that you find interesting and you believe your peers should know more about than they presently do.

Your paper should <u>summarize</u> what happened, answering the questions *Who? What? Where? When?* and <u>synthesize</u> different perspectives on the event. You should include an initial account of the event from a newspaper as well as information from the most recently published journal article or book about the event, reporting how scholars past and present or eye witnesses have interpreted the significance of the event.

Rhetorical Situation: Assume that your paper will be published in the *Journal of Popular Culture*. Your task is to make the narrative and commentary interesting and relevant to your audience.

Ronny's Reflections

During my research, I found different and interesting topics that I could have used. However, we have been dealing with the topic of the human rights movement in class, and it came to mind that this topic would be interesting and attractive to my audience. In the beginning I wanted to discuss the relationship of drugs and athletes, but I felt my audience would be more receptive to another topic. I decided the 1968 Olympic Games seemed more suitable.

To study and make a conclusion from this topic was not easy. All the information and sources that I found were too broad. I had a hard time finding specific information on what happened. My goal was to give my audience a general and specific idea of this huge event. One of the problems I dealt with was finding a specific and accurate source. Most of my other sources only gave me general information. I needed to find a newspaper article that discussed this topic as soon as it occurred. I found it in a microfilm of *The New York Times* in the Library of Texas A&M University. During the revision of my first draft, I realized that I had to be more specific in certain patterns concerning the main idea because it is a historical event and my audience needs to know as much information as possible. With help from my peer comments, I can improve on many of my weaknesses.

Ronny Jimenez

Ms. Li

English 104

04 Dec. 2000

A MOMENT IN TIME: THE 1968 OLYMPIC GAMES

We live today in a society that has changed with the passing years. We have learned how to live in harmony. We have learned to respect each other and society. All these changes are consequences of a series of infinite moments that took place several years ago in America. In America today, all kinds of people exist and are trying to subsist as a nation. There was a time when America also held a great tension between whites and blacks. During the time of the 1960s, the human rights movement took place. It was a struggle led by the great leaders of our time, including Dr. Martin Luther King. I believe that the mission of equality was correct. However, we find that ordinary people also fought for human rights. Among them were two black Americans who in their protests made a controversial statement for the world to see. These two Americans are Tommie Smith and John Carlos.

This historic event took place at the 1968 Olympic games held in Mexico City. Tommie Smith and John Carlos won the 200-meter dash, They set a new world record, winning first and third place, respectively. Smith and Carlos were not only athletes, but activists. They were part of an organization called the Olympic Project for Human Rights, or OPHR. After they had received their medals, and the United States national anthem began, both started a silent protest. According to a *New York Times* article, "2 Accept Medals Wearing Black Gloves," they raised their fists, wearing black gloves and bowing their heads together, in representation of the black power salute. At that moment Smith was wearing a black scarf that represented black pride. Both athletes wore black stockings that represented poverty. They did this as a gesture to protest racial discrimination in the United States. The silver medallist, Norman, was the only white man on the podium during the ceremony. After this, he put on a civil rights button of OPHR in support of their protest against racial discrimination.

In the *Augusta Chronicle* interview Tommie Smith states, "It was an act of courage" because nobody would have dared to do this in the Olympic Games. Something had to be done."According to Smith, the left-hand glove and the right-hand glove together presented "Black Unity." "People are getting closer and closer together," said Smith. It was a nonviolent act that gave light to a period where public demonstration was very important. It was done "to make people aware," stated Smith in his *Augusta Chronicle* interview. Both athletes immediately were suspended and banned by the Olympic Committee from the Olympic Games for life. Furthermore, most of the media banned Smith and Carlos for their "civil disobedience" and labeled their behavior as a "juvenile gesture."

However, as time passed, the media that once criticized them named their protest as one of the most important events in the human rights movement. After they were suspended, they had to hide in their town, San Jose. After the protest their lives were in danger. According to an interview given by Smith to the *Augusta Chronicle*, he stated that "we were there for human rights. I have no regrets, I had no regrets, I will never have any regrets." They were supporting, and at the same time facing, what they believed was true. The year of 1968 was perhaps the most crucial moment in the U.S. human rights movement. It was the year that

Dr. Martin Luther King and Robert F. Kennedy were assassinated. It was a time when (most of) the government of Alabama was against its own black people, and some part of the church demanded peace, but on hands of racist people. Smith and Carlos stood together in fighting for what they believed, and changed people's way of thinking. Nowadays we can find articles, newspapers, magazines, and fighters for this glorious cause. Many of the fighters were ordinary black people. Smith and Carlos were honored in 1999 to commemorate the 30th anniversary of their protest. In that glorious moment, Smith and Carlos showed to the world that people can get together and participate without regard of race or color, and things can be done in a pacific way, and all this hatred, injustice, and discrimination can be stopped.

We must remember that being in, and maintaining a society is about taking care of yourself and the people around you. The most important thing we have to do is to stand together against the problems in the future, just as Tommie Smith and John Carlos stood together. We must fight for our beliefs and our rights to be human beings.

WORKS CITED

"2 accept Medals Wearing Black Gloves" <u>New York Times</u>
    17 Oct. 1968: Ht.
<u>Encyclopedia Britannica</u> nd. 7 Sep. 2000
<<u>http~//www.britannica.com/bcom/eb/ldxref/2/</u>
    <u>0,5716,364550,00.htmI</u>>
"Tommie Smith: No regrets over '68 protest." <u>Augusta</u>
    <u>Chronicle</u> 19 May. 2000 7, Sep.
2000 <<u>http://augustachronicle.com/stories/052098/</u>
    <u>spo 124.shtm</u>>

EXERCISE: COLLABORATING WITH YOUR PEERS

Working in pairs or in groups, share the paper on road rage you revised following suggestions and checklists in this chapter. Share a copy of the original paper as well. Ask your classmates to evaluate your revision, commenting on passages that show improvement. Identify any features of the paper that create problems with coherence. Finally, ask for suggestions for further revision and improvement.

EVALUATING PUBLISHED WORKS

You evaluate published works for better understanding of the work and your reaction to it; to find out what makes it special, unique, or ordinary; and sometimes, out of curiosity, to understand how a piece of writing achieves an effect. You see this kind of evaluation in book reviews in magazines and journals. As a critic writes in a magazine column, a student writes for classmates and members of the academy. When you critique a work for an academic audience, you should be prepared to judge it against specific standards of criticism scholars use. When you focus on issues of gender, psychology, or social class, your analysis may yield something you might not otherwise see.

When you evaluate published works, begin by previewing. As you read and annotate, analyze the rhetorical situation, the relationships of the writer to the subject and intended readers. Use the questions posed in Chapter 1 as a starting point:

- Who is the writer?

QUESTIONS FOR ANALYSIS

Audience Awareness

- What terms or concepts does the writer explain?
- Does the writer create distance between the writer and intended readers or does the writer establish a close relationship with intended readers? How does the writer establish this relationship?
- Does the writer make the subject relevant to readers? If so, how?

Organization and Content

- What does the title make you think the article will be about?
- Does the writer offer a thesis statement?
- Does the writer rely on an implied thesis?
- What kind of organizational plan does the writer follow? For example, does the writer move from specific to general? general to specific?

- Does the text include content that would be confusing or unclear to the intended audience?
- Is the content sufficiently thorough, or are there gaps? Is it one-sided? simplified?
- What kinds of examples, illustrations, statistics, original observation, or expert testimony does the writer provide?
- How does the writer conclude his or her ideas?
- Does the conclusion connect with the beginning without being too mechanical?

Style

- How would you characterize the style? For example, is it formal or informal?
- Is the writer's style appropriate for the rhetorical situation?
- Does the writer create vivid imagery for the reader? How?
- Does the writer convey to the reader a sense of authority? How?

- What is the writer's attitude toward the subject?
- What is the writer's level of knowledge about the subject?
- Who is the intended audience?
- What is their level of knowledge about the subject?
- In what medium did the source appear?
- What is the context (social, political, intellectual) that shapes what the writer says and how the writer envisions the intended audience?

Taking note of your initial response is also important. Your analysis of the work may or may not prove this initial response valid, but it is important to consider what we sometimes call a "gut reaction." It usually informs your evaluation. A close reading and analysis of the work will either reinforce this reaction or help you move beyond it to a deeper understanding, and possibly appreciation, of the work.

WRITING A CRITIQUE

In order to write a critique, you have to understand the work you are critiquing. A thorough understanding usually requires multiple readings and extensive annotation. Use your annotations and responses to the "Questions for Analysis" above to generate ideas for the various parts of a critique: introduction, summary of the work, analysis of the work, evaluation and any recommendations, and conclusion. You will find different organizational plans in published critical reviews, and if you have experience writing critical reviews, you may want to follow another plan. If you haven't written a formal critique, you should find the following guidelines useful.

GUIDELINES FOR WRITING A CRITIQUE

Introduction

- Identify the title of the work you are critiquing.
- Identify the author and any pertinent information about him or her.
- Identify the thesis if it is stated. If it is implied, explain what the thesis seems to be.
- Explain the writer's purpose in writing.
- Identify intended readers.
- Give a brief explanation of the work's importance or relevance.
- State your thesis. Your thesis might indicate whether you agree or disagree with the writer's thesis, whether the writer fulfills his or her purpose, and whether you recommend the source to your intended readers.

Summary of the Work

- In one or two paragraphs, summarize the main points that support the writer's thesis.

Analysis of the Work

- Support your thesis with discussion of such matters as content, organization, and style.
- Point out strengths and weaknesses.

Evaluation and Any Recommendations

- Discuss your understanding of and assumptions about the subject.
- Explain why you agree or disagree with the writer.

Conclusion

- Come back to your thesis: Restate it, or provide a quotation from the work that allows the reader to see a clear relationship between your thesis and your evaluation.

A word of caution: For most writers, summarizing is easier than evaluating. The summary should be limited to approximately 25 percent of the body of the paper. The rest of the paper should concentrate on analysis and remarks explaining the basis of your evaluation.

Review your critique, using the questions above and the "Checklist for Revisions" earlier in this chapter. Keep your intended readers in mind. You want your critique to be a coherent whole instead of a series of short responses to the "Questions for Analysis."

READINGS FOR PRACTICE: WRITING A CRITIQUE

Preview, read, and annotate the articles that follow. Consider the relationship of each writer to his subject and intended readers. Then answer the questions for analysis above. You will use your annotations and analysis of each article to complete several writing assignments, including a critique.

In "Maybe All of Us Should Be Leery of Mickey Mouse," an editorial, Carlos Fuentes discusses the Disney Corporation's acquisition of the ABC television network in 1995.

MAYBE ALL OF US SHOULD BE LEERY OF MICKEY MOUSE

CARLOS FUENTES

THE absorption of Capital Cities/ABC by Disney is a business deal motivated by profit—or, if you wish, greed—but also by hunger for power.

As a business deal it could claim to be value-neutral, but because of the kind of business deal it is, it cannot claim to be innocent.

When an entertainment giant buys an information giant, you can bet your Mickey Mouse cap on who is going to define the whole operation. Information will suffer, entertainment will flourish.

We are, argues Neil Postman, the New York University educator and social critic, *Amusing Ourselves to Death*—to quote his insightful book title.

To be sure, the ABC-Disney deal is one giant step forward in the march toward a grinning death, death by slapping your knee in delight, a smiling death acted out by smiling robots who, little by little, are being deprived of their right to choose, discriminate, criticize or even rebel against what they are receiving and the way they are receiving it.

Not that there is anything inherently evil in good old entertainment.

The danger lies in its supplanting important, meaningful information.

It does this first by offering the viewer so much information that he or she can come to believe that being informed so much means being well-informed.

We now know this is not the case and also that after all these years it will be supremely difficult to undo the damage.

More and more people all over the world are convinced that abundance of information equals quality of information. They haven't the need—or the means—to search for what's left in the shadows while the sun of a few giant conglomerates selects and showers its beams on us all.

The second, more subtle arrangement, I fear, is a fatal postponement of a greatly needed relationship between the audiovisual media and their viewers.

The printed word, over the centuries—be it literature, politics or journalism—has developed a self-critique, expressed through the same medium used to communicate: the written word.

Impunity in the verbal media has traditionally been checked by verbal critics, that is, criticism in kind. That means readers are privy to what is being expressed about what they read.

But the audiovisual universe lacks precisely this critical, leveling, balancing factor. It is, in fact, blessed with impunity because it is not well criticized by audiovisual means.

Responsible TV journalism is an off-shoot of responsible print journalism. To have Walter Cronkite, Peter Jennings or Ted Koppel, you first needed Walter Lippmann, James Reston and Tom Wicker. Can the Koppels and Jenningses survive the onslaught of entertainment?

Well before the Disney takeover, some noted ABC journalists already had gone elsewhere, convinced that serious discussion of issues, documentaries, probing—even muckraking—were out of favor in the context of speculators, game shows, show-biz gossip and heartrending public confessions.

Just look at the policies of media moguls such as Rupert Murdoch, who censor themselves in overseas markets so as to flatter authoritarian governments—notably in Asia. Disney's Michael Eisner practically promised Beijing that if political reportage made them angry, they could get Donald Duck instead, and nobody the wiser.

Only two years ago a second battle of Manassas was won just when Eisner wanted to invade the famous Civil War battlefield in Virginia with a Goofy theme park but was stopped

in his tracks by the much-despised liberal elite.

But a taste of things to come emerged this month when Charles Gibson, ABC's respected *Good Morning America* host, asked his new bosses, Eisner and Thomas S. Murphy, if journalism and entertainment were compatible.

Murphy shot back: Aren't you proud now to be a member of the Disney family?

In other words, aren't you proud to be a member of the Third Reich?

"Madam," says a character in Jean Giraudoux's *The Madwoman of Chaillot,* "We are the press. You know our power. We fix all values. We set all standards. Your entire future depends on us."

That candid assertion, which sounds pretty quaint today, should be paired with another by the nefarious industrialist, Andrew Undershaft—a character in George Bernard Shaw's *Major Barbara,* who says: "I am a millionaire. That is my religion."

He said a mouthful.

In a world being ripped apart by religious, racist, nationalist and tribal fundamentalisms, we are now giving the place of honor to the fundamentalism of the marketplace—a quasi-religious conviction that, if merely left to itself, the market will work things out.

This hand-of-God faith has its own ayatollahs. Their church is profit, their altar greed, their host a merger, their prayer a monopoly, their halo a Mickey Mouse cap.

Who's afraid? I am.

Source: Carlos Fuentes, "Maybe All of Us Should Be Leery of Mickey Mouse," *Houston Chronicle.* 20 August, 1995: Section C.

EXERCISES: READING AND RESPONDING

1. What is Fuentes' purpose in writing this article?
2. What is the writer's stance on the Disney Corporation's acquisition of ABC? What reasons does he give? Do you agree or disagree with his stance on this issue? Explain why or why not.
3. How would you describe Fuentes' tone? Cite passages to illustrate your answer.
4. What kind of evidence does Fuentes offer to illustrate his claim that "information will suffer; entertainment will flourish."
5. Fuentes alludes to historical events and works. Does he provide a context for these allusions?
6. Op-ed pieces like this one are written with the purpose of informing and convincing readers. Did you learn anything from reading Fuentes' editorial? If your answer is *yes*, identify passages that offered you new information.
7. Fuentes expresses concern about our ability to sift through the overload of information that confronts us in order to reach the truth:

   "More and more people all over the world are convinced that abundance of information equals quality of information."

   Explain why you agree or disagree that the "abundance of information" makes people feel as if they have received accurate information.

EXERCISE: THINKING CRITICALLY

Review "Maybe All of Us Should Be Leery of Mickey Mouse"and your annotations. Identify passages you would use as quotations, passages you would paraphrase, and passages you would summarize in a critique. Be prepared to explain your rationale for each selection.

COLUMBUS CRACKS AN EGG

STEPHEN JAY GOULD

Was the great voyager also a heavy-handed trickster?

The moment of truth—put up or shut up—has arrived. It is September, and this column has a lead time of three months. I either write about Christopher Columbus now or I miss the opportunity to note the most important quincentennial of my lifetime. Five hundred one just doesn't have that nice, even ring that we associate with celebrations.

Obviously, since I have delayed to the last possible moment, I have experienced no burning desire to address this subject. My reluctance does not arise from any doubt about the importance of the event, or of its relevance to natural history, but only from a widely shared feeling of personal ambivalence toward the value and meaning of Columbus's Bahamian landfall. History is full of horror, and we prefer to commemorate rare moments of light. I did not note, in 1983, the 500th anniversary of Torquemada's leadership of the Spanish Inquisition, so why should I celebrate, nine years later, an expedition that led to even more bloodshed and chauvinism (and was, incidentally, not unrelated to Torquemada's success)?

I am scarcely alone in my ambivalence, and this greatest opportunity for a white man's patriotic outburst has been a muted thing indeed. The usual, and entirely valid, reason for subdued acknowledgment arises from the treatment of indigenous peoples by their European conquerors—a panoply ranging from enslavement to genocide, with occasional islands of decency. For a natural historian, the further theme of environmental rape and pillage only adds to the profound feeling of ambiguity. While fully allying myself with these reasons for doubt, I would rather emphasize another set of home-grown factors, all too rarely discussed (and often not even mentioned) in popular statements of reluctance to celebrate.

Fourteen hundred ninety-two was an amazing year in Spain, a moment of triple coincidence. We may now be marking Columbus's quincentenary, but 1992 is also the 500th anniversary of military victory over the Moors and of the expulsion of all Jews from Spain—and the three events are complexly intertwined, for this is a causal coincidence, not a fortuitous array of simultaneous happenings. Moreover, Columbus's expedition ranks last in time among the three, and was partly a consequence of the other two, not a prod.

The marriage, in 1469, of Ferdinand of Aragon (roughly east Spain) and Isabella of Castile (roughly west Spain) began a train of events that led to both increased power and, in a term now tragically in vogue, to "ethnic purification" for a white and Catholic Spain. Isabella's victory in her war of succession against Afonso V of Portugal, and Ferdinand's accession to the throne of Aragon, following the death of his father, John II, in 1479, established a powerful joint monarchy, committed to the expansion of power and territory and the contraction of the ethnic and religious diversity that had marked the Iberian peninsula for centuries.

The Encyclopædia Britannica's article on Spanish history notes: "With its large Moorish and Jewish populations, medieval Spain was the only multiracial and multireligious country in Western Europe, and much of the development of Spanish civilization in religion, literature, art, and architecture during the later Middle Ages stemmed from this fact" (quoted from the 1980 edition, before contemporary terminology of "political correctness" came into vogue—so don't blame this claim on early 1990s fashion).

But the *reyes catolicos* (the Catholic kings), as Ferdinand and Isabella were called, struggled to terminate this diversity and succeeded in the Columbian year of 1492. The campaign against the Moors, who had held power for nearly 800 years and had once ruled almost all of Spain, had been proceeding for centuries. The final conquest of Granada and its Alhambra, with the capitulation and exile of Boabdil, the last Muslim ruler, ended a long process of conquest and removed the last handhold of Islamic temporal power in Western Europe (although the Turks besieged Vienna in 1683). Aided greatly by internecine warfare within the Moorish ruling family, Ferdinand and Isabella prevailed and received the keys to Granada from Boabdil on January 2, 1492 (in medieval walled cities with gates, keys to towns were more than symbolic). According to legend, the weak ruler (derisively called *el rey chico,* or "the little king," by the Spaniards) took one last look over his shoulder and burst into tears as he departed into exile. His powerful mother responded with the most viciously sexist one-liner in history: "Cry like a woman for what you could not hold as a man."

As for the Jews, Ferdinand and Isabella had obtained a papal bull from Sixtus IV for setting up an Inquisition in 1478. (Sixtus later regretted his decision when he understood the ferocity of the institution he had permitted and the ecclesiastical powers that he had given away.) The Inquisition itself—and this is widely misunderstood today—did not persecute professing Jews because it was established to root out heresy *within* Catholicism. Its ardor turned instead to the so-called *conversos,* or Jewish converts to Catholicism, whose successes and large numbers (some 300,000) had frightened the older establishment. In a mixture of paran-cia and expediency (for the property of those convicted was confiscated and redistributed), the inquisitors searched for "Judaizing practices" among the *conversos* as signs of their insincerity and their conspiracy to usurp the church from within. They used a variety of techniques that became a textbook for such later organizations as the S.S. and K.G.B., including networks of informers (who looked for such signs as failure of *converso* neighbors to buy adequate amounts of pork, or lack of chimney smoke emerging on Saturdays), interrogation with no right to counsel and no opportunity to confront hostile witnesses, and of course, torture and burning.

But when Tomás de Torquemada (ironically, from a *converso* family himself) became head of the Inquisition in 1483, be began to badger Ferdinand and Isabella about the professing Jews (who may have numbered close to 200,000). As this well- and long-established community retained such a focal role in arts and commerce, the monarchs were at first reluctant to follow Tocquemada's advice. But their growing power and success, particularly in victory over the Moors, boosted their confidence and their narrow piety, and they issued an order for the expulsion of all lews in the same focal year of 1492. Thus began the diaspora of the Sephardic (Spanish) Jews, first largely into Portugal (where many were killed or forcibly converted in 1498) and thence to more accepting Muslim countries (where many still live today, or at least until recent migration to Israel), and to a few pockets of relative toleration in Europe, notably the Netherlands where, among many others of note, the great philosopher Spinoza lived and worked.

A few days after the final departure of the Jews in July, Columbus set sail on August 3. I do not, of course, claim that the eventual, crucial patronage of Ferdinand and Isabella (after so much dithering over so many years) arose directly from their "cleansing" of both Muslim and Jew from their lands, but these prior events of 1492 surely set a climate of narrow piety and aggressive expansionism that greatly boosted support for Columbus's plans. In any case. I cannot, both as a Jew and as a general celebrator of diversity and its cultural benefits, view Spain in 1492 as an object of whole-hearted commemoration.

And yet, I really don't want to bypass something so important by an almost cowardly silence. I therefore take recourse in two of my own traditions. If I cannot celebrate the broad generality, let me look for a tiny little something about Columbus (which may then cascade by implication to a statement of wider worth), and let me go, once again, to my intellectual hero Charles Darwin for inspiration.

In his autobiography, Darwin writes about his excitement in formulating the principle of natural selection as a young man in 1838. But he then chides himself for having ignored a crucial problem that any evolutionary theory must resolve (we will return to the nature and identification of this problem at the end). Darwin writes:

> But at that time I overlooked one problem of great importance; and it is astonishing to me, except on the principle of Columbus and his egg, how I could have overlooked it and its solution.

Now this is a famous quotation in the Darwinian brotherhood; it is cited over and over again, and I have been encountering it throughout my professional life in numerous guises. But something about this statement always bothered me: I didn't understand the reference to Columbus and his egg—and no one ever bothered to explain it by commentary or footnote. As a young man, and with the usual diffidence of those years, I hypothesized my own stupidity and shut up. That is, I assumed that everyone else grasped something I ought to know, and that one day I'd figure it out. Better not embarrass myself by asking. As I got older and learned the ways of the world, I realized that if I didn't comprehend the line, maybe no one else did either—and the fact that every citationist passed by Columbus's egg in silence could just as well signify ignorance as comprehension. Yet Darwin's mention is so off-the-cuff that he, at least, must have regarded Columbus's egg as a schoolboy tale known to all. But times change, and the folk wisdom of one generation may be oblivion to the next. Will our children relish the details of Woody and Mia; do we even remember much about Joe DiMaggio and Marilyn Monroe or Grace Kelly and the Prince of Monaco or Edward VIII and Ms. Simpson?

Cambridge, Massachusetts, is a funny place. The town is not so rarefied and intellectual as some folks think, but it certainly provides a great advantage if you want to pursue Columbus's egg by the art of survey. I began by asking several of my contemporaries, and not a soul had ever heard of Columbus's egg. So I queried some older American colleagues on the theory that Darwin had cited a former school-boy's tale, now extinct. None of them had a glimmer. As a last effort, I then approached some older colleagues who had spent their childhoods in prewar Europe, conjecturing that Darwin might have cited folk wisdom that never crossed the ocean. I finally got some return, but no solution. Two of my colleagues (neither English, but both continental) remembered such a story but could not recall the details.

So I gave up, and Columbus's egg remained in limbo for me—there are, after all, more important matters demanding attention during our short sojourn in this vale of tears. Then, as so often happens, the solution dropped into my lap when I wasn't looking. The scene switches to the spring equinox of 1989. The editorial and letters column of the *New York Times* are buzzing with an exchange about an old (and truly foolish) chestnut—the issue of whether or not one can balance an egg on its end during the equinoxes, but on no other day

(now how many of you have encountered that one!). A Mr. Louis Marck—bless his soul—contributed the following letter on March 26, not only resolving Columbus's egg, but also acknowledging the failure of the story to penetrate our culture:

> In "It's Spring. Go Balance an Egg" (editorial March 19), you say that cheaters "crack the shell to create a flat bottom." According to a tradition strangely unknown in this country, one person who did that very thing, not as a cheater, but to prove a point, was Christopher Columbus.
>
> My German dictionary of quotations places the apocryphal incident in 1493, at a banquet given in honor of Columbus by Cardinal Mendoza. When the difficulty of his voyage of discovery was put into question. Columbus challenged his interlocutors to balance an egg. When they failed, he did it by cracking the shell.
>
> In German, as well as Spanish, "the egg of Columbus" has become proverbial for solving a difficult problem by a surprisingly simple knack or expedient.

Fine. A welcome solution. But why have I chosen this obscure item of Columbiana for my essay on this quincentenary? I may not particularly like the man, and I may feel nothing but ambivalence in contemplating his achievements, but I am both too vain and too conscious of duty to blow an essay by mock celebration of a triviality. The image is as colorful as the expression is clichéd:

I will not cut off my nose to spite my face. No, I actively like the story of Columbus's egg and find it wonderfully illustrative of an important principle of science and intellectual life in general. Columbus's egg is an emblem for a different kind of ambiguity that we all must face.

Did Columbus achieve a fair solution of the puzzle that he himself had set? He asks his dinner companions to balance an egg. They assume that they may not destroy the object as they attempt to stand it on an end—and they fail as the egg rolls back each time. Columbus cracks the shell at its bottom, and the egg stands. I'm sure that he fractured the shell ever so gently—just enough to achieve a sufficiently flat bottom. But he still destroyed the egg. Does the destruction of an object count as a fair solution to a puzzle posed about it? Were Columbus's dinner guests unoriginal, obtuse, or bovine—or were they just properly respectful? And does such respectful-ness always indicate a hidebound resistance to innovation?

The story of Columbus's egg is, of course, a metaphor about creativity and its meaning. Any true creator must wield a mallet against an accepted framework. The word *iconoclast,* after all, means "image breaker." We reserve the primary niches in our intellectual pantheon for great iconoclasts: For Galileo, fracturing a limited, earth-centered universe; for Darwin, shattering a system of created, immutable species. Our great intellectual revolutions are never simple infusions of knowledge into a previous void; they are always exercises in destruction and replacement.

But the dark figure, the fallen angel of mindless, truly anti-intellectual destruction always waits in the wings, carefully watching any potential episode of iconoclastic creativity, trying to impart the small nudge that pushes a potential intellectual triumph into the abyss of thoughtless destruction. The frenzied mob that cries for the blood of old privilege is no better than the king's polite executioner. The rabble who cursed and spat at Lavoisier on his way to the guillotine might just as well have been the henchmen of Torquemada tightening the rack or the thumbscrews.

Consider the classical example of a "clever" response that overstepped the boundary and substituted thoughtless destruction for genuine resolution—the story of Alexander and the Gordian knot. In 333 B.C. after victories in Asia Minor and as he began a campaign that would defeat Darius and the Persian Empire, Alexander marched to Gordium, the capital of Phrygia (now in central Turkey). There he was shown the famous Gordian knot, an enormously complex configuration (with a hidden end) that lashed the chariot of Gordius, ancient founder of the city, to a pole. According to legend, the man who untied the Gordian knot would conquer all of Asia. Alexander took one look at the knot, drew out his sword, and cut it clean through. (If you don't like tales from antiquity, consider the best modern example from one of the Indiana Jones movies. Jones is challenged by a muscular local hero, who takes out his sword and puts on a long preliminary display by graceful and pyrotechnical brandishing of his preferred weapon. Jones withdraws his gun and promptly plugs his adversary between the eyes.)

For that matter, I'm not so sure we should be celebrating the original iconoclasts by incorporating their name in such a favorable way into our language. The iconoclasts objected to veneration of icons or images of human faces, citing an interpretation of the biblical prohibition in the Ten Commandments against worshiping graven images (Exodus 20:4). (Traditional Islamic and Jewish religious art avoids images for the same reason.) The iconoclastic movement twice won power, only to be reversed within the Byzantine Empire during the eighth and ninth centuries. Ironically, the Christian art of Constantinople was ravaged twice—both times by Christians. First, by the iconoclasts during their temporary ascendancy; second, by the armies of the Fourth Crusade who, having failed in their objective of capturing Jerusalem, turned their marauding attention to Christians of another stripe. The Latin rulers of Byzantium (1204–1261) plundered the city, destroyed its art and even melted down most bronze statues for coin. When Mehmed II took Constantinople for the Turks in 1453, he did not engage in the wholesale destruction of Byzantine art, which he admired. Islamic worship precluded veneration of human figures, so when many Christian churches were converted to mosques, the great Byzantine mosaics were often plastered over, rather than ripped apart—and so, thankfully, we may still enjoy them today, as restored in such shrines as Hagia Sophia and the museum of the former Kariye mosque (Saint Savior in Chora under the Byzantines).

Alexander's assault upon the Gordian knot remains one of the most ambiguous events in our history or legends. Some have praised Alexander, either for seeking novel solutions apart from expected pathways or simply for taking decisive action when the situation demanded an immediate response. But intellectuals have generally read the story in a deeply negative way, and I must align myself with my own tribe in this case.

The quick and violent fix, particularly one that destroys the very object that set the puzzle, must be viewed as the antithesis of our best mental functioning. I do not say that all worthy intellectual activity must follow the silly stereotype of ponderous contemplation (the professor knitting his brow and chewing on the end of his glasses). Brilliant insights are often the antithesis of calm and may be sudden or even violent. But a revolutionary solution to a problem must at least honor the processes of thought and not belittle our mentality for the sake of expediency.

At least I can document this negative use of Alexander's example over several centuries of commentary in my own field of geology. In 1690, Thomas Burnet called for a naturalistic rather than a miraculous interpretation of the Flood by attacking those who would simply attribute the excess water to God's creating power: "They say in short, that God Almighty created waters on purpose to make the deluge, and then annihilated them again.... This is to cut the knot when we cannot loose it." And, in one of the most famous passages in all geological writing, Charles Lyell excoriated the miraclemongers with the same image in 1833: "We see the ancient spirit of speculation revived, and a desire manifested to cut, rather than patiently to untie, the Gordian knot."

Now I admit that cracking an egg at a banquet may not be so drastic as severing a venerated object at the outset of a war.

But Columbus's solution still evokes the whiff of the philistine. Cracking the bottom was clever, but it violated the rules in a manner that strikes me as destructive of a legitimate game.

How then shall we define that most precious, yet most elusive, property called creativity? I don't know the answer of course. But we can at least state some properties and specify some criteria. The most historically potent and positive form of creativity must occupy the middle ground between strong respect for accepted norms and accumulated knowledge and Alexander's or Columbus's tactic of destroying rules and objects for an immediate and narrow victory. Maximally useful creativity will surely not arise from the immobilization of the obsessive t-crosser and i-dotter, but the waste and carelessness of a brilliant scholar who refuses to build upon the fruitful work of others, or even acknowledge past tradition (if

only to break it), rarely yields much of use either. Let me tell one personal story about a man who, in my opinion, strayed too close to the Columbian end of this spectrum. Many people regard Richard Feynman as the greatest scientific genius of recent times. Perhaps so; as I said, I hardly know what the term means. But I do think that Feynman's anti-scholarly approach led him to waste a great deal of time, at the very least (and he died too young, with too much undone). Despite his stunning raw mental power, Feynman was a self-proclaimed and vigorous philistine. He simply would not consult anyone else's work or acknowledge that anything already in the literature might be worth his attention. He insisted on working everything out for himself from first principles.

One may admire the audacity, but what an inefficient system. The world, after all, is not entirely inhabited by morons, and some conclusions of quality can be found in published sources. Several years ago, I visited CalTech to give a lecture and spent the night in a suite that Einstein had occupied. In the best conceivable follow-up, my host told me the next morning that Richard Feynman wanted to have breakfast with me because he had "figured out some things about evolution" and wanted to discuss them with me (tell them at me would be more accurate, as it turned out). I was delighted, of course, for I had never met the man and knew him only by his incandescent reputation. We sat for three hours, long past closing time for bacon and eggs. I was fascinated but also disturbed.

Feynman told me that he had reached some conclusions about evolution that were probably important and no doubt novel—all by reasoning from basic principles of Darwin's theory of natural selection. Well, he had figured out about half a dozen things, and they were all correct (so far as we know). But I was as dumbstruck as I have ever been in my intellectual life. Every one of his conclusions can be found in chapter one of any elementary evolution textbook. They were all figured out more than a hundred years ago, mostly by Darwin himself. (Feynman, for example, had rediscovered Darwin's principle of sexual selection in both versions of male combat and female choice.) I said to him, "Dick, that's all well and true, but we really do know these things; they are the basis of our science; didn't you ever encounter them in your readings?" He replied that he had read nothing, on purpose.

Now Feynman could get away with such an antischolarly approach because be was so brilliant, and because the method had served him well. But he had frittered some time away in this case—and I would certainly not recommend this tactic to ordinary mortals, even highly intelligent and creative ones. My colleague Sid Coleman spoke of Feynman's willful ignorance of past work (quoted by James Gleick, *New York Times Magazine,* September 20. 1992):

> I'm sure Dick thought of that as a virtue, as noble. I don't think it's so. I think it's kidding yourself. Those other guys are not all a collection of yo-yos. Sometimes it would be better to take the recent

machinery they have built and not try to rebuild it, like reinventing the wheel. Dick could get away with a lot because he was so goddamn smart.

The intellectual version rarely produces real injury, and the cracked egg probably didn't spoil Cardinal Mendoza's dinner. But the destructive side of exploration can cause painful, palpable harm when the object involved is an inhabited land rather than an abstract concept.

I must recall the other column I once considered writing for the quincentenary. I wanted to illustrate the biological importance of taxonomic diversity by pointing out that I could personally solve the old debate about Columbus's Bahamian landfall if only he had collected a single *Cerion* shell (they live right at the coastline) as he stepped off the boat. Several islands have been proposed as the spot that Columbus called San Salvador, most historians accept Wailing (now officially called San Salvador), but Cay Sal and several other spots have their defenders. *Cerion,* the focus of my personal research, is a highly diverse land snail with absolutely distinctive populations on each of the proposed islands. A single snail marked "This is the first thing I picked up when I landed on October 12, C. C." would settle the issue forever.

But then I thought, what irony! We know the distinctness of each island's *Cerion* because humans have never bothered them, and they have suffered no extinction or transportation. We have not disturbed these snails because they have absolutely no impact upon us: they are not agricultural pests and they taste terrible. They do not fight back; they cannot be enslaved, they know nothing of gold. But humans are exploitable, and their original Bahamian diversity was shattered in the wake of a man whom legend honored because he broke an object to illustrate his ability to manipulate it, and who sailed as emissary of a nation that had just purged the twin sources of its internal diversity.

Let us return then, in conclusion, to the subject of Darwin's attention when he cited the story of Columbus and his egg. What was the "one problem of great importance" that he had overlooked? Ironically again, Darwin identified the missing piece in his system as an explanation of *diversity*. Darwin realized that his original (1838) version of natural selection only told how one population might evolve into another of different form, but not how diversity might be produced—that is, how one population might branch into two descendants. He wrote, just after citing Colum-

bus's egg: "The problem is the tendency in organic beings descended from the same stock to diverge in character as they become modified."

Darwin now understood that he would not have a complete theory until he could explain the origin of species, the process of making new twigs on life's bush—the source of the stunning variety that is both the glory and the staying power of life on earth. And so Darwin celebrated and sought to explain the very property that Spain had eliminated at home and Columbus diminished abroad—the diversity that is our ballast, our anchor, our only safe mooring in the flood of time. We either preserve this nurturing variety, or ultimately, we may intone a requiem for all humanity with Shakespeare's words for Hamlet (using a Columbian style of fracture): "Now cracks a noble heart. Good night, sweet prince."

Stephen Jay Gould teaches biology, geology, and the history of science at Harvard University.

Source: Stephen Jay Gould, "Columbus Cracks an Egg," *Natural History.* Dec. 1992: 4–11.

EXERCISES: READING AND RESPONDING

1. What is Gould's purpose in writing this essay?
2. Gould frequently defines terms for readers. Cite at least three examples. What do these definitions suggest about the writer's perception of his intended audience?
3. Who is the implied audience? How would you describe Gould's relationship to his audience? Cite specific passages that establish the relationship you describe.
4. How would you describe the writer's tone?
5. In your opinion, why does Gould rely frequently on parenthetical statements? What do these statements suggest about the writer's relationship to his readers?

6. How does Gould organize his article?

7. In your opinion, is this a well-organized essay? Does Gould conform to the conventions of organization you expect a writer to follow? Cite specific passages that illustrate your response.

8. How does Gould develop ideas? Does he rely on narration, analogy, comparison and contrast, cause and effect?

9. Does Gould accomplish his purpose? Explain why or why not.

EXERCISES: THINKING CRITICALLY

1. Review Gould's article and your annotations. Identify passages you would use as quotations, passages you would paraphrase, and passages you would summarize in a critique. Be prepared to explain your rationale for each selection.

2. Use the checklists for revision in this chapter to review and revise a rough draft of your critique.

3 Use the Guidelines for Editing in this chapter to edit your critique

EXERCISES: FOCUS ON WRITING

1. Write a summary of each article.

2. Identify each writer's thesis and paraphrase it.

3. Write a letter to the editor of the publication in which each article appeared. Explain whether the article was meaningful or confusing to you or whether you agree or disagree with the writer.

4. Select one of the articles above and write a critique.

EXERCISE: COLLABORATING WITH YOUR PEERS

Working in pairs or in groups, exchange drafts. Read and discuss the drafts and make suggestions for revision.

Chapter 5

Analyzing Argument

The Boss knew all about the so-called fallacy of the *argumentum ad hominem*. "It must be a fallacy," he said, "but it is shore-God useful. If you use the right kind of *argumentum* you can always scare the *hominem* into a laundry bill he didn't expect."

—*Jack Burden's observation about Willie Stark in Robert Penn Warren's* All the King's Men

THE PURPOSE OF ARGUMENT

Our lives are affected every day by the outcomes of arguments, formal presentations or informal conversations in which we attempt to resolve issues on which we disagree. Arguments take place in editorials and letters to the editor; in stockholder, club, or faculty meetings; in pamphlets, flyers, advertisements; in art, music, or literature; in scholarly books and journals and professional conventions and meetings; and in college classrooms, student union lounges, and campus hangouts. Turn on television or radio talk shows and you hear people arguing about all kinds of controversial issues—social, political, and economic; local, national, and international. On television, you'll also find shows such as *Washington Week in Review* or *Politically Incorrect* in which a panel of four or five people argue about a specific issue, all trying to persuade each other and viewers that their perspectives are valid.

While arguments take different forms, *constructive* arguments are usually governed by rules or conventions that establish "fair play." For example, judges and juries require lawyers to adhere to rules of the court, and judges who listen to debate teams expect debaters to observe time limits and to speak in order. At a city council meeting, two opposing factions follow *Robert's Rules of Order* as they negotiate for a solution to a problem. In the classroom or at the dinner table with friends or family, you aren't constrained by formalities when you argue. Still, you probably make sure that everyone gets a voice in the conversation. As you know, if the conversation turns into a shouting match and people get mad, issues usually aren't resolved and there is no satisfactory or productive outcome of any kind. In order to have a *constructive* argument, you need two or more perspectives on an issue for which there is no agreement or consensus, someone to advance different perspectives, an environment conducive to an exchange of ideas, common ground between the opposing perspectives, and an audience to respond to the exchange of ideas.

While we usually think of argument as discourse intended to convince or persuade, arguments can have other outcomes, too. In fact, many end in standoffs, and such arguments aren't necessarily in vain. On the contrary, they may result in subtle changes in the participants and their positions, or in a better understanding of the opposition and of the complexity of the issues. The important point here is that arguments facilitate the exchange of ideas. Through arguments we

- Discover on what points we agree and disagree.
- Negotiate change or compromise.
- Inquire about and gain a better understanding of an issue.
- Reconcile different perspectives.
- Call our readers or listeners to action.
- Convince our readers or listeners to modify or rethink their point of view—or to accept the point of view we favor.

And sometimes when we argue, we learn information that makes us change our minds about a perspective we originally advocated or opposed. A case in point is the World Health Assembly's 1980 decision to eradicate smallpox. Meeting in 1999 in Geneva, the 191 members that make up the organization voted for the third time to postpone the eradication, citing the need for further research. According to *The New York Times*, the Assembly's decision "reflects a major shift in thinking about the virus" and "highlighted rare political common ground between the United States and Russia." The common ground the United States and Russia share is the belief that more research is needed. The research and the conversation that results from it may very well convince the World Health Assembly to rescind altogether the decision it made in 1980.

WHY WE ANALYZE ARGUMENTS

In a democracy where there is free exchange of ideas, all the functions of argument become especially important. And because argument is so important, so is the ability to analyze those functions and articulate their validity. In other words, citizens in a democracy need to be able to think for themselves—to question, examine, refute, and be specific about why they agree or disagree on an issue. You want to develop the ability to analyze an argument to determine where it is effective, where it falls short, where it breaks down in logic, and where it works on your emotions, your understanding of logical connections, or your sense of ethics.

Another reason for analyzing argument is to understand how other writers develop effective arguments. Academic discourse typically has as its aim persuading readers to accept what the writer offers as valid, well-founded, sound, logical, accurate, authoritative, or conclusive. Writers use many techniques to persuade readers, and you need to recognize these techniques. For example, you should understand how writers order their arguments. If a writer begins by assuming a general principle and cites specific examples that support it, the writer is using deduction. If a writer begins by citing specific examples and drawing a conclusion from them, the writer is using induction. Writers make choices when they choose either one of these methods, and you should be prepared to understand how each method facilitates an effective argument. You'll read more about induction and deduction in Part Two.

The discussion in this chapter suggests several strategies for analyzing arguments. One of the most important is to give serious consideration to a perspective that is radically different from you own. You can't write off perspectives you reject as unworthy of any consideration or examination. It's important to pay close attention to detail and to analyze why a perspective you disagree with is received positively by other people. In other words, for a sympathetic reader, what makes the perspective effective, interesting, or convincing?

Analyzing Persuasive Appeals

Academic discourse typically has as its aim persuading readers to accept what the writer offers as valid, well-founded, sound, accurate, authoritative, or conclusive. While we expect academic writers to build logical cases to support their theses, it's important to understand that scholarly writing uses many techniques to appeal to readers:

Appeal to Logic

Logical appeals focus on well-reasoned ideas and clear rationales. For example, in a discussion about euthanizing animals held in a local community shelter, a writer focuses on statistics from the last two years and argues that the numbers clearly suggest that the current level of donations now make it possible to cease the practice of euthanizing animals. Funds are available to keep the animals alive and put them up for adoption. When you cite statistics, examples, precedent, recognized authority, laboratory experiments, or testimony, you appeal to your readers' sense of reason or logic.

Appeal to Authority

Appeals to authority focus on the credibility or authority of the writer—or the writer's *ethos*. Readers have to accept writers as trustworthy and serious about their purpose in writing; otherwise, they probably will not consider seriously any arguments writers advance. To establish credibility, a writer demonstrates good will toward readers and respect for their opinions. Equally important is showing that an argument is based on practicality and good sense. A writer has to convince readers that he or she is a person of good character. Imagine readers' reactions if a writer were to resort to name calling or sarcasm in a plea for the local shelter to quit euthanizing animals. If a writer has an attitude or shows contempt for readers, that writer runs the risk of offending readers and losing credibility. Even with a well-reasoned argument, if a writer appears to lack sincerity, readers will have serious doubts about the writer's *ethos* (the word *ethics* comes from the word *ethos*). Writers use a variety of strategies to establish their credibility-for example, in academic writing, thorough research and careful editing play a role in establishing a writer's credibility.

Appeal to Emotions

Emotional appeals focus on readers' feelings: anger, sympathy, fear, apprehension, or happiness, for example. Imagine one last discussion of euthanizing animals at the local shelter. The writer, arguing against euthanizing animals, offers two stories: In the first, a family is very relieved and overjoyed when they claim their beloved pet dog after he has been held in the local shelter for five days. In the second, a family is very distressed when they learn that their beloved pet dog was euthanized according to standard policy after being held in the shelter for five days. This writer tugs at the heartstrings. The emphasis is on emotions. Appeals to emotions can be very persuasive, but once the moment passes and the reader has had time to get over an emotional reaction or to think it through, the power of the emotional appeal often diminishes.

Logical Fallacies

When you analyze writing that aims primarily to persuade, you should be on the lookout for arguments that rely on faulty or deceptive logic. For example, you write a note to one of your professors and argue that the grade on your last essay exam would have been ten to twenty points higher if you had had your lucky rabbit's foot with you the day of the exam. You're arguing for a conclusion that lacks logical support. Was the grade on the exam the result of bad luck or lack of adequate preparation? You've oversimplfied the situation. You need to study more. In another approach, you try to persuade the same professor to change the format of your next exam. You argue that essay exams are too difficult to complete in a one-hour exam period because students have to write under limited time constraints. In this circular line of reasoning, you don't get to the heart of the difficulty. Why is the essay more difficult than multiple choice? Does it call for a higher line of thinking? Does it require keener analytical skills? Does guesswork play a role in one and not in the other? You beg the question when you claim that a timed essay is difficult because students don't have enough time. In a final attempt, you argue that no one else in the professor's department gives essay exams, so why should your class be subjected to them? This is just another version of an argument you've probably used with your parents: *Everyone else is doing it, so why can't I?* You're jumping on the bandwagon and drawing the conclusion that if everyone is doing something, it must be okay.

Sometimes inadvertent, other times deliberate, logical fallacies can help persuade readers who aren't analyzing the argument carefully. Advertising and political rhetoric provide some of the best examples of the use of logical fallacies. For example, a recent television ad begins with a group of men walking through an airport quietly chanting messages of peace and love. They wear saffron-colored robes and their heads are shaved. Another group of men watching a football game on an airport TV monitor offers to share a popular snack chip with the chanters. In the next frame, the chanters are transformed into aggressive football fans. One or two sport rainbow wigs; the group sings the Notre Dame fight song; and in the background two men turn somersaults, like cheerleaders. The snack chip has transformed the chanters into good-old-boy party animals. The advertiser associates the snack chip with people enjoying themselves. You see this kind of advertising all the time. The messages are simple, but full of logical flaws: Buy this product—it will make you more attractive to the opposite sex. Buy this product—you will enjoy good times with friends and family. Buy this product—you will climb the corporate ladder and get a better job. Buy this product—it will eliminate stress, worry, fatigue, depression, anxiety, etc.

Real-life politicians are not above using the same tactics that got Willie Stark elected governor of a fictional gulf coast state. In Robert Penn Warren's 1946 novel, *All the King's Men*, Willie begins his career believing that people would "only listen to argument and language that was grand and bright." In his first campaign for governor, Willie's speeches are "awful ... full of facts and figures he had dug up about the running of the state" (71). As he develops into a win-at-all-costs politician, Willie becomes an expert at audience analysis—at recognizing what people want and need to hear and at motivating crowds, even if he has to resort to logical fallacies and skewed reasoning. He understands full well that if his constituents don't *think* about the content of his speeches, rhetorical effect alone, the skillful use of language that acts upon the audience, will be enough to move them to action.

To the observant reader, logical fallacies suggest laziness or faulty reasoning. If you know your readers will analyze your argument, looking for weaknesses or for skewed logic, you don't want to include something that will send up red flags. Some of the common logical fallacies include the following:

- *Ad hominem (against the man) argument:* The writer attacks an individual instead of an issue.
  EXAMPLE: Why should we take campaign reform seriously? One of its main supporters is under investigation for shady real estate investments. [The real issue should be campaign reform instead of the person being investigated.]

- *Hasty generalization:* The writer reaches a conclusion based on flimsy or inadequate evidence.
  EXAMPLE: The majority of baby-boomers show no concern about the problems we will eventually face with the Social Security system. It's clear that they could care less if future generations enjoy a decent retirement. [The writer can't support this last statement.]

- *Begging the question:* The writer offers circular reasoning by simply rewording the claim.
  EXAMPLE: Taxing the poor is wrong because it is taxing people who have very little money. [This statement is illogical because it says that taxing the poor

is wrong because the poor are poor. The writer hasn't explained why taxing the poor is wrong].

- *Oversimplification:* The writer simplifies a complex situation.
  EXAMPLE: The disciplinary problems teachers face today will disappear when our children are allowed to pray in school. [The writer concludes that prayer alone will solve disciplinary problems, but without demonstrating how.]

- *Either-or fallacy:* The writer reduces a complex issue to only two choices and suggests that one is correct and the other wrong.
  EXAMPLE: President Clinton is either a national hero or a national disgrace. Evidence clearly suggests the latter. [The writer offers no middle ground, only two extremes.]

- *Bandwagon appeal:* The writer claims that everyone is doing something or embracing a particular perspective on an issue and that that perspective is therefore the correct one.
  EXAMPLE: The governor's education advisers are for school vouchers; Hispanic and African American leaders are for them as well. Clearly, vouchers are the best solution. Everyone should support school vouchers. [The writer bases the conclusion on the claim that everyone is for vouchers, and offers no other evidence.]

- *Slippery slope:* the writer suggests that one event will lead to a chain of events that will result in disaster.
  EXAMPLE: Making English the nation's official language would do away with language diversity. Is the eradication of cultural diversity far behind? And with that loss, are our rights to other freedoms safe from challenge? Will democracy prevail? [The writer suggests that establishing a national language would start a chain of events.]

- *Non sequitur (does not follow)*: The writer draws a conclusion that does not follow from the evidence.
  EXAMPLE: If students spend three evenings a week in the campus library, it goes without saying that they will make good grades.

- *Post hoc ergo propter hoc fallacy ("after this, therefore because of this"):* The writer offers a cause-and-effect relationship based on faulty reasoning.
  Example: The number of illegal immigrants coming to Texas increased dramatically in the 1980s. At the same time, the number of people on welfare increased. Therefore, illegal welfare resulted from the increase in immigration. [The writer hasn't established a cause-and-effect relationship.]

- *Strawman:* The writer introduces a counterargument, but makes it seem weaker than it actually is. The weak version makes refutation easy for the writer.
  EXAMPLE: A candidate for congress discusses her opponent's stance on government regulations on cutting timber in national forests. Speaking to members of the logging industry, the candidate claims her opponent is a *tree*

hugger, when in fact the opponent is a well-informed environmentalist. The label *tree hugger* diminishes the opponent's positon. It suggests that a person acts on uninformed emotion with little consideration for other perspectives . The congressional candidate makes her argument seem strong by making her opponent's argument weaker than it actually is.

One of the points Part One of this book makes repeatedly is that revision and multiple drafts give you a chance to develop ideas, rethink the content of a paper, and revise with your intended readers in mind. When you write argumentative papers, it's easy to begin with hasty generalizations, oversimplification, or slippery slope arguments. These logical fallacies are a way to get ideas down on paper, but they aren't appropriate if your goal is to develop a logical argument. By taking a paper through multiple drafts and reading your own work with a critical eye, you should be able to recognize logical fallacies and revise passages that rely on them. For readers who will evaluate and analyze your writing, you want to develop logical, sound, and rational arguments.

EXERCISES: THINKING CRITICALLY

1. Review letters to the editor published in your campus or local newspaper. Identify any logical fallacies writers employ in their letters. Be prepared to explain whether you think the logical fallacies help advance the writer's argument or hinder the argument.

2. Write a letter to the editor of your campus or local newspaper about a local issue. Include at least three logical fallacies. Share your letter with your classmates. Ask them to identify the logical fallacies and to explain whether they would recommend revising the letter to correct the logical fallacies or leaving the logical fallacies as they are.

Analyzing Rhetorical Strategies

The ancient Greeks and Romans defined rhetoric as the *art* of using language to persuade. The way a skilled writer puts words together, delivering phrases that are pleasing to our eyes and ears, can be as persuasive as the appeals to our senses of reason or ethics. Eloquence is a rhetorical strategy, a technique for persuading a reader to accept or believe something. While rhetorical strategies and eloquence are not unique to argumentative discourse, they usually are an important feature, and sometimes can be more important—more persuasive to intended readers—than reason or logic.

Chances are, you recognize artful—or eloquent—language when you hear it, because it is pleasing to the ear. When you read it, eloquent language is pleasing to the eye because it follows patterns that create balance and parallelism (phrasing that repeats the same structure; for example, "I came; I saw; I conquered."). Or it repeats patterns that provide emphasis on ideas and make information clear and easy for the mind to process.

In the excerpt below from President John F. Kennedy's televised address announcing the 1963 Civil Rights Bill, these patterns are underlined. Notice the effective parallel sentence structure:

> We are confronted primarily with a moral issue. It is <u>as old as the Scriptures</u> and is <u>as clear as the American Constitution.</u>

The underlined phrases create eye and ear patterns that have a rhetorical effect on the reader or listener because these patterns are similar in shape and pleasing in sound. While it's difficult to explain exactly why these patterns can be highly effective persuasive devices, it is easy to cite examples. One of the best illustrations comes from the closing arguments of the O.J. Simpson trial when defense attorney Johnny Cochran cautioned the jury repeatedly: "If it doesn't fit, you must acquit!" This line, with its ear (notice the rhyme) and eye patterns (notice the balance of the two clauses) reminded jurors of the dramatic moment when the prosecuting attorney had Simpson try on the gloves found at the murder scene of his ex-wife, Nicole Brown, and her friend, Ronald Goldman. The gloves, presumably those of the murderer, did not fit. Cochran offered his admonition repeatedly. Let's consider alternate versions of this line:

> Because the glove found at the murder scene does not fit Mr. Simpson, you must not find him guilty.

> You saw Mr. Simpson try on the gloves, and they didn't fit, so he must be innocent of the charges.

> The law requires the prosecution to prove that the defendant was guilty beyond a reasonable doubt, and the gloves found at the murder scene do not fit Mr. Simpson, so you must not find him guilty.

These three sentences are much longer than the short sentence Cochran used. Notice that in the eye-ear pattern sentence, Cochran captures the main idea expressed in the longer sentences, and in the short version, he creates rhythm, rhyme, and balance. "If it doesn't fit, you must acquit" captures the listener's attention. The longer sentences, on the other hand, make the point, but do so ploddingly, without eloquence or style.

Was "If it doesn't fit" an effective argument? Whether your answer is yes or no, understand that Cochran used this line as a rhetorical argument, relying as much on stylistic technique as logical appeal—relying, you might even argue, more on stylistic technique than logical appeal.

You are probably familiar with other brief admonitions, rhythmic, balanced sentences so frequently quoted that no one has to explain the argument each presents:

> Ask not what your country can do for you, ask what you can do for your country.

> Don't ask; don't tell.

> Just say no!

Once again, we find ear-pattern sentences that offer eye patterns as well. One way to recognize eye-pattern sentences is to stack the parts of the sentence that create the patterns:

Ask not what your <u>country can do for you</u>,
ask what <u>you can do for your country</u>.

Don't ask;
don't tell.

Just
say
no!

What do these sentences have in common? First, each one is a command (an imperative sentence). Second, each one is balanced. We can see the balance and the flip-flop of phrasing in the first sentence when we stack the sentences.

The ear and eye patterns in these isolated sentences are easy to recognize. How difficult is it to recognize eye patterns within a paragraph or an entire essay? Actually, this kind of analysis isn't as difficult as you might think. Typically, we give word patterns (alliteration, assonance, consonance) and figurative language (metaphors, similes) more consideration when we study literature than we do when we study nonfiction prose. As "Letter From Birmingham Jail," included in Chapter 11 illustrates, an effective argument may employ any number of stylistic devices that make it a powerful expression.

When you analyze rhetorical strategies, pay attention to passages that are meaningful to you. Take note of passages that you find forceful, thought-provoking, fluent, articulate, and persuasive. You should expect to encounter irony, hyperbole, understatement, rhetorical questions, allusions, similes, and metaphors. You will also discover eye patterns and sentence patterns that create balance and rhythm, and you should find repetition of words and phrases for rhetorical effect.

RHETORICAL STRATEGIES AND CONTENT

A word of caution: In effective papers, rhetorical strategies and content must walk hand-in-hand. When writers rely on rhetorical flourishes and ignore content, they may have nothing but empty rhetoric (a charge commonly leveled at politicians—meaning *it sounds good, but says nothing*). If writers or speakers concentrate only on content and ignore rhetorical strategies, they may have a text that expresses important ideas; however, those ideas may be difficult for the reader or listener to follow because the style is clumsy, awkward, mundane, or inexact.

FOCUS ON STUDENT WRITING: Three Analyses

Read "Blood-Curdling to Make Rounds with Dr. Death," an op-ed piece by Jeff Hooten that appeared in the *Houston Chronicle*. Then discuss the analyses by Eric, Stacey, and Whitney. Do you agree or disagree with points the student writers make about Hooten's rhetorical strategies? Are there points the student writers overlook that you would mention in an analysis of this article? What are those points? Why are they important?

BLOOD-CURDLING TO MAKE ROUNDS WITH DR. DEATH

JEFF HOOTEN

Jack Kevorkian insists he is not obsessed with death.

During his medical residency, Kevorkian donned a black arm band and asked to work the night shift because more patients died then. He carted around a camera to photograph patients' eyes at the moment of death. Co-workers nicknamed him Dr. Death, and he jokingly called his late-night quest "the death rounds." This is detailed in *Appointment With Doctor Death*, the book by Detroit reporter Michael Betzold.

But Kevorkian is not obsessed with death.

An accomplished artist, Kevorkian's paintings are filled with detached organs and severed heads. Maggots, blood and bullets. Skulls and suffering. Cannibalism. His artistic rendering of Christmas shows Santa's boot crushing a baby lying in a fireplace. Religion is a favorite target: In a painting titled *Give Us This Day*, a half-man/half-baby is shown eating the flesh off a decomposing corpse.

But he's not obsessed with death.

Early in his career, Kevorkian advocated medical experimentation on death row inmates. He has since expanded on the idea by suggesting that condemned prisoners be allowed to auction off their organs. At one point, he proposed that anyone sentenced to more than three years in prison be given the option of assisted suicide.

Over at Pontiac General Hospital, he experimented with transfusing blood from corpses into live patients. (Former guinea pig Neal Nicol once got such a severe case of hepatitis from cadaver blood that his eyeballs turned orange.) Kevorkian even mixed cadaver blood with his own and used it to paint the frame for one of his works.

But he's not obsessed with death.

Public support is high for Kevorkian's crusade. According to a recent Gallup poll, about 75 percent of Americans now favor physician-assisted suicide. To many Americans, Kevorkian is a compassionate if eccentric man who wants nothing more than to end people's suffering. But do those same Americans know the Jack Kevorkian who once tried to organize an exhibit of Adolf Hitler's art-work; the Kevorkian who said carbon monoxide gives corpses a "lovely rosy glow"; the Kevorkian who said Jesus Christ would have been better off dying in the back of his rusty van?

Kevorkian has been generating corpses at an accelerated pace since May, when he was acquitted for a third time of violating Michigan's ban on assisted suicide. In mid-August, Kevorkian broke his own record by performing four so-called "medicides" in a week. "Now be really feels he's off and running, and no one can stop him," said Yale Kamisar, a University of Michigan constitutional law professor and expert on the issue of assisted suicide. "It's unlikely that he'll ever be convicted unless he makes a mistake."

Mistake? Take the case of Rebecca Badger, Kevorkian suicide No. 33. This 39-year-old mother of two was depressed and in pain. Her doctors diagnosed her with multiple sclerosis. On July 9, Kevorkian "treated" her. One problem. Badger didn't have MS.

Just five weeks after Badger's death, Kevorkian "assisted" 42-year-old Judith Curren. Kevorkian attorney Geoffrey Fieger said Curren suffered from chronic fatigue and immune-deficiency syndrome, as well as the muscle disorder fibromyalgia. But the Oakland County medical examiner said be could find no evidence of any disease in Curren. Even if he had, none of Curren's maladies is considered fatal.

The Oakland County, Mich., medical examiner said he did find that Curren likely was worn out from carrying 269 pounds on a 5-foot, 1-inch frame. Curren probably experienced depression—90 percent of chronic fatigue sufferers do. She took potentially addictive drugs. Reports also surfaced widely that Curren had accused her husband of domestic abuse, prompting speculation that she was looking to escape a bad marriage. So what if Curren in fact wasn't terminal? "It has nothing to do with lethality, it's quality of life" Kevorkian said on *Dateline NBC*.

Will Dr. Death ever quit? After his third acquittal, Kevorkian said the only way to stop him would be to burn him at the stake.

Opponents of physician-assisted suicide say Kevorkian is a bizarre man on the fringe of medical practice. Rita Marker, executive director of the International Anti-Euthanasia Task Force, said Kevorkian already has reset the boundaries of acceptability in the United States. In comparison with Kevorkian, a suicide doctor with a Marcus Welby-like demeanor will suddenly seem eminently reasonable.

"There will be those who will be Kevorkian with class," Marker said. "They will look respectable. They will sound respectable Their patients will be just as dead."

Welcome to the slippery slope.

Source: Jeff Hooten is an associate editor of *Focus on the Family's Citizen* magazine. This is excerpted from the magazine's October issue.

Eric's Analysis

Mr. Hooten deftly uses several subtle rhetorical tactics in order to, well, upset his readers and destroy any faith they might have had in Dr. Kevorkian. From the very first sentence, Mr. Hooten uses the rhetorical device of repetition in order to make his point. By offering up example after example of Dr. Kevorkian's eerie idiosyncrasies, and then following them with the statement "But he's not obsessed with death," the writer confronts the reader head-on with an obvious contradiction. But there is no hesitation on the reader's part as to which side of the argument to believe. With his stone-faced delivery, and almost sarcastic tone, the author brings out a loathing for Kevorkian and persuades the reader to take his side.

Stacey's Analysis

Hooten utilizes resourceful word choice to complete his devilish impression of Dr. Death. In addition to the sarcasm used in his repetitive phrasing, Hooten places sarcasm throughout the article. For example, he describes Kevorkian, with his paintings of "detached organs and severed heads," as "an accomplished artist." Later, Hooten writes that "Kevorkian broke his own record" in assisted suicides. And when describing the details of Kevorkian's cases, Hooten chooses the satirical words *treated* and *assisted*. The humorous tone of Hooten's sarcasm drives the reader to accept and to believe Hooten's loathing of Kevorkian. Moreover, Hooten conveys Kevorkian's own words to the reader in order to identify Kevorkian as an evil man. In the first paragraph, Hooten tells the reader how Kevorkian "jokingly called his late-night quest 'the death rounds.'" However, nothing compares to the powerful response evoked by Kevorkian's statement that "the only way to stop him would be to burn him at the stake." With these words, Hooten clearly demonstrates the witchcraft and the madness of Kevorkian's work.

Whitney's Analysis

The most obvious rhetorical technique in the article, which follows specific examples concerning the gruesome and morbid practices of Jack Kevorkian, is the recurring statement, "Jack Kevorkian insists he's not obsessed with death." In the article, Hooten speaks of Kevorkian photographing patients' eyes "at the moment of death" and using blood from corpses along with his own to paint picture frames for his artwork. By illustrating the baseness of Kevorkian's hobbies, Hooten has identified him as a disturbed man, and is attempting to stir the emotions of the reader. Hooten successfully makes his point by following these unsettling examples with the statement concerning Kevorkian's obsession with death.

By carefully selecting his words and phrasing of sentences, Hooten portrays Kevorkian as a man who is void of all emotion. Hooten alleges that in relation to Kevorkian's third acquittal in Michigan, "Kevorkian has been generating corpses at an accelerated rate since May." The reference to death in such a flippant manner causes the reader to view Kevorkian as a robot who is incapable of any thought or remorse about his actions. Hooten uses the word *generating* to give the sentence a very cold and empty feeling. The use of this pivotal word impresses upon the reader that Kevorkian is almost inhuman and treats life and his patients with little respect.

Two Systems of Analysis

For further practice in analyzing arguments, use the Toulmin and classical systems. Both are presented here to provide you with different approaches for analysis. Notice that each uses different terminology and asks you to use different approaches in examining how writers develop arguments. Even if you favor one system over the other, it's important to understand both and to use both to examine arguments thoroughly.

Using these two systems, you should be prepared to differentiate between papers in which a writer states a position and supports it and papers that develop arguments—examination of both sides of an issue.

The Toulmin System

In the late 1950s, philosopher Steven Toulmin developed a system of analyzing arguments that examines a writer's data (facts offered as support), warrants (general principles, often unstated, that support a connection between the data and claim), and claim (the conclusion the writer wishes to reach in an argument); or, in a simplified version, the writer's

- Claim (thesis)
- Qualifications of the claim (qualifiers, adverbs and adjectives, limit claims; words such as *usually*, *occasionally*, *typically*, *normally*, and *sometimes*)
- Data (reasons, evidence, statistics, opinions, facts, or examples offered to support the claim)
- Warrants (assumptions the writer may not state outright but assumes readers understand and share; values; general accepted beliefs)
- Backing (additional evidence that supports the warrant)
- Counterarguments and response (arguments that would challenge the claim)

Using the Toulmin system will help you determine how logical an argument may or may not be. Questions to ask when you analyze a source using the Toulmin system include the following:

- What is the writer's claim/thesis? Is it stated or implied? If it is implied, put the writer's claim/thesis in your own words.
- Does the writer qualify the thesis? (Identify the qualifiers and any exceptions the writer makes to the claim.)
- What assumptions does the writer make about readers' values or beliefs?
- What reasons does the writer offer to support the claim? (Identify and evaluate the reasons. Do the reasons seem to be valid? pertinent? questionable?)
- What kinds of evidence does the writer offer? (Does the evidence clearly support the claim?) Evaluate the evidence.
- Does the writer offer counterargument and response to the counterargument?

To illustrate how the Toulmin system works, read "Invasion of the Tree Snakes and Other Coming Infestations" and the writer's analysis that follows the article.

INVASION OF THE TREE SNAKES AND OTHER COMING INFESTATIONS

THEODORE GIDEONSE

It's midnight on Guam, and an eight-foot-long brown tree snake has just emerged from a toilet bowl. After hours of slithering through sewage pipes, she's hungry. She slides across the bathroom floor into the room where a baby lies sleeping. The snake slithers up into the crib, and then under the boy's blanket. Her jaws clamp down on his fingers. The boy screams. His father bolts into the room, grabs the slinky monster and throws it out an open window.

There are so many snakes on Guam they're literally crawling out of the woodwork. In some areas there are as many as 13,000 per square mile, and they eat everything they can sink their teeth into. Eventually, many biologists think, the infestation is going to spread to Hawaii, which is just a short flight away. "It's only a matter of time," says Tom Fritts, a research biologist with the U.S. Geological Survey. "Hawaii could be devastated," agrees Julie Savidge of the University of Nebraska. In this century much has been made of vanishing species; in the next millennium we may be even more alarmed about rapidly expanding ones.

The ecological equation is simple. When there are too many predators, not enough resources and a great deal of competition, an animal population dies out. But when the opposite occurs, the population explodes. This can be every bit as bad. When the brown tree snake arrived on Guam in the cargo of a military plane 50 years ago, the ecosystem wasn't ready for the reptilian assault. The snake had no natural competitors or enemies. Virtually every forest songbird on Guam is snake droppings now.

The situation will get worse as trade, shipping and tourism bring stowaway animals—a snake in a shipping crate, a mosquito in a suitcase—to new habitats. And native species run rampant can be as much of a problem as alien intruders. "What humans do is make the environment worse for a number of species and make it much better for some," notes ecologist James Brown of the University of New Mexico, The white-tailed deer, for example, has been thriving in second-growth forests and is now a suburban pest.

Opportunistic animals aren't pests just to us: they can be their own worst enemy. The lesser snow geese of Canada are so overpopulated they're destroying their own habitat. Over the past three decades, the population has risen from 800,000 to almost 3 million. Advances in agriculture have enabled the geese to arrive at their breeding grounds in better condition, leading to higher rates of reproduction. As these huge flocks of birds nest on the west coast of Hudson Bay, they grub intensively, upturning soil and pulling out plants by their roots. The land has been ravaged. "The Arctic is a fragile ecosystem," says Bob Trost of the U.S. Fish and Wildlife Service. "It may take upwards of a century to come back to a productive state." There are two options: the geese will find another nesting ground and destroy it, or they will run out of food and land and their population will crash.

Managing these booms is difficult. Encouraging recreational hunting is one option, though it's unlikely to make a large dent. More efficient methods, like killing animals en masse, tend to prompt public outcry. Nobody much cares for tree snakes, but keeping them from leaving Guam is ultimately more important than eradicating them. The USDA is using snake-sniffing dogs to check outgoing cargoes.

The most natural method of controlling outbreaks is biological control—bringing in a predator or enemy. Recently the USDA introduced the phlorid fly to help cull the pesky fire ant, which has long been stinging Southerners and sucking the sap out of soybeans. The fly implants its larvae in the ant, eventually killing it. But this method has its dangers, too. When Australian authorities released a virus targeting wild rabbits, they ended up killing many domesticated bunnies as well. And some scientists say the virus could spread to humans. Maybe that's what you get for playing God.

Source: Theodore Gideonse, "Invasion of the Tree Snakes and Other Coming Infestations," *Newsweek* 28 Jul. 1997: 13.

Writer's Analysis

Claim: Stated thesis—In this century much has been made of vanishing species; in the next millennium we may be even more alarmed about rapidly expanding ones.

Qualifier: We *may* be *even more* alarmed (than we have been previously).

Warrant: Overpopulation is equally as devastating as extinction.

Data:

1. Trade shipping and tourism will bring stowaway animals to new habitats that are not ecologically prepared to deal with them.

Evidence:

- Statistics—Brown tree snakes in Guam: "as many as 13,000 a square mile."
- Songbird population in Guam has been wiped out.
- Expert testimony—Tom Fritts, research biologist with the U.S. Geological Service: Only a matter of time until brown tree snakes reach Hawaii.
- Expert testimony—Julie Savidge, University of Nebraska, "Hawaii could be devastated."

2. Native species run rampant can be as much of a problem as alien intruders.

Evidence:

- The white-tailed deer is now a suburban pest.
- The lesser snow geese of Canada are destroying their own habitat.

3. Managing the booms in a species' population is difficult.

Evidence:

- Killing is not an option because of public protests.
- Trying to contain a species in one country is also difficult.

Counterargument: We might not have to worry about overpopulation of a species if we used biological control, as the introduction of the phlorid fly to control fire ants illustrates.

Response: Biological control has its dangers: a virus targeting wild rabbits in Australia killed many domesticated bunnies; scientists believe the virus could spread to humans, too.

Writer's Notes

The reasons seem to be valid; the evidence relies on two examples: brown tree snakes in Guam and snow geese in Canada. The example of the tree snakes is frightening and seems slightly sensational. While this kind of minimal evidence may be sufficient for readers of *Newsweek,* it would not be sufficient for an academic paper. The writer does not say whether examples of population control that have been effective outnumber examples of population control that have had tragic results.

Now, with this analysis completed, we can go back and determine the data, claim, and warrants.

Data: The populations of several species are currently out of control.

Claim: In the next millennium we may be even more alarmed about rapidly expanding species than we are now.

Warrants: People should be as concerned about overpopulation as they are about extinction.

Ecological balance can be upset when non-native species are introduced.

Backing: When there are no predators, available resources, and competition, a species' population will explode.

International trade and travel presently allow for transporting species to areas that are not ecologically prepared for them.

Solutions to overpopulation of a species may be dangerous to existing species and unacceptable to animal rights groups.

In the past, we have "played God" with species' population control.

Writer's Note: While evidence is thin, the writer has constructed a logical argument.

The Classical System

The classical system is named for the formula the ancient Greeks and Romans used for organizing orations. These orations required an introduction, a thesis statement, support for the thesis, acknowledgment of counterarguments, and a conclusion. The version outlined below is, of course, a simplified version of the formula. We can analyze an argument by answering questions about how writers introduce and conclude their ideas, support their theses, and address their intended readers.

Introduction

- Is the introduction inviting? interesting? routine? What makes it so?
- Does the writer establish common ground with the reader? How?

Thesis

- Does the writer announce his or her purpose in a thesis statement?
- Is the thesis implied?
- Is the thesis sufficiently narrowed?

Background

- Does the writer provide a clear context for the topic?
- Does the context establish the significance of the topic?

Support for the thesis

- Does the writer offer as major points of support personal experience? citations from scholarly studies? statistics?
- Does the writer appeal primarily to readers' logic, ethics, or emotion?
- Does the writer offer adequate support? Are any points of support noticeably underdeveloped?

Audience Analysis

- Do examples, illustrations, or statistics appear to be appropriate for the intended audience?
- Does the writer define terms as needed?

Content

- Does the text include lines of reasoning that are clear and accessible?
- Does the argument rely on logical fallacies?
- Do you find the content to be predictable, general, specific?
- Does the medium limit content?

Style

- Is the style clear and precise? heavy-handed and pedantic? dry and stuffy? informal and chummy?
- Does the writer create vivid imagery for the reader? How?
- Does the writer convey to the reader a sense of authority? Cite passages that illustrate your evaluation.

Conclusion

- Does the conclusion tie up any loose ends?
- Does it recommend a course of action?

The following is another analysis of the *Newsweek* article "Invasion of the Tree Snakes and Other Coming Infestations," this time using the classical system:

Writer's Notes:

Introduction

The brief narrative in the first paragraph engages the reader's attention. Speculation on the spread of the brown tree snakes to Hawaii establishes a common concern:

Thesis

The thesis is stated in the last sentence of the second paragraph. The thesis is rather broad. The writer begins with a specific example and draws a generalization (the thesis) from that example and other examples cited in the article.

Background

The second paragraph supplies a context and the significance of the topic: the infestation of brown tree snakes will probably spread from Guam to Hawaii.

Support for the thesis

The writer offers a few statistics: 13,000 brown tree snakes per square mile in Guam; population of the lesser snow geese in Canada has increased, over three decades, from 800,000 to almost 3 million. The writer also cites experts: a research biologist with the U.S. Geological Survey, someone associated with the University of Nebraska (the reader can't tell exactly what this person's qualifications are—graduate student? faculty?); someone with the U.S. Fish and Wildlife Service.

The writer establishes a logical argument: If modern modes of travel have allowed the brown tree snake to be transported to a habitat where the population can explode, the same thing can happen with other species. Paragraph 3 establishes a cause-and-effect relationship between too many or two few predators, too many or two few resources, and too much or too little competition. Even more effective, though, is the writer's appeal to the reader's sense of fear. The example of the brown tree snakes is much more alarming than the example of the lesser snow geese. Other appeals to emotions are evident in the description of the lesser snow geese destroying their habitat and eventually running out of food and land. Very disturbing is the image of snake-sniffing dogs policing outgoing cargoes from Guam. Also, in the last paragraph, the writer appeals to the reader's emotions with the description of domesticated bunnies being killed by a virus targeted to kill wild rabbits. The writer also appeals to the reader's sense of ethics with the discussion of ways to control overpopulation. A lot of people will find mass killing objectionable. Overall, the emotional appeals are the strongest.

The writer asserts that white-tailed deer are suburban pests, but offers no examples, personal testimony, or statistics.

Overall, support for the thesis is sufficient for a lay audience.

Audience Analysis

The writer defines one term—*biological control.* The ideas seem clear; nothing in the article is confusing. The brief narrative in the first paragraph illustrates good audience analysis. It whets the reader's curiosity.

Content

Content is clear. The content of the article is limited by constraints of the magazine. The writer cites a total of four examples of overpopulation, though. If the reader isn't convinced that overpopulation can be as serious a problem as underpopulation, the article should at least make the reader think seriously about the writer's claims.

Style

The writer's style is appropriate for the rhetorical situation. At the end of the last paragraph, he shifts to direct address of the audience, suggesting that even advocating interference with population control puts all of us, not only scientists, in the role of playing God.

The writer conveys a sense of authority when he cites examples, statistics, and expert testimony.

Conclusion

The concluding paragraph ends with a strong emotional appeal—the idea that possible solutions to the problem of overpopulation will be a threat to man. The last sentence provides an ethical appeal. The writer uses persuasive techniques effectively and gives the reader a sense of closure with the last sentence.

As these two examples illustrate, using either system, you may end up with a set of notes longer than the article itself. That's okay, though. The more thorough your analysis of a source, the better your understanding will be of the argument and counter argument and of the writer's ability to present each one effectively.

READINGS FOR PRACTICE: READING AND WRITING ABOUT ROCK

Chapter 4 included an organizational plan for writing a critique. You can use a similar plan for analyzing a writer's argument. If you don't have experience writing analyses of arguments, use the following guidelines. But don't feel locked in to this order. You may want to experiment with different ways to discuss your analysis.

Introduction

- Identify the title of the work you are critiquing.
- Identify the author and any pertinent information about him or her.
- Identify the thesis/claim, if it is stated, and any qualifiers. If it is implied, explain what the thesis seems to be.
- Explain the writer's purpose in writing.
- Identify intended readers.
- Give a brief explanation of the importance or relevance of the issue.
- State your thesis. Your thesis might indicate whether you agree or disagree with the writer's thesis, whether the writer fulfills his or her purpose, and whether you recommend the source to your intended readers.
  - I. Summary of the work
    - In one or two paragraphs, summarize the main points that support the writer's thesis.
  - II. Analysis of the work
    - Using either Toulmin or the classical system, analyze the writer's argument.
    - Support your thesis with discussion of such matters as the writer's use of persuasive appeals, organization, and rhetorical strategies.
    - Point out any logical fallacies or weak evidence to support claims.
  - III. Evaluation and any recommendations
    - Discuss your understanding of and assumptions about the subject.
    - Explain why the writer's argument is or is not worthy of consideration.

Conclusion

- Come back to your thesis—restate it; or provide a quotation from the work that allows the reader to see a clear relationship between your thesis and your evaluation.

Preview, read, and annotate the following articles.

ENDANGERED ROCK

CAMILLE PAGLIA

Rock is eating its young. Rock musicians are America's most wasted natural resource.

Popular music and films are the two great art forms of the 20th century. In the past 25 years, cinema has gained academic prestige. Film courses are now a standard part of the college curriculum and grants are routinely available to noncommercial directors.

But rock music has yet to win the respect it deserves as the authentic voice of our time. Where rock goes, democracy follows. The dark poetry and surging Dionysian rhythms of rock have transformed the consciousness and permanently altered the sensoriums of two generations of Americans born after World War II.

Rock music should not be left to the Darwinian laws of the marketplace. This natively American art form deserves national support. Foundations, corporations and Federal and state agencies that award grants in the arts should take rock musicians as seriously as composers and sculptors. Colleges and universities should designate special scholarships for talented rock musicians. Performers who have made fortunes out of rock are ethically obligated to finance such scholarships or to underwrite independent agencies to support needy musicians.

In rock, Romanticism still flourishes. All the Romantic archetypes of energy passion, rebellion and demonism are still evident in the brawling, boozing bad boys of rock, storming from city to city on their lusty groupie-dogged trail.

But the Romantic outlaw must have something to rebel against. The pioneers of rock were freaks, dreamers and malcontents who drew their lyricism and emotional power from the gritty rural traditions of white folk music and African American blues.

Rock is a victim of its own success. What once signified rebellion in now only a high school affectation. White suburban youth, rock's main audience, is trapped in creature comforts. Everything comes to them secondhand, through TV. And they no longer have direct contact with folk music and blues, the oral repository of centuries of love, hate, suffering and redemption.

In the 1960's, rock became the dominant musical form in America. And with the shift from singles to albums, which allowed for the marketing of personalities, it also became big business. The gilded formula froze into place. Today, scouts beat the bushes for young talent, squeeze a quick album out of the band and put them on the road. "New material is stressed. Albums, featuring cover tunes of classics, as in the early. Rolling Stones records are discouraged.

From the moment the Beatles could not hear themselves sing over the shrieking at Shea Stadium in the mid-60's, the rock concert format has become progressively less conducive to music-making. The enormous expense of huge sound systems and grandiose special effects has left no room for individualism and improvisation, no opportunity for the performers to respond to a particular audience or to their own moods. The show, with its army of technicians, is as fixed and rehearsed as the Ziegfeld Follies. Furthermore, the concert experience has degenerated. The focus has switched from the performance to raucous partying in the audience.

These days, rock musicians are set upon by vulture managers, who sanitize and repackage them and strip them of their unruly free will. Like sports stars, musicians are milked to the max, then dropped and cast aside when their first album doesn't sell.

Managers offer all the temptations of Mammon to young rock bands: wealth, fame and easy sex. There is not a single public voice in the culture to say to the musician: You are an artist, not a money machine. Don't sign the contract. Don't tour. Record only when you are ready. Go off on your own, like Jimi Hendrix, and live with your guitar until it becomes part of your body.

How should an artist be trained? Many English rock musicians in the 60's and early 70's, including John Lennon and Keith Richards, emerged from art schools. We must tell the young musician: your peers are other artists, pass and future. Don't become a slave to the audience, with its smug hedonism, short attention span and hunger for hits.

Artists should immerse themselves in art. Two decades ago, rock musicians read poetry, studied Hinduism and drew psychedelic visions in watercolors. For rock to move forward as an art form, our musicians must be given the opportunity for spiritual development. They should be encouraged to read, to lock at paintings and foreign films, to listen to jazz and classical music.

Artists with a strong sense of vocation can survive life's disasters and triumphs with their inner lives intact. Our, musicians need to be rescued from the carpetbaggers and gold-diggers who attack them when they are young and naïve. Long, productive careers don't happen by chance.

Camille Paglia, author of "Sexual Personae," is professor of humanities at the University of the Arts.

Source: Camille Paglia, "Endangered Rock," *New York Times.* 16 Apr. 1992: A 23.

ROMANTICIZING ROCK MUSIC

THEODORE A. GRACYK

If now we reflect that music at its greatest intensity must seek to attain also to its highest symbolization, we must deem it possible that it also knows how to find the symbolic expression for its unique Dionysian wisdom.
—Nietzsche, *The Birth of Tragedy*

To the extent that theorists are willing to treat rock music as art, most of them consider it popular art rather than fine art. But several recent writers contend that rock music is a manifestation of the aesthetics of Romanticism and as such can be understood in terms of the same categories that are applied to artists who produce fine art. We are invited to conclude that rock musicians deserve the same respect as such poets as Wordsworth and Byron and such musicians as Chopin and Liszt, because the accomplishment of the Rolling Stones is of the same type as that of these nineteenth-century precursors. The major obstacle to admitting that rock musicians are important artists is supposedly the common confusion of a commercial product ("pop" music) with rock music.

Another manifestation of the aesthetics of Romanticism is the idea that rock music is not fine art, but rather modern urban folk music.[1] As one rock critic put it, "It is just because they didn't worry about art that many of the people who ground out the rock-and-roll of the fifties—not only the performers, but all the background people—were engaged (unconsciously, of course) in making still another kind of art, folk art."[2] Again, a distinction is to be made between popular art, an inauthentic exploitation of the masses, and this modern folk art. Yet another position, to be considered at length in this essay, brings the two strands together in the claim that rock possesses the virtues of Romantic art while drawing much of its power from its folk music roots.

Tied to each of these positions is an attempt to bring rock music into the domains of art and aesthetic education. (At present, academic attention on rock is almost entirely sociological in perspective.) While I sympathize with attempts to locate an aesthetic of rock music, I do not believe that Romanticism is the right model. And it is an even greater mistake to believe that rock musicians should be trained according to the model for educating other artists.

I

The boldest and most uncompromising of those who would romanticize rock is Camille Paglia. She contends that it is time to accept rock musicians as legitimate artists and to treat rock as we treat other arts, supporting it directly with government subsidies and private grants and indirectly through special college scholarships. Paglia calls for a return to rock's past glories, when the music was rebellious, vital, and pulsating with "surging Dionysian rhythms."[3] It turns out that, like Nietzsche, she does not regard the masses as capable of appreciating true art when they encounter it. But unlike Nietzsche, she does not give us any sense that the highest art will be a fusion of the Dionysian and Apollonian strains.

Paglia's argument is worth considering because it adopts, without criticism, the prevailing story of rock music. Except for her proposal that we treat rock musicians as full-fledged artists, she depends on common assumptions, so common that most rock fans would probably applaud her endorsement and ignore the distortions, half-truths, and stereotypes. The story is this: "The pioneers of rock were freaks, dreamers and malcontents" who drew on an authentic tradition of "white folk music and African American blues." The sixties were rock's golden age, when rock musicians drew their inspiration from poetry and Eastern religions. (She doesn't point out that groups like Steppenwolf, Mott the Hoople, and Steely Dan got their names from literary works, but I assume that that's the sort of thing she has in mind.) Above all, rock musicians were the inheritors of Romanticism. They were outlaws, "storming from city to city on their lusty, groupie-dogged trail." Because she regards them as sensitive artists, Paglia here brushes over the fact that she's really talking about their sexual exploitation of women, many of them underage.

But rock soon fell victim to capitalism. Market forces corrupted rock. Paglia offers three pieces of evidence. First, the authentic source is lost; neither fans nor musicians have direct knowledge of folk music and blues, "the oral repository of centuries of love, hate, suffering and redemption." Second, live performance has atrophied, leaving no room for spontaneous musical expression or artist-audience interaction. Once it was a performing art, with the focus on the performance. Now it is a mere show—fully rehearsed and with no room for artistic spontaneity—and an excuse for partying. Third, greedy and manipulative managers exploit innocent young artists, turning them from self-expression to pandering to crass commercial interests, "milking" them for profit in exchange for "wealth, fame and easy sex." Knowingly or not, Paglia is paraphrasing

Bob Geldof's remark that people join rock bands for "three very simple rock and roll reasons: to get laid, to get fame, and to get rich."[4]

Her remedy? Divorce rock from the commercial marketplace. We should provide an escape from the commercial interests that divert rock artists from serious music making. Like classical musicians, rock musicians must relocate to colleges and universities. (Was Bob Dylan ahead of his time when, on his debut, he introduced a traditional song as having been acquired among the fair fields of Harvard?) Supported by government and private grants, prestige and artistic freedom will follow, compensating the musicians for the lost wealth, fame, and sex. After all, Paglia notes, both Keith Richards and John Lennon attended English "art schools." Never mind that they were barely able to obtain passing grades and that the schools were as much trade schools as art institutes; perhaps we should instead be satisfied that Mick Jagger went to the London School of Economics and Lou Reed studied with poet Delmore Schwarz. Complementing their musical studies with art history and literature, a liberal arts education will guide rock musicians' spiritual development, and rock will recover as the "authentic voice of our times."

Charming as this is, it disintegrates when we go through it one claim at a time. Let us start with the pioneers of rock as Romantic archetypes. Paglia offers no examples, but obvious cases would have to include Bill Haley, Elvis Presley, Chuck Berry, Little Richard, Bo Diddley, Carl Perkins, Buddy Holly, Jerry Lee Lewis, Fats Domino, and Ray Charles.[5] While this may be a list of freaks and dreamers, their dreams were mostly about making hit records and a lot of money. They were hardly malcontents, unless being an African American or poor Southern white in the nineteen-fifties automatically qualified one. If anything, they represent the American underclass of the period, seeking respectability in money and fame. Perhaps Paglia is thinking of the sixties and its political posturing, but at that point we are already far from the folk and blues roots that she identifies as the source of their authenticity and expressive power.

The rebellion of rock's pioneers was of the James Dean variety, strictly adolescent. If we are to believe any of the prevailing *sociological* analysis of rock, it tells us this:

> What mattered about rock'n'roll in the 1950s was its youth; its expression of a community of interest between performer and audience; and its account of a generation bound by age and taste in a gesture of self-celebration, in defiance against the nagging, adult routines of home and work and school.... rock'n'roll stardom soon became a matter of the youth voice and the youth song, so that Elvis Presley became rock'n'roll's superstar because he so clearly *represented* his listeners and Chuck Berry became the most successful R & B performer to adapt its loose limbed lyrics to the interests of the white, teenaged record-buyer.[6]

It was also rooted in a very American desire for material comforts like a sharp wardrobe (blue suede shoes immediately come to mind) and a pink Cadillac. Paglia complains that rock's original rebellion has been reduced to "high school affectation." Yet search as we might through early rock, the only *social* protest comes mainly from Chuck Berry, and it was *very* high school: "School Days," "Too Much Monkey Business," and "No Particular Place to Go." The Coasters' "Yakety Yak" and Eddie Cochran's "Summer-time Blues" likewise gave voice to teens' railing against parental authority. There is occasional social commentary, but it is fairly mild, as in the undercurrent of black pride in Chuck Berry's "Brown Eyed Handsome Man" or the Coaster's "Shopping for Clothes" and "Framed" (both written by the white production team of Leiber and Stoller).

Her complaint is also odd in light of analyses given by Nik Cohn and Carl Belz. Writing in the late sixties, Cohn reflected the prevalent British enthusiasm for rock and American "pop" *as* reflections of America. He praised rock because it voiced teen concerns; the best popular music, he wrote, "is all teenage property and it mirrors everything that happens to teenagers in this time, in this American 20th century. It is about clothes and cars and dancing, it's about parents and high school."[7] Carl Belz, defending a view of rock as modern folk music, praised Chuck Berry for "unconsciously" expressing the "ordinary realities of their world: ... cars, girls, growing up, school, or music."[8] Rock's decline started, on these analyses, when the Beatles and others turned to self-expression and musical experimentation for its own sake. The point is not whether Cohn and Belz are right and Paglia is wrong; both seem rather simplistic. The point is that to many at the time, rock and roll had always been the music of teenagers, and only later did it develop affectations toward art. So Paglia's alternative story of rock's decline, as a shift from genuine rebellion to high school values, sounds like selective memory that focuses on the late 1960s rather than rock's first decade as the point for all comparisons. As such, it is too hopelessly slanted to form the basis for any argument that appeals to rock's special strengths.

It is also hard to believe that only *subsequent* rock musicians were corrupted by money, fame, and sex. If rock's pioneers had any consistent message, it was a desire for sex. As critic Dave Marsh says of Buddy Holly's 1957 hit "Oh Boy," "Edgy and excited, he sings the opening way too fast.... But as he jitters along, the cause of Buddy's nervousness becomes clear: He's about to get laid. Probably for the very first time."[9] There is Hank Ballard's widely banned "Work with Me, Annie," Elvis Presley's cover of "Good Rockin' Tonight," Chuck Berry's less overt "Carol," and hundreds of others that relied on innuendo to make their point. Anyone who has seen Martin Scorsese's *The Last Waltz* knows that easy sex could be a powerful incentive to becoming a rock musician. In one of the interview sequences, Robbie Robertson and the others who were to become The Band confess that they hit the road with Canadian rockabilly singer Ronnie Hawkins because he promised them more groupies than Frank Sinatra had.

As for fame, when the musicians who became three-fourths of the Beatles were depressed and ready to throw in the towel, John Lennon rallied them with a chant. He would say, "Where are we going, fellows?" and they answered, "To the top, Johnny" in American accents, followed by, "Where is that, fellows?" and, "To the toppermost of the poppermost."[10] In other words, they were going to the top of the record (pop) charts. Why the faked American accents? Because, as Lennon said, "Elvis was the biggest. We wanted to be the biggest, doesn't everybody? ... Elvis was the thing. Whatever people say, he was it."[11] Paglia's complaints about managers who take advantage of innocent young musicians date from this same period; Britain's *Daily Worker* made precisely the same criticisms in 1963.[12] Keith Richards and Mick Jagger have made no secret about the degree to which their manager, Andrew Oldham, manipulated the press to achieve notoriety and fame for the Rolling Stones.

Finally, even the sixties musicians that Paglia specifically singles out as purer and artistically truer than those of today, the Beatles and the Rolling Stones, were infiltrated by Philistines who worried as much about their bank accounts as they did about their spiritual development. The Stones had difficulty recruiting drummer Charlie Watts because he refused to quit his day job and its steady paycheck, and bass player Bill Wyman was chosen as much for his having a good amplifier as for his artistic potential. They were unwilling to fulfill the Romantic stereotype of the starving artist. Stu Sutcliffe served as the Beatles' bass player before Paul McCartney; Lennon convinced his art school friend to buy a bass and join because he *looked* the part. A wretched musician, he played his first audition with his back to the promoter in an effort to hide his ineptitude. Ringo Starr later joined as drummer with the expectation of salting away enough money to open a hairdressing parlor when the group lost its popular appeal. Of course, Paglia might dismiss such anecdotes because they involve nonwriting members of rhythm sections, whereas her focus is squarely on the singers and songwriters. But she thereby neglects the very players who give rock its Dionysian rhythms.

The greatest distortion in Paglia's argument is probably the idea that early rockers had some "direct" connection with an authentic oral tradition which accounts for their expressive power. To begin with, there were few "white folk music" sources for rock. Rock's pioneers knew hillbilly and country in a commercial form. Chuck Berry's first record, "Maybellene" (1955), was a simple rewrite of a country standard, "Ida Red." And most of what the early rockers knew of music—black or white—was obtained secondhand, from records. For the white rock and rollers in particular, the primary noncommercial source was gospel music. When Elvis Presley walked into Sun Records in 1953 and taped two songs (purportedly as a birthday gift to his mother, although her birthday was months away), he covered the Ink Spots. When producer Sam Phillips invited Elvis to audition in January of 1954, Elvis chose two country tunes, also learned from records. At their next meeting, Elvis ran through a broader repertoire, "heavy on the Dean Martin stuff. Apparently he'd decided, if he was going to sound like anybody, it was gonna be Dean Martin."[13] So much for "direct contact" with rural traditions on the part of rock's first great popularizer.

The recordings of Buddy Holly are another good case in point. Holly was immortalized by his death in an airplane crash. (Touring the Midwest in January and February of 1959, he and Ritchie Valens and the Big Bopper [J. P. Richardson] chartered a light plane and flew ahead after a gig in Clear Lake, Iowa, so that they could get some laundry done before the next night's show in Minnesota.) Virtually everything that Holly ever put on tape has been released, most of it in a box set *The Complete Buddy Holly* (MCA Records, 1979). Holly was one of the first rockers to have some control over production and, like Chuck Berry, but unlike Elvis Presley, founded his career on his own songs. Nonetheless, much of Holly's recorded legacy consists of cover versions of earlier songs. Many were rock and roll hits that had just been released by *other* rock pioneers: the Robins' (later the Coasters) "Smokey Joe's Cafe," Carl Perkins's "Blue Suede Shoes," Chuck Berry's "Brown-Eyed Handsome Man," Little Richards's "Slippin' and Slidin'," Fats Domino's "Blue Monday." He continued this practice right to the end. One of the very last things he recorded, on a tape recorder in his New York apartment, was a haunting version of Mickey and Sylvia's 1955 hit "Love Is Strange." His other sources were country; his first business card advertised "Western and Bop," and his early radio performances in Lubbock covered the music of Hank Williams, Flatt and Scruggs, and the Louvin Brothers.

Finally, consider Paglia's complaint that live performance has lost its spontaneity and communication and has become a rehearsed and meaningless show. She points to the Beatles' stadium performances as the point of decline. How so? When the Beatles earlier played the cellars of Hamburg's red-light district, singing American hits in Liverpool accents to drunk Germans, was the setting really all that conducive to genuine artistic expression? By all accounts, including the one tape recording made in Hamburg, they played brutal rock and roll for up to six hours a night. And the mix of beer and amphetamines that kept them going hardly made them sensitive to the audience or to their own development as "artists." Paul McCartney had it right when he described it as "noise and beat all the way."[14]

Where Paglia claims that the audience-artist bond was severed by the complexity and expense of ever larger sound systems, coupled with increasingly elaborate special effects, it was certainly these very things that first made rock concerts into something more than party music. The elaborate improvisations of Cream, the Grateful Dead, and the rest of the San Francisco scene, Led Zeppelin and Jimi Hendrix, all came in the five years *after* the Beatles abandoned the stage for the studio. And their achievements depended on superior sound systems; improvisational rock was hardly possible when the musicians had no stage monitors and the cheap amplification system distorted the music into a dull roar, with a sound mix that put the tinny vocals far out in front. Concerts as we understand them today, as extended performances by one or more artists, were rare events before the advent of the modern sound system. In rock's early days, the audience usually saw a specific singer or act as part of a "package" show featuring a half dozen acts, each performing two or three songs and then making way for the next group and its performance of selected hits.

Rather than modern counterparts of Wordsworth, Coleridge, Shelley, Keats, and Byron, rock musicians have always had crass commercial motives, playing dance music to mostly teen audiences. Their direct musical sources were commercial recordings by earlier musicians, and their lyrics featured heavy doses of innuendo but little in the way of overt rebellion and, prior to 1965, almost nothing in the way of personal expression. None of this is offered with the intention of denigrating rock musicians. But if we are considering the claim that rock is either folk or fine art, the available facts count heavily against such status.

II

I have outlined the historical distortions of Paglia's story in order to clear the stage for the main thrust of her proposal: "Rock music should not be left to the Darwinian laws of the marketplace.... For rock to move forward as an art form, our musicians must be given an opportunity for spiritual development." Having constructed a selective history that postulates an "authentic" tradition with a subsequent commercial distortion, she thinks that rock has a legitimate claim to being a true art form. But even if successful rock musicians have actually been those who could adapt to the commercial demands of entertainment, Paglia is advocating that rock can be fine art if the musicians can be freed from these commercial constraints. Paglia might have quoted composer Roger Sessions for support: "The artist's values are not, and cannot be, those of the market. If one must think of him as writing *for* anyone, the answer is ... he is writing for all who love music."[15] If modern composers have lost out to popular music, Sessions argues, it is mainly the fault of audiences who have become too lazy to listen with sympathy and understanding. In the same vein, Paglia recommends that rock artists write for posterity, not the commercial audience.

Paglia believes that rock, purged of its economic dependence on a fickle and immature audience, will be recognized as the equal (or better) of current painting, sculpture, and serious composed music. She never explicitly says so, but her only standard of artistic achievement is rooted in her own acceptance of the aesthetics of Romanticism and its assumptions about the goals and value of art. I will argue that this line of argument is of no use if one wants to bring rock music and musicians into academia.

In the story she tells of rock's decline, Paglia singles out the following features as having been lost: individualism, spontaneity, energy, passion, and rebellion. Paglia has accepted Josiah Royce's "creed" of the Romantic artist: "Trust your genius; follow your noble heart; change your doctrine whenever your heart changes, and change your heart often."[16] It is also clear that she does not regard the artist's role as one of reflecting society. Disdaining the trivial concerns of the "white suburban youth" who are rock's primary audience, she believes that serious rock focuses on "dark" emotions, demonism, and spirituality. In Paglia's controversial book *Sexual Personae,* she contends that despite its commercialism, American radio proves that we "still live in the age of Romanticism." The Rolling Stones "are heirs of stormy Coleridge."[17] Other writers have analyzed rock in the same terms:

> In part because of its contradictions, the best way to understand rock and roll is to see it as a twentieth-century popular expression of Western romanticism. In fact, rock may even by the last gasp of romanticism in this anxious materialistic and scientific age. More than any other contemporary cultural form, rock captures the central elements of the romantic spirit: its individuality, freedom, and rebellion, ... its exultation of emotion, physicality, and imagination, and its relish of contradictions, extremes, and paradoxes.[18]

The most detailed attempt to link rock and Romanticism is Robert Pattison's *The Triumph of Vulgarity,* subtitled "Rock Music in the Mirror of Romanticism." Pattison contends that rock "is a unique integration of Romantic mythology and American blues."[19] Like Paglia, he identifies the Rolling Stones as the greatest rock band ever. (The Beatles, we are left to presume, are just not demonic enough.)

Unlike Paglia, Pattison does not endorse Romanticism, and he is sometimes condescending toward his subjects. While he is aware that the Romantic myths are espoused by rock musicians, he does not regard them as anything but myths. With particular attention to the idea of rock's "primitive" sources, he believes that rock artists themselves have adopted the doctrines of nineteenth-century Romanticism. He contends that the "vulgar mode" of Romanticism is the cultural force behind rock, "and the Sex Pistols come to fulfill the prophecies of Shelley."[20] His argumentation amounts to quoting extensively but selectively from rock lyrics, putting rather too much weight on rock's supposed pantheism as the primary evidence of romanticist influences. A more serious weakness is a tendency to equate rock's mythology, as expressed in its lyrics, with the forces actually driving it; he likes to quote obscure groups like the Fall and then to assure us that in "describing themselves, they describe all rockers."[21] Yet there is every reason to believe that the attitudes of most rock lyrics are posturing and image-making for commercial purposes and that many of the musicians are themselves perfectly aware of this.

There is also a tendency toward circularity. Anything that does not reflect Romanticism is written off as nonrock, so Pattison does not recognize soul and other black popular music as rock. Black music "has supplied the raw materials, but there is no reason to suppose that blacks share the Romantic preoccupations necessary for rock."[22] But it is absurd to think that such preoccupations are *necessary* for rock. When the Beatles covered black musicians like Chuck Berry and Little Richard, and when the Rolling Stones covered Chuck Berry and Otis Redding, they were not taking "raw materials" from black musicians and transforming them. They were taking songs from musicians whom they admired as models of rock musicianship. On Pattison's thesis, what are we to make of Aretha Franklin's late-sixties work with producer Jerry Wexler (backed by several white musicians), or of Sly and the Family Stone, Little Feat, the Allman Brothers, the Doobie Brothers, Bruce Springsteen's E Street Band, and other racially integrated groups? Do the white members supply the requisite romanticist mythology to transform the black musicians' contributions into rock?

I do not deny that as an aesthetic program Romanticism enshrined many of the values that are popularly attributed to rock. As a reaction against Enlightenment classicism and its emphasis on "intellectual" values of order, structure, precision, and technical polish, Romanticism first surfaced in serious music with the *Sturm und Drang,* flowered with program music and tone poems, and peaked with Wagner's music drama and chromactic explorations. The new values were "emotional" and were manifested overtly in change, excess, personal meanings, ambiguity, and idiosyncratic structures. But even if we can construct a case that the same conflict of values is present in any contrast of serious music with rock, parallels do not show causality.

The problem with the whole line of analysis is that *most* opinions about music sound like *some* aspect of Romanticism, if only because of the general presumption that music is preeminently concerned with the expression of emotion. These characteristics all fit jazz as easily as rock. In fact, with writers like Paglia and Pattison we may have a case of critical history repeating itself. Those who link Romanticism and rock sound like earlier writers on jazz who found in jazz the same characteristics that are now attributed to rock, particularly the uncompromised and spontaneous nature of the performance and the freedom and instinctive self-expression of the performer.[23] And these values were often espoused by jazz performers themselves.

Consider Billie Holiday. Not exactly known for her art school background or reading of Byron and Shelley, she denied having any influences except the records of Bessie Smith and Louis Armstrong:

> If you find a tune and it's got something to do with you, you don't have to evolve anything. You just feel it, and when you sing it other people can feel something too. With me, it's got nothing to do with working or arranging or rehearsing.... But singing songs like "The Man I Love" or "Porgy" ... When I sing them I live them again and I love them.[24]

However much this sounds like Wordsworth's formula that poetry is a spontaneous overflow of emotions "recollected in tranquility," we have no reason to regard Lady Day as influenced by Wordsworth. Likewise, we have no reason to regard rock as an expression of Western Romanticism. As Peter Kivy has so carefully documented, most of these ideas about music were first advanced in the seventeenth and eighteenth centuries.[25] It might be better to regard

romanticist aesthetics as a generalization to all the arts of assumptions that had long been held of music, in which case rock has no special connection to Romanticism.

Furthermore, Paglia's account of rock music is fraught with the same internal tensions that characterize Romanticism, particularly in relation to the folk tradition that she praises as a source of power in early rock. To the extent that such traditions have survived in Western culture in our century, oral folk traditions are communal rather than individual artistic creations, and they reflect the community rather than the personal self-expression of the Romantic genius. Yet Paglia criticizes rock musicians who cater to or reflect the values of the audience. The idea of a "folk" dimension in rock is also present in her ideal of an authentic and spontaneous interaction between performer and audience, but this conflicts with the reality that rock fans are self-consciously aware that they are members of a distinct subculture, and of distinct subcultures within rock.[26]

It is no surprise that Paglia tries to find a link between rock and folk music. One of Romanticism's several themes was a glorification of the rural "folk" and of their collective art as a less intellectual, more spontaneous, and thus purer mode of expression. When the Rolling Stones imitated black American singers in a self-conscious blues purism, they were indeed behaving like many Romantic composers. Chopin and Dvo[[rcaron]]ák borrowed musical materials from their native folk traditions, and Wagner and Mahler adopted folk poems and myths as texts. But the aesthetics of Romanticism are fraught with internal contradictions, among them the fact the very process of appropriating these sources contradicts the desired spontaneity and authenticity of expression, no less for rock musicians than for nineteenth-century composers.[27]

According to Peter Wicke, the aesthetic values imparted to British rockers who attended art schools led to a calculated bohemianism and intellectual snobbery. Among those who articulated their aesthetic principles, pop art and then situationism appear to be the most prominent influences. Their preoccupation with the authenticity of their self-expression precluded their participation in any sort of community with their audience, and in fact they were often aware of the distance between their own privileged status and the working-class lives of most of their audience.[28] These attitudes may even have worked against direct political activism on the part of British rockers. Prior to the Beatles' single "Revolution" (1968), British rock lyrics stayed away from anything overtly political, whereas the American charts had featured political material since 1965.

Rock recreates Romantic contradictions in another way when the ideology of artistic freedom comes up against the reality that the musicians are engaged in a commercial enterprise. Within the actual context of the nineteenth century, Romanticism glorified the sensitivity and sensibility of the individual artist/genius; but the requisite artistic freedom had its price in the commercialization of music. We might even say that when Romanticism valued both individuality and folk traditions, it did so in conscious opposition to the standardization and industrialization of the emerging bourgeois capitalism. Thus Paglia has nothing but disdain for those who get their rock from MTV. A parallel is present within the rock audience; fans of hardcore express contempt for mainstream audiences who imitate their slam-dancing and thus strip it of its "underground" status.

Yet it was bourgeois capitalism and the opportunity for self-promotion that provided the composer's freedom. When earlier composers like Bach or Handel supported themselves with pupils and commissioned works, their music was largely utilitarian, written for specific occasions: Bach's masses and chorales, Handel's oratorios with their religious texts and his *Water Music* and *Royal Fireworks Music*. Beethoven solidified the shift from the composer-for-hire to the composer-as-entrepreneur, with works sold to publishers rather than commissioned by royal patrons. Concerts became moneymaking ventures, designed to please the bourgeois crowd who can afford the fee. Beethoven was attuned to the need to please the audience, repeating movements of symphonies when the concert audience called for it and showing off with piano improvisations when challenged. He could also be sensitive to criticism, withdrawing and replacing the final movement (the *Grosse Fugue*) of the String Quartet in B-flat Minor when the audience at its premiere reacted negatively.

At the other end of the spectrum, Wagner scraped together funding for his music dramas by a combination of self-promotion and spectacle. Wagner was keen to wrap himself in Beethoven's mantle, conducting the latter's Ninth Symphony at the 1872 dedication of Bayreuth. But Beethoven's willingness to meet the audience half-way had given way to Wagner's self-conscious Romanticism. Stubborn and uncompromising, his vision required absolute control of his creations, and he was vicious to anyone who criticized him. The result was precisely the opposite of Paglia's ideal performance as an audience-artist interaction that features improvisation and spontaneity. Ideally, the audience comes to the Bayreuth festival theater and listens to the *Ring* cycle in a hushed silence, broken only by the turning of pages as devoted Wagnerites follow the score. In short, there is no spontaneity of any kind; the Bach mass had found its secular parallel.

Which of these artists represents Paglia's ideal? Her advice to rock musicians, "Don't become a slave to the audience" and "Don't tour" (study art instead), points to Wagner and not to Beethoven or to Romantics like Berlioz, Chopin, and Liszt, who more or less invented the modern promotional tour. More pointedly, she expects rock to combine two artistic goals that have been at odds ever since Romanticism cobbled them together. On the one hand there is the development of the individual artist, cushioned from and thus impervious to commercial demands. But this sort of autonomy is unlikely to foster energy, rebellion, and the emotional power of rock's pioneers. On the other hand there is the emotional power of the folk tradition, where the music emerges from the community in a way that blurs the line between creator and audience. But the communal nature of the folk process fits uncomfortably with the self-conscious

artistry of the trained professional; training rock musicians at colleges and universities is not likely to connect rock with centuries of folk music.

Finally, Paglia is recommending that rock musicians trade the vicissitudes of commerce for a system of artistic patronage. But are commercial demands always an artistic kiss of death? Paglia links popular music and film as the two great art forms of our time, but film has fared quite well without much institutional support. Paglia is really recommending that rock shouldn't remain popular music any longer, that is, a commodity designed for consumption by masses of listeners of varying degrees of musical knowledge. Rock musicians are to regard themselves as fine artists and to train accordingly. Putting aside the conflict with folk ideology, such ideas fail to address how rock music would retain its identity apart from its popular base. Romanticism has a healthy strain of artistic elitism that is antithetical to rock, and patronage is likely to reinforce that strain in rock. While I would not go as far as Nietzsche did, he captures the problem involved when he attacks Romanticism: "The artist who began to understand himself would misunderstand himself: he ought not to look back, he ought not to look at all, he ought to give."[29] Can rock deliver on its own terms if its artists are successful at the transformations that Paglia recommends?

We should also consider the likely consequences of treating rock like the other arts. Funding through grants, scholarships, and the like is increasingly limited, so the proposal could cover only a fraction of the ten thousand or more artists who release rock recordings each year (many of these being groups of several members). In practical terms, freeing artists from traditional commercial concerns means that *most* rock music will remain exactly what it is anyway: product for popular consumption. So the scheme is likely to split rock into two camps. One will carry on as before, and the other will consist of artists with grants, afforded the freedom to follow their own muse. (This would reverse the current process, where *mature* successful artists like Dire Straits, George Harrison, the Grateful Dead, Bruce Springsteen, and the Rolling Stones can wait five years between records and tours, producing what they like when they choose to do so.) But the select few who would be singled out for support will face the same problems that already occur in a patronage system. While there is intense competition for scarce resources, very little of the money is risked on artists whose work is genuinely avant-garde, and less still on those whose work is highly political in content. One has difficulty imagining the Clash or rappers N.W.A. and Ice-T getting a grant under Paglia's scheme. Training rock musicians at colleges and universities is likely to result in music that parallels the output of similarly trained jazz and classical musicians: highly accomplished, technically excellent, and intellectually challenging music that values extreme polish, individuality, experimentation, and novelty for their own sake as well as continuous progressive change. But there is little reason to think that the music produced by these musicians is going to connect with the general public and conquer the top ten. (If we were talking about music with commercial potential, Paglia, would lose her basic premise that commercial demands corrupt the music.)

Although those involved with the fine arts do not like to say so, there is also a fundamental unfairness to this system, particularly if we are funding artists who are not interested in producing music that the general public wants to hear. As Jeremy Bentham argued, the arts "are useful only to those who take pleasure in them," and to the extent that public patronage is set up to further arts which lack widespread appeal, we are instituting a regressive tax, "laying burdens on the comparatively indigent many, for the amusement of the comparatively opulent few."[30] We do this with other arts in the United States, with mixed success. Consider the National Endowment for the Arts (NEA). In recent years we have seen an overt politicization of the patronage system as politicians on the right have demanded that public funding be restricted to art that expresses mainstream values. Yet by operating within the sphere, of mass entertainment, rock music has gradually loosened the bonds of censorship. The Rolling Stones had to sing "Let's Spend the Night Together" as "Let's Spend Some Time Together" on the Ed Sullivan Show in 1967, a form of self-censorship difficult to imagine in the 1990s. Stephen Sondheim recently rejected an NEA grant because of the restrictions involved, preferring the freedom of artistic free enterprise. Why advocate a patronage system that is just as likely to control and censor artistic expression as to encourage it?[31]

As Ezra Pound said, "Music rots when it gets *too far* from the dance. Poetry atrophies when it gets too far from music."[32] While teachers and literature professors like to think that schools and colleges have some special ability to bring poetry and literature to the masses, there is plenty of evidence that "good" literature is not what the masses want. It is not even what most college students and graduates want, as junk fiction and "Calvin and Hobbes" collections repeatedly top the sales lists of college bookstores. I do not mean to put down junk fiction and comics, but there is little reason to think that poetry has much meaning for the majority of people. It has gotten too far from music, and most of the "serious" music composed in our century has gotten too far from the dance. In my more cynical moments I believe that both are mainly produced by college professors for other college professors (they seem to make up most of the audience when I attend local "new music" concerts). Academics, however well meaning, are the last group to keep rock rooted in the syncopated and danceable rhythms that have made it one of America's most successful exports. If the lyrics to rap have vitality, it may be because they aren't composed by college students who have immersed themselves in great literature.

If there is any element of Romanticism that we ought to keep out of art education, it is the notion of the artistic genius as a superior soul requiring special nourishment, for this is probably one of the great obstacles to full enjoyment and participation in the arts by large numbers of our students. Why inject elitism into popular culture, where students engage at least one form of art without anxiety or feelings of inferiority? Romanticism is a poor model for understanding the achievements of rock music, and it is worse yet as a justification for treating rock music as we now treat the fine arts.

Theodore A. Grayck is Associate Professor of Philosophy at Moorhead State University. He has most recently published in the *Musical Quarterly, the International Philosophical Quarterly,* and the *British Journal of Aesthetics.*

Notes

1. An interesting variation of this thesis is defended in Richard Shusterman, "The Fine Art of Rap," in his *Pragmatist Aesthetics* (Oxford: Blackwell, 1992), pp. 201–35. Shusterman's argument focuses on showing that rap is the form of popular music which best exemplifies a postmodern aesthetic; for this reason, his version avoids endorsing rap as folk music.
2. Robert Christgau, "Rock Lyrics Are Poetry (Maybe)," in *The Age of Rock,* ed. Jonathan Eisen (New York: Random House, 1969), p. 232.
3. Camille Paglia, "Endangered Rock," *The New York Times,* Thursday, 16 April 1992, p. A23. Reprinted in Camille Paglia, *Sex, Art, and American Culture* (New York: Vintage Books, 1992), pp. 19–21. Unless otherwise credited, all further quotations from Paglia are from this editorial, which was widely reprinted.
4. Quoted in *Melody Maker,* 27 August 1977; quotation disseminated in Tony Angarde, *The Oxford Dictionary of Modern Quotations* (New York: Oxford University Press, 1991), p. 89.

5. In *Sexual Personae* (New York: Vintage Books, 1990), Camille Paglia does offer parallels between Elvis Presley and Lord Byron; most of them are physical similarities such as their early deaths and enlarged hearts.

6. Simon Frith, "Popular Music 1950–1980," in *Making Music,* ed. George Martin (New York: William Morrow, 1983), p. 24.

7. Nik Cohn, *Pop from the Beginning* (United Kingdom: Weidenfeld and Nicholson, 1969), p. 133.

8. Carl Belz, *The Story of Rock,* 2d ed. (New York: Oxford University Press, 1972), p. 64.

9. Dave Marsh, *The Heart of Rock and Soul* (New York: Plume, 1989), pp. 474–75.

10. John Lennon, quoted in David Sheff and G. Barry Golson, *The Playboy Interviews with John Lennon and Yoko Ono* (New York: Berkley Books, 1981), pp. 170–71.

11. John Lennon quoted in Jann Wenner, *Lennon Remembers* (San Francisco: Straight Arrow Books, 1971), p. 70; interview conducted in December 1970.

12. "Working Class?" *Daily Worker,* 7 September 1963, p. 5.

13. Quotation of Marion Keisker, who was present at the sessions; Ed Ward, in *Rock of Ages* (New York: Rolling Stone Press/Summit Books, 1986), pp. 78–79.

14. Quoted in Geoffrey Stokes, *The Beatles* (New York: Rolling Stone Press/Times Books, 1980), p. 45.

15. Roger Sessions, *Questions about Music* (New York: W. W. Norton, 1970), p. 11.

16. Quoted in Frederick B. Artz, *From Renaissance to Romanticism: Trends in Art, Literature, and Music, 1300–1930* (Chicago: University of Chicago Press, 1962), p. 227.

17. Paglia, *Sexual Personae,* p. 358.

18. Quentin J. Schultze, et al., *Dancing in the Dark* (Grand Rapids, Mich: William B. Eerdmans, 1991), p. 164.

19. Robert Pattison, *The Triumph of Vulgarity* (Oxford: Oxford University Press, 1987), p. 63.

20. Ibid., p. xi.

21. Ibid., p. 10.

22. Ibid., p. 64.

23. See Andy Hamilton, "The Aesthetics of Imperfection," *Philosophy* 65, no. 253 (1990), pp. 323–40; and Ted Gioia, *The Imperfect Art* (New York: Oxford University Press, 1988), pp. 19–49.

24. Billie Holiday with William Dufty, *Lady Sings the Blues* (New York: Penguin, 1984), p. 39. There is a certain irony here for anyone who wants to fit Holiday into the Romantic archetype, since she is talking about commercial songs by white composers.

25. See chaps. 3–5 of Peter Kivy, *Sound Sentiment* (Philadelphia: Temple University Press, 1989); this incorporates his earlier book *The Corded Shell.*

26. See Simon Frith, *Sound Effects* (New York: Pantheon, 1981), pp. 202–34.

27. Attempts to legitimize rock by association with folk music first arose among rock critics; see Simon Frith, "'The Magic That Can Set You Free': The Ideology of Folk and the Myth of the Rock Community," in *Popular Music,* vol. 1,

ed. Richard Middleton and David Horn (Cambridge: Cambridge University Press, 1981), pp. 159–68.

28. Peter Wicke, *Rock Music: Culture, Aesthetics, and Sociology,* trans. Rachel Fogg (Cambridge: Cambridge University Press, 1990), chaps. 5 and 7.

29. Friedrich Nietzsche, *Will to Power,* trans. Walter Kaufmann and R. J. Hollingdale (New York: Vintage/Random House, 1968), p. 429 (section 811).

30. Jeremy Bentham, "Reward Applied to Art and Science," *The Works of Jeremy Bentham,* vol. 2, ed. John Bowring (New York: Russell & Russell, 1962), p. 253.

31. See Edward C. Banfield, *The Democratic Muse* (New York: Basic Books, 1984).

32. Ezra Pound, *ABC of Reading* (Norfolk, Conn.: New Directions, n.d.), p. 61.

Source: Theodore A. Gracyk, "Romanticizing Rock Music," *Journal of Aesthetic Education.* 27.2 (Summer 1993): 43–58.

EXERCISE: THINKING CRITICALLY

Following the format used in the writer's analyses above, use the Toulmin and classical systems to develop a set of notes that will help you analyze each source. Before you use either system to analyze a source, use the questions posed in Chapter 1 as a starting point:

- Who is the writer?
- Who is the intended audience?
- What is the writer's purpose in writing?
- When was the source written?
- In what medium did the source appear?
- What factors (social, political, economical) might be at play to influence readers to accept the writer's argument?

EXERCISES: FOCUS ON WRITING

1. Write a paper agreeing or disagreeing with Paglia's stance.
2. Write a letter to the editor of the *Journal of Aesthetic Education.* Agree or disagree with Gracyk.
3. Write a critique of "Endangered Rock." Select an audience that would have a serious interest in music.
4. Write a critique of "Romanticizing Rock Music." Select an audience that might not appreciate rock music.
5. Select an argumentative article on a topic that interests you and write a critique. Submit an annotated copy of the article, preliminary notes, and drafts with the copy to be graded.

Chapter 6

Writing Research Papers

Play with the "quotes" by all means—selecting, rejecting, thinning, transposing their order, saving a good one for the end. Just make sure that the play is fair. Don't change any words or let the cutting of a sentence distort the proper context of what remains.

—*William Zinsser, quoted in Gertrude Himmelfarb's*
"The Right to Misquote"

While you write research papers primarily to meet course requirements and to gain new knowledge about a topic, a secondary purpose is learning how to do research—that is, knowing where to find timely, pertinent, reliable sources on a given topic. In a world where information develops daily in volumes difficult to imagine, knowing how to find useful, reliable information on a given subject is a specialized skill. You may have already discovered the value of good research skills for planning a vacation, purchasing a new vehicle, tracing your family tree, reading about the side effects of a new medication, considering a new major, or adopting a new pet. While it's possible to get information on topics like these by talking to friends, family, peers, or colleagues, you'll encounter situations when it's advisable or necessary to weigh information gained informally against published information. When such a situation arises, you want to know how to find credible and authoritative information.

Sometimes, the search for information is just for fun. If you're lucky, you've experienced the enjoyment of an afternoon or evening in the library or on the Internet exploring and investigating a topic that captures your interest. You don't have to turn in note cards or write a paper for this kind of research. It's an activity for personal enrichment, and it can be rewarding and satisfying.

While your motivation for doing research will vary, it's safe to predict that you will do research in your academic and professional careers, and for personal reasons too. Assignments in your composition course will give you practice in doing library research and using both paper and electronic sources, in searching the Internet, and possibly in conducting research in the field (doing interviews, gathering information through questionnaires, observing or measuring something). Because you want to gain as much experience as possible in all kinds of research, make it your personal goal to pursue sources of information that are new or unfamiliar to you. Discover the benefits of field research on a local issue. Learn how to use the Internet. Spend time in the campus library. Get acquainted with the full resources of the reference section, learn how to use boolean terms to search electronic databases, look at old microfilms of old newspapers, or just find a comfortable spot and read a magazine or a book. You never can tell where or when you'll discover a new idea that sparks your interest and demands inquiry and research.

DEVELOPING A TOPIC

Topic selection is itself a unique kind of problem-solving activity. When you have the freedom to develop a topic on your own, how do you find a question to answer, a problem to solve, or an issue or argument to investigate before you make a recommendation? Most writers claim that their writing is more effective when they write about topics that interest them than it is when someone else stipulates topic selection. So, if you have the opportunity to select a topic, find one that is interesting, thought-provoking, engaging, and exciting to you. A good place to start is to take inventory of what you know and what you want to know. Consider investigating

- Your major
- Political issues
- Social issues
- Historical topics
- Ethical issues
- Local issues

You may know a great deal about a subject already from reading, traveling, working, participating in clubs or special interest groups on or off campus, surfing the Internet, or pursuing a hobby or sport. You can develop a topic from your own personal inventory by asking questions about people, issues, or events that seem to be unanswered, that have multiple interpretations or conflicting or confusing answers, or that present a specific problem that remains unsolved. Or you can identify some aspect of your topic that is debatable or controversial. If your own personal inventory doesn't help you develop a topic, use library sources and the Internet to generate ideas.

Before you begin to search the Internet or the library, think about specific words and phrases that will help you find information about your topic and try to identify

- Key terms associated with your topic
- Individuals whose names are associated with your topic
- Ethical, intellectual, historical, political, or social issues associated with your topic

Using the Internet

The Internet is a system of computer networks linked to each other that allows you to search the World Wide Web (Web), a hodgepodge of material—general and specialized—provided without any kind of editorial guidance. Anyone with access to a computer and an understanding of how to post information is able to publish on the Web. As a result, you can find everything on the Web: scholarly papers and journals, photo galleries with pictures of someone's beloved pet poodle, newspapers and magazines—in other words information that may be reliable or questionable, or even misleading and false. Even though it's primarily a tool for disseminating information, the equivalent of the office water cooler or the backyard fence, the Internet gives us instant access to information, and for that reason, you'll probably want to use it.

Even if your instructor has asked you to avoid citing Internet sources in papers, the Web is still a valuable research tool. You can use it to develop ideas for topics and to get a good overview of your topic. And your preliminary research can make library research more focused than if you were starting from scratch.

When you have search terms in mind, go to one of the search engines made available by your web browser—for example, Yahoo!, Lycos, Excite, Alta Vista, Infoseek, or WebCrawler—and enter a term. These search engines will take you to Web pages that mention your search term. Yahoo!, for example, brings up approximately nine category matches and just under 300 site matches for the search term *Titanic*. These matching pages include everything from information posted by the *Titanic* Historical Society to an entry from *Britannica Online* to a page posted by the Titanic Deck Chair Rearrangement Corporation, a business devoted to "Gonzo Marketing."

More often than not, the dilemma you'll encounter when you use web browser search engines is finding a kind of smorgasbord of category matches and matching pages. While each one includes the search term in the title, it may not apply to your topic. In short, search engines don't discriminate. They simply identify what's out there. Let's consider another example. Intending to develop a topic on some aspect of biological warfare, Mike used Yahoo! to search for information on anthrax. The search engine found links to anthrax, the disease normally associated with animals, but it also brought up pages on the musical group Anthrax. After consulting pages in the category match listed under Health > Diseases and Conditions > Anthrax, Mike tried to find information about the recent controversy over mandatory anthrax vaccinations for military personnel by using the terms *anthrax vaccinations*. This search term brought up over 2000 matching pages that gave Mike access to newspaper articles, releases from the U.S. Department of Defense and other news agencies, an encyclopedia entry, talking points, individual homepages, and university news pages. A quick check of approximately 25 matching pages confirmed that required anthrax vaccination for military personnel was a good topic for an argumentative paper. It also confirmed that research with web browser search engines was not sufficient for an academic research project. While it yielded an overwhelming number of matching pages, many of them were clearly pages posted by individuals who wanted to vent their frustration or pages that appeared to offer reliable information but that failed to provide the source of the information, the date, or a contact person.

GUIDELINES FOR SELECTING INTERNET SOURCES

If your assignment allows you to cite Internet sources, give them the same careful examination you would give printed material. First, consider your assignment:

- Who is the intended audience for the paper you are writing?
- Is your purpose to inform or to persuade?
- What kinds of sources will your intended readers value?
- What kinds of sources might undermine your credibility?
- What kinds of sources would establish your credibility?

Second, ask yourself the following questions:

- Does the source offer information pertinent to the topic you have chosen?
- Are there features that suggest the source is primarily or to some degree self-promotional for an individual or a company?
- Does the source include the name of the individual who created it? A way to contact that individual? The date when information was published or updated?
- Do graphics dominate, making the text secondary or insignificant?
- Does the text include documentation? Is it well-written?
- Can you readily establish the rhetorical situation?
- Would an academic audience consider this source reliable and appropriate?

Mike's experience with the search terms *anthrax* and *anthrax vaccinations* is not unusual. Because search engines look for exact matches, you should expect results to include links that will not be useful to you. If you narrow your term, as Mike did, you have a better chance of getting matches related to your topic than you do with a term that isn't narrowed. The important point is that web browser search engines will support, but not replace, library research.

EXERCISE: GOING ON-LINE

To practice using search engines, enter one of the terms listed below on Yahoo!, Lycos, Excite, Alta Vista, Infoseek, or WebCrawler. Be prepared to report to your peers the search engine you used, the number of sources you found, and the kinds of sources you found. Finally, explain what kind of information the source includes about the author or publisher, and whether the source lists a date or a way to contact the author or publisher.

Topics for Investigation on the Web

- Little Father Time, a character in *Jude the Obscure*
- Censorship and Literature
- Treatment of Lyme Disease
- World Series Scandal of 1919
- Release of Wolves into Yellowstone Park
- Conscientious Objectors
- Berlin Airlift
- Eradication of Smallpox
- Ethics and Science
- Ebonics
- Statistics on Teenage Suicide
- The "Who was Shakespeare?" Debate
- Regulation of Children's Programs on TV
- Yangtze River Dam
- Roswell UFOs
- Barbara Jordan's Participation in the Impeachment of President Nixon
- People for the Ethical Treatment of Animals
- Oklahoma City Bombing
- Simon Wiesenthal Center
- Statistics on Date Rape
- Gulf War Syndrome

Using the Library

Libraries can be intimidating and mysterious places if you don't know how to access information. You have to understand how different kinds of reference systems and parts of the library work—reference materials, the library card catalog, electronic databases, paper indexes, microfilm copies of journal and newspaper articles, for example. If your library offers orientation sessions, be sure to sign up for one. And get acquainted with the reference librarians, one of the best resources libraries offer. Because they help students with all kinds of research projects, reference librarians can help you if you have trouble finding information. Don't hesitate to ask for help.

Reference Materials

The library reference section houses general and specialized encyclopedias, yearbooks, almanacs, and indexes. Because these sources need to be available to library patrons at all times, they are usually restricted to in-house use. Most of the material in the reference section will be from print sources; however, an increasing number of reference books are appearing on CD-ROM.

General Encyclopedias

For an overview of your topic, a general encyclopedia is a good place to start, even if you don't use it as an actual source. Some encyclopedias include a bibliography at the end of entries, giving you additional sources to investigate.

Academic American Encyclopedia

Encyclopedia Americana International Edition

Encyclopedia Britannica

Collier's Encyclopedia

World Book Encyclopedia

Specialized Encyclopedias

Specialized reference books cover a wide range of topics. The list below is not comprehensive; however, it illustrates the diversity of specialized encyclopedias and reference works:

Encyclopedia of American Biography

Encyclopedia of American Education

Encyclopedia of American History

Encyclopedia of American Journalism

Encyclopedia of American Music

Encyclopedia of American Political History

Encyclopedia of American Scandal

Encyclopedia of Analytical Science

Encyclopedia of Animal Rights and Animal Welfare

Encyclopedia of Anthropology

Encyclopedia of Applied Ethics

Encyclopedia of Modern Social Issues

Encyclopedia of Native American Legal Traditions

Encyclopedia of Propaganda

Scribner's Encyclopedia of American Lives

Contemporary Authors

Webester's Biographical Dictionary

Almanacs and Yearbooks

For information on current events, statistics, or demographics, consult yearbooks and almanacs. These are also general and specialized, some focusing on international matters, others on issues that pertain to a specific country or state. They are updated frequently in order to provide the most recent information available. Some examples include:

Information Please Almanac (atlas and yearbook)

The Wall Street Journal *Almanac*

The People's Almanac

The New York Times *Almanac*

International Yearbook of Industrial Statistics

Health Care Almanac and Yearbook

*The International Yearbook of Environmental and Resource Economics,
1997/1998*

Indexes
Use indexes to find information in newspapers, magazines, and journals.

Readers' Guide to Periodical Literature

General Science Index

Humanities Index

Business Periodicals Index

Social Sciences Index

Major newspapers such as *The New York Times*, *Los Angeles Times*, *Times* of London, *Washington Post*, and *The Wall Street Journal* also have indexes.

Abstracts
Abstracts are summaries of journal articles. Electronic databases frequently include abstracts of sources to provide users with an overview. As the titles below suggest, abstracts are most frequently published by subject areas

Biological Abstracts

Historical Abstracts

Physics Abstracts

Linguistics and Language Behavior Abstracts

Card Catalogs
A card catalog records titles and call numbers of a library's holdings: books, newspapers, journals, electronic holdings, and audiovisual materials. You are probably aware that the old wooden card catalogs with the long pull-out drawers full of typed cards are becoming a thing of the past. College and university libraries are switching to on-line card catalogs, and forming consortiums or networks that provide students with access to local libraries off campus or to a library on another campus. This kind of collaboration is to your advantage. It expands available resources.

Print catalogs arrange book titles by author, title, and subject. Electronic catalogs use these same terms for searches, but offer other search options as well—for example, key words searches or searches using Library of Congress Subject Headings. The reference section of your library should have a copy of the *Library of Congress Subject Headings* (LCSH), a three-volume reference book that lists, as the title suggests, specific terms for broad subject headings—for example, under *biological warfare*, you would find terrorism, agents, vaccines, environment. If you have a topic in mind, but can't think of search terms, consult the LCSH.

If your library has a print catalog, ask if it has more than one catalog. Occasionally, separate catalogs are devoted to special collections. If your library has both print and on-line catalogs, be sure your check both. Sometimes they don't include the same titles.

Guidelines for Selecting Sources

Writers establish their credibility in a number of ways—for example, demonstrating audience awareness, eliminating surface errors, following guidelines for proper documentation, offering readers interesting and relevant content. The sources you cite also work for or against you in establishing credibility. If you were writing an academic paper arguing for the legalization of marijuana, for example, you would want to use the most recent sources published. If you limited sources to publications that appeared in the late 1970s or early 1980s, your readers might understandably ask why you relied on dated sources. By the same token, if you are writing about a historical event, sources published at the time the event took place would be appropriate. Notice that in "Black American Perceptions of the *Titanic* Disaster" (Chapter 1), Robert Weisbord cites several sources published in 1912, the year the *Titanic* went down on her maiden voyage.

When you select sources, consider the following questions:

- What kinds of sources does your assignment require?
- What kinds of sources will your intended readers value?
- What kinds of sources might undermine your credibility?
- What kinds of sources will establish your credibility?

SELECTING ELECTRONIC SOURCES

If your assignment allows you to cite electronic sources, give them the same careful examination you would give printed material.

- Does the source offer information pertinent to the topic you have chosen?
- Are there features that suggest that the source is primarily or to some degree self-promotional for an individual or a company?
- Does the source include the name of the individual who created it? A way to contact that individual? The date when the information was published or updated?
- Do graphics dominate, making the text secondary or insignificant?
- Does the text include documentation? Is it well-written?
- Can you readily establish the rhetorical situation?
- Would an academic audience consider this source reliable and appropriate?

Selecting Printed Sources

- Does the source offer information pertinent to the topic you have chosen?
- What does the source tell you about the writer's credentials?
- Is the source recent or dated?
- Is the source published by a popular press? academic press?
- Will your intended readers be familiar with the author?
- Is there any reason your intended readers might not recognize the source as reliable?

Sources to Avoid

- Abstracts (a summary of a source written by someone other than the author). You should use the actual source, not the abstract.
- Sources that are confusing or too complex for you to understand.

EXERCISE: READING AND RESPONDING

For a topic you are considering, check each of the following and record the authors, titles, and call numbers of three sources, if sources are available:

- General encyclopedia
- Specialized encyclopedia
- Yearbook or almanac
- Newspaper
- Card catalog

EXERCISE: COLLABORATING WITH YOUR PEERS

In formal articles and essays, documentation in notes and works cited furnishes readers with information about sources. Working in groups, select one of the readings listed below:

"If We Have It, Do We Use It?" (Chapter 1)
"Black American Perception of the *Titanic* Disaster" (Chapter 1)
"Priceless Legacy of the *Titanic*" (Chapter 1)
"'Road Rage' Tied to More Traffic Deaths" (Chapter 3)"
"Columbus Cracks an Egg" (Chapter 4)
"Romanticizing Rock Music" (Chapter 5)

Review the selection and list the kinds of sources the writer uses. Be prepared to answer the following questions:

- Does the writer cite sources at the end of the piece?
- Does the selection offer readers a good variety of sources, or does the writer rely primarily on one kind of source—newspapers, books, or academic journals?

- Does the writer refer primarily to sources aimed at a general readership?
- What do the kinds of sources suggest about the intended audience's level of knowledge?

DEVELOPING A WORKING BIBLIOGRAPHY

A working bibliography is a record of sources you identify for a research project. We call this a *working* bibliography because you will add and delete entries as your research progresses. Notecards or a small notebook, a kind of a library journal, are convenient ways to keep up with notes on your research. No one can tell you how many sources you will need for a working bibliography. Even though assignments designate a required number of sources, you'll probably look at two or three times that number in order to find the best sources on your topic. For example, some sources will provide an overview or first impression and help you develop a topic, but you may decide not to use them as actual sources in your paper. A good rule of thumb is to identify twice as many sources as your assignment requires. By doubling your sources, you can avoid doing additional searches for information if you discover that two or three sources duplicate information or that a source provides you with a good overview of information but not with anything significant enough to cite in your paper. Eventually, the working bibliography will become the Works Cited page for a paper, but it should go through several revisions in the process.

Figure 6.1 is an example of a working bibliography. In a working bibliography, record library call numbers after each bibliographical citation. If you have questions about the kind of information you need to record for journals, newspapers, Internet sources, or books, consult the instructions for bibliographical citations in Chapter 7. Remember, careful record keeping means you'll avoid making trips to the library solely for the purpose of finding bibliographical information you should have recorded on the first visit.

Working Bibliography

Abbasi, Anisa. "Fake Fat." Letter. *New Scientist* 4 Oct.
    1997: 49. Q1.N52.

Berg, Francie M. *Health Risks of Weight Loss.*
    Hettinger: Healthy Weight Journal. 1995.
    RM222.2B448.

Canedy, Dana. "Selling Weight Loss From a Bottle." *New
    York Times* 14 Feb. 1997, late ed.: D1 + . N425.

"Controversies in Obesity." "Nutrition Today
    Newsbreaks" *Nutrition Today* May/June 1993: 4–5.
    W. Campus RA784.N83.

Czajka-Narins, Dorice M., and Ellen S. Parham. "Fear of
    Fat: Attitudes Toward Obesity." *Nutrition Today*
    Jan./Feb. 1990: 26–32. RA784.N83.

Grunwald, Lisa. "Do I Look Fat to You?" *Life* Feb. 1995:
    58–74. AP2.L54715.

Gura, Trisha. "Uncoupling Proteins Provide New Clue to
    Obesity's Causes." *Science* 29 May 1998:
    1369–1370. Q1.S35.

Hill, James O., and John C. Peters. "Environmental
    Contribution to the Obesity Epidemic." *Science*
    29 May 1998: 1371–1373. Q1.S35.

Hittner, Patricia. "Dying To Be Thin." *Better Homes and
    Gardens* Aug. 1997: 84 + . NA7100.B45.

"Is It Time For a Fat Tax?" *Psychology Today* Sept./Oct.
    1997: 16. BF1.P83.

Jeffery, Robert W., and Simone A. French. "Epidemic
    Obesity in the United States: Are Fast Foods and
    Television Viewing Contributing?" *American
    Journal of Public Health* Feb. 1998: 277–280.
    RA421.A41.

Kassirer, Jerome P., and Marcia Angell. "Losing Weight—
    An Ill-Fated New Year's Resolution" Editorial.
    The New England Journal of Medicine 1 Jan. 1998:
    52–54. R11.B7.

Kleiner, Kurt. "Diet Drugs Go Through Thick and Thin."
    New Scientist 28 Mar. 1998: 22. Q1.N52.

National Task Force on the Prevention and Treatment of
    Obesity. "Long-Term Pharmacotherapy in the
    Management of Obesity." *Journal of the American*

FIGURE 6.1 *(continued on next page)*

Medical Association 18 Dec 1996: 1907–1915.
R15.A48.

Nemeth, Mary. "Body Obsession." *MacLean's* 2 May 1994:
45–49. AP5.M2.

Parham, Ellen S. "Is There a New Weight Paradigm?"
Nutrition Today July/Aug. 1996: 155–161.
RA784.N83.

Polivy, Janet. "Psychological consequences in food
Restriction." *Journal of the American Dietic
Association* June 1996: 589–592. RM214.A6.

Sloan, Elizabeth A. "One Big Fat Market." *Food
Technology* Apr. 1998: 28. TP370.F63

Taubes, Gary. "As Obesity Rates Rise, Experts Struggle
to Explain Why." *Science* 29 May 1998: 1367–1368.
Q1.S35.

Wickelgren, Ingrid. "Obesity: How Big a Problem?"
Science 29 May 1998: 1364–1367. Q1.S35.

FIGURE 6.1 *(continued)*

DEVELOPING AN ANNOTATED BIBLIOGRAPHY

We've used the term *annotation* to refer to notations in a text, recording your first impressions or any questions that came to mind as you read. An annotation is also an explanation or a comment. The annotated bibliography is a preliminary assignment to a research paper. It lays a solid foundation for the paper that will follow. It is a formal paper with an introduction stating the purpose and scope (an indication of how broad or narrow your study will be) of a research project, followed by a bibliographical citation and annotation for each source you intend to use in your paper. A statement about the value of the source—why it is important to the paper—frequently accompanies the annotation. The introduction to Amy's annotated bibliography, "Finding the Cure for Obesity: A Select and Annotated Bibliography," and five of her annotations provide an example. We refer to the annotated bibliography as a *select* bibliography because it doesn't list everything you find on your topic, as the working bibliography does. The annotated bibliography lists only those sources that will help you support your thesis and develop ideas.

FINDING THE CURE FOR OBESITY

SELECT AND ANNOTATED BIBLIOGRAPHY

Obesity has become a controversial problem in the United States. Because the causes of obesity are disputed, a cure for the problem has been difficult to find. While diet pills, changing the environment, food restriction diets, and changing genes and proteins have all been looked at as ways to combat the problem of obesity, nondiet techniques are the most successful for improving the mental and physical health of obese patients. In my research paper, I will use data from research to discredit the effectiveness and safety of diet medication. Also, I will provide evidence that changing the environment requires cooperation between all aspects of society, and that sufficient data does not support the claim that altering the environment would affect the obesity epidemic. My sources also point out that diet may actually lead to weight problems. Nondiet techniques encourage the patient to accept himself and not to feel limited by his weight. This technique also emphasizes improved psychological health. The introduction for my research paper will contain statistics that emphasize the extent of obesity in American society especially in adult women. This accentuates the reasons obesity is regarded as such a tremendous issue in the United States. The paper will then go on to prove that nondiet methods are the safest, most reasonable, least expensive, and most effective way to treat obese women.

Abbasi, Anisa. "Fake Fat." Letter. *New Scientist* 4 Oct.
      1997: 49.

In her letter to the editor of *New Scientist,* Anisa Abbasi reiterates the findings in John Blundell's report that occurs on pages 7 and 24 of the September 20, 1997 issue of *New Scientist.* Appetite suppressants

are not only ineffective when trying to lose weight,
but they are also linked with causing "primary
pulmonary hypertension" and should therefore not be
used. One of the most prolific examples of this is the
recent discovery that dexfenfluramine and fenfluramine,
two popular appetite suppressant drugs, could possibly
contribute to heart valve problems. Fat substitutes are
also disregarded as an effective way to lose weight
because these substitutes often interfere with the
uptake of vitamins into the bloodstream. Vitamin
deficiency will make patients more susceptible to
cancer, heart disease, problems with blood clotting,
and also vision impairment. Patients should not
endanger their health merely to conform to society's
pressure to be thin. The letter is important because it
summarizes doctors' concerns over current weight loss
medication and therefore provides one argument against
the use of drugs to lose weight.

Canedy, Dana. "Selling Weight Loss From a Bottle." *New
      York Times* 14 Feb. 1997, late ed.: D1 + .
    As a writer for *The New York Times,* Dana Canedy
explores whether weight loss drugs should be marketed
by weight loss clinics. Recently, institutes such as
Jenny Craig, that had before encouraged more nondiet
techniques such as exercise and balanced meals, started
to prescribe diet pills. Consumer demand for the
medication is forcing weight loss programs to prescribe
the pills in order to make a profit. This type of
"medically supervised" treatment has revenues at $1.9
billion and an increase is expected this year. Critics,
however, worry that the potential for profit will cause
doctors to prescribe these pills for people who just
want to lose a few pounds, or that doctors at these
clinics will not take the time to know the patient and
to follow their progress. Advocates of diet centers

selling weight loss drugs say that it is effective when combined with their program of exercise and sensible eating. Because there are so many different weight loss clinics available to the consumer, many clinics must sell the drugs in order to be competitive. One company, Weight Watchers, has decided not to sell the medication stating that they are not a medical organization and that the drugs do not go with their current program. Other critics cite addictiveness, side effects such as nervousness, sleep disorder, and pulmonary hypertension, and uncertainty about long term effects as reasons not to prescribe the drugs. Although this article mainly examines whether doctors in a weight loss clinic should be able to prescribe medication, it brings up important statistics on consumer demand for the product, and it explains that sometimes the company's well-being can have priority over the health of the patient. This will be used as an argument against the safety of diet pills.

Czajka-Narins, Dorice M., and Ellen S. Parham. "Fear of
      Fat: Attitudes Toward Obesity." *Nutrition Today*
      Jan./Feb. 1990: 26-32.

     Dr. Dorice Czajka-Narins and Dr. Ellen Parham, professors at Northern Illinois University, examine society's negative attitude toward fat. This attitude can be found in children as young as five years old, and this attitude is more harmful to women because of society's tendency to judge women on appearance. The idea that fat is unattractive and harmful to the body can lead to psychological problems because of social discrimination. Slenderness is often linked with success, intelligence, and capability. Even professionals in the weight loss field display society's negative attitude. Doctors view obese patients negatively because most times the doctors are not able to cure the patient. Television and magazines play an important part in encouraging this negative attitude and also in encouraging activity that can lead to obesity. Television depicts eating as an activity that has no negative consequences. Magazines and television alike use slender models, and they are also the place to find advertisements for diets and other weight loss techniques. This constant media influence to be thin is often times linked to the growing occurrences of eating disorders in America. An estimated 75% of female American adolescents view themselves as overweight. Slenderness is not only associated with attractiveness; during times of plenty, it is also linked with higher class society. Slenderness is also viewed as healthy and as a sign of control over oneself. Because of society's perceptions, many people, especially women, have low self-esteem and feel that they must diet in order to meet society's expected weight. According to magazine surveys, many women claimed losing weight would make them a happier person. Although women as a whole are obsessive about weight, the preoccupation with appearance is also becoming evident in men and children. This article is co-written by the same author of "Is There a New Weight Paradigm?". This article proves that an effective method for obese patients to gain self-esteem is important and necessary. It also discusses the society's perception of obesity which ties into another type of cure I will discredit in paper #4: changing the environment and our culture.

Grunwald, Lisa. "Do I Look Fat to You?" *Life* Feb. 1995:
      58-74.
     This article answers several important questions concerning the preoccupation with body image and weight loss in America. Although we as Americans are bombarded

with information on diets and with models encouraging us to be thin, we are also constantly shown fattening foods and other temptations. This paradox often leads to confusion over what is best for the body. Obesity is linked to serious health problems, but Surgeon General C. Everett Koop points out that many of these problems can be lessened significantly with only modest weight loss. The prevalence of obesity in the United States can be attributed to what Yale University's Kevin Brownell notes as a "toxic environment." Society, through advertisement and technology, is responsible for Americans' lack of exercise and tendency to eat fattening foods. However, research is currently studying an obesity gene that has been found in mice which may prove that some humans have a genetic inclination to be obese. Other researchers are proposing the set-point theory. Even after weight is lost, dieters usually return to the size that they were before the diet. This could possibly be explained because the body has a tendency to stay at a natural weight. If this is the case, the only way to lose weight and keep it off would be to change one's rate of metabolism. Others claim that dieting causes fat because weight cycling can slow metabolic rates. Exercise, however, can raise metabolism and is also responsible for improving self-esteem. Along with exercise, diet pills are also being used as a way to combat obesity. A drug combining phentermine and fenfluramine, and also Orlistat and Prozac have all been used to lose weight. Like the article "Fear of Fat" states, preoccupation with weight is often more prevalent with women, and weight is even an issue for children. This often leads to eating disorders by the teenage age. This article is helpful because it covers a wide variety of issues including the causes of obesity and possible treatments for each different cause.

Gura, Trisha. "Uncoupling Proteins Provide New Clue to
        Obesity's Causes." *Science* 29 May 1998:
        1369–1370.

    This article explains current research on a type of
protein that might contribute to obesity. Researchers
recently discovered the first "uncoupling proteins"
(UCPs) in humans. Originally found in bears, UCPs raise
the resting metabolic rate. Although the research is
incomplete, if it is proven that UCPs do play an active
role in metabolism, obesity and its causes and treatment
will be better understood. UCPs could become a popular
alternative to current weight loss medication. While
UCPs act in muscle and fat, other weight loss treatments
alter substances in the brain. Three human UCPs have
been found within the last year, but extensive research
is still underway. If research can show how the UCPs
function, and if they can then be forced to work a
little harder, researchers may have found the answer
needed to lose weight. This article explains the most
current research in the search for finding a cure for
obesity, but the research is incomplete.

The intended reader for the annotated bibliography is usually the instructor. The assignment serves two purposes: It lets your instructor know whether you have drafted a thesis, identified the required number of sources, and selected appropriate sources for your topic and intended readers. It provides a preview of sorts, illustrating that you have selected recent, relevant, and integrated sources (sources that address one another directly) for a paper on your topic. The assignment requires you to summarize each of your sources, so when you have completed it, you should be thoroughly familiar with your topic and ready to start organizing and drafting a paper. Notice that Amy mentions the introduction to her research paper. She had a preliminary outline in mind when she wrote the annotated bibliography. Outlines aren't required for annotated bibliographies; however, getting as much of the preliminary work completed as possible is an advantage. It allows you to discuss your plans for your paper in specific terms. Check with your instructor if you have questions about adding to or deleting sources from the annotated bibliography. Assignments in this chapter will give you practice in compiling an annotated bibliography.

    Use the tentative title for your paper as the title of the annotated bibliography, and underneath the title write "A Select and Annotated Bibliography." The entry for each source will include a bibliographical citation following a specific style such as

MLA or APA and an annotation that summarizes the source and comments on its value. Summaries should inform the reader of each source's thesis, aim, audience, and scope. You should avoid quotations.

Examples below illustrate two ways to write summaries. The easiest way to tell the difference in these two is to consider whether the writer focuses on the author and what he or she does (descriptive) or on the information in the source (informative). It is possible to combine these two kinds of summary. Ask your instructor if your annotations should be primarily informative or descriptive.

Descriptive Summary

Clayton, Lawrence. "Forrest Carter/Asa Carter and Politics." *Western American Literature* 21 (1988): 19–26.

In his article, "Forrest Carter/Asa Carter and Politics," Lawrence Clayton, professor of English at Hardin-Simmons University, discusses the achievements of writer Forrest Carter, author of several books, the most famous of which is *The Outlaw Josey Wales*. Clayton provides details about Carter's life and discusses what appears to be a political agenda that runs through Carter's novels and his autobiography. Clayton concludes more or less by evading the question of whether Carter played a big joke on the literary community or whether he experienced a transformation that would give his "autobiography," *The Education of Little Tree*, some validity.

Informative (primarily)

Clayton, Lawrence. "Forrest Carter/Asa Carter and Politics." *Western American Literature* 21 (1988): 19–26.

Asa Carter, a political activist who favored states' rights and opposed integration, invented an identity to support his new image when he changed his name to Forrest Carter in the early '70s, gave up politics, and published *Gone to Texas*, *Watch for Me on the Mountain*, and his "autobiography," *The Education of Little Tree*. This double identity may seem insignificant to a reader interested only in Carter's entertaining adventure stories. However, for the reader who recognizes the ardent political criticism clearly manifested in Carter's fiction and autobiography, the double identity explains the recurring criticism throughout Carter's work of a government that does not protect its citizens, of corrupt political officials, and of the tendency of government bureaucracy to meddle in people's lives. Why Carter changed his name and his identity is not known. One point is clear, however: Mr. Carter was adept at storytelling and adept at creating a fictional identity that many people believed to be true. This source is important because it discusses the political criticism that readers may ignore in *The Education of Little Tree*.

EXERCISE: THINKING CRITICALLY

Identify passages in either example above that could be eliminated because they repeat information or because they are so vague or general that they have little meaning for the intended reader.

For one of the readings in the previous chapters, write an informative summary and a descriptive summary. Working in pairs or in groups, share your summaries with your peers and ask them to identify which summary is informative and which one is descriptive.

TAKING NOTES

If you wrote research papers in high school or if you have done research for other college-level courses, you may already have a preference for note taking. Some writers prefer note cards, others record notes in computer files, and others opt for a yellow legal pad or sheets of notebook paper. Whatever your preference, careful note taking can help you understand your topic, achieve a good synthesis of sources in your paper, and avoid plagiarism. Confusion at the note-taking stage—getting one author confused with another, failing to mark direct quotations, writing down incorrect information—can result in major problems when you draft a paper. By following strategies for effective note taking, you should be able to avoid these kinds of problems.

The availability of copy machines in libraries has made photocopying a preferred method of note taking. You read about annotating and highlighting sources in Chapter 2. While highlighting is a good method for marking important ideas and annotating a good way to engage the text, neither will suffice completely for taking notes—putting ideas in your own words by summarizing or paraphrasing original passages. It's handy to work from photocopies, up to a point; however, if you develop the ability to work from your own notes, you won't be at a loss when the copy machine is broken or when you aren't allowed to photocopy a source, and you will probably have a thorough understanding of your topic that you might not have if you rely completely on photocopies . Because note cards are the easiest method to illustrate, the following discussion refers to them; if you are already committed to computer files or notes recorded in a tablet, journal, or on loose-leaf notebook paper, you can still adapt the suggestions made here to your method of taking notes.

Before you begin working on notes, review your working bibliography. Be sure you have a complete bibliographical citation for each source. In the left-hand margin of your working bibliography, enter a number (1, 2, 3, 4, 5,...) or letter (A, B, C,...) that will correspond to your notes. In the sample note card, (Figure 6.2), the writer notes in the right-hand corner that the source is number 3, an article by Marcia Barinaga, "Researchers Broaden the Attack on Parkinson's Disease," that appeared in *Science* on January 27, 1995. A subject heading identifies the topic covered in the note. Below this information, the writer paraphrases a passage from the article and notes the page number. On another note card, the writer records a quotation from source 3, and notes the page number. Notice that the writer has followed suggestions in Chapter 3 by noting the nature of information recorded on each card: "paraphrase" and "direct quotation."

Treatements   #3

Presently, there is no cure for Parkinson's,
but researchers are working on ways to treat
the disease. The most controversial
treatment uses fetal tissue to replace brain
neurons affected by the disease. The
treatment has raised political and ethical
problems.

Paraphrase

Encouraging Developments   #3

GDNF-glial derived neurotrophic factor
prevents the death of dopaminergic neurons.

According to Lars Olson and Barry Hoffer,
"direct injections of GDNF into the brains
of rats and mice can save dopaminergic
neurons that have been damaged ..."

Direct Quotation

FIGURE 6.2

As you work on notes, develop the habit of double-checking each note carefully. Be sure you have

- Keyed it to the working bibliography
- Recorded a page number or numbers from the original source
- Labeled it correctly—paraphrase, summary, direct quotation
- Recorded information accurately

Double-check against the original, taking special note of page numbers and any statistics you might have recorded. Transposing numbers can be a common problem.

If you scanned sources quickly when you compiled your working bibliography, the note-taking stage of the paper should help you weed out sources that are inappropriate (above or below readers' level of understanding; repetitive—same information found in other sources; lacking in credibility; dated) and identify sources that will be important to your paper. Questions to ask as you review each source and take notes are the following:

Does the source

- Support or challenge my thesis?
- Support or challenge points made in other sources?
- Offer statistics, tables, or illustrations that will support or challenge my thesis?
- Offer expert testimony that will support or challenge points made in other sources? Note the experts' names.
- Include direct response to one of my other sources?
- Reinforce important ideas or arguments in my argument or counterargument?
- Refer to specific studies or individuals mentioned in my other sources?

SYNTHESIZING SOURCES

Papers that draw on multiple sources to support a thesis offer readers a *synthesis*— a coherent whole built from several parts. When you synthesize, you include two or more sources in a paper. There is no simple formula for synthesizing. It is a kind of joining together of ideas from two or more writers. You synthesize sources to demonstrate that several studies support a claim you are making or to present a claim someone else has made and to dispute the claim by offering other writers' arguments against it. Think of synthesis as selecting who is allowed to participate in a panel or roundtable discussion.

Frequently, writing assignments stipulate how many sources you should use; sometimes an assignment even requires specific kinds of sources. For example, an assignment for a position paper on an ethical issue of your choice requires a minimum of three sources and must include a newspaper article, an article from a magazine, and information from a book. Or an assignment for an extended research paper calls for a minimum of ten sources, no more than one-third from the Web. Instructors typically include requirements for the number and types of sources because they want you to refer to different kinds of information and to practice synthesizing sources.

A good way to develop an understanding of how to synthesize sources is to analyze how other writers manage this task. Papers that string sources together without regard to how those sources work to develop ideas usually create a *pastiche*—several parts that make up a medley rather than creating a whole. Writers who understand how to synthesize sources understand that sources can work together to create a coherent whole, to support important points, and to avoid generalizing. For example, let's look at three paragraphs from Amy's paper. After exploring her topic through clustering and reading what other writers had written on the topic, Amy developed the following thesis:

> Although medical experts are considering and have had some success with diet pills, changing the environment, food restriction diets, and genetic alterations, a

nondiet technique that combines health awareness with improved physical and psychological health is currently the safest, cheapest, and most effective long-term method available.

Amy's intended readers were her peers in her first-year composition class.

FOCUS ON STUDENT WRITING: Amy's Paper

Other cures that medical experts have attempted, such as diet medication, have had limited success, but this success has come at a high cost to both the individual's pocketbook and physical health. Consumers spend millions of dollars each year on diet pills. Statistics gathered by the National Task Force on Obesity projected that, in 1995, approximately 1.1 million prescriptions would be written for the weight-loss drug fenfluramine alone ("Long Term Pharmcotherapy" 1907). Despite the popularity of diet medication, experts are now warning customers about the possible side effects and also the ineffectiveness of certain pills. Extensive research on the long-term effect of using weight-loss medication has shown that although weight is lost while the pill is being taken, the patient regains the weight as soon as the medication is stopped ("Long Term Pharmcotherapy" 1909). Many people argue that the patient should just stay on the medication. However, not only would this be expensive, it could be unsafe. Newspaper articles, such as Dana Candey's "Weight Loss from a Bottle," carried by the New York Times, as well as articles in women's magazines have made the public aware that specific popular weight-loss drugs have been linked to an increased risk for serious health conditions involving the heart (D1 +). According to the National Task Force, "information of the safety and efficacy of drug combinations in the treatment of obesity is extremely limited" and is therefore not recommended ("Long Term Pharmcotherapy" 19130.

Another suggested cure for obesity is the traditional restricted diet. Although this may work for some people, research has shown that dieting in itself may lead to excessive eating. Dr. Janet Polivy explains in the Journal of the American Dietetic Association that research conducted during World War II has shown that soldiers who were on limited rations became preoccupied with food. When food was available, men who had before had normal eating habits, binged. Food restriction is the same principle that diets rely on. One reason for the ineffectiveness of diets may be that the dieter feels psychologically deprived from food. This could cause dieters to become increasingly preoccupied with food and develop a tendency to binge (589-591).

Dieting is also extremely difficult because of the society that we live in. Along with information on diets and the perpetual pressure to be thin, Americans are bombarded with fattening foods and other temptations. As James Hill and John Peters point out in Science, we have large amounts of food available to us at a reasonable cost (1371). Advances in technology have also made us more of a passive society. Because of computers and other technological advancements, we have everything we need at our fingertips, and the requirements for physical activity have greatly decreased (Hill 1372). Hill and Peters suggest "curing the environment" in order to combat obesity. By making portion sizes smaller, increasing the availability of low-fat, nutritious food, and by creating incentives for physical activity, Hill and Peters claim we will be taking the first step in stopping obesity (1372). However, Gary Taubes, also writing in Science, points out that sufficient data do not support the claim that obesity is caused by environmental factors: "Both

dietary intake and physical activity are very hard to
measure on a population-wide scale" (1368). Furthermore,
restricting certain foods because they are high in fat,
could cause binge eating as it did to the World War II
soldiers Dr. Janet Polivy describes. While cutting back
seems like good advice, changing a person's environment
could end up encouraging the obesity problem rather than
curing it.

Some medical experts argue that obesity may not
have anything to do with an individual's eating habits
or environment; obesity may be caused by a glitch in a
person's genetic makeup. According to <u>Life,</u> researchers
in 1994 found a genetic mutation in obese mice. This
mutated gene may change metabolism and also keep "the
brain free from knowing the stomach is full" (64). This
mutation may also be present in humans, resulting in
some people having an uncontrollable tendency to gain
weight. However, a genetic mutation would not explain
the recent increase of obesity in America. James Hill
and John Peters point out that our genes have not
changed over the past twenty years, although the
percentage of obese people has increased dramatically
during that time period (1307).

Amy cites two sources in the first paragraph, one in the second; in the third,
she cites two and refers to one she mentioned in the second paragraph; and in the
fourth paragraph, she cites two. Notice how she uses sources to support her topic
sentence in paragraph 1: Information from "Long-term Pharmocotherapy in the
Management of Obesity," an article that appeared in the *Journal of the American
Medical Association,* and a newspaper article from *The New York Times* support
Amy's claim that the success of diet medication has "come at a high cost to both
the individual's pocketbook and physical health." In the next paragraph, she refutes
the claim that restricted dieting is effective by citing a study published in the *Journal of the American Dietetic Association.* Her topic sentence tells the reader that
"research has shown that dieting in itself may lead to excessive eating." And in the
third paragraph she uses three sources to demonstrate why dieting is difficult. Hill
and Peters tell us one thing. The other two sources offer different perspectives.

EXERCISES: READING AND RESPONDING

1. Would you advise Amy to revise any of her topic sentences? For each topic sentence, explain why or why not.
2. Would you advise Amy to cite additional sources in any paragraphs? Explain why.
3. Cite passages that demonstrate for you that Amy is or is not achieving her purpose in writing.
4. Cite passages that demonstrate that Amy is aware of her intended readers' needs and expectations.

EXERCISES: THINKING CRITICALLY

1. Working in groups or in pairs, examine "Black American Perceptions of the *Titanic* Disaster" in Chapter 1, and discuss how the writer incorporates sources into the article. To do this, identify the writer's thesis and topic sentences. Does the writer use sources to report information? to illustrate a point? to support a claim? to present a claim the writer refutes?
2. Review Steffany's paper in Chapter 2 and Ronny's paper in Chapter 3. Be prepared to explain how these writers use sources in their papers. Do they paraphrase or quote to illustrate a point? support a claim? present a claim they refute?

Strageties for Synthesizing Sources

While there is no formula for synthesizing, there are some strategies for putting yourself in a good position to offer readers an effective synthesis of sources. One of the most important is understanding your purpose in writing. Another is narrowing a topic sufficiently. For example, instead of writing a position paper on legalizing marijuana, which is a very broad topic, you narrow the scope, focusing on the position that marijuana should be made available to people undergoing chemotherapy to relieve nausea. With this narrowed focus, you know to use sources that discuss this aspect of legalizing marijuana. Understanding what kinds of sources readers will value and find informative is also important. Would your readers find an article from the *Journal of the American Medical Association* more authoritative than an article in *Time* or *Newsweek?* Would the article from *Time* or *Newsweek* help you explain a complex concept? As you read and annotate sources, draft a tentative thesis and topic sentences, the major points that will support the thesis. In each paragraph in a paper, you must decide if your purpose in developing ideas is best served by allowing only one person to speak or by bringing several individuals to the conversation and allowing your audience to hear how they agree or disagree with, validate or deny, one another.

Once you have a sense of purpose—that is, when you know what you want the paper to accomplish—you need to develop a game plan for using sources. Your game plan should help you to weed out sources that are inappropriate (above or below readers' level of understanding; redundant; lacking in credibility; dated) and identify sources that will be important to your paper. Sources that are important are those that support or challenge your thesis or main points or that support or challenge points made in other sources you're using.

You'll practice synthesizing sources as you work on assignments in Part Two. When you research a topic, you shouldn't expect to use every source you find. Expect to discard some information as you read and review sources. You want to be sure your sources are closely connected. You'll read about focal points in Chapter 8, common concerns or direct responses from one source to another. To present a clear, coherent research paper, you'll need to find sources that offer your readers an interesting and relevant discussion. Handling sources effectively is the mark of a mature writer. Make understanding how to synthesize sources one of your goals.

Chapter 7

Documenting Sources

Journalists sometimes have morally good reasons for shielding their sources.
Scholars never do. Scholars are not like God, creating out of nothing. Nor are
they Lone Rangers, going it alone. Footnotes are reminders that scholarship
is an intrinsically communal enterprise—building on, revising or replacing
the work of predecessors. History as we know it would not exist without
source notes. Neither would philosophy, which even in its most original
involves a dialogue with thinkers dead and alive.

—*Kenneth L. Woodward, "In Praise of Footnotes"*

THE PURPOSE OF DOCUMENTATION

Kenneth L. Woodward admits that footnotes are an "endangered species." Internal
documentation and endnotes, sometimes called source notes, have taken their
place. As their name suggests, endnotes follow a text. They provide either copyright
information or information that isn't central to a writer's discussion. These notes
can be important to the reader if they provide points of clarification. For example,
in Chapter 1, Robert Weisbord lists six notes at the conclusion of "Black American
Perception of the *Titanic* Disaster." He uses them to define a term, identify individuals he interviewed, direct readers to additional information in newspapers, and
illustrate the extent of the *Titanic* image in black American history with the example of the Joe Louis vs. Max Schmelling bout. In Chapter 5, Theodore A. Gracyk uses
a different system of documentation in "Romanticizing Rock Music." His notes list
works cited and occasionally offer comments such as pointing out that Camille
Paglia "offer[s] parallels between Elvis Presley and Lord Byron."

As articles by Weisbord and Gracyk illustrate, most scholarly publications use
a system of internal documentation that identifies the work by title or the author's
name and directs readers to specific pages where a passage can be found. This internal documentation is linked to a list of bibliographical citations alphabetized or
listed numerically. If the writer includes endnotes, they appear after the text and
before the bibliographical citations. If there are no endnotes, the list of bibliographical citations follows the text.

Unfortunately, a one-size-fits-all system of documentation that you could use in any subject area isn't available—or, for that matter, appropriate. Every scholarly field has a recommended style for internal documentation and bibliographical citations. This documentation serves several purposes. Most importantly, it acknowledges a writer's indebtedness to the works of others. Without appropriate documentation to indicate that a writer is summarizing, paraphrasing, or quoting other writers' works, a paper misrepresents whose words or ideas are on the page; the writer is guilty of plagiarism. Documentation also directs readers to sources. For example, in a book on media and presidential elections, *Power and the Media*, a student finds data from a survey reported in *American Historical Review*. Questioning the way the survey was conducted and how the data were interpreted, the student decides to look at the complete survey. Internal documentation in a chapter in *Power and the Media* directs the student to a "Works Cited" page. It provides a bibliographical citation for the article in *American Historical Review*: author's full name, title of the article, date of publication, volume and page numbers. With this information, the student can retrieve the article. Even if it's difficult to imagine someone consulting sources in one of your papers, you'll need to provide all the information a reader would need to find your sources. This full disclosure contributes to your credibility. Done correctly, documentation establishes you as a member of a specific discourse community and demonstrates audience awareness. If you take the creative route, listing a partial citation, or providing all the necessary information but not in the proper order, you can undermine your credibility. Your problems with following a specific style of documentation will be noticeable—like too many surface errors in a text. At some point, readers invariably wonder if you didn't know enough or care enough to correct the problems.

Because you are a *reader* as well as a writer, it is beneficial to understand the different conventions of the many styles of documentation. Most likely, you'll have to learn several styles throughout your academic career. Instructors in the sciences, for example, will expect you to follow the *CBE Manual* (Council of Biology Editors), *The ACS Style Guide* (American Chemical Society), or *AIP Style Manual* (American Institute of Physics). If you enroll in a linguistics course, your instructor will ask you to follow the style of documentation outlined by the Linguistic Society of America. And if you submit an article to an academic journal, the editor would probably ask you to use the *Chicago Manual of Style*.

MLA AND APA

This chapter shows you how to document sources using the Modern Language Association (MLA) and American Psychological Association (APA) styles, which are used primarily in academic papers written in the humanities and social sciences, respectively. The guidelines offered here are not comprehensive. They provide examples of bibliographic citations for the kinds of sources cited in this book. For guidelines on expression of ideas, punctuation, spelling, headings, and other stylistic matters, you'll need to consult one of the following:

- The Modern Language Association's Web site ·<http:www.mla.org>
- One of the MLA publications on style:

Gibaldi, Joseph. *MLA Handbook for Writers of Research Papers*. 5th ed. New York, 1999. (Intended for high school and undergraduate writers.)

Gibaldi, Joseph. *MLA Style Manual and Guide to Scholarly Publishing*. 2nd ed. New York: MLA, 1998. (Intended for graduate students and scholars.)

- The APA style manual:

The Publication Manual of the American Psychological Association (5th ed.) Washington, D.C.: APA, 2001.

- Guidelines on MLA or APA style provided by the Purdue University Online Writing Lab <http://owl.english.purdue.edu>

SELECTING A STYLE OF DOCUMENTATION

Because the humanities and social sciences value specific details in bibliographic citations and internal documentation, you'll find slight differences in MLA and APA styles. The examples below, both bibliographical citations for a book by a single author, illustrate some of these differences:

MLA Style: Lack, Paul D. <u>The Texas Revolutionary Experience: A Political and Social History, 1835–1936</u>. College Station: Texas A&M UP: 1992.

APA Style: Lack, P. D. (1992). <u>The Texas revolutionary experience: A political and social history 1835–1836.</u> College Station, TX: Texas A&M University Press.

MLA lists the date at the end of the entry. APA lists it immediately after the author's name. Notice the way the author's name, the book's title, the city of publication, and the publisher are listed in each entry. Format—indentation of the second line in MLA and of the first line in APA—also differs. While APA offers students the option of formatting references with hanging indents (first line begins at the left margin and subsequent lines are indented five spaces), the examples in this chapter show the paragraph indent on the first line with subsequent lines beginning at the left margin. The paragraph indent can be easier to format on a word processor than the hanging indent.Bibliographical entries for magazines, journals, newspapers, and other sources vary slightly from one style to the other just as these entries do.

As you document papers that refer to sources in the case studies in Part Two, consult the guidelines included in this chapter. In addition to citing sources, you need to understand how to handle

- Internal documentation
- Short and long quotations
- Bibliographical citations

THINKING CRITICALLY
ABOUT DOCUMENTATION

The style of documentation you use should mesh with your subject and audience. If your instructor doesn't designate a system of documentation to use, ask yourself the following questions before selecting MLA or APA as you write about the case studies in Part Two:

- Is the subject I am researching a subject discussed in the humanities, social sciences, or sciences?

  Humanities: Use MLA.

  Social sciences: Use APA.

  Sciences: Use either MLA or APA.

- Do a majority of my sources rely on one of these two systems?

  Sources use primarily or exclusively MLA: Use MLA.

  Sources use primarily or exclusively APA: Use APA.

  Sources use other systems of documentation: Use either MLA or APA.

- If I were to submit my paper for publication, would I submit it to a journal concerned with the humanities, social sciences, or sciences?

  Humanities: Use MLA.

  Social sciences: Use APA.

  Sciences: Use either MLA or APA.

GUIDE TO DOCUMENTATION

This chapter includes MLA and APA guidelines for the following: (page numbers indicate where these topics are covered within the chapter).

Internal Documentation

Both MLA and APA use internal or parenthetical documentation in the text to direct readers to bibliographical citations listed at the end of the paper. This documentation includes the author's name and page numbers (some electronic sources are exceptions) for the passage being summarized, paraphrased, or quoted. It may also include the date a source was published. Place parenthetical documentation as close as possible to the passage you are citing.

Use internal documentation to acknowledge

- Quotations
- Other writers' opinions, theories, or unique perspectives offered in your paraphrases or summaries
- Statistics
- Tables, figures, or illustrations from your sources

The following guidelines explain how to handle internal documentation. The source cited is *The Texas Revolutionary Experience* by Paul Lack.

General Format

MLA: If the author isn't mentioned in the text, the author's last name and page number—no punctuation in between—appear in parenthesis at the end of the passage quoted, paraphrased, or summarized. If internal documentation falls at the end of a sentence, hold the end punctuation and place it after the parenthesis.

> One historian claims that the "list of those who
> braved the assault on the Alamo should also include
> four or five Bexarenas and nine dependent children
> who had accompanied their husband-father-protectors
> into the fort" (Lack 197).

MLA: If the author's name is mentioned in the text, place only the page number(s) in parentheses.

> Historian Paul Lack claims that the "list of those
> who braved the assault on the Alamo should also
> include four or five Bexarenas and nine dependent
> children who had accompanied their husband-father-
> protectors into the fort" (197).

MLA: If you have more than one source by a writer or sources by writers who share the same surname, provide an abbreviated version of the title of the work. Place the abbreviated title between the writer's name and the page number, in parenthesis.

> One historian claims that "from the early months of
> the year through September 1835, Texas charted a
> spasmodic course toward revolution" (Lack, *Texas Rev.*
> *Exp.*, 17).

APA: If the author isn't mentioned in the text, the author's last name, the date of publication, and the page number(s) appear in parenthesis following the passage you summarize, paraphrase, or quote.

> One historian claims that the "list of those who
> braved the assault on the Alamo should also include
> four or five Bexarenas and nine dependent children
> who had accompanied their husband-father-protectors
> into the fort" (Lack, 1992, p. 197).

APA: If the author is mentioned in the text, include the date in parenthesis after the author's name and the page number(s) in parentheses at the end of the passage or sentence.

> Historian P. Lack (1992) claims that the "list of
> those who braved the assault on the Alamo should also
> include four or five Bexarenas and nine dependent

> ## Thinking Critically about Documentation
>
> One of the editing skills you should develop is double-checking biblio-graphical citations to make sure you have listed all the required informa-tion in the proper order following conventions of punctuation and capitalization. Also, check internal documentation carefully to be sure spelling of authors' names and book titles is consistent and that page numbers cited in internal documentation for articles match up with any page numbers listed in bibliographical citations.

```
           children who had accompanied their husband-father-

           protectors into the fort" (p. 197).
```

APA: If you have more than one article by a writer or articles by writers who share the same surname, include the writer's first initial in addition to the year of publication.

```
           One historian claims that the "list of those who

           braved the assault on the Alamo should also include

           four or five Bexarenas and nine dependent children

           who had accompanied their husband-father-protectors

           into the fort" (P. Lack, 1992, p. 197).
```

Long and Short Quotations

Short quotations   Incorporate short quotations (see length requirements below) into a paper by double spacing them in the text. Place quotation marks around the quoted passage. Whenever possible, hold internal documentation until the end of the sentence.

MLA: Quotations of no more than four lines.

```
           Richard Hoffer, who covered this incident for Sports

           Illustrated, explained that Ron Weaver's "deception

           was born out of a whim and carried out rather

           clumsily. There were no doctored transcripts, no

           conspiracy on the part of coaches or schools, and

           hardly any thought of where this might lead" (27).
```

APA: Quotations of less that forty words.

> Richard Hoffer (1996), who covered this incident for *Sports Illustrated*, explained that Ron Weaver's "deception was born out of a whim and carried out rather clumsily. There were no doctored transcripts, no conspiracy on the part of coaches or schools, and hardly any thought of where this might lead" (p. 27).

Block quotations   For quotations longer than four lines (MLA) or more than thirty-five words (APA), start the quotation on a new line and double-space it in a freestanding, indented block. Do not place quotation marks around the passage. Include internal documentation at the end of the passage.

MLA: Four lines or more: Indent ten spaces.

> In a feature story for *Sports Illustrated*, Richard Hoffer analyzed the success of Ron Weaver's hoax:
>
> > The deception was born out of a whim and carried out rather clumsily. There were no doctored transcripts, no conspiracy on the part of coaches or schools, and hardly any thought of where this might lead. Possibly it was the purity of motive that kept this thing on rails as long as it did, because there is not much evidence planning kept it in motion. (37)

APA: Thirty-five words or more: Indent five spaces.

> In a feature story for *Sports Illustrated*, Richard Hoffer (1997) analyzed the success of Ron Weaver's hoax:
>
> > The deception was born out of a whim and carried out rather clumsily. There were no doctored transcripts, no conspiracy on the part of coaches or schools, and hardly any thought of where this might lead. Possibly it was the purity of motive that kept this thing on rails as long as it did, because there is not much evidence that planning kept it in motion. (p. 37)

Indirect Quotations

When one source cites another (for example, a book on medical ethics quotes a passage from *Scientific American*), you have a direct source and an indirect source.

MLA: Include a tagline in the text and internal documentation that includes the abbreviation *qtd. in*, the last name of the author of the direct source, and the page number.

> Hillel Schwartz, author of *The Culture of the Copy*, claims that "both [imposture and impersonation] may be impeccably costumed, yet in the final dressing down, impostors want attention and love, and we betray them; impersonators want our money, [and] our secrets, . . . and they betray us" (qtd. in Gibson 56).

APA: Refer to the direct and indirect sources in the tag line.

> Gibson (1997) prefaces her discussion of impostors with remarks from Schwartz, 1998 *The Culture of the Copy*. Schwartz claims that "both [imposture and impersonation] may be impeccably costumed, yet in the final dressing down, impostors want attention and love, and we betray them; impersonators want our money, [and] our secrets, . . . and they betray us" (p. 56)

Bibliographical Citations

At the end of the text on a separate page, provide full bibliographical citations for all sources cited in your paper. Full citations vary by source, but in general include the author's or editor's name, title of the work, date of publication, city of publication, and name of the publisher. In MLA style, this list is entitled *Works Cited*; in APA style, the list is entitled *References*. List citations alphabetically by author or, for unsigned sources, by title; double-space each entry.

General Format for Books

Author's name: MLA provides the author's full name, last name first for alphabetizing.

APA lists the author's last name followed by the first initial.

Both MLA and APA list names of two or more authors in the same order as they appear on the title page.

Capitalization of the title:	MLA capitalizes everything except articles, conjunctions, and prepositions.
	APA capitalizes the first word and any proper nouns.
City of publication:	MLA lists only the city.
	APA includes city and state if the city is not well-known or if it could be confused with another city by the same name. For publications outside of the United States, list the city and country.
Publisher:	MLA abbreviates publishers' names.
	APA drops unnecessary words or abbreviations such as *Co., Company, Inc., Publishers*.
Format:	MLA indent five spaces from the left margin on the second line and any subsequent lines of an entry.
	APA indents five spaces from the left margin on the first line of an entry.
	Both MLA and APA double-space entries.

Book with one author

MLA: Clayton, Lawrence. <u>Watkins Reynolds Matthews: A
             Biography</u>. Abilene: Hardin-Simmons UP, 1990.

1. Begin with the author's name, as it appears on the title page, last name first.
   - Omit titles or degrees—for example, *Matt Sherwood, Ph.D.*, appears as *Sherwood, Matt*.
   - List any suffixes that are part of a name: *Octavus Madison Eaves, Jr.*, appears as *Eaves, Octavus Madison, Jr.*
2. Give the full title of the book, including any subtitle, underlined or italicized.
3. List the city of publication, publisher's name, and year of publication as this information appears on the title page or the copyright page (usually the back of the cover page).
   - If more than one city is listed on the title page, use the name of the first city listed.
   - Include an abbreviation of the country for cities outside of the United States:

Crewkerne, England:	*Crewkerne, Eng.*
Brussels, Belgium:	*Brussels, Belg.*
Salzburg, Austria:	*Salzburg, Aus.*

4. Separate the name of the city and the publisher with a colon.
5. Use an abbreviation of the publisher's name:

   Texas A&M University Press: Texas A&M UP

Addison Wesley Longman: Longman

Gale Research Inc.:   Gale

Government Printing Office: GPO

6. Separate the name of the publisher and the date of publication with a comma.

7. Be sure the citation ends with a period.

APA: Clayton, L. (1990). <u>Watkins Reynolds Matthews:</u>
<u>A biography.</u> Abilene, Texas: Hardin-Simmons
University Press.

1. Begin with the author's last name followed by the initial of the first name or initials of the first and middle names.

2. Give the date of publication in parenthesis followed by a period.

3. Give the title, capitalizing the first word, the first word of the subtitle, and any proper nouns; underline or italicize the title.

4. List the city and state where the book was published, and publishing company.

5. Separate the city of publication from the publishing company with a colon.

6. Be sure the citation ends with a period.

Book with two or more authors

MLA: Killingsworth, M. Jimmie, and Jacqueline S. Palmer.
<u>Ecospeak: Rhetoric and Environmental Politics in</u>
<u>America</u>. Carbondale: Southern Illinois UP, 1992.

1. Reverse the order of the first author (last name first) and list the other authors' names first name first.

2. Separate the names with a comma and place the word *and* before the last name.

APA: Killingsworth M. J., & Palmer, J. S. (1992).
<u>Ecospeak: Rhetoric and environmental politics in</u>
<u>America.</u> Carbondale, IL: Southern Illinois
University Press.

1. List the last name and initial(s) of each author, last name first.

2. Separate the names with a comma followed by an ampersand.

Edited book

MLA: Downs, Fane, and Robert W. Sledge, eds. *Pride of Our*
Western Prairies: McMurry College 1923-1988.
Austin: Eakin, 1989.

1. Treat the editor as you would an author.
2. Place a comma after the name or names and include the abbreviation for editor, *ed,* or for editors, *eds.*

> **APA:**   Downs, F., & Sledge, R. W (Eds). (1988). <u>Pride</u>
> <u>of our western prairies: McMurry College 1923–1988.</u>
> Austin: Eakin.

1. Place the abbreviation for editor, *Ed.,* or for two editors, *Eds.,* in parenthesis.

Article or chapter in an edited book

> **MLA:**   Neal, Maureen. "Abdominal Conditions and Other
> Cretins of Habit: Hyperfluency and the
> Acquisition of Academic Discourse." <u>Attending</u>
> <u>to the Margins: Writing, Researching, and</u>
> <u>Teaching on the Front Lines</u>. Ed. Michelle Hall
> Kells and Valerie Balester. Portsmouth:
> Heinemann, 1999: 74–89.

1. Begin with the name of the author of the article or chapter and follow with the title of the article or chapter in quotation marks.
2. List the title of the book, followed by the abbreviation *Ed.* and the name(s) of the editor(s).
3. Follow the date of publication with the page numbers of the article or chapter.

> **APA:**   Neal, M. (1999). Abdominal conditions and other
> cretins of habit: Hyperfluency and the acquisition
> of academic discourse. In M. H. Kells & V. Balester
> (Eds), <u>Attending to the Margins: Writing,</u>
> <u>Researching, and Teaching on the Front Lines</u> (pp.
> 74–89), Portsmouth, NH: Heinemann.

1. Begin with the last name and initial(s) of the author of the article or chapter followed by the date of publication in parenthesis and the title of the article or chapter.
2. Place the word *In* before the initials and last name(s) of the editor(s), and follow with the abbreviation *Ed* in parenthesis.
3. List the title of the book and, in parenthesis, the page numbers for the article or chapter.

Article in a reference book

MLA: "Barbara Jordan." *Black Women in America: An*

   Historical Encyclopedia. Ed. Darlenne Clark

   Hine. Vol. I. Brooklyn: Carlson, 1993.

   653-659.

1. If the article is signed, begin the entry with the author's name; if the article isn't signed, begin with the title of the entry in quotation marks.
2. After the title of the reference book, place *Ed.* before the names(s) of the editor(s).
3. For reference works that are not well-known, provide full publication information: number of volumes, revised edition, or other information.
4. For reference works that are well-known and revised periodically, omit the city and publisher; list only the edition and year.

APA: Barbara Jordan (1993). *In Black women in America:*

   An historical encyclopedia. Ed. Darlenne Clark Hine.

   (Vol. I., pp. 654-659), Brooklyn: Carlson.

1. If the article is signed, begin the entry with the author's name; if the article is not signed, begin with the entry title.
2. Place the word *In* before the title of the reference book, and place the abbreviation *Ed.* before the name of the editor.
3. In parenthesis, list the volume and write *p.* or *pp.* and give the page numbers.

An introduction, preface, foreword, or afterword

MLA: Marquez, Gabriel Garcia. Introduction. The Circle of

   Life: Rituals from the Human Family Albums. Ed.

   David J. Cohen. Harper: San Francisco, 1991.

1. After the name of the author, list the part being cited.
2. After the title of the book, write the name of the author.
3. For an edited book, follow the title with *Ed(s).* and the name(s) of the editors.

APA: Marquez, G. G. (1991) [Introduction]. The

   Circle of Life Rituals from the Human Family Albums.

   Ed. David J. Cohen. Harper: San Francisco.

1. After the date, list the part being cited in brackets.

Report from a private organization

MLA: Committee on the Administration of Justice. Inquests

   and Disputed Killings in Northern Ireland.

```
Belfast: Committee on the Administration of
Justice, 1992.
```

1. Begin with the name of the organization.
2. List the title.
3. List the city, publisher, and date.

> **APA:**   Committee on the Administration of Justice.
> (1992). <u>Inquests and disputed killings in Northern</u>
> <u>Ireland.</u> Belfast: Author.

1. Begin with the name or the organization that published the report.
2. If the publisher is the author, use the word *Author* after the name of the city of publication.

General Format for Articles

Follow the guidelines below for articles in newspapers, magazines, or scholarly journals.

Author's name:	MLA provides the author's full name, last name first for alphabetizing.
	APA lists the author's last name followed by the first initial.
Title of article:	MLA places the title in quotation marks and capitalizes everything in the title except articles, conjunctions, and prepositions.
	APA does not place the title in quotation marks. APA capitalizes only the first word in the title and any proper nouns.
Name of periodical:	Underline or italicize the name of the periodical
	MLA capitalizes everything except articles, conjunctions, and prepositions.
	APA capitalizes the first word and any proper nouns.
Publication information:	MLA lists the volume and/or date followed by the page numbers of the article.
	APA lists the volume after the title and underlines or italicizes both.
Page numbers:	MLA and APA require page numbers for the entire article, not just the page(s) you used.
Format:	MLA indents five spaces from the left margin on the second line and any subsequent lines of an entry. Both MLA and APA double-space entries.

Article in a popular magazine

MLA: Tumulty, Karen. "Buy One, Get One Free." <u>Time</u> 7 Sep. 1999: 34.

1. After the title of the magazine, list the day, month, and year of publication followed by the page number(s).

APA: Tumulty, K. (1999, September 7). Buy one, get one free. <u>*Time*,</u> 154, 34.

1. List the year, month, and day of publication after the author's name.
2. After the title, list the volume number and the page number(s).

Article in a scholarly journal that pages each issue separately Use this format for journals that begin each issue on page 1.

MLA: Gladden, Samuel L. "Sebastian Melmoth: Wilde's Parisian Exile as the Spectacle of Sexual, Textual Revolution." <u>Victorians Institute Journal</u> 28.5 (2000): 23–28.

1. After the title of the journal, list the volume number and issue number separated by a period, and give the year of publication in parenthesis followed by a colon and the page number(s).

APA: Gladden, S. L. (2000). Sebastian Melmoth: Wilde's Parisian exile as the spectacle of sexual revolution. <u>Victorians Institute Journal, 28</u> (3) 23–28.

1. Underline or italicize the title of the journal and the volume number.
2. Give the issue number in parenthesis after the volume number.

Article in a scholarly journal with continuous pagination Use this format for journals that begin pagination where the previous issue left off (for example, one issue extends from 1–235; the next issue extends from 236–435.

MLA: Keep, Christopher. "The Cultural Work of the Type-Writer Girl." <u>Victorian Studies</u>. 40 (1997): 401–426.

1. After the title of the journal, give the volume number and, in parenthesis, the year of publication and the page number(s) of the complete article.

APA: Keep, C. (1997). The cultural work of the type-writer girl. <u>Victorian Studies, 40,</u> 401–426.

1. Underline or italicize the title of the journal and the volume number.

Article in a newspaper

MLA: Goode, Erica E. "New and Old Depression Drugs are found Equal." New York Times 19 Mar. 1999, late ed.: A1 + .

"Storm Clouds Building in Congress." (1998, 25 September) New York Times 27 8 Nov. 1998, late ed.: B18 + .

1. If the article is signed, begin with the author's name; if it is unsigned, begin with the title of the article.
2. Give the name of the newspaper exactly as it is appears on the front page.
3. After the date, give the edition if listed.
4. If sections are paginated separately, give the section and the page.
5. If sections are numbered and not part of the pagination, use the abbreviation *sec.* after the date, and give the section number.

APA: Goode, E. E. (1999, March 19). New and old depression drugs are found equal. New York Times, pp. A1, A7–8.

Storm clouds building in Congress. (1998, September 25). New York Times, pp. 18B, 19B, 20B.

1. For unsigned articles, begin with the title.
2. For articles appearing on discontinuous pages, list all page numbers, separated with a comma.

Letter to the editor or signed editorial

MLA: Eastwood, Clint. Letter. New York Times 16 Oct. 1991: A24.

1. After the author's name, write *Letter* or *Editorial*.
2. After the date, list the section and page number(s).

APA: Eastwood, C. (1991, October 16) [Letter to the editor]. New York Times, p. A24.

1. Treat an editorial as an article in a newspaper.
2. If the letter has a title, follow it with *Letter to the editor* enclosed in brackets.
3. Place the abbreviation *p.* or *pp.* after the name of the newspaper and give the section and page number(s).

Review of a film

MLA: King, Florence. Rev. of <u>Braveheart</u>, dir. Mel Gibson. <u>National Review</u> 20 Apr. 1998: 64.

1. Place *Rev of* before the title of the film.
2. Place *dir.* before the director's name.

APA: King, F. (1998, April 20). <u>Braveheart</u> [Review of the film <u>Braveheart</u>]. *National Review, 50*, 64.

1. After the title of the film, enclose in brackets *Review of the film* and the film's title.
2. Underline or italicize the title of the magazine or journal and the volume number.

Review of a book

MLA: Long, Kenneth O., Jr. "Cow Jumped Over the Moon." Rev. of <u>Bovine Respiratory Disease: A Symposium</u>, Raymond W. Loan, ed. *Abilene Reporter News* 1 Apr. 1984: 13.

1. Place *Rev of* before the title of the book.
2. Place a comma after the name of the book and write *by* and the author's or editor's name.

APA: Long, K. O., Jr. (1994, April 1). Cow Jumped Over the Moon. [Review of <u>Bovine respiratory disease: a symposium</u>]. A*bilene* <u>Reporter News,</u> 13.

1. After the title of the article, enclose in brackets *Review of* and the book's title. Underline or italicize the title.
2. Underline or italicize the title of the magazine, journal, or newspaper.

Other Sources

Unpublished letter

MLA: Wallace, Lew. Letter to Susan Arnold Elston Wallace. 22 Jun. 1888. Lew Wallace Papers. General Lew Wallace Museum. Crawfordsville, Indiana.

1. Give the author's name followed by *Letter to* and the name of the recipient.
2. After the date, list the owner of the letter and the city and state.

APA: Wallace, L. (1888, June 22) [Letter to Susan Arnold Elston Wallace]. General Lew Wallace Museum. Crawfordsville, Indiana.

1. After the date, enclose in brackets *Letter to* and the recipient's name; list the owner of the letter and the city and state.

Personal interview

MLA: `Holladay, Robert E. Personal interview. 16 Apr.`
`1996.`

1. Cite the kind of interview, personal or telephone.

APA: `Holladay, R. E. (1996, April 16). Personal`
`interview.`

Scholarly project, professional, or personal site*

MLA: `Martin Luther King, Jr., National Historic Site's`
`Online Visitor Information Center. 11 Apr.`
`2000. Martin Luther King, Jr., National`
`Historic Site Interpretive Staff. 3 Mar. 2000`
`<http://www.nps.gov/malu/frames/frames.htm>`

1. Begin with the title of the database or page, underlined or italicized.
2. Give the name of the editor if one is provided.
3. List publication information: date the information was posted or updated and the name of a webmaster or sponsoring institution.
4. Give the date of access and the web address.

APA: `Martin Luther King, Jr., National Historic Site's`
`Online Visitor Information Center. (2000, April 11).`
`<http://www.nps.gov/malu/frames/frames.htm> (2000,`
`March 3).`

E-mail

MLA: `Baker, James A. "Aggie Critic." Email to Bill`
`Carroll. 12 Feb. 2000.`

1. List the name of the sender, the title of the subject line, a description of the message that includes the name of the recipient, and the date of the message.

APA: `APA style encourages writers to cite references`
`to e-mail in the text instead of in the list of`

---

*Citations for electronic sources, like those for paper sources, should provide enough information for a reader to retrieve the source. If you looked at an on-line publication that is also available in print and there is no difference in the two versions, cite the print form. If there is a difference (for example, the on-line version is abbreviated or it doesn't include pagination), cite the on-line version.

references. For an e-mail from James A. Baker to
Bill Carroll, the citation would include the
initials and surname of the communicator, the
notation <u>personal communication,</u> and the exact date
of the communication: (J. A. Baker, personal
communication, February 12, 2000).

ADDITIONAL GUIDELINES FOR COMPILING A LIST OF WORKS CITED

1. Check all information (especially spelling, volume numbers, and year of publication) against the original source.
2. Ignore *A*, *An*, and *The* when you alphabetize unsigned sources.
3. Alphabetize two or more works by the same author as follows:

     MLA: Alphabetize by title.

     APA: List by year of publication, with the earliest year first.

4. Alphabetize two or more authors with the same surname, as follows:

     MLA: List by alphabetical order of the first name or inital.

     APA: List by alphabetical order of the first initial.

5. Close each citation with a period.
6. Include pagination on the *Works Cited* or *Reference* pages (last name and page number for MLA; an abbreviated version of the title and page number for APA).

FOCUS ON STUDENT WRITING: Examples of MLA and APA

Marcus Frye and Candace Davis wrote the sample papers that follow, which illustrate MLA and APA style, respectively.

Both students wrote in response to the assignment below, a requirement for their first-year composition course. Notice how both writers incorporate sources into the text and synthesize sources within paragraphs. Annotations point out conventions of each style.*

Overview   Research is a process of investigation—of reading, writing, and thinking that incorporates you (the researcher) into a conversation, whether it is about RBIs in major-league baseball, ecological damage caused by offshore oil drilling, or

---

*The papers have been edited for inclusion in this chapter, but not extensively.

who should be elected president. While it is possible to argue from the basis of unsubstantiated opinion, you are likely (especially when facing an educated audience) to end up with egg on your face. Making a claim and sustaining an argument backed up by credible and current research is the keystone of academic discourse and your ultimate success as a college student. In an academic context, a brash claim *might* make for a good introduction, but it had better be backed up with good research or your reputation (and grade) will suffer. The point of this assignment is to demonstrate that you have learned the conventions of written academic discourse, that you are capable of doing scholarly research, and that you can construct an argument that is effectively supported by that research. In other words, it's your opportunity to prove that you can play the game, walk the walk, and talk the talk of the university discourse community.

Objective   You should be able to write a midlength paper that synthesizes, analyzes, or interprets credible, academic sources gathered in the library or on the Web to present a coherent, well-organized argumentative essay. Argue your perspective on an issue, using the research you've gathered to provide relevant background information and to aid you in developing your argument. You must recognize the opposition's arguments and address them. You must demonstrate that you have a thorough understanding of the various perspectives surrounding an issue, especially those in opposition to your own. The thesis of the paper should clearly state your own position/perspective on the issue under discussion.

Audience   Your audience should be a group of students and professors with an interest in your topic. Assume that they know the structure of the issue but have not yet decided (and therefore must be convinced) to agree with your position.

Sample MLA Paper

```
            The Road to Change
                    by
              Marcus Fryer


          Professor Matt Sherwood
             English 104-571



            12 December 2000
```

MLA offers the option of including a title page that lists in the following order the title of the paper, your name, your instructor's name, the name and number of the course, and the date (day, month, and year). Center this information one-third of the way down the page and double-space between items.

*Prompt developed by Jim Baker and Susan Murphy

Pagination for the first page of text starts ½ inch from the top of the page. The writer's name and the page number appear on page.

Fryer 1

Marcus Fryer

Mr. Sherwood

English 104-571

12 December 2000

Heading: Your name, name of your instructor, course title, number and section, and date. Start 1 inch from the top of the page.

The Road to Change

Center title above the text

Indent ½ inch or five spaces

Of all the things we use every day, automobiles are probably the most prevalent and useful. Without vehicles, we would be greatly limited in the distance that we could travel daily from our home, affecting our work and our personal lives. The automobile has made our lives better in many ways, including the fact that without the automobile to facilitate interstate traffic, we would have to grow more of our food at home and we would have less time to spend doing what we want and working in jobs we enjoy. According to James MacKenzie in The Keys to the Car, "Over the past century, petroleum-powered motor vehicles have revolutionized how and where countless millions of Americans live, work, and travel" (1). The problem lies in the fact that these vehicles that we have grown so dependent upon are slowly choking our planet. The current situation that our vehicles put us in threatens us in three distinct ways. First of all, they have caused air pollution to grow to

Tag phrase introduces quotation; parenthetical documentation includes only the page number when the title is included in the text.

Leave 1-inch margin on both sides
of the page and also at the bottom

dangerous levels in some of this country's
largest cities. Secondly, the use of gas-
powered cars has caused the United States
to grow to be overly dependent on other
nations for their exported oil. Lastly,
the carbon dioxide from our cars has
caused, over the years, global warming to
take place, which, if left unchecked,
could cause great natural disasters to our
country. What all of these things show is
that an alternative must be found to
combat the negative effects of gas-powered
cars on our environment.

There are many different options
available for alternate fuel types for
automobiles, including methanol,
electricity, and natural gas. Each option
has strengths and weaknesses, but the one
with the fewest weaknesses and most
strengths is the use of electricity.
Electric cars are currently being developed
by many different car companies, including
Ford and Honda, both domestically and
overseas. A book by the International
Energy Agency, <u>Electric Vehicles:
Technology, Performance and Potential</u>,
explains that "EV [electric vehicle]
development has accelerated rapidly over
the past few years. More capital and
manpower than ever before are now being
invested in technical advances" (7).

Opponents to the use of electric
vehicles claim that at this time electric
vehicles can't perform as well as the

Brackets indicate an
addition by the writer.
The addition is
necessary because of
the abbreviation.
When you use
abbreviations readers
won't recognize,
provide the full name
or term in parenthesis
when you use your
own words and in
brackets when the
abbreviation appears
in quotations.

When you
incorporate a partial
quotation into the
text, the quotation
and whatever
precedes it must be
a grammatically
correct sentence.

Fryer 3

standard gas-powered vehicle. Though this is true, electric vehicles are quickly catching up to standard cars. At this time, the EVs that are commercially available can travel between 50 and 80 kilometers in the city between having their batteries fully charged, and can attain a top speed of 70-90 km/h (IEA 8). Granted, this isn't as good as most, if not all, of the gas-powered vehicles available, but it is good enough to get the job done. Though it is not common, there are EVs that are capable of going much faster. In Oregon every year there is an Electric Car Crag Race, with contestants going from 0 to 125 mph in 10.5 seconds (Munoz 3).

When the text doesn't mention the title of the source, include the title (abbreviated version for long titles) in parenthetical documentation before the page number.

When you cite statistics, include documentation.

Though this is not the norm yet, it shows that it is possible, and will be plausible within a few years. Also, within a few years, EVs are going to be up to spec with standard vehicles. Noting both of these facts, it shouldn't be a hard decision to see why sacrificing a few miles (or kilometers) per hour is worthwhile to help preserve our environment and to make our country more independent of its energy needs.

Facts show that there exists a good relationship between petroleum use and electrical production. In "Potential of Electric Vehicles in Present and Future Transportation Systems," Brown, Barber, and Kirk say that the use of electricity

Tag phrases provide a context for the reader in a paragraph that synthesizes two sources.

Fryer 4

would supplement the use of gasoline in
automobiles well. "In the United States,"
they say, "the transportation sector uses
63% of the total petroleum consumption.
The fraction of electricity generated from
petroleum is only 5%" (9). This shows that
if electricity were used more often in
vehicles, there would be a drastic
reduction in the amount of petroleum used.
If we could reduce the amount of petroleum
that we use, then the United States would
be much better off. Reducing our
dependence on other countries would put
the United States in a better position in
world politics. Also, prices at the gas
pump would no longer be at the whim of
another country's oil production regime,
helping U.S. consumers. Electric vehicles
are also responsible for cleaning up our
water supply. Econogics Inc., an
environmental company, published an
article stating that

Quotation is modified by the insertion of brackets. This information makes the partial quotation clear.

[EVs] reduce water pollution by
virtue of reducing the amount of
petroleum products being produced,
transported, stored, used and
disposed of [in the water supply]....
EVs produce far less waste heat than
combustion engines (also known as
heat engines), so they reduce the
amount of heat pollution being
produced.

For quotations of four lines or more, indent 1 inch or ten spaces and double space. Do not place quotation marks around the quotation.

Opponents of the use of electric cars
raise many valid points. Many see their

Fryer 5

vehicles as an expression of themselves, whether it is a sporty yellow race car or a large SUV. These vehicles are not available in electric form yet, thus making them less appealing to many. The individuals who own these small, fast cars or large, loud tanks see them as a way to express themselves and what they like. The solution to this is that if consumers begin buying more of these automobiles from car makers, then there can surely be a way to customize these vehicles to their owner's liking once they are mass-produced. Thus, by buying these new EVs, consumers with certain preferences for their cars would only be helping the eventuality of customizable electric cars.

The use of electric vehicles will revolutionize the way we get around and the way that our world is run. It is through the use of these vehicles that cities choked with pollution will be free again to stand tall in clean, fresh air. EVs will make it possible to reduce the amount of pollution in the water supply, making it safe for all to drink water again. Finally, EVs will reduce the amount of petroleum that the United States has to import, making our country more self-sufficient. The combination of these facts makes the use of electric vehicles a necessary given for our future.

The writer concludes with his own words. He restates thed thesis and the main points that support it.

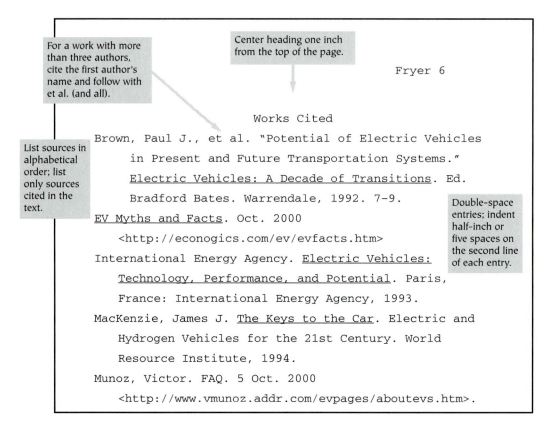

For a work with more than three authors, cite the first author's name and follow with et al. (and all).

Center heading one inch from the top of the page.

Fryer 6

Works Cited

Brown, Paul J., et al. "Potential of Electric Vehicles in Present and Future Transportation Systems." <u>Electric Vehicles: A Decade of Transitions</u>. Ed. Bradford Bates. Warrendale, 1992. 7-9.

List sources in alphabetical order; list only sources cited in the text.

<u>EV Myths and Facts</u>. Oct. 2000
    <http://econogics.com/ev/evfacts.htm>

International Energy Agency. <u>Electric Vehicles: Technology, Performance, and Potential</u>. Paris, France: International Energy Agency, 1993.

Double-space entries; indent half-inch or five spaces on the second line of each entry.

MacKenzie, James J. <u>The Keys to the Car</u>. Electric and Hydrogen Vehicles for the 21st Century. World Resource Institute, 1994.

Munoz, Victor. FAQ. 5 Oct. 2000
    <http://www.vmunoz.addr.com/evpages/aboutevs.htm>.

Sample APA Paper

Place the abbreviated title and page number 1/2 inch from the top and 1 inch from the right-hand margin.

Safety of 1

The Safety of Our Fellow Drivers
Candice Davis
Professor Matt Sherwood
English 104
December 11, 2000

Center title, name, instructor's name, course number, and date on the page. Double-space between item.

Center title. Double-space and begin the text.

Safety of 2

The Safety of Our Fellow Drivers

When I drive down the highway, I am usually cautious of my speed and the speed of others, and I observe traffic signs warning me and my fellow drivers of construction, reduced speed, and sharp turns. I consider myself to be a cautious driver, and I am always "aware of my surroundings." Despite all these precautions, I always get nervous, as I'm sure most others do, when I'm near a motorcyclist driving without a helmet. They always make me nervous because I know that these drivers are not as well protected as they should be. Vehicle accidents cannot be predicted, so just as a precaution, motorcycle drivers should feel just as obligated to wear helmets as drivers of cars are to wear seat belts. A few years ago, drivers would hardly ever pass a motorcyclist without a helmet, and now it seems like passing a motorcyclist with a helmet is unusual. A helmet should be a necessity when riding a motorcycle. Many head injuries occur during wrecks that can be less severe, if not prevented, if a helmet is worn. So why is it that motorcyclists do not wear helmets?

One problem is that helmets are not required to be worn in some states. According to a recent study by the United States Department of Transportation (2000), "At the end of 1992, twenty-five

states and the District of Columbia had
universal helmet use laws in effect"
(p. 6). This means that in these twenty-
five states, helmet use is required at all
times, regardless of age. The problem
occurs in the twenty-five states that do
not have the universal helmet law. In
these states, helmet use is required for
motorcyclists under the age of twenty-one,
and, in three of the twenty-five states,
there is no law requiring helmets
(Department of Transportation, 2000). The
only solution to this problem would be to
require all motorcyclists to wear helmets
in all fifty states. This requirement
would cause the death rate in motorcycle
accidents to decrease and cause the
severity of the injuries to decrease as
well (National Highway Traffic Safety
Administration, 1998).

   Many motorcyclists choose not to wear
helmets for several reasons. Some claim
that helmets prevent the driver from
hearing very well. Others claim that the
helmet blocks the driver's peripheral
vision. Still others claim that the way
helmets are made cause head and neck
injuries. According to several studies,
all these claims have been proven false.
Helmets do not prevent the driver from
hearing well. With a helmet, the sounds
heard from the outside environment are not
as loud as they would be without a helmet,
but they occur in the same proportions
(National Highway Traffic Safety

The name of the source is mentioned in the text and the year is included in parenthesis. The page number follows the quotation.

The title and the year note the source for statistics.

Safety of 4

Administration, 1996). In other words, the driver would still be able to distinguish certain sounds from one another when driving with a helmet. Helmets also do not affect the driver's visual range.

Tag phrases provide a context for the reader in a paragraph that synthesizes two sources.

According to a study, Motorcycle Helmets, by the National Highway Traffic Safety Administration (1996), "Less than 3% of the peripheral vision is limited." This study maintains that drivers can turn their heads a little more to see anything that might be blocked by a helmet. Finally, it reports that, in most cases, helmets do not cause injuries. If an injury is caused, it is relatively minor compared to the injury that could have been caused if the driver was not wearing a helmet.

Tag phrases provide a context for the reader in a paragraph that synthesizes two sources.

According to another study by the National Highway Traffic Safety Administration, Motorcycle Safety (1999), "Safety helmets save lives by reducing the extent of head injuries in the event of a crash" (p. 6). So why not wear a helmet, even if it is not required by law? Between 1984 and 1995, helmet use saved the lives of more than 7,400 motorcyclists (National Highway Traffic Safety Administration, 1996). Motorcycle drivers can have up to a 73% decline in death rates if they wear helmets (National Highway Traffic Safety Administration, 1998). Even if helmets are not required in some states, motorcyclists should save their own lives by wearing a helmet.

An even better solution would be for the government to require helmet use among all motorcyclists. By requiring motorcyclists to wear helmets, more drivers would feel obligated to wear helmets. In states that carry the universal law, 98% of motorcyclists wear helmets, and in states not requiring helmets, 34% to 54% have been found to wear helmets (National Highway Traffic Safety Administration, 1996). Helmet laws and helmet use have a direct effect on each other. If the law is enforced, more riders will wear helmets, and vice versa. In 1997, for example, the state of Texas did away with the required age law anyone under the age of twenty-one is required to wear a helmet) (Department of Transportation, 2000). After the law changed, helmet use dropped from over 90% to below 70% (Department of Transportation, 2000). If the laws aren't enforced, the motorcyclists will not abide by them, and the number of deaths due to motorcycle accidents well remain steady. This number will not decrease unless the government steps in and requires that all fifty states approve of the universal helmet law.

Some people might raise the objection that issuing a law that requires drivers to wear helmets is not respecting their rights as individuals. They claim that they have the right to choose whether or not they wear a helmet. Motorcycle helmet laws, however, are put into place to protect the individual drivers (National Highway

Traffic Safety Administration, 1998). When
people get into a car, the first thing they
need to do is put on a seat belt. It
becomes a habit. For motorcyclists, a
simple thing, such as putting on a helmet,
could be a habit, too.

Helmet laws are an important part of
all drivers' lives, no matter if they
drive a car or a motorcycle. Every state
needs to have the universal helmet law in
place to protect citizens. It could mean a
matter of life and death.

Center the heading
and list sources in
alphabetical order.

References

Department of Transportation. (2000 September).
Evaluation of Motorcycle Helmet Law Repeal In Arkansas
and Texas Retrieved October 7, 2000: http://www. nhtsa.
dot. gov.

National Highway Traffic Safety Administration,
Department of Transportation. (1996). Motorcycle Helmets.
(Serial No. DOT HS 807 603"—P.[8]). United States.

National Highway Traffic Safety Administration,
Department of Transportation. (1999). Motorcycle Safety.
(Serial No. DOT HS 807 709"—P.[4]). United States.

National Highway Traffic Safety Administration,
Department of Transportation. (1998). Without
Motorcycle helmets We All Pay the Price. (Serial No.
DOT HS 808600). United States.

Start each entry with a paragraph
indent. The second and any
subsequent lines begin at the next
margin. Double-space between entries.

PART TWO
Case Studies

Chapter 8

The Case Study Method

Sir Ernest Heavywether's speech in opening the case for the defence was not
a long one, but it was backed by the full force of his emphatic manner. Never,
he said, in the course of his long experience, had he known a charge of
murder to rest on slighter evidence. Not only was it entirely circumstantial,
but the greater part of it was practically unproved. Let them take the
testimony they had heard and sift it impartially.

—*Agatha Christie,* The Mysterious Affair at Styles

CASE STUDIES
The Inductive Method

A case study is a problem—hypothetical or real—presented in narrative form or in
a series of sources. The method you'll use to solve the problem in a case study is
read, evaluate, analyze, and synthesize. In a way, you are an investor weighing the
evidence that supports a claim. Like the jury listening to Agatha Christie's Sir
Ernest Heavywether, you have to consider the facts in a case study and "sift …
[them] impartially."

Case studies, as you might guess, originated in the study of law. In the late
1800s, Professor Christopher C. Langdell, Dean of the Harvard Law, school revised
the curriculum, believing that students would benefit from examining actual legal
situations rather than studying law in the abstract. Eventually, Langdell's case study
method gained widespread use in law schools. This method isn't confined to the
study of law. It's used across the disciplines—especially in business, education, and
political science. This method of study is appropriate in any course that requires
evaluation, analysis, and synthesis. It lends itself to individual work, collaborative
activities—especially class discussion—and different kinds of writing assignments.
And it allows for multiple interpretations instead of right or wrong answers.

The case studies in Part Two focus on specific problems or issues drawn from
real life. They'll take you from a specific case to issues that fit into a broad context

of related concerns. For example, the case study on Mexican artist Diego Rivera looks at the destruction of a mural Rivera painted in Rockefeller Center in 1932. The main issue at the heart of this incident, censorship, is a broad, general topic on its own, but a narrowed, focused topic in the Rivera case study. The movement from specific scenarios to broad issues is intended to facilitate invention and give you ideas for developing writing topics on your own.

Focus and Connection

The primary differences between a case study and a chapter of readings on a broad topic—for example, global warming, legalization of drugs, affirmative action—are the focus and integration of the sources. In each case study, you'll encounter a specific event or issue and you'll read sources that provide a sustained, coherent conversation—that is, writers examine specific issues that are central to the case or they actually respond to or cite one another. You'll see how writers addressing different discourse communities report information, take a position on a topic, negotiate differences, attempt to reconcile opposing points of view, and develop arguments. The case studies are intended to illustrate how using sources with similar focal points supports effective academic writing. As you develop your own topics, you should seek sources that have strong connections to one another and similar focal points. The case studies illustrate this concept and offer strategies for research.

Applying Critical Thinking Skills

You'll use the critical thinking skills you read about in Part One to address reading and writing assignments in each case study. Readings vary in purpose and audience. You'll find entries from reference books; articles from popular magazines, newspapers, and academic journals; Web pages; chapters from books; letters; and interviews. Think of these multiple sources as layers of information that take a topic from an overview for a very broad audience to a thorough, complete analysis aimed at a specialized group of readers. Readings provide different perspectives and rhetorical situations. An important problem-solving exercise in these case studies is evaluating sources. You'll encounter repetition, contradictions, ambiguities, skewed logic, and errors. You'll also find examples of effective writing that illustrate audience analysis, thorough development of ideas, effective argumentative techniques, good support for a thesis, and sound principles of organization.

In addition to reading, you'll complete informal and formal writing assignments as you work on case studies; you'll write to articulate your understanding of a topic, your perspective on an issue, or your stance in an argument. While writing assignments vary in purpose and include assignments for reflection, your primary aims will be the aims of academic writing: to inform or to persuade readers. You'll summarize and analyze readings, provide overviews of issues, reflect on your understanding of a situation, take a stand on an ethical issue, and develop arguments. You'll read, analyze, evaluate, and write to support a thesis. You'll read to become familiar with each case study, evaluate the information, analyze the problem, and address it in a paper that synthesizes sources and examines issues and multiple perspectives of the case.

Cases and Tasks

Your primary task in this practice chapter is to learn how to use the case study method. As you move from one case to another, you'll focus on a specific task in each chapter—for example, exploring a topic, listening to writers' voices, creating a historical context for a topic, reconciling different perspectives, and developing an argument. And you'll carry out a wide range of reading and writing tasks that will prepare you to draft and revise in-class and out-of-class writing assignments. You'll reflect on what you know about a topic, explain what you've learned from sources in the case studies, and synthesize sources in assignments that address a variety of rhetorical situations. Writing assignments cover a wide range: short and long papers, documented papers, letters to the editor, journal entries, and annotated bibliographies.

ORGANIZATION
Chapter Introductions

Each chapter in Part Two begins with an introduction that includes a preview of the case study and discussion of the primary task you'll be expected to complete as you work on the case. The introduction also places the case study in a broad context by introducing you to related issues and to ideas you can develop into research topics. Think of the introduction as the starting line—a place to begin reflecting on issues and exploring how you react to them initially. We've defined the case study method as read, evaluate, analyze, and synthesize. Reflection is also an important activity. You'll read other writers' opinions and you'll need to formulate your own opinions.

The Case Study

Sources in each case study discuss controversial issues and ethical problems and introduce you to the "players" in the case. In the five case studies in Part Two, you'll meet "jungle doctor" Dr. Thomas Anthony Dooley, an American hero in the late 1950s and early 1960s; Iva Toguri, who allegedly used the name Tokyo Rose as a radio announcer during World War II; civil rights leader Dr. Martin Luther King, Jr.; AIDS activist Jeff Getty; and Mexican artist Diego Rivera. Their stories are located in American culture of the present and past—from the early 1990s to as far back as the 1930s—and their experiences are connected to issues—political, social, and ethical—that are relevant to our lives today: the vulnerability of individuals caught up in international incidents, the ethics of outing homosexuals, the importance of understanding the past, the ethics of using animals in medical research, the controversy over art with political overtones. The focus on related issues that begins in the introduction continues through the case study, and connects it to a wide range of concerns. Case studies in Chapters 9–13 conclude with a selection on contemporary perspectives.

Primary and Secondary Sources

You'll refer to primary and secondary sources to construct a narrative in each case study. *Primary sources* are original sources: historical and government documents; data generated by observable events; personal interviews; surveys and questionnaires; original work by a writer of poetry or fiction; letters; journals or diaries; or any kind of firsthand account. *Secondary sources* are sources generated by primary sources. Works that discuss the sinking of the *Titanic* typically include original sources such as firsthand accounts from survivors and records from the White Star line, the company that owned the ship. These accounts rely on secondary sources as well: newspaper articles that reported information after the ship was lost or books that analyzed some aspect of the *Titanic* disaster. Academic writing usually includes both primary and secondary sources. Robert Weisbord's article in Chapter 1, "Black American Perception of the *Titanic* Disaster," for example, cites an interview with two survivors (primary source) as well as sources that interpret and analyze African-American folklore (secondary sources). The movie *Titanic* is a secondary source if your goal is research on the sinking of the ocean liner, but it's a primary source if your goal is to examine movies directed by James Cameron.

The case studies illustrate how other writers employ primary and secondary sources. It's important to you as a student doing research and evaluating sources to understand the difference between primary and secondary sources. If you know that a primary source is available and that it will be significant in a paper you are writing, consult it before you look at secondary sources. That way, your initial reactions aren't influenced by anyone else. You start fresh and explore your own ideas. Secondary sources should provide you with points of support or points of divergence—that is, ideas for you to challenge, evaluate, or interpret in a new way

Reading Case Studies

It's important to read all of the sources in a case study—primary and secondary—and to develop a thorough understanding of each case and all its complexities. Even if you're familiar with the issues, you'll want to follow the case study method in its proper order: Read, evaluate, analyze, synthesize. One of the common problems students experience is trying to jump the gun—taking a stand on an issue before reading about it, or starting writing assignments before understanding a case completely. The best way to read a case study is to read and annotate two or three sources in one sitting. That way, you'll have time to reflect on your reading. Activities described below will help you explore case studies and develop a thorough understanding of them:

Case Study Activities

Each case includes research assignments that ask you to augment sources in this book with additional library or web sources. While these assignments provide practice in research methods, they are not essential to understanding case studies, addressing problem-solving activities, or completing writing assignments. Each case provides sufficient information to be used on its own and numerous activities to help you understand the case. For example, questions for discussion call on you to share ideas about reading assignments with your classmates. Writing assignments in each case are intended to help you understand the issues and give you practice in writing for a variety of purposes and intended readers. These assignments vary from reflective and informal writing to documented papers in which you take a position on an issue, provide an overview, or develop an argument. Short writing assignments lay the groundwork for longer writing assignments. Think of the short writing assignments as avenues that take you into the heart of the case and facilitate articulation of your perspective on the issues. Two activities that will prepare you to write documented papers on the cases are freewriting and note taking.

Freewriting   Freewriting requires writing without pause during a specified time span—for example, five to ten minutes or more. This nonstop writing allows you freedom to record ideas without concern for form or surface errors. As the name suggests, freewriting can take any form—brainstorming; reacting to readings, for example, saying what you like or don't like about them; making connections with readings and ideas that come to mind. The possibilities are endless. The object is to explore your thoughts and generate ideas. You are the primary audience for your freewriting. Designate a notebook, file folder in your computer, or paper file folder for freewriting. As you work on the case studies, try freewriting after you read the introduction to a chapter. If you aren't familiar with the topic, consider first impressions, connections you make after reading the overview, questions you expect the case study to answer, or perspectives you anticipate finding.

Taking notes   The case studies are a good place to practice taking and organizing notes. Your notes should include

- *Analysis of rhetorical situations.* Note the primary aim of each source and explain the relationship of the writer to the subject and intended readers.
- *Answers to reporter's questions.* Who? What? Where? When? Why?

    Who? Be sure major "players" are clearly identified. Like the list of characters that prefaces a play, note individuals and the role they play in the case, the opinions they express, or the questions they raise.
    What? What is the case about? What is the main issue at the heart of the case?
    Where? When? Why? Answers to these questions will help you place the case in a specific historical, social, or political context.

- *Key terms and concepts.* Identify key terms and concepts and define them in your own words. This also gives you a chance to practice paraphrasing.

- *Time lines.* After you've read all the sources, compile a list of events in chronological order. An important part of understanding a narrative is making sense of the sequence of events. Create a timeline for each case study, noting month, date, and year of important events. Timelines will vary in detail.

- *Notes on multiple perspectives.* Each case study presents more than one perspective: For example, the articles on road rage in Chapter 3 give us two perspectives: (1) documented cases of aggressive driving suggest that road rage is a serious problem, and (2) statistics prove that road rage cannot be verified. Keep track of perspectives as you read and annotate. Use a system of highlighting in a specific color to mark passages where you find people agreeing or disagreeing with each other. Or create headings on a sheet of paper noting sources that take a stand for or against an issue, that play the role of negotiator, that present an overview, that offer solutions or ask questions.

- *Notes on focal points.* Examine sources and note how they share points of concern, discuss the same issues, respond directly to each other, or cite each other. For example, in the road rage articles, focal points include statistics on traffic accidents, definition of the term *road rage*, and profiles of aggressive drivers. Take a close look at focal points. They'll help you identify issues and understand the complexities of the case.

- *Summaries and bibliographical citations.* A sound method of testing your understanding of a reading is to summarize it. For practice, write bibliographical citations for each source you summarize.

Writing Assignments

At the end of each case, you'll find suggested writing assignments on the case study and assignments on related topics. The case study assignments range from freewriting activities to assignments that ask you to synthesize sources in the case study. These assignments do not require outside research, but you may want to include your own research on the topic. After you have annotated sources and completed a series of writing assignments similar to those described in this chapter, you'll be prepared for in-class and out-of-class writing assignments. Some of the assignments specify a rhetorical situation; others ask you to select your audience and determine your purpose in writing. For assignments that require documentation, you'll need to refer to Chapter 7.

Writing assignments that require library research follow the case study writing assignments. These assignments are topics related to issues raised in the case study. The suggested related topics reverse the inductive approach. From a broad, general topic, you'll develop writing assignments to complete on your own. You'll narrow the scope, identify a purpose in writing, and designate an audience. A section on brainstorming asks you to add to the list of related topics. As you work on the case studies, you'll probably have ideas of your own that develop from class discussion or your take on an issue. Add these ideas to the "brainstorming" list.

CASE STUDIES

- Center discussion on a specific issue.
- Offer sources that show connections to each other.
- Call for collaboration and discussion.
- Provide multiple perspectives.
- Raise ethical issues.
- Require decision making and critical thinking skills.

ON-LINE COURSE EVALUATIONS
Preview

The practice case study on page 291 of this chapter asks you to read sources about on-line course evaluations. It discusses an on-line evaluation system developed for students at Texas A&M and the University of Texas and presents students' and professors' perspectives on course evaluations. It also discusses the repercussions of having a consumer attitude toward higher education. One of the questions you'll need to consider as you work on this case is whether an on-line evaluation system that reserves students' anonymity further democratizes higher education or pressures faculty to give high grades and abandon rigorous course requirements.

In "What the Numbers Mean: Providing a Context for Numerical Student Evaluations of Courses," Paul A. Trout, associate professor of English at Montana State University, speculates that as many as 80 percent of colleges and universities utilize standardized in-house course evaluations that ask students to rank their professors in areas of overall knowledge of a subject, teaching effectiveness, organization, accessibility, and fairness in grading. Students often have opportunity as well to provide written responses to a faculty member. Trout explains that although reliability and validity of standardized evaluations have been studied for the last twenty years, no one seems to agree on whether they should be used in cases of promotion, retention, or salary increases. Until the advent of the Internet, student evaluations were typically used in house, seen most frequently by administrators or committees determining such matters as tenure, promotion, and raises. For students, gaining access to evaluations was difficult because if they were published they were selectively distributed. With the Internet, students have created their own systems of evaluation and made their comments about professors a matter of public record. For example, the students rank professors on a scale of 1 to 5 and justify their rating with a comment about their experience in the course. The anonymous comments range from recommendations such as "I learned more in this class than in any other; be sure to take a class with this professor" to comments that advise "avoid this professor at all costs—too much work, picky exams, strict attendance policy." Professor Trout believes that in-house written student evaluations send a clear underlying message: "Teach us less; require less." This case study asks you to think about the underlying messages on-line evaluations send.

In theory, the Texas A&M/University of Texas web site is intended to help students shop around and select faculty instead of taking pot luck. In practice, will this web site and others like it also have unintended effects on higher education? Might they lead, for example, to easier exams? fewer papers? lower standards? more jokes in class? Carol Iannone, who teaches at New York University's Gallatin School of Individualized Study, and Mark Edmundson, Professor of English at the University of Virginia, maintain that in-house written course evaluations promote an "ethos of consumerism" that is turning education into a commercial enterprise that caters primarily to entertaining students and keeping everyone happy. Will college and university faculty feel more pressure from on-line course evaluations than they have from standard in-house evaluations? And if so, what will the effects of this pressure be?

FOCUS ON RELATED ISSUES:
TECHNOLOGY—A "FAUSTIAN BARGAIN"

While the Internet and the personal computer are relatively new technological innovations, they have had profound effects on education, ranging from the manner in which students take notes (laptop or handheld computers) to the manner in which they take classes (distance education), to the construction of classrooms. Computer terminals decenter the classroom, and shift class discussion from verbal exchange to synchronized interchanges. Not too long ago, library holdings determined an institution's rating. These days we're more likely to rate educational facilities by the extent of their wiring—that is, whether they provide faculty and students with ready access to databases, e-mail, and Internet resources.

Social critic Neil Postman urges readers to consider the role of new technology in education and cautions that the discussion should take place "without the hyperactive fantasies of cheerleaders" (41). He also offers ten principles he believes students should learn about technology and its uses. Read the following excerpts from Postman and then use these principles to develop ideas for writing assignments.

Consider Postman's principles as you read about on-line course evaluations. Suggested writing assignments at the end of the case study ask you to use the ideas you generate on technology for papers you research on your own.

EXERCISE: GOING ON-LINE

If you have access to a computer, look at the on-line course evaluation sites below to get an idea of how they are set up and what students say in their evaluations:

<http://www.pickaprof.com>
Texas A&M University and University of Texas

<http://www.retrosoft.com/cte/umn>
University of Minnesota

<http://members.primary.net/~place/umsl_rate.htm>
University of Missouri St. Louis

<http://www.retrosoft.com/cte/sfsu/browse/teachers/depts/au.htm>
San Francisco State University

THE END OF EDUCATION

NEIL POSTMAN

The computer and its associated technologies are awesome additions to a culture, and they are quite capable of altering the psychic, let alone the sleeping habits of our young. But like all important technologies of the past, they are Faustian bargains, giving and taking away, sometimes in equal measure, sometimes more in one way than in another. It is strange—indeed shocking—that with the twenty-first century so closely on our heels, we can still talk about new technologies as if they were unmixed blessings, gifts, as it were, from the gods. Don't we all know what the combustion engine has done for us and against us? (41)

....

1. All technological change is a Faustian bargain. For every advantage a new technology offers, there is always a corresponding disadvantage.

2. The advantages and disadvantages of new technologies are never distributed evenly among the population. This means that every new technology benefits some and harms others.

3. Embedded in every technology there is a powerful idea, sometimes two or three powerful ideas. Like language itself, a technology predisposes us to favor and value certain perspectives and accomplishments and to subordinate others. Every technology has a philosophy, which is given expression in how the technology makes people use their minds, in what it makes us do with our bodies, in how it codifies the world, in which of our senses it amplifies, in which of our emotional and intellectual tendencies it disregards.

4. A new technology usually makes war against an old technology. It

competes with it for time, attention, money, prestige, and a "worldview."

5. Technological change is not additive; it is ecological. A new technology does not merely add something; it changes everything.

6. Because of the symbolic forms in which information is encoded, different technologies have different *intellectual* and *emotional* biases.

7. Because of the accessibility and speed of their information, different technologies have different *political* biases.

8. Because of their physical form, different technologies have different *sensory* biases.

9. Because of the conditions in which we attend to them, different technologies have different *social* biases.

10. Because of their technical and economic structure, different technologies have different *content* biases.

Source: Neil Postman, *The End of Education* (New York: Vintage, 1995) 41, 192–93.

EXERCISE: FOCUS ON WRITING

Before you read what other writers have to say about on-line course evaluations, devote ten to fifteen minutes to freewriting. Before you begin, review the preceding overview of the case and discussion of technology and education. What does the title of the case study, "Education.com," suggest to you? Explain how technology has had positive and negative effects on education. Cite specific examples from your own experience. Identify areas of study or school activities that are simplified or complicated or otherwise changed by new technology.

Education.com:
A Case Study for Practice

So what happens to those in-class evaluations we fill out, anyway? Some committee somewhere looks 'em over and files them in a dusty file cabinet?

Screw that. We want to know what our classmates think of classes and professors. What they really think. Who's hot, who's not. And we, the students, want an unbiased forum in which to express ourselves. Hence, we run the show, we say what we want, and we allow everyone access to the information.

> —*Introduction to Course and Teacher Evaluations*
> *Web page, University of Minnesota. Available at*
> *<http://www.retrosoft.com/cte/umn/>*

PICKAPROF

In April 2000, two Texas A&M University students, Chris Chilek and John Cunningham, unveiled "Pickaprof," a web site that made information previously confined to offices within Texas A&M University and the University of Texas accessible to the student body and public in general. They also provided a forum for ranking and evaluating faculty. Disclaimers explained that the web site was not associated with either university. The local newspaper in College Station, where Texas A&M is located, featured an article on Pickaprof.

PROFESSORS GRADED ON STUDENT-RUN SITE

JOHN KIRSCH

Wondering if that chemistry professor you'll have this fall is really a Doctor Death when it comes to grading students?

No problem.

Just sign on to pickaprof.com, a new student-run Web site that gives historical grade distribution data and other useful information on Texas A&M University professors.

Type in the prof's last name and first initial, click on "go," and up comes a bar chart breakdown of how the professor grades on average. In some cases, you can even get anonymous comments by former students, praising a good faculty member or criticizing individual faculty members.

"A lot of people base their class decisions on it," said Alba Almudena, an A&M junior majoring in international relations.

The site seems to be catching on. Since its official launch April 5, it's had more than 1 million hits, said Chris Chilek, an A&M student who runs the site with John Cunningham.

Which isn't to say the two busy Aggies have tapped into yet another Internet mother lode of riches right here in College Station.

In fact, they've yet to find a way to actually make money off the site, and are thinking of posting ads—if they can get any for the free service.

"You got any ideas?" Cunningham jokingly asked a reporter over a burger and fries at Duddley's Draw.

The information the two have compiled has been available previously, but in less accessible form. And national Web portals offer information about A&M professors, along with their colleagues around the country.

Chilek and Cunningham said their site gives the most complete information. And like true Aggies, they're thinking big. The site also provides information on University of Texas professors, and the two students hope to provide data on professors all over the country at some point.

All of this has drawn mixed reactions from faculty at A&M. Paul Busch, a marketing professor, said he supports the project as a way to pro-vide useful information, particularly to freshmen who aren't yet plugged into the Aggie grapevine.

Busch said Cunningham developed the Web site as part of a marketing assignment.

"It seems to me that it is making available information that already exists. They're putting it in a more convenient form. I don't have a problem," Busch said.

Tom Wehrly, a statistics professor and speaker of the faculty senate, had a more critical view.

"It's a mixed blessing. It has information that if used in context could be useful," Wehrly said. "If students use it as their only criteria, I would say it is not very good."

Chilek and Cunningham freely admit that their online information source can't replace the actual experience of sitting in a classroom with a real live professor.

"There's no way that a Web site could give someone that kind of complete information," Cunningham said.

"But we're doing our darndest to get close," said Chilek.

They said they screen out obvious personal attacks by students on individual faculty members.

William Perry, the executive associate provost at A&M, said pickaprof.com needs to be used cautiously like any other information source, online or off.

"Students just need to intelligently use all those sources," said Perry.

So far, Cunningham and Chilek have been able to get grade distribution information through the Texas Public Information Act and they said they expect to continue to do that at both A&M and UT.

There may or may not be a cloud on their horizon.

On April 5, A&M President Ray Bowen approved a faculty senate resolution that recommends that the university stop compiling class grade distribution lists, primarily out of concern over ventures such as pickaprof.com.

Perry said it isn't clear what impact that may have on Chilek and Cunningham. For their part, the two Aggie entrepreneurs said they expect to keep building the site. They noted that pickaprof.com operates off a Houston server, so it's independent of A&M.

"It's a fair thing for students to know. I don't think it's something that should be locked away." Chilek said.

Source: John Kirsch, "Professors Graded on Student-Run-Site," *Bryan-College Station Eagle* 27 Apr. 2000: A1.

EXERCISES: FOCUS ON WRITING

1. Use "Professors Graded on Sudent-Run Sites" to answer the reporter's questions:

   - Who?
   - What?
   - Where?
   - When?
   - Why

2. Summarize "Professors Graded on Sudent-Run Sites" and write a bibliographical citation for it.

3. Summarize "Professors Graded on Sudent-Run Sites" perspectives of students and faculty reported in Source 2.

While Chilek and Cunningham claim that their web site is intended to help students make educated choices when they register for classes, it's not too difficult to imagine anonymous on-line course evaluations as a venue for disgruntled students to vent their frustration. One concern of in-house evaluations is that in the hands of students who are unhappy with grades, course evaluations become a tool for getting even with a professor rather than for offering constructive feedback. In 1998, for example, Randal C. Archibold called course evaluations "Payback time" in an article that appeared in the *New York Times*.

PAYBACK TIME: GIVE ME AN 'A' OR ELSE

RANDAL C. ARCHIBOLD

Every year at about this time, just as classes are winding down, college professors begin handing out a test that could be the most important of the course.

Most important, that is, for them. It is the student evaluation.

Colleges and universities have greatly increased the use of student evaluations in recent years, and now there is concern that their widespread use may contribute to grade inflation.

"Grading leniency affects ratings," said Anthony Greenwald, a psychologist at the University of Washington. "All other things being equal, a professor can get higher ratings by giving higher grades."

Mr. Greenwald and a colleague, Gerald Gillmore, analyzed 600 course evaluations at the university and concluded that the assessments were flawed and often misused.

Their study, published last year in The Journal of Educational Psychology, showed that math and science instructors "suffer the worst under the current evaluation system and are at the bottom of the ratings because they teach tough courses, give lower grades and demand a lot of hard work," Mr. Greenwald said.

Grades have been rising at all colleges and universities but especially at elite institutions.

Not That Much Smarter

Princeton University, for example, reported in February that 83 percent of the grades between 1992 and 1995 were A's or B's, compared with 69 percent between 1973 and 1975. This occurred in the absence of compelling evidence that students were that much better prepared, according to a university report.

What is clear is that during the same time period student evaluations became much more important, according to a recent survey by Peter Seidin, a professor of management at Pace University. In 1973, 23 percent of the 600 institutions he surveyed said they used student evaluations as a factor in tenure, promotion or salary decisions. Today, the proportion has grown to 88 percent, he said.

"There is no other source as widely used as the student rating to evaluate teaching," said Mr. Seldin.

Used at some colleges since the early part of the century, student evaluations bloomed in the 1960's as a response to restive students clamoring for a greater say in their education.

They vary in form; some ask students to rate teachers on a scale of 1 to 5 on such things as lecture preparation, the helpfulness of course materials, rapport with students and fairness of grading. Others ask for written comments. Some allow both.

The results usually are distributed to the instructor and the department head. Some universities summarize the findings and make them available to students in a catalog.

At a few institutions students provide their own rating service. The Harvard Crimson newspaper's Confi-Guide, written by anonymous contributors, offers a sometimes irreverent take on the value of particular courses.

An entry on a political philosophy course reads: "The material is dry. Very dry. So dry that it's hard to imagine anything else being more difficult to get through without falling asleep. Lectures, therefore, are painful at times."

Published on and off for 70 years—and on-line in its latest incarnation—it competes with the university's official "CUE Guide," a compendium of statistics and observations about courses culled from official student evaluation forms.

The Confi-Guide has been known to "upset people a good bit," said Michael Andrade, a junior who is president of the Harvard Crimson. But the CUE Guide, he said, has the opposite problem. "The CUE guide is facts buried in objectivity," Mr. Andrade said.

William McKeatchie, an emeritus psychology professor at the University of Michigan at Ann Arbor who is widely regarded as the dean of evaluation researchers, said the preponderance of research shows that teachers who earned high ratings by students also earned high marks from peers, neutral observers and other evaluators.

Imperfect Measure

The evaluations are often the best—if imperfect—measure of teaching ability. Professor McKeatchie said. Still, he has reservations about their widespread use.

Colleges often set arbitrary standards for evaluation results without considering the nature of the course, the specific circumstances involved, such as the number of students in the course," he said. "It's like an intelligence test. They are misused a lot."

Source: Randal C. Archibold, "Payback Time: Give Me an 'A' or Else," *New York Times* 24 May 1998: 5 WK [*The Week in Review*].

EXERCISES: READING AND RESPONDING

1. Determine the rhetorical situation for the in-house course evaluations professors give to students at the end of the semester. Is there a secondary audience? If you have completed in-house course evaluations and included a written response, explain whether you considered a secondary audience.

2. Whom do you think students envision as their primary audience when they complete course evaluations? Explain why you agree or disagree with Archibold's description of course evaluations as "payback time."

3. Identify the different perspectives on course evaluation Archibold presents. Explain whether you agree or disagree with these perspectives.

4. Explain whether you agree or disagree with the claim that high grades or leniency results in high course evaluations.

EXERCISE: GOING ON-LINE

Look at the *Harvard Crimson Confi-Guide* on grades:
<http://www.thecrimson.harvard.edu/configuide/gradesgame.shtml>.

What does this information suggest about students' assumptions about their education? learning? academic achievement?

In "The Professor's Lament," Carol Iannone, a faculty member at New York University's Gallatin School of Individualized Study, claims that "these are unhappy times for" faculty in higher education. One of the main reasons, she explains is the "consumer expertise" that empower students when they see themselves as being "buyer[s] in a buyer's market."

THE PROFESSOR'S LAMENT

CAROL IANNONE

It is hardly news that these are unhappy times for the American professor. Thanks to a combination of factors—tighter university, budgets, deferred retirements, the demands of affirmative action—good jobs have all but dried up in many academic fields. Colleges increasingly staff their classrooms by drawing on a poorly compensated proletariat of "adjuncts": hapless Ph.D.'s who have not yet given up on the possibility of securing a full-time position, or even a coveted tenure-track post.

Of late, a new grievance has been added to the list. As one educator recently lamented in the *Christian Science Monitor,* colleges these days have become "youth resorts," complete with "pools, hockey rinks, catered meals, student centers, [and] television rooms." Worse, complains another in the *Chronicle of Higher Education,* our institutions of higher learning are more eager to please students than to instruct them. Because of a new emphasis on student-friendly pedagogy, the professor has become "a congenial traffic officer, ... a 'guide on the side' rather than a 'sage on the stage.'" As *The New York Times* reported earlier this year, the signs of this trend include not only grade inflation—of Weimar-like proportions—but the growing importance of student evaluations in assessing professors for retention and promotion.

On many American campuses, it would now seem, the kids are in charge. But this is no accident. "Democratizing" the university was, after all, a chief aim of the campus protests of the 1960's, led in many instances by the same men and women who today constitute the professoriate. And it is also no surprise that, faced with the unpleasant consequences of their youthful desires, some of these tenured radicals should now be having second thoughts. Unfortunately, these second thoughts stop far short of where they should lead.

A prime example of the phenomenon I have in mind is an extraordinarily revealing article by Mark Edmundson, a professor of English at the University of Virginia, which appeared late last year in *Harper's.* Disturbed by his most recent experience with the anonymous, standardized evaluation forms that his students fill out at the end of each semester, Edmundson writes with soul-baring candor about the state of his profession and liberal-arts education in general.

It is not that Edmundson himself fears bad evaluations. On the contrary, he assures us, he knows that once his students have finished rating him on a scale of 1 to 5 and scribbled some remarks about his abilities in various categories, he will find yet again that, by their standards, he is a success: his course will be commended as "enjoyable," and he will be praised for being "interesting," for his "relaxed and tolerant ways," for his "sense of humor and capacity to connect the arcana of the subject matter with current culture."

Indeed, it is this very success that distresses him, smacking as it does of "calm consumer expertise" on their side, salesmanship and hucksterism on his. The very forms on which his students register their reactions are "reminiscent of the sheets circulated after the TV pilot has just played to its sample audience in Burbank." They reflect the "serene belief" that the function of a teacher, not to mention the function of what he teaches, is "to divert, entertain, and interest."

This "ethos of consumerism," Edmundson argues, pervades the contemporary university, where faculty and administration relations with students are invariably conducted in "a solicitous, nearly servile tone." Before they are even admitted as freshmen, students are "flooded with advertising, pictures, testimonials, videocassettes,

CD-ROM's," all designed to lure them to campus. Once safely enrolled, they are kept satisfied by permissive grading (especially in the humanities), easy requirements for majors, and the option of withdrawing from a class well after the semester has begun. Students are "shocked," says Edmundson, "if their professors don't reflexively suck up to them."

The result has been to create an academic Lake Wobegone, a place, Edmundson writes, "where almost no one fail[s], everything [is] enjoyable, and everyone [is] nice." The only thing lost amid all this complacency is "an education that matters."

And what has brought us to this pass? Demography, Edmundson avers, bears some of the blame. Having expanded to accommodate the postwar baby boom, universities now find themselves in fierce competition to attract the members of a smaller college-age population; as a consequence, today's students are buyers in a buyer's market.

The chief culprit, however, is not demography but "American culture writ large"—a culture that has become "ever more devoted to consumption and entertainment, to the using and using up of goods and images." Edmundson admits that the capitalist system is not the only factor at work here. Some responsibility also falls on the radicals of his own 1960's generation, whose idealistic search for pleasure and gratification devolved into a mere quest for commodities, thus stoking the very system they so ardently wished to overturn.

What is clearly not at fault for the crisis of liberal-arts education, in Edmundson's view, is the "democratization" the radicals of the 60's brought to student-faculty relations—something he does not even so much as mention. He does, however, discuss another related development that also came in with the 1960's and their aftermath: the "peculiar ideas" that travel under the banners of multiculturalism, deconstruction, feminism, and queer theory. Indeed, Edmundson is himself among the promoters of these new ideas, having edited a collection of essays, *Wild Orchids and Trotsky* (1993), intended to showcase outstanding examples of just such cutting-edge scholarship.

Edmundson concedes that many of the new theories have been taken too far and have had a leveling effect both on learning itself and on students' attitudes toward the educational enterprise. Multiculturalism has degenerated into uncritical ethnic celebration. So-called "cultural studies" have brought the tawdriest effusions of popular culture into the classroom. And thanks to deconstruction, students of literature have been turned into "sophisticated debunkers," rejecting all claims of greatness and genius. Still, he hastens to conclude, these unfortunate developments are not the real source of the problem. "It's not that a left-wing professorial coup has taken over the university," he writes. Rather, on American campuses "left-liberal politics have collided with the ethos of consumerism," and the "consumer ethos is winning."

For anyone with experience in today's colleges, much in Edmundson's account will strike a deep chord of recognition. Consumerism has become the controlling ethos of the university, and he captures its spirit with vulgar precision when he says that professors have had to learn "never to piss the customers off."

And yet customers and the consumer mentality were not invented yesterday; they have always been with us, and so have those who decry their effects on the human spirit. To go back no farther than the late 40's and early 50's, works like *The Man in the Gray Flannel Suit* and *The Lonely Crowd* warned Americans that they were in danger of losing their souls to things and goods, to status and acquisition. In those days, however, the universities somehow remained largely untouched by what Carlyle called the culture of "profit and loss," managing for the most part to form a refuge for pursuing the life of the mind.

Edmundson himself provides a glimpse of these institutions as they once were, recalling with fondness the no-nonsense college catalogues he perused as a high-schooler, with their implicit and unapologetic assumption that the university operated on teachers' terms. Those teachers believed, not without reason, that they were introducing students to what was best and most lasting in their cultural tradition, works that embodied such truth and beauty as human beings are capable of approximating. Instruction in this tradition was regarded as both morally and intellectually edifying— as well as a necessary prerequisite to testing, challenging, and refining what had been handed down over the generations.

But this is—precisely—the understanding of liberal education that students were rebelling against in the 1960's when they demanded a curriculum more "relevant" to their own experience, an experience they understood to consist by and large of oppression at the hands of authority. The old books—the "canon"—were part and parcel of that authority. Only by casting them aside, or by learning to read them through the lens of the new, liberationist credos, could one begin to call oneself educated. In the course of the 1970's, with the arrival at American universities of various pseudo-sophisticated theories imported from France and Germany, the slogans of the 1960's became transformed into the now-familiar vocabulary of the undergraduate seminar: Eurocentrism, logocentrism, phallocentrism, marginality, alterity, hegemony, indeterminacy, and all the rest. Today it is commonplace in the humanities to hear morality, language, even reason itself dismissed as tools of elite privilege, while the word *truth* is almost universally consigned to question-begging quotation marks.

In the classroom, this revolution has had predictable consequences. Taught that there are no truths above them, and no timeless works with which they must be acquainted, students now simply search for what pleases, much as they might at the local shopping mall. Since nothing is or can be defended as priceless, everything has its price, and sooner or later, everything goes on sale.

Edmundson, invoking a favored shibboleth of today's academic radicals, lamely proposes that today's teachers learn to "subvert" the new consumerist attitudes of their students. That is hardly likely to happen unless teachers have something to fill the void, unless they can direct students to books and thinkers whom they firmly believe to be intrinsically worthy of attention, and unless they are prepared to defend that belief. Until that day arrives, students will go on playing the role that has been assigned to them by their elders, including professors like Mark Edmundson who are frank enough to acknowledge the wasteland they inhabit but cannot bring themselves to repudiate the ideas—their ideas—that have so plainly brought it about.

Source: Carol Iannone, "The Professor's Lament," *Commentary* 5 Nov. 1998: 54–56.

EXERCISES: READING AND RESPONDING

1. Identify Iannone's thesis.

2. In your opinion, does the evidence she presents provide adequate support for the thesis? Explain why or why not.

3. Identify the different sources Iannone synthesizes.

4. At what point does she mention course evaluations? What is her perspective on course evaluations?

5. Iannone reacts to an article by Mark Edmundson. On what points does she agree and disagree with Edmundson?

6. What is Edmundson's perspective on course evaluations?

7. Explain whether you agree or disagree with the unnamed educator Iannone cites who claims that institutions of higher learning are more eager to please students than to instruct them. Cite examples from your own experience or observation that support or challenge this claim.

8. Define the term "ethos of consumerism" as it is used in Iannone's article.

9. Whom does Iannone hold responsible for the ethos of consumerism? Explain whether you agree or disagree with Iannone's explanation of the effects of the "ethos of consumerism."

10. In your opinion, are universities "democratized?" If your answer is *yes*, explain how the Internet and course evaluations might have contributed to a democratized college or university. If your answer is *no*, speculate on what it would take to democratize colleges and universities.

11. Do appeals to logic, ethics, or emotions dominate Iannone's article?

EXERCISES: FOCUS ON WRITING

1. Devote ten to fifteen minutes to freewriting. Explain whether you agree or disagree with Iannone's perspective on the present state of higher education, or use this exercise to determine your stance on the issues raised so far about student evaluations and the current state of higher education.

FOCUS ON RELATED ISSUES:
AMERICAN CULTURE—DUMBING UP
OR DUMBING DOWN?

Several sources in the case study bemoan the present state of higher education and claim that standards are lower, grade inflation higher, and requirements less rigorous than they were twenty years ago. If higher education were in a decline, one might reason, it would logically follow that American culture would suffer the same fate. In a May 24, 1999, essay in *Time*, "In Fact, We're Dumbing Up," Pico Iyer writes, "In certain respects the country around us seems to be dumbing up, presenting us on a daily basis with texts and thoughts that give no indication of a nation suffering from attention deficit disorder"(100). She cites recent publications on the best-seller list—Harold Bloom's scholarly work on Shakespeare and a book on the compilers of the Oxford English Dictionary—as evidence. While she admits that the contemporary imagination is on the verge of being impoverished, she rejects the notion that we've abandoned the classics, rejected the humanities, and privileged theme parks over museums and retreats that offer stillness and time for reflection.

Is American education and therefore American culture dumbing up or dumbing down? Try to support Iyer's perspective and identify individuals, events, publications, trends, and anything else you're aware of that provide evidence that we're dumbing up.

---

2. Summarize "Give me an 'A"or Else" and "The Porfessor's Lament" and write bibliographical citations for each source.

3. Read the article by Mark Edmundson that Iannone refers to in her article: Mark Edmundson, "On the Uses of a Liberal Education I: As Lite Entertainment" *Harper's* 295 (Sept. 1997): 39–49.

   Compare passages in Edmundson's article to summaries, paraphrases, and direct quotations in Iannone's article. Explain whether Iannone offers an accuate account of Edmundson's stance or whether her account includes some inaccuracies.

In a 1999 article in the *New York Times*, Ian Zack sounded the alarm about on-line course evaluations. This article generated two letters to the editor. They are included here after Zack's article.

TO PROFESSORS' DISMAY, RATINGS BY STUDENTS GO ON LINE

IAN ZACK

John Moriarty, a 21-year-old business major at the University of Texas, was eager to enroll in a marketing course whose "syllabus sounded really intriguing."

But first, like many collegians, he sat down at his computer, logged on to the Internet and availed himself of a new on-line resource: course evaluations written anonymously by other students.

The critiques, in the style of brief movie reviews, said the professor in question was distant, his research outdated and his lectures uninspiring. And if the mini-commentaries were not blunt enough; the numerical ratings were, hovering around 2 on a scale of 1 to 10.

"I thought, 'Oh, boy, that's probably not a good course to take.'" Mr. Moriarity recalled.

And so it goes at colleges across the country. As students sign up for fall classes, they are turning the tables on the teachers who have long held sway over their grade point averages and job prospects. Emboldened by the communal power and the democratic ethos of cyberspace, they are heading to Web sites where they can lambaste professors they deem poor, sing the praises of those they like and scout out courses before adding them to their schedules.

Some of these sites are "official," maintained by the college itself. Others are run by student organizations or even individual students. And in at least one case, computer access to course evaluations has become a commercial venture.

Many professors are uneasy about the trend, fearing that the evaluations will be used as retribution by bad students or, as one faculty member put it, become like "Nielsen ratings for higher education." Some worry, too, that universities will begin using them when deciding on raises and promotions.

"Faculty are suspicious of numerical evaluations because they reflect popularity and enthusiasm of delivery more than they reflect the knowledge of the professor or the professor's high academic standards," said Mark Goor, a special-education professor at George Mason University in Fairfax, Va., where a course evaluation Web site went up this spring.

"Typically faculty with high standards will get low evaluations because students get angry at them." Professor Goor added, in a criticism common among faculties.

Actually there is nothing much new in themselves about student course evaluations. For decades, students have filled out their official course evaluation forms with a No. 2 pencil on the final day of the semester. In most cases, though, these are seen only by the professor and the administration, which uses them to assess its faculty and provide the members some feedback.

But some universities, like George Mason and Northwestern, now have their own official rating Web sites. And elsewhere, unofficial sites run by students have sprung up, fed by reviews from anonymous classmates.

What makes professors especially uneasy is that although some of the Web sites can be viewed only by those using their university's server, the critiques' presence on the Internet most often makes them accessible to a vast public. And the reviewer reaching that vast public could well be a disgruntled student eager to even the score for some real or imagined slight. In fact, since the reviewer is anonymous, it may be that he has not even taken the course he is pillorying.

George Mason has one of the more polite sites, created by the provost's office at the insistence of student leaders. It provides only numerical ratings, on a professor's course preparation, grading fairness and motivation, for example.

Students at Virginia Tech, on the other hand, created their own Web site last year after failing to persuade administrators to release official course evaluations. That site offers student commentaries on hundreds of courses. It also lists grade distributions, so that students can determine in advance how many A's, B's and F's a particular professor is likely to give. The students who maintain the site buy the grade statistics from the university for several hundred dollars a year.

Some of the reviewers at the Virginia Tech site pull few punches. Of a biology class, for instance, one student wrote, "Break out the coffee and Vivarin cause this one can bore a tick off a dog." Another student said of a computer science professor: "He constantly scolds and attempts to verbally intimidate students. He constantly rambles on and on about his supposed expertise, however it was never availed to the class."

Students who read such reviews say they typically take them with a grain of salt, and there are a fair share of positive, even stellar, reviews as well.

Still, Kathy K. Franklin, an assistant professor of higher education at the University of Arkansas at Little Rock, says the "student as consumer" approach underlying the critiques may paint a false picture of what is happening of value in the classroom.

"Consumers typically will not tell a retailer, 'Gee, you did a good job today,'" Professor Franklin said. "But let the least little thing go wrong, and they'll tell you in a heartbeat. If evaluations are negative and broadcast publicly, then you'll have faculty who will never do anything creative again."

Professor Franklin, who studies student attitudes toward college, also noted that popular teachers were not always the best teachers, or the ones with the most lasting impact.

"Education is not a joy ride," she said. "It is not a thrill park experience."

Some professors have even raised the prospect that evaluations that seem to amount to personal attacks might be deemed libel, and in fact Web site creators have sought legal advice before going on line. In one case, professors at the City College of San Francisco threatened, but did not file, a suit against students who had created a course evaluation site, according to the Student Press Law Center, a Washington group that advises student media organizations on legal matters.

Source: Ian Zack, "Ratings by Students Go On-Line," *New York Times* 1 Sep. 1999: 9B.

PROFESSOR SMITH'S ADVICE TO COLLEGES

MARK BERNKOPF

To the Editor:

A few professors seem concerned about Web sites that publish student evaluations of their teaching (news article, Sept. 1). Perhaps they should approach this feedback with an open mind and greater confidence.

Adam Smith, himself a university lecturer, might well have lauded

this market force. In his day, professors at some British universities were paid directly by their students; Smith believed that this practice encouraged high-quality instruction.

Student feedback is, of course, subjective. Yet so are all such evaluations—including grades. On-line publishing of student evaluations might bring some balance to the longtime tradition of "publish or perish." Research has a vital role at our universities. Ultimately, however, a university cannot be a place of light, liberty and learning without good teaching.

MARK BERNKOPF

Arlington, Va., Sept. 2, 1999..

Source: Mark Bernkopf, "Professor Smith's Advice to Colleges," letter. *New York Times* 5 Sep. 1999: 10.

STUDENTS AS CONSUMERS

ANOUAR MAJID

To the Editor:

"To Professors' Dismay, Ratings by Students Go on Line" (news article, Sept. 1) alludes to the troubling trend of thinking of students as consumers. To the extent that students prefer to be entertained, such an analogy holds true. But there is a crucial difference between selling candy or clothes in a store and teaching. While teachers must do their best to excite students in learning, they do not "sell" knowledge. The acquisition of knowledge is ultimately a self-generated activity and cannot be bought.

It may well be that students shaped by the prevailing consumer ethos find it hard to pay for something that they ultimately have to do. Though college administrators designate students as consumers in an attempt to empower them and recognize their rights, the analogy may create expectations that could undermine the learning process. Students are not consumers; they are learners.

ANQUAR MAJID

Portland, Me., Sept. 2, 1999

The writer is an associate professor of literature at the University of New England.

Source: Anouar Majid, "Students as Consumers," letter. *New York Times* 5 Sep. 1999: 10.

EXERCISES: READING AND RESPONDING

1. Identify the different perspectives on on-line course evaluations Zack presents. Explain whether you agree or disagree with these perspectives.

2. What is the composite picture of students' attitudes toward on-line course evaluations created in this article? What is the composite picture of faculty reactions to on-line evaluations?

3. What assumptions does Zack make about his intended readers? Cite specific passages that illustrate your response.

4. Griffin Davis talks about students being empowered and using the Internet to make "choices about how they spend their money." Explain whether you consider yourself a consumer and whether you consider a college course a product for sale.

5. On what points do the letters to the editor agree and disagree with Zack?

6. What new points do these letters raise?

7. Explain whether you agree or disagree with Bernkopf and Majid.

EXERCISE: FOCUS ON WRITING

Summarize "To Professors' Dismay" and the letters by Mark Bernkopf and Anouar Majid, and write bibliographical citations for each source.

The associate editor of *The Daily Texan*, the student newspaper published at the University of Texas, wrote the following article shortly after Zack's article was published.

FAIL YOUR TEACHER

BRIAN WINTER

Some professors don't like to be graded.

In the Sept. 1 edition of *The New York Times*, George Mason University professor Mark Goor vented his displeasure over the posting of teacher evaluations on the internet. "Faculty are suspicious of numerical evaluations because they reflect popularity and enthusiasm of delivery more than … knowledge of the professor or the professor's high academic standards."

So a numerical grade doesn't always accurately reflect performance? Ah, sweet irony. Welcome to our world.

While these scores certainly do not provide a totally comprehensive evaluation of a professor's teaching ability, they can be a valuable, informative tool during class registration. By accessing the results of course-instructor surveys on the Internet, students may learn whether a class is taught by a dynamic lecturer or a burned-out product of the tenure system. Attempts to restrict the availability of these surveys would diminish a valuable resource and thus violate the consumer rights of students.

Professors didn't really get too jumpy about their end-of-semester "final exam" until a couple years ago when their students' tirades started showing up online. Before the proliferation of the Internet, students just filled in Scantron bubbles and scrawled some remarks with a No. 2 pencil. While these evaluations did factor into tenure considerations, at least universities didn't widely release the results to the general public, especially students.

Now, when choosing their classes, students can simply log on to the Internet and read every rant and rave about any given professor. Teachers especially bite their nails about the numerical grades, which ask students to score their instructors on a variety of different areas, from course content to office hour availability.

Exasperated professors point out that the best instructors aren't always the most popular ones. True enough, but contrary to their belief, most students are smart enough to recognize the difference between "tough" and "oppressive," or "knowledgeable" and "monotonous." Students talk all the time about that class that's "really hard, but totally worth it."

Online course-instructor surveys are best used as one tool out of many when choosing classes. Combined with other available resources, students can actively better their education by selecting a popular, well-respected professor. For those instructors scared by the Information Age, the only remaining question is: What have you got to hide?

Source: Brian Winter, "Fail Your Teacher," *The Daily Texan* 9 Sep. 1999.

In the following article published in *College Student Journal*, Stephen B. Fortson and William E. Brown, professors in the College of Education an d Human Services at Wright State University, look at graduate students' course evaluations.

BEST AND WORST UNIVERSITY INSTRUCTORS: THE OPINIONS OF GRADUATE STUDENTS

STEPHEN B. FORTSON AND WILLIAM E. BROWN

Abstract

One hundred and fifteen graduate level students were asked to identify a variable that most influenced their choice of "best" instructor. They were also asked the same question about their "worst" instructor. Each respondent was then asked to describe their "best" and "worst" instructor in one sentence. These responses were categorized into common themes. Using a variety of teaching methods, a sense of humor, and good course organization were perceived as most influencing "best" choice. Poor course organization was the characteristic that most influenced students' choice of their "worst" instructor.

Introduction

In the 1990's Americans have become very conscious of the quality of the goods they consume. The practice of being a conscious consumer has also extended into the realm of higher education. What this means for institutions of higher learning and their faculty is that students are concerned with getting the highest quality instruction for their money.

Most colleges and universities use course evaluations to determine the quality of teaching of their instructors. These questionnaires are often given just prior to or following the final examination. Many students have difficulty focusing on the

Focus on Related Issues:
Anonymity and Rhetorical Situations

In Chapter 1, you read about the relationships between the writer, intended readers, and the subject that create the communication triangle. In electronic communication, writers frequently have the opportunity to remain anonymous to their readers. How does anonymity affect a rhetorical situation? Does it dissolve the traditional concept of a discourse community? In particular, think about how electronic communication changes how we construct ourselves in a rhetorical situation as readers and writers. Does it create a raceless, classless, genderless community? What does a discourse community gain when identities are hidden? What does it lose? Should we be concerned about the level of anonymity on the Internet? Should we be concerned that the push for regulation of the Internet will eventually make anonymity difficult?

strengths and weaknesses of their instructors at that particular time because of anxieties related to their final grade. This research effort sought to obtain reliable, valid, and useful information on the characteristics of the best and worst instructors in one graduate program.

Review of Literature

The literature on teaching evaluation is extensive (Broder & Dorfman, 1994; Feldman, 1978, 1988; Cohen, 1981; Alciatore & Alciatore, 1979). A central point of investigation in most of these studies is the validity of student evaluations. There are several variables that can impact the validity of student's evaluations of their instructors. Some examples of these variables include the confidentiality of the evaluations, secondary motivations, and cultural, gender, and/or age bias. Another important factor is the potential mismatch between what students consider good teaching versus the professor's perceptions of good

teaching. These issues of validity and perception can create problems in the evaluation process for both students and instructors.

The response of institutions of higher learning and researchers to the issues of bias have varied. Some institutions and researchers have argued that the issue of bias is overstated, and common in the process of any subjective evaluation (Kulik & McKeachie, 1975). Other researchers and institutions have resorted to additional methods of evaluation, such as peer review, course revision and updating, and measures of student achievement: (Marlin & Niss, 1980; Broder & Dorman, 1994).

Given the consumer driven society that exists today in western society, most institutions would be very hesitant to eliminate student evaluations completely, in spite of the inherent problems with bias and perception. Furthermore, having insight into which characteristics graduate students like and dislike about their professors can be helpful in tailoring a teaching style that is student oriented. This current study looks at eight central instructor characteristics and ask students to describe which qualities made their instructor either the best or worst in their degree program.

Procedure

One hundred and fifteen graduate education students were asked to identify one classroom variable they felt most represented their "best" professor [see Figure 8.1]. Each student was then asked to state, in one sentence, what made that instructor their "best" choice [see Figure 8.2].

The same eight choices in Figure 8.1 were then presented as antonyms and students were asked to identify the one classroom variable that epitomized their worst professor [see Figure 8.3]. Finally, the students

Number of Students	%	Category
24	21	1. Good course organization.
2	2	2. Fair grading procedure.
3	3	3. Good textbook selection.
1	0	4. Course material was not too difficult.
4	3	5. Course material was not too easy.
42	37	6. Instructor's variety of teaching methods.
35	30	7. Instructor's sense of humor and the class was enjoyable.
5	4	8. Instructor was available for help.

FIGURE 8.1 Categorized Responses to "What made this instructor your best choice?"

Number of Students	%	Category
17	15	1. Lectures were interesting.
9	8	2. Instructor was competent.
11	10	3. Course was well organized.
3	3	4. Grading methods were fair.
9	8	5. Instructor used a variety of teaching methods.
5	4	6. Instructor used "real life" examples.
8	7	7. Instructor was humorous and made learning fun.
5	4	8. Instructor presented the material clearly.
11	10	9. Instructor could relate to students.
5	4	10. Instruction was directly related to work experiences.

FIGURE 8.2 Categorized Responses to "What made this instructor your best choice?"

were asked to state in one sentence, what made that instructor their "worst" choice [See Figure 8.4].

Figures [8.1 and 8.3] simply contain a count of the number of students who chose one of the eight variables which describe their "best" and "worst" instructor. Figures [8.2 and 8.4] are the result of categorizing the student responses as they appeared. Some subjectivity is recognized in this categorization process.

Summary

Eighty-seven percent of the sample chose the following three variables to describe their best professor [see Figure 8.1]. Those variables were: 1) instructor used a variety of teaching methods; 2)

Number of Students	%	Category
48	42	1. Poor course organization.
10	9	2. Unfair grading procedures.
0	0	3. Poor textbook selection.
5	4	4. Course material was too difficult.
2	2	5. Course material was too easy.
32	28	6. Instructor limited in variety of teaching methods.
13	11	7. Instructor did not have a sense of humor and class was not enjoyable
3	3	8. Instructor was not available for help outside of class.

FIGURE 8.3 Categorized Responses to "What made this instructor your worst choice?"

Number of Students	%	Category
9	14	1. Instructor was boring.
16	25	2. Poor course organization.
5	6	3. Instructor did not know course material.
3	5	4. Instructor spent too much time lecturing on irrelevant material
3	5	5. Unfair grading procedure.
9	14	6. Instructor could not relate to students.
8	12	7. Instructor taught straight from the textbook.
6	9	8. No variety in teaching method.
2	3	9. Instructor was narcissistic.
3	5	10. Course material was presented in an unclear fashion.
2	3	11. Instructor let students do most of the teaching.

FIGURE 8.4 Categorized Responses to "What made this instructor your worst choice?"

instructor had a sense of humor and the class was enjoyable; and 3) instructor had good course organization. These results are similar to those of Brown, Tomlin and Fortson (1996) who used the same methodology to study undergraduate student preferences of "best and worst" professor. In the earlier study, 87% of the respondents also preferred these three variables (Brown et al., 1996).

When the "best" responses were categorized after being written in sentence form (see Figure 8.2), 17 students preferred an instructor who was interesting, while 22 students (11 each) said that the most important characteristic was "good course organization" and "the instructor could relate well to students." In comparing the results in Figure [8.2] to that of the earlier study of Brown et al. (1996), it seems that the majority of undergraduates and graduates alike, identified characteristics that related to instructional variety, enthusiasm, motivation, and concern for student success as their main criteria. From the results of these studies, clearly both graduate and undergraduate students connect teaching excellence to how well a course is organized, and presented.

The "worst" instructor choice (see Figure 8.3) was dominated by the variable, "Poor course organization." Forty-one percent of the students surveyed selected this variable as the characteristic they least liked in an instructor. Undergraduate students in the Brown et al. (1996) study seem to concur with their graduate counterparts, in that 41% of them also choose poor course organization as the variable they liked the least. Students in this study also cited "limited variety of teaching methods" as a major factor in the selection of the worst instructor.

When categorizing the one sentence descriptors of the "worst" professor, most students varied in what they described as poor instruction (see Figure 8.4). Again, poor course organization was listed as a major problem by 25% of the sample. Fourteen percent of the students said that "the instructor being boring" was a major consideration for worst instructor, while another 14% said that an "inability to relate to students" was the reason for their choice.

When considering graduate or undergraduate students, professors must address some core issues in their instruction. Students seem to want instructors who can organize their course material, use a variety of teaching methods, and can inject humor into their lectures.

While clearly course organization is a goal worthy of all university professors, variety in teaching methods and humor involves other factors. Typically, it takes an experienced instructor to incorporate both variety and humor into their teaching style. Furthermore, neither humor nor variety are necessities in the delivery of academic information. However, those professors concerned about keeping their students interested and engaged should also consider developing these attributes.

When considering the importance of student evaluations, professors must begin to address the needs of their students. In the 1990's, the mere transfer of knowledge is not enough, students want to be entertained, understood, and motivated while they learn. Instructors who can fit this "bill" will be rated higher than those who cannot. The significance of these student preferences for professors is that if you want to be perceived as a good instructor by your students, you must go beyond the essential delivery of course content. In other words, it is not what you teach, but instead, how you teach.

References

Alciatore, R. T. & Alciatore, P. L. (1979). Consumer reactions to college teaching. Improving College and University Teaching. 27(2), 93–95.

Broder, J. M. & Dorfman, J. H. (1994). Determinants of teaching quality: What's important to students? Research in Higher Education. 35(2), 235–249.

Brown, W., Tomlin, J. & Fortson, S. (1996). Best and worst university teachers: The opinion of undergraduate students. College Student Journal. 30(4), 431–434.

Cohen, P. A. (1981). Student rating of instruction and student achievement: A meta-analysis of multi-section validity studies. Review of Educational Research. 51(3), 281–309.

Feldman, K. A. (1978). Course characteristics and college students' ratings of their teachers: What we know and what we don't. Research in Higher Education. 9(3), 199–242.

Feldman, K. A. (1988). Effective college teaching from the students' and faculty's view: Matched or mismatched priorities. Research in Higher Education. 30(6), 291–344.

Kulik, J. A., & McKeachie, W. J. (1975). The evaluation of teachers in higher education. In F. N. Kerlinger (ed.), Review in Higher Education 3, 210–240.

Marlin, J. W. & Niss, J. F. (1980). End-of-course evaluations as indicators of student learning and instructor effectiveness. Journal of Economic Education 11(2), 16–27.

Source: Stephen B. Fortson and William E. Brown, "Best and Worst University Instructors: The Opinions of Graduate Students," *College Student Journal* Dec. 1998: 572–76.

EXERCISES: READING AND RESPONDING

1. Explain how "Best and Worst University Instructors" differs from other sources in format, organization, content, and tone. How do you account for these differences? Identify any other differences you perceive in this source and others in the practice case study.

2. Other sources in the practice case study focus on undergraduates' response to course evaluations. Explain how Fortsom and Brown does or does not reinforce issues raised in other sources.

3. Review the data Fortson and Brown present. Explain whether they validate, contradict, or raise questions about claims other sources make.

4. Fortson and Brown explain that several variables affect the validity of course evaluations. Identify the variables they discuss. Explain whether you agree or disagree that these variables affect validity of course evaluations. Can you think of other variables the authors omitted?

5. The evidence this source presents is different from evidence included in other sources. Explain whether you consider this evidence credible and reliable.

6.Summarize "Fail Your Teacher" and "Best and Worst University Instructors" and write bibliographical citations for each source.

EVALUATING AND ANALYZING THE CASE STUDY

EXERCISES: THINKING CRITICALLY

1. Identify the rhetorical situation for each source in the practice case study.

2. The Pickaprof web site is a primary source for this case study. Identify any other sources in the case study that are primary sources. Identify secondary sources. Be prepared to explain why you classify a source as one or the other.

3. "To Professors' Dismay, Ratings by Students Online" is a focal point in the practice case study. Notice that it's mentioned in other sources. Remember, focal points can be recurring issues, people who are quoted in different sources, studies cited in one or more sources, or books and articles referred to in several sources. Review sources in this case and identify focal points or connections that link one source to another

4. Make a list of key players in this case. Be prepared to share your list with your classmates.

WRITING ABOUT THE CASE STUDY

EXERCISES: FOCUS ON WRITING

1. Imagine that someone at your college or university has started an on-line faculty evaluation system. Write a letter to the editor of your school newspaper explaining why you would or would not encourage students to post evaluations.

2. Conduct a survey that asks students if they think of themselves as consumers and of courses as products when they register for courses. Survey at least fifty to seventy-five students. Write a paper that reacts to Carol Iannone's article, "The Professor's Lament." Summarize the article, and explain why you believe students do or do not express an "ethos of consumerism." Use the results of your survey to support your claims.

3. In a paper that cites a minimum of three sources from the practice case study, write a paper that presents at least two perspectives on on-line course evaluation.

4. In a paper that cites a minimum of five sources from the practice case study, develop an argument that supports one of the following claims:

   • The on-line course evaluation system that reserves students' anonymity is a device to further democratize higher education.

   • The on-line course evaluation system is a device to pressure faculty into giving high grades and abandoning rigorous course requirements.

WRITING ABOUT RELATED ISSUES

EXERCISES: FOCUS ON WRITING

1. Select a topic from the list below or develop a similar topic. In a paper that cites a minimum of five library sources, explain how this technological innovation is used in higher education, when and why it was adopted, and why it is or isn't a "Faustian bargain."

   Brainstorming: Technology and Education
   - On-Line Library Card Catalogs
   - Electronic Data Bases in Libraries
   - Telephone Course Registration
   - Distance Education
   - Computer Classrooms
   - Surveillance Cameras
   - Televised Conferences
   - Copy Machines
   - Calculators
   - Spell-Check
   - Palm PilotsSurveillance Cameras

2. In a paper that cites a minimum of five sources, explain why you agree or disagree with one of Neil Postman's ten principles of technology (Source 1). Refer to a specific technology in your argument. Think of specific kinds of technology for the broad categories listed below.

   Brainstorming: Technology
   - Safety
   - Security/Law Enforcement
   - wireless
   - Laser
   - Exercise
   - Entertainment
   - Agriculture
   - Military
   - Home and Garden
   - Medical
   - Energy

3. One of the related issues in the practice case study is authorial anonymity. Select a book published anonymously that created controversy because of authorial anonymity. Explain whether the identity of the work was ever revealed and why the author chose to publish anonymously.

Chapter 9

Exploring a Topic

If a man will begin with certainties, he shall end in doubts; but if he will be content to begin with doubts, he shall end in certainties.

—*Francis Bacon,* The Advancement of Learning

READING, WRITING, AND EXPLORING

At some point in your academic career, you've probably been assigned a topic you knew little or nothing about or you've selected a topic primarily because it sounded interesting and you wanted to learn more about it. In either scenario, you start at ground zero, a point at which your understanding of the central issues is minimal or perhaps limited. Your goal is to reach a point where you can discuss the topic intelligently, write about it confidently, and marshal pertinent sources together in a paper that meets your readers' needs and invites them to consider your stance. To achieve this goal, you need to explore your topic—that is, examine it from as many different angles as possible. You consult sources to ask questions; to compare claims, data, and evidence; to identify important issues and individuals; to consider how writers' prejudices and biases influence their stance; and, finally, to place the topic within your own frame of reference and to determine your stance on it. When you hold a topic up to this kind of scrutiny, you make it your own. Writing is part of the process. You write to articulate ideas, to formulate a thesis, to summarize what you've read, to explain your opinions, and to synthesize sources. The activities you practiced in Chapter 8—freewriting and taking notes that include analyses of rhetorical situations, focal points, and multiple perspectives—are all helpful strategies for exploring a topic. The case study in this chapter asks you to practice these activities and to augment them with additional activities that will make your exploration thorough and complete.

In many ways, exploring an unfamiliar topic is like exploring an unfamiliar place: You have to scout the territory and learn the lay of the land; if you don't get your bearings, you're lost. Think about the first time you visited a large metropolitan area or university campus. You probably relied on maps, guides, diagrams, signs, directions from someone familiar with the territory, or a guided tour by a friend to learn your way around. Even with some kind of orientation—a tour of the city or a visit to campus landmarks—the full resources of a new place don't become clear until you explore, observe, and investigate on your own. And the larger the city or campus, the more time it takes to learn what's available, where things are located, and how they're run. The same principle is at work when you explore a topic. A thorough, well-planned exploration requires visiting and revisiting your sources and drafting your paper many times. You read to preview sources and to learn what other writers have to say about your topic. You analyze rhetorical situations, narrow your topic, and examine arguments. You write and revise to explore and develop your ideas. You read your drafts with your intended readers in mind, looking for ways to make your ideas clear and accessible and your language and style appropriate for the rhetorical situation. Most importantly, you explore a topic as a reader and a writer, and you determine what the topic means to you and how you'll make it clear and relevant to others.

This chapter asks you to explore events from the past: the arrest and trial of an American citizen, Iva Toguri, who was found guilty of treason and eventually pardoned. You'll find similarities and differences among the accounts of Iva's ordeal, and you'll have to determine if one version is more reliable than the other. You'll read and annotate sources and use the case study method to see what kind of composite picture of issues and individuals emerges. You'll need to look at the strengths and limitations of the different sources, and look at whether the limitations result from the author's bias, your lack of context or information, or the source itself—its genre, its purpose, or the time the source was published. This kind of analysis will help you account for any differences the sources provide.

PREVIEW: IVA TOGURI, ORPHAN ANN, AND TOKYO ROSE

When World War II ended, the United States Army and the FBI identified Iva Toguri as the legendary Tokyo Rose, a radio announcer who broadcast propaganda to Allied troops in the Pacific during the war. Iva Toguri was born in Los Angeles to Japanese immigrants. Stranded in Japan when war broke out, she worked for Radio Tokyo and under the name Orphan Ann read radio broadcasts written by Allied POWs. These broadcasts were in fact her effort to sabotage Japanese propaganda. But was Toguri also Tokyo Rose? She admitted to being Tokyo Rose, but later alleged the admission was false and had been made because she was poor and wanted to claim the $2,000 the American press offered for an exclusive interview with Tokyo Rose. Convicted in 1949, Toguri served six years in prison, and, in 1977, received a presidential pardon from Gerald Ford, the first-ever pardon for treason. Because a pardon forgives a crime but does not clear an individual of guilt, friends and supporters of Toguri have suggested that a pardon is not enough and that Iva Toguri should at the very least receive a national apology. For example, Dafydd Neal Dyar, who has crated a web page, "Sayonara, 'Tokyo Rose' Hello Again, 'Orphan Ann,'" explains that Iva Toguri was "unjustly tried, convicted, fined, and imprisoned for broadcasting as Tokyo Rose" and proposes that she be offered an official apology for the injustice she suffered. As you work on this case study, explore reasons for and against Dyar's proposal, as well as your stance on the issue of a national apology.

GETTING STARTED
Strategies for Exploring

Haphazard or random ventures in which you pursue only one perspective on an issue can be interesting, but there's no guarantee they'll give you a sufficient understanding of the topic to make your writing about it coherent, logical, informed, and appropriate for your readers. When you explore a topic—somewhat familiar or completely unfamiliar—you need a plan. Strategies for exploring a topic include

- Reading and recording first impressions and connections you make between the topic and other events or issues.
- Annotating and noting such matters as:

  Scope: How broad or narrow is the topic?
  Issues: What are the central issues? What are the related issues?
  Persuasive appeals: What kind of dominant appeal emerges from you sources?
  Facts and opinions: How is information presented?
  Inconsistencies or contradictions: How do you account for either one?
  Perspectives: How many are there? How do they differ? How are they similar?
  Relevance: Why is the topic relevant to you? How can you make it relevant to your intended readers?

- Determining your stance on the topic.
- Writing about the topic informally: What kinds of ideas will freewriting yield? brainstorming on paper? drafting a letter to the editor?

When you hold a topic up to this kind of scrutiny, you make it your own. Don't be surprised if your opinions or reactions change as you research your topic and read about it, especially if the issue is one you knew little about initially. A thorough understanding of a topic's complexities can lead you to reverse your first impressions. This kind of switch in perspectives need not mean you're vacillating mindlessly; on the contrary, it is usually the result of becoming well-informed and making educated choices.

Even at the beginning of a research project, you sometimes take a stance on a topic before you read much about it. It's important to explore your stance, whether it's formed on intuition, a hunch, hearsay, or informed reading. In informal terms, you need to understand "where you are coming from": You should examine the influences that lead you to embrace a particular position. For any issue that you react to quickly with a strong opinion, ask yourself the following questions:

- Is my reaction based on emotion? ethical considerations? personal experience? political convictions? general knowledge about the topic?
- How well-informed am I about the issue? Does my understanding of the issue come from conversations with friends and family? television or radio? Internet? personal experience? classroom instruction or discussion?

EXPLORING A TOPIC

When you explore a topic, you read initially for an overview of the topic. Thereafter, you read and write

- To discover ideas, central issues, and related issues
- To understand different points of view
- To examine facts, statistics, and evidence
- To evaluate sources that discuss the topic
- To formulate questions of your own
- To determine your stance

FOCUS ON RELATED ISSUES: THE ROLE OF THE MEDIA IN SHAPING PUBLIC PERCEPTION

When the Japanese American Citizens League (JACL) came to the defense of Iva Toguri, it discussed long-standing stereotypes of Asian women as a contributing factor to the legend of Tokyo Rose.

THE LEGEND OF "TOKYO ROSE"

NATIONAL COMMITTEE FOR IVA TOGURI,
JAPANESE AMERICAN CITIZENS' LEAGUE

Pre-World War II Stereotypes

Historic stereotypes about Japanese Americans in general, and Asian women specifically, created an atmosphere whereby war-weary soldiers and civilians could easily transfer their fantasies and hostilities to a real person. Negative images of Japanese Americans originated in the 1890s, when the first sizable number of immigrants from Japan arrived in the United States and became targets for anti-Asian prejudice previously directed against Chinese pioneers. The anti-Japanese feelings were fueled by Japan's empire building in Asia (Taiwan in 1895, Sakhalin in 1905, Korea in 1910, Manchuria in 1931), and the newspapers were full of stories implying Japanese Americans were the outpost for an ever expanding Japanese empire. The newspapers depicted Japanese Americans as being unassimilable and incapable of loyalty to the United States because somehow their ancestral ties to Japan would predominate. This theme was later expressed by Lt. General John L. DeWitt, military chief of the Western Defense Command: "A Jap's a Jap. It makes no difference whether the Jap is a citizen or not. He's still a Jap and can't change." The anti-Japanese elements were very influential and succeeded in passing numerous state and federal laws discriminating against Japanese and Japanese Americans. By 1942, the negative stereotypes were so well implanted in the public's consciousness that there was practically no protest over the mass incarceration of American citizens based solely on a presumption of disloyalty.

The image of the seductive and sinister Asian woman emerged during the height of anti-Chinese agitations during the 1880s, and became particularly prominent when Japan became a military power in the 1930s. Hollywood movies and newspaper cartoons confused and combined Chinese and Japanese images into a general "oriental" stereotype, and Asian women were portrayed as exotic, sexy, and smart, but always determined to corrupt the morality of white American men.

Source: National Committee for Iva Toguri, Japanese American Citizens' League, "The Legend of 'Tokyo Rose,'" Iva Toguri (d'Aquino): Victim of a Legend (San Francisco: 5ACL, 1975).

One of the central issues in the Tokyo Rose case is the role of the media in shaping public perception of Iva Toguri during her arrest and trial. During the 1940s, radio broadcasts and daily newspapers were the dominant media. As you work on this case study, think about the role television, the Internet, radio, newspapers, and magazines have in public perception of people, events, and issues that are newsworthy. More diversified and widespread today than before World War II, the media is a powerful tool that influences almost every facet of our lives: politics, fashion, entertainment, education, consumerism, travel, medical practices, scientific research, and so on. We rely on the media for news—the more timely, the better. Television cameras, radio, and the Internet bring us live coverage from courtrooms, senate hearings, locker rooms, backstage, the battlefield, state funerals, royal weddings, awards ceremonies, search-and-rescue missions, and hurricanes and other natural and manmade disasters. Are the news reports we hear and see primarily the work of an impartial free press reporting factual information, or is a good deal of it hype created to further careers and generate sensationalism?

What was the media's role in the arrest, trial, and imprisonment of Iva Toguri? Was one branch of the media more successful than others in influencing the American public? Working on your own, explore our understanding today of the media's role in shaping our perceptions of one of the following: legal issues, scientific experiments, political races, high-profile trials, technological innovations, or some other newsworthy event or issue.

EXERCISE: FOCUS ON WRITING

Before you read what others have to say about Tokyo Rose, write for ten to fifteen minutes and explain your understanding of *treason:* Define the term, explain why it's a serious offense, record examples that come to mind of treasonous acts, and explain what you consider appropriate punishment for the crime.

Case Study 1:
An Apology for Tokyo Rose

"Where is the U.S. fleet?" jeered Tokyo Rose ... "I'll tell you where it is, boys. It's lying at the bottom of Pearl Harbor"

> —*quoted in* U.S. Submarine Operations in World War II

"I do not believe that those who brought about the execution of Mata Hari [WWI spy] believed that she was guilty—only expendable—and I am not convinced that the persecution of Iva Toguri [Tokyo Rose] was conceived in the spirit of justice.... What matters is to set the record straight. President Ford did the decent thing and pardoned her.... Now the time has come to go further, and to acknowledge her innocence"

> —*Russell Warren Howe,* The Hunt for Tokyo Rose

"The Tokyo Rose story is a dwindling sidelight on the history of the Pacific war. But it is a powerful reminder to Americans today of the dangers of racism and the need for true justice."

> —*Edwin O. Reischauer in the introduction to* Tokyo Rose: Orphan of the Pacific

---

UNITED STATES CONSTITUTION, ARTICLE 3, SECTION 3, CLAUSE 1

"Treason against the United States shall consist only in levying war against them, or in adhering to their enemies, giving them aid and comfort. No person shall be convicted of treason unless on the testimony of two witnesses to the same overt act, or on confession in open court."

THE LEGEND OF TOKYO ROSE

A chapter from *They Called Her Tokyo Rose* introduces the controversy about Iva Toguri. Read and annotate the chapter and see if you can determine Gunn's position on the guilt or innocence of Iva Toguri.

A WILD NIGHT ON OAHU

REX GUNN

It was a wild night on Oahu—the night of December 7, 1941. In the stunning aftermath of the Sunday attack by Japanese carrier planes on Pearl Harbor, the *Honolulu Advertiser* issued an extra, containing rumors.

Readers were warned to be "on the watch for parachutists reported in Kalihi ...," for "a party of saboteurs that had been landed on northern Oahu, distinguished by red discs on their shoulders ...," for "parachute troops sighted off Barber's Point," and for a man of "unannounced nationality" apprehended in the Punch Bowl, "carrying a basket of pigeons."[1]

With the darkness and the rumors had come the first blackout under martial law in Hawaii. Nervous guards triggered machine-gun blasts aimed at wind-blown litter, dogs, cats, anything that moved. GI trucks with their headlights masked by blue cellophane groped their way through unlighted streets.

Few facts were known. Strict censorship was imposed. Among the GI's in Hawaii, Japanese-Americans were presumed to have had something to do with the fantastic success enjoyed by the attacking pilots. There was talk of huge arrows carved in sugar cane fields, pointing the way to Pearl Harbor.

In the wake of the shocking news, submariners, cruising in U.S. submarines in the waters below the Philippines as far as the South China Seas tuned in on Radio Tokyo. They heard many announcers trumpeting news of the Japanese victory at Pearl Harbor. The cold, hard voice of one woman in particular caught their attention. She was introduced over short wave as "Madame Tojo." Speaking in excellent English, she delivered taunts about the location of the American fleet.

"Where is the United States fleet? I'll tell you where it is, boys. It's lying at the bottom of Pearl Harbor!"[2]

Early on the morning of December 11, 1941, one of those taunts via short wave from Radio Tokyo was picked up by a U.S. submariner, and he recorded it in the ship's log. He wrote:

"'Where is the United States fleet?' jeered Tokyo Rose.... 'I'll tell you where it is, boys. It's lying at the bottom of Pearl Harbor.'"[3]

As far as anyone has been able to learn from a review of wartime U.S. Navy logs it was the first time that the name, "Tokyo Rose," had been recorded. It was obvious that the recorder had used license in his "quotation" because he had added in the log entry that the announcer had been introduced by a "jiujitsu rendition of 'It's Three O'Clock in the Morning ...'".[4]

Clearly, the submariner was allowing his imagination to roam.

Where did he get the name, "Tokyo Rose?"

There is no way to be sure. According to Army Air Corps Major Joseph Gervais, the name Tokyo Rose first was used by construction workers on Saipan in connection with the disappearance of aviatrix Amelia Earhart on a round-the-world flight in 1937.[5]

Gervais said the name was applied to a lanky woman captive of the Japanese—a woman with red hair and freckles. According to various reports among the workers, Gervais added, the woman called Tokyo Rose had gone to Radio Tokyo as a captive propagandist or had fallen sick and died to be buried in an unmarked grave on Saipan or had been beheaded and buried in a secret grave.

The rumor that a captive Amelia Earhart had become a radio propagandist was persistent. It was officially investigated by the U.S. Army during the war and in the post-war occupation of Japan.[6]

Perhaps the name was linked to Amelia Earhart, but the creation of Tokyo Rose need not necessarily have been linked to any actual person. Roses abound in American popular song and folklore, i.e., *Rambling Rose, Mexicali Rose, Rose of Washington Square, The Yellow Rose of Texas, Rosie the Riveter, My Wild Irish Rose, Sweet Gypsy Rose,* ad infinitum. It wasn't really necessary that the submariner had to be thinking of any actual broadcaster to come up with a name like Tokyo Rose.

Two months later (in February, 1942), the name was linked to a tale about red submarines—a pirate fleet of submarines—in the South China Seas. Once again, the recording was done in a submarine log (the *U.S.S. Seadragon*). When they heard a woman announcer from Radio Tokyo promising "Death to the red submarines!" the crew of *Seadragon* had a big laugh. The joke, they said, was on Tokyo Rose. The *Seadragon* was the only red submarine in the Pacific, and she was red because her black paint had peeled off and she hadn't been able to make port to get another paint job. So, her red-lead undercoat was showing, and when she had entered Soerabaja Straits, *Seadragon* had looked like a boiled lobster.[7]

One month later, Tokyo Rose was recorded in the log of another U.S. submarine (*Seawolf*) as the sub cruised off Java, headed for Christmas Island.[8]

By then, Tokyo Rose quotations among the growing U.S. forces in the Pacific were legion. One concerned a famous American ace of the war, Navy Lt. Edward H. (Butch) O'Hare, who had shot down five Japanese planes on February 20, 1942. After Butch O'Hare was given a hero's welcome back in the states, *Yank Magazine* quoted Tokyo Rose, and in the quotation something new was added (another nickname) linking the Pacific siren to the most infamous English traitor at Radio Berlin—Lord Haw Haw.

"The Japs jeered. Butch O'Hare was a one-battle fighter, they said. He was afraid to return to the Pacific. Tokyo Rose, Japan's Lady Haw Haw, declared he was probably dead."[9]

By April, 1942, American fortunes in the Pacific war were at low ebb. The Philippines, Guam, Wake Island, the Solomon Islands, New Britain, Malaya, and Java had fallen to the Japanese. Captive allied forces by the thousands were shuffling through Pacific ports. Many died. All were uncertain whether they ever would be free again. The last American resistance in the Philippines was being worn down at Bataan and Corregidor. Those were grim days for Americans in the Pacific.

Recalling those days, a correspondent who was saved from capture on Bataan by a last-minute rescue via submarine (AP's Clark Lee) wrote:

> *"The story that Radio Tokyo invariably knew every move made by the American Army is one of the most persistent of the war. It began shortly after Pearl Harbor, and as far back as April, 1942, when a group of us escaped from Bataan and reached Australia, we were told that Radio Tokyo had reported our arrival and had said, 'Glad you made it to Australia. We'll be down after you before long.'*
>
> *"When a fighter squadron or a bomber group moved to a new base, dozens of people reported that* Tokyo Rose *had said, 'Hello, there, you boys of the Three Hundred and Nineteenth. Hope you'll enjoy the Philippines more than you did New Guinea.'"*
>
> *"Every new transfer was supposed to be announced by Tokyo the day it was made. However, I never found anyone who actually had heard such broadcasts himself. It was always the guy in the next tent."*[10]

Lee, eventually, would be the man who would file a sensational post-war story on "the one and only Tokyo Rose" as an American traitor.

So, Bataan fell. Corregidor fell, and to be an American GI stationed at one of the endangered outposts west of Hawaii was to live in fear. From our pre-war state of confidence, in which we had pictured ourselves as protected by "invincible Pearl Harbor,"[11] we had been alarmed by one defeat after another, stretching almost 3,000 miles from the Philippines to Midway. Now, each one of us knew, the next large land mass to fall to the Japanese (unless the crippled U.S. Navy could stop them in mid-ocean), would be the Hawaiian Islands.

Daily, we watched the skies for reassuring swarms of American war planes. Surely, we thought, we would be reinforced so that we could gain air supremacy over the Japanese. But we watched in vain. No swarms of planes were sent—not even a trickle. American air power was being directed to the European Theatre. It occurred to each of us that he, too, might be sacrificed to the higher priority for American arms in the European Theatre.

By the end of May, 1942, Tokyo Rose "quotes" were credited with virtually every rumor about American troop movements in the Pacific. The legend winged far ahead of any actual propaganda from Radio Tokyo. Tokyo Rose had grown to formidable authority as the Dragon Lady—Tojo's girl Friday.

According to the GI's, the whole shooting match was being broadcasted by Tokyo Rose. She knew everything—knew which outfit was moving to which island—knew when and why. And as likely as not she would call the C.O. by name and rank. When she promised planes a hot reception, they got one; and when she forecasted bombings, we got bombed.

That was the original, authentic, GI Tokyo Rose—a news caster, not a disc jockey or a torch singer, not a nostalgia peddler as she later was pictured to be. Prior to the Battle of Midway (June 4–6, 1942), there was nothing playful about her. We credited hers as the voice of our daily fears. Her roll call of our outfits on the move sounded like the crack of doom. We figured that all of us had about as much chance to get back home alive as the men of Torpedo Squadron Eight had to get back to the *Hornet*. She was no joke. The laughter she caused was grim and bitter. She was the victorious enemy.

After the U.S. Navy turned back the Japanese fleet at Midway, Tokyo Rose continued to be the unofficial greeter at virtually every island occupied by Allied forces, and her messages continued to be grim.

"Hey, you GI's on Guadalcanal!... Your island is mined with TNT. Anyone still there after the next 24 hours will be blown sky high."[12]

"Greetings to the bloody butchers of Guadalcanal. Welcome to Cape Gloucester We've been expecting you."[13]

"This program is dedicated to the Jolly Rogers, the 90th Bomb Group. I know you are moving from Dobodura to Nadzab, New Guinea on January 17th, and I will have a reception

committee there waiting for you."[14]

"Congratulations, Commander Perry, on your safe landing [on Abemama in the Gilberts]. But you will be sorry if you don't leave soon or now."[15]

But the victories in the new battles were ours now. At last, we were on the winning side. Hundreds of thousands of fresh American troops and swarms of friendly planes were arriving in the Pacific. With them came a fresh image of Tokyo Rose. The GI attitude toward "her" became increasingly playful.

When seabees were building an airfield on Saipan in the summer of 1944, so the story went, Tokyo Rose came on the air and said, "Confidentially, boys, your strip is showing."

When a general's house caught fire in the Aleutians while the general was en route to the states in a plane, Tokyo Rose beamed a special message to the general's radio operator, telling the crew to return to the Aleutians so that the general could save his home.

Another Aleutian story attributed to Rose was a thank-you broadcast for the use of an air base photo lab, entered one night by members of a Japanese submarine crew who sneaked ashore to develop some pictures of geisha girls.

Still another story current in Seventh Army Air Corps circles told of an admiral's special swimming pool on Lady Slipper Island off Kwajalein, built from war materials by seabees and "staffed" by U.S. Army and Navy nurses. On moonlit nights, so the tale went, crews returning from bombing missions could see the nude nurses swimming about in the admiral's pool.

Meanwhile, by the spring of 1944, Roses by many other names had sprung up before microphones not only at Radio Tokyo, but at Manila, in Indonesia, Java, and at Shanghai. None was introduced as Tokyo Rose. But at the receiving end, all were called Tokyo Rose.

A New York Times article described the new Tokyo Rose as an entertainer and spread her fame to millions of new readers. The headline read:

'TOKYO ROSE' A HIT
WITH U.S. SOLDIERS

"If a radio popularity poll could be taken out here among American fighting forces a surprisingly large number of votes would go to 'Tokyo Rose' and other of the programs beamed from the Land of the Rising Sun.

"Tokyo programs might even be voted first place …

"Tokyo is entertaining. Tokyo gives the listeners comedy and good dance music…. The men say they get the most music from the five Tokyo programs they hear regularly."[16]

Obviously, Tokyo Rose was getting a new image. But the *New York Times* article had raised more questions than it had answered about that image. It had not named "the five programs heard regularly" from Radio Tokyo, and had not even mentioned the red-hot mama of Japanese radio—the low-moaning, torch singing woman sometimes called "Myrtle" and at other times "Margie" at Radio Manila.

She came on with "Auld Lang Syne" by Guy Lombardo and went off with an equally nostalgic version of "Aloha," sandwiching in between pitiful condolences for all of "you boys" who were dying out there in the muck and jungle while their wives and sweethearts at home were out with 4-F's and defense workers, spending the big money.

Finally, the U.S. Army had decided to find out what was actually being broadcast to Allied forces by Japanese sirens in the Pacific. To do that job, the Office of War Information had sent to Australia late in 1943 a Hollywood movie writer, Lieutenant Colonel Ted E. Sherdeman, head of Armed Forces Radio.

Sherdeman had another mission, too. Once he had analyzed who or what was meant by Tokyo Rose, and what she was doing that was so popular among GI's in the Pacific, he meant to lure away her audience, using GI talent.

Sherdeman quickly identified the old Tokyo Rose legend as centering on "Madame Tojo" of Radio Tokyo, and the new playmate legend as focused on a woman, a newcomer with a staccato voice like a WAC drill sergeant, who called herself "Orphan Ann" on the previously all-male "Zero Hour."

The "Zero Hour" was beamed on the 19 and 25-meter bands at 6:00 p.m. (Tokyo Time) to catch GI's as they lined up for chow in the Central and South Pacific.

It opened with "Strike up the Band" and closed with a peppy version of "Goodbye Now." The music stayed peppy with a lot of marches and semi-classical stuff by the Boston Pops orchestra.

To lure away Orphan Ann's audience Sherdeman created the "Sarong Network" or "Mosquito Network," using GI disc jockeys such as "Boondock Barney" and "Gizmo" on Armed Forces stations at Eniwetok, Kwajalein, Saipan, Guam, etc.

But shipping space aboard transport planes and ships was scarce, and the GI disc jockeys were hard put to get late recordings from the states. So, their music libraries were no more up to date than Radio Tokyo's. And in spite of the Armed Forces Radio efforts, the legendary Tokyo Rose continued to lead the hit parade in the Pacific, with "Madame Tojo" leading the pack of actual broadcasters as news announcer and "Orphan Ann" of "Zero Hour" in the spotlight as disc jockey.

Meanwhile, at the same time that Tokyo Rose had made the big time in the *New York Times,* news of the Pacific siren filtered into Radio Tokyo via a Swedish magazine story, reprinted from the New York articles. Prior to April, 1944, the actual broadcasters at Radio Tokyo never had heard of Tokyo Rose. Now, they looked about among themselves with a wild surmise. Somebody among them apparently had become famous. Who was she?

Notes, Periodicals, Bibliography

1. *Honolulu Advertiser,* Extra Edition, December 7, 1941.
2. Fumi (Foumy as some writers spelled it) Saisho was a former University of Michigan student who became Radio Tokyo's principal female announcer and one of Shigetsugu Tsuneishi's interpretors. She went to work at Radio Tokyo in 1938 and broadcast as "Madame Tojo" throughout the war.
3. Roscoe, Theodore. *U.S. Submarine Operations in World War II.* Annapolis, Maryland, United States Naval Institute, 1949.
4. *Ibid.*
5. Klaas, Joseph, and Gervais, Joseph. *Amelia Earhart Lives.*
6. Morissey, Muriel (Amelia Earhart's sister). *Courage Is The Price.* George Palmer Putnam, Amelia's husband, made a three-day trek to reach a Marine Corps radio station near the coast of China, where broadcast reception from Radio Tokyo was loud and clear. Mrs. Morissey wrote of Putnam's reaction, "After listening to the voice for less than a minute, GP said decisively, 'I'll stake my life that ... is not Amelia's voice.'"
7. _____, *U.S. Submarine Operations in World War II,* p. 71.
8. *Ibid.*
9. *Yank* Magazine, Pacific Edition, Aug. 20, 1943.
10. Lee, Clark. *One Last Look Around.* (Duell, Sloan, and Pierce, New York), 1947, p. 90f.
11. The phrase, "Invincible Pearl Harbor," became a journalist's cliche in prewar days. Predictions abounded that if the Japanese should attack U.S. forces in the

Pacific (presumably, such an attack would have started in the Philippines), the U.S. navy would crush the Japanese navy within a matter of weeks.

12. The quotation was repeated commonly among men of the First U.S. Marine Division on Guadalcanal in August, 1942.

13. Another quotation passed among First Division Marines at Cape Gloucester, New Britain, December 26, 1943.

14. Repeated among members of the 90th Bomb Group, Fifth U.S. Army Air Force during their move from Dobodura to Nadzab, New Guinea, January 17, 1944.

15. Commander Perry led a flight of Marine planes to their new base on Abemama, Gilbert Islands, December 29, 1943.

16. *New York Times,* March 27, 1944 (bylined George F. Horne).

Source: Rex Gunn, "A Wild Night on Oahu, They Called Her Tokyo Rose," (Author, Santa Monica: 1977), 1–5.

EXERCISES: READING AND RESPONDING

1. Notice that this is a self-published book. Explain whether you consider self-published books reliable sources of information.

2. Summarize Gunn's explanations for the origin of the name Tokyo Rose. Then explain whether any of these explanations seem credible and why or why not.

3. Summarize at least two different perspectives on the image of the legendary Tokyo Rose.

4. Summarize Gunn's perspective on "Orphan Ann."

5. How does Gunn suggest that the media shaped public perception of Tokyo Rose?

"TOKYO ROSE" A HIT WITH U.S. SOLDIERS

GEORGE F. HORNE

FORCES IN PACIFIC, IMMUNE
TO PROPAGANDA, ENJOY OUR MUSIC
ON JAPANESE RADIO

Espiritu Santo Atoll, March 20 (Delayed)—If a radio popularity poll could be taken out here among American fighting forces a surprisingly large number of votes would go to "Tokyo Rose" and other of the programs beamed from the Land of the Rising Sun to the advancing American bases in the south and southwest Pacific.

Tokyo programs might even be voted first place, but unfortunately the popularity rating has little if any bearing on our morale, and as propaganda they are efficient only in the sense of being good entertainment. The consensus is that American fighting men are pretty impervious to propaganda, and that is probably a good thing, too, for otherwise they might be a victim of, our own, home brand of propaganda, some of which, according to officers stationed here, is pretty bad and might work in reverse.

But Tokyo is entertaining. Tokyo gives the listeners comedy and good dance music. The comedy comes when the "commercial" is plugged. Tojo, of course, is the sponsor, and the announcer, almost always speaking smooth English, puts his product over very nicely. The boys listen but they do not buy despite the fact that the oil is applied pretty lightly and sometimes there will be thirty minutes of first class. American dance music without a single interruption for the commercial plug. The men say they get the best and the most music from the five Tokyo programs they hear regularly.

It will go something like this:

"Hello, our American friends. Don't you wish you were back home again, back with your wives, sweethearts, children? It's too bad you are out here, away from all that means so much to you and to enter a war in which you are not interested or concerned."

The Tokyo radio, it turns out, thinks America is a wonderful place and it understands how the boys must be longing for it. The Tokyo radio is extremely sympathetic and tries to ease the heart pain by sending over some soothing music. Then the music comes from the best American and English name bands.

There are not many programs back home that will give you thirty minutes of entertainment without breaking in every few minutes to say life cannot be complete, culturally speaking, without daily applications of heavenly rose water eyewash. That is why the programs that reach the boys down here from "Uncle Sugar," which is their way of saying the United States of America, could be a lot better and so could the movies. At least there could be a lot more of the good ones, which of course we have.

They do not want to hear a single program about how evil and dumb the enemy is or a single "back the attack" program. They are backing it already. They would like to hear more dance bands, light love stories, light musical comedies. In film form they would like newsreels, not of war but shots showing familiar streets and scenes at home, and animated cartoons and films showing the best football and baseball games of the year. They will probably continue to listen to Tokyo Rose, but no one at home need worry about that.

Source: George F. Horne, "'Tokyo Rose' a Hit with U.S. Soldiers," *New York Times* 27 Mar. 1944: 4.

TOKYO ROSE STIRS PHILIPPINE MIRTH

On Radio She Tells of
Times Square Gloom as News
Lights Flashed Our 'Naval Defeat'

Advanced Headquarters, on Leyte, Oct. 29—As the Japanese defeat mounts Japanese official propaganda becomes increasingly tenacious. American and Philippine listeners here in Leyte laughed tonight when Tokyo Rose, broadcasting in English, said:

"The Americans' great naval defeat caused great gloom in New York when news was flashed in lights around THE TIMES building in Times Square."

It is to be wondered how long Japanese-conquered territories will believe this increasingly mendacious tale when our forces continue to make leaps of hundreds of miles forward and our Navy always reappears as strong as ever and closer and closer to Japan after each "defeat" by the Tokyo radio.

Tokyo Continues to Talk

The Japanese Domei agency directed an English-language wireless dispatch to North America yesterday claiming that "twenty-two Japanese bombers and fighters" had shot down fourteen American "carrier-based fighters early yesterday morning" in the vicinity of Tacloban, on Leyte Island.

The unconfirmed overseas transmission, recorded by the Federal Communications Commission, declared that the Japanese planes had been "on their way to a raiding mission against enemy positions at Tacloban" when they encountered the American planes and, "during the course of the hot serial combat that ensued shot down all of the enemy aircraft."

The dispatch added that "our loss was one plane that failed to return to its base."

Domei transmitted another English-language dispatch, admitting that Japanese forces on Leyte had "finally abandoned" the airfields at Tacloban and Dulag but claimed that "all military installations were destroyed and enemy forces had to pay a heavy price."

Domei asserted that "a fleet of Japanese airmen have already blasted seventy enemy planes on these fields," but complained that the "enemy stubbornly continues to send more planes."

It then went on to describe the fighting on Leyte, declaring that "a commanding height in the western part of Leyte Island is still firmly in our hands," and adding that "with the enemy desperately trying to secure control of the air by seizing the airfields at Dulag and the outskirts of Burauen, the center of the fighting on Leyte is now shifting to the south of these two areas."

Later Domei claimed in an English-language transmission to North America that Japanese planes on Friday night and Saturday morning had sunk "eleven more large-sized enemy transport vessels" that were "attempting to send reinforcements" to American troops on Leyte.

Source: "Tokyo Rose Stirs Phillipine Mirth," *New York Times.* 30 Oct. 1944: 3

EXERCISES: READING AND RESPONDING

1. Explain whether the newspaper articles suggest that Tokyo Rose was a serious threat to American morale during the war. What kind of evidence is cited? Explain why it does or does not appear to be reliable.

2. Explain whether you think the newspaper articles are reliable sources.

3. Explain whether you would agree or disagree (and why) with the claim that for morale purposes of their own, these articles were underplaying the effect of Tokyo Rose's influence.

4. Summarize the information newspapers provided about the effect of Tokyo Rose's broadcasts during the war.

5. Identify any focal points in "A Wild Night on Oahu," "'Tokyo Rose' a Hit with U.S. Soldiers" and "Tokyo Rose Stirs Philippine Mirth."

6. Use the three sources listed in question five to begin answering the reporter's questions: Who? What? When? Where? Why?

In "Japanese Overseas Broadcasting: A Personal View," by Namikawa Ryo, includes excerpts from scripts housed in the National Archives. The editor of *Film & Radio Propaganda in World War II* includes the following information about Ryo:

> A graduate of the Faculty of Law of Tokyo University, he joined the International Section of the Japan Broadcasting Corporation in 1931. After World War II broke out, he became a member of the Cabinet Information Bureau. After the war, he pursued an academic career as Professor of Drama and English Literature at Nihon University, Tokyo.

"JAPANESE OVERSEAS BROADCASTING: A PERSONAL VIEW"

NAMIKAWA RYO

At the beginning of 1943, just before the Japanese retreat from Guadalcanal and the German's crushing defeat at Stalingrad, Colonel Tsuneishi instructed Sawada Shinnojō, the chief of the 2nd Section of NHK, to form the *Zensen-han* (Front line unit), composed of Nisei, Charles Cousens, Wallace Ince and Norman Reyes, to operate a series of 'strategic broadcasts'. This project was under the direction of the 8th Section of the Daihonei; the Information Bureau of the Cabinet could not interfere in the content of the programmes. Sawada independently selected a team of about ten members which included Hideo Mitsushio as its leader, Kenneth (Kenkichi) Oki, graduate of New York University, Kenichi Ishii, and Shinichi Oshitari, a musician and graduate of the American University; Miss June Suyama, Miss Kuth, Sumi Hayakawa and other girls worked as typists and announcers. The manuscripts written by the members were not subjected to censorship for the army trusted them. Even Colonel Tsuneishi had confidence in this team which was responsible for producing a 75-minute programme called 'Zero Hour'. Directed at the Allied forces in South-east Asia and the South Pacific, it began at 6 o'clock every evening. The opening announcement, 'This is Zero Hour from far Japan', by the

Philippino Norman Reyes was followed by 'Strike up the Band' and fifteen minutes of classic music, five minutes of news, fifteen minutes of popular music, another five minutes' news, a short talk or fifteen minutes of Jazz and so on. Messages were read from war prisoners mailed to Tokyo from various parts of the Japanese occupied South Pacific, records were played by 'Orphan Ann' (Ikuko Toguri—better known as 'Tokyo Rose' to her listeners), news taken from US shortwave broadcasts and edited by the American, Wallace Ince, and 'Jazz stories' by Norman Reyes were also inserted.

The following are excerpts from scripts kept in the National Archives in Washington. They were recently copied by Akira Suzuki, a former staff member of TBS (Tokyo Broadcasting System).

Zero Hour

1st voice: This is the Zero Hour calling in the Pacific, and for the next 75 minutes we're going to take you through music as you like it, sweet and hot and otherwise, music from all over the world, and a thought for the day, sometimes even two thoughts for the day. First, let's have the fighting news for the fighting men.

(News)

5th voice/woman, 'Tokyo Rose': Hello you fighting orphans in the Pacific! How's tricks? This is 'after her weekend Ann' back on the air strict under […] hour. Reception O.K? Well it [should] be because this is 'all request night'. And I've got a pretty nice programme for my favourite lit-

tle family, the wandering Marine […] of the Pacific islands. The first request is made by none other than the boss and guess what? He wants Bonney Baker, and 'My resistance is so low'. Now, what taste you have sir, she said. (Music). And now, that Hot Ruby Carr, our second request is sent in by […] request number twenty nine. He wants Tony Martin, of all people, to help him forget the mosquitos and dirty rifles. Well, you know obliging Annie. Tony Martin and 'Now It Can Be Told'. (Music). This is Monday, washday for some, lots of cleaning for some and for the others, just another day for play. Let's all get together and forget those washday blues, with Kay Kaiser, Sonney Mason and all the playmates, so come join the parade you boneheads! (Music). Well, well, a new telegram, signed just M.S.S. and he wants a song also from our famous melody, R. L. Hum, well, Miss Bonnie Baker with the usual in the background, and the song, 'Shhh-baby's Asleep'. Quiet now everyone. (Music).

(Omission)

1st voice: This is the Zero Hour calling in the Pacific. We've just had it sweet, and in a moment we're going to have it hot. But in the meantime there are these news highlights.

2nd voice: Honolulu was alive with rumours, all of them wrong. It was rumoured that the closely guarded navy command where the president stayed was to be the site of a meeting with Churchill or Chiang Kai-Shek or both. Actually the whole affair was an American huddle. To the reporter who asked the president about an Anglo-American meeting,

Roosevelt replied that Churchill is not in Honolulu, nor is he expected in Waikiki. A Churchill conference, he said, is a question for future determination. Roosevelt said he will report to the nation on his Pacific trip, his first war journey. He said he has no time for political campaigning in the usual sense, but said that he will report to the people from time to time.

Roosevelt ordered the seizure of Midwest truck companies involved in an eight-day strike, and that they would be operated by the Office of Defence Transportation until the dispute was settled. The War Labour Board, which found itself powerless to solve the controversy in which one hundred eight companies refused to pay a directed seven cents an hour wage increase, and twenty-five thousand drivers went on strike.

The Australian war brides have arrived in San Francisco, forming the largest contingent of Australian wives of American servicemen. There were 296 wives carrying 72 babies. Australian sources have announced that there's plenty more, a larger number than there were in 1942. Already some babies of these brides have travelled to the United States. Another batch of 134 brides are awaiting transportation, and 200 others have applied for permit to enter the United States.

1st voice: You have just heard the news highlights for tonight. This is the Zero Hour calling in the Pacific. We've had it sweet and now ...

3rd voice: Hey boss! What are we gonna [do] about Watanabe?

1st voice: Have we received any pictures from the International Red Cross?

3rd voice: That's just what I'm worried about ...

1st voice: Six thirty P.M. and here again to American Fighting men in the Pacific, once again the music from homeland brings you 'Swinging music for Syncopating Smoothies' ...

(Music)

How'd you like to be back in Los Angeles tonight, dancing at Coconut Grove with your best girl? How would you like to be parked with her in Griffith Park listening to the radio?

How'd you like to go the comer drug store tonight, and get an ice cream soda?

I wonder who your wives and girl friends are out with tonight. Maybe with a 4F or a war plant worker making big money while you are out here fighting and knowing you can't succeed.

Wouldn't you California boys like to be at Coconut Grove tonight with your best girl? You have plenty of Coconut Groves, but no girls.

As one can see the programme's soft tone and humour aimed to stimulate war-weariness, nostalgia and pessimistic view of war. I do not know whether this can be regarded as 'strategic broadcasting', and it is hardly likely that this sort of programme was effective in actually reducing the fighting spirit of the Allies in the South Seas. American newspapers reported that Japan's war-weariness campaign seemed to be talked about by soldiers in some places, but Colonel Tsuneishi himself recognised that it was only the first step in Japan's strategy. The war developed so rapidly that 'Zero Hour' could not achieve its intended effect. 'Tokyo Rose' later participated in the unit. Her husky and sexy voice fitted exactly the mood of the aching heart, lovesickness and solitude of the orphan she was meant to portray. The messages from prisoners of war mailed to the station from Japanese-occupied areas of the South Pacific, however, did have an effect and were received with great concern by their families. The International Red Cross co-operated in this project. Many letters came to NHK after the war thanking it for this programme. The way of speaking and the contents of 'Zero Hour' were soft and dreamy, not like the threatening manner of speaking adopted by 'Lord Haw Haw' in Germany and Ezra Pound in Italy. I think the reason for this difference in the nature of propaganda may lie in the difference in the traditional and national characters of the nations.

Source: Namikawa Ryo, "Japanese Overseas Broadcasting: A Personal View." *Film & Radio Propaganda in World War II,* ed. K R M Short (Knoxville: U. of Tennessee, 1983): 324–27.

EXERCISES: READING AND RESPONDING

1. Describe the rhetorical situation in this script.
2. Summarize the main points of the script.
3. Explain how you interpret the script: Is it primarily demoralizing propaganda? innocuous banter? entertainment? some combination of all three? Be prepared to point to specific passages that support your interpretation.
4. On what points does this source agree with other sources cited in this case study? On what points does this source contradict other sources?
5. Summarize the perspectives this source presents.
6. Explain why you do or do not consider Namikawa Ryo a reliable source.

EXERCISE: THINKING CRITICALLY

1. Write for a minimum of ten to fifteen minutes and explore your stance on one of the following questions:
   a. Do the sources you have read suggest that Tokyo Rose was guilty of treason?
   b. During the war, what role did the media play in shaping Americans' perception of Tokyo Rose?
   c. Do Iva Toguri and Tokyo Rose appear to be one and the same?
2. Review the sources included to this point and identify focal points or connections that link one source to another.

1. Working in pairs or in groups, construct a time line using the sources you have read so far.
2. Make a list of key players in this case. Be prepared to share your list with your classmates.

"Peace of the Roses" reports the arrest and imprisonment of Iva Toguri.

PEACE OF THE ROSES

A prim University of California graduate, her hair in pigtails, sat in the first-floor dining room of the Bund Hotel in Yokohama last week and answered newsmen's questions in a Betty Boopish voice. She was Iva Ikuko Toguri, 29, known to thousands of Pacific-based GI's as "Tokyo Rose."

Iva, who was born on the Fourth of July in Los Angeles, claimed she was not a traitor to the United States because her program was nothing more than good entertainment. She refused to answer several questions and labeled one reporter's query as "stupid." The daughter of an uprooted Californian, now a Chicago grocery-store owner, she went to Japan in the summer of 1941 "to visit a sick aunt." When caught by the war she turned to radio "for the experience." She was arrested and taken into custody by MP's after the Yokahama interview, but her fate remains undecided because she is married to a Portuguese and therefore has dual, or triple, citizenship.[1]

But the discovery of Miss Toguri by no means clears up the Tokyo Rose mystery:

Her name is a GI invention, not a Japanese one. There has never been a "Rose" on the Japanese air waves. To soldiers in Hawaii and the Aleutians she was a nameless girl newscaster. To others, farther west, she was the coy and melting mistress of ceremonies on The Zero Hour, a propaganda show.

Miss Toguri was on the Zero Hour. But far from claiming full credit, she admits she was only one of four feminine announcers. Furthermore, she denies any propagandic cooing about home and hot dogs. Asked if she had not used the phrase "forgotten men," she said no. She had never heard it except in the 1932 Presidential campaign.

---

[1]Portugal grants citizenship to wives of citizens. American-born Japanese have dual citizenship, which many retain because Japan disinherits any who renounce their loyalty to Japan. A question still exists whether Miss Toguri renounced her birthright of American citizenship.

To add to the confusion, on Aug. 7 the Navy Department, indulging in a bit of horseplay, awarded a citation to Tokyo Rose for "contributing greatly to the morale" of United States armed forces in the Pacific. But the Navy failed to specify which Rose.

Source: "Peace of the Roses," *Newsweek* 17 Sep. 1945: 96–97.

EXERCISES: READING AND RESPONDING

1. Summarize the perspectives this article presents.
2. How does this article differ in tone from "Japanese Overseas: Broadcasting a Personal View"? Try to account for any differences.
3. Explain whether you believe this article is primarily informative or persuasive. Be prepared to defend your response by citing passages from the article.
4. What kind of composite picture of Iva Toguri does this article present?
5. What focal points does this article share with other sources from the 1940s?

ARREST AND TRIAL

When the war ended in 1945, American journalists searched Japan for the woman known as Tokyo Rose. Through a contact at the Domei News Agency, Clark Lee, a reporter with the International News Service, and Harry Brundidge, of *Cosmopolitan* magazine, managed to meet Iva Toguri. A coworker had suggested that Iva and several other women fit the description of Tokyo Rose. Brundidge and Lee offered $2,000 for an exclusive interview with Tokyo Rose. After Iva told her story, *Cosmopolitan* refused to pay the $2,000 not wanting to give money to a traitor. "Her Neck in a Noose," Chapter 7 in Lee's *One Last Look Around,* is a report on Iva Toguri's claim to be Tokyo Rose.

HER NECK IN A NOOSE

CLARK LEE

For twenty-five years of her life, Iva Ikuko Toguri, a Los Angeles-born American girl of Japanese ancestry, kept her nose clean and stayed out of trouble. Then—for the sum of $6.66 monthly—she deliberately sold her services to a country with which the United States of America was at war and thus laid herself open to charges of treason.

Iva, who is also known as Tokyo Rose, was one of the first prizes of our occupation of Japan. There is a possibility that she may die for her crimes. But if the dimpled, soft-voiced Los Angeles girl ever does dangle from the gallows it will be a gross miscarriage of justice unless the next scaffold holds the frail, arthritic figure of an eighty-three-year-old American missionary known as "Mother" Topping.

Both Iva Ikuko Toguri and Mrs. Genevieve Faville Topping committed the same crime—if it is held to be a crime—of broadcasting radio programs aimed at weakening the fighting spirit of their fellow Americans in the war against Japan. Both worked for a Japanese victory; Iva for pay. Mother Topping for free. Tokyo Rose's programs were at least entertaining to our troops—and there the parallel ends. Iva was arrested for her sins and at this writing faces indictment by the Los Angeles grand jury, while Mrs. Topping is still presiding benevolently over her missionary nest in Tokyo and trying to convince American soldiers that the Japs were forced into an economic war that was no fault of their own.

What saved Mrs. Topping from arrest and trial may have been, in addition to her age, her close friendship for the Japanese "Christian leader" Kagawa. Kagawa, after the surrender, became a great favorite of certain of the American occupation authorities who chose to ignore his violent anti-American broadcasts during the war. The "Christian," who with some reason had accused American soldiers of all kinds of atrocities, emerged as a "Liberal" leader and an active figure, while a *Stars and Stripes* writer who dared to expose his wartime activities got into severe difficulties with the American authorities. Kagawa continued to move around Japan, associating with his old missionary friends, while the man who attacked him. Corporal Bernard Rubin of *Stars and Stripes* was investigated by the Counter-Intelligence Corps on a "loyalty" check and exiled to Okinawa.

Tokyo Rose was the fall guy, rather than some other of Tokyo's broadcasters, because she was the best-known voice from Japan during the war. She had a tremendous following among GIs who listened to her program of recorded American music on Radio Tokyo's "Zero Hour," especially in the days before our own Army set up its broadcasting equipment on recaptured Pacific islands. Next to Tojo, hers was the most familiar enemy personality and there was great curiosity among our soldiers as to the identity of the Oriental Lady Haw-Haw. Various rumors had identified her as a girl from the Hawaiian Islands, a beautiful German, a St. Louis woman married to a Japanese and a Eurasian Mata Hari. The best guess made by Americans, as they heard her slangy inflection coming over the air to their foxholes, was that she was American.

Because of the widespread curiosity as to her identity, there was a race between American correspondents to try to locate her. We happened to find her first and sneaked her into the Imperial Hotel with her husband, a Portuguese-Japanese named Phillip d'Aquino who worked in Domei.

"Are you Tokyo Rose?" we asked.

"Yes," the girl said, "the one and only Tokyo Rose."

She was a little nervous at first, as she sat on the bed holding her husband's hand. She was a pleasant-looking girl, but by no stretch of the imagination a siren; her long braids made her look nearer twenty than the ten more years to which she readily confessed. She was wearing blue slacks tucked into American-made zippered rain shoes, to compromise with the ugly Japanese mompei-style garment, and a yellow blouse and a reddish vest. Her teeth were straight and white, and when she smiled you noticed a small mole on her upper lip.

"It looks like I'm on the spot," she said in a low, well-modulated voice. You could tell that she hadn't yet made up her mind just what to do about it—whether to tell everything or keep silent. She went on, "I don't think I should talk to you. When the story is published I'll be arrested."

What she really wanted, we quickly found out, was a contract, promising her some money, signed before she told her story. When that preliminary was over, we sent for some tea, and while we were drinking it she debated with herself how much to tell. Finally, I believe, it was her vanity that decided her to give the full story. After all, she was thinking, I am an international figure known to millions of American GIs and sailors. I have become world famous during the war. This story will be in nearly every paper in America and in one of the biggest magazines, and my picture will be everywhere.

And so, talking on for hour after hour, she told us her story—that of a woman who was scholarly, intelligent in most matters, and fully capable of exercising judgment, who had sold out her country, with little regard for the consequences, for the sum of $6.66 monthly and for no other reason, motive, or reward.

In the case of Iva Ikuko Toguri, born in Los Angeles on July 4, 1916, there was no question of a smoldering resentment against her native land, no incident that had made her feel an alien. She had never been called "you dirty Jap." She liked life in the United States and hated the restrictions in wartime Japan, where she had been trapped by the war's outbreak while visiting relatives. Yet, night after night, she sat down to write and broadcast a script deliberately designed to make her compatriots lose their will to go on fighting. She attacked their morale by telling them their wives and sweethearts at home were out with 4Fs—something many of them guessed anyway but didn't like to hear on the radio. She created Allied disunity by telling the Australian soldiers, "Diggers, the Americans are taking all your women." And through it all Iva always felt herself still American, still looked forward to going home to Los Angeles and her family and old friends there, and steadfastly refused to sign a paper renouncing her American citizenship in favor of naturalization as a Japanese.

Sipping our tea in the Imperial but not smoking "on account of my voice, you know," Iva talked like a mixture of adolescent bobby-soxer and college professor. Her father, Jun, had come to the United States in 1899 and her mother a year later. Her father was a prosperous importer and exporter and her mother, unusually advanced for a Japanese woman of her times, had wanted to become a doctor. There were three other children, Fred, a UCLA graduate and now a businessman, June, twenty-five, and Inez, nineteen. All of them were well educated.

"It was unheard of for a woman of my mother's generation to study medicine," Iva said, "and her ambition centered in me. I planned to become a doctor, like seven of my cousins in Japan, but finally decided on zoology." At school, she became a crackerjack in microscopic technique, joined scientific societies at UCLA, and on weekends camped out in the desert with student paleontologists looking for the Miocene horse which roamed in the Barstow region 3,000,000 years ago. The biggest day in her life each year was Independence Day, the birthday of the United States of America and of Iva Ikuko Toguri. Of all the birthdays the one she remembers most was July 4, 1941, the day before she sailed on the "Arabia Maru" of the OSK line, wearing a new suit made by her sister June and carrying presents of stockings, candies, sugar, and fruit, to visit her mother's ailing sister in Japan. Her aunt and uncle, cousins and friends met her at the pier in Yokohama. Everything Japanese seemed strange to her. She had never been in a Japanese home and couldn't speak the language, so she entered a missionary school to learn it. The food was strange, too. She couldn't eat rice and was beginning to lose weight when her uncle went to the police and by special permission had her ration changed to bread. Iva decided, after a few months, to go home.

She wrote her family and told them, "Japan is no place for an American-bred person to live. The sooner I can come home, the better." To her sister she wrote of the contrasts between the two countries, describing how the Jap school kids had to march and drill, how discourteous the Japanese were on public conveyances, and how annoying the police restrictions that required her, as a foreigner, to report for questioning every few days.

She was packing to go home in November when suddenly all shipping was halted. Pearl Harbor was a complete surprise to her. "My uncle came in and said, 'We are at war with America. I heard it on the radio.' The shock was so great that I can never explain it in words."

She watched the Doolittle raiders fly over Tokyo with mixed emotions. "I stood there and prayed that the anti-aircraft fire wouldn't hit them, but at the same time I didn't want them to hit me. If it came to a choice between the two, I wanted the planes to be shot down." I know how she felt.

After a few months, Iva began worrying about money. She had $500 but was starting to eat into her savings. So she moved into a boarding house, continued school, and in July of 1942 got work in the English department at the Domei news agency. "I suppose," she said, "that working for Domei was just as much treason—if I am guilty of treason—as was my later broadcasting as Tokyo Rose. Domei paid me one hundred and thirty yen monthly." Her tuition was one hundred yen monthly, leaving only thirty yen for food and board, and in July of 1943 she gave up school.

It was while Iva was with Domei that the friend she had made through the missionary school. Mother Topping, went on the air with the first of her seven broadcasts to America. Perhaps that gave Iva the idea of becoming a radio star, too. In any case, she applied for a job with Radio Tokyo and was accepted in August, 1943, and given work as a typist and script arranger. One evening, two Allied prisoners at Radio Tokyo, Captain Ted Wallace, alias Ince, an American who had been one of the "Voices of Freedom" from Corregidor, and Major Cousens, an Australian, suggested to Iva that she take part in the Zero Hour program.

They outlined what they wanted, "A girl with a definite voice personality … a happy-go-lucky style, just talking to the fellows. Imagine they are the kids from next door in Los Angeles and sort of talk to them." Iva asked, "How much?" "One hundred yen [$6.66] monthly." "I'll take it," she said. "I can live on that plus my Domei salary and hang onto what's left of my five hundred dollars."

Iva caught on quickly. Soon she was writing her own scripts and inventing her own characters, the stars being a boy-friend named Abe (she said no religious angle was intended) and a good-looking sergeant of whom Abe was jealous. As the Victrola ground out nostalgic tunes, she would pretend to dance with the sergeant and then tell Abe to run get them glasses of cold beer. She would imagine the GIs sitting in the jungles, sweating under the tropical sun and swatting flies. Then she would play cooling music. "Compared to what other hard-working girls were getting at the station," she said, "my job was easy. Just face the mike and go home. I was rather selfish, in a way."

Unlike some of the other Radio Tokyo programs, Zero Hour was never gruesome. The approach was pally and the propaganda was not too obvious. The theme was homesickness, and since this was so, it did not matter that the most recent musical recordings were late 1941. After the B-29 raids started, one of the plane crews parachuted some new records over Tokyo intended for Iva, but she never got them. So she stressed the nostalgic quality of the music she played.

Iva first learned she was famous about a month after she went on the air. Before that several Nisei girls had done the announcing but it was not until she took over that a dispatch came through from Switzerland telling how the American soldiers listened to Tokyo Rose. "Everybody in the station began to call me that, and notes were left on my desk addressed to Tokyo Rose. I never used the name on the air, though." She had to fight off others in Radio Tokyo who wanted to horn in on this popular program.

After a while she got control of the entire Zero Hour, and right up to the end she continued her programs, claiming great American defeats and Japanese victories, in accordance with instructions from the Tokyo War Office. Shrewdly, she burned her scripts ten days before the surrender, unaware that official American listening posts had made complete recordings of her programs in preparation for her trial some day.

Did she regret having turned traitor for $6.66 a month, I asked Tokyo Rose. "I haven't any particular feeling," she said dispassionately. "It was an education. If it weren't for the war I never would have faced the mike, learned radio technique, and had the thrill of listening to my own voice recorded." So the war did some good after all: Iva Toguri got a thrill out of it. "I have no feeling of being a traitor," she went on. "My husband often warned me to quit but you can't just do that. Even if I quit a year ago it would have been the same. If I'm guilty now I was guilty then. I often thought I was doing wrong but I felt I was providing as much fun as propaganda for the GIs."

The neat little girl smoothed out her pigtails, finished the last of a fresh batch of tea, and rose to go. She signed an autograph, laughingly, to "Harry Brundidge and Clark Lee, who may have put my head in a noose today." She was very chipper about it. You could tell she didn't believe such a thing could ever really happen to her. After all, you can't hang anybody for learning mike technique and having the thrill of hearing her recorded voice played back to her. Americans, Iva felt sure, would understand that.

Later, I asked six American GIs here and there in Japan what they thought should be done to Tokyo Rose. Three of the answers were unprintable. Two, slower workers, said. "I'd sure like a date with her." One thought she should be punished. "What the hell," the five GIs said, "she gave us a lot of good music and we laughed at her propaganda. Lots of us thought she was on our side all along. We got a big bang when she welcomed our unit to the different islands every time we'd move."

The story that Radio Tokyo invariably knew every move made by the American Army is one of the most persistent of the war. It began shortly after Pearl Harbor, and as far back as April, 1942, when a group of us escaped from Bataan and reached Australia, we were told that Radio Tokyo had reported our arrival and had said, "Glad you made it to Australia. We'll be down after you before long." When a fighter squadron or a bomber group moved to a new base, dozens of people reported that Tokyo Rose had said, "Hello there, you boys of the three hundred and nineteenth. Hope you'll enjoy the Philippines more than you did New Guinea." Every new transfer was supposed to be announced by Tokyo the day it was made. However, I never found any one who actually heard such broadcasts himself. It was always a guy in the next tent. For what it is worth, Tokyo Rose told me that the Japanese War Office had never furnished her such intelligence information, and it does seem reasonable that if the Japs did have such a reliable espionage setup, they would have kept that fact to themselves.

A few days after our interview with her, little Iva went to jail.

No such fate was in store for Mrs. Genevieve Fayville Topping who, in the tone of a minister's wife addressing the church women's club, had made seven overseas broadcasts to her sister Americans. "I tried to persuade the women of America," Mrs. Topping explained, "to move anyone and everyone to the realization that it was possible to negotiate peace if the Americans would only halt their atrocities." Jap atrocities? Mother Topping had never heard of them and was sure the Christian Japanese were incapable of committing them.

"Mother's" attitude is by no means unique among American missionaries.

There were others who remained in Japan during the war who broadcast appeals to their fellow Christians to cease fighting against Japan's "just crusade." One American woman on the Tokyo Women's Hour turned on the tears in this fashion: "Yesterday I was rummaging about the closets and I came across some dusty photographs taken in America ... memories of past joys, hopes and fears.... My daughter piped up and said, 'Do you think Edward's father, whose picture is there, will fly over here and throw bombs on us?' I looked at my children and couldn't answer."

Other missionaries like the Rev. Theodore F. Walzer, who returned to the United States by diplomatic exchange ship, were unshaken in their conviction that the Japs were really very nice people. Talking to fellow exchangees—American reporters who had undergone six months' imprisonment—Walzer warned, "If you send back stories about what the Japanese did to you, you will be playing them a dirty trick." At Laurenço Marques, where the Japanese exchange ship "Asama Maru" shifted its passengers to the "Gripsholm," and vice versa, a group of American missionaries massed on the after-deck of the "Gripsholm" waved their handkerchiefs to the Japs on the "Asama," and shouted "Banzai! (Long live Japan!)." The Japs responded by singing a war song.

Talking to reporters after the surrender, Miss Elizabeth Kilburn, one of the followers of Mother Topping and of Kagawa, shrugged off the latter's vicious anti-American broadcasts. "Those were violent times," she said. "I was in an internment camp and I said violent things in my heart when American planes bombed Tokyo. You can't understand unless you were under the liquid fire of the American planes. If I could have reached a radio, I would have said violent things to the Americans, too."

Reminded that the Japs had done a bit of bombing here and there, Miss Kilburn gave her tardy advice that after Pearl Harbor America should have turned the other cheek. "Does one wrong," she inquired, "deserve another? Anyway, Japan didn't even start it." To which Mother Topping added sagely, "It was an economic war. The poor Japanese were taken from their homes and forced to fight."

Source: Clark Lee, "Her Neck in a Noose," *One Last Look Around* (New York: Duell, 1947) 84–91.

EXERCISES: READING AND RESPONDING

1. At what point in the article does Lee offer his position on Iva Toguri's activities during the war? What is his position?

2. How does Lee support his position? Cite at least three points of support.

3. At what point in the article does Lee provide a narrative of Iva Toguri/Tokyo Rose's activities during the war? From the first six sources included in this case study, identify accounts that confirm Lee's report and accounts that contradict it.

FOCUS ON RELATED ISSUES: PROPAGANDA BROADCASTING IN WORLD WAR II

In the preface to *Film & Radio Propaganda in World War II*, K. R. M. Short points out that "'propaganda,' 'information,' and 'education' were much the same thing in the wartime context; they meant *persuasion* by whatever method was most applicable to the purpose in hand." Consider the components of a rhetorical situation that make propaganda such as radio broadcasts effective. What kind of relationship must broadcasters have with their intended audiences? with the subject? What kind of relationship must listeners have with the subject? with the broadcaster? What conditions must be present to make propaganda effective? Based on the information on radio propaganda in "Japanese Overseas Broadcasting: A Personal View," do you find that war propaganda appealed primarily to logic, ethics, or emotions?

According to Masayo Duus, author of *Tokyo Rose: Orphan of the Pacific*, of the twelve people indicted for treason after World War II, seven had participated in enemy radio propaganda broadcasts. Tokyo Rose was one of many radio broadcasters accused of spreading propaganda. Second to Tokyo Rose in notoriety was Axis Sally. Working on your own, explore sources that report information on other radio broadcasters who broadcast programs for Germany, Italy, or Japan.

---

4. Lee says that Tokyo Rose was the "fall guy" because she was the best-known voice from Japan during the war. Does he explain whether the rest of the article seems to support this claim?

5. Lee frames this chapter with references to Mother Topping, offering the stories of both women so that the reader can compare and contrast their activities. Explain whether you consider this frame an appeal to readers' logic, ethics, or emotions.

6. Identify passages in the article where Lee seems sympathetic to Iva Toguri and passages where he seems unsympathetic.

7. What kind of composite picture of Iva Toguri does Lee present?

ACCUSATIONS OF TREASON

Six weeks after her interview with Lee and Brundidge, Iva Toguri was arrested and placed in jail for over a year. No formal charges were ever made. After her release, she and her husband lived in Tokyo. She applied for a U.S. passport in 1947 because she wanted to return to the United States to see her family and to be sure the child she was expecting would have U.S. citizenship. When the press reported that the woman known as Tokyo Rose had applied for an American passport, a media campaign began opposing Iva's return, and the hunt for Tokyo Rose escalated. Iva was arrested again in 1948 and transported back to the United States to stand trial for treason.

TOKYO ROSE'S AID TO JAPAN PICTURED

LAWRENCE E. DAVIES

PROSECUTION AT TREASON TRIAL
ASSERTS SHE VOLUNTEERED
FOR 'NEFARIOUS PROPAGANDA'

San Francisco, July 6—The role of Tokyo Rose as a propagandist for Japan in the Pacific war was pictured today by the prosecution in the treason trial of Mrs. Iva Toguri D'Aquino as a "glamorous job" performed "gladly" by the American-born defendant "without duress or compulsion."

Opening the Government's case in a ninety-minute address, Tom DeWolfe, a special Assistant Attorney General, told the six men and six women jurors that Mrs. D'Aquino voluntarily sought work broadcasting for Radio Tokyo to American troops in the South Pacific.

She engaged in "nefarious propagandistic purposes," he asserted, after being "distinctly told" that the "zero hour" broadcast on which she appeared was "part of the Japanese Government's program of psychological warfare against the United States."

Moreover, Mr. DeWolfe said, the evidence to be presented by the prosecution during the next three weeks would show that Mrs. D'Aquino, introducing herself on the air as "your favorite playmate and enemy, Orphan Ann," sought and received "increased emolument" while she "talked chitchat" and "broadcast propaganda" to troops addressed as "boneheads and suckers."

Trial Expected to Last Weeks

The morning session was fully occupied with the prosecution's opening statement, at the end of which Theodore Tamba of the defense staff told Judge Michael J. Roche that he would reserve his own statement until the prosecution finished its case. Each side expects to take about three weeks.

While Mr. DeWolfe leisurely outlined his case, emphasizing to the jurors that Mrs. D'Aquino must be looked upon as innocent until all the evidence was in, the defendant sat at first with complete outward composure, eyes usually downcast. As he continued, however. Mrs. D'Aquino grasped a pencil and began writing vigorously. She continued making notes almost until he had ended his speech with these words to the jury.

"I now say to you that the United States Government believes that after you have given consideration to all evidence presented by both parties, you will come to no other conclusion than that the material allegations in the indictment have been proved to your satisfaction beyond reasonable doubt."

Prosecutor Defines Treason

He told the jurors that treason was a "heinous crime" and cited the treason statute as saying in substance "that whoever owing allegiance to the United States Government adheres to the enemy and gives the enemy aid and comfort is guilty of treason."

Proof would be given, Mr. DeWolfe said, that Mrs. D'Aquino was first used on the "Zero Hour" program as "listener bait" so that American troops would "not be bored." But later, he asserted, she told the soldiers they had lost "all" their ships and made other statements "intended to impair the capacity of the United States to wage war upon its enemies."

Pointing to a loudspeaker and reproducing equipment in the court room, the attorney said it would be used, if the court permitted, to reproduce four records monitored at Portland. Ore., by the Federal Communications Commission. All,

include broadcasts by Mrs. D'Aquino, it is alleged. The defense has announced that it will object strenuously to their reproduction. The jury box and press table have been equipped with earphones.

The first prosecution witness was Richard J. Eisenhart of Rochester, N. Y., employed in the purchasing department of the Eastman Kodak Company. He testified that he served as corporal of the guard at Yokohama Prison when Mrs. D'Aquino was incarcerated there in the fall of 1945 and asked a fellow guard to obtain an autograph of the prisoner for him a few weeks later.

Wayne Collins, chief of defense counsel, questioned Mr. Eisenhart closely about the guards' alleged use of clubs and about any exertion of pressure in getting the autograph. The witness, who said he accompanied the area guard to Mrs. D'Aquino's cell and watched her sign her name and add Tokyo Rose in quotation marks, denied that guards in the prison were armed.

Source: Lawrence E. Davies, "Tokyo Rose's Aid to Japan Pictured," *New York Times* 7 Jul. 1949: 14.

TOKYO ROSE'S CHIEF DOUBTED HER EFFECT

San Francisco, July 12 (AP)— The Japanese colonel who directed Tokyo propaganda broadcasts during the war didn't have much good to say about their effectiveness.

Shigelsugu Tsuneishi had charge of prisoner-of-war broadcasts. The Government brought him here as a

witness against Mrs. Iva Toguri D'Aquino, native American, charged with treason for her Tokyo Rose broadcasts on Colonel Tsuneishi's "zero hour" shows.

But under questioning by defense attorneys, Colonel Tsuneishi conceded that he wasn't satisfied with, the program's effectiveness as a propaganda instrument.

The defense picked on this angle diligently. The defense argument has been that the Tokyo Rose broadcasts were innocent.

So Wayne Collins defense attorney, tore into the Government witness. Was it not true, he asked, that in consequence of lack of military success, "you did not try to convert to a propaganda program?"

Colonel Tsuneishi spoke thoughtfully in Japanese. The interpreter translated:

"It was unfortunate, but the opportunity did not present itself to present a real, true, propaganda broadcast as I wished to."

United States Attorney Frank Hennessy told newsmen at recess that "the effectiveness of the propaganda does not mitigate the offense, of course."

Source: "Tokyo Rose's Chief Doubted Her Effect," *New York Times* 13 Jul. 1949: 11.

EXERCISE: THINKING CRITICALLY

Review the list of focal points you compiled for the first five sources in this case study. For "Peace of the Roses," "Her Neck in a Noose," "Tokyo Rose's Aid to Japan Pictured," and "Tokyo Rose's Chief Doubted Her Effect," identify focal points or connections that link one source to another.

EXERCISES: COLLABORATING WITH YOUR PEERS

1. Working in pairs or in groups, review the time line you constructed using Sources 2–5. Using Sources 6–9, make any necessary additions to your time line.

2. Review your list of key players from Sources 2–5. Using Sources 6–9, make any necessary additions to your list. Be prepared to share your list with your classmates.

EXERCISE: GOING ON-LINE

"Sayonara, 'Tokyo Rose' Hello Again, 'Orphan Ann,'" a web page created by Dafydd (David) Neal Dyar, is available at <http://www.dyarstraights.com/orphan_ann/orphanan.html>. Read Dyar's account of Iva Toguri's broadcasts, arrest, trial, and imprisonment. Are there details in this account of Iva Toguri's years in Japan, her arrest, and trial that do not appear in other sources in this case? What focal points do you find between this source and other sources in the case study? What kinds of appeals does Dyar make?

In January 1954, *American Mercury*, a popular, influential magazine that scrutinized American politics, published "America's First Woman Traitor," by Harry T. Brundidge. As you read and annotate, think about the stance Brundridge takes and how it compares to Clark Lee's account of Iva Toguri's confession.

AMERICA'S FIRST WOMAN TRAITOR

HARRY T. BRUNDIDGE

There's a tiny gardener in the Federal Reformatory for Women in the old village of Alderson, West Virginia. Fellow prisoners know her best for two things: her green thumb with flowers and vegetables, and for always standing at rigid attention when the national anthem is played.

Her name is Iva Toguri d'Aquino and she's doing a ten-year stretch. The name today means little or nothing, but in the last war her voice and her recorded music were known to hundreds of thousands of service men throughout the Pacific.

She would play sweet, nostalgic records—and then feed them sour propaganda designed to undermine their morale. She would laughingly tell them that while her music was sweet, it was not half so good as the music to which their wives and sweethearts were dancing with the big 4F's and war workers back home, while *they* were giving their sweat, blood, and lives at sea, on the beaches and in the jungles. For Iva Toguri d'Aquino, the tiny gardener of Alderson, is "Tokyo Rose"—*the first American woman ever to be convicted of treason.* Here, for the first time in any publication, is the inside story of "Rose." The writer played a role in the entire drama. The only other man who knew and shared it with me was Clark Lee, of International News Service.

Our part in the drama began on Okinawa in August, 1945. Lee and I sat on the stone wall guarding the entrance to an ancient burial tomb. We were bathed in the yellow light of a tropical moon.

The war was over—almost. Japan was to be occupied. This was "Occupation Day Minus One." I looked at Lee, and he looked at me. We'd been buddies together around the world for a long, long time. Back in 1939–40, as fellow war correspondents, we had followed the fortunes of the Japanese Army throughout North, Central and South China.

I said to Lee, "Want to make a deal?"

"Sure," he answered. "What kind of a deal?"

"Well," I went on, "we've lived in Japan. We know something about the people. We know that when Hirohito told 'em to quit, they quit. I feel certain that most of the armed forces, and all of the civilian population, have folded, and that it would be perfectly safe for us to dash to Tokyo the minute we land in Japan. The hottest story in Japan today is: Who is Tokyo Rose? Let's find out and get her. Our old Japanese friends will help us."

"Okay," said Lee, "it's a deal."

Lee and I, and eleven other correspondents, were awaiting the "big call" from Colonel "Tex" McCreary, who was flying us to Atsugi, Japan. A sergeant aroused us. We checked our .45's and other gear and were jeeped to the air strip. The atmosphere was tense. General Robert Eichelberger, the hero of Buna, told us he hoped there wouldn't be a fight when we reached Japan. There was of course the possibility we were being led into a trap for slaughter. Maybe the Kamikaze pilots would crash their planes into our formations. Men of Eleventh Airborne were climbing into the bowels of giant C-54's. Lee and I climbed into McCreary's B-17.

Now at dawning we saluted majestic Mount Fuji and thirty minutes later were on the ground at Atsugi. We had only a few troops on the ground—and there were eighteen divisions of fully armed Japanese troops in the Atsugi-Yokohama-Tokyo area. The C-54's kept coming in, unloading troops, and taking off for another load. As each cargo was discharged the newcomers joined their fellow troopers in spreading out to form a perimeter of defense. Our fears were quickly dispelled. There were plenty of Kamikazes on hand— but propellers had been removed. And there was a reception committee of grinning, hissing, bowing Japanese with iced beer and sandwiches and Buddha alone knows where they got the meat. There was a hot breakfast in the Kamikaze barracks and a motor pool with scores of ancient, prewar cars, with civilian drivers wearing hastily inscribed arm bands.

We looked over the banged-up cars in the motor pool.

"What are we waiting for?" asked Lee.

We picked a 1935 Plymouth because it had a lovely green paint job and a Japanese businessman driver who grinned when we told him we wanted to sneak to Tokyo. Our

officer insignia got us past the M.P.'s at the airport gate, just as the Eleventh Airborne was pulling out for Yokohama. The forty-mile dash to Tokyo was underway.

We registered at the Imperial Hotel (to the amazement of all our old Japanese friends there) and went to work. We found Leslie Yamashita, newspaperman and old friend, and told him we wanted to find Tokyo Rose. Now, "Rose" had never used that pseudonym in here broadcasts. The name had been pinned on her by our G.I.'s and later was adopted by her fellow workers in sending her memos at Radio Tokyo. But Yamashita knew all about her—and promised to produce her.

There was a knock on the door of our suite in the Imperial on that hot, humid morning of September 1, 1945. Our Number One Boy ushered in Yamashita, escorting a young woman in slacks, a blouse, and pigtails tied with a red ribbon; and a solemn-faced young Portuguese-Japanese half-caste. Yamashita, with the Japanese flair for drama, said: "This is Iva Ikuko Toguri—your 'Tokyo Rose'—and this is her husband, Philip d'Aquino." (The girl who had sold out her country married the half-caste in an effort to change her nationality and avoid a treason charge.) "We shall have tea," Yamashita continued, "and then I shall withdraw."

We had tea.

"Are you really 'Tokyo Rose'?" I asked as we sipped.

"The one and only," she smiled.

After tea we got down to cases. She had a story to tell—and sell. We made a deal. I would pay her $2,000 for a full confession signed by her, which I would ghost-write for *Cosmopolitan* magazine. In return she and her husband were to go to a secluded rural village and hide out from other correspondents (and our Army's G-2 and CIC) until after publication of the confession. Failure to comply would nullify the agreement. Now I was in business.

Rose talked for hours, with Lee' making notes on the portable. It was the story of an intelligent, scholarly young woman who had sold out the country she really loved for the country (Japan) she really hated, for $6.60 monthly and, by wartime conditions in Japan, a "soft" living. Instead of going into a munitions factory and sticking it out she, with no regard for consequences, elected to become America's first woman traitor.

She was born in 1916—on the Fourth of July—of a high-class California Japanese family. She had every educational advantage and many social advantages unusual to West Coast Nisei.

She related the story of her graduation from UCLA' in 1941, and how, following "the biggest fire-works display ever given me on my birthday," she sailed for Japan, second class, on the following day, July 5, 1941. She didn't want to go, and went only because some family emissary had to go to Tokyo to attend the illness of her mother's sister. Her mother was ill too, and her father too busy, and so she was elected.

Rose told of her dislike for Japan, rice, and relatives; how she tried to get back home; was caught in the war; needed a job; and how, after doing stenographic jobs, she listened to the wiles of a former U.S. Army captain—and became a traitor. The captain—a former radio commentator—had been taken prisoner on Corregidor and rushed to Tokyo where he became? "Radio Tokyo's" top anti-American propagandist. He taught Rose the trade, wrote her scripts, and began her sweet music and sour propaganda.

At long last "Rose" finished her story. We had seventeen pages of typewritten notes.

Lee hurried away to Atsuki to file a piece of the story. Before he left I gave him a cable to *Cosmopolitan,* my magazine, stating that I had the traitor's confession. With Lee's departure I began writing that article. I worked throughout the night.

Then things happened, fast!

Lee got back to the Imperial with a long face and handed me a cable. My editor was astounded that I would offer an article by a traitor and demanded an explanation. Back in Yokohama, some 250 correspondents were laughing up their sleeves at the cable, which was made public.

In the meantime, I learned that "Rose" had been talking to Army officers, and thus invalidated her agreement with me. So when Lee arrived, I handed over the story—and his INS editor was thrilled when he received the material which Lee had broken down into a series. *I kept the seventeen pages of typewritten notes which Lee had recorded.*

Rose was arrested. She was locked up for a long time, and finally released while the investigation continued.

Time and place changed. On a Sunday evening in February, 1948, Silliman Evans, publisher of the Nashville *Tennessean,* and the writer were sitting in our suite in the Wardman Park Hotel, in Washington. We had a Monday morning appointment with the Attorney General, then Tom Clark, concerning matters in Tennessee. We were listening to the radio. A news broadcast asserted that the Department of Justice (from Clark's office) had announced that no treason case could be made against Tokyo Rose because Brundidge had lost the seventeen-page confession made to Lee and Brundidge. I was red-hot because that original confession was reposing in my New York apartment.

I called my friend, J. Edgar Hoover, and told him I *had* the original and he made plans to have it picked up. Next morning, after we had finished our Tennessee business, Clark asked me if I would go to Tokyo. He asked if I could get Rose to sign that original statement. I said I would and I could. Soon thereafter I took off in a military plane for Tokyo. With me was John B. Hogan, an assistant to the Attorney General.

In Tokyo, Hogan gathered a large number of Japanese witnesses against Rose—mostly former associates at Radio Tokyo. Then, at last, we were ready to talk to our little traitor. She was sitting on a bench, outside a large conference room on the fifth floor of GHQ, reading yesterday's edition of *Stars and Stripes*. She looked up as we came in, recognized me, extended a hand and said: "Hello, Mr. Brundidge." I introduced Mr. Hogan, who got down to business. He handed her the typewritten notes of her confession to Lee and me.

"Do you remember this?" Hogan asked.

"I think so."

"What is it?"

"I'm quite sure it is the statement I made to Mr. Brundidge and Mr. Lee when they talked to me in the Imperial Hotel in September, 1945, before the Occupation."

"Will you read it?"

"Of course, if you want me to. I've read it before."

Rose read all the seventeen pages.

"Is that a true statement?"

"It was true when I made it and it's true now."

"Will you sign it?"

"Certainly." And she did.

Then she smiled at me and said: "I've told you everything because, win or lose, I want to go home. When do you think I'll be tried?"

I could only shake my head in the negative.

"Well," she said, "the sooner the better."

Again, there is a shift of scenes. This time to San Francisco. It was September, 1948. Rose, following our report to the Attorney General, had been arrested and shipped back to her native California. As the Army transport docked she was turned over to the U.S. Deputy Marshals. A grand jury was in session. Lee and I were called. We told all we knew about Rose. Her original statement to us— now signed by her—was offered in evidence. And then Lee and I poured it on the Army captain who taught Rose her broadcasting business.

The jury demanded that the prosecutors write an indictment not only of Rose but of the Army officer. Hogan and the others pointed out that the Army officer was not within the jurisdiction of the court and therefore could not be indicted. *The jury went on a strike, adjourned, and refused to indict Rose.* It was only after the prosecutors promised to eventually bring about an indictment—somewhere— of the Army officer (a promise never kept) that Rose was indicted.

A year later she went to trial in San Francisco. On September 30, 1949, she was convicted as a traitor and sentenced to a prison sentence of ten years and a fine of $10,000.

So the tiny gardener with the green thumb continues her labors at the Alderson Reformatory. And Rose might be interested in knowing that there is no disposition in Washington to let her out for good behavior. The officials think she got off cheap.

What ever happened to the Army captain who taught Rose her trade? Instead of being tried, he was promoted to major, a rank he still holds in the United States Army! Name furnished on request.

Source: Harry T. Brundidge, "America's First Woman Traitor," *American Mercury* Jan. 1934: 37–41.

EXERCISES: READING AND RESPONDING

1. What assumptions does Brundidge make about his readers' attitudes toward Iva Toguri? What are his claims? What evidence does he offer to support those claims?

2. Does this article seem to appeal primarily to ethics, emotions, or logical reasoning? Cite passages that support your answer.

3. Many passages in this article talk about the writer and his role in bringing Iva Toguri to trial. What kind of persona (see Chapter 1) results from these passages? Cite specific passages that explain your response.

4. Do the descriptions of Iva Toguri and her husband differ in any way from descriptions offered in other sources you have read so far? If your answer is yes, explain how. If your answer is no, identify two other sources that offer similar descriptions.

5. Brundidge uses the frame of Iva working in her garden. Explain whether you consider the frame an appeal to logic, ethics, or emotions.

6. Compare Brundidge's article to Clark Lee's chapter, "Her Neck in a Noose". For example, compare the descriptions of Iva and her husband. Are there points on which these sources differ? On which points do they agree?

7. Does the account of Brundidge's interview with Iva Toguri seem more reliable than Lee's? or vice versa? Explain why or why not.

8. The article is peppered with references to Iva Toguri's "selling out" and being a "traitor." Review the article and find passages that include word choice that contributes directly to a composite picture of Iva Toguri.

9. What kind of composite picture of Iva Toguri does the reader find in this article?

A PARDON FOR IVA TOGURI

In October 1949, Iva Toguri was found guilty of treason and sentenced to ten years in prison and a fine of $10,000. The first request for a presidential pardon came in 1954. Eventually, the JACL became involved. In 1975, the National Committee for Iva Toguri, part of the JACL, published *Iva Toguri (d'Aquino): Victim of a Legend*. The epilogue to that pamphlet and the resolutions adopted by the JACL in 1974 follow.

IVA TOGURI (D'AQUINO): VICTIM OF A LEGEND

NATIONAL COMMITTEE FOR IVA TOGURI,
JAPANESE AMERICAN CITIZENS' LEAGUE

Epilogue

During her trial in 1949, there were no organized groups supporting Iva Toguri. While Japanese Americans may have sympathized with her predicament, there was very little they could effectively do to help while their own position in American society was under attack. As their hard struggle to gain fundamental rights progressed, Japanese Americans warmed up to the idea of supporting Iva Toguri, but it was an excruciatingly slow evolution. In 1957, William Hosokawa suggested in the Japanese American Citizens League (JACL) newspaper: "Perhaps it is time to acknowledge that she does indeed exist, and say firmly that we are interested in seeing that she gains justice." In 1969 proposals were initiated within JACL in support of Iva Toguri and also in 1974 a resolution was adopted by the National Council of the Japanese American Citizens League (JACL) committing support for her (see appendix E). Now the largest national human rights organization representing Americans of Japanese ancestry with 30,000 members throughout the United States is supporting Iva Toguri.

The general public also had difficulty supporting Iva Toguri during her trial. McCarthyism was beginning to sweep the country in 1949, and most people withdrew from involvement in controversial cases. Congressional committees started investigating alleged communists in government and the movie industry, loyalty oaths were imposed on college professors and the espionage trial of Judith Coplon and perjury trial of Alger Hiss were in progress (Hiss was recently readmitted to the practice of law). When the severe repression subsided a bit in 1957, a small support committee was formed in San Francisco during Iva Toguri's deportation hearing, but people were still afraid to become involved.

Wayne M. Collins, Jr., has lived with the Toguri case since childhood, and when his father died he took over as Iva Toguri's attorney and chief advocate. He is planning to file another petition for executive clemency with the President of the United States. With the support of the American people, Iva Toguri has a good chance to redeem her name and regain her precious American citizenship. Iva Toguri deserves justice. She has suffered enough.

Appendix E

National Japanese American Citizens League Resolution

Adopted by the National Council on July 27, 1974 at the 23rd Biennial National Japanese American Citizens League Convention in Portland, Oregon.

WHEREAS, Iva Toguri was the victim of wartime hysteria and became a scapegoat for her alleged role as "Tokyo Rose" for those forces which sought to foster vengeance and national retribution; and

WHEREAS, Iva Toguri suffered imprisonment, embarrassment, and physical and mental anguish for alleged acts of treason; and

WHEREAS, it is now apparent that much of the evidence and the conduct of her trial were highly questionable and prejudicial and that in view of the motivations and climate of public hysteria at the time of the trial the verdict is a blot on the integrity of American jurisprudence;

NOW, THEREFORE, BE IT RESOLVED that the Japanese American Citizens League, meeting at its 23rd Biennial National Convention in Portland, Oregon, July 23 to 27, 1974, recognize that Iva Toguri was unjustly tried and convicted in the aftermath of World War II;

BE IT FURTHER RESOLVED that the JACL offer to Iva Toguri and her family its belated apology for long silence and inaction;

BE IT FURTHER RESOLVED that the JACL use its leadership, manpower, and resources to correct the miscarriage of justice in Iva Toguri's case by seeking all executive or other remedies available under the law;

BE IT FURTHER RESOLVED that the JACL personally contact Iva Toguri to apprise her of the action of the National Council, and to ask whether she desires, consents to, or accepts any help from the National organization.

Source: National Committee for Iva Toguri, Japanese American Citizens League, "Iva Toguri (d'Acquino): Victim of a Legend" (San Francisco: JACL, 1975).

Edward H. Levi served as attorney general during Gerald Ford's administration. "In the Matter of the Application for Pardon of Iva Ikuko Toguri D'Aquino" is the heading of Levi's letter to the president, summarizing Iva Toguri's case and recommending a presidential pardon. This unpublished letter is made available courtesy of the Gerald R. Ford Presidential Library.

IN THE MATTER OF THE APPLICATION FOR PARDON OF IVA IKUKO TOGURI D'AQUINO.

The President
　　Sir:
　　This petitioner was convicted in the United States District Court for the Northern District of California of treason and on October 6, 1949, was fined $10,000 and sentenced to ten years' imprisonment. The judgment was affirmed by the Court of Appeals for the Ninth Circuit in 1951 and the Supreme Court denied certiorari in 1952. The Supreme Court thereafter denied petitions for a rehearing on several occasions.
　　Petitioner began service of her sentence in 1949. She was released from prison with credit for good time in 1956. Subsequent deportation proceedings were terminated and she was released from supervision by expiration of sentence in 1959. She completed payment of the fine in 1975.
　　The offense for which she requests pardon occurred between 1943 and 1945 when petitioner, in her late twenties and a United States citizen born of Japanese parents, willfully supported and gave aid and comfort to the Imperial Japanese Government, then at war with the United States. Specifically, she was accused of working as a radio announcer and broadcaster of recorded music in the short-wave radio broadcasting station of the Broadcasting Corporation of Japan, which was engaged in beaming propaganda to members of the Armed Forces of the United States and their allies in the Pacific. Her broadcasts apparently drew large audiences and she became well known in the press and among Allied military personnel as "Tokyo Rose." She has no other arrest record.
　　Petitioner explains that she was unable to return to the United States after the outbreak of World War II and that she had no intention of committing treason against the United States when she accepted employment as a typist by the Broadcasting Corporation of Japan and subsequently participated in the broadcasts with Allied war prisoners. While the broadcasts generally were believed to have been designed to weaken the Allied will to fight, she has stated that her participation was confined to non-political commentaries introducing non-political musical recordings. Moreover, she states that she was told at the time that broadcasting orders came from the Japanese Army and must be obeyed. Petitioner's presence in Japan at the outbreak of war between the United States and Japan was the result of her travelling to Japan to visit a sick relative in the Summer of 1941. It appears that prior to Pearl Harbor she made some unsuccessful attempts to return to the United States.
　　Born in Los Angeles in 1916, petitioner has lived in Chicago since her release from prison in 1956. She married Felipe Jairus D'Aquino, a Portuguese of Japanese extraction, in 1945 in Japan. No children were pro-

duced by this marriage. Petitioner's husband left the United States for Japan in 1949 and apparently has never returned. She has worked in Chicago since 1956 in her father's business, the J. Toguri Mercantile Company, an importer of Japanese merchandise. Since her father's death in 1972, she has worked long hours managing the business. She apparently inherited substantial family assets, enabling her to complete satisfaction of her fine. She appears to be financially secure and maintains an excellent credit standing.

Business associates, a family physician, references and others familiar with petitioner's post-conviction conduct and activities characterize her as a warm and sincere individual and a highly regarded, honest and competent businesswoman of good character and reputation. Without exception, these individuals, neighbors and others indicate that petitioner leads a quiet, business-oriented life and is worthy of a pardon.

United States District Court Judge Alfonso J. Zirpoli, who as a private attorney represented a witness at petitioner's trial, has advised the present United States Attorney that he believes petitioner was selected for prosecution to serve as an example and that her conviction rested heavily upon the conditions prevailing at the time. Noel E. Story, now a senior trial attorney in the Justice Department who was involved as a Department representative after World War II in several treason cases and who interviewed and cross-examined over 50 persons who furnished depositions on petitioner's behalf in connection with her treason trial, believes that her treasonable intent was considerably less clear and convincingly demonstrated than in other treason cases in which he participated. He strongly recommends favorable pardon consideration.

Petitioner's previous pardon application was denied in 1969 because of the adverse recommendation of the then United States Attorney and the nature and seriousness of the crime. Noting Judge Zirpoli's views and petitioner's recent satisfaction of the fine, the present United States Attorney recommends that the instant petition be granted. The trial judge and the prosecuting United. States Attorney are deceased.

Now 60, petitioner requests pardon of her only criminal offense as an aid in the restoration of her civil rights and to facilitate foreign travel. In the 21 years since her release from prison she has led a completely law-abiding, productive and useful existence. I believe that her post-conviction conduct and reputation have been sufficiently meritorious to justify her forgiveness. In the circumstances, and based upon the many favorable recommendations of concerned citizens, Government officials and the present United States Attorney, I recommend that she be granted a pardon.

Respectfully,
Edward H. Levi
Attorney General

Source: Edward H. Levi, Letter to President Gerald R. Ford. Gerald R. Ford Library 12 Jan. 1977.

EXERCISES: READING AND RESPONDING

1. The language in this letter differs somewhat from the language in the other sources. What kinds of terms or phrases do you find in the letter that are not used in other sources? Explain how the words and phrases you identified create a tone in the letter. Then explain how the tone of the letter differs from the tone of "America's First Woman Traitor."

2. This letter concludes with the writer's position—a recommendation for a pardon. How does the writer support this position? What kinds of evidence does he cite?

EXERCISE: THINKING CRITICALLY

Review the list of focal points you have compiled so far. For the last three sources, "America's First Woman Traitor," "Iva Toguri (D'Aquino): Victim of a Legend," and "In the Matter of Application...," identify focal points or connections that link one source to another.

EXERCISES: COLLABORATING WITH YOUR PEERS

1. Working in pairs or in groups, review the time line you constructed. Referring to Sources 10–12, make any necessary additions to your time line.

2. Review your list of key players. Review the last three sources, and make any necessary additions to your list. Be prepared to share your list with your classmates.

FOCUS ON RELATED ISSUES: SCAPEGOATS

Several of the sources you've read argue that Iva Toguri was a scapegoat, an innocent individual singled out to take blame for a problem. Scapegoats— individuals or groups of people—can be found in just about every social context, from the schoolyard to the international scene. For example, people against gun control argue that the NRA is the scapegoat in the Columbine shootings; a CBS news report asks whether Wen Ho Lee, accused of passing information about U.S. nuclear secrets to China, is a scapegoat or a spy; another news report claims the media has made President Clinton the scapegoat in the breakdown of the World Trade Organization talks held in Seattle in 1999. Can you think of situations—local, national, or international— where an individual or a group is made a scapegoat? If you aren't familiar with origins of the term *scapegoat*, consult a reference book for an explanation of the history behind the practice of scapegoating.

Find a copy of William Holman Hunt's painting *The Scapegoat*, on the Web or in your library. Without looking at sources that discuss the painting, do a freewriting exercise for ten to fifteen minutes exploring what you see in the picture, how you interpret it, and finally whether you believe the arrest and trial of Iva Toguri made her a scapegoat.

CONTEMPORARY PERSPECTIVES: NATIONAL APOLOGIES

While Nicolaus Mills doesn't address the Tokyo Rose case directly, he touches on the issue of formal apologies and when they are and aren't appropriate. His op-ed piece appeared in the *Houston Chronicle* in April 2000. Before you read it, take a look at Dafydd (David) Neal Dyar's web page, "Sayonara, 'Tokyo Rose' Hello Again, 'Orphan Ann'" available at <http://www.dyarstraights.com/orphan_ann/orphanan.html>.

HOW FAR BACK CAN AN APOLOGY GO AND STILL BE CREDIBLE?

NICOLAUS MILLS

Pope John Paul II surprised the world with a Lenten sermon in which he apologized for the sins committed by the Roman Catholic Church against Jews, fellow Christians, women and various indigenous people over the last 2,000 years. This was not the first time John Paul II had apologized for the failings of the church. In his 1998 document "We Remember: A Reflection on the Shoah," he addressed the failure of many Catholics to help Jews during the Holocaust. But nothing John Paul II or earlier popes have done constituted an apology on the magnitude of this pope's recent apology.

In his plea for a "purification of memory," the pope has done more than move the church into new territory. Rather, his actions have brought into focus the degree to which the public apology has become part of contemporary culture.

In the United States, what has helped to pave the way for this development is the surge in popularity of the talk show and tell-all memoir. These entertainments have made the most humiliating personal revelations commonplace and, in turn, made the public apology seem far less jarring than it was for earlier generations.

But just as important—for America and the world at large—is the combined impact of two historical developments. The first is the Holocaust and the principle established at the Nuremberg Trials of 1945–46 that leaders are accountable for the actions of their governments and cannot avoid moral responsibility by saying they were taking orders. The second is the rise of multiculturalism and the widespread acceptance by both blacks and whites of how pervasive racism has been in the West, especially in the United States. As a consequence, the public apology has gone from an action no government leader nor politician would think of taking to an action that seems consistent with contemporary reality.

The significance of this change cannot be over-estimated. In our private lives we take apologies for granted. We make them for breaking a promise or arriving late for a dinner party. But public apologies are a different matter. Historically, they have been few and far between. It is as if over the years we had come to accept at face value the Greek proverb, "From the time they invented 'I'm sorry,' honor was lost."

Generals traditionally made it a habit never to apologize for killing enemy soldiers or even civilians. Neither Julius Caesar in his commentaries on the Gallic Wars nor Napoleon Bonaparte in his memoirs ever apologizes for his bloody deeds. Even in the U.S. Civil War, where the dead on both sides were Americans, apologies are conspicuously absent in the celebrated memoirs of such leading military figures as Ulysses S. Grant and William T. Sherman.

Apologies are also absent in the great confessional literature of the past. From St. Augustine to Jean Jacques Rousseau, any number of writers acknowledged the awful deeds they had done and, in the process, begged forgiveness from God. But these same writers did not make it a practice to apologize directly to those they hurt. Instead, they contented themselves with apologias—explanations quite different from apologies—for their bad behavior. We don't find in these public confessions the kind of direct apology to a wronged individual that occurs in a novel such as *Huckleberry Finn,* for example, when Huck, after playing a mean trick on the slave Jim, makes the decision to "humble" himself and say he is sorry.

Despite the fact that we have no shared, historic code on what constitutes a genuine public apology, we still believe we can tell one when we see it. Particularly over the last decade, we have come to regard a public apology as authentic when it has the following qualities: First, the apology is not self-serving. It does not come when the apologist is under such pressure to acknowledge his faults that an apology leaves him better off. Second, the apology is directed at whomever has been damaged and does not allow the apologist to save face by a generalized admission of wrongdoing or confession to a higher power that substitutes for a personal apology. Third, the apology is accompanied by reparations or, if they are not possible, by an implicit promise to halt the conduct that made the apology necessary.

We have not come to treat all public apologies as equal. For example, voters were particularly skeptical of President Clinton's apology for lying about his relationship with Monica S. Lewinsky. After months of doing his best to conceal his relationship, the president's apology seemed little more than an attempt to get out from under public criticism. The same widespread skepticism is true of the reaction of baseball fans to Atlanta pitcher John Rocker's apology for his comments about hating the idea of taking the subway to Shea Stadium in New York, because it would mean sitting next to gays, immigrants, welfare mothers and people with AIDS. Rocker's tepid apology seemed designed only to allow him to continue his baseball career and minimize his fine and suspension by the baseball commissioner.

But in the last 15 years public apologies far more complex than Clinton's or Rocker's have gained acceptance. Near the end of his life, Alabama's segregationist Gov. George C. Wallace abandoned the racism that had characterized his political career and, on the 30th anniversary of the 1965 Selma-to-Montgomery march, apologized for his past deeds. His repentance was accepted by many civil-rights leaders he had hurt, including Rep. John Lewis, D-Ga, former head of the Student Nonviolent

Coordinating Committee, who praised Wallace for trying to mend the fabric of America.

The same pattern is true on an international level. In 1990, Czech President Vaclav Havel made history by apologizing to the 3.25 million Sudeten Germans expelled from Czechoslovakia at the end of World War II. It was a subject on which Havel might have been quiet, given Nazi atrocities, but in apologizing for what tiny Czechoslovakia had done, Havel was, essentially, making the point that no nation can claim purity.

Nine years later, U.N. Secretary-General Kofi Annan made a similar admission with regard to the United Nations and the genocide it failed to stop in Rwanda. He declared, "On behalf of the United Nations, I acknowledge this failure and express my deep remorse." Annan's apology reflected his desire to reach out to the Tutsi victims of genocide and acknowledge that even an organization devoted to peacekeeping can be guilty of great ethical lapses.

What remains open to debate is how far back in time a public apology can extend and still be credible. It is one thing for the Roman Catholic Church to apologize for the sins its "children" committed over a span of 2,000 years. But the Havel example notwithstanding, for nations and public figures, apologies for the wrongs done by previous generations are difficult—especially when they impose a burden on the young. The question becomes, "Just what does the current generation owe?" In recent years, for example, it has been hard for the Japanese to deal with new revelations about the crimes their soldiers committed in World War II during the "rape" of Nanking. They have not wanted to apologize to the Chinese and reopen old wounds. Similarly, in the United States, the idea that the country should apologize for the wrongs of slavery, as TransAfrica founder Randall Robinson argues in his recent book, *The* *Debt: What America Owes to Blacks,* by paying reparations to African-Americans, has drawn minimal support, even in liberal circles.

What is certain, however, is that, as long as there are groups who believe they can trace their current difficulties to wrongs done in the past, the public apology will occupy a central place in the culture of the new century.

Source: Nicolaus Mills, "How Far Back Can an Apology Go and Still Be Credible?" *Houston Chronicle* 2 Apr. 2000: C4.

EXERCISES: READING AND RESPONDING

1. Summarize Mills' explanation of why the "public apology has become part of our contemporary culture."

2. Explain why you agree or disagree with the qualities Mills lists for identifying a genuine public apology.

3. Mills focuses on apologies to groups of people. Identify specific passages you would use in a paper arguing for a national apology to Iva Toguri. Identify passages you would use it in a paper arguing against a national apology to Iva Toguri.

4. Summarize Mills' perspective on public apologies. Explain whether you agree or disagree with him.

5. Mills' article is on an issue related to the case study. Explain why you would or would not add points in this article to your list of focal points in sources in this case study.

6. If a public apology were made to Iva Toguri, should it come from the present generation or the generation of World War II?

7. What issues does Mills raise that would make good topics for exploring and developing into research assignments?

EVALUATING AND ANALYZING THE CASE STUDY

EXERCISES: THINKING CRITICALLY

1. Identify the rhetorical situation for each of the sources included in the case study.

2. The letter from former Attorney General Edward H. Levi is a primary source for this case study. Identify any other sources in the case study that are primary sources. Identify secondary sources. Be prepared to explain why you classify a source as one or the other.

3. Whether or not Tokyo Rose was a myth is one of the focal points in the case study. Review sources and identify other focal points or connections that link one source to another.

4. Working in pairs or in groups, construct a time line for the case study.

5. Make a list of key players in this case. Be prepared to share your list with your classmates.

WRITING ABOUT THE CASE STUDY

EXERCISES: FOCUS ON WRITING

Freewriting

1. Write for fifteen to twenty minutes on your impressions of the case study. Answer the reporter's questions—*who? what? where? when? why?* and *how?* Touch on any controversial perspectives.

2. Write for fifteen to twenty minutes, and explain who or what influenced sentiment about Tokyo Rose from 1945 to 1947.

3. Write for fifteen to twenty minutes, and explain who or what influenced sentiment about Iva Toguri from 1947 to 1977.

4. Write for fifteen to twenty minutes, and explore your position on whether or not the United States owes Iva Toguri a formal apology. Identify anything you have read, heard, seen, or experienced that influences your stance.

Evaluating Sources

5. Imagine that your assignment is to write a biographical sketch of Iva Toguri. Write a memo to your instructor that provides bibliographical citations and summaries of sources in the case study. After each summary, include a paragraph or two commenting on how the source compares with other sources in the composite picture of Iva Toguri. Conclude with comments on the strengths or limitations of the source. For sources that have limitations, try to account for them.

6. Imagine that your assignment is to write a paper that provides an overview of the issues at play in this case study. Write a memo to your instructor that identifies the issues and provides bibliographical citations and summaries of sources in the case study. After each summary, include a paragraph or two commenting on how the source compares with other sources in the discussion of issues. Conclude with comments on the strengths or limitations of the source. For sources that have limitations, try to account for them.

Writing Letters

7. Draft a letter to the Japanese American Citizens League explaining why you favor or oppose an apology for Iva Toguri.

8. Draft an op-ed piece for your campus or local newspaper summarizing Iva Toguri's story and explaining why you agree or disagree with Dyar's plea for a public apology for Toguri.

Writing Discovery Drafts

9. Review the discussion of discovery drafts in Chapter 2. Draft a paper that explains why Iva Toguri was in Japan when World War II broke out, summarizes her activities as "Orphan Ann," and explains when, where, and why she was arrested for broadcasting under the name Tokyo Rose.

10. Draft a paper that explains the media's role in the arrest, imprisonment, and trial of Iva Toguri.

11. Draft a paper that takes a position on whether or not the United States should issue a public apology to Iva Toguri.

Writing for an Academic Audience

12. Using your freewriting exercises and discovery drafts, write a paper that summarizes two perspectives on whether Iva Toguri was guilty of making treasonous broadcasts to American GIs during World War II. Your aim is to inform intended readers. You should incorporate a minimum of five sources from this case study in your paper.

13. Using your freewriting exercises and discovery drafts, write a paper that explains the media's role in the arrest, trial, and pardon of Iva Toguri. You should incorporate a minimum of six sources from this case study in your paper.

14. Using your freewriting exercises and discovery drafts, write a paper that defends your stance on the issue of issuing a national apology for Iva Toguri. You should incorporate a minimum of six sources from this case study in your paper.

WRITING ABOUT RELATED ISSUES

EXERCISES: FOCUS ON WRITING

1. **National apologies:** Official apologies from the U.S. government are made by the president, and they tend to come when the individuals who carried out any injustice are no longer on the scene. On May 16, 1999, for example, President Clinton made an emotional national apology to five men who survived the U.S. Public Health Service's secret experiments on

black men in Macon County, Alabama, conducted from 1932 to 1972. The experiments, known as the Tuskegee Study of Untreated Syphilis, allowed an estimated 400 black men to go untreated when they thought they were receiving free medical care and when standard methods of treating the disease were available. Never told they were part of a study, and never informed they had syphilis, the survivors received $10 million for damages after the study was made public, but no apology. President Clinton acknowledged that the apology was "so long in coming." Speaking to survivors, relatives of victims, health officials, and members of the Black Congressional Congress, he stated, "What was done cannot be undone, but we can end the silence. We can stop turning our heads away, we can look at you in the eye and finally say, on behalf of the American people, that the United States government was shameful, and I am sorry."

Working on your own, identify a situation that called for or that currently calls for a formal apology from a head of state. If you are reporting on an apology that has been made, explain whether it seems justified. If you are reporting on an apology that is being considered, explain why you think it should or should not be issued. Draw on a minimum of five sources.

2. **Brainstorming:** Write a paper that takes a position on an issue associated with one of the topics listed below or a topic that you've developed as you read the Tokyo Rose case study. You'll need to narrow your topic sufficiently. Your paper should cite a minimum of five sources, and it should be aimed at an academic audience.

Brainstorming

- Incarceration of Japanese Americans During World War II
- The Role of Women in the War Effort
- Stereotyping Minorities
- Treatment of Japanese Americans after the War
- American or British Propaganda During World War II
- Contributions by Minorities to the War Effort
- Scapegoats
- The Media's Influence on a Recent or Historical High-Profile Trial
- The Media's Portrayal of a Controversial Public Figure
- The Media's Response to an International Event
- The War in the Pacific

3. Write a paper that explains the process one must go through to secure a pardon at the federal level. Explain why pardons are usually given and identify to whom they have been given or identify an individual who is asking for a pardon and argue for or against that person's case.

Chapter 10

Listening to Writers' Voices

Ever since I was first read to, then started reading to myself, there has never been a line read that I didn't *hear*. As my eyes followed the sentence, a voice was saying it silently to me. It isn't my mother's voice, or the voice of any other person I can identify, certainly not my own. It is human, but inward, and it is inwardly that I listen to it.

—*Eudora Welty,* One Writer's Beginnings

"HEARING" WRITERS' VOICES

When we talk about a writer's *voice*, we refer to the writer's attitude, level of formality or informality, word choice, and sentence structure. The combination of these elements can make a distinctive impression on readers, imparting a sense of an actual personality behind the voice and establishing the writer as knowledgeable and credible. If you completed the postcard exercise in Chapter 1, you demonstrated your ability to address a variety of rhetorical situations, using different voices in brief notes to family and friends. As you work on developing a voice of your own that is appropriate for academic writing, you want to develop the ability to recognize voices that will lend credibility and authority to a paper when you incorporate them into the text. This chapter asks you to listen to writers' voices and to determine what features create voices of reason, authority, integrity, or experience to readers. In papers written from sources, you'll use other writers' voices to support your theses, provide examples or illustrations, support or refute an argument, provide testimony, or cite precedent. You'll use Case Study 2: The Public and Private Life of Dr. Thomas Anthony Dooley III, to consider how writers rely on other writers' voices to accomplish their purpose in writing.

The voices you hear on any controversial topic usually offer different perspectives, attitudes, interpretations, and evaluations, even if they're in agreement. If they don't agree with each other, the conversation takes on an edge as an argument develops and the tactics of point-counterpoint develop. You're probably familiar with situations that bring different voices together in arguments. Consider the many roundtable discussions you see on television featuring reporters, news commentators, lawmakers, or a variety of well-known personalities discussing newsworthy, controversial events. Each one brings a different voice to the conversation. If the voices were all the same, the program wouldn't be very interesting. This kind of programming owes its success in part to the dynamics at play in the different stance of each participant on whatever subject is open to discussion. Another appeal this kind of programming offers is each participant's understanding of how to communicate effectively with one another and the studio or viewing audience, primary and secondary audiences, respectively.

For writers, the equivalent of the televised roundtable discussion takes place in a variety of forums: newspapers, articles, and books. In a body of research compiled from these forums, you "hear" different voices. In the Tokyo Rose case study in Chapter 9, for example, you heard voices from the past and present, the voice of an organization, the voice of a government official, and reporters' voices as well. You heard both strong conviction and deep cynicism about Iva Toguri's innocence. And you heard expressions of indignation and admiration, as well as calls for negotiation. These voices give the case study a texture, like material with a rough weave: If you close your eyes and run your hand across it, you feel irregularities—the surface is alternately smooth and ragged. It's a stark contrast to a smooth piece of silk that has a consistent texture throughout.

READING AND "LISTENING"

What a writer has to say—content— is usually your primary consideration the first time you read a source. In subsequent readings, think about expression—that is, *how* writers present ideas and how they succeed or fail in creating a distinctive voice. Your critical reading skills play an important role in whether you recognize irony, cynicism, sarcasm, reverence, enthusiasm, skepticism, passion, solemnity, and other tones in a writer's voice. Case Study 2 includes multiple voices and rhetorical situations: writers' accounts of their personal experiences; their knowledge of an individual; their close observations of, or strong convictions about, a person or an issue; or their scholarly research on an individual. As you read and annotate sources, you should identify each voice you hear. Is it the voice of an individual? institution (university, religious group, the government)? anonymous publisher (unsigned articles in newspapers or magazines; unsigned entries in an encyclopedia)? or corporation (annual reports)? Then assess the writer's voice. Is it consistent? uneven? controlled? uncontrolled? inflated? rational? annoying? engaging? sarcastic? appropriate or inappropriate for the rhetorical situation? Does the writer speak from a position of authority? Does the writer show evidence of bias or prejudice? Overall, is the writer's voice strong? weak? effective or ineffective? What makes it so? Answers to these questions help you evaluate sources and determine whether to use them and how to use them in writing assignments.

THREE VOICES, ONE SUBJECT

To understand how word choice and sentence structure create a writer's voice, examine the following descriptions of Florence Nightingale from *Encyclopedia Britannica,* Lytton Strachey's *Eminent Victorians*, and Rafael Sabatini's *Heroic Lives*. Each excerpt is taken from the writer's introductory paragraph. As you read, try to determine the writer's attitude toward Florence Nightingale and speculate on the writer's purpose in writing. Also, decide how you would characterize each writer's voice; is it respectful? serious? neutral? reverent? facetious? ironic? earnest? Be prepared to cite specific words and phrases that create the voice you hear in each selection.

Nightingale, Florence (1820–1910), an Englishwoman, is generally accepted as being the originator and founder of modern nursing. Of almost equal importance are her achievements in the field of public health, especially those relating to the sanitary condition of hospitals and barracks, while by her example, her personality, and her attainments she did more than perhaps any other one woman to bring about the emancipation of women.

Encyclopedia Britannica.

Everyone knows the popular conception of Florence Nightingale. The saintly, self-sacrificing woman, the delicate maiden of high degree who threw aside the pleasures of a life of ease to succour the afflicted, the Lady with the Lamp, gliding through the horrors of the hospital at Scutari, and consecrating with the radiance of her goodness the dying soldier's couch—the vision is familiar to all. But the truth was different. The Miss Nightingale of fact was not as facile fancy painted her. She worked in another fashion, and towards another end; she moved under the stress of an impetus which finds no place in the popular imagination. A Demon possessed her. Now demons, whatever else they may be, are full of interest. And so it happens that in the real Miss Nightingale there was more that was interesting than in the legendary one; there was also less that was agreeable.

Strachey, Lytton. *Eminent Victorians.* New York: Putnam, 1918. 135.

Some of Florence Nightingale's most ardent admirers in her own day compared her with Joan of Arc.

It is no detraction from the merit of either of those heroines to say that no parallel exists.

On the one hand, we have a peasant girl acting upon an instinctive impulse, driven and guided by an inner voice which assumes to her simple mind an objective character, taking up a task that properly belongs to the other sex.

On the other hand, we have a lady, delicately nurtured and carefully educated, pursuing a reasoned course in a province entirely feminine.

In common they possess a selfless devotion to a cause and to the service of an ideal, so unstinting that it is not to be daunted by any personal sacrifice. They have it also in common that each was under the necessity of overcoming at the outset barriers of prejudice and opposition before which souls less altruistic would have fainted, and that each, in the sphere of her activity, left behind her, as all heroes leave, an inspiration to posterity.

Sabatini, Rafael. *Heroic Lives*. Freeport: Books for Libraries, 1971. 363.

Now consider the purpose of each writer. The purpose of the reference-book description of Miss Nightingale is to provide information. Notice the absence of descriptive passages. Here the tone is neutral. You can probably tell from the tone of the Strachey entry that the title *Eminent Victorians* is ironic. His purpose is to topple Victorian sacred cows, using biographical essays that set the record straight about the lives of an "ecclesiastical [Henry Edward Manning, Cardinal in the Catholic Church], an educational authority [Dr. Thomas Arnold, headmaster of Rugby], a woman of action [Miss Nightingale], and a man of Adventure [General Gordon, who led British troops in the defense of Khartom]." Notice the words he uses to describe Miss Nightingale and the verbs he uses to create images of her. Strachey's Florence Nightingale is a busy lady. The title of Sabatini's book, *Heroic Lives*, is in earnest; his purpose is to present Richard Lionheart, Saint Francis of Assisi, Joan of Arc, Sir Walter Raleigh, Lord Nelson, and Florence Nightingale as heroes. The tone of the excerpt—notice the words he uses to describe Miss Nightingale and the strategy of contrasting Joan of Arc with Miss Nightingale ("on one hand" and "on the other hand")—illustrates Sabatini's reverence for his subject.

SYNTHESIZING WRITERS' VOICES

Several of the sources in this book illustrate how writers incorporate multiple voices into a text. For these sources, you'll need to do more than identify the voices. Consider whether a writer lets you hear other writers' voices directly or indirectly. Quotations, for example, give you a chance to hear another writer's voice. Paraphrases and summaries, however, filter a writer's voice and allow you to hear it indirectly through another writer. You'll also need to reflect on the author's attitude toward voices he or she synthesizes in a text, and record your impressions. For example, what tone does the writer use to introduce voices that agree with the ideas or arguments the writer supports? Does the writer suggest that these voices are reasonable? well-informed? sensible? authoritative? Does the writer include voices of dissension? What tone does the writer use when he or she introduces or takes issue with voices of dissension? Does the writer suggest indirectly or state outright that voices of dissension are uninformed, biased, or prejudiced? If the writer attempts to discredit voices of dissension, does the writer characterize these voices as unreasonable? irrational? absurd? Overall, does the synthesis of other writers' voices suggest that the writer has selected voices that fully address an issue, providing readers with sufficient information? Do you suspect that the writer has omitted or overlooked voices that should be heard if readers are to examine a topic or issue thoroughly?

When you synthesize sources, you don't want to use voices at random, incorporating other writers' voices just for the sake of citing a required number of sources. If you use other writers' voices haphazardly, your readers will notice. Nor do you want to incorporate inappropriate voices into a paper. You can compare careless or haphazard source selection with choosing the well-meaning, enthusiastic, but off-key soprano and tenor as soloists from the choir. Their voices attract notice, but not for the right reasons. The Introduction included an excerpt from a student paper on animal experimentation, illustrating a reader's failure to identify irony in a writer's voice and the problem that resulted when a writer unknowingly synthesized a facetious voice in a research paper. If the writer fails to "hear" the facetious voice, you might ask whether the writer also fails to "hear" sincerity, conviction, irony, earnestness, or humor.

When you develop the ability to "listen" to writers' voices and to identify techniques writers use to convey meaning and purpose, you can use other writers' voices to help you achieve your purpose in writing. By listening to your own voice as a writer, you can detect passages that sound unsure or that "hedge" on issues, as well as passages that strike the note of authority and credibility. In general, a writer establishes an authoritative, credible voice by

- Having a thorough understanding of a topic
- Having a clear sense of what he or she seeks to accomplish (to describe, to explain, to persuade)
- Having a clear sense of who the intended readers are—what they value (sense of humor, seriousness, conformity, nonconformity); what they share in common (gender, age, political affiliation, level of education, social class, economic background, occupation); what goals they have; how they may use the information the writer offers
- Having a clear sense of the emphasis (appeals to logic, emotions, ethics) that will engage and motivate readers
- Having a clear sense of what readers will consider appropriate and inappropriate expression of ideas (usage standards, jargon, specialized language, key terms)

The case study that follows asks you to "listen" to writers' voices as they discuss the public and private lives of Dr. Thomas Anthony Dooley III. As you "listen," try to determine what features create voices of reason, authority, partiality, integrity, prejudice, or experience.

LISTENING TO WRITER'S VOICES

As a reader, you "listen" to voices in a text to

- Understand fully the relationships between writers and their subjects and intended readers.
- Identify the strategies that succeed or fail in influencing readers' opinions.
- Determine if a writer's voice is appropriate to quote, summarize, or paraphrase.

PREVIEW: THOMAS ANTHONY DOOLEY—AMERICAN HERO

Dr. Thomas Anthony Dooley III was a well-known figure to the American public in the 1950s and early 1960s. He resigned from the navy in 1956, ending a career as a navy doctor that included service in Vietnam, where he treated the health problems of thousands of refugees fleeing communist rule. As a civilian, he returned to Southeast Asia and founded MEDICO (Medical International Cooperation), which was funded by volunteer support. In 1960, a Gallop Poll named him one of the ten most admired Americans. Dooley died of cancer in 1961, at the age of thirty-four.

As you read and annotate sources in the case study that follows, pay particular attention to writers' discussion of Dooley's resignation from the navy. His own account, as well as others published from the 1950s until 1989, fails to mention that he was forced to resign from the navy because he was homosexual. In *The Catholic Counterculture in America 1933–1962,* James Terrance Fisher provides an explanation:

A CATHOLIC ERRAND IN THE WILDERNESS: TOM DOOLEY IN LAOS AND AMERICA, 1956–1961

JAMES TERRANCE FISHER

Dooley seemed well on his way toward his avowed ultimate goal, the Surgeon Generalship of the Navy. Thus it was no small shock when one evening in February 1956 he told his mother: "I'm resigning from the Navy, and I'm going to Laos." It was as simple as that.

Dooley's abrupt resignation from the Navy—effective March 28, 1956—was linked to his sexuality. He was apparently charged with involvement with a group of homosexual officers stationed at Yokosuka in 1954 and 1955. People who knew him as an adolescent report that he began having sexual relations with men, at the latest, while a student at St. Louis University High School. Amidst the

insular, conformist atmosphere at Notre Dame, he was widely perceived as "queer," although that term did not necessarily indicate active homosexuality. Homosexuality was obviously not considered an appropriate topic for conversation among Catholics; in clerical journals it was gingerly treated as a perversion of natural law; what Dorothy Day termed the "most loathsome" of sins. One of Dooley's St. Louis classmates recalled that his own Irish-Catholic mother, an educator, believed that homosexuality was something which "only happened in hell."

In 1959 the FBI began an inquiry into the circumstances surrounding Dooley's resignation from the Navy. An FBI memorandum of December

11, 1959, reported that the Office of Naval Intelligence "had conducted an investigation of Dooley while Dooley was in the Navy and that Dooley had been permitted to resign from the Navy for the good of the service in order to avoid a general court-martial.... Dooley had been interviewed concerning allegations of homosexuality at which time he admitted to ONI a long history of that trait.

In a March 9, 1960, memorandum concerning an invitation to J. Edgar Hoover to appear at an interfaith gathering honoring Dooley and others, a bureau agent explained that "Dooley was discharged from the Navy because of homosexuality" and concluded that "certainly the Director would not desire to appear on a program with Dooley." Hoover readily concurred.

Source: James Terrance Fisher, "A Catholic Errand in the Wilderness: Tom Dooley in Laos and America, 1956–1961," *The Catholic Counterculture in America 1933–1962* (Chapel Hill: U. North Carolina P. 1989) 167–168.

Randy Shilts used the story of Dooley's forced resignation from the military as the introductory and concluding chapters to *Conduct Unbecoming: Lesbians and Gays in the U.S. Military: Vietnam to the Persian Gulf.*

EXERCISE: FOCUS ON WRITING

Before you read what others say about privacy issues, spend ten to fifteen minutes exploring your own ideas about this topic. What kinds of privacy issues concern you? What do you consider the biggest threat to an individual's privacy?

FOCUS ON RELATED ISSUES: PRIVACY PROTECTION

George Orwell's vision of the future in the novel *1984* predicted that Big Brother would be watching us. In truth, in the twenty-first century we may not know who is watching—or why. There is a good case to be made that personal privacy is slipping away rapidly in a "need to know" culture equipped with the technology to intrude into our personal lives in ways we may never suspect. Someone can learn a lot about you by accessing any number of records you may assume are private: medical, financial, military, legal, and academic records; work history; and consumer credit information, to name a few. Sophisticated electronic systems collect, assess, and distribute information, making it possible to create extensive records on anyone with a Social Security number or a driver's license. The kind of information these systems gather may be used primarily for seemingly innocuous purposes— for example, providing or selling information to telemarketers. However, for households bombarded with telemarketers' unsolicited phone calls, the loss of privacy is a nuisance. While we may be thankful for rapid information

FOCUS ON RELATED ISSUES (continued)

FOCUS ON RELATED ISSUES *(continued)*

systems that allow law enforcement agencies to track criminals and post all-points bulletins on missing children or suspects, the sophistication of technology in the information age is, in many ways, a double-edged sword. It isn't difficult to find examples of identity theft, fraud, and other abuses.

The Electronic Privacy Information Center and Privacy International identify globalization, modern information systems, and multimedia as three of the greatest threats to individual privacy. They also define four areas of privacy protection:

1. *Information privacy,* which involves the establishment of rules governing the collection and handling of personal data such as credit card information and medical records

2. *Bodily privacy,* which concerns the protection of people's physical selves against invasive procedures such as drug testing and cavity searches

3. *Privacy of communications,* which covers the security and privacy of mail, telephones, e-mail, and other forms of communication.

4. *Territorial privacy,* which concerns the setting of limits on intrusion into the domestic and other environments such as the workplace or public space.*

As a possible topic for library research, consider some aspect of privacy. Use the issues raised here as a starting point to narrow and shape a topic that will be appropriate for a documented paper.

---

*Privacy and Human Rights: An International Survey of Privacy Laws and Developments. Electronic Privacy Center and Privacy International, 25 April 2000. <http://www.privacy international.org/Survey/Overview.html#Heading2>

Case Study 2:
The Public
and Private Lives of
Dr. Thomas Anthony
Dooley III

The outing of the dead presents a different dilemma. There are no privacy issues here: under American law, the dead have no right to privacy. That's how it should be."

— *Randy Shilts, "Is 'Outing' Gays Ethical?*

The personal and historical forces that helped compose the mystery of Dr. Tom Dooley—including the dark romance of his secret life as a "compromised" homosexual, beholden to elements of the U.S. intelligence community—ranged far beyond the conventional limits of his religious background and identity....

—*James T. Fisher,* Dr. America: The Lives of Thomas A. Dooley 1927–1961

IN PRAISE OF DR. DOOLEY

In 1961, the U.S. Senate and House of Representatives passed a joint resolution approving a gold medal to be awarded posthumously to Dr. Thomas Anthony Dooley III. The record of public bills approved by the Senate during the 87th Congress, first session, includes a general statement indicating that the proposal to honor Dooley had received "widespread and bipartisan support," a summary of Dr. Dooley's life, and several letters to the Honorable A. Willis Roberston, Senate Chairman on Banking and Currency supporting the award to Dr. Dooley. The Senate records indicate that neither the State nor Treasury Departments offered objection to the joint resolution. Included in the record is a letter from Senator Hubert H. Humphrey.

LETTER FROM HUBERT H. HUMPHREY TO THE HONORABLE A. WILLIS ROBERSTON, SENATE CHAIRMAN ON BANKING AND CURRENCY

U.S. Senate
Committee on Government Operations
May 10, 1961

Hon. Willis Robertson,
Committee on Banking and Currency,
U.S. Senate, Washington, D.C.

Dear Senator: I am advised that your committee will consider Senate Joint Resolution 64, which I introduced, to authorize the President of the United States to award posthumously a medal to Dr. Thomas Anthony Dooley III.

Dr. Dooley was a great American and a great humanitarian. Through Medico, the medical organization he co-founded, the people in the teeming jungles of southeast Asia not only were given the medical care they so vitally needed, but also were exposed to the wondrous personality of this deeply religious and inspiring young man. "Dr. Tom" as he was called by those who loved him, put into action what so many of us often idealistically talk about, that is, compassionately aiding people less fortunate than ourselves.

Born in St. Louis, Dr. Dooley attended the University of Notre Dame. He served 2 years as a Navy corpsman during World War II, after which he enrolled at St. Louis University Medical School where he was graduated in 1953 and rejoined the Navy for his internship.

As you know, although suffering from cancer which claimed his life the day after his 34th birthday, Dr. Dooley insisted on returning to Laos where, from the proceeds of his three books, he established two hospitals. These were turned over to the Laos Government.

Dr. Dooley, during his short lifetime, earned the respect and admiration of peoples throughout the world through his selflessness and Christ-like charity.

I was pleased to see that the House Banking and Currency Committee on May 9 favorably reported Congressman Reuss' House Joint Resolution 306, which is a companion measure to my Senate Joint Resolution 64, and I urge the Senate committee to act similarly in Senate Joint Resolution 64. Sincerely,

Hubert H. Humphrey

Source: Published in Rep. 257 from the Committee on Banking and Currency submitted by Senator George Bush: 87th Congress, 1st session, Washington: GPO, 1961.

1. Describe the voice you hear in the letter. Cite specific words or phrases that create the voice you described.
2. What is the writer's stance toward his subject?
3. What kinds of appeals does Senator Humphrey use?
4. What claims does he make about Dr. Dooley?
5. What assumptions does Senator Humphrey reveal in this letter?

TOM DOOLEY: JUNGLE DOCTOR

Dr. Tom Dooley wrote about his experiences as a navy and civilian doctor in Laos and Vietnam in three books: *Deliver Us From Evil* (1956), *The Edge of Tomorrow* (1958), and *The Night They Burned the Mountain* (1960). The following is a chapter from *The Edge of Tomorrow*.

"BUT I HAVE PROMISES TO KEEP"

THOMAS ANTHONY DOOLEY

High above the Pacific, flying westward in a luxury airliner, the night passes swiftly. Passengers put away their books and briefcases; one by one, the reading lights wink out. Lulled by the monotonous beat of the engines, the Honolulu-bound vacationers and the businessmen bound for Tokyo and Manila slumber peacefully.

But I am the sleepless traveler, my mind filled with memories that are more captivating than dreams. I close my eyes and recall that wretched refugee camp in Haiphong in the Spring of '55. Operation Cockroach the Navy called us—one young Navy doctor, still professionally wet-behind-the-ears; four young enlisted men who had only a few months' training as hospital corpsmen; and a half-million filthy, diseased, muti-

lated Asians fleeing from the godless cruelties of Communism.

That was North Viet Nam during what was ironically called the "Passage to Freedom." That was where Dooley really came of age.

How many times have I told that story? I told it not only in the pages of *Deliver Us from Evil,* but whenever and wherever I could find Americans who were willing to listen. But, at least, it was never told in vainglory. For what we *did* in dying Haiphong was far less important than what we *learned* there.

We had seen simple, tender, loving care—the crudest kind of medicine inexpertly practiced by mere boys—change a people's fear and hatred into friendship and understanding. We had witnessed the power of medical aid to reach the hearts and souls of a nation. We had seen it transform the brotherhood of man from an ideal into a reality that plain people could understand.

To me that experience was like the white light of revelation. It made me proud to be a doctor. Proud to be an American doctor who had been privileged to witness the enormous possibilities of *medical aid* in all its Christlike power and simplicity. Was that why the foreign-aid planners, with their billion-dollar projects, found it difficult to understand?

I preached so ardently that my folks began to worry. "Look, Dooley," my friends would say, "you've had adventure enough. When are you going to settle down?" My mother reminded me of all the things I had always wanted, and now might have. A home, a wife, kids, a nice medical practice, maybe a few fine hunting horses. My old medical mentor told me I'd better get on with my post-graduate training if I hoped to be a good orthopedic surgeon.

How could I make them see that things would never be the same?

I remember those lines by Robert Frost that kept echoing in my mind during those fretful days:

The woods are lovely, dark and
   deep,
But I have promises to keep,
And miles to go before I sleep.

I knew the promises I had to keep. I knew that the keeping of them would take me many miles, back to Southeast Asia, to the very edge of tomorrow, where the future might be made—or lost.

One evening in February 1956, after I had been home from Asia only a few months, I went to a dinner at the Vietnamese Embassy in Washington, D.C. This night I had a premonition that all hope of returning to Indo-China with a medical team of my own would hinge on whatever happened at that dinner.

Regretfully, I was aware that I could not go back to Viet Nam. The north was now locked behind the Bamboo Curtain. I was not needed in the south where the medical teams of the Filipinos' Operation Brotherhood were already doing a wonderful job. Where else could I operate and utilize my knowledge of Indo-China? Cambodia? Laos? Would I, as an American, be welcome there in view of the ticklish political situation?

To help me find an answer to these questions, my good friend, Ambassador Tran Van Chuong of Viet Nam, had arranged a dinner party for me to which he had invited a number of Cambodian and Laotian diplomats. Late that evening I was still talking about the kind of medical mission I had in mind—small, privately financed (mostly out of my own pocket), without any government or church sponsorship or obligations. The team would consist only of myself and a few of the young Americans who had served with me in North Viet Nam.

We would be plain Americans working among the plain people of the country, wherever we were needed, in paddy fields and villages, in jungles and mountains. Perhaps, if we did a good job, we might inspire other Americans, doctors and laymen, to follow our example of international cooperation on a people-to-people basis.

The Cambodians listened, politely non-committal. But I saw that the Laotian ambassador, the Hon. Ourot Souvannavong, was following me with keen interest.

"But, Dr. Dooley," he asked, "why should you, a young man just released from your naval duty, with a career before you, choose to make this sacrifice? Obviously, you have much to offer. But what do you stand to gain?"

Once more, I tried to explain my deep conviction that medical aid, offered on a people-to-people basis, could form lasting bonds of friendship between East and West. If this was true, we American doctors had a duty to perform. Since I had served in Southeast Asia and had seen the need, the duty for me as an individual was inescapable. Besides, I was young, unattached, free to go wherever I was needed.

Suddenly, I remembered something that big, hardboiled Boatswain's Mate Norman Baker had once said in answer to a somewhat similar question. Gambling on my ability to translate Baker's homespun American into French, I explained how Baker had groped for words to explain our motives, and then blurted out:

"Aw, hell, sir, we just want to do what we can for people who ain't got it so good!"

The Cambodians raised their eyebrows and smiled—Baker's words had hit the mark. But Ambassador Souvannavong beamed, and from the way he shook his head in frank admiration I could practically read his mind: These incredible Americans!

"Dr. Dooley," he said, "my country would be honored to receive your mission. Will you come to see me at the Embassy in the morning?"

The following day, seated in his study, the Ambassador gave me a briefing on social and political conditions in the Kingdom of Laos. He began by telling me why medical teams like mine were needed there. For the entire population of about two million, he said, Laos had only *one* doctor who was a medical graduate by western standards. He watched my astonishment with a sad smile.

"Oh, we have a few young men we call *médecins indochinois*," he added. "They are graduates of the *lycée* who have had a little medical training. But for the vast majority of our sick people there are only the witch doctors and the sorceress." (The *lycée* is roughly equivalent to an American junior high school.)

Then the Ambassador explained that the one doctor in Laos was his nephew, Dr. Oudom Souvannavong, who was also the Minister of Health. "I am sure he will welcome you, and give you all the help you need," he said. "And I must warn you, Doctor, that you will need help and guidance. You will find everything in my country difficult, possibly dangerous."

We stood before a huge wall map, and the landlocked Kingdom of Laos, which extends down the middle of the Indo-China peninsula, reminded me of a long bony finger, with the huge knuckle attached to the red hand of

China and the fingertip poking into Cambodia and South Viet Nam.

Ambassador Souvannavong pointed to the northwest province bordering on China and Burma. For the first time I noticed a name that was to haunt me—Nam Tha.

"If you go up here, where you will be needed most," he said, "you may face considerable danger. Nam Tha is isolated, the people are poor, disease is rampant. The political situation is delicate—very difficult for a Westerner to understand."

I looked at the map, and was struck by the fact that Nam Tha lies almost on a straight line due west of the tragic city of Haiphong in North Viet Nam—perhaps 500 miles as the vulture flies. The two adjoining provinces had become the temporary haven of the Communist-led Pathet Lao under the terms laid down by the Geneva Conference of 1954—the same conference that had partitioned Viet Nam and committed Cambodia and Laos to a "neutralized" status in Indo-China.

I said we were willing to take our chances, but I also promised to be discreet. Ambassador Souvannavong shook my hand warmly, and assured me that he had confidence in me.

"Many times before," he said, "white men have come to help us. But always they had other motives—colonization, trade, even our religious conversion. I really believe your motive is purely humanitarian. That will make your mission unique in my country," he said. Then, with a twinkle in his eye, he added: "And, also, for some of my people, a trifle hard to believe."

To give my mission legal status, Angier Biddle Duke, president of the International Rescue Committee, arranged to have us taken under the aegis of the IRC, which enjoys worldwide respect. I took another look at the bank account in which I had been salting away the proceeds from my book and lecture tour, and said a prayer. Then, profiting by my experience in Viet Nam, I again made the rounds of the pharmaceutical companies and surgical supply houses with my hat in hand.

Their understanding and generosity overwhelmed me. The Charles Pfizer Company gave me over $100,000 worth of antibiotics. Johnson & Johnson supplied bandages and surgical dressings. The A. S. Aloe Company of St. Louis, Mo., donated a complete line of surgical instruments and equipment, and the Aloe employees passed the hat and presented me with a handsome check!

The Mead Johnson Company give me a bill of lading for a huge supply of vitamins and protein extract, and Mr. Johnson wrote out his personal check for $5,000. Walt Disney presented us with a sound projector and a collection of Disney movies for the children of Laos. The Willys Company presented us with a jeep, especially constructed for rough-country operations. (We later named the vehicle Agnes, after my mother.)

I went to Abercrombie & Fitch in New York and ordered a lot of essential equipment—cookstoves, lanterns, sleeping bags, etc. The bill was staggering. When the salesman learned the nature of my mission, he excused himself and disappeared into a vice-president's office. He came back with the bill slashed to a fraction of the original amount.

One day in Washington, D.C., I was waiting to testify at a hearing of the International Rescue Committee concerning free Viet Nam's role in Asia today. A dynamic little woman, who was very late, sat down beside me in the last row and whispered, "Has Doctor Dooley given his speech yet?" I smiled and said, "No, but he should be great." She nodded and said, "I have been chasing that man halfway around the country." "Why?" "I want to give him five thousand pounds of protein." At that moment I was called as the next speaker. We met afterwards in the corridor and it turned out that she was the affable Miss Florence Rose, executive secretary of the Meals for Millions Foundation. She did give me five thousand pounds of their multi-purpose food, which was directly responsible for saving hundreds of lives in my mountain hospital during the following year.

The U. S. Navy did not let me down. They agreed to transport the tons of medicines, food and equipment that I had accumulated, even though I was now a civilian. They transferred this for me to South Viet Nam, at a tremendous saving to my mission.

I spent several weeks going in and out of the various American agencies in Washington concerned with work in Asia. The International Cooperation Administration promised me a great deal, sincerely and genuinely, but the end result coming from their men-on-the-scene in Laos, turned out to be very little. However, I.C.A. in Washington helped me greatly in the earlier planning stages. So did the United States Information Agency, which pledged a battery-run tape recorder.

During this period I met Mrs. Raymond Clapper, widow of the famous war correspondent killed in Korea. Mrs. Clapper is the head of the CARE offices in Washington, D.C. By guiding my steps, introducing me to people, and just being a good friend, Mrs. Clapper became a sort of midwife to the birth of Operation Laos of the International Rescue Committee. (Incidentally, CARE has an excellent midwife kit, in appearance much like the flight bags which air travelers carry; it was Mrs. Clapper's idea that CARE donate about fifty kits to the graduates of the midwife classes that I planned to inaugurate. Later in my story you will learn the good use to which they were put.)

But I had left the most difficult phase of the plan—lining up my men—until the last. All along I had been counting on Norman Baker, Peter Kessey, and Dennis Shepard, the most devoted and dependable of the enlisted men who had been with me in North Viet Nam. This wasn't going to be easy. Denny Shepard, newly married, was taking his premed at the University of Oregon. Pete Kessey was attending pharmacy school in Austin, Texas. Baker, also a bridegroom, was still in the Navy. Would they as civilians return to that part of Asia where they had seen such wretchedness?

However, Pete and Denny responded to my call promptly and enthusiastically. Baker's ship was somewhere at sea; several weeks passed before I could get in touch with him. Then one day, in Washington, I received a long-distance call from Baker in San Diego. When I told him about Operation Laos, his roar could be heard from coast to coast, even without the help of AT&T.

"What! Back to Indo-China? Are you crazy? Why, you slave-driving fool—sir—you couldn't pay me to go back into that hellhole! Besides, my wife wouldn't stand for it! Hell, no—not a chance!"

There was an awkward silence. I just let him simmer down. Then....

"Hello ... You still there, Doc? Listen, you don't really need *me,* do you? What makes you think we can do any real good out there? And there's something you seem to have forgotten. (*Hearty chuckle.*) Little Old Baker is still the pride and joy of Uncle Sam's Navy!"

I assured him that I needed him, that Operation Laos was one helluva big challenge, and that I was pretty sure I could get him out of the Navy on an early discharge. I could hear him grumbling and meaning.

"Aw, whatehell, Doc, sure, I *volunteer!* But Priscilla's going to divorce me for this, sure as shootin'!"

(Bless her heart, Priscilla Baker did nothing of the sort. She went right ahead with a project I didn't know about at the time—having their baby.)

In July, 1956, after a short seven months in America, I started on my return trip to Asia. I lectured in Hawaii, Japan, Hong Kong, and then flew to the Philippines to speak with the founders of Operation Brotherhood. From them I could glean much for my own mission, for we had really borrowed the whole idea of non-governmental, non-sectarian medical service to foreign nations from this Filipino endeavor.

My men followed behind me, and we were to meet in the Philippines.

On a sweltering day in August I stood in the Manila airport watching a plane glide down through the heat haze rising from the runway. It taxied around, and the door swung open. Out stepped Pete Kessey, our lean and hungry looking Texan, followed by 200-pound barrel-cheated Baker (flexing his muscles, as always), and then quiet, serious Denny Shepard. How very young they looked! Pete and Denny were 25. Baker was still only 21. Yet they were more mature and dependable than most men twice their age.

We had about an hour's wait before leaving for Saigon, which was to be our "staging area." The boys plied me with questions. What kind of gear did we have? How had I ever high-pressured the Navy into hauling the four tons of stuff to Saigon? Where did we go from there? What kind of place was Laos? ("Yeah, man," groaned Baker. "I can see now that this means living on C-rations and holding 24-hour sick-call!")

When we were back aboard the plane, the talk turned serious. I got out my map and explained that, if my plans went through, we would operate up north in the province of Nam Tha. Denny gave a long, low whistle of surprise. He had a bundle of notes and clippings, and knew as much about Laos as I did.

I told them about the flying trip I had made to Hong Kong to meet Oden Meeker, a dynamic young American, who had served in Laos with CARE during the famine of 1954. Oden strongly favored the plan to operate in Nam Tha. It was a critical area, he said, the most isolated part of Laos, and politically the most vulnerable. "Those mountain people have rarely seen a white man," said Oden. "They have no allegiance to the central government. They're just ripe for the Commie treatment."

The boys listened solemnly. Then Baker said: "Look, Doc, you've got to level with us. What are the odds on this setup? I'm a married man now. So is Denny. Fact is, Priscilla's going to have a baby. Besides. I never did like the sound of those Chinese prison camps!"

Well, I said, the odds were about standard for that part of the world. No better, no worse. We'd been in tough spots before, but we had done our jobs, and come through with our hides intact. Baker hooted.

"Oh, we sure did—only you forget that we had the U.S. Navy back of us last time!"

I let that pass, and switched to the kind of job we had to do. We wouldn't be "showing the flag" so much this time, as we had in Haiphong; we'd be showing American face to a lot of Asians who had been told that American white-men didn't give a damn. I reminded them of what we had learned in Haiphong, and invited them to think of what we could accomplish by working among people on the village level in Laos.

Pete Kessey spoke up. "Doc, it looks to me like you expect to accomplish an awful lot in a short time. You know we only signed on for six months. You think we can do a job by then? And what happens to you when we pull out?"

That was the one part of the plan that had me worried, but I couldn't admit it. After six months, I said, I'd be able to play it by ear. I told them about the *médecins indochinois*. Maybe I could train a few young Lao to serve as assistants. And I also had a scheme in mind for getting a few replacements from the States.

They sensed that I was whistling in the dark. Baker declared that this was the screwiest part of the whole setup. Pete just shook his head. I was glad when Denny Shepard broke it up.

"This is one devil of a time to be talking about going home," he said. "We're not even there yet!"

Source: Thomas Anthony Dooley, "But I Have Promises to Keep," *The Edge of Tomorrow* (New York: Farrar, 1958) 133–140.

EXERCISES: READING AND RESPONDING

1. Identify passages in the chapter that create the persona of Dooley as humanitarian, patriot, and jungle doctor, respectively. Analyze how Dooley creates each persona.

2. Besides Dooley's voice, how many other voices do you hear in this chapter? Who are the other voices? How do these voices complement Dooley's voice?

3. What kind of rhetorical effect does the parenthetical statement "mostly out of my pocket" have? Explain why the statement would or would not have the same effect without the parentheses?

4. Find the passages that describe Dooley's resignation from the navy. What explanation does he offer for his resignation?

5. Dooley explained his motivation for returning to Southeast Asia as a missionary doctor by quoting a "hard-boiled Boatswain's Mate, Norman Baker, who once said, 'Aw, hell, sir, we just want to do what we can for people who ain't got it so good!'" What rhetorical effect would this explanation have on Dooley's intended readers? Speculate on Dooley's reasons for using this quotation rather than a more genteel, eloquent explanation.

6. Identify passages in the chapter that cause you to believe in or doubt Dooley's sincerity. Also, identify passages that establish Dooley as a credible source about his own experiences. Identify any passages that make you doubt that Dooley is a credible source.

7. The entry on Dooley in the *New Encyclopedia Britannica* (1992) states that "some of ... [Dooley's] colleagues in Asia regarded him as an egotist who allowed medical services to deteriorate while he engaged in self-promotion." Identify any passages in the chapter that refute or validate this claim.

When Admiral Arleigh Burke retired in 1961, his stint as chief of naval operations was the longest in the history of the U.S. Navy. His three terms hold the record to date. In 1956, he offered the following tribute to Dooley.

FOREWORD TO *DELIVER US FROM EVIL*

ADMIRAL ARLEIGH BURKE

The United States Navy has always been proud of its men, proud of their character, of their American ideals and convictions.

The heart of the Navy is found in its men—skilled, imaginative, courageous, alert, enthusiastic and kindly men. No organization in the world depends so much upon the individual initiative of its men as do we in the Navy.

The Navy is essentially a combat organization but one whose primary purpose is to support our government to the utmost both in peace and war. As a result, Navy men must continuously train thousands of other men to accomplish skillfully a myriad of undertakings. The Navy's training program is a never-ending chain. It teaches the real meaning of service to one's fellow men. It also teaches men to become technically proficient and to utilize the most modern tools in existence.

Today's naval traditions have been built by generations of men like young Doctor Dooley who have served their country well under arduous and challenging circumstances. The American sailor is ofttimes (as was Doctor Dooley) confronted with situations in which proper courses of action could not have been pre-planned or pre-determined.

Therefore in his training, whether as line officer, doctor or boatswain's mate, each individual must have pre-pared himself to assume responsibility and to act in accordance with his best judgment. Every Navy man must know that the life of his ship, and the success of his country, may sometimes depend upon his willingness and his ability to act boldly and independently for the common good.

Hence sailors will read with pride, as will all Americans, the courageous exploits of the young lieutenant, Doctor Dooley. His humanitarian actions are the kind of good deeds that will remain indelibly impressed in people's hearts—good deeds that neither propaganda nor brainwashing will ever stain.

Through the tireless work of his small naval unit in the huge refugees camps of the hostile and turbulent North Viet Nam country, he has won for America the love and admiration of thousands and thousands of refugees who passed through these camps on their historic march to freedom.

Lieutenant Dooley, a naval med-ical officer on independent duty, con-tributed greatly to the welfare of mankind and to an understanding of the fundamental principles of the United States, as he participated in this epoch-making period of world history. In DELIVER US FROM EVIL he has written that story with freshness, clarity and force. It is a story that will be told and re-told.

It is a story of which the United States Navy is proud.

Source: Admiral Arleigh Burke, foreword, *Deliver Us From Evil* (New York: Farrar. 1956) 7–8.

EXERCISES: READING AND RESPONDING

1. When a writer contributes a foreword to a book, what is his or her primary purpose?
2. Would you characterize Admiral Burke's voice as the voice of an individual or the voice of an institution (speaking on behalf of the U.S. Navy)?
3. What does Burke's voice convey about his attitude toward his subject?
4. Underline passages that seem to be Burke's opinion. Circle passages that seem to be fact. Is the foreword primarily fact or opinion?

Creating a Geographical Context

In "But I Have Promises to Keep," Dooley describes Laos: "We [Dooley and Laotian Ambassador Souvannavong] stood before a huge map, and the landlocked Kingdom of Laos, which extends down the middle of the Indo-China peninsula, reminded me of a long bony finger, with the huge knuckle attached to the red hand of China and the fingertip poking into Cambodia and South Viet Nam." To create a geographical context for Dooley's adventures in Southeast Asia, find Laos, Vietnam, Nam Tha, and Haiphong on the map in Figure 10.1.

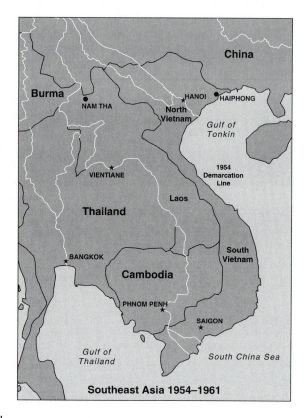

Southeast Asia 1954–1961

FIGURE 10.1

Dooley's obituary appeared on the front page of *The New York Times*, January 19, 1961. As you annotate Dooley's obituary, which follows, listen to the voices you hear commenting on Dooley, and note the facts reported about Dooley's life.

DR. DOOLEY DEAD; BUILT LAOS CLINICS

Dr. Thomas Dooley, the medical missionary, died here last night at Memorial Hospital. Death by cancer, which he calmly awaited for two years, came at 9:40 P.M.

Dr. Dooley, famed for work in establishing hospitals in Laos, was 34 years old Tuesday. He was visited then by Cardinal Spellman, who said yesterday:

"I tried to assure him that in his thirty-four years he had done what very few have done in the allotted scriptural life span."

The patient also received hundreds of birthday messages including a telegram from President Eisenhower.

'Accomplished So Much'

"It must be a source of heartened gratification," the President said, "to realize that in so few years you have accomplished so much for the good of distant peoples and have inspired so many others to work for all humanity."

Dr Dooley underwent surgery for chest cancer at Memorial Hospital in 1959, but returned to his work in Laos, although he knew that the disease was likely to recur. He was forced to return to Memorial Hospital last month.

In an article written for *The New York Times Magazine* in 1958, Dr. Dooley summed up his work in Laos as follows:

"I believe that it behooves those of us to attempt to aid in a foreign land to be content with small achievements. We must not attempt to build dynasties. We must try to build at the level of the people, or just one step ahead, always planning it so that the Asian can ultimately take over."

The statement reflected the will of the author but not his driving personality. The physician not only was a medical missionary but also an author, lecturer, gadabout and indefatigable promoter. In five years, starting with his medical work among refugees streaming from Communist-held North Vietnam in 1954, the often brash young doctor achieved international fame.

By 1960 a Gallup Poll showed that he was one of the ten most-admired Americans.

He agreed with his critics that he practiced "nineteenth century medicine" in his remote jungle hospitals in northern Laos a few miles from the Chinese border. By that, Dr. Dooley meant that despite such modern drugs as penicillin, his style of medicine was relatively simple compared with present-day techniques in this country. The various young American volunteers who worked with him in Laos did not have medical degrees.

Dr. Dooley was the driving force behind Medico, an organization that collects funds and sends medical teams to establish hospitals and clinics in the world's least developed countries.

Raised $850,000

He was credited with personally raising $850,000 for Medico. He made lecture tours, appeared on television and promoted Medico constantly, traveling to this country from his Laos base many times. In addition, he turned over royalties from his best-selling books for Medico programs.

Thomas Anthony Dooley 3d was born Jan. 17, 1927, in St. Louis, one of five brothers. In 1944 he entered the University of Notre Dame but dropped out to enter the Navy as a hospital corpsman. After the war he went back to Notre Dame and eventually received his medical degree at St. Louis University in 1953.

In the Navy again in 1954, he was serving as a volunteer medical officer in the Vietnam area at the time that former French colony was partitioned into Communist and non-Communist areas. Dr. Dooley's care for nearly 600,000 refugees from the Communist area won acclaim. The Navy awarded him the Legion of Merit. And The Washington Post in an editorial said of his refugee work: "It was the ultimate example of effective person-to-person contact with a foreign people."

Dr. Dooley's best-selling book. "Deliver Us From Evil," was based on his experience in caring for the 600,000 refugees in camps at Haiphong. He was a Navy lieutenant at the time.

Home again in 1956, he resigned from the Navy and, with three medical corpsmen who had worked with him at Haiphong, returned to the Far East to set up a hospital in Laos.

He described it as a small village hospital on stilts. It was at Nam Tha. The Laotian Government supplied canoes to transport equipment. In 1958 Dr. Dooley turned over the hospital to Laotians and established a new one twenty miles across the mountains at Muong Sing. He also had planned a third hospital in Laos.

Dr. Dooley also wrote "The Edge of Tomorrow" and "The Night They Burned the Mountain," based on his Laotian experiences. He held the highest national decoration of South Vietnam and was the first American to be decorated by the Kingdom of Laos. He also received the highest Laotian medal—the Order of a Million Elephants and the White Parasol.

Universally admired in the United States, Dr. Dooley was a controversial figure among Americans working in the Far East. Physicians criticized him as a "hit and run" doctor who gave snap diagnoses and was absent from his hospital too often. Many complained of an overbearing ego and said he was insensitive to the feelings of others. Laotian children revered him, and before his illness he often rough-housed with them.

As for his ego, Dr. Dooley once said: "After all, like most humble Irishmen, I think I'm practically faultless."

In 1959 he fell and bumped his chest. Later he felt a growing lump in his chest. It was diagnosed as sarcoma, a fast-spreading cancer. He flew to New York for a successful operation for removal of the malignancy. Weeks later he was back on the job in Laos. But he was afflicted anew with a serious ailment in his vertebrae.

At Hong Kong in December, 1960, he was fitted with a steel and leather harness stretching from his shoulders to his hips. He called it his "iron maiden."

Dr. Dooley, a bachelor, is survived by his mother, Mrs. Agnes Dooley, and two brothers, Malcolm and Edward. At his death his mother was en route to her home in St. Louis. The funeral will take place there.

Source: "Dr. Dooley Dead; Built Laos Clinics," *New York Times* 19 Jan. 1961.

EXERCISES: READING AND RESPONDING

1. Whose voices do you hear directly in the obituary?
2. Explain the connotations with the following words included in paragraph 9: "gadabout," "indefatigable promoter," "brash."
3. Why do you think the obituary mentions Dooley's ego and other physicians' criticism?
4. Characterize the voice of the writer.

EXERCISES: THINKING CRITICALLY

1. In one or two paragraphs addressed to a peer who is considering writing a paper explaining why Dooley was one of the ten most admired Americans in 1960, explain which of the sources above is the most informative for someone learning about Dooley's accomplishments for the first time. At the end of your explanation, provide a bibliographical citation for each source.
2. Paraphrase Senator's Humphrey's letter (Source 2), and Admiral Burke's foreword (Source 4). Then determine whether these sources would be used most effectively indirectly (your paraphrase) or directly (quotation) in the assignment listed in the next exercise.
3. Using at least three of the sources you have read so far, write a biographical summary of Dooley. Your intended readers are a group of premed students interested in humanitarian efforts in medicine. They are not familiar with Dr. Dooley's story.

OUTING: A PHENOMENON OF THE 1990s

The term *outing* was coined by *Time* magazine in 1990 when Michelangelo Signorile wrote a story, "The Secret Gay Life of Malcolm Forbes." Forbes, a millionaire who died in 1990, never publicly acknowledged his homosexuality. Signorile's article appeared in *Outweek*. Since 1990, Signorile and *Outweek* have outed other gay celebrities, and the media has debated the ethics of their revelations. In a 1991 article, *Newsweek* explained that "uncloseting gays was once a tactic of right-wing homophobes and other haters. Not so in the age of outing."

The two articles that follow examine the ethical problems of outing the living and the dead. After you have read and annotated both articles, make a list of claims for and against outing. Be prepared to discuss whether these claims are substantiated by evidence.

"OUTING": AN UNEXPECTED ASSAULT ON SEXUAL PRIVACY.

DAVID GELMAN

GAY ACTIVISTS ARE FORCING
OTHERS OUT OF THE CLOSET

In the 1962 movie "Advise and Consent" based on Allen Drury's best-selling novel, a United States senator commits suicide when political rivals threaten to expose his one youthful homosexual escapade. On television, the movie seems a bit dated now. Americans, since the '60s, have opened their minds sufficiently to tolerate a few openly homosexual office holders. But the operative word is "few." Even after decades of gay activism, many homosexuals consider it the better part of valor to keep their sexual preference hidden, whether from their families or from a world that can still hurt them badly for being "different." Thus the threat of exposure continues to create serious distress.

Lately the greatest threat has come from homosexuals themselves, in the form of a controversial new tactic called outing. At AIDS rallies, in public lectures, in interviews and in their newspapers, gay activists are publicizing the names of alleged homosexuals who have chosen to hide their sexual preference. By bringing recalcitrants into the open, the activists say, they will swell the ranks of role models for young gays and help lift the curse of secrecy from homosexual life. Writer Michelangelo Signorile, for example, regularly salts his column in *OutWeek*, a New York-based gay weekly, with the names of

alleged gays, including prominent entertainment figures. "Come out while you can ..." he taunted recently.

Born out of frustration at the slow pace of gay progress, the practice has created a sharp split among movement factions. Feelings run high, especially among those selected for exposure. "I am disgusted by these AIDS terrorists," says syndicated columnist Liz Smith, a favorite target. "I may be a gossip columnist, but I do respect the right of people not to tell me 'everything,' and I reserve the same right for myself."

Many moderates bristle at the assault on privacy by a movement that has fought bitterly for that right. "It's philosophical rape," says Stuart Kellogg, former editor of the Advocate, the country's largest gay-oriented publication. "If we don't want policemen coming into our bedrooms, we have to safeguard other people's privacy, too." Even the moderates, however, tend to favor exposing politicians who hide their own gay proclivities while aligning themselves with homophobic legislation. Last year Rep. Barney Frank of Massachusetts, a professed homosexual, threatened to expose gay Republican congressmen unless GOP officials stopped falsely hinting that House Speaker Thomas Foley was gay. The Republicans promptly backed off the innuendo.

Signorile touched off the current outing debate with a story purporting to detail the secret homosexual life of Malcolm Forbes, after the publishing tycoon died last February. Some mainstream papers, such as the *Los Angeles Times* and *USA Today*, picked up on the story and others didn't. Since then, commentators have pondered what the press's position should be. "Whatever the cause," wrote media critic Fred Friendly in The Washington Post, "do we journalists have the ethical or moral prerogative to strip away anyone's privacy, unless there is an overriding … justification?"

Justification takes many forms. A *New York Times* story on the outing controversy dutifully quoted *OutWeek* editor Gabriel Rotello deploring the media "code of silence" on gays. But the story alluded to the weekly's article on Forbes as being about "a famous businessman who had recently died." The paper, explains Times spokesman Anthony Sprauve, "has a strong ethical belief that any individual's sex life is his own business."

Yet the *Times* and other newspapers appeared to show no such compunction in carrying stories about the escapades of real-estate magnate Donald Trump. As gays note, the bouts of ethical hand wringing seem to crop up only where homosexuality is involved. The implicit assumption is that adultery is more acceptable.

Built-in Bias:

There are further complications. Newspapers that reported the Forbes disclosures appeared to accept the legalistic view that the dead cannot be libeled. But does that close the discussion? What about the unwelcome notoriety for his family? On the other hand, to raise that question slanders the very idea of homosexuality. Is it a disgrace by definition? Would it be the same as calling the deceased a philanderer or a drunk? Gay organizations insist the straight world's very approach to the subject is warped by such built-in bias.

The issue is clearly riddled with booby traps. Suzanne Braun Levine, editor of the *Columbia Journalism Review*, sees similarities to the dilemma often encountered in rape stories. "By not revealing the name of the victim we perpetuate the idea that rape is a stigma," she says. "By revealing the name we expose the victims to harassment and trauma." The zealots might stop to consider that analogy before they proceed with their plan to haul all gays, ready or not, out of the closet. The worst thing about outing, says Thomas B. Stoddard, head of the Lambda Legal Defense Fund, is that "it looks mean and nasty. That doesn't advance the gay movement at all."

Source: David Gelman, "'Outing': An Unexpected Assault on Sexual Privacy," *Newsweek* 30 Apr. 1990: 66.

EXERCISES: READING AND RESPONDING

1. Is the writer's purpose to inform or to persuade? Cite specific passages that illustrate your answer.

2. What are the ethical issues Gelmen raises about outing?

3. Suzanne Braun Levine compares outing to the dilemma reporters encounter in rape stories. Explain why this analogy does or does not seem valid.

4. Characterize the voice you hear in this essay.

Randy Shilts was a national correspondent for the *San Francisco Chronicle* when he died in 1994. One of the first reporters to cover the gay community for a major newspaper, he's also credited with being one of the first journalists to call attention to the AIDS epidemic.

IS "OUTING" GAYS ETHICAL?

RANDY SHILTS

In more polite times, gay organizers and journalists generally agreed that homosexuals in the closet had a right to stay there if they didn't choose to publicly acknowledge their sexuality. It was an unspoken rule.

With the AIDS epidemic now causing a significant depopulation of gay men in major urban areas, however, the times have become less congenial for covert homosexuals. Both gay newspapers and militant AIDS activists have launched a campaign of "outing"! publicly revealing the sexual orientation of people who'd rather keep it quiet.

The controversy over outing recently erupted in force when the sexual activities of a famous, deceased millionaire were documented in a New York City gay newspaper. Over the past year, various AIDS groups have also circulated fliers announcing that several national and local politicians were gay. They did this after the officials took actions that the activists considered inimical to the fight against AIDS.

For journalists and gay leaders themselves, these tactics present a panoply of ethical quandaries.

Most mainstream daily newspapers have refused to name those exposed in gay newspapers and AIDS protests. In most cases, this has made sense. The outings of the politicians, for example, were based on nothing more than gossip and did not contain the factual substantiation that would warrant reporting in a legitimate news story.

Moreover, none of the politicians thus far exposed by outings have engaged in rabidly anti-gay politicking. By the standards of most journalists, such hypocrisy would warrant a public outing, because the politicians themselves would have already asserted that homosexuality was an issue that demanded intense public scrutiny.

The outing of the dead presents a different dilemma. There are no privacy issues here: under American law, the dead have no right to privacy. That's how it should be.

Some newspaper editors maintain that they would not reveal even a deceased person's homosexuality because they always refrain from discussing sex lives. But that just isn't so. In the most recent case, the late millionaire's heterosexual affairs with some of the world's most celebrated women were the stuff of news coverage for more than a decade. Many newspapers included the information in their obituaries.

It seems then that the refusal of newspapers to reveal a person's homosexuality has less to do with ethical considerations of privacy than with an editor's homophobia. In my experience, many editors really believe that being gay is so distasteful that talk of it should be avoided unless absolutely necessary.

This has left us with newspapers that often are more invested in protecting certain people than in telling the truth to readers. In Hollywood and New York, hundreds of publicists make their living by planting items in entertainment columns about whom this or that celebrity is dating. Many of these items are patently false and intended only to cover up the celebrity's homosexuality.

Moreover, many newspaper writers and editors know full well that this is the case and merrily participate in the deceptions. Editors who would never reveal a public figure was gay are routinely lying to their readers by implying the same person is straight.

It is in rage against this hypocrisy—and in desperation over the ravages of AIDS—that the trend of outing was born. In major urban areas around the country, the homosexual community must watch helplessly as AIDS decimates the gay male population. Meanwhile, just about every eminent body studying the Government's response to the AIDS crisis has agreed that it is woefully inadequate.

Just about everyone also agrees that the response to the epidemic is so pathetic because gay men comprise the largest population struck by AIDS—and gay men are largely viewed as degenerate reprobates. In truth, of course, lesbians and gay men are to be found among the most respected public figures in every field of American society.

Gay organizers hope that if more Americans knew this, the nation might see a better response to the AIDS epidemic. Fewer people might die. That's a major reason why outing started. That's also why it will become more pronounced, as more people die and frustration among AIDS activists grows.

At the same time, outing presents gays with their own moral quandaries. In outing politicians, gay activists often have acted more from vindictiveness over a particular vote than from a genuine desire to enlighten the public. Outing threats are political blackmail. And what happens if religious conservatives threaten to reveal a politician's homosexuality if he or she doesn't vote a certain party line? Outing is a powerful political weapon that can cut both ways.

Gay activists counter that young gay people have a right to role models of successful gay adults. That's true, but someone who is only public because he or she has been hauled from the closet is certainly no paragon of psychological integration.

As a journalist, I cannot imagine any situation in which I would reveal the homosexuality of a living person who was not a public official engaged in voracious hypocrisy.

Yet, as someone who has chosen to be open about being gay, I have nothing but disdain for the celebrated and powerful homosexuals who remain comfortably closeted while so many are dying. Most of these people have nothing to lose by stepping forward and they could do much to instruct society about the contributions gays daily make to America.

As I watch my friends die all around me, a certain part of me hopes against all hope that the outing stories now appearing in the press may do something to stop the avalanche of death around me.

Source: Randy Shilts, "Is 'Outing' Gays Ethical?" *New York Times Magazine* 12 Apr. 1990: A23.

EXERCISES: READING AND RESPONDING

1. How does Shilts develop his argument?
2. What kinds of appeals does he make?
3. What kinds of evidence support his claims?
4. Explain why his argument is or is not convincing?

FOCUS ON RELATED ISSUES: DON'T ASK; DON'T TELL

Currently the U.S. military follows the Don't Ask; Don't Tell policy, implemented during the Clinton administration. Some people consider this policy hypocritical, enforcing a kind of double life that certain gay activists find reprehensible. Gay soldiers can't reveal their sexual orientation; if they do, they're discharged. Other people support the policy and argue that for the morale of the troops and for national security as well, the Don't Ask; Don't Tell policy is appropriate.

Working on your own, examine sources that discuss this policy. Review the claims, data, and evidence each side presents, and analyze the strengths and weaknesses of their arguments using the Toulmin systems of analysis (Chapter 5). Refer to answers to the following questions as you work on narrowing your topic:

- What kinds of appeals does each side make in their arguments?
- Does the policy govern conduct or status?
- Has it stopped discrimination against gays in the military?
- Who has challenged the policy?
- What were the results of their challenges?
- What role did negotiation play in the development of this policy?

5. What ethical issues does Shilts raise about outing?

6. Characterize the voice you hear in this essay.

EXERCISE: THINKING CRITICALLY

Paraphrase Shilts' article. Review your version and determine whether any passages are more emphatic in Shilts' voice than in your paraphrase. Mark those passages, and keep a copy of your paraphrase to refer to when you draft writing assignments at the end of this case study.

In 1993, St. Martin's Press released Randy Shilts' *Conduct Unbecoming: Lesbians and Gays in the U. S. Military*. Of the cases cited in Shilts' book, Dr. Tom Dooley's was the most familiar to readers.

OUTING DR. DOOLEY

WHAT TOM DOOLEY REALLY WANTED

RANDY SHILTS

August 1954

On a balmy August morning in 1954, it was not only the story of Tom Dooley's life that lay beyond the bow of the USS *Montague,* it was the story of the next quarter century of American history. But this was not what Dooley saw as he stood at the rail, contemplating his Temporary Assignment Duty (TAD) as medical officer of the *Montague*. Ahead, shimmering in the morning sun like an emerald, was a country few Americans had heard of then, a place variously called Tonkin or Annam or Cochin China, but which in the past dozen or so years had become known by a new name, Vietnam.

A twisted tale lay behind Dooley's abrupt transfer from his job in the American military hospital at Yokosuka, Japan, but the twenty-seven-year-old was not aware of it at the time. When orders for the first TAD of his career came through for the *Montague*. Dooley had taken them to be propitious, since his initials were TAD. Friends credited Dooley with an uncanny kind of prescience: Dooley claimed to know two things about his future—that he was meant to accomplish some great task in his lifetime and that he would die young.

Dozens of small gray landing craft pulled alongside the *Montague*. Slowly, hundreds of weary Vietnamese took their first steps up the gangplank. Within a few hours, the ship held more than two thousand refugees, clutching their belongings close while they warily eyed the strange American sailors. Operation Passage to Freedom had begun.

The division of Vietnam had been announced, carving out one Vietnam that would be comprised of two "zones of temporary political influence" divided by the 17th parallel. In the north, the Vietminh would run things "temporarily"; in the south, the government would be aligned with the West. The plan called for free elections in both sectors by 1956, and a reunited Vietnam.

The West had reneged on numerous promises to their colonials, so the Vietminh never believed they would willingly let go of South Vietnam. And the Communists had as bad a record for providing free elections, so the West never believed they would willingly let go of North Vietnam. Therefore, a lot of people in the new "temporary zone" of North Vietnam were eager to flee to South Vietnam. This was particularly true of anyone who had links to the French, whom the Vietminh detested.

Catholics were especially nervous, since they were suspect to the nationalists for having taken up the colonizers' religion. The Catholic solution was Operation Virgin Mary, a campaign coordinated by the U.S. Central Intelligence Agency and the Catholic Church in which priests told their congregations that the Virgin Mary was leaving the north to live in the south, and if they wanted to be saved they had better go south, too. Getting all these people south became the mission of the United States Navy's Operation Passage to Freedom.

One million refugees were expected to board the handful of Navy

ships supplied for the task. The Navy quickly converted the cargo holds of a half dozen auxiliary cargo attack, or AKA, ships into huge warehouses with food, sleeping, and toilet facilities for their human cargo. They did not anticipate the miserable health problems that attended their passengers. Tending these health problems became the job of the *Montague*'s health officer, Lieutenant (junior grade) Tom Dooley.

As he watched the first refugees crawl over the gang rail of the USS *Montague* on the morning of August 14, 1954, he was stunned to see how many were diseased. Though he had not been a stellar medical student, he soon recognized symptoms of tropical maladies he had studied just two years before at St. Louis University medical school: yaws and smallpox, leprosy and elephantitis, malaria, and, of course, malnutrition. The voyage from Haiphong to the mouth of the Saigon River took two days. Among the 2,061 refugees, Dooley recorded four births and two deaths. In his meticulous diaries, he also recorded many worries. The operation threatened to expose American sailors to a panoply of microbes to which they had no immunity. As more Catholics crowded into Haiphong, their squalid living conditions were bound to create even more health problems. Already 150,000 had come to Haiphong to board the American transports; hundreds of thousands more were expected. The prospects of epidemics of bubonic plague and cholera headed the list of Dooley's fears.

At the end of the first voyage, he pleaded for better medical screening of refugees before they were loaded onto ships from the south. The admiralty saw the wisdom of the suggestion and appointed Dooley medical officer for Task Force 90, the unit that would monitor the refugees' health conditions. Dooley set up his medical shop at the refugee camps and burst into a flurry of activity that astounded his Navy colleagues and would leave him revered for decades by hundreds of thousands of Vietnamese.

Deciding it was his job to define his mission, Dooley resolved that no refugee should leave Haiphong until he or she had been thoroughly screened for all tropical diseases and appropriately treated. He wrote to American pharmaceutical companies for cases of antibiotics. Pan Am Airlines sent ten thousand bars of soap. Seeing the publicity value in helping the young doctor, corporations across the country soon began donating supplies. To ensure that the pesky chain of command did not interfere with his plans, Dooley always sent his requests and solicitations through Red Cross mail runs rather than by military mail delivery.

Every time a new American ship entered Haiphong harbor, Dooley launched out to greet it, demanding every available bandage, hemostat, and medication. Dooley's most effective tool was his chutzpah. If he needed equipment that a ship commander was reluctant to turn over, Dooley blustered that he spoke for the admiral and *that* was an order—whether it was true or not.

Though the Navy had intended for Dooley to run a single processing station, he quickly established a network of clinics that treated between three and four hundred people a day. At his various camps, a population of fifteen thousand refugees was always waiting for vaccinations, antibiotic treatments,

and screening for communicable diseases. Before long, Dooley insisted on offering surgery to those refugees in need of urgent treatment. Meanwhile, he directed his staff to collect stool samples, insects, and even rats for laboratory studies of indigenous diseases. The United States "never knew where it had to fight next," he said, and the studies of local ailments could benefit troops in the future.

To give the entire effort a patriotic spin that the military brass would have to endorse, Dooley repeated the same phrase with each pill he dispensed and every disease he cured: *Dai la My-quoc Viet-tro.* "This," he told his patients, "is American aid." To the Vietnamese, he became known simply as *Bac Sy My,* "the American doctor."

In his off-hours, Dooley also started writing long letters about his work to his widowed mother in St. Louis, who passed a few of them on to local newspapers. His easy style and dramatic flair soon caught the attention of newspaper editors nationwide, as well as Navy Commander William Lederer, who was working as public-affairs aide to Admiral Felix Stump. When he stumbled across Dooley in Haiphong, he suggested the young lieutenant keep a diary of his Vietnam experiences and stop by Lederer's home in Honolulu on his way back to the United States. There might be a book in Dooley's experience.

Haiphong was to be an "open zone," allowing debarkation only until May 1955, and with each month the area in which the Vietminh would allow Americans to operate grew smaller. In the last months, Dooley was down to three Navy corpsmen to tend the thousands of ailing Vietnamese under his care. After supervising the treatment of 610,000 refugees in nine months, Dooley left on one of the last boats out of Haiphong, with his diary and the Vietnamese who now venerated him.

By now, the Navy realized that it had gained a precious public-relations asset with *Bac Sy My*. Operation Passage to Freedom had failed to garner the publicity the U.S. government had expected, but the memoirs of the young Navy doctor offered a rare chance to recoup. Dashingly handsome, with a square jaw, sparkling blue eyes, and thick black hair, Dooley also made a striking appearance when giving public lectures and on the new medium of television.

On a visit to South Vietnam before returning to the United States, President Ngo Dinh Diem awarded Dooley the highest honor South Vietnam could bestow on a foreigner, the "Officier de l'Ordre National de Vietnam." The only other two Americans so honored were a general and an admiral, the commanders of Operation Passage to Freedom. On the tarmac of Hickam Air Force Base in Honolulu, Dooley received the Legion of Merit, the youngest doctor in Navy history to be so honored. Navy Surgeon General Lamont Pugh wrote what was for Dooley the most meaningful praise: "It is my earnest hope that some day you may become Surgeon General of the Navy, not merely because you say that is what you want to be, but because I will leave that office soon with a sense of contentment that it will be in the most worthy and 'can do' hands if it ever reaches yours."

In Hawaii, Lederer, who would gain greater fame a few years later as coauthor of *The Ugly American*, helped Dooley fashion his diary into a book, *Deliver Us from Evil*. Early drafts did not please the publisher, who complained they were not dramatic enough, so later drafts included colorful embellishments. Dooley's devout Catholicism also influenced the book. Refugees streamed into the harbor in little sampans that flew the golden-keyed flag of the Vatican, Dooley wrote. As biographer Diana Shaw later noted, Dooley's readers could come away from his writing with the impression that the Vietnamese were overwhelmingly Catholic.

Even more troubling were the book's unsubstantiated allegations of Communist atrocities. According to one story, Vietminh soldiers crammed chopsticks into the ears of children who had heard a priest recite the Lord's Prayer, tearing their eardrums. In another account, Dooley related that Catholic teachers who had taught the Gospel had had their tongues pulled out with pliers.

All these episodes were news to everyone who had worked with Tom Dooley. As people associated with the refugees' medical treatment later pointed out, the tales of atrocity were inarguably fiction.

They were fiction, however, that played very well in the frenzied anti-Communist mood of the mid-1950s. Few words could have been more pleasing to the American Catholic establishment, which was, to a large extent, the domestic American patron of President Diem. Dooley soon struck up a personal relationship with New York's John Cardinal Spellman, the most vociferously anti-Communist cleric in the nation. More than promoting anticommunism and rhapsodizing about heroic Vietnamese Catholics, the book was a paean to the United States Navy. "Everything we did because the Navy made it possible for us to do," Dooley wrote in the book's afterword. "A finer lot of men cannot be found on this earth."

The Navy reciprocated the admiration. Chief of Naval Operations Admiral Arleigh Burke wrote in his foreword to the book, "Today's naval traditions have been built by men like young Dr. Dooley who have served their country well under arduous and challenging circumstances.... It is a story of which the United States Navy is proud."

After being excerpted in *Reader's Digest, Deliver Us from Evil* shot up the best-seller list. Dooley made Gallup poll's list of the men most admired in the United States. Much in demand as a speaker, he repeated the stories of Communist aggression in hundreds of personal appearances around the country, but he offered his own, very nonmilitary prescription for solving them. Only American kindness could "wash away the poisons of Communist hatred," he argued. The efforts in Haiphong had built "a quiet pride in our hearts at being American.... We brought not bombs and guns, but help and love."

These recommendations were rather sentimental for the cold warriors in the Pentagon, but such ideas were easily overlooked. Many were girding, even then, for an armed confrontation with Communist aggressors in Southeast Asia. From their point of view, President Roosevelt had given away Eastern Europe at Yalta, and President Truman had "lost" China to the Communists. Korea had been saved, but aggression continued in Laos and Vietnam. Vietnam was the place to draw the line against the enemy, and most Americans had heard of Vietnam by now because of Tom Dooley.

And this was what made the events in the first months after Tom Dooley's return from Vietnam so problematical.

Dooley's friend Navy Lieutenant Commander Ted Werner had seen the paperwork on the desk of the crusty old admiral who headed the military hospital in Yokosuka. Homosexuality was running rampant on the medical staff and an investigation was demanded. The admiral wanted nothing to do with the messy business of a homosexual purge. Rather than have such revelations come to light on his watch, he proceeded to transfer the suspects elsewhere, where somebody else would have to deal with it. That was how one of the suspects, Tom Dooley, had ended up on the USS *Montague*.

Once Dooley was back from Vietnam, however, the rumors surfaced again. Though a stirring speaker, Dooley was, in private, extraordinarily effeminate. Rumors streamed into the Office of Naval Intelligence that the famous young doctor was homosexual, and this time a very thorough investigation followed. Of course, it had to be handled delicately. This was a man who, according to what the Chief of Naval Operations said in a book now a best-seller, was the epitome of what was good in the U.S. Navy. Any publicity would be as embarrassing to the Navy as to the doctor himself.

The Navy fretted over how to rid itself of Dooley without bringing undue attention to the circumstances. The Office of Naval Intelligence suggested two possible routes of obtaining his severance from the Navy. First, the Navy could attempt to obtain a straightforward confession. "While there is always the possibility that interrogation will fail to bring forth a confession of guilt, past experience indicates that few homosexuals refuse to admit their activities when skillfully interrogated," the ONI said. The other option was to plant an ONI agent at the hotel bar where Dooley was staying so he could be solicited by the doctor. "A trained and skillful agent, carefully avoiding any possibility of entrapment or homosexual involvement, would be a capable witness to verbal statements and overt actions by subject … (which) would most probably result in the latter's complete confession of homosexual tendencies and activities."

The details of the confrontation between the ONI and Tom Dooley have been lost to history. Within two weeks, however, Dooley announced that he was resigning his commission in the Navy to return to Southeast Asia and continue his work tending the sick. He arranged a mission with the Laotian government and the Navy flew medical supplies to the remote outpost of Muong Sing, where Dooley opened his first hospital.

Tom Dooley's story did not end with his forced resignation from the Navy; it had only begun. In the following years, he would become more famous than he had ever been in the service, much to the chagrin of the military, which always worried that the secret of his resignation might become public. Dooley worried about it, too, and he worried that others might learn of the words spelled out, all in capital letters, on his separation papers: UNDESIRABLE DISCHARGE. Changing these words and getting his discharge upgraded to honorable became a crusade for the rest of his life.

Like so many others of his generation, Tom Dooley had done everything he could to overcome the singular defect that in his eyes made him less than human. His entire life, it seemed, was an effort to compensate for this, and everything good and everything evil that he did can be traced back to the shame he carried over his homosexuality. The Catholic Church had said he could not see the face of God because of his sin, so he struggled to be the best Catholic he could be, performing acts of kindness and obediently following the ideology of the Church. He had been told he could not be a good sailor if he was homosexual, so he set out to be a great sailor, and, it seemed, nearly succeeded. He had been told he could not be a great American, so he had tried to be the best American he could, fighting his country's enemies and gaining the United States new friends. He would even lie if his lies would be good for the country, and lie he did. He did all of this—for his God, for the Navy, and for his country—and, in the end, it did not help.

Perhaps that is why in his final years he struck out on a more independent path. He no longer repeated the tales of Communist atrocities he had told in the mid-1950s. Now he grew sharply critical of U.S. policies that were drawing Southeast Asia closer and closer to war. The U.S. military seemed to care only for the political credentials of Asian leaders, not for whether they were actually improving the lot of their citizens. In files from the Central Intelligence Agency and the Federal Bureau of Investigation, government agents complained that Dooley had become "extremely disparaging of U.S. propaganda techniques and their results" and "highly critical of the official American community ... [and] particularly of official lack of interest in 'the Laotian people.'"

Dooley's old friend Ted Werner, who had left his commission as a Navy fighter pilot to fly Dooley between his hospitals, remembered that on the doctor's last trip to Asia, in late 1960 when tensions were rising, he had met with embassy officials to warn against considering a ground war in that region. The basis of American infantry power, the tank, would be useless on this terrain, he had said. The enemies here would not fight like European ground armies but, rather,

would take to the jungle once they had inflicted casualties. And the United States would be fighting for governments that did not have popular support. These were governments that did not care for their people, Dooley said, only for their own power.

But by now, everyone in the Asian capitals knew that the CIA and the military brass were pushing for war. All through the Eisenhower years, the numbers of military advisers in Vietnam had been climbing. The embassy officials listened politely to Dooley, but Werner could see they had no intention of heeding his advice. It did not jell with American policy. The United States had never lost a war in its nearly two-hundred-year history, and it did not intend to lose one to a bunch of rice-growing, slant-eyed peasants barely out of the Stone Age.

Besides, everybody knew, Tom Dooley was dying. The brass were seeing him only as a courtesy—and less as a courtesy to Dooley than to the Asians who worshiped him.

Source: Randy Shilts, "What Tom Dooley Really Wanted," *Conduct Unbecoming: Lesbians and Gays in the U.S. Military* (New York: St. Martin's, 1993) 21–27.

EXERCISES: READING AND RESPONDING

1. How would you describe Shilts' voice? What does it reveal about his attitude toward his subject? toward his intended readers?

2. What kind of assumptions do you think Shilts made about his intended readers' attitudes toward gays and lesbians in the military?

3. Determine whether the facts Shilts reports validate or contradict facts presented in other sources in this case. Highlight passages in the chapter that appear to be Shilts' opinion.

4. Shilts claims that the navy realized it had a valuable public relations asset in Dooley. What evidence does he offer to back this claim?

5. Explain why this introductory chapter would or would not motivate you to read *Conduct Unbecoming*.

Focus on Related Issues: U.S. Involvement in Vietnam

A large part of the Tom Dooley story centers on his work as a "jungle doctor" in Vietnam. His biographer, James T. Fisher, claims that "no American played a larger role in announcing the arrival of South Vietnam as a new ally whose fate was decisively bound to that of the United States. Dooley's enormously popular 1956 account of his work in Vietnam, *Deliver Us From Evil*, quite literally located Vietnam on the new world map for millions of Americans" (*Dr. America* 34–5).

Conflict in Southeast Asia began in 1954, when the Geneva Conference provisionally divided Vietnam at lat. 17° N into the Democratic Republic of Vietnam. Up until 1954, the country had been under French colonial rule. Escalating from a Vietnamese civil war, the conflict turned into limited international involvement in 1961 when South Vietnam signed a military and economic aid treaty with the United States. U.S. support troops began arriving in 1961 and left in 1972. Despite massive U.S. military aid, the South was unable to defeat communist troops in the North. U.S. casualties during the era of direct involvement were high—more than 50,000 dead. The heavy emotional, psychological, and physical toll the conflict took on survivors was high as well.

Working on your own, develop a topic on some aspect of the Vietnam conflict for a documented paper.

TOM DOOLEY'S HONORABLE DISCHARGE

RANDY SHILTS

January 20, 1961
St. Patrick's Cathedral, New York

It was a bitter cold day in New York, but hundreds had come for the funeral. President Eisenhower had sent a message of condolence. The Pope had authorized a special pontifical requiem mass.

It seemed that all of America attended Dr. Tom Dooley in the weeks before he died. Newspapers published near-daily reports on the status of his health. Dooley himself issued optimistic statements that he was feeling fine, but in the last week he deteriorated rapidly. Cardinal Spellman was a frequent visitor in spite of his aides' discouraging the visits, warning of rumors that Dooley was a homosexual. There were rumors about the Cardinal as well.

Nevertheless, the two remained close friends. It was Spellman who had introduced Tom Dooley to John

Kennedy, and Kennedy, citing inspiration from Dooley's work, would found the Peace Corps on March 1.

The Surgeon General of the Navy made an official visit to Dooley's bedside two days before he died to present him with what he had sought since he had been separated from the Navy years before—his honorable discharge. But most of his friends believed Dooley was too sedated to be aware of the largely symbolic gesture.

Dooley died on the day before John Kennedy's swearing-in as President of the United States. It is unclear whether he knew that his country had forgiven him at last.

Years later, Retired Lieutenant Commander Ted Werner recalled the last moments he spent with Dooley, saying good-bye at the airport in Vientiane, Laos. Werner knew that Dooley was returning to America to die; if his work had not required that he remain in Laos to fly for Dooley's group, he would have accompanied him.

It was a strange afternoon, Werner remembered, because Dooley, who rarely discussed his sexuality with anyone, confided in him about the disgrace he had felt when he was discharged from the Navy. It was a disgrace that had followed him

ever since, he said, and he knew that if, after his death, it became known what he had been discharged for, then all the good that he had accomplished in his lifetime would be forgotten. "All they'll remember is that I was queer," he told Werner.

This was, after all, the message Dooley and millions of other homosexual Americans had heard for generations. No matter what good deeds he did, his God would damn him; no matter how well he championed patriotism, his country would disgrace him. This ultimately was the point of the armed forces' regulations—they had little to do with military goals and everything to do with a culture enforcing millennia-old taboos. No matter what the content of his character, Dooley, like millions of others, would always be identified as queer; they were unworthy.

As Dooley prepared to board the Pan Am flight that had been outfitted to receive him on a gurney, he said good-bye to Werner, and recited a part of his favorite poem to his friend:

"The woods are lovely, dark and deep," he said,

"But I have promises to keep,
And miles to go before I sleep,
And miles to go before I sleep."

Source: Randy Shilts, "Tom Dooley's Honorable Discharge," *Conduct Unbecoming: Lesbians and Gays in the U. S. Military,* (New York: St. Martin's, 1993) 735–36.

EXERCISES: READING AND RESPONDING

1. Highlight passages in the chapter that appear to be Shilts' opinion.
2. The last stanza of Robert Frost's "Stopping by Woods on a Snowy Evening" is used in several sources in the case. Read the entire poem and explain why you think Shilts ends the chapter—and his book—with these lines.
3. Identify and characterize other voices you hear in this chapter.

4. Explain why Shilts is or is not credible.

5. Speculate on Shilts' rationale for framing his book with the story of Tom Dooley.

The *Los Angeles Times Magazine* identified Diana Shaw as a "writer and a researcher for the movie industry" when they published her article on Tom Dooley.

THE TEMPTATION OF TOM DOOLEY

DIANA SHAW

HE WAS A HEROIC JUNGLE DOCTOR OF INDOCHINA IN THE 1950S. BUT HE HAD A SECRET, AND TO PROTECT IT, HE HELPED LAUNCH THE FIRST DISINFORMATION CAMPAIGN OF THE VIETNAM WAR.

One night last spring I lay sleepless and sweltering in the dying city of Haiphong, North Viet Nam, asking myself the question that has taunted so many young Americans caught in faraway places: "What in the hell am I doing here?"... Out there, in the makeshift refugee camp I had set up with U.S. Army tents, were more than 12,000 wretched, sick and horribly maimed Vietnamese, most of them either very young or very old. They were fleeing from the Communists of North Viet Nam, hoping to reach the doubtful security of Saigon. Before they came, more than 300,000 others had already passed through the camp....

I was treating diseases that most of my classmates would never encounter in a lifetime's practice, performing operations which the textbooks never mention. What do you do for chil-dren who have had chopsticks driven into their inner ears? Or for old women whose collarbones have been shattered by rifle butts? Or for kids whose ears have been torn off with pincers?... At Notre Dame the priests had tried valiantly to teach me philosophy. But here in this Communist hellhole I had learned many more profound and practical facts about the true nature of man.... I knew now why organized godlessness can never kill the divine spark that burns within even the humblest human.

In April, 1956, most Americans got their first glimpses of Vietnam through the eyes of a 27-year-old naval officer named Tom Dooley. The fevered, patriotic prose of his book, "Deliver Us From Evil," filled 27 pages of *Reader's Digest* with a first-hand account of Operation Passage to Freedom, the U.S. Navy boat-lift moving refugees from newly communist North Vietnam to the soon-to-be-democratic South.

The 1954 Geneva accords that ended French occupation of Vietnam had divided the country at the 17th Parallel and given U.S. Navy Task Force 90 a little less than a year to move an anticipated 1 million political refugees. It was an extraordinary undertaking, complicated by rains, high winds and debilitating heat. The population of Dooley's Haiphong camp swelled way beyond the task force's ability to handle it as the operation moved ever-growing numbers of refugees, housed them at the port, examined them for contagious discuses and deloused them with DDT.

To many readers, Dooley's book seemed to be more than a compelling chronicle of this operation; it reflected the sensibilities and concerns of a Cold War humanitarian and idealist. "All in Viet Nam dream and strive for freedom," he had written, "the people who toil in the rice fields with backs bent double and faces turned to the brackish mud, the naked children playing in the monsoon, the little fruit sellers in the arroyos of the markets and the poor with amputated arm or hand outstretched. They have one dream: Freedom."

The New Yorker's reviewer, responding to such passages, declared it was as much poetry as documentary. And readers began passing the hat to answer Dooley's appeal for American aid in Vietnam. "My meager resources in Indochina did not win the people's hearts," he wrote, "though they helped. What turned the trick were those words *Day La Vien Tro My* (This is American aid')—and all that those words conveyed. I believe that in the long run such plain help can be the decisive factor in bringing about a victory for all the sacred things we stand for."

But Dooley's urgent pleas for aid were deliberately, strategically overblown. Although he may have been sincere in his desire to vanquish communism and help the Vietnamese, his crusade became, ultimately, integral to a covert CIA disinformation campaign. And the result of his propaganda, taken to its extreme interpretation, was no less than U.S. involvement in the Vietnam War.

Dooley was a lanky young man with a remarkable resemblance to Gary Cooper and a propensity for exaggeration. He liked to tell people that his middle initial A stood for Anheuser, and that he was a scion of the brewing family. In fact, the A stood for Anthony, and his father was a railroad foundryman, a hard drinker who hoped that his namesake would become a prizefighter. But the younger Dooley was a flamboyant *bon vivant* who had stunned his friends and family by choosing to go into medicine. A Catholic, he may have chosen the profession largely a penance for his self-indulgence and other aspects of his character that didn't square well with his church. He was brilliant but had no discipline, attending—but not graduating from—Notre Dame, then staying at the bottom of his class at St. Louis University Medical School, which admitted him on a special waiver. He would have flunked out of medical school if the dean, Melvin Casberg, had not been a family friend, and willing to press the administration board to let Dooley stay. "Tom did not fit well in the straitjacket of academic life," recalls Casberg, towering man with a resonant voice and gentle manner. "I told him. Think, if you would only harness that energy, all the good you could do.'"

Dooley entered the Navy from medical school, spending a year at Camp Pendleton before being sent to Japan. When Operation Passage to Freedom needed a French speaking medical officer, he was transferred to Task Force 90.

He arrived in Haiphong as refugees were being loaded—thousands at a time—onto ships making the 700-mile trip south to Saigon. And he threw himself into his work with such vigor and conviction that he became known, perhaps facetiously but not without respect, as "the doctor who won the war in Indochina."

Dooley was decorated twice before leaving Vietnam: once in Saigon, by South Vietnamese President Ngo Dinh Diem, who gave him the highest commendation his country could bestow on a foreigner, and then by the U.S. Navy, which made him the youngest officer to receive the Legion of Merit, its highest peacetime honor.

Dooley distinguished himself in another way as well. While the "situation reports" commonly filed by medical commanders were blunt and straightforward accounts of the day's work, Dooley's were eloquent. The brass recognized that his chronicles, enlivening the dry details with dramatic descriptions and impassioned patriotic commentary, could boost morale. They sent them throughout the fleet so that everyone, from corpsmen to vice admirals, could read them.

Among those impressed with his writing was William Lederer, eventually renowned as co-author, with Eugene Burdick, of the book "The Ugly American." Lederer was a press officer, attached to the admiralty, and he appreciated the public relations potential in bringing Dooley's work to a wider audience. Who wouldn't be moved by the story of a young doctor who had fought communism with penicillin or disarmed the communist Viet Minh with a smile? Lederer suggested that Dooley write a book.

Such a book would be just the tool the Navy needed to make Operation Passage to Freedom a success. Officially, the operation had a simple objective—moving hundreds of thousands of refugees and getting French weapons out of reach of the communists. But more important was its classified purpose: to create a strong constituency in South Vietnam for Diem, who had next to none. Catholic, like the reviled French, and just back from three years of exile in the United States, Diem was subject to suspicion that he was a puppet of his American mentor, Cardinal Francis Spellman, as well as the French and the U.S. Department of State.

The operation was a two-part attempt to bolster Diem. First, there was a psychological-warfare campaign organized by the CIA's Edward Lansdale, aimed at frightening northern Catholics into fleeing south. This phase, involving such scare tactics as bombings falsely attributed to the Viet Minh and pamphlets warning that Catholics would be tortured or slain under communist leader Ho Chi Minh; was meant to stock the South with people who would vote for Diem and support his administration.

Phase 2 involved generating international press coverage of the flight of refugees. Of course, it would appear that the Catholics were leaving the North in spontaneous reaction to the ascendance of the Viet Minh. No one would know that their migration had been provoked by an American intelligence operation. Rather, the press would be encouraged to spotlight Saigon as the Ellis Island of the Fast and Diem as the last great hope for Indochina.

Together, the psychological warfare and publicity for the American-assisted evacuation would provide internal and external support for a weak, minority president who wouldn't stand a chance without it. But the press had not come through. Distracted by the war for independence in Algiers, the media largely had ignored the whole operation.

In Dooley, the Navy found a media magnet. He was not only handsome and eloquent but also confident that vanquishing communism in Asia was a matter of showing people the benefits of the American way of life, and he could express this in a spirited, captivating and infectious way. The Navy granted him a leave to write his book. Dooley, an ambitious dreamer, soon had visions of parlaying any resulting publicity into a position as Navy surgeon general. And the Navy was prepared to distinguish his accounts with an official imprimatur. But they were not prepared to deal with the discovery that he was a homosexual.

That discovery, and the Navy's threats to expose or censure him, would turn Dooley into a frightened pawn of U.S. policy-makers who were laying the groundwork for U.S. military involvement in Vietnam. Together, the Navy and Tom Dooley would create a great American hero—and a great American deception.

From the outset, Dooley's ambition made him a man who was eager to please. And while he may have set out to meticulously record his experiences in "Deliver Us From Evil," he was encouraged throughout the writing process to make his story more dramatic, something he was happy to do. He met frequently with Lederer, and several times while the book was in production he also met with Spellman, heady stuff for a former altar boy from St. Louis. What his mentors wanted, it seemed, was a vivid story that would make it impossible for Americans to ignore what they both perceived to be the crisis taking shape in Vietnam. His editors had the same idea, responding to an early draft by requesting "a more dramatic and impressive picture of a young doctor suddenly faced with a colossal job—at once a doctor with tens of thousands of patients, an administrator of a difficult physical plant under heartbreaking conditions, etc. etc."

The result was a highly charged piece of writing that put his book on the bestseller list, taking Vietnam from the edge of American awareness to the core of its consciousness—and making Tom Dooley a hero.

The book told of how he had treated children whose feet had been crushed to "moist bags of marbles" by soldiers, and of a priest who had had nails driven into his skull in a mockery of the crown of thorns of Jesus—sensational atrocities that found their way into the book reviews and into the hearts of readers.

The atrocities, he wrote, "seemed almost to have a religious significance. I was accustomed by now to patching up emasculated men and women whose breasts had been mutilated and even little children without fingers or hands. But more and more I was learning that these punishments were linked to the refugees' belief in God."

In one long passage, he described a priest who, he said, had been hung by his feet and beaten for defying a Viet Minh order to stop saying Mass at night. When Dooley encountered him, he was "lying on a bamboo stretcher, writhing in agony, his lips moving in silent prayer. When I pulled away the dirty blanket, I found that his body was a mass of blackened flesh from the shoulders to the knees. The belly was hard and distended, and the scrotum swollen to the size of a football. I gave him a shot of morphine and inserted a large needle in the scrotum in an attempt to draw off some of the fluid."

Dooley provided a compelling catalogue of horrors. But, as U.S. officials knew early on, the horrors were completely unsubstantiated. None of Dooley's correspondence, official or personal, describes the atrocities, that, in his book, he attributes to the communists. There are no corroborating accounts in the war diaries kept by Navy commanders nor in anything Dooley wrote during the operation.

The many letters be had mailed home from Haiphong describe dismal conditions to be expected as a consequence of a protracted war—squalor, disease and battle-related injuries. But there was no mention of atrocities, says Lederer, who now lives in Peacham, Vt., because "those things never happened. The atrocities he described in his books either never took place or were committed by the French. I traveled all over the country and never saw anything like them." And he didn't see Dooley's accounts of the atrocities until after the book came out.

Norman Baker of Santa Fe Springs, who had been a corpsman under Dooley in Haiphong, says much the same thing. "If I'd found a priest hanging by his heels with nails hammered in his head, I'd have the whole camp hearing about it," he says. "If those atrocities had occurred, human nature would make you talk about it at the time." Curiously, Dooley never had.

Perhaps more understandable was the way be exaggerated his own importance in the relief effort—so much so that when his book came out, he became known as "Dr. America." In truth, says Lederer, "he did some good stuff out there, but be was one of many"—and some were angered by his report. Onetime Voice of America reporter Ann Miller of Fountain Valley was one of 50 civil servants who sent a letter to Dooley's publisher, Farrar, Straus & Cudahy, protesting Dooley's egocentric account, saying "he exaggerated his role in the refugee, camps at the expense of the people who were working with him, many of whom did just as much, if not more, than he did."

Dooley's descriptions encouraged one more fundamentally flawed perception. He implied that most Vietnamese, like most of the refugees, were Catholic, when, in fact, fewer than 10% were. "The adults had children on their backs and by the hand, and even the older kids toted babies," he wrote. "Across their shoulders they carried balance poles with shallow baskets at either end. There they had their meager belongings—clothing, rice bowls, heirlooms and, invariably, a crucifix."

The reason for the distortion was obvious. It would be hard to muster support for Diem in a country where he was at odds with 90% of the population and was considered a relic of a French regime despised by those wanting independence. By writing as though the Catholics' fears of persecution were shared by all Vietnamese, Dooley made a compelling case that Americans should be actively concerned for the fate of that country. As journalist Robert Scheer would observe in an article published 10 years later. "Tom Dooley's major achievement ... was to convince the American public that the U.S. must come to the aid of these people and to help them maintain their freedom under God and Diem."

The protests about the book's veracity were ignored. Tom Dooley's editor, Robert Giroux, had an idea that the book wasn't, strictly speaking, true. "But" he says, "it had the essence of truth." And given the Cold War climate, he observes, that was just as good.

The Navy, for its part, had wholeheartedly endorsed the book—Adm. Arleigh A. Burke, Chief of U.S. Naval Operations, had even written the introduction. If the Navy had any qualms about the truth of Dooley's accounts, they went unexpressed. And the book, when it was released, was a runaway bestseller.

When Dooley returned from his book leave, he was given a desk job at Bethesda Naval Hospital instead of being put back on active duty. Baffled, he volunteered for a lecture tour to spread the word about what Operation Passage to Freedom had accomplished. And when the tour was abruptly canceled in Seattle three months later, he learned why the Navy had not returned him to his old post: It had received a tip that Dooley was gay.

During his tour, detectives from the Office of Naval Intelligence had tailed Dooley, and their final report runs to 700 pages. It represents hundreds of hours spent rifling through his briefcase, engaging him in leading and suggestive conversations and listening at bars and hotel-room doors. At the Statler Hotel in New York, Dooley was observed entering the bar. "He [Dooley] immediately stood beside a young fellow in civilian clothes," the informant reported, "and struck up a conversation, the following statements of which were overheard:

"Subject [Dooley]: 'Are you married? Are you a Roman Catholic? Do you go to church often?

"... Subject and civilian left the bar and proceeded to subject's room."

If Navy investigators had simply wanted to prove Dooley was homosexual, what they produced was overkill. It seems they were after more—proof that his conduct would damage the Navy. Proof, in other words, that he wasn't fit to serve.

The youngest officer to have received the Legion of Merit would be discarded without honor, but also without the public humiliation that usually accompanies such a dismissal.

Customarily, the Navy casts off homosexuals in a deliberately demeaning manner—stripping them of their bars in front of an assembly of officers and enlisted men. But the Navy couldn't dismiss Dooley that way. In fact, it couldn't even acknowledge that it had let him go. It had decorated the man and endorsed his book, and both would be worthless to them if the young doctor's sexual orientation were known. So Dooley and the officers charged with his dismissal concocted an alibi, Dooley would announce that he was leaving the Navy in order to serve the people of Vietnam in his own way.

"The brass say I'm more Navy now that I'm out than when I was in," Dooley wrote to console his mother, though he couldn't have wanted her to understand exactly what he meant by that. The Navy could ruin him now. The investigations had destroyed his dream of becoming Navy surgeon general. And, with a simple lapse of discretion, it could devastate any dreams he might replace it with.

The Navy had no intention of dissociating itself from Dooley.

The best-selling author never disappeared from the public eye. Farrar, Straus & Cudahy sent Dooley on a promotional tour, and he won over audiences wherever he went. He was especially eager to appeal to those with enough money and influence to help him return to Vietnam—he was ready to go back.

Despite the publicity and accolades, and for all the spirit and good humor he showed before a crowd. Dooley had been living with humiliation since the Navy had discharged him, says Ted Werner, a longtime

friend and, briefly. Dooley's pilot in Laos. Dooley had become accustomed to praise and admiration during the evacuation, and now he felt rejected and betrayed, his patriotism in question. "The Vietnamese loved him." Werner says, "and Dooley would want to be where he was so loved and appreciated."

Early in Dooley's promotional tour, he stopped at the Willard Hotel in Washington to address the lobbying group American Friends of Vietnam. There, he met two men who could help him get back to Vietnam: Leo Cheme and Angier Biddle-Duke, Cheme, a longstanding member of the President's advisory board on intelligence, was president of the International Rescue Committee, an organization devoted to helping certain political refugees escape persecution. Among the refugees the group had assisted was Ngo Dinh Diem, finding him sanctuary with Spellman, then arranging his return to Saigon as an "unofficial" adviser. Biddle-Duke, chairman of the IRC, agreed with Cheme that Dooley would be an asset to their campaign to win more U.S. support for their protege.

Dooley thought his popularity—his celebrity—would free him from the Navy's grasp. But he was wrong. Cheme and Biddle-Duke knew about the Navy's intelligence report, and what they knew—and what they observed for themselves—made them nervous. Dooley was often indiscreet; he might, if left on his own, inadvertently give himself away and sabotage the very campaign he was meant to advance. They asked Gilbert Jonas, a publicist and executive secretary of their allied group,

American Friends of Vietnam, to spend two days with him—to help him stifle the "telltale" mannerisms and to bring him up to date on foreign policy objectives.

Jonas recalls that Dooley was a quick but stubborn study. "He thought our goals and means were too complicated. He really believed we could fight off the communists with apple pie and Louisville sluggers." Dooley did indeed think that squelching communism was a simple matter of providing people with things many Americans take for granted, such as decent food, housing, medical care. "If America as a nation ignores the Asian's physical needs while handing him pious platitudes, we justify the communists' characterization of our religion as 'the opiate of the people' and 'pie in the sky by and by,'" he had written. And now he planned to go back to South Vietnam, to prove his theory and show up the Navy at the same time.

But the International Rescue Committee had something else in mind, and Dooley, dependent on its sponsorship, couldn't make a move without it. At an IRC dinner, ostensibly in his honor, Dooley was told that Operation Brotherhood, a CIA-trained Filipino medical corps, already had Vietnam's health-care needs covered. Then he was introduced to the ambassador from Laos, Ourot Souvannavong who invited him to open a clinic near his capital city, Vientiane.

The ambassador made a good case for coming to his country; the communist Pathet Lao was gaining strength, and the Geneva accords barred foreign armies from the nation. The Patient Lao were saying that the Vientiane administration was slavishly bound to the colonialist United States. The government wanted to fight that image with a visible, effective demonstration of U.S. good will.

The "suggestion" that Dooley go to Laos, made at a dinner arranged by potential sponsors, smacked of coercion. He wasn't in a position to defy them or to deny them anything. Both his affiliation with the rescue committee and his need to overcome the shame of his discharge for "less than honorable" reasons made him beholden to people who had the power to make him or break him and who would exploit his penchant for exploiting himself.

One of those people was Edward Lansdale, the CIA's chief "psychological warfare" operative in Vietnam. Lansdale knew about Dooley's discharge and his desire to return to Indochina. He had also watched Dooley on the docks in Haiphong and knew that, with his energy and humor, he could be an effective "agent of influence," a propaganda vehicle. Lansdale said he believed that Dooley would be useful in Laos, and it was he who passed this on to the rescue committee, which, in turn, brought in the Laotian health minister to make his appeal.

Dooley's "independent mission" to Laos, then, was not independent of the CIA or the Navy. Dooley was too much of a loose cannon to be trusted with substantial intelligence responsibilities, but as an eloquent anti-communist committed to peace by means of human services, he could be counted on generally to fire in the right direction. Dooley was useful as a spokesman and a symbol, and, to some degree, as a spy and a courier. In return for his support, the Navy wanted "situation reports." Likewise, the rescue committee asked him to dispatch weekly "Letters from Laos."

The CIA asked him for help of a different order. The agency wanted him to take weapons, along with his pharmaceutical supplies and surgical gear, so he could bury caches of arms that agents could use to mobilize local militia. His task would be to promote his clinics as outposts of peace, all the while covertly preparing for battle and giving induction exams to Laotian boys to clear them for service in the militia. Dooley's clinics were early mobilization efforts—in a part of Indochina that was meant to be neutral.

Much of Dooley's Vientiane clinic project was a sham. Dooley's assistants were untrained and unqualified to give him the kind of help he would need to operate a legitimate clinic. His medicine chest was full of pills and elixirs that had been donated by Pfizer, a drug manufacturer, because they had expired and were no longer legal to sell in the United States. Yet feature stories in Life, Look, Newsweek and Time presented Dooley as an ideal role model in features titled "The Splendid American," "Do-it-Yourself Samaritan" and "The Schweitzer of Asia." (According to Ann Miller, Schweitzer was not flattered by the comparison. He considered Dooley a dilettante and a charlatan.)

Dennis Shepard, who spent several months with Dooley as a volunteer in Laos, remembers that Dooley would round up as many of his former patients as he could whenever potential sponsors came to tour the clinic, giving the impression that he had a full and active hospital. In fact, he handled few cases, and the hospital was largely empty. According to Shepard, Miller and others, local CIA officers came by often to find out if Dooley had picked up anything about the movement of Chinese troops. They also came, Shepard remembers Dooley telling him, to ensure that the weapons Dooley had brought up with his medical supplies were well-hidden and secure. Shepard adds that he thought Dooley, always after a way to inflate his, importance, may have been bluffing. But home movies Dooley took of his move to Nam Tha show a boatload of rifles, jealously guarded by his escorts—armed members of the Laotian militia.

According to Ted Werner, Dooley exaggerated too much to be really useful to the CIA. "They would ask me to report on certain things when I was up there visiting Dooley, which was an indication to me they weren't relying on him in that sense," he says. Yet the weapons cache made the clinic an outpost of sorts, in contrast to its publicized purpose.

And the clinic *was* publicized. It made sensational copy, as this lead from a New York Daily News story suggests: "I have come halfway around the world to report one of the most dramatic stories in modern medicine. An incredible journey in Laos to within five miles of the Red Chinese border took me to the primitive land where Dr. Thomas A. Dooley operates a hospital at Nam Tha."

Before long, Dooley had become a familiar and favorite guest on radio and television talk shows, including the popular programs hosted by Arthur Godfrey and Jack Paar. He had his own radio show, broadcast over KMOX. St. Louis, ostensibly recorded each week in Laos. But according to Werner, who was present at several recording sessions, Dooley often set up his tape recorder during idle moments—wherever he happened to be—and improvised his "true" stories of life at the clinic while Werner and others faked ambient jungle sounds. Dooley was even the celebrated guest on "This is Your Life." Once again, his audience was deceived. While the program usually lured the celebrant on a ruse. Werner says that Dooley's appearance was made with his knowledge and direction. Unwitting viewers didn't know that Dooley's reaction—utter surprise—wasn't spontaneous.

In short, Dooley was everywhere—and more often in the United States than with patients in his clinic. He had the kind of celebrity typically associated with television and movie stars. Naturally, this drew some unsettling inquiries as well.

Several months after he had arrived in Laos, Dooley's mother wrote him that Hollywood columnist Hedda Hopper and others were making snide allusions regarding Dooley's departure from the Navy. His mother offered to do anything she could to stop the rumors—including calling the FBI to investigate their origin and arrest the instigators. He fired off a telegram to her, ordering her to do nothing. "This would be gravest error," he wrote. Surely it would; she would learn the truth.

Dooley followed up the telegram with a rambling letter saying he had known all along that his abrupt resignation would start rumors. But, he went on, no one who had read his book or heard him speak would believe such nonsense, implying that everyone knew that to be homosexual was blatantly at odds with being the man of action he was. The "slur on his family name" came with being a public figure; the fact that anyone should even bother to malign him was a measure of how big he had become. "I can take it, mother," he wrote, "and you should buck up and take it, too."

The rumors died before most people heard them, killed off by those who had invested in his image. The Navy issued denials—restating that Dooley had resigned from the Navy only to continue his humanitarian work in Indochina. And Life ran a three-page spread, replete with photographs of the good doctor at work and at play. Churches, schools, and corporations went on with fund drives for Dooley, while Reader's Digest bid with other publications for exclusive rights to his next piece.

Within a year, Dooley came home, swinging through the country to solicit support. He had it in mind to franchise himself, to set up a foundation called MEDICO (Medical International Cooperation) to sustain a network of clinics throughout the developing world. He also intended to move farther north in Laos, near the Chinese border, so that he would be close to the action—if any developed.

But during his move north, Dooley fell, knocking his shoulder and raising a lump that wouldn't recede. A few weeks later, he asked a visitor, the late William Van Valin, then a surgical resident, to remove the lump. Van Valin, jittery about operating on the famous doctor, performed the procedure nevertheless. "I did it under local," he said, "and Tom was wide awake and alert when I pulled the thing out of his chest." The "thing" was a wad the size of a golf ball, and pitch black. "Tom knew it was cancer, and that it was malignant."

Dooley dawdled before going home for more extensive surgery, and there are many who interpret the delay as a death wish. After all, Tom Dooley was fundamentally at odds with the very institutions and individuals sustaining him—the church and the U.S. government. He knew he could count on them only as long as he was useful to them. Dr. Vincent J. Fontana, medical director of the New York Foundlings Hospital, remembers having dinner with Dooley when he came to New York for treatment. "We were sitting in a restaurant, and Dooley said. 'Nobody loves me,'" Fontana recalls.

He reacted with astonishment. "You get letters every day, from all over the world," he says he told Dooley. "Everyone loves you." But Dooley shook his head. Nobody could possibly love him, he thought, because nobody knew him. If they knew him, they would find him loathsome.

"Tom Dooley was never able to integrate his sexuality into his life in the way that many gay men in the professions were able to do back then," Fontana observes, "He gave in to the stigma and isolated himself."

Dooley parlayed his cancer treatment into a public-relations event. He invited CBS News to film his operation at New York's Sloan Kettering Medical Center, and the network dispatched cameras. On film, in contrast to the grave, stentorian CBS commentator Howard K. Smith, Dooley, painfully thin and wearing a bathrobe, was calm and straightforward. He has agreed to have his surgery broadcast, he said, to comfort other cancer victims and to promote MEDICO. The resulting footage, titled "Biography of a Cancer," was broadcast nationally on April 21, 1960, and ended on a sanguine note. On television, Dooley's doctor told him he would survive for years. In fact, Dooley knew that he had a year, at most, to live.

Dooley's popularity soared after the show. By 1961, he ranked third on the Gallup poll's list of the 10 men most admired by Americans, behind President Dwight D. Eisenhower and the Pope. He received hundreds of thousands of dollars for MEDICO, which was to be his living legacy.

In December, 1961, Dooley, emaciated, bent and insensible with pain, checked back into Sloan Kettering, where be celebrated his 34th birthday. According to Fontana, who was Spellman's physician at the time. Spellman went to see Dooley despite warnings from his advisers, who worried that it might lend credence to rumors about the cardinal's sexual orientation. Navy Surgeon General Bartholomew Hogan went to see Dooley as well, bringing with him a copy of Dooley's new discharge. The record would show, he told Dooley, that he had resigned with a grade of "honorable," not his original "less than honorable." And so it does.

On the day Tom Dooley died, his clinic in Laos was overrun by the Pathet Lao.

Thousands turned out for Dooley's funeral, in the snow, in St. Louis. President John F. Kennedy awarded him a posthumous Medal of Freedom. But given the demands of U.S. policy objectives and events in Vietnam and Laos. Dooley's message, that we need "works of peace," would have to be abandoned. The United States was preparing for war. And so he—or who he was meant to be— had to make way. He had served his purpose; the public now cared about a part of the world it had known nothing about before Dooley started pleading on its behalf.

Few doubted Dooley's motives as they were presented by him and the press—the selflessness that made him remain a bachelor so that he could dedicate himself entirely to this cause. It seemed to them it must be a worthy cause indeed that would inspire him to sacrifice a promising career in the military so that be might devote himself to it. "He was a national hero and a national hazard." Lederer says. "It was his mammoth ego, his need for recognition, that helped get us into that mess over there."

Diana Shaw is a writer, and a researcher for the movie industry.

Source: Diana Shaw, "The Temptation of Tom Dooley," *Los Angeles Times Magazine* 15 Dec. 1991: 43–46 + .

EXERCISES: READING AND RESPONDING

1. Describe Shaw's voice.

2. Is the Dooley persona she presents different from the persona presented by Shilts? If your answer is yes, explain how each writer presents a different persona.

3. What assumptions does Shaw make about her intended readers?

4. Highlight passages that appear to be Shaw's opinion. Do these passages seem to be primarily positive or negative opinions about Dooley?

5. Identify voices she includes in the essay that support her opinion. Identify voices that offer opinions that differ from Shaw's.

6. What other voices besides Shaw's do you hear in this article? Are these voices credible?

7. What information does Shaw report about Dooley's resignation from the navy and the explanation he provided his mother about his resignation that other sources in this case—especially the chapter by Tom Dooley—do not include?

James Terrance Fisher is recognized as the first major biographer of Tom Dooley. In the following article, he reviews Randy Shilts' book, *Conduct Unbecoming*.

TOM DOOLEY'S MANY LIVES: NOBODY'S PLASTER SAINT

JAMES TERRANCE FISHER

Randy Shilts's *Conduct Unbecoming: Gays and Lesbians in the U.S. Military* (St. Martin's Press, $27.95, 784 pp.) is no ordinary book. Rushed into print to influence the raging debate over the status of gays in the military, its dust jacket proclaims. "Once in a generation comes a book that can change the world." The recent announcement that Shilts is suffering from AIDS only adds to the poignant urgency surrounding his message, that gays have served proudly and well in the U.S. military only to find themselves harassed, reviled, and persecuted simply for being themselves.

The best-known victim of military homophobia in *Conduct Unbecoming* is Thomas A. Dooley, the jungle doctor of Laos and folk here to millions of American Catholics in the late 1950s. While Dooley's ordeal comprises but a small part of Shilts's vast exposé, the book is framed by Dooley's story for maximum dramatic effect. Shilts describes the U.S. Navy's frenzied investigation of Dooley's sexuality while Dooley was on the American lecture circuit in early 1956, promoting *Deliver Us from Evil,* the best-selling, highly embellished account of his role in the Navy's 1954 "Operation Passage to Freedom," which transplanted over 600,000 Catholics from North Vietnam to the new regime of Ngo Dinh Diem in the South. Fearing a scandal that would diminish its own prestige, the Navy hounded Dooley into confessing his homosexuality following a campaign of surveillance and perhaps entrapment by Office of Naval Intelligence (ONI) operatives who bugged Dooley's phone and eavesdropped on his hotel room conversations.

Dooley's homosexuality has been no secret for years. It was first reported in an academic book I wrote in 1989 (*The Catholic Counterculture in America, 1933–1962*). At the time I felt it sufficient to describe the circumstances of Dooley's ouster from the Navy and indicate the role this forced resignation played in determining his future relationships with American personnel in Laos, where he went as a private citizen in 1956 to establish village clinics. Yet Dooley's career remains shrouded in mystery, and Shilts dramatically purports to expose the secret campaign that wrecked his life.

Shilts's first mistake in *Conduct Unbecoming* is an overreliance on the work of Diana Shaw, whom he misidentifies as a "biographer." Shaw, a researcher for the film industry, published an article on Dooley in the *Los Angeles Times Magazine* in

December 1991 which was riddled with factual errors. (For example, she dismissed Dooley's "Vientiane clinic project" as a "sham"; while it is true he never worked in Vientiane, his village clinics were no sham.)

Shilts describes Shaw's heroic pursuit of the secret Navy file on Dooley: "from the first time Diana Shaw attempted to retrieve Dooley's official Navy records, it was clear that the service had something to hide." Actually, the ONI report is readily available to scholars who will simply pay a visit to the Naval Operational Archives in Washington and request the documents. In relying upon a single journalist's questionable work and a couple of interviews. Shilts has made a remarkable number of errors in his brief but central discussion of the Tom Dooley case, from calling Cardinal Francis Spellman "John" to elaborately setting Dooley's funeral Mass at Saint Patrick's Cathedral. (It actually occurred a thousand miles away in Saint Louis.)

When I first began researching Tom Dooley's life and works I was often annoyed by the embarrassingly saccharine hagiographies that pervaded the Catholic press during his lifetime and even in the years since his death from melanoma in 1961. I sought out more critical treatments of his career that would help establish his significance beyond the confines of the preconciliar Catholic subculture. Yet I discovered that works by bitter ex-Catholics and New Leftists that claimed to expose Dooley's links to the CIA, or that held him responsible for the Vietnam War, were only secular equivalents of the religious hagiographies: they contained little of value concerning the real Tom Dooley. Shilts's discussion is, in its way, as misleading and mistaken as the most garish Dooley tributes in *The Sign or St. Anthony Messenger* in 1958. Shilts's claim that "everything good and everything evil that he did can be traced back to the shame he carried over his homosexuality" reduces Dooley to the sum of his sexuality for polemical reasons and is no more justified than the ill-fated campaign for his canonization.

Dooley's story is extraordinary, maddeningly complex, as I have learned in the course of research for a biography I am currently writing. Having interviewed nearly two hundred of his friends and associates, I can attest that the contradictions in the man's character multiply exponentially even as we seek some definitive conclusions in his compelling, tragic journey to celebrity and sainthood. Shilts appears content to present a cardboard Dooley as gay martyr in order to promote his own important cause, but there is no evidence that Dooley would have been in any way interested in serving as a symbol of oppression.

Shilts writes: "The Catholic church had said he could not see the face of God because of his sin, so he struggled to be the best Catholic he could be, performing acts of kindness and obediently following the ideology of the church." In fact several of Dooley's gay friends insist he was convinced that God had made him homosexual and that, since he was considered highly attractive, his sexuality was offered as a gift to others. There are also those who assert that he was indeed tormented by his sexual orientation and that he dealt with it by acting as though he were another person during his often anonymous sexual encounters. Still another individual recalled making a sexual advance toward Dooley only to be told: "I'm in a state of grace, so I don't do that anymore." The point is simply that we have absolutely no documentary evidence of Dooley's own thoughts or feelings about his sexuality or the state of his soul. He was at once hugely egocentric and unintrospective, at least in the thousands of letters he wrote in haste from remote corners of Asia.

Dooley constantly sought to restore the faith of others in the church without revealing much of his personal situation, other than to state that he did not know how anyone could live without belief in God. He seemed aware that his own life was less important than the impact he might have on others because of his charisma and the powerful mystique of service generated by his work in Laos. Anyone hoping to understand Tom Dooley must first concede that we can only see him through the infinitely variegated perspectives of others. In this respect he is perhaps the first postmodern saint, continually shifting in his appearance as we seek to discover some deeper reality. I can understand why Randy Shilts needed to tell his limited version of Dooley's story, but I must also lament Dooley's continuing misuse by those less interested in understanding than enlisting him in personal crusades, however legitimate they may be.

Tom Dooley was nobody's martyr. He was an arrogant, supremely self-confident, and in many ways profoundly compelling individual who believed he was destined to perform a special errand in God's wilderness. He totally ignored Navy protocol and rarely did anything he did not want to do, perhaps, according to some of his gay friends, because he enjoyed the patronage of well-placed homosexuals in the Navy Medical Corps. One reading of the ONI report supports a theory that Dooley wanted out of the Navy and enjoyed enraging the top brass with his antics, since they had fallen for the largely fabricated version of recent history he presented in *Deliver Us from Evil* (one of their spies was more upset by Dooley's ignorance of Navy terminology than by his sexual behavior). Tom Dooley may not have been a saint, but he was no patsy either. He is much too interesting and his work too important to play a cameo role in a political melodrama he would probably have dismissed as unworthy of his cosmic grandeur.

JAMES T. FISHER

James T. Fisher is an associate professor of American Studies at Yale University.

Source: James Terrance Fisher, "Tom Dooley's Many Lives: Nobody's Plaster Saint," Rev. of *Conduct Unbecoming* by Randy Shilts, *Commonweal* 21 May 1993: 6–7.

EXERCISES: READING AND RESPONDING

1. Characterize Fisher's voice. What does it reveal about his attitude toward his subject? toward his intended readers?

2. In your opinion, does Fisher write from a position of authority? Cite passages that illustrate your answer.
3. On which points about Dooley do Fisher and Shilts agree?
4. On which points about Dooley do Fisher and Shaw disagree?
5. Does Fisher's version of the Dooley persona differ in any way from Shilts' version?

CONTEMPORARY PERSPECTIVES

While several biographies of Tom Dooley were published following his death in 1961, James T. Fisher's *Dr. America: The Lives of Thomas A. Dooley 1927–1961*, was the first biography to put Dooley's life in the broad context of politics, religion, and celebrity.

DELIVER US FROM DOOLEY

JAMES T. FISHER

Since all of the published accounts of Dooley's lecture tour confirmed the impression that this gifted young man in navy dress blues was destined for greatness, it is profoundly jarring to compare the public adulation he received in the winter of 1956 with unpublished accounts of his activities, emanating from sources of a very different nature. A navy press officer who attended the doctor's lecture before the King County Medical Society in Seattle on March 15 witnessed a less savory side of Lieutenant Dooley. "While Dr. Dooley's remarks were interesting in general," he noted in a memorandum to the navy's Public Information Office, "it is felt that his presentation on this occasion was a disservice to the Navy." The press officer complained that Dooley resorted to "off color humor" in his talk, including jokes about circumcisions, mention of a "tall flat-chested Navy nurse" to whom he had lent his car during the refugee operation ("when I got back eleven months later, the car had 45,000 miles on it and the Navy Nurse looked like she had about 35 on her"), and such quips as "every time I broke wind [Norman] Baker saluted—we were a sharp outfit."[52]

The press officer objected to Dooley's criticisms of both French and American policies in Indochina. He was also incensed at Dooley's "poor use of Navy terms": Admiral Sabin and his staff "were called the 'heirarchy' [sic]"; Dooley described highly specialized naval craft simply as "boats." Despite Dooley's growing reputation as a sparkling after-dinner speaker, the press officer reported that during the talk, "many of the audience left ... at the conclusion of the address, forty to fifty people left. Only one question was asked."[53]

The navy had a question of its own for Lieutenant Dooley. The press officer was probably unaware that his report contributed to an ongoing, exhaustive investigation of Dooley's sexual behavior that was to result in his forced resignation from the service, effective March 28, 1956. On January 26 the chief of naval personnel had ordered the director of naval intelligence to initiate an "appropriate investigation" to determine whether Dooley "has homosexual tendencies," and if so, to determine "the extent of his homosexual activities."[54]

The rumors had begun at Yokosuka in the summer of 1954: one of Dooley's closest gay friends even claimed that Tom was assigned to the Vietnam refugee operation in retaliation for seducing the son of an admiral at the base. Dooley was without question a homosexual as well as the victim of a navy witch hunt. Although some of his admirers have sought to place Tom in the category of people with homosexual "tendencies" who do not necessarily act on their sexuality, he was in fact an extraordinarily active gay man who was considered one of the great underground sex symbols of his era—a figure well-known in sophisticated gay circles as far-flung as Hollywood, Washington, D.C., and the capitals of Southeast Asia.[55]

Dooley's ardent homosexual life had begun amid the dramatic social transformations wrought by World War II, which greatly influenced what the historian John D'Emilio called

"the social expression of same-sex eroticism. The war years allowed the almost imperceptible changes of several generations, during which a gay male and lesbian identity had slowly emerged, to coalesce into a qualitatively different form. A sexual and emotional life that gay men and women previously experienced mainly in individual terms suddenly became, for the war generation, a widely shared collective phenomenon."[56]

As a devout Catholic of the 1940s and 1950s, Dooley was expected to suffer for his sexuality; a psychiatrist who briefly lived in Laos (just after Dooley's death) and was apprised of Tom's life style was convinced that he died of guilt manifest as melanoma. Yet there are powerful counterclaims to this conventional narrative. Historian George Chauncey, in his study of gay New York culture between 1890 and 1940, convincingly dispelled what he called the "myths" of "isolation, invisibility, and internalization" that have dominated perceptions of urban gay life in the prewar era. Tom Dooley found a well-established subculture awaiting him when he began acting on his homosexuality in the early 1940s: his sexuality most definitely was not divorced from his social life.[57]

Tom had spent the summer of 1952 as a medical intern at the naval hospital in Bethesda, Maryland. One day he was picked up on a streetcar by a German airline steward who took him directly to the home of one of the leading lights of the Washington gay community. Dooley quickly became a favorite of a group that included theater people and musicians, Rock Hudson's future manager, and a man who went on to become a renowned omelette chef.

Dooley was recalled as "a most mesmerizing person" and "one of the most charming people you could ever meet," an emotional, spontaneous young man who brightened his surroundings and the lives of all around him. In that world, where homosexuals referred to each other as "friends of Bertha's" or "friends of Dorothy," or some other variation on the theme, Dooley was considered extremely desirable; according to one of his friends, he offered his sexuality as a gift to those he considered less attractive than himself. This individual recalled with exceptional clarity a conversation in which Dooley bluntly dismissed the Catholic Church's teaching on homosexuality as simply wrong. There was even then a certain mystical quality to Dooley's sex appeal, with his wild, undisciplined streak and his sparkling presence that friends insist distinguished him from other conventionally attractive men. Dooley would "drink like a fish" while playing the tunes of Gershwin and Porter (occasionally interspersed with darker classical melodies) at elegant rounds of parties.[58]

Yet if he consorted with a cosmopolitan gay elite as part of his ambition, Dooley also allegedly found time to engage in the kind of behavior guaranteed to confirm the navy's equation of homosexuality with criminal behavior. The "joyous way of looking at life" that Tom's friends recalled so vividly of the summer of 1952 is notably absent from the ONI report. The navy's informants portray Tom Dooley as a manipulative, even predatory character. One pickup reported that after they had sex, he suggested they get together again while Dooley was in New York, but Tom's "reply to that was that he was 'not here to make friends.'"[59]

Notes

52. Press Officer to Public Information Officer, March 16, 1956, Thomas A. Dooley Office of Naval Intelligence (ONI) file. Operational Archives, NHC.
53. Ibid.
54. Chief of Naval Personnel to Director of Naval Intelligence, January 26, 1956, Dooley ONI file, Operational Archives, NHC.
55. Interview with Ted Werner, January 6, 1992.
56. John D'Emillo, *Sexual Politics, Sexual Communities: The Making of a Homosexual Minority in the United States, 1940–1970* (Chicago, 1983), 38: see also Allan Bérubé, *Coming Out under Fire: The History of Gay Men and Women in World War Two* (New York, 1990).
57. Seymour Cholst, M.D., personal correspondence, May 19, 1986. George Chauncey, *Gay New York: Gender, Urban Culture, and the Making of the Gay Male World, 1890–1940* (New York, 1994), 2–6.
58. Interview with R. C., January 7, 1991; O.S., personal correspondence, October 12, 1992.
59. Report of surveillance of Tom Dooley in New York, February 4, 1956, Dooley ONI file, Operational Archives, NHC.

Source: James T. Fisher, "Deliver Us from Dooley," *Dr. America: The Lives of Thomas A. Dooley 1927–1961* (Amherst: U. of Massachusetts P., 1997) 81–89.

EXERCISES: READING AND RESPONDING

1. Whose voices do you hear directly and indirectly in this chapter?

2. Is the Dooley persona Fisher presents similar to or different from the Dooley persona presented by Shilts? Shaw?

3. Fisher claims that "Dooley's credibility was virtually nonexistent". In this chapter, how does Fisher demonstrate that Dooley lacked credibility? Whose voice demonstrates this point clearly?

4. Describe Fisher's stance on Dooley and on the ONI investigation.

5. Explain whether you find Fisher to be a credible or unreliable source.

6. Does Fisher's chapter give you a context for the Tom Dooley story that Shilts and Shaw do not provide for their readers? Cite specific passages that provide this context. Do these passages offer political, social, historical, intellectual, ethical, or some other kind of context?

7. Shilts, Shaw, and Fisher discuss Dooley's sexual orientation. In your opinion, are these writers using their respective media responsibly and ethically?

EXERCISE: GOING ON-LINE

Investigate other contemporary views on Tom Dooley or on the ethics of outing by looking for Internet sources.

EVALUATING AND ANALYZING THE CASE STUDY

EXERCISES: THINKING CRITICALLY

1. Identify the rhetorical situation for each source in the case study.

2. The letter from Senator Humphrey is a primary source for this case study. Identify other sources in the case study that are primary sources. Identify secondary sources. Be prepared to explain why you classify a source as one or the other.

3. *Conduct Unbecoming* is a focal point in the case study. Notice that it's mentioned in other sources. Review sources in this case and identify people, events, and issues that are focal points or connections that link one source to another.

EXERCISES: COLLABORATING WITH YOUR PEERS

1. Working in pairs or in groups, construct a time line for this case study.

2. Make a list of key players in this case. Be prepared to share your list with your classmates.

WRITING ABOUT THE CASE STUDY

EXERCISES: FOCUS ON WRITING

Freewriting

1. Write for fifteen to twenty minutes on your impressions of the case study. Answer the reporter's questions—*who? what? where? when? why?* and *how?*—and touch on issues that are controversial.

2. Write for fifteen to twenty minutes on public and private lives of individuals (other than entertainers or athletes) who find themselves in the public eye. How much is the public entitled to know about a person's life? Refer to the case study to illustrate your points.

3. Write for fifteen to twenty minutes on the voices you hear in this case study. Which voice makes the strongest impression? Why? Identify voices that seem credible and any voices that lack credibility.

Writing Letters

4. Assume that you read Shilts' editorial the day it appeared in *The New York Times*. In a letter to the editor of *The New York Times*, agree or disagree with Shilts' claim that outing is ethical.

5. Revise your letter responding to Shilts' claim. This letter will go to your campus or local newspaper.

Library Assignments

6. Agnes Dooley wrote about her son's accomplishments in *Promises to Keep: The Life of Doctor Thomas A. Dooley* (New York: Farrar, 1962). If your library has this book, read Chapter 4, "Towards the Edge of Tomorrow" (pp. 157–170), and write a paper analyzing how Mrs. Dooley's voice conveys authority, objectivity, bias, assumptions, and prejudices, and how other writers' voices contribute to her purpose.

7. Check the following indexes for at least one other book review of *Conduct Unbecoming*:

   Book Review Digest

   Book Review Index

   The New York Times Book Review Index

   An Index to Book Reviews in the Humanities

   Make a photocopy of the review and summarize it. Be prepared to explain whether the review identifies Shilts' purpose in writing *Conduct Unbecoming* and whether or not the review suggests that Shilts' account of Dooley's resignation and last days is reliable and credible.

8. Check the following indexes for at least one other book review of *Dr. America: The Lives of Thomas A. Dooley. 1927–1961*:

    Book Review Digest

    Book Review Index

    The New York Times Book Review Index

    An Index to Book Reviews in the Humanities

    Make a photocopy of the review and summarize it. Be prepared to explain whether the review suggests that Fisher offers a reliable, credible voice.

    Writing for an Academic Audience

9. Revise the biographical summary you wrote for the premed students interested in humanitarian efforts in medicine. In your revised draft, you should cite at least five sources in this case. This time your intended readers are the premed faculty as well as their students.

10. Select one of the sources listed below and write a documented essay focusing on how a writer's voice conveys authority, objectivity, bias, assumptions, and prejudices, and how other writers' voices contribute to the overall credibility and success—or lack of credibility and success—of a text.

    "What Tom Dooley Really Wanted"

    "But I Have Promises to Keep"

    "The Temptation of Dr. Tom Dooley"

    "Deliver Us From Dooley"

11. In a documented essay, compare and contrast Diana Shaw's voice in "The Temptation of Tom Dooley" with James T. Fisher's voice in "Tom Dooley's Many Lives: Nobody's Plaster Saint" and the excerpt from "Deliver Us From Dooley." In your opinion, which one of these sources is more reliable than the other? Identify any features or passages that support your opinion.

12. In a documented essay citing at least two sources in this case study, summarize two perspectives on the ethics of outing. Your aim is to inform and to allow readers, members of the academic community who are interested in ethical issues, to determine their own stance on the subject.

13. In a documented essay, citing a minimum of five sources in this case study, write a paper that answers the question: *Are there circumstances in which it is ethical to "out" an individual who wishes to keep his or her sexual orientation a secret?* You may cite sources you've found on your own, as well.

WRITING ABOUT RELATED ISSUES

EXERCISES: FOCUS ON WRITING

1. Working with two or three of your peers, survey a minimum of 100 students and ask: *Are there circumstances in which it is ethical to "out" an individual who wishes to keep his or her sexual orientation a secret?* Ask respondents

to begin with a yes or a no answer. If they elaborate, take notes on their responses. In addition to recording respondents' answers, record information about their age and gender. After you have completed your survey, tabulate the responses your group has accumulated and discuss how you interpret the numbers your survey has generated. Summarize the results of your question-naire and explain what conclusions you draw from the results.

2. In a documented essay, summarize two perspectives on an ethical issue of your choice. Conclude your essay with remarks on how the issue may be resolved or why it may never be resolved. Your purpose is to inform your readers, giving them specific information about the issues.

3. Working with two or three of your peers, develop a question that asks about a privacy issue. Then survey of a minimum of 100 students or members of your community. Be sure you ask a question that can be answered by a yes or a no. In addition to recording respondents' answers, record information about their age and gender. After you have completed your survey, tabulate the responses your group has accumulated and discuss how you interpret the numbers your survey has generated. Summarize the results of your question-naire and explain what conclusions you draw from the results.

Brainstorming: Questions about privacy issues might include the following:

- Should insurance companies be notified when medical tests reveal whether or not an individual has a genetic disease?
- Should state colleges and universities notify parents when their children have been issued citations for minor-in-possession or driving while intoxicated?
- Should employers or insurance companies be notified when an individual tests positive for AIDS?
- Should neighborhoods be notified when parolees move in who have been convicted of rape or molesting children?
- Should adopted children have access to the names and addresses of their birth mothers if the mother has asked that those records remain sealed?
- Should professors post students' grades even if individual grades are difficult to identify?
- Should the government implement a law that assigns Americans an identifi-cation code to track their medical history?
- Should states be allowed to require driver's license applicants to submit to thumbprinting or fingerprinting?
- Should the state and federal governments be allowed to use biometrics (fingerprints, retinal scanning, voiceprints, finger imaging) as a unique identifier (like the Social Security number) for people participating in welfare programs?
- Should hidden surveillance cameras be allowed in schools?
- Should hidden surveillance cameras be allowed in the workplace?
- Should hidden surveillance cameras be allowed in businesses?

4. For one of the questions above, identify library sources and Web sources. Then write a documented essay citing a minimum of five sources that

summarize two perspectives on the issue. Conclude your essay with remarks on how the issue may be resolved or why it may never be resolved. Your purpose is to inform your readers, giving them specific information about the issue you selected. If you completed a survey, you may use it as a sixth source.

5. Write a documented paper that examines privacy rights another country offers its citizens. Focusing on one specific area—for example, collection and dissemination of personal information, disclosing financial or medical information, wiretaps, or surveillance—compare and contrast these rights to those of U.S. citizens.

6. Write a paper that discusses the success or failure of the Don't Ask; Don't Tell policy.

Chapter 11

Creating a Context

It can hardly be denied that cultural context and situational context determine text. In this large sense, no text is autonomous—it exists within a biographical and historical stream.

—*James Kineavy*, A Theory of Discourse

THINKING ABOUT READERS' NEEDS

When writers write about subjects that are unfamiliar to their readers, confusion will inevitably result if readers aren't provided with sufficient context—an explanation that helps them understand the subject. In Chapter 1, you read about the necessity of identifying context in a rhetorical situation—that is, recognizing the circumstances that prompted a writer to write and categorizing a piece of writing. As a writer, you'll need to consider your readers' needs and identify places in a piece of writing that require some kind of context to help them follow your ideas. Depending on the subject, readers need different kinds of contexts—social, historical, scientific, political, economic, intellectual, and so on. Depending on their knowledge about a subject, context will be brief or extended. Providing readers with a sufficient context for a subject is like putting a jigsaw puzzle together. Audience analysis will help you determine the amount of detail your readers need. If they have a sufficient grounding in a subject, you might say that they have only a few pieces of the puzzle missing. If they have little or no background in the subject, your job is make the odd-shaped pieces of history or politics fit together to form a clear and coherent picture. You'll practice audience analysis when you complete writing assignments in the case study in this chapter, "Letter from Birmingham Jail."

CONTEXTUALIZING A SUBJECT

How you contextualize a subject will vary according to the subject itself, the medium you have selected, and the discourse community you address. Graphics— pictures, charts, graphs, or tables—may be helpful and appropriate. You have to be prepared to rely entirely on the written word alone, though, employing any combination of the modes of development: narration, description, comparison and contrast, definition, classification and division, analogy, cause and effect. More than likely, you will most frequently use narration (telling what happened) and description. To create a context for a topic, you'll also employ your skills in summarizing, paraphrasing, and quoting other sources. You have to exercise judicious selection of detail, always with your intended readers in mind.

In "Columbus Cracks an Egg" (Chapter 4), Stephen J. Gould uses a variety of rhetorical strategies to establish both historical and ethical contexts for readers as he tries to answer the question *Was the great voyager also a heavy-handed trickster?* Notice that he doesn't begin by telling readers that 500 years ago, Columbus sailed from Spain and claimed the new world he discovered for King Ferdinand and Queen Isabella. Instead, in the first three paragraphs, Gould sets up his ambivalence about Columbus; in paragraph 2, he parallels Torquemada's leadership during the Spanish Inquisition to Columbus' rape and pillage of the people and environment of the New World. Then, in the fourth paragraph, he sets up a context for the discussion that follows by telling the reader that the "military victory over the Moors, and the expulsion of Jews from Spain" and Columbus' discovery of the new world are three "completely intertwined" events. Using narration, he tells readers what happened when Ferdinand and Isabella "struggled to terminate diversity." Remember, Gould's intended audience has an interest in history, but the text illustrates his assumption that his readers need details about events that are not as familiar to them as the achievements of Christopher Columbus.

In "Maybe all of us should be leery of Mickey Mouse," (Chapter 4) Carlos Fuentes assumes that readers will be familiar with the acquisition of ABC News by the Walt Disney Corporation. His editorial comes on the heels of several days of headlines and news features about Disney's purchase of ABC News. Notice the quick reference to the acquisition. Fuentes doesn't hash out when and where it occurred or who was involved. He doesn't get bogged down with too much detail, either. Instead, he gets to his main point quickly: Entertainment is taking over the news. As this article illustrates, events and issues that are covered extensively by the media may need very little if any context. Historical topics, on the other hand, or highly specialized topics will require some kind of grounding for readers.

STRATEGIES FOR PROVIDING CONTEXT

While there is no set formula for how to provide context, we can predict placement of context: Because it provides readers with "background information" or a frame of reference, it should preface discussion of an issue or event it explains. You may need to provide a context for ideas, issues, or events at various stages in a paper, so we can't say that context is *always* provided in the first or second paragraph of a paper. Think of context as information that can capture, enhance, and sustain your readers' understanding of—and interest in—a topic.

To determine what kind of background information or context you need to provide on a topic, you should develop a profile of your topic and your intended readers by answering the following questions:

Analyzing the Topic

- Does the topic fall into the category of popular culture, or is it highly specialized?
- Has the topic been discussed by the popular press or media recently?
- Is the topic of high, low, or medium interest to intended readers?
- Is the topic controversial?
- Do sources use pictures, graphics, or statistics to create a context for the topic?
- How do other writers set up a context for the topic?

Analyzing Intended Readers

- Will readers respond to this topic with interest? indifference?
- Would readers' personal or professional experience, level of education, general or specialized interest in a subject provide them with some knowledge or frame of reference?
- If readers have no background or frame of reference for the topic, what is the best strategy for making the topic relevant and interesting to them?

While you are second-guessing your intended readers, this kind of topic/audience analysis is important for two reasons: First, you want your readers to understand your topic. Sufficient and appropriate background information will help them follow your line of reasoning or train of thought. Second, you want your intended readers to sense that you have a good grasp of the rhetorical situation. In other words, you understand your topic and your readers. This understanding should enable you to write with clarity and authority.

PREVIEW: DR. KING'S LETTER

Dr. Martin Luther King's "Letter from Birmingham Jail," written in 1963, was a response to a group of white clergymen who wrote a public statement criticizing King for "unwise and untimely" demonstrations that disrupted life in downtown Birmingham, Alabama. Today Dr. King's letter is regarded as one of our most important historical documents—an eloquent statement about nonviolent civil disobedience and the unjust laws that enforced segregation throughout the South.

It might surprise you to know that "Letter from Birmingham Jail" did not receive widespread publication in 1963. *Time* magazine ran a brief excerpt from the "Letter" in its January 3, 1964, issue, and included the observation that "although in the tumble of events then and since, it never got the notice it deserved, it may yet live as a classic expression of the Negro revolution of 1963". Case Study 3 asks you to focus on the events that took place in Birmingham, Alabama, during the spring, summer, and fall of 1963. Sources in this case study illustrate how writers provide readers with a context intended to help them understand a complex series of events,

---

Focus on Related Issues: Past and Present

In *Why History Matters*, Gerda Lerner, a leading historian on women's history, writes:

> A meaningful connection to the past demands, above all, active engagement. It demands imagination and empathy, so that we can fathom worlds unlike our own, contexts far from those we know, ways of thinking, and feeling that are alien to us. We must enter past worlds with curiosity and with respect. When we do this, the rewards are considerable.
>
> History, a mental construct which extends human life beyond its span, can give meaning to each life and serve as a necessary anchor for us. It gives us a sense of perspective about our own lives and encourages us to transcend the finite span of our lifetime by identifying with the generations that came before us and measuring our own actions against the generations that will follow. By perceiving ourselves to be part of history, we can begin to think on a scale larger that the here and now. We can expand our reach and with it our aspirations. It is having a history which allows human beings to grow out of magical and mythical thought into the realm of rational abstraction and to make projections into the future that are responsible and realistic.
>
> These aspects of history also lead to misuse. We construct symbolic communities, based on ethnicity, religion, race or any other kind of distinguishing mark, setting ourselves apart from those different from us, in order to find and enhance our own identity. We look to a past community, our "folk" of whatever definition, and our stories weave a collective myth into our narrative.*

As you work on this case study, consider how information about the struggle for civil rights in 1963 enlightens your understanding of the struggle for civil rights today. Think about individuals and organizations who work to ensure that all Americans are guaranteed civil rights. Who are they? Why is it important to remember their stories? Why is it important to honor their memories? What kind of struggles do they presently face?

Working on your own, investigate an event that furthered civil or human rights and develop it into a topic for a paper that reports what happened, who was involved, and why the event is significant. Keep in mind that you'll have to provide context—historical, social, or political—for whatever audience you select.

*Gerda, Lerner *Why History Matters: Life and Thought* (New York: Oxford UP, 1997) 117.

and a context that explains how city and state politics forced a group of citizens to organize and respond to—and change forever—laws that allowed segregation and discrimination.

After you have read firsthand accounts as well as more recent analyses of the period written with the advantage of hindsight, you should understand why the "Letter" is regarded as a landmark in the civil rights movement. One of the writing assignments in this case study asks you to write a documented paper that provides readers with a historical context for the "Letter from Birmingham Jail." In other words, your task is to help readers understand the events that lead up to King's incarceration and the political forces that were in place in 1963.

EXERCISE: FOCUS ON WRITING

Before you read what others say about King's "Letter from Birmingham Jail," spend ten to fifteen minutes freewriting to explore your own ideas about civil rights. What comes to mind when you think about the term *civil rights*? What documents guarantee civil rights in the United States? Are there rights an individual is guaranteed by the international community? What are the major civil rights issues today in this country? in other countries? Why is King regarded as one of America's most important historical figures?

Case Study 3:
"Letter from Birmingham Jail"

We shall overcome, we shall overcome
We shall overcome someday.
Oh deep in my heart, I do believe
That we shall overcome someday.

We'll walk hand in hand, we'll walk hand in hand
We'll walk hand in hand someday.
Oh deep in my heart, I do believe
That we shall overcome someday.

We shall live in peace, we shall live in peace
We shall live in peace someday.
Oh deep in my heart, I do believe
That we shall overcome someday.

We shall brothers be, we shall brothers be
We shall brothers be someday.
Oh deep in my heart, I do believe
That we shall brothers be someday.

The truth shall make us free, truth shall make us free
The truth shall make us free someday.
O deep in my heart, I do believe
That we shall overcome someday.

We are not afraid, we are not afraid
We are not afraid today.
O deep in my heart, I do believe
That we shall overcome someday.

(Author unknown.)

THE "ABSENCE OF JUSTICE"

In the spring and summer of 1963, Dr. Martin Luther King, Jr., president of the Southern Christian Leadership Conference (SCLC), led civil rights protests in Birmingham, Alabama, against segregation. According to the *New York Times*, civil rights leaders' minimum demands included "removal of racial restriction in downtown snack bars, public facilities, and stores; adoption of nonracial hiring practices for such posts as salesgirls and secretaries; and formation of a biracial committee to carry on continuing negotiations for further desegregation." Charging that promises on these matters had been made but never fulfilled, civil rights leaders organized massive demonstrations witnessed by the nation through media coverage. When television cameras brought into American homes pictures of police officers using dogs and fire hoses against demonstrators, a national outcry took place. "The Birmingham Manifesto," dated April 3, 1963, outlines the African-American community's goals for the protests:

BIRMINGHAM MANIFESTO

IN 1963, A SERIES OF EVENTS IN BIRMINGHAM, ALABAMA, MADE KNOWN THE PLIGHT OF AFRICAN AMERICANS TO THE NATION AT LARGE. BLACK CITIZENS WERE ARRESTED EN MASSE DURING PEACEFUL DEMONSTRATIONS—DEMONSTRATIONS WHICH WERE CRUSHED BY POLICE DOGS AND FIREHOSES. THE MANIFESTO, DATED APRIL 3, 1963, EMBODIED THE HOPE OF THE AFRICAN-AMERICAN COMMUNITY IN BIRMINGHAM THAT LAW, ORDER, AND PEACE WOULD SOMEHOW PREVAIL.

The patience of an oppressed people cannot endure forever. The Negro citizens of Birmingham for the last several years have hoped in vain for some evidence ... [of the] ... resolution of our just grievances.

Birmingham is part of the United States and we are bona fide citizens. Yet the history of Birmingham reveals that very little of the democratic process touches the life of the Negro in Birmingham. We have been segregated racially, exploited economically, and dominated politically. Under the leadership of the Alabama Christian Movement for Human Rights, we sought relief by petition for the repeal of city ordinances requiring segregation and the institution of a merit hiring policy in city employment. We were rebuffed. We then turned to the system of the courts. We weathered set-back after set-back, with all of its costliness, finally winning the terminal, bus, parks and airport cases. The bus decision has been implemented begrudging and the parks decision prompted the closing of all municipally-owned recreational facilities with the exception of the zoo and Legion Field ...

We have always been a peaceful people, bearing our oppression with superhuman effort. Yet we have been the victims of repeated violence, not only that inflicted by the hoodlum element but also that inflicted by the blatant misuse of police power.... For years, while our homes and churches were being bombed, we heard nothing but the rantings and ravings of racist city officials.

The Negro protest for equality and justice has been a voice crying in the wilderness. Most of Birmingham has remained silent, probably out of fear. In the meanwhile, our city has acquired the dubious reputation of being the worst big city in race relations in the United States. Last fall, for a flickering moment, it appeared that sincere community leaders from religion, business and industry discerned the inevitable confrontation in race relations approaching. Their concern for the city's image and common-weal of all its citizens did not run deep enough. Solemn promises were made, pending a postponement of direct action, that we would be joined in a suit seeking the relief of segregation ordinances. Some merchants agreed to desegregate their restrooms as a good faith start, some actually complying, only to retreat shortly thereafter. We hold in our hands now, broken faith and broken promises. We believe in the American Dream of democracy, in the Jeffersonian doctrine that "all men are created equal and are endowed by their Creator with certain inalienable rights, among these being life, liberty and the pursuit of happiness.

Twice since September we have deferred our direct action thrust in order that a change in city government would not be made in the hysteria of a community crisis. We act today in full concert with our Hebraic-Christian traditions, the law of morality and the Constitution of our nation. The absence of justice and progress in Birmingham demands that we make a moral witness to give our community a chance to survive. We demonstrate our faith that we believe that the beloved community can come to Birmingham. We appeal to the citizenry of Birmingham, Negro and white, to join us in this witness for decency, morality, self-respect and human dignity. Your individual and corporate support can hasten the day of "liberty and justice for all." This is Birmingham's moment of truth in which every citizen can play his part in her larger destiny ...

Source: "Birmingham Manifesto," *Reference Library of Black Americas,* Ed. Kenneth Estell, Vol. 1 (Detroit: Gale, 1994) 191–92. 5 vols.

EXERCISES: READING AND RESPONDING

1. Identify passages of the "Manifesto" that provide a context for the civil rights movement.
2. According to this document, why was the "Negro protest for equality and justice ... a voice crying in the wilderness"?
3. How do the authors of the "Manifesto" create an ethos?
4. Characterize the voice you hear in this document. What does it reveal about the writer's attitude toward the subject and audience?

EXERCISE: THINKING CRITICALLY

Summarize the terms of the "Manifesto."

In an introduction to their book, *The Rhetoric of the Civil-Rights Movement,* Haig A. and Hamida Bosmajian explain the effect pictures of the Birmingham demonstrations had on the entire nation.

INTRODUCTION TO *THE RHETORIC OF THE CIVIL-RIGHTS MOVEMENT*

HAIG A. AND HAMIDA BOSMAJIAN

Through the news media the entire nation saw Birmingham police unleashing police dogs upon children and using high-pressure fire hoses against demonstrators. Arthur Waskow has pointed out the national impact of this violence directed against the demonstrators:

On May 4, a notable news photograph appeared all over the world, showing a Birmingham police dog leaping at the throat of a Negro schoolboy. If there was any single event or moment at which the 1960s generation of "new Negroes" can be said to have turned into a major social force, the appearance of that photograph was it. Intense pressure upon President John F. Kennedy to initiate federal action began to be applied the moment that photograph appeared, and both financial and political support for all organizations in the civil rights movement multiplied at once.

The effect of this photograph illustrates the rhetorical function of

---

FOCUS ON RELATED ISSUES: THE RHETORIC OF PICTURES

In 1972, the picture of nine-year-old Phan Thi Kim Phuc running naked from her village after a napalm attack became a searing image of the horrors of the war in Vietnam. An image of pain, agony, and helplessness, it said a great deal about war, even without words to accompany it. Although the air strike was carried out by the Vietnam Air Force, the photograph became one of many indictments of American involvement in Southeast Asia. It won a Pulitzer Prize for AP photographer Nick Ut.

Images in newspapers and magazines are often used because they have a rhetorical effect on readers. They tell a story, illustrate a claim, or make an appeal more vividly than a text does. Consider the rhetorical function of images you see every day in newspapers and magazines, on television, or on the Web. Select one that you find particularly effective in having a rhetorical effect, and write a paper that provides a context for the picture and analyzes the elements of the photograph that create a rhetorical effect.

a picture. Apparently where persuasive speeches and articles and books had not persuaded some Americans to give financial and political support to the civil-rights movement, the visual images of peaceful demonstrators abused by the Birmingham police did bring support.

Source: Haig A. and Hamida Bosmajian, Introduction, *The Rhetoric of the Civil Rights Movement,* (New York: Random House, 1969) 14–15.

EXERCISE: THINKING CRITICALLY

Paraphrase the Arthur Waskow quotation in the introduction to *The Rhetoric of the Civil-Rights Movement.* Share your paraphrase with your classmates and determine if it is a fair and accurate paraphrase.

THE FIGHT FOR CIVIL RIGHTS:
TIME LINE

1954—Supreme Court hears *Brown vs. Board of Education.* Oliver Brown and other black parents challenge the "separate but equal" policy that allows for segregation of schools. The Court refuses to uphold the "separate but equal" policy.

1955—Montgomery Bus Boycott. In Montgomery, Alabama, Rosa Parks refuses to give her seat on a public bus to a white woman. Civil rights leaders organize a boycott of the bus system in Montgomery and bring national attention to segregation.

1957—An angry mob objects when nine black students try to enroll in Little Rock High School in Arkansas. President Eisenhower orders that the students be admitted.

1962—James Meredith tries to enroll at the University of Mississippi. Governor Ross Barnett challenges the Supreme Court's ruling.

1963—Media coverage of demonstrations in Birmingham bring national and international attention to the civil rights movement.

August 28, 1963—Over 200,000 people gather in the nation's capitol. Martin Luther King, Jr., delivers his "I Have a Dream" speech.

1964—President John F. Kennedy introduces the Civil Rights Bill of 1964. The bill empowered the federal government to act against segregation.

1964—Martin Luther King, Jr., receives the Nobel Peace Prize.

In "Alabama: 1960–1963," James Reston responds to the September 15 bombing of the Sixteenth Street Baptist Church in Birmingham. Anthony Lewis explains that the blast injured fourteen Negroes and killed Cynthia Wesley, 14; Denise NcNair, 11; Carol Robertson, 14; and Addie Mae Collins, 14.

ALABAMA: 1960–1963

JAMES RESTON

WHY, THE NATION WONDERED, WAS BIRMINGHAM SO DRIVEN TO STRIFE? AND WHEN, THE WORLD WONDERED, WOULD THE UGLY, UNGOVERNABLE TURBULENCE END? JAMES RESTON ATTEMPTED TO FIND ANSWERS IN A *TIMES* ARTICLE PRINTED ON SEPTEMBER 20TH:

The striking thing about Birmingham to an outsider is that it seems so advanced industrially and so retarded politically. It has seized the scientific revolution and rejected the social revolution of our time. Accordingly, it is engaged in a remarkable and hazardous experiment: it is trying to back full speed into the future.

The visible and audible symbols of the city dramatize this paradox. It lies in a long valley surrounded by lovely flowering hills. Above the forest of smoking chimneys stands on a peak a vast stainless-steel statue of Vulcan, like some hideous modernistic monster out of the German Ruhr. Yet down below in the city the symbols are not of the fires of the future but of the fires of the past. The Confederate flag is painted on the cars and helmets of Governor George Wallace's state troopers, now very much in evidence here, and the biggest clock in town booms out across the city from the tower of the Protective Life Insurance Company a few bars of "Dixie" before it strikes each hour. Look to the industrial future, says the gleaming Vulcan. "Look away, look away, look away, Dixie Land," chimes the clock.

That Birmingham should have become the symbol of southern defiance adds to the paradox, for it did not come out of the tradition of the old agrarian, slave-holding, plantation South. It was not even incorporated until December, 1871, in the decade after the war between the states; it was populated from the North more than almost any southern city, and its commercial and industrial ties now run to New York and Pittsburgh rather than to Atlanta or New Orleans.

Like most industrial cities it does have a tradition of putting private interests above public interests and it does have a history of violence. It was for many years an overgrown mining camp, populated by rough men from all sections of the country. Convict labor from the state prisons worked in the mines until the early 1920's, and National Guardsmen first went on strike patrol during the coal miners' walkout here in 1894. Thus Birmingham is not like any other city in the country. Industrially it is ahead of much of the North; politically it is behind most of the urban South. It pays its Negroes better and in some ways treats them worse than most southern towns, partly because it suffers from some of the worst aspects of both industrialization and segregation.

No generalization about Birmingham is safe, but its history does help suggest one possible explanation about the present attitude of many of its most influential leaders. This is not a city dominated by inherited wealth. More than in most southern cities, Birmingham's commercial and industrial leaders are self-made men, with the self-made man's feeling that others can be just as successful too if they will only work.

Many white leaders here created their own fortunes, others are managers under pressure from northern headquarters to produce the maximum at the minimum cost. As human beings, they are probably no better or worse than business leaders in other cities, but there is something in the history and atmosphere of this place, some relationship between the idea of the supremacy of the dollar and the supremacy of the white man, that has made them feel they could hold out longer against social change. It isn't that they wanted more than other white leaders in Atlanta and elsewhere, but merely that in this particular city they thought they could get away with demanding more.

The result is that the leaders of Birmingham are trapped for the time being in the struggle. For the more they have delayed making concessions to Negro equality, the more the Federal Government has dramatized their dilemma, and the more the Negroes have demanded, and the more business the city has lost. The death of the four Negro children in this week's bombing of a Negro church has merely brought all this to a head. It has shocked the community, but there is little evidence that it has changed the convictions of the white leaders about what they regard as the proper (separate) relations between the races. They merely seem a little more convinced now that the continued uproar here is not good business, and Birmingham wants good business, even if it has to obey the federal law to get it.

Source: James Reston, "Alabama: 1960–1963," *Portrait of a Decade: The Second American Revolution,* ed. Anthony Lewis and the *New York Times* (New York: Random House, 1964) 198–99.

EXERCISES: READING AND RESPONDING

1. Lewis explains that James Reston attempted to answer the question *Why ... was Birmingham so driven to strife?* because the "world wondered, would the ugly, ungovernable turbulence end." What are three of the reasons Reston offers for the strife in Birmingham?

2. What are the "visible and audible" symbols of the city?

3. According to Reston, how did Birmingham differ from other Southern cities?

4. Identify passages that provide a geographical, political, social, economic, or historical context for the events that took place in Birmingham in 1963.

EXERCISE: THINKING CRITICALLY

Paraphrase paragraphs 2, 4, and 6 in Reston's article. If you were using any one of these paragraphs in a documented paper describing the civil rights movement in Birmingham in 1963 , would you use your paraphrase, quote the original passage, or use some combination of paraphrase and quotation? Be prepared to explain your choices.

EXERCISE: GOING ON-LINE

Identify web sites devoted to either the "Letter from Birmingham Jail" or the bombing of the Sixteenth Street Baptist Church. Write a critical review of one of these sites.

Dan Carter, professor of history at Emory University, has served as president of the Southern Historical Association and received the Bancroft Prize in History for the best book in American History, *Scottsboro*. In "The Threads Ran Through," he describes the city of Birmingham as it was on the brink of protests by the Southern Christian Leadership Conference.

THE THREADS RAN THROUGH

DAN CARTER

While George Wallace taunted the Kennedy administration, the city of Birmingham erupted in the largest series of civil rights demonstrations in the nation's history. By the time the confrontation on the streets of Birmingham and the standoff between George Wallace and the federal government had reached an awkward resolution in early June 1963, all of the cautious assumptions that had guided the Kennedy administration in dealing with issues of race and politics had been swept aside. A year later, Burke Marshall sat and struggled to summarize the late-night conferences at the Justice Department and in the White House, the urgent telephone calls, the hurried flights back and forth to Alabama. If disorder ruled his memories, Marshall remained certain of one fact: there were "threads that ran through" the events that had unfolded in Tuscaloosa, Montgomery, and the chaos of Birmingham.[22]

Two years earlier, the *New York Times*'s Harrison Salisbury had visited Birmingham to prepare a profile of the state's largest city. "I had worked for years in Russia and behind the Iron Curtain," he recalled, but nothing had prepared him for the surreal atmosphere of this Deep South center of iron and steel production. Here in America he found a city in which decent, well-meaning, respectable citizens dismissed the most cautious criticisms of white oppression as evidence of "Communist sympathies," a city in which most whites supported or fastidiously turned their gaze away from a brutal system of absolute white supremacy maintained by "the whip, the razor, the gun, the bomb, the torch, the club, the knife, the mob, and police and many branches of the state's apparatus."[23]

There had been brief moments of hope for better days. Driven to desperation by the Depression, Birmingham's blue-collar coal, iron, and steel workers briefly forged alliances that cut across racial lines, but the faltering effort at biracial unionism collapsed after the war. When the last of the ore mines closed in the early 1950s, and U.S. Steel ended nearly a half-century of expansion, a coalition of local and absentee-owned corporations joined hands with an economically and racially threatened white lower middle class to create a political system personified by the fiery public safety commissioner, Eugene (Bull) Connor.

Connor and his lesser-known fellow city commissioners supported a political and economic system based on low wages (a race-discriminatory wage paid blacks even less than whites, and both were well below the national average), low taxes, and limited government services. Connor ran the police department like a plantation (he called his favorite cops "my

nigguhs") and he tolerated blacks only if they were willing to grovel or to assume the role of "Sambos" and "Aunt Jemimas."[24]

Wartime labor shortages had forced steel plants and ore mills to hire black workers in slightly higher-paying jobs, and they began to look for housing outside Birmingham's compact and dilapidated African-American communities. In late 1946, a black forty-three-year-old drill operator at the Ishkooda ore mines used his life savings of $3,700 to purchase a frame house on the racial-boundary line of the white working-class community of Fountain Heights. Local Klansmen gave Sam Matthews one warning: they painted a skull and crossbones on the front of the empty house. When he refused to abandon his plans, vigilantes broke into the vacant house and dynamited it on the night of August 18, 1947. No one could have anticipated that the destruction of Sam Matthews's home would be the first of more than fifty bombings directed against blacks over the next sixteen years. By the mid-1950s, people in Birmingham routinely referred to the Fountain Heights community as Dynamite Hill.[25]

From 1948 to 1965, blasts shattered more than two hundred black churches and homes, as well as synagogues, in the Deep South, but far more bombs exploded in Birmingham than in any other city. Dozens of men in the Steel City, as the Federal Bureau of Investigation soon discovered, were familiar with explosives and skilled in their illicit use.

City commissioners made it clear from the outset that the black victims, by directly or indirectly challenging the racial status quo, had no one to blame but themselves. When the Birmingham chapter of the NAACP complained to city officials in 1948 that Police Commissioner Connor had made little visible effort to investigate the explosions, Connor arrested the most recent victim and accused him of destroying his own home in order to help "those subversives who created this situation."[26]

What began as a violent tactic to prevent black neighborhood expansion soon became a favorite weapon to terrorize civil rights activists. And so long as the bombers directed their skills against bona fide integrationists—so long as the main effect was property damage and intimidation—civic élites made little effort to curb their police commissioner. Beginning in the 1920s and 1930s, middle- and upper-income whites had moved across Red Mountain into separate suburban municipalities: Mountain Brook, Homewood, and Vestavia Hills. After they rejected a proposed merger with Birmingham in 1958, white suburbanites hunkered down behind what one resident bluntly called their Maginot Line, safe from the uncomfortable dangers of school integration and economic competition. Geographically just over the mountain from Birmingham, they lived in a world a thousand miles distant from the back alleys and streets of the Steel City's black and white working-class communities.[27] In 1958, a black neighborhood watch apprehended three Klansmen seconds after they had bombed two homes on Dynamite Hill. One of the homeowners had actually seen the men lighting the fuse seconds before the blast; city police finally had terrorists—caught red-handed—in custody. But the *Birmingham News* dismissed the incidents as "harmless explosions" that were "probably" set by blacks in the neighborhood. The police, said the *News,* should be far more concerned about the Negroes who had "ganged up" on the white suspects. Connor refused to hold the three Klansmen.[28]

While the bombers plied their trade at night, scarcely a week went by without an account of the police shooting a black suspect, or a brief report, buried in the back pages of the *Birmingham News* or *Post-Herald,* on the death of a black person in custody. Inevitably, a perfunctory investigation would clear the gun-wielding police officer. Occasionally, community leaders murmured disapproval when police beat or abused a particularly inoffensive black man or woman. But most of the business and professional leaders who ruled Birmingham turned a blind eye to the excesses of Connor and his fellows, giving them a free hand to create one of the most brutal police forces in the nation. Fred Shuttlesworth did not exaggerate when he said that, for black people, Birmingham in the 1950s and early 1960s was "very close to hell itself; the Johannesburg of the South."[29]

Despite Connor's record, George Wallace never faltered in his support. In the spring of 1963, the Alabama governor went out of his way to encourage the police commissioner's hard-line response to civil rights demonstrations, and during Birmingham's critical mayoral election in

March and April, he embraced Connor with unseemly enthusiasm. Even after Birmingham voters elected the more moderate Albert Boutwell as mayor, Wallace used the lame-duck Connor to try to sabotage any rapprochement between blacks and whites in the city. A quarter-century later, Wallace diffidently suggested to his official biographer that his "good friend Bull Connor was a little too abrasive," but that was as far as he could bring himself to go in criticizing his old ally.[30]

The prospect of storming Bull Connor's citadel seemed less daunting than outright suicidal to Martin Luther King's Southern Christian Leadership Conference (SCLC), still reeling from the embarrassment of its failed 1961–62 antisegregation campaign in Albany, Georgia. If demonstrations mushroomed into widespread violence, they could easily destroy King as a national spokesman and deliver a devastating setback to a civil rights movement that had gained precarious national support only by shielding its defiance behind the public relations armor of

nonviolence and martyrdom. Where there was danger, however, there was also opportunity. The fall of Birmingham would electrify the movement and rebuild the battered fortunes of the SCLC.

Civil rights leaders briefly delayed the beginning of demonstrations so as not to affect the outcome of an April 6 election in which a new city charter replaced the old mayor-commissioner government with a new mayor-council organization. The old mayor, hard-line racist Arthur Hanes, along with Bull Connor and his fellow commissioners, insisted that they should be allowed to serve out their terms. The newly elected Boutwell was forced to launch a court battle to assume office. In the meantime, Connor remained in control of the police. Whether Boutwell or Hanes was mayor seemed irrelevant to the movement's leaders; both were committed to maintaining the racial status quo. Within hours of the runoff election, sit-ins took place at half a dozen lunch counters; police arrested twenty-one demonstrators. The siege of Birmingham had begun.[31]

Notes

22. Robert Kennedy and Burke Marshall, JFK interview, 107.
23. Letter from Harrison Salisbury to author, July 20, 1991; *New York Times,* April 12, 1960.
24. Nunnelley, *Bull Connor,* 9–68.
25. Eskew, "But for Birmingham," 101–102.
26. Ibid., 118.
27. Morgan, *A Time to Speak,* 59.
28. Eskew, "But for Birmingham," 202.
29. Garrow, *Birmingham, Alabama, 1956–1963,* 140. Even for Connor, his response to the bombing of three black Birmingham churches in January of 1963 was an audacious exercise. At one of the three churches, a member of the congregation smelled the burning dynamite fuse and sounded the alarm. Con-

nor immediately issued a statement announcing that "We know that Negroes did it." The proof, he said, was the fact that witnesses "saw Negroes running from the churches." *Birmingham Post-Herald,* February 1, 1963; *New York Times,* February 1, 1963.

30. Lesher, *George Wallace,* 195.
31. *Birmingham Post-Herald,* April 4, 1963.

Source: Dan Carter, "The Threads Ran Through," *The Politics of Rage: George Wallace, the Origins of the New Conservatism, and the Transformation of American Politics,* (New York: Simon, 1995).

EXERCISES: READING AND RESPONDING

1. How did Harrison Salisbury describe Birmingham?
2. Carter explains how racial division escalated from the 1940s to the early 1960s. Summarize his explanation.
3. According to Carter, what attitude did the Birmingham newspapers take when numerous bombings took place in black neighborhoods?
4. What details does Carter include to illustrate Fred Shuttlesworth's comparison of Birmingham to Johannesburg?
5. What role did Bull Connor play in city politics?
6. What role did Albert Boutwell play in city politics?
7. How did the mayoral election affect the civil rights demonstrations?
8. Identify passages that provide a geographical, political, social, economic, or historical context for the events that took place in Birmingham in 1963.

Dan Carter explains that civil rights demonstrators had held back for months "for fear of giving Connor campaign ammunition". In January 1963, King announced that he would lead demonstrations in "the most thoroughly segregated big city in the U.S."; however, he went on a sixteen-city speaking tour from January 16 to March 29, and postponed taking action in Birmingham until after the April 2 elections. The following sources explain how the mayoral election affected the protests in Birmingham.

"BULL" AT BAY

Eugene (Bull) Connor is an unprepossessing figure—a fleshy man of 63 with jug ears, nagging sinuses, a glass eye, and a bellowing style that dates to an early job reading the baseball ticker aloud in a poolroom. But Connor is as much a giant in Birmingham as the cast-iron statue of Vulcan, god of the forge, atop Red Mountain just outside town. Both are monuments—Vulcan to the city's steel economy and Connor to her standing as the biggest, toughest citadel of segregation left in the Deep South. As commissioner of public safety, Ole Bull ran the police force. And Connor's cops carried out a fiat he once laid down: "We ain't gonna segregate no niggers and whites together in this town."

But Birmingham toppled one of her twin monuments last week, retiring Bull Connor after 21 years in City Hall and picking a softer-spoken, business-as-usual segregationist to run the town.

Civic leaders had been increasingly worried about the city's lagging growth and her image as a racial powder keg. Under their prodding last year, voters scrapped the government setup under which Connor had flourished—a troika of city commissioners—and adopted a mayor-and-council plan. Connor ran for mayor. But, in last week's run-off election, he lost by 8,000 votes to former Lt. Gov. Albert Boutwell.

Images

Boutwell built his campaign around a pledge to build a new civic image for Birmingham, Connor scoffingly labeled him "The Image" and charged that Boutwell would permit token integration of the city schools. And, though Ole Bull disowned such tactics, racist leaflets were scattered about. (Sample: a cartoon of a Negro standing at the city limits in an Ole Miss cap and gown, saying, "I'se de new image.") But civic leaders and both daily newspapers backed Boutwell; so, grudgingly, did Negroes. Connor carried the

blue-collar precincts 2 to 1, but the coalition proved too much for him.

NEW DAY DAWNS FOR BIRMINGHAM, the News headlined the morning after. But it had not quite arrived. For one thing, a conflict in state laws made it uncertain whether Boutwell would move into city hall next week—or not until 1965, when the present commissioners—including Connor—finish their terms. For another, Negroes picked the day after the election to launch their first frontal assault in a year on apartheid in Birmingham.

For months, they had held back for fear of giving Connor campaign ammunition. But now, Martin Luther King flew in from Atlanta with his top aides to lay "non-violent" siege to what he called "the most thoroughly segregated big city in America." Teaming up with Birmingham's Rev. Fred Shuttlesworth, they drafted a bill of demands: lunch-counter integration and equal job opportunity in downtown stores, a timetable for school desegregation, appointment of a biracial committee to discuss race problems. King, meanwhile, rounded up a somewhat undermanned "non-violent army" of 250 Negroes and sent squads on forays at downtown lunch counters.

Connor was waiting, with a vow to "fill the jail full ... as long as I am at city hall." At Britt's department store, the manager asked the Negroes to leave, then called in Connor's cops. Twenty demonstrators were arrested for trespassing; next day they drew the maximum penalties—$100 and 180 days. But some stores simply shut down their counters, abandoning them to the demonstrators. Connor was miffed that these stores hadn't called him. "We had to let them sit in," he railed. "It's a disgrace." Even so, by the end of the week, Connor's bag of arrests numbered more than 75.

Needle-points

There were other dissenting voices. Boutwell, furious, decried "racial agitation" and added a needle-pointed prediction that King & Co. would "fold their tents and silently fade away, leaving behind them the problems they have created." Indeed, some white liberals thought King should call a 30-day truce and leave town until they can sound out Boutwell's readiness to enter quiet negotiations. Even

among Negroes, some questioned King's timing. Besides, the generals of King's army were having some trouble recruiting troops. About 500 Negroes sat fanning themselves in St. James Baptist Church one night while King and Shuttlesworth sent out the call. But only 54 walked down to the altar to sign up.

King, however, was committed, and he had his own notion of timing. With the Easter shopping season in progress, he urged Negroes not to buy new outfits and to come to church Easter Sunday in blue jeans. And he vowed to stay on. "The time is always wrong for some people," he said. "The cup of endurance has run over." And the slender Shuttlesworth echoed: "This is Birmingham's moment of truth."

Source: "'Bull' at Bay," *Newsweek* 15 Apr. 1963: 29–30.

EXERCISES: READING AND RESPONDING

1. How does this source characterize Bull Connor?
2. Why did Connor lose the mayoral election?
3. Why did the mayoral election fail to result in a "new day in Birmingham"?
4. According to this source, why had the black community held back from protesting for a year?
5. What prediction did Boutwell make about King?
6. Identify passages that provide a political, social, economic, or historical context for the events that took place in Birmingham in 1963.

In "The Birmingham Story: Segregation is Teetering Under Fire," published May 26, 1963, in the *New York Times*, Foster Hailey observed that Birmingham's "two newspapers carried only brief articles on the demonstrations. The only time the racial turmoil achieved page one was when someone denounced 'outside agitators' who were said to be stirring up the peace-loving local Negro community". The following article illustrates Hailey's claim.

BOUTWELL URGES ALL
TO AVOID DISCORD HERE

Mayor-elect Albert Boutwell yesterday urged Negro citizens "to think long and hard before committing themselves to follow the questionable leadership of strangers—people whose sole purpose is to stir inter-racial discord here."

Boutwell warned, "These outsiders will desert, as they have in other localities, once they have worked their mischief, and leave our local citizens to pay the penalty of discord, in an atmosphere of tension that did not exist before they came."

He added. "I want to point out to all of our citizens, that these strangers have never won a victory anywhere in the kind of struggle they are trying to foment here in Birmingham."

The head of Birmingham's new mayor-council government, slated to take office the middle of this month, assured the people of Birmingham he had confidence in the effectiveness of solving problems peacefully, with people and law enforcement officers working together.

"Demonstrations and sit-ins can accomplish absolutely nothing," Boutwell said. "I scarcely need to tell Birmingham citizens of either race that this is an attempt to stage a show—to make national headlines. The strangers here in the city responsible for these demonstrations are interested only in the headlines that help them raise money for themselves and their hate campaigns—not in the welfare of their people.

"Birmingham must not give these outsiders opportunity for personal glory or martyrdom.

"I urge everyone, white and Negro, to go calmly about their daily lives and ignore what is now being attempted here and what will certainly fail if we maintain good judgement and calm minds."

Boutwell reminded citizens that the new government has problems on other fronts—unemployment and a transit strike—to mention a few that demand immediate action.

Source: "Boutwell Urges All to Avoid Discord Here," *Birmingham Post-Herald* 5 Apr. 1963: 1.

The *Birmingham Post-Herald* also championed opposition to the demonstrations and "outside agitators" in editorials.

SEND THE TROUBLE-MAKERS AWAY!

If the Negroes responsible for the demonstrations which have shattered the tranquility of our community for more than a week are really interested in improving the lot of the Negro they will send the trouble-makers away and put an end to the lawlessness they have fostered.

These demonstrations have accomplished nothing constructive. On the other hand they have created racial friction, risked the possibility of serious trouble and made it impossible to continue such efforts as were being made to solve some of the problems which confront us.

Most of our citizens, white and colored, have conducted themselves commendably indeed. They have refused to get excited or be stampeded to rashness by the efforts of these outsiders.

Our law enforcement agencies likewise have won the admiration, respect and appreciation of the public for the manner in which they have handled themselves under very trying circumstances.

Let's continue to keep our heads. These trials too in time will pass.

Source: "Send the Trouble-Makers Away!" *Birmingham Post-Herald* 15 Apr. 1963: 10.

EXERCISE: THINKING CRITICALLY

Using the sources you have read so far, write a documented paper that summarizes the effect the city elections of April 2, 1963, had on the demonstrations. Cite a minimum of three sources.

King and the Reverend Ralph Abernathy were arrested during a demonstration on Good Friday, April 13, 1963. King was kept in solitary confinement until Monday afternoon, when Attorney General Robert F. Kennedy intervened on King's behalf after learning that Coretta Scott King had not heard from her husband since his incarceration. In addition to calling federal attention to the civil rights demonstrations in Birmingham, King's arrest motivated supporters to raise money for his campaign. Actor and singer Harry Belafonte raised over $5,000 during the weekend King spent in solitary confinement.

An article published in *Newsweek* reports King's arrest and explains that it will be left to history whether Connor or King experiences a victory as a result of the arrest.

CONNOR AND KING

All week long the opposing generals kept their distance across the no-man land that divides the races in steel tough Birmingham, Ala. Each day Martin Luther King sent detachments of Negroes downtown to picket, pray and demonstrate against segregation. Each day, burly Eugene (Bull) Connor, Birmingham's lame-duck public-safety commissioner, marshaled his police force and packed King's men off to jail.

For Connor, it was a virtuoso performance in the jail-'em-all school of tamping down the Negro revolt. It had only one flaw—the accidental arrest of Al Hibbler, the blind Negro jazz singer in a party of twenty demonstrators. Connor ordered him freed at the jailhouse door. "Folks at the jail work for their food and you can't work," he told the disappointed Hibbler next day. "I can sing," Hibbler protested. "There's no place at the jail for entertainers," Connor shot back. His press notices for the week were mixed, but Connor never put much stock in newspapers. "The trouble with America," he snorted, "is Communism, socialism, and journalism."

While King waited, the arrests thinned his "civil-rights army." Some Negroes were grumbling about his strategy. And more bad news came at 1:15 a.m. Thursday, as King and some aides sat up sipping coffee: they had been enjoined from further demonstrations.

King plainly needed a dramatic gesture. The next afternoon, dressed for jail in workshirt and jeans, he met 300 Negroes at Zion Hill Church. "This may be my thirteenth arrest," he told them. "We shall overcome." Their ranks swelling past 1,000, the Negroes headed Downtown behind King, marching toward his facedown with Bull Connor. It came as the marchers wheeled off seventeenth Street onto Fifth Avenue. A police motorcycle buzzed across their path. King and a lieutenant, Rev. Ralph Abernathy, fell to their knees. With Connor calling the signals, officers pulled them up by the arms and marched them to the paddy wagons with 52 other demonstrators. With the arrest, the antagonists, Connor and King, each had what he wanted. It was left to history to say which man would have the victory.

Source: "Connor and King," *Newsweek*. 22 Apr. 1963: 28–29.

EXERCISES: READING AND RESPONDING

1. Explain whether "Connor and King" helps you understand the political context that led up to King's "Letter."

2. Summarize the perspectives included in the article.

3. Characterize the different voices you hear in the article. What do these voices tell you about the speakers' attitudes toward the civil rights protests?

4. Characterize the voice of the writer. What does it reveal about the writer's attitude toward Connor? King?

After King was arrested, eight white clergyman from Alabama published a statement in the *Birmingham News* objecting to the demonstrations.

PUBLIC STATEMENT BY EIGHT ALABAMA CLERGYMEN

We the undersigned clergymen are among those who, in January, issued "An Appeal for Law and Order and Common Sense," in dealing with racial problems in Alabama. We expressed understanding that honest convictions in racial matters could properly be pursued in the courts, but urged that decisions of those courts should in the meantime be peacefully obeyed.

Since that time there had been some evidence of increased forbearance and a willingness to face facts. Responsible citizens have undertaken to work on various problems which cause racial friction and unrest. In Birmingham, recent public events have given indication that we all have opportunity for a new constructive and realistic approach to racial problems.

However, we are now confronted by a series of demonstrations by some of our Negro citizens, directed and led in part by outsiders. We recognize the natural impatience of people who feel that their hopes are slow in being realized. But we are convinced that these demonstrations are unwise and untimely.

We agree rather with certain local Negro leadership which has called for honest and open negotiation of racial issues in our area. And we believe this kind of facing of issues can best be accomplished by citizens of our own metropolitan area, white and Negro, meeting with their knowledge and experience of the local situation. All of us need to face that responsibility and find proper channels for its accomplishment.

Just as we formerly pointed out that "hatred and violence have no sanction in our religious and political traditions," we also point out that such actions as incite to hatred and violence, however technically peaceful those actions may be, have not contributed to the resolution of our local problems. We do not believe that these days of new hope are days when extreme measures are justified in Birmingham.

We commend the community as a whole, and the local news media and law enforcement officials in particular, on the calm manner in which these demonstrations have been handled. We urge the public to continue to show restraint should the demonstrations continue, and the law enforcement officials to remain calm and continue to protect our city from violence.

We further strongly urge our own Negro community to withdraw support from these demonstrations, and to unite locally in working peacefully for a better Birmingham. When rights are consistently denied, a cause should be pressed in the courts and in negotiations among local leaders, and not in the streets. We appeal to both our white and Negro citizenry to observe the principles of law and order and common sense.

Signed by:

C. C. J. Carpenter, D.D., LL.D., *Bishop of Alabama*

Joseph A. Durick, D.D., *Auxiliary Bishop, Diocese of Mobile, Birmingham*

Rabbi Milton L. Grafman, *Temple Emanu-El, Birmingham, Alabama*

Bishop Paul Hardin, *Bishop of the Alabama-West Florida Conference of the Methodist Church*

Bishop Nolan B. Harmon, *Bishop of the North Alabama Conference of the Methodist Church*

George M. Murray, D.D., LL.D., *Bishop Coadjutor, Episcopal Diocese of Alabama*

Edward V. Ramage, *Moderator, Synod of the Alabama Presbyterian Church in the United States*

Earl Stallings, *Pastor, First Baptist Church, Birmingham, Alabama*

Source: "Public Statement by Eight Alabama Clergymen," *Birmingham News* n.d: N.pag.

LETTER FROM BIRMINGHAM JAIL

MARTIN LUTHER KING, JR.

April 16, 1963

My Dear Fellow Clergymen:

While confined here in the Birmingham city jail, I came across your recent statement calling my present activities "unwise and untimely." Seldom do I pause to answer criticism of my work and ideas. If I sought to answer all the criticisms that cross my desk, my secretaries would have little time for anything other than such correspondence in the course of the day, and I would have no time for constructive work. But since I feel that you are men of genuine good will and that your criticisms are sincerely set forth, I want to try to answer your statement in what I hope will be patient and reasonable terms.

I think I should indicate why I am here in Birmingham, since you have been influenced by the view which argues against "outsiders coming in." I have the honor of serving as president of the Southern Christian Leadership Conference, an organization operating in every southern state, with headquarters in Atlanta, Georgia. We have some eighty-five affiliated organizations across the South, and one of them is the Alabama Christian Movement for Human Rights. Frequently we share staff, educational and financial resources with our affiliates. Several months ago the affiliate here in Birmingham asked us to be on call to engage in a nonviolent direct-action program if such were deemed necessary. We readily consented, and when the hour came we lived up to our promise. So I, along with several members of my staff, am here because I was invited here. I am here because I have organizational ties here.

But more basically, I am in Birmingham because injustice is here. Just as the prophets of the eighth century B.C. left their villages and carried their "thus saith the Lord" far beyond the boundaries of their home towns, and just as the Apostle Paul left his village of Tarsus and carried the gospel of Jesus Christ to the far corners of the Greco-Roman world, so am I compelled to carry the gospel of freedom beyond my own home town. Like Paul, I must constantly respond to the Macedonian call for aid.

Moreover, I am cognizant of the interrelatedness of all communities and states. I cannot sit idly by in Atlanta and not be concerned about what happens in Birmingham. Injustice anywhere is a threat to justice everywhere. We are caught in an inescapable network of mutuality, tied in a single garment of destiny. Whatever affects one directly, affects all indirectly. Never again can we afford to live with the narrow, provincial "outside agitator" idea. Anyone who lives inside the United States can never be considered an outsider anywhere within its bounds.

You deplore the demonstrations taking place in Birmingham. But your statement, I am sorry to say, fails to express a similar concern for the conditions that brought about the demonstrations. I am sure that none of you would want to rest content with the superficial kind of social analysis that deals merely with effects and does not grapple with underlying causes. It is unfortunate that demonstrations are taking place in Birmingham, but it is even more unfortunate that the city's white power structure left the Negro community with no alternative.

In any nonviolent campaign there are four basic steps: collection of the facts to determine whether injustices exist; negotiation; self-purification; and direct action. We have gone through all these steps in Birmingham. There can be no gainsaying the fact that racial injustice engulfs this community. Birmingham is probably the most thoroughly segregated city in the United States. Its ugly record of brutality is widely known, Negroes have experienced grossly unjust treatment in the courts. There have been more unsolved bombings of Negro homes and churches in Birmingham than in any other city in the nation. These are the hard, brutal facts of the case. On the basis of these conditions, Negro leaders sought to negotiate with the city fathers. But the latter consistently refused to engage in good-faith negotiation.

Then, last September, came the opportunity to talk with leaders of Birmingham's economic community. In the course of the negotiations, certain promises were made by the merchants—for example, to remove the stores' humiliating racial signs. On the basis of these promises, the Reverend Fred Shuttlesworth and the leaders of the Alabama Christian

Movement for Human Rights agreed to a moratorium on all demonstrations. As the weeks and months went by, we realized that we were the victims of a broken promise. A few signs, briefly removed, returned; the others remained.

As in so many past experiences, our hopes had been blasted, and the shadow of deep disappointment settled upon us. We had no alternative except to prepare for direct action, whereby we would present our very bodies as a means of laying our case before the conscience of the local and the national community. Mindful of the difficulties involved, we decided to undertake a process of self-purification. We began a series of workshops on nonviolence, and we repeatedly asked ourselves: "Are you able to accept blows without retaliating?" "Are you able to endure the ordeal of jail?" We decided to schedule our direct-action program for the Easter season, realizing that except for Christmas, this is the main shopping period of the year. Knowing that a strong economic-withdrawal program would be the by-product of direct action, we felt that this would be the best time to bring pressure to bear on the merchants for the needed change.

Then it occurred to us that Birmingham's mayoral election was coming up in March, and we speedily decided to postpone action until after election day. When we discovered that the Commissioner of Public Safety, Eugene "Bull" Connor, had piled up enough votes to be in the run-off, we decided again to postpone action until the day after the run-off so that the demonstrations could not be used to cloud the issues. Like many others, we waited to see Mr. Connor defeated, and to this end we endured postponement after postponement. Having aided in this community need, we felt that our direct-action program could be delayed no longer.

You may well ask: "Why direct action? Why sit-ins, marches and so forth? Isn't negotiation a better path?" You are quite right in calling for negotiation. Indeed, this is the very purpose of direct action. Nonviolent direct action seeks to create such a crisis and foster such a tension that a community which has constantly refused to negotiate is forced to confront the issue. It seeks so to dramatize the issue that it can no longer be ignored. My citing the creation of tension as part of the work of the nonviolent-resister may sound rather shocking. But I must confess that I am not afraid of the word "tension." I have earnestly opposed violent tension, but there is a type of constructive, non-violent tension which is necessary for growth. Just as Socrates felt that it was necessary to create a tension in the mind so that individuals could rise from the bondage of myths and half-truths to the unfettered realm of creative analysis and objective appraisal, so must we see the need for nonviolent gadflies to create the kind of tension in society that will help men rise from the dark depths of prejudice and racism to the majestic heights of understanding and brotherhood.

The purpose of our direct-action program is to create a situation so crisis-packed that it will inevitably open the door to negotiation. I therefore concur with you in your call for negotiation. Too long has our beloved

Southland been bogged down in a tragic effort to live in monologue rather than dialogue.

One of the basic points in your statement is that the action that I and my associates have taken in Birmingham is untimely. Some have asked: "Why didn't you give the new city administration time to act?" The only answer that I can give to this query is that the new Birmingham administration must be prodded about as much as the out-going one, before it will act. We are sadly mistaken if we feel that the election of Albert Boutwell as mayor will bring the millennium to Birmingham. While Mr. Boutwell is a much more gentle person than Mr. Connor, they are both segregationists, dedicated to maintenance of the status quo. I have hope that Mr. Boutwell will be reasonable enough to see the futility of massive resistance to desegregation. But he will not see this without pressure from devotees of civil rights. My friends, I must say to you that we have not made a single gain in civil rights without determined legal and nonviolent pressure. Lamentably, it is an historical fact that privileged groups seldom give up their privileges voluntarily. Individuals may see the moral light and voluntarily give up their unjust posture; but, as Reinhold Niebuhr has reminded us, groups tend to be more immoral than individuals.

We know through painful experience that freedom is never voluntarily given by the oppressor; it must be demanded by the oppressed. Frankly, I have yet to engage in a direct-action campaign that was "well timed" in the view of those who

have not suffered unduly from the disease of segregation. For years now I have heard the word "Wait!" It rings in the ear of every Negro with piercing familiarity. This "Wait" has almost always meant "Never." We must come to see, with one of our distinguished jurists, that "justice too long delayed is justice denied."

We have waited for more than 340 years for our constitutional and God-given rights. The nations of Asia and Africa are moving with jetlike speed toward gaining political independence, but we still creep at horse-and-buggy pace toward gaining a cup of coffee at a lunch counter. Perhaps it is easy for those who have never felt the stinging darts of segregation to say, "Wait." But when you have seen vicious mobs lynch your mothers and fathers at will and drown your sisters and brothers at whim; when you have seen hate-filled policemen curse, kick and even kill your black brothers and sisters; when you see the vast majority of your twenty million Negro brothers smothering in an airtight cage of poverty in the midst of an affluent society; when you suddenly find your tongue twisted and your speech stammering as you seek to explain to your six-year-old daughter why she can't go to the public amusement park that has just been advertised on television, and see tears welling up in her eyes when she is told that Funtown is closed to colored children, and see ominous clouds of inferiority beginning to form in her little mental sky, and see her beginning to distort her personality by developing an unconscious bitterness toward white people; when you have to concoct an answer for a five-year-old son who is asking: "Daddy, why do white people treat colored people so mean?"; when you take a cross-country drive and find it necessary to sleep night after night in the uncomfortable corners of your automobile because no motel will accept you; when you are humiliated day in and day out by nagging signs reading "white" and "colored"; when your first name becomes "nigger," your middle name becomes "boy" (however old you are) and your last name becomes "John," and your wife and mother are never given the respected title "Mrs."; when you are harried by day and haunted by night by the fact that you are a Negro, living constantly at tiptoe stance, never quite knowing what to expect next, and are plagued with inner fears and outer resentments; when you are forever fighting a degenerating sense of "nobodiness"—then you will understand why we find it difficult to wait. There comes a time when the cup of endurance runs over, and men are no longer willing to be plunged into the abyss of despair. I hope, sirs, you can understand our legitimate and unavoidable impatience.

You express a great deal of anxiety over our willingness to break laws. This is certainly a legitimate concern. Since we so diligently urge people to obey the Supreme Court's decision of 1954 outlawing segregation in the public schools, at first glance it may seem rather paradoxical for us consciously to break laws. One may well ask: "How can you advocate breaking some laws and obeying others?" The answer lies in the fact that there are two types of laws; just and unjust. I would be the

first to advocate obeying just laws. One has not only a legal but a moral responsibility to obey just laws. Conversely, one has a moral responsibility to disobey unjust laws. I would agree with St. Augustine that "an unjust law is no law at all."

Now, what is the difference between the two? How does one determine whether a law is just or unjust? A just law is a man-made code that squares with the moral law or the law of God. An unjust law is a code that is out of harmony with the moral law. To put it in the terms of St. Thomas Aquinas: An unjust law is a human law that is not rooted in eternal law and natural law. Any law that uplifts human personality is just. Any law that degrades human personality is unjust. All segregation statutes are unjust because segregation distorts the soul and damages the personality. It gives the segregator a false sense of superiority and the segregated a false sense of inferiority. Segregation, to use the terminology of the Jewish philosopher Martin Buber, substitutes an "I-it" relationship for an "I-thou" relationship and ends up relegating persons to the status of things. Hence segregation is not only politically, economically and sociologically unsound, it is morally wrong and sinful. Paul Tillich has said that sin is separation. Is not segregation an existential expression of man's tragic separation, his awful estrangement, his terrible sinfulness? Thus it is that I can urge men to obey the 1954 decision of the Supreme Court, for it is morally right; and I can urge them to disobey segregation ordinances, for they are morally wrong.

Let us consider a more concrete example of just and unjust laws. An unjust law is a code that a numerical or power majority group compels a minority group to obey but does not make binding on itself. This is *difference* made legal. By the same token, a just law is a code that a majority compels a minority to follow and that it is willing to follow itself. This is *sameness* made legal.

Let me give another explanation. A law is unjust if it is inflicted on a minority that, as a result of being denied the right to vote, had no part in enacting or devising the law. Who can say that the legislature of Alabama which set up that state's segregation laws was democratically elected? Throughout Alabama all sorts of devious methods are used to prevent Negroes from becoming registered voters, and there are some counties in which, even though Negroes constitute a majority of the population, not a single Negro is registered. Can any law enacted under such circumstances be considered democratically structured?

Sometimes a law is just on its face and unjust in its application. For instance, I have been arrested on a charge of parading without a permit. Now, there is nothing wrong in having an ordinance which requires a permit for a parade. But such an ordinance becomes unjust when it is used to maintain segregation and to deny citizens the First-Amendment privilege of peaceful assembly and protest.

I hope you are able to see the distinction I am trying to point out. In no sense do I advocate evading or defying the law, as would the rabid segregationist. That would lead to anarchy. One who breaks an unjust law must do so openly, lovingly, and with a willingness to accept the penalty. I submit that an individual who breaks a law that conscience tells him is unjust, and who willingly accepts the penalty of imprisonment in order to arouse the conscience of the community over its injustice, is in reality expressing the highest respect for law.

Of course, there is nothing new about this kind of civil disobedience. It was evidenced sublimely in the refusal of Shadrach, Meshach and Abednego to obey the laws of Nebuchadnezzar, on the ground that a higher moral law was at stake. It was practiced superbly by the early Christians, who were willing to face hungry lions and the excruciating pain of chopping blocks rather than submit to certain unjust laws of the Roman Empire. To a degree, academic freedom is a reality today because Socrates practiced civil disobedience. In our own nation, the Boston Tea Party represented a massive act of civil disobedience.

We should never forget that everything Adolf Hitler did in Germany was "legal" and everything the Hungarian freedom fighters did in Hungary was "illegal." It was "illegal" to aid and comfort a Jew in Hitler's Germany. Even so, I am sure that, had I lived in Germany at the time, I would have aided and comforted my Jewish brothers. If today I lived in a Communist country where certain principles dear to the Christian faith are suppressed, I would openly advocate disobeying that country's antireligious laws.

I must make two honest confessions to you, my Christian and Jewish brothers. First, I must confess that over the past few years I have been gravely disappointed with the white moderate. I have almost reached the regrettable conclusion that the Negro's great stumbling block in his stride toward freedom is not the White Citizen's Counciler or the Ku Klux Klanner, but the white moderate, who is more devoted to "order" than to justice; who prefers a negative peace which is the absence of tension to a positive peace which is the presence of justice; who constantly says: "I agree with you in the goal you seek, but I cannot agree with your methods of direct action"; who paternalistically believes he can set the timetable for another man's freedom; who lives by a mythical concept of time and who constantly advises the Negro to wait for a "more convenient season." Shallow understanding from people of good will is more frustrating than absolute misunderstanding from people of ill will. Lukewarm acceptance, is much more bewildering than outright rejection.

I had hoped that the white moderate would understand that law and order exist for the purpose of establishing justice and that when they fail in this purpose they become the dangerously structured dams that block the flow of social progress. I had hoped that the white moderate would understand that the present tension in the South is a necessary phase of the transition from an obnoxious negative peace, in which the Negro passively accepted his unjust plight, to a substantive and positive peace, in which all men will respect the dignity and worth of human personality. Actually, we who engage in nonviolent direct action are not the creators of tension. We merely bring to the surface the hidden tension that is already alive. We bring it out in the open, where it can be seen and dealt with. Like a boil that can never be cured so long as it is covered up but must be opened with all its ugliness to the natural medicines of air and light, injustice must be exposed, with all the tension its exposure creates, to the light of human conscience and the air of national opinion before it can be cured.

In your statement you assert that our actions, even though peaceful, must be condemned because they precipitate violence. But is this a logical assertion? Isn't this like condemning a robbed man because his possession of money precipitated the evil act of robbery? Isn't this like condemning Socrates because his unswerving commitment to truth and his philosophical inquiries precipitated the act by the misguided populace in which they made him drink hemlock? Isn't this like condemning Jesus because his unique God-consciousness and never-ceasing devotion to God's will precipitated the evil act of crucifixion? We must come to see that, as the federal courts have consistently affirmed, it is wrong to urge an individual to cease his efforts to gain his basic constitutional rights because the quest may precipitate violence Society must protect the robbed and punish the robber.

I had also hoped that the white moderate would reject the myth concerning time in relation to the struggle for freedom. I have just received a letter from a white brother in Texas. He writes: "All Christians know that the colored people will receive equal rights eventually, but it is possible that you are in too great a religious hurry. It has taken Christianity almost two thousand years to accomplish what it has. The teachings of Christ take time to come to earth." Such an attitude stems from a tragic misconception of time, from the strangely irrational notion that there is something in the very flow of time that will inevitably cure all ills. Actually, time itself is neutral; it can be used either destructively or constructively. More and more I feel that the people of ill will have used time much more effectively than have the people of good will. We will have to repent in this generation not merely for the hateful words and actions of the bad people but for the appalling silence of the good people. Human progress never rolls in on wheels of inevitability; it comes through the tireless efforts of men willing to be co-workers with God, and without this hard work, time itself becomes an ally of the forces of social stagnation. We must use time creatively, in the knowledge that the time is always ripe to do right. Now is the time to make real the promise of democracy and transform our pending national elegy into a creative psalm of brotherhood. Now is the time to lift our national policy from the quicksand of racial injustice to the solid rock of human dignity.

You speak of our activity in Birmingham as extreme. At first I was rather disappointed that fellow clergymen would see my nonviolent efforts as those of an extremist. I began thinking about the fact that I stand in the middle of two opposing forces in the Negro community. One is a force of complacency, made up in part of Negroes who, as a result of long years of oppression, are so drained of self-respect and a sense of "somebodiness" that they have adjusted to segregation; and in part of a few middle-class Negroes who, because of a degree of academic and economic security and because in some ways they profit by segregation, have become insensitive to the problems of the masses. The other force is one of bitterness and hatred, and it comes perilously close to advocating violence. It is expressed in the various black nationalist groups that are springing up across the nation, the largest and best-known being Elijah Muhammad's Muslim movement. Nourished by the Negro's frustration over the continued existence of racial discrimination, this movement is made up of people who have lost faith in America, who have absolutely repudiated Christianity, and who have concluded that the white man is an incorrigible "devil."

I have tried to stand between these two forces, saying that we need emulate neither the "do-nothingism" of the complacent nor the hatred and despair of the black nationalist. For there is the more excellent way of love and nonviolent protest. I am grateful to God that, through the influence of the Negro church, the way of nonviolence became an integral part of our struggle.

If this philosophy had not emerged, by now many streets of the South would, I am convinced, be flowing with blood. And I am further convinced that if our white brothers dismiss as "rabble-rousers" and "outside agitators" those of us who employ nonviolent direct action, and if they refuse to support our nonviolent efforts, millions of Negroes will, out of frustration and despair, seek solace and security in black-nationalist ideologies—a development that would inevitably lead to a frightening racial nightmare.

Oppressed people cannot remain oppressed forever. The yearning for freedom eventually manifests itself, and that is what has happened to the American Negro. Something within has reminded him of his birthright of freedom, and something without has reminded him that it can be gained. Consciously or unconsciously, he has been caught up by the *Zeitgeist,* and with his black brothers of Africa and his brown and yellow brothers of Asia, South America and the Caribbean, the United States Negro is moving with a sense of great urgency toward the promised land of racial justice. If one recognizes this vital urge that has engulfed the Negro community, one should readily understand why public demonstrations are taking place. The Negro has many pent-up resentments and latent frustrations, and he must release them. So let him march; let him make prayer pilgrimages to the city hall; let him go on freedom rides—and try to understand why he must do so. If his repressed emotions are not released in nonviolent ways, they will seek expression through violence; this is not a threat but a fact of history. So I have not said to my people: "Get rid of your discontent." Rather, I have tried to say that this normal and healthy discontent can be channeled into the creative outlet of

nonviolent direct action. And now this approach is being termed extremist.

But though I was initially disappointed at being categorized as an extremist, as I continued to think about the matter I gradually gained a measure of satisfaction from the label. Was not Jesus an extremist for love: "Love your enemies, bless them that curse you, do good to them that hate you, and pray for them which despitefully use you, and persecute you." Was not Amos an extremist for justice: "Let justice roll down like waters and righteousness like an ever-flowing stream." Was not Paul an extremist for the Christian gospel: "I bear in my body the marks of the Lord Jesus." Was not Martin Luther an extremist: "Here I stand; I cannot do otherwise, so help me God." And John Bunyan: "I will stay in jail to the end of my days before I make a butchery of my conscience." And Abraham Lincoln: "This nation cannot survive half slave and half free." And Thomas Jefferson: "We hold these truths to be self-evident, that all men are created equal ..." So the question is not whether we will be extremists, but what kind of extremists we will be. Will we be extremists for hate or for love? Will we be extremists for the preservation of injustice or for the extension of justice? In that dramatic scene on Calvary's hill three men were crucified. We must never forget that all three were crucified for the same crime—the crime of extremism. Two were extremists for immorality, and thus fell below their environment. The other, Jesus Christ, was an extremist for love, truth and goodness, and thereby rose above his environment. Perhaps the South, the nation and the world are in dire need of creative extremists.

I had hoped that the white moderate would see this need. Perhaps I was too optimistic; perhaps I expected too much. I suppose I should have realized that few members of the oppressor race can understand the deep groans and passionate yearnings of the oppressed race, and still fewer have the vision to see that injustice must be rooted out by strong, persistent and determined action. I am thankful, however, that some of our white brothers in the South have grasped the meaning of this social revolution and committed themselves to it. They are still all too few in quantity, but they are big in quality. Some—such as Ralph McGill, Lillian Smith, Harry Golden, James McBride Dabbs, Ann Braden and Sarah Patton Boyle—have written about our struggle in eloquent and prophetic terms. Others have marched with us down nameless streets of the South. They have languished in filthy, roach-infested jails, suffering the abuse and brutality of policemen who view them as "dirty nigger-lovers." Unlike so many of their moderate brothers and sisters, they have recognized the urgency of the moment and sensed the need for powerful "action" antidotes to combat the disease of segregation.

Let me take note of my other major disappointment. I have been so greatly disappointed with the white church and its leadership. Of course, there are some notable exceptions. I am not unmindful of the fact that each of you has taken some significant stands on this issue. I commend you, Reverend Stallings, for your Christian stand on this past Sunday, in welcoming Negroes to your worship service on a nonsegregated basis. I commend the Catholic leaders of this state for integrating Spring Hill College several years ago.

But despite these notable exceptions, I must honestly reiterate that I have been disappointed with the church. I do not say this as one of those negative critics who can always find something wrong with the church. I say this as a minister of the gospel, who loves the church; who was nurtured in its bosom; who has been sustained by its spiritual blessings and who will remain true to it as long as the cord of life shall lengthen.

When I was suddenly catapulted into the leadership of the bus protest in Montgomery, Alabama, a few years ago, I felt we would be supported by the white church. I felt that the white ministers, priests and rabbis of the South would be among our strongest allies. Instead, some have been outright opponents, refusing to understand the freedom movement and misrepresenting its leaders; all too many others have been more cautious than courageous and have remained silent behind the anesthetizing security of stained-glass windows.

In spite of my shattered dreams, I came to Birmingham with the hope that the white religious leadership of this community would see the justice of our cause and, with deep moral concern, would serve as the channel through which our just grievances could reach the power structure. I had hoped that each of you would understand. But again I have been disappointed.

I have heard numerous southern religious leaders admonish their worshipers to comply with a desegregation decision because it is the law, but I have longed to hear white ministers declare: "Follow this decree because integration is morally right and because the Negro is your brother." In the midst of blatant injustices inflicted upon the Negro, I have watched white churchmen stand on the sideline and mouth pious irrelevancies and sanctimonious trivialities. In the midst of a mighty struggle to rid our nation of racial and economic injustice, I have heard many ministers say: "Those are social issues, with which the gospel has no real concern." And I have watched many churches commit themselves to a completely otherworldly religion which makes a strange, un-Biblical distinction between body and soul, between the sacred and the secular.

I have traveled the length and breadth of Alabama, Mississippi and all the other southern states. On sweltering summer days and crisp autumn mornings I have looked at the South's beautiful churches with their lofty spires pointing heavenward. I have beheld the impressive outlines of her massive religious-education buildings. Over and over I have found myself asking: "What kind of people worship here? Who is their God? Where were their voices when the lips of Governor Barnett dripped with words of interposition and nullification? Where were they when Governor Wallace gave a clarion call for defiance and hatred? Where were their voices of support when bruised and weary Negro men and women decided to rise from the dark dungeons of complacency to the bright hills of creative protest?"

Yes, these questions are still in my mind. In deep disappointment I have wept over the laxity of the church. But be assured that my tears have been tears of love. There can be no deep disappointment where there is not deep love. Yes, I love the church. How could I do otherwise? I am in the rather unique position of being the son, the grandson and the great-grandson of preachers. Yes, I see the church as the body of Christ. But, oh! How we have blemished and scarred that body through social neglect and through, fear of being nonconformists.

There was a time when the church was very powerful—in the time when the early Christians rejoiced at being deemed worthy to suffer for what they believed. In those days the church was not merely a thermometer that recorded the ideas and principles of popular opinion; it was a thermostat that transformed the mores of society. Whenever the early Christians entered a town, the people in power became disturbed and immediately sought to convict the Christians for being "disturbers of the peace" and "outside agitators." But the Christians pressed on, in the conviction that they were "a colony of heaven," called to obey God rather than man. Small in number, they were big in commitment. They were too God-intoxicated to be "astronomically intimidated." By their effort and example they brought an end to such ancient evils as infanticide and gladiatorial contests.

Things are different now. So often the contemporary church is a weak, ineffectual voice with an uncertain sound. So often it is an archdefender of the status quo. Far from being disturbed by the presence of the church, the power structure of the average community is consoled by the church's silent—and often even vocal—sanction of things as they are.

But the judgment of God is upon the church as never before. If today's church does not recapture the sacrificial spirit of the early church, it will lose its authenticity, forfeit the loyalty of millions, and be dismissed as an irrelevant social club with no meaning for the twentieth century. Every day I meet young people whose disappointment with the church has turned into outright disgust.

Perhaps I have once again been too optimistic. Is organized religion too inextricably bound to the status quo to save our nation and the world? Perhaps I must turn my faith to the inner spiritual church, the church within the church, as the true *ekklesia* and the hope of the world. But again I am thankful to God that some noble souls from the ranks of organized religion have broken loose from the paralyzing chains of conformity and joined us as active partners in the struggle for freedom. They have left their secure congregations and walked the streets of Albany, Georgia, with us. They have gone down the highways of the South on tortuous rides for freedom. Yes, they have gone to jail with us. Some have been dismissed from their churches, have lost the support of their bishops and fellow ministers. But they have

acted in the faith that right defeated is stronger than evil triumphant. Their witness has been the spiritual salt that has preserved the true meaning of the gospel in these troubled times. They have carved a tunnel of hope through the dark mountain of disappointment.

I hope the church as a whole will meet the challenge of this decisive hour. But even if the church does not come to the aid of justice, I have no despair about the future. I have no fear about the outcome of our struggle in Birmingham, even if our motives are at present misunderstood. We will reach the goal of freedom in Birmingham and all over the nation, because the goal of America is freedom. Abused and scorned though we may be, our destiny is tied up with America's destiny. Before the pilgrims landed at Plymouth, we were here. Before the pen of Jefferson etched the majestic words of the Declaration of Independence across the pages of history, we were here. For more than two centuries our forebears labored in this country without wages; they made cotton king; they built the homes of their masters while suffering gross injustice and shameful humiliation—and yet out of a bottomless vitality they continued to thrive and develop. If the inexpressible cruelties of slavery could not stop us, the opposition we now face will surely fail. We will win our freedom because the sacred heritage of our nation and the eternal will of God are embodied in our echoing demands.

Before closing I feel impelled to mention one other point in your statement that has troubled me profoundly. You warmly commended the

Birmingham police force for keeping "order" and "preventing violence." I doubt that you would have so warmly commended the police force if you had seen its dogs sinking their teeth into unarmed, nonviolent Negroes. I doubt that you would so quickly commend the policemen if you were to observe their ugly and inhumane treatment of Negroes here in the city jail; if you were to watch them push and curse old Negro women and young Negro girls; if you were to see them slap and kick old Negro men and young boys; if you were to observe them, as they did on two occasions, refuse to give us food because we wanted to sing our grace together. I cannot join you in your praise of the Birmingham police department.

It is true that the police have exercised a degree of discipline in handling the demonstrators. In this sense they have conducted themselves rather "nonviolently" in public. But for what purpose? To preserve the evil system of segregation. Over the past few years I have consistently preached that nonviolence demands that the means we use must be as pure as the ends we seek. I have tried to make clear that it is wrong to use immoral means to attain moral ends. But now I must affirm that it is just as wrong, or perhaps even more so, to use moral means to preserve immoral ends. Perhaps Mr. Connor and his policemen have been rather nonviolent in public, as was Chief Pritchett in Albany, Georgia, but they have used the moral means of nonviolence to maintain the immoral end of racial injustice. As T. S. Eliot has said: "The last temptation is the greatest treason: To do the right deed for the wrong reason."

I wish you had commended the Negro sit-inners and demonstrators of: Birmingham for their sublime courage, their willingness to suffer and their amazing discipline in the midst of great provocation. One day the South will recognize its real heroes. They will be the James Merediths, with the noble sense of purpose that enables them to face jeering and hostile mobs, and with the agonizing loneliness that characterizes the life of the pioneer. They will be old, oppressed, battered Negro women, symbolized in a seventy-two-year-old woman in Montgomery, Alabama, who rose up with a sense of dignity and with her people decided not to ride segregated buses, and who responded with ungrammatical profundity to one who inquired about her weariness: "My feets is tired, but my soul is at rest." They will be the young high school and college students, the young ministers of the gospel and a host of their elders, courageously and nonviolently sitting in at lunch counters and willingly going to jail for conscience' sake. One day the South will know that when these disinherited children of God sat down at lunch counters, they were in reality standing up for what is best in the American dream and for the most sacred values in our Judaeo-Christian heritage, thereby bringing our nation back to those great wells of democracy which were dug deep by the founding fathers in their formulation of the Constitution and the Declaration of Independence.

Never before have I written so long a letter. I'm afraid it is much too long to take your precious time. I can assure you that it would have been much shorter if I had been writing from a comfortable desk, but what else can one do when he is alone in a narrow jail cell, other than write long letters, think long thoughts and pray long prayers?

If I have said anything in this letter that overstates the truth and indicates an unreasonable impatience, I beg you to forgive me. If I have said anything that understates the truth and indicates my having a patience that allows me to settle for anything less than brotherhood, I beg God to forgive me.

I hope this letter finds you strong in the faith. I also hope that circumstances will soon make it possible for me to meet each of you, not as an integrationist or a civil-rights leader but as a fellow clergyman and a Christian brother. Let us all hope that the dark clouds of racial prejudice will soon pass away and the deep fog of misunderstanding will be lifted from our fear-drenched communities, and in some not too distant tomorrow the radiant stars of love and brotherhood will shine over our great nation with all their scintillating beauty.

Yours for the cause of Peace and Brotherhood,

Martin Luther King, Jr.

AUTHOR'S NOTE: This response to a published statement by eight fellow clergymen from Alabama (Bishop C. C. J. Carpenter, Bishop Joseph A. Durick, Rabbi Hilton L. Grafman, Bishop Paul Hardin, Bishop Holan B. Harmon, the Reverend George M. Murray, the Reverend Edward V. Ramage and the Revered Earl Stallings) was composed under somewhat constricting circumstances. Begun on the margins of the newspaper in which the statement appeared while I was in jail, the letter was continued on scraps of writing paper supplied by a friendly Negro trusty, and concluded on a pad my attorneys were eventually permitted to leave me. Although the text remains in substance unaltered, I have indulged in the authors prerogative of polishing it for publication.

Source: Martin Luther King, Jr., "Letter from Birmingham Jail," *Why We Can't Wait* (New York: Harper, 1963). 77–100.

EXERCISES: READING AND RESPONDING

1. How does King use analogy to justify his presence in Birmingham?
2. How does King address the charge of being an outside agitator?
3. Why does King claim that nonviolent civil disobedience is needed?
4. What kinds of distinctions does King make between just and unjust laws?
5. What are the four basic steps in a nonviolent campaign?
6. How does King answer the charge that he "didn't give the new city administration enough time to act"?
7. How does King demonstrate that segregation laws are unjust?
8. How does King use analogy in his argument for nonviolent civil disobedience?

9. How does King use analogy to defend his role as an extremist?

10. Explain whether King's linking of his own disillusionment with the status quo of social justice with the disillusionment young people feel with organized religion is an effective or ineffective argumentative strategy.

11. Characterize the voice you hear in the "Letter." What does it reveal about the writer's attitude toward the subject and audience?

12. At what point does King provide a context for readers?

FOCUS ON RELATED ISSUES: "I HAVE A DREAM"

Dr. Stephen E. Lucas of the University of Wisconsin-Madison, and Dr. Martin J. Medhurst of Texas A&M University have compiled a list of the top 100 speeches of the twentieth century. Dr. Martin Luther King's "I Have a Dream Speech," delivered in Washington, D.C., August 28, 1963, is ranked number one.

King spoke to an estimated crowd of 250,000 when he delivered his speech from the steps of the Lincoln Memorial. Television and radio stations broadcast the event to the nation. Working on your own, find a copy of this speech and write a documented paper in which you analyze the rhetorical strategies and provide a context for the speech.

CONTEMPORARY PERSPECTIVES

In "Up From Jim Crow," Vern E. Smith and Matthew Murr write about the city of Birmingham. The title of the article refers to laws that enforced racial segregation, which were passed from the 1880s to the 1960s.

UP FROM JIM CROW

VERN E. SMITH AND MATTHEW MURR

After all the years they echo still, the boom of dynamite and the rain of glass through the autumn leaves— just as some of the leading citizens of Birmingham, Ala., feared when, in the aftermath of the calamitous summer of 1963, they seriously debated changing the name of their city. Since then there have been deadlier crimes, but few conceived and carried out with such a purity of malice as the Sunday-morning bombing of the

16th Street Baptist Church that killed four young girls. And few had such far-reaching, if unintended, consequences. The church bombing was meant to intimidate demonstrations by people then politely called "Negroes," and usually something else, where the beatings, dogs and fire hoses deployed by Public Safety Commissioner Bull Connor had failed. Instead, it galvanized the demonstrators, and the rest of the country as well, helping to set the stage for the great Civil Rights Act the following year that set the nation on the tumultuous and still unfinished course of racial reconciliation.

Birmingham long ago lost the distinction of being "the most segregated city in America," in the words of no less an authority than Martin Luther King Jr. The lunch crowd at the Fish Market downtown is a mix of black and white students, blue-collar workers, white businessmen and immigrant nurses from the nearby medical complex—an ordinary scene, except in its stark contrast to Section 369 of the city's original segregation rules ("It shall be unlawful to conduct a restaurant ... at which white and colored are served in the same room"). There is little to set Birmingham apart, in its demographics and its problems, from other cities its size (population about 255,000): a clutch of downtown office buildings fed by highways, surrounded by a patchwork of mostly black working-class neighborhoods and enveloped by mostly white upper-middle-class suburbs. There is a small but growing population of Latino immigrants, who are being eagerly courted with social services and language classes by both the Roman Catholic diocese and some of the area's Protestant churches. Blacks make up about two thirds of the city's population—and 96 percent of the public-school students.

But race relations are an inescapable preoccupation for the people of Birmingham, a burden they carry with them even when they leave the South. "When I tell people I'm from Birmingham, I get responses like, 'You can walk down the street?'" says Karima Wilson, a sophomore at Swarthmore College outside Philadelphia. Birmingham has a prodigious infrastructure of groups dedicated to improving race relations—Leadership Birmingham and Peace Birmingham and Operation New Birmingham and the Community Affairs Committee, whose Unity Breakfast on Martin Luther King Day attracts as many as 2,000 participants. Three years ago, while returning from an interracial conference in Mobile, a white lawyer named James Rotch composed a renunciation of prejudice that has become known as the Birmingham Pledge ("... I will strive daily to eliminate racial prejudice from my thoughts and actions ..."). It's been signed by 70,000 people, including Bill and Hillary Clinton, although Mayor Bernard Kincaid has so far demurred. Kincaid, Birmingham's second black mayor, says he would be happy to sign a pledge that specified some concrete actions, such as mentoring a black child or inviting a member of another race over to your house for dinner. His stance is an embarrassment to some white civic leaders and the harmony-minded editorial board of The Birmingham News. But in how many other cities would interracial dinner parties become a political issue? "Race is on our minds all the time here," says Cathy O. Friedman, a businesswoman who serves on the Birmingham Pledge Advisory Board.

Having been born long after the end of legal segregation doesn't excuse you from having to think about it, either. Civil rights history is a central part of Alabama's ninth-grade curriculum, and every school for miles around makes an obligatory trip to the Civil Rights Institute, a museum and study center in a Civil Rights Historic District that embraces the restored 16th Street church and the nearby park where demonstrators memorably clashed with Connor's thugs. Teenagers have their own network of interracial clubs, at the summit of which is Camp Anytown, a weeklong retreat sponsored by the National Conference for Community and Justice. It brings together people like Caleigh Rathmell, a high-school senior from the affluent suburb of Mountain Brook, and Richard Winchester, a senior at A.H. Parker, Birmingham's original, century-old Negro high school—long "desegregated," except for the near-entire absence of white students. The distance between them was demonstrated by an exercise at Camp Anytown in June. The participants formed a line and stepped forward or back to indicate agreement with statements such as "I go to a good school in a wealthy neighborhood" or "There were days when my family didn't have enough money for food." "Eventually it came to the point where everyone was spread out and I was in the front, feeling

ashamed, and I turned around and Richard was in the back, standing tall and proud," Rathmell recalled. The two have stayed friends. But "we keep in touch mainly through the telephone because he has a difficult time getting here without a car, and the area where he lives is not very comfortable for me, unfortunately," Rathmell says.

What the two youngsters have discovered is that all the good will in the world can't bridge the gaps of income, class and power that still separate whites and blacks (and, increasingly, Hispanics). "Birmingham is still almost two communities," says the Rev. Fred Shuttlesworth, a leader in the civil-rights movement who survived two bombings at his old church. The city first elected a black mayor, Richard Arrington, in 1979, but Shuttlesworth points out that after the first of his five elections Arrington never got more than 12 percent of the white vote. And many blacks suspect that when the white power structure couldn't dislodge Arrington in an election, they tried other means—such as a federal investigation into allegations of corruption. Arrington was not indicted and never defeated, although whites voted in large numbers against his chosen successor last year, helping to elect Kincaid. But it was partly to smooth relations with the black community that federal officials reopened the long-dormant investigation into the church bombing. Former Ku Klux Klansman Robert (Dynamite Bob) Chambliss had been convicted in 1977, but it was widely believed that he didn't act alone. Earlier this year the evidence gathered by the FBI was presented to a state grand jury, and two alleged accomplices, Thomas Blanton Jr., 62, and Bobby Frank Cherry, 70, were indicted on murder charges. U.S. Attorney Doug Jones, under a special appointment by Alabama Attorney General Bill Pryor, will try the case personally.

The same themes, of power and class, are played out every day on the streets, patrolled by a police force that hired its first black officer in 1966. Police Chief Mike Coppage remembers how, as a rookie in the mid-'70s, he was corrected by a veteran officer after he failed to correctly address an elderly black man on the street. "Don't call him sir!" the older cop barked, rapping Coppage on the knuckles with his club. "You tell him, Get over here right now!" Coppage, who succeeded a black chief and commands a force that is more than half black, can enforce a code of respect and civility on his troops. But he also must enforce the law in a city where demographics alone dictate that the majority of perpetrators, as well as victims, will be black. The Rev. Abraham Woods, a longtime civil-rights activist, believes blacks are the victims of racial profiling in traffic stops, but after several nights spent riding with cops on patrol, it's apparent to an outsider that at least part of the problem has to do with the economics of car maintenance. Being poor is actually against the law, if it means you can't afford to fix a broken taillight. "If I pull you over, I've got to have a reason," says Field Training Officer Erick Hall. "A broken taillight is a reason." The issue is so sensitive that when the state authorized cops to ticket drivers without seat belts last year, it required them to keep track of recipients by race. Figures show that blacks are getting seat-belt tickets roughly in proportion to their population—but that doesn't satisfy Woods, who thinks the tickets should reflect the ratio of white to black drivers, which includes suburbanites who drive downtown to their jobs. But even he agrees that if blacks and the police are arguing over how to interpret statistics on traffic stops, they've come a very, very long way from Bull Connor's dogs.

And so has someone like Robert Holmes, who remembers how as a teenager he and his brother once had to physically restrain their father from rushing downtown to shoot the dogs. Robert Holmes Sr., who dug ditches for the Alabama Gas Co., saw on the news the demonstrators fleeing German shepherds and bolted for the door. "We held him because we didn't want him to be killed," says his son, who now has his own job in the utilities industry, as vice president for ethics and business practices of Alabama Power Co. Holmes has an engineering degree from the University of Alabama-Birmingham, which didn't even exist in the 1960s but enrolled a freshman class last year that was roughly 30 percent black, making it by far the most successful campus among major state schools in achieving diversity. The university's rise as a medical-technology center has helped drive the city's transformation, economically and socially. Birmingham is "light-years from where we were" back in the early '60s, says Holmes. That assessment is shared by another prominent black citizen, Shelley Stewart, 70, who parlayed a job as a radio announcer into ownership of the station, as well of as an advertising agency and other businesses—but remembers well how the richest black man in Alabama in the 1950s, A. G. Gaston, had to go to the kitchen door of a Chinese restaurant to get an order of chop suey, because he couldn't be seated in front. Today, says Stewart, "a black man can go to any restaurant, he can check into any hotel he wants to, and that's a big change. But he can't afford to check out. And that's a big change that's still to come."

Source: Vern E. Smith and Matthew Murr, "Up From Jim Crow," *Newsweek* 18 Sep. 2000: 42–46.

EXERCISES: READING AND RESPONDING

1. Characterize the voice you hear in this article. What does it tell you about the writers' attitude toward the subject and audience?
2. Characterize two of the two voices quoted in the article. What perspectives about Birmingham do the speakers enforce?
3. At what points in the article do the writers provide readers with a historical, political, or cultural context for information? What does the context suggest about readers' familiarity with the subject?
4. Smith and Murr explain that "Birmingham long ago lost the distinction of being 'the most segregated city in America.'" What evidence do they offer to illustrate that "Birmingham is 'light-years from where [it was] back in the early '60s'"? What evidence do they offer to illustrate that Birmingham is still racially divided?
5. According to this article, what are the major issues facing Birmingham today?
6. In your opinion, is the purpose of this article *primarily* to advance an argument or provide information? Explain your response by citing specific passages from the article.
7. If you believe the writers' primary purpose is to provide information, identify at least five different kinds of evidence they provide.
8. If you believe writers' primary purpose is to advance an argument, what kinds of appeals are at work in the article?

EVALUATING AND ANALYZING THE CASE STUDY

EXERCISES: THINKING CRITICALLY

1. Identify the rhetorical situation for each source in the case study.
2. King's letter is a primary source for this case study. Identify any other sources in the case study that are primary sources. Identify secondary sources. Be prepared to explain why you classify a source as one or the other.

3. Bull Connor is one of the focal points in this case study. Notice that he's mentioned in other sources. In order to understand what happened in Birmingham in 1963, you have to know something about him. Review sources in this case and identify other people, events, and issues that are focal points or connections that link one source to another.

EXERCISES: COLLABORATING WITH YOUR PEERS

1. The time line included in the case study gives you an overview of the civil rights movement. Working in pairs or in groups, construct a time line for the events in Birmingham in 1963.
2. Make a list of key players in this case. Be prepared to share your list with your classmates.

WRITING ABOUT THE CASE STUDY

EXERCISES: FOCUS ON WRITING

Freewriting

1. Write for fifteen to twenty minutes on your impressions of the case study. Answer the reporter's questions—*who? what? where? when? why?* and *how?*—and touch on issues that are controversial.
2. Write for fifteen to twenty minutes recording what you have learned from the case study that would help you provide a historical or political context for readers who weren't familiar with the case.

Writing Letters

3. Write a letter to your college or university's newspaper that provides readers with a historical context for "Letter from Birmingham Jail." Your letter should also explain why readers need to be aware of the historical context.
4. Photocopy a newspaper or journal article that has a rhetorical effect. In a letter to the editor of the publication in which the picture appeared, comment on the effect you think the picture had on readers.

Writing for an Academic Audience

5. For *Southern Cultures*, a journal published by the University of South Carolina Press, write a documented paper that provides a historical context for the "Letter from Birmingham Jail." Your paper should cite a minimum of five sources.
6. Pictures usually accompany articles in *Southern Cultures*. If you have identified pictures that would provide readers with a context for the "Letter," write a letter to the editor that describes each picture and explains where it should be placed in the text and what kind of rhetorical effect you think the picture will have on readers.
7. Design a web page that would give readers a social context for the "Letter." Submit the text to accompany the page. The text should cite a minimum of five sources from this case study. In addition, submit a memo in which you identify any pictures you would use and explain why you have chosen them.

The pictures may come from this case study or from your independent library research.

8. Select one of the following and explain how King uses it effectively throughout the "Letter":
   - Appeal to logic
   - Appeal to emotions
   - Appeal to ethics
   - Definition
   - Rhetorical questions
   - Irony
   - Allusion
   - Similes and metaphors

   You will submit your paper to the *Southern Speech Communication Journal*. Readers may not be familiar with the events that led to the composition of the letter, so provide a brief context. If you use any sources from this case study or from the library, provide appropriate documentation.

WRITING ABOUT RELATED ISSUES

EXERCISES: FOCUS ON WRITING

1. For a current issue that is being discussed in newspapers and news magazines, find at least five sources that discuss the issue. Aim for different rhetorical situations—for example, a front-page newspaper article, a letter to the editor, an editorial, an article in one of the weekly magazines, or pictures in newspapers or magazines. Select an audience within the academic community and provide a context for the issue and identify the rhetorical strategies that appear in the sources you selected. If certain strategies are repeated in two or more sources, comment on why these strategies seem to be used.

2. Spike Lee's 1997 production for HBO, *4 Little Girls*, documents the bombing of the Sixteenth Avenue Baptist Church. View the video and write a paper that summarizes the documentary, explains how Lee provides viewers with a context for this event, and leads to a recommendation about whether or not students interested in the civil rights movement would benefit from watching the documentary.

3. In a paper of 800–1,000 words using five to eight library sources, provide a historical context for King's "I Have A Dream" speech for an audience of your choice.

4. Using the top 100 list or *Vital Speeches of the Day*, a journal that publishes noteworthy speeches, find a speech you would like to share with your peers. Make a copy of the speech, annotate the text, and draft a paper of 500–600 words in which you analyze the speaker's rhetorical strategies. Be sure you provide readers with a context for the speech you selected.

5. Select an event from the past (at least 30 years ago) that took place in 24 hours or less. Write a documented paper citing a minimum of five sources. Your paper should provide an audience of your choice with a context for the event. Explain the event's social, historical, political, or intellectual significance.

Brainstorming: Focus on American Politics

Beating of West Point Cadet Johnson Chestnut Whittaker

Assassination of John F. Kennedy

Assassination of Robert F. Kennedy

Assassination of Dr. Martin Luther King, Jr.

Attempted assassination of George Wallace

Arrest of Rosa Parks

The National Guard at Little Rock Central High School

George Wallace Stands in the Schoolhouse Door

Sit-In Protest at Woolworth's Lunch Counter, Greensboro, North Carolina

James Meredith Enrolls at the University of Mississippi

Murder of Medgar Evers

Bombing of the Sixteenth Street Baptist Church, Birmingham, Alabama

Murder of Malcom X

Chapter 12

Reconciling Different Perspectives

> When there are persons to be found, who form an exception to the apparent unanimity of the world on any subject, even if the world is in the right, it is always probable that dissentients have something worth hearing to say for themselves, and that truth would lose something by their silence.
> —*John Stuart Mill,* On the Liberty of Thought and Discussion

FINDING MIDDLE GROUND

When you reconcile differences of opinion, you settle disputes or bring different perspectives into agreement. For example, consider the debate over drivers using cell phones. One side argues that we engage in many different activities when we drive—eating and drinking, finding stations on the radio or changing a CD, or looking at a road map. There's not any difference, this side claims, in performing these activities while driving and talking on the phone while driving. The opposition maintains that talking on cell phones distracts drivers, taking their attention away from the road, more so than checking radio stations or talking to children in the backseat. Obviously, reconciling these two perspectives won't be easy. We can predict an outcome, though: (1) Drivers will be prohibited by city, state, or the federal government from talking on cell phones while driving; (2) drivers will have no restrictions placed on them concerning talking on cell phones while driving; or (3) drivers will be allowed to have cell phones in their vehicles, but will have some restrictions on when they use them. Option 3 is a compromise, a combination of 1 and 2. Think about how we persuade people to accept compromises.

Let's assume that you're writing about this issue for a broad general audience. You should expect your readers to embrace one of the first two perspectives discussed above. How do you lead them to middle ground, away from a pro or con position and toward an understanding of how to look at this issue in a new way? You have to know the subject well and look for common ground.

471

In the brief sketch of the talking and driving issue, we've focused on the differences between the two perspectives. One way to reconcile opposing perspectives is to understand what both sides have in common and to use that information to develop a plan or solution. Both sides, you might reasonably assume, value safety. What kinds of safety precautions should drivers take if they use cell phones while driving? Would both sides agree to restrictions only on the use of cell phones in heavy traffic? What else would these two sides agree upon? Would they accept a proposal including a component on cell phones and driving in driver education programs or an ad campaign emphasizing the dangers of distraction on the road, similar to ad campaigns that educate people on drinking and driving?

As a reader, you often reconcile different perspectives in an informal manner after evaluating and analyzing sources. Sometimes you operate on intuition or a felt sense of what is a justifiable or acceptable way to negotiate differences in perspectives. In this scenario, however, you have only yourself to consider. As a writer addressing an audience, reconciling different perspectives involves considering your readers' understanding of the issues and any biases or assumptions they may have. Readers need an opportunity to explore all perspectives, so when you write to reconcile perspectives, you don't want to present a one-sided picture to your audience. Your review of perspectives should be comprehensive, furnishing readers with a complete picture of the issues and a thorough understanding of the topic. After reviewing perspectives, you should propose a way to bring them into agreement— for example, you could propose a compromise, issue a call to action, or suggest a solution to a problem. Whatever form of resolution you offer should be one your readers will accept or, at the very least, regard seriously. You'll practice analyzing your readers' perspectives and reconciling different opinions and attitudes as you work on the case study in this chapter, Xenotransplantation.

Strategies

To reconcile different perspectives, you have to analyze and develop arguments. And you have to respect your intended readers' commitment to their perspectives, recognizing the old adage about being able to lead a horse to water. If you anticipate difficulty in "getting the horse to drink" (still playing on the metaphor here), one option is simply to provide readers with information. Stress the importance of reconciling differences, but encourage readers to reconcile differences on their own— and hope they will answer your call to action. Consider this strategy when a situation or issue is extremely complex and not easily resolved. Another strategy is to provide an overview of the perspectives and conclude with resolutions your sources suggest. If you were writing about cell phones and driving, you might encourage readers to accept recommendations from the National Safety and Transformation Board. Using this approach, you would provide information for your readers and emphasize how other writers' ideas will work. And another strategy is to reconcile differences in perspectives by reviewing the issues and arguing that a plan or proposal you have devised is more practical, acceptable, or workable than others.

ANALYZING SOURCES

Several sources included in Case Study 4 are models of published writers' attempts to reconcile different perspectives. You can expect to agree with some of the resolutions they offer and disagree with others. Questions to consider as you examine these sources are the following:

- Does the writer present a clear context for different perspectives?
- Does the writer offer a comprehensive account of different perspectives?
- Does the writer omit or minimize pertinent information?
- Does the writer fabricate, distort, or magnify information?
- Does the writer present information that other sources confirm?
- Does the writer document sources?
- Does the writer offer a resolution that sources support?

To reconcile either slight differences or outright contradictions in opinion, you'll have to seek a comprehensive overview of available information. This overview is important. It will help you determine what you believe to be the most acceptable way to resolve conflicting perspectives.

RECONCILING DIFFERENT PERSPECTIVES

You have several options when you attempt to reconcile different perspectives. You can

- Propose a compromise.
- Issue a call to action.
- Suggest a solution.
- Offer readers sufficient information so that they can reconcile the differences on their own.

PREVIEW: THE JEFF GETTY CASE

On December 14, 1995, doctors at San Francisco General Hospital transplanted bone marrow taken from a seven-year-old baboon from the Southwest Foundation for Biomedical Research in San Antonio, Texas, into Jeff Getty, a thirty-eight-year-old AIDS patient. If the experiment worked, Getty's doctors theorized, the baboon bone marrow, which is resistant to HIV and AIDS, would repair Getty's weak immune system. Getty survived the operation without complications. His health improved afterward, largely because of the treatments that preceded the operation. The Getty/baboon marrow transplant, however, raised questions about possible health hazards associated with cross-species transplantation, and perhaps more importantly, questions about the ethical dilemma of using animals for spare parts for humans. Editors of *Nature Biotechnology* wrote:

> Replacing human tissue with animal cells and organs clearly raises issues that some people will find threatening. Spare-parts surgery, using organs or cells from animals, challenges our notions of humanness, our sense of distinctness from other species. It is easy to find sympathy for those who are repelled by xenotransplantation—even if that repulsion has visceral rather than cerebral roots.

FOCUS ON RELATED ISSUES: THE LIMITS OF SCIENCE

In Chapter 3, you read about Dolly, the first mammal cloned from the cell of an adult donor. Since 1997, scientists have cloned mice, cattle, more sheep, and most recently, genetically identical piglets, designed specifically to be spare parts for humans. With businesses sporting names like Genetic Savings and Clone popping up to offer cloning for a fee, how far away are we from human clones? One theory is that if the scientific community has the know-how, someone will try it, regardless of any laws or policies that prohibit it.

After researchers announced their success with Dolly, a report from the Institute of Philosophy and Public Policy discussed the ethics of human cloning:

> The successful cloning of an adult sheep, announced in Scotland this past February, is one of the most dramatic recent examples of a scientific discovery becoming a public issue. During the last few months, various commentators—scientists and theologians, physicians and legal experts, talk-radio hosts and editorial writers—have been busily responding to the news, some calming fears, other raising alarms about the prospect of cloning a human being. At the request of the President, the National Bioethics Advisory Commission (NBAC) held hearings and prepared a report on the religious, ethical, and legal issues surrounding human cloning. While declining to call for a permanent ban on the practice, the Commission recommended a moratorium on efforts to clone human beings, and emphasized the importance of further public deliberation on the subject.

Who should be responsible for formulating public policy on cloning? The scientific community? the legal community? politicians? What are some common assumptions about cloning that are true? false? Working on your own, develop a topic on cloning for a documented paper.

The baboon bone marrow transplant was an experiment in *xenotransplantation,* the transplanting of animal organs into humans. Case Study 4 investigates different perspectives on the issue of using spare parts from animals. As you read and annotate sources, take special note of the various perspectives on cross-species transplants. What are the opinions of members of the medical community? What are the opinions of animal rights activists? What are the opinions of ethicists? What are the opinions of individuals who think a transplant would improve their health? You should be prepared to summarize, analyze, and synthesize these opinions in writing assignments. In addition, you should be prepared to write a paper that examines different perspectives on this issue and reconciles differences in the perspectives.

EXERCISE: FOCUS ON WRITING

Before you read what others say about xenotransplantation, spend ten to fifteen minutes freewriting to explore your own ideas about the topic. What is your initial reaction to it? What ethical issues does it bring to mind? If you were a candidate for an organ transplant, how would you react if you knew the donor was a baboon or pig?

Case Study 4:
Xenotransplantation

I collected bones from charnel houses; and distributed, with profane fingers, the tremendous secrets of the human frame. In a solitary chamber, or rather cell, at the top of the house, and separated from all the other apartments by a gallery and staircase, I kept my workshop of filthy creation; my eyeballs were starting from their sockets in attending to the details of my employment. The dissecting room and slaughter-house furnished many of my materials; and often did my human nature turn with loathing from my occupation, whilst, still urged on by an eagerness which perpetually increased, I brought my work near to a conclusion.

—*Victor Frankenstein in Mary Shelley's* Frankenstein

USING ANIMALS AS SPARE PARTS

In Source 1, "Surgeon's Quest for Life: The History and Future of Xenotransplantation," Rebecca Malouin traces experiments with xenotranplantation back to the sixteenth century. Malouin was a junior at the University of Michigan when she wrote the paper for an advanced biology class. In 1994, *Perspectives in Biology and Medicine*, a scholarly journal out of the University of Chicago Press, published Malouin's paper.

SURGEON'S QUEST FOR LIFE: THE HISTORY AND FUTURE OF XENOTRANSPLANTATION

REBECCA MALOUIN

None but those who have experienced them can conceive of the enticements of science. In other studies you go as far as others have gone before you, and there is nothing more to know; but in a scientific pursuit there is continual food for discovery and wonder.

Frankenstein in Mary Shelley's
Frankenstein [1]

Introduction

The consumption of this "continual food for discovery and wonder" proved destructive for Victor Frankenstein, yet enabled him to reveal the "secret of life." Analogies may be drawn between young Dr. Frankenstein and his contemporary counterparts, surgeons specializing

476

in transplantation. Such surgeons also search for a way to extend life and, in the process, occasionally lose a life—the life of the patient. The similarity ends there. Frankenstein lacked professional, psychological, and moral support, landmarks of the medical establishment today and, consequently, lost control of his experiment and, finally, his life. Scientists today, as hungry for discovery as young Frankenstein, must abide by many, strictly enforced guidelines allowing them to pursue the secret of life without incurring similar unfortunate results. Transplant surgeons experiment within a protective structure that reduces the magnitude of mistakes and, therefore, allows them to advance by learning from prior failures. Such advancements have fed the field of transplantation so that it has metamorphosed into xenotransplantation, or transplantation between dissimilar species. Due to the novelty of xenotransplantation, medical precedents, procedural guidelines, and public opinion have not been firmly established so that claims of immortality and uncontrolled experimentation have "run rampant." Xenotransplantation has matured quite recently, though, much like other specialties in the medical profession, and through a supportive media and public understanding, may be the next frontier in the quest for the "secret of life."

The Past

The history of xenografting before the 1960s was a history of misunderstanding. The techniques and theories culminating in attempts at xenotransplantation reflect the popular social and scientific ideas of the period. Gasparro Tagliacozzi of Bologna (1547–1599), one of the first to record information regarding xenografting, related grafting, the "binding [of] two persons," to agriculture and the grafting of plants [2]. He concluded that difficulty would arise in xenografting due to the "problems ... involved relating to the individual humoral constitution of the body of both man and animal" [2]. The strength of the myth of the unicorn found in a cavern in Lascaux, France, painted 20,000 years ago and incorporating characteristics of many species, may have continued to taint the scientific reasoning of this period for, as Dubernard and Flyer recognize in *Principles of Organ Transplantation,* "especially intriguing to the mind of the human has been the idea of endowing himself or herself with certain characteristics of various animals by transplantation of the appropriate part" [3]. Tagliacozzi concluded in his works concerning the feasibility of xenografting that "difficulties are so great that good judgment suggests success would be remote" [2].

During the seventeenth century, the transfusion of blood from animals to humans began after Harvey's demonstration of the circulation of blood and his treatise on the heart [2]. The blood of lambs was transfused into a boy in 1667, and shortly after into a healthy man for reasons "more by curiosity than by necessity" [2]. Miraculously, a patient of Jean Baptiste Denys who had been subject to similar medical treatments, "awakened ... wonderfully composed and in his right mind" although "he pist a large glass full of such black Urine that you would have said it has been mixed with soot" [4]. The adverse prognoses of most of the experiments were not reported to the degree that is expected now with the current knowledge of incompatibility. This may be accounted for by the novelty of the experiments, the severity of the original dysfunction, and the absence of continual observation or "follow-up" [2].

In 1667, Richard Lower transfused the blood of a lamb into Arthur Coga, a Bachelor of Divinity at Cambridge University [4]. Coga stated in response to his choice of the source of blood that "Sheep's blood possess a symbolic relationship with the blood of Christ, since Christ is the lamb of God" [2]. His statement reflects the persistent view of blood and organs as entities capable of possessing and transferring the special attributes of their original possessor. The combination of mythical and religious interpretations greatly influenced this novel procedure. During the eighteenth century, though, John Hunter (1728–1798) disputed his popular opinion, arguing instead that "the blood of one animal could be transferred to another since all living matter is similar in nature" [2]. His view, although incorrect, displays the slow evolution of scientific thought in its progress toward eventual autonomy from mythical, and to some extent, religious influences.

James Blundell (1790–1877), an obstetrician, discovered the actual incompatibility of heterologous blood through repeated animal experiments involving dogs transfused with the blood of sheep [2]. As a result, enografting stopped during the beginning of

the nineteenth century. In 1857, Charles-Edouard Brown-Sequard (1817–1894) "set back progress by declaring that the blood of any one species was not toxic to that of another far removed" after transferring the defibrillated blood of various mammals into dogs without observing any adverse reactions. Henry Gradle (1855–1941) of the United States also attempted the transference of blood of heterospecific mammals by injecting lamb blood into a tubercular patient, but with disastrous results [2]. Consequently, during the end of the nineteenth century, "transfusion once more fell into disfavor," and xenografts were not attempted [2].

A Scientific Explosion

During the first half of the twentieth century, scientific discoveries progressed at a rate unparalleled in previous history. Lister's production of antisepsis and the consequent ability to perform aseptic surgery prompted a new wave of transplantation[5]. Beginning in 1900. Shattuck and Landsteiner discovered the principles and basic chemical mechanisms of blood incompatibility [2]. Tissue and cellular differences between species were noted, and concepts such as "'sympathetic' differences or differences in biochemical constitution" became popular [5].

The new fields of evolution, genetics, and biochemistry also influenced various physicians' opinions as evident in the statement of famed Chicago physiologist Charles Clarke Guthrie (1880–1963) who said, in regard to previous xenotransplantations, that "there may be no evidence that any of the original tissue survive" [6]. The new scientific view incorporated reductionism and specificity, focusing upon the details of the surgery and the sources of incompatibility, as opposed to the general theories of humors and chimeras previously expressed. Some chose to disregard this scientific information, though, such as the physicians performing repeated unsuccessful xenografts at the Rockefeller Institute of Medical Research before World War I, "[doing] so much in their turn to discredit organ transplantation" [2].

In 1923. Carlos Williamson observed the underlying principles in transplanted organ failure and developed the basic biological principle of "rejection" [5]. By the end of World War II, "the immune system ... [had] come to be understood as a mechanism which attempts to distinguish between 'self' and 'nonself' to protect the former from the latter" [5]. This understanding paved the way for Emile Holman's discovery in the 1950s that rejection is a result of antibodies. In 1960, MacFarlane Burnet and Peter Medawar were awarded the Nobel Prize for their studies inducing a newborn animal to permanently tolerate foreign bodies [5].

A New Era of Transplantation

Armed with such a vast array of knowledge and a newly developed arsenal of immunosuppressants, surgeons began once again to transplant organs with some degree of confidence. During the 1960s, the first successful allografts as well as slightly improved xenografts were performed in the United States. Kidney trans-

plants led the parade of various primate-to-human xenotransplants. Thomas Starzl states in his article, "The Future of Xenografts," that "the demonstration ... that renal allotransplantation was routinely feasible with azathioprine prednisone therapy created a ... [human] organ shortage crisis" [7]. Keith Reemtsma and Starzl independently began investigating kidney xenografts, Reemtsma focusing on chimpanzees and Starzl focusing on baboons, after Dr. Claude Hitchcock performed a kidney xenotransplantation of a baboon on a sixty-five-year-old woman in 1963 that functioned for four days [7]. Each of the kidneys transplanted by Reemtsma functioned for a short period with dieresis except for one from a chimpanzee with an incompatible blood group, while the baboon kidney transplanted by Starzl functioned dialysis-free for ten to sixty days[8]. One of Reemtsma's transplanted kidneys survived nine months, a success rate that has not been repeated since [7, 8].

In 1964, the first heart xenograft was performed by Hardy and Chavez, involving a chimpanzee heart transplanted into a sixty-eight-year-old man [9]. No record of the use of immunosuppressants exists, and the heart functioned for only two hours. [8] The second heart xenograph involved a baboon heart inserted into a twenty-five-year-old woman in South Africa [10]. The heart functioned for eight hours [10]. The third attempt, performed by the same team, incorporated the use of a chimpanzee heart transplanted into a sixty-year-old man [10]. The man lived for four days and, upon examination of the heart during the autopsy, the surgical team found evidence of acute rejection [10].

During the late 1960s, Starzl performed the first chimpanzee-to-human liver transplants with moderate success [11]. Although the longest survived only nine days, postmortem observations of the liver displayed much less evidence of rejection than with kidney transplant, and it was felt that the patient's death had not been the direct result of hepatic failure due to rejection" [8, 11].

The importance of the choice of donor species surfaced during these early experiments. The difference between the terms "heterograft" and "xenograft" was expounded upon in journals such as *Transplantation Proceedings,* in 1969, and earlier in the *New England Journal of Medicine* in 1965) [12, 13]. The journals stressed that "heterograft" be "used to designate grafts along the lines of species, genus and family" while "xenograft" apply "to transplants between individuals of greater genetic disparity, such as grafts across ... order, class, phylum and kingdom" [13]. Experiments such as Reemtsma's and Starzl's established the relationship between closely related species and the length of graft survival. Reemtsma's longest surviving chimp kidney transplant lasted nine months while Starzl's longest functioning baboon kidney transplant lasted only sixty days [8]. During the same period, the maximum functioning of a pig kidney xenograft had been discovered to be only 375 minutes [12]. As stated in *Transplantation Proceedings,* "[transplantation of organs between] closely related species follow functional, immuno-logical and pathological patterns that are similar to those [of] homografts".

New insights into the mechanisms of organ transplant incompatibility also surfaced between the 1960s and 1980s as a result of the new experiments and discoveries in biochemistry. Chimpanzees were typed as human blood groups *A* or *O* using antigroup typing sera, and baboons were classified as *A, B* or *AB* through similar tests of blood and saliva [14]. High doses of immunosuppressant therapy were available and used to fight the vigorous rejections resulting from the baboon-to-man xenografts [8]. Methods of detecting malfunctions in the newly transplanted organs had advanced to such a level that detailed serological studies such as those detecting specific 'antispecies' antibodies were possible [15]. Discoveries in xenotransplantation had progressed at such a rapid rate that Sir Peter Medawar, a recipient of the Nobel Prize, stated, "Of the use of heterografts I can say only this: that in the laboratory we are achieving greater success with grafts between species today than we achieved with grafts within species fifteen years ago. We shall solve the problem of using heterografts one day if we try hard enough, and maybe in less than fifteen years" [16].

The Legacy of Baby Fae

Close to fifteen years later, in 1984, the method and practice of xenotransplantation were revealed to the public through the emotionally charged, ethically debated "Baby Fae" case. During the 1970s, there were few attempts at xenografting while scientists studying biochemistry searched for the perfect immunosuppressant. Baby Fae, a newborn girl with "hypoplastic left heart syndrome," received a "baboon cardiac orthotopic transplantation" on October 26, 1984; the operation was performed by Dr. Leonard Bailey at Loma Linda Medical Center [17]. The event stimulated public debate concerning the ethics, procedure, and general necessity of the operation as well as an investigation into the patient's general role and rights in xenotransplantation.

Stephen Gould, a renowned evolutionary biologist at Harvard University, questioned Bailey's choice of a baboon as an organ donor in his article "The Heart of Terminology" [18]. He stated "I believe that Bailey performed an indefensibly improper experiment from the standpoint of evolutionary homology…. Rejection is a function of genealogical closeness, not morphological appearance … through conceptual error [Baby Fae] was not given her best chance" [18].

Other critics agreed that Baby Fae was not given her best chance of survival, not due to evolutionary theory, but through the "blatant negligence of Dr. Bailey. They reasoned that Loma Linda did not attempt to search for a feasible human donor for the transplant; the availability of a two-month old donor at the time, was cited as further proof that the doctor's first priority was not to save the life of Baby Fae. An article in *Nature* states that "Bailey … even acknowledged that a human donor had not been sought because, simply, the purpose of his experiment was to see if the baboon heart would work" [19]. Such opponents of Dr. Bailey believed the

doctor failed to adhere to the ancient dictum *primum non nocere*.

Alexander Morgan Capron wrote in an editorial concerning the case that "the public receives a distorted view about the process by which scientific knowledge and useful technology actually unfold [and that] may be misled about the usefulness of techniques like the baboon-heart transplant technique used on Baby Fae" [20]. The public awareness in the case is evident and surprisingly found in such nonmedical sources as Paul Simon's song "Boy in the Bubble" in such verses as "Medicine is magical and magical is often with … the baby with the battle with the heart … don't cry baby, don't cry, don't cry" [18]. The fact that the public received information about the case does not necessarily imply that the information was misrepresented, or that they were "misled" however.

Proponents of xenotransplantation and supporters of Bailey defend Bailey's decision to use a baboon heart. The human donor heart available was never tested and may have been incompatible [19]. Keith Reemtsma, the head of the team performing kidney xenografts in the 1960s, supported Bailey on the basis of the information available at the time. Reemtsma felt that the previous successful primate kidney grafts, the fact that a newborn may be more likely to accept a graft than an adult, and the much improved immunosuppressants were sufficient incentives to perform the operation [21]. He also acknowledged the role of the media and the public reaction to the operation by stating "Science and news are, in a sense, asymmetrical and sometimes antagonistic. News emphasizes the uniqueness, the immediacy, the human interest ... [while] ... science emphasizes verification, controls, comparisons, and patterns". [21]

Bailey was also supported by colleagues at a meeting mentioned in the *Journal of the American Medical Association* where "speakers, including Bailey, said that the only convincing ethical justification for pursuing the xenograft approach is the continuing scarcity of human hearts" [22]. Following the Baby Fae case, surgeons "stress[ed] xenografts as a bridge to keep alive infants with hypoplastic left-heart syndrome until a compatible human donor can be located" [22].

Once again social opinions influenced and interfered with scientific endeavors. The role of the patient and the importance of consent were discussed in depth in the aftermath of the Baby Fae ordeal. Some opponents disagreed with the use of an infant in such an experimental operation; among them was Capron who argued for "a model of successive approximations ... try[ing] to get down to the least vulnerable child-subjects for procedures designed and tested to involve the least possible risk" [20]. Capron concluded that physicians "[must] never advanc[e] their research at the expense of the child by foregoing an alternative treatment that offers a better chance" [20].

Even the procedure for obtaining the consent of Baby Fae's parents drew unfavorable responses. George Annas attacked Dr. Bailey as well as many of the pioneer xenograft surgeons, including Dr. Hardy, who performed the first heart transplant, and Dr. Reemtsma, who transplanted chimp kidneys. He noted that "subjects in xenograft experiments have 'traditionally' been drawn from [the impoverished] population" [23]. Perhaps this is true, but many impoverished people cannot afford preventive care and a disproportionate number compared to other populations may be in need of such drastic surgery. Also, even with an alternative treatment, the fact that a procedure may lengthen a life and, incidentally, be free should appear attractive to people of any socioeconomic class. Perhaps people who could afford such an operation choose to do so without publicity and, as a result, their surgeons were neither required nor permitted to disclose the procedure to the public due to the privacy of the physician-patient relationship.

Annas also disputes the validity of the informed consent obtained by Bailey [23]. He describes a verbal portrayal by Bailey of a seven hour explanation to Baby Fae's parents in which Bailey "spent hours talking to them very candidly and very frankly ... show[ing] them a film and giv[ing] them a slide show" [23]. By comparing this oral interpretation to a *People* magazine interview with the parents, Annas deduced that the father was not actually present for this particular presentation by Bailey [23]. He then concluded that "It is unclear that either of the parents ever read or understood the consent forms, but it is evident that the father was not involved in any meaningful way in the consent process" [23]. At the time of the publication of Annas's article, the consent form was a "Loma Linda Top Secret Document" [23]. Consequently, Annas could not have known definitively by the information given in his article whether the parents' consent was not, indeed, informed. Exposés of xenotransplantation cases such as Annas's, while meant only to protect patients' rights, may hinder the progress of science at the expense of society.

Animal Exploitation?

The other life lost during the Baby Fae operation also received much attention. The baboon who sacrificed his heart and his life, Goobers, was also mourned, and articles were subsequently written concerning the ethical treatment of animals during xenotransplantation. In his article, "The Other Victim," Tom Regan [24] warned that "as Darwin saw, and as we should see, the psychology of such creatures differs from ours in degree, not in kind ... Goobers was somebody, a distinct individual ... experienc[ing] ... a life whose quality and duration mattered to him, independently of his utility to us." Nelson [25] draws parallels between the use of primates in experiments and the use of Jewish people or people of color, reminding us that, "As the history of medical research in the nineteenth and early twentieth century reveals, we have been more than willing to subject those who have 'clearly less value' to the rigors of research" Nelson believes that current proponents of xenografting fail at "any serious attempt to balance [the] cost against the debt incurred to the victims of those grafts."

Various philosophies are drawn upon in developing a logical justification for the continual use of primates and other animals in experimentation, and xenografts in particular. One writer attempts to "balance the cost against the debt incurred by the victim" drawing from Rawl's philosophy of "reflective equilibrium" through "moral balancing." Cartwright [26] claims that "the greater the good and the less valuable the animals, the more likely the practice is to be justified ... [and that] the case of xenografting would seem to be the strongest [compared to eating and experimenting upon animals] since here the purpose of the practice is to save directly the life of an identifiable human being." Further, he supposes that "what underlies the sense that xenografting is morally worse than eating animals is that the latter is in some sense natural while the former is not" [26].

The Near Future

The concluding statement in Cartwright's article, "What science has so remarkably brought us to respect we may find it increasingly difficult to allow science to exploit" [26], directly relates to the current wave of xenotransplantation, and the use of nonprimates as organ donors. Cartwright theorizes that the "judgment [to use an animal] ... increases in strength the less important the animal is" [26]. Because such animals as pigs are already enormously consumed as food and clothing, their use in xenografting would already be ethically justifiable. That ninety million pigs are slaughtered annually for human consumption in the United States should "minimize [any] criticism" [27]. Also, as explained in the article "The Pig as Organ Donor for Man."

> Considerable similarities exist between certain pig organs and those of man, both anatomically and physiologically, namely, size, dietary habits, digestive physiology, kidney structure and function, respiratory rate, pulmonary physiology, coronary artery distribution and hemodynamics, propensity to obesity, susceptibility to disease, and social behavior. [27]

Also, pigs grow rapidly, "offering organs suitable for even the largest of adult humans" [27]. Pigs need little space to breed, require low-cost maintenance, and produce large litters.

Diseases such as Epstein-Barr virus, various strains of herpes, human immunodeficiency virus type 1, and Ebola virus may be found in primates and transferred to the recipient of a diseased organ [28, 29]. The risk of such infection is less with pigs because they may be raised easily in a germ-free environment. [27]

Currently, British scientists are "developing a plan to insert parts of human genes into fertilized sow eggs to create 'transgenic pigs'" [30]. The technology of genetic engineering has already advanced to such a level in agriculture and animal breeding. Since the late 1980s, scientists have "microinjected [fusion genes] into a pronucleus of an ovum" that have been "integrated into the pig genome" [31]. The pigs have, consequently, "transmitted the fusion gene as an autosomal dominant trait to about half of their progeny"[31]. Thus, a human-genic pig could be produced and reproduced in the near future.

In a recent xenograft attempt following the Baby Fae transplant, Susan Fowler, a twenty-six-year-old woman suffering from autoimmune hepatitis, received a pig liver transplanted by Dr. Leonard Makowka at Cedars-Sinai Medical Center after a failed attempt to locate a human donor [32]. Makowka claimed that the "pig liver transplant was a scientific success [due to] ... the fact that Fowler's brain returned to normal size and function as the pig liver took over blood cleansing and metabolizing functions of her own damaged organ," including bile production [33]. Unfortunately, just as surgeons prepared to replace the pig liver with a human donor liver, Fowler died.

Dr. Arthur Caplan, director of the Biomedical Ethics Center at the University of Minnesota, stated in a newspaper article following Fowler's death that "There's absolutely no basis in basic research for trying a pig liver in a human being given the difference in biology between people and pigs ... [and that] the gap in biology ... is too large to morally justify subjecting any human being to a transplant organ from a pig" [32]. This gap may have been a deterrent only a few years ago, but with immunosuppressants, such as Cyclosporin A, and the medical technology available, such as breeding transgenic pigs, such operations soon may be feasible and justifiable.

In the case of Fowler and the recent baboon liver xenografts performed by Starzl, the deaths of the patients were not a direct result of any malfunctioning in the livers. Starzl, like Makowka, observed that the liver xenografts functioned well, concluding that, "there was little evidence of hepatic rejection by biochemical monitoring or histopathological examination. Products of hepatic synthesis, including clotting factors, became those of the baboon liver with no obvious adverse effects" [34]. In Starzl's published article relating the case, he wrote of finding baboon DNA in the patient's heart, lung, kidney, and two lymph nodes as "evidence of the chimerism that we believe is integral to the acceptance of both xenografts and allografts." Starzl felt that his overindulgence of immunosuppressants, such as cyclophosphamide, probably influenced and affected the patient's death. [34]

The fear of "hyperacute rejection," a process just recently understood and revealed in depth, prompted Starzl's overuse of immunosuppressants as well as Caplan's assertion of the impossibility of xenografting. During the past ten years, many articles have attempted to explain this process, although the exact causes of the various rejections are still debated. As Auchincloss stated in his extensive review of xenografts in 1988, "it is unknown whether the greater difficulty in prolonging xenografts is the result of quantitatively stronger cell-mediated rejection or of qualitatively different, perhaps unrecognized, mechanisms of rejection" [35]. Although many of the "qualitatively different" mechanisms are now known, their degree of influence on rejection remains unknown. [15]

A Polish team of surgeons, in an article recently published in the *Journal of Heart and Lung Transplant,* outlined the exact causes of hyperacute xenograft rejection while discussing the transplantation of a porcine heart into a man. The first, most severe and immediate reaction to the xenograft involves the host body's preformed antibodies' attack upon the donor's antigens [36]. If the patient survives this phase, the second stage, which lasts days as opposed to hours, begins [36]. The second stage relates to the host cells' reaction and defensive attack upon the new organ, which is usually a result of insufficient immunosuppressants. [36] The recent discovery of preformed antibodies or "circulating antibodies that can agglutinate red blood cells of the donor species," occurs more often in discordant species, or species more phylogenetically distant, prompting the sentiment that humans, without a doubt, would reject nonprimate organs [15]. Concordant species also possess natural antibodies directed against foreign antigens, however, and this is evident in the history of nonhuman primate-to-human transplants and allografts. The specific mechanisms and components involved in rejection are beyond the scope of this paper.

As the exact nature of hyperacute rejection becomes understood and the roles of natural antibodies, complement (a separate process that aids antibodies), endothelial cell antigens, and natural killer cells become known, the method of xenotransplantation may be improved so that the lives of those requiring organs may be prolonged enough to secure human donors. The question raised by Bailey in the *Journal of the American Medical Association* in 1987 is yet unanswered as to "what happens when you have a functioning xenograft and then an allograft comes along" [22]. Perhaps, as Nelson contends in his article opposing xenografts "[we should] figure better ways to engage in altruism of the human community, until at least it strikes us all as mighty peculiar that anyone would want to hang on to her organs after death, when she has no conceivable use for them" [25]. Xenografts have enlightened and facilitated the progress toward the day when allografting can be carried out with fewer complications. For, as Frankenstein declares during the height of his excitement over his scientific studies at Ingolstadt, "… with how many things are we upon the brink of becoming acquainted, if cowardice or carelessness did not restrain our inquiries?" [1]. The courage and insight of xenograft surgeons such as Reemtsma, Starzl, and Bailey have acquainted us with the "secrets" of life, yet more food exists to fuel further discoveries.

References

1. Shelley, M. *Frankenstein.* London: Penguin Books Ltd., 1985, pp. 55–265.
2. Saunders, J. B. A conceptual history of transplantation. In *Transplantation,* edited by J. Najarian and R. Simmons. Philadelphia: Lea and Febinger, 1972, pp. 3–22.
3. Dubernard, J. M.; Flyer, M. W. Xenografts. In *Principles of Organ Transplantation,* edited by M. W. Flye. Philadelphia: Harcourt Brace Jovanovich Inc., 1989. pp. 612–633.
4. Lamb, D. *Organ Transplantation and Ethics.* London: Routledge, 1990, pp. 111–112.
5. Lyons, A.; Petrucelli, R. J. *Medicine: An Illustrated History.* New York: Henry H. Abrams, 1987, pp. 1–616.
6. Guthrie, C. C. Applications of blood vessel surgery. In *Blood Vessel Surgery.* New York: Longman's, Green and Co., p. 113, 1912.
7. Starzl, T. The future of xenotransplantation. *Surgical Resident's Newsletter.* 3(10):2–11, 1992.
8. Council on Scientific Affairs. Xenografts: review of the literature and current status. *JAMA.* 254:3353–3357, 1985.
9. Hardy, J. D.; Chavez, C. M. The first heart transplant in man: developmental animal investigation with analysis of the 1964 case in light of current clinical experience. *Am. J. Cardiol.* 22:772–781, 1968.
10. Barnard, C. N.; Wolpowitz, A.; Losman, J. G.; et al. Heterotopic cardiac transplantation with a xenograft for assistance of the left heart in cardiogenic shock after cardiopulmonary bypass. *S. Afr. Med. J.* 52:1035, 1977.
11. Starzl, T. Orthotopic heterotransplantation. In *Experience in Hepatic Transplantation.* Philadelphia: W. B. Saunders Co., pp. 408–421, 1969.
12. Reemtsma, K. Heterotransplantation. *Transplant. Proc.* 1(1):251–255, 1969.
13. Reemtsma, K. Heterograft versus xenograft (letter to the editor). *N. Eng. J. Med.* 272:380, 1965.
14. Wiener, A. S.; Moor-Jankowski, J. Blood groups in anthropoid apes and baboons. *Science.* 142:67–68, 1963.

15. Platt, J. L.; Vercellotti, A. P.; Dalmasso, A. P.; et al. Transplantation of discordant xenografts: a review of progress. *Immunol. Today.* 11:450–457, 1990.
16. Medawar, P. Sir Peter Medawar's views on transplantation. *British Med. J.* 1:373, 1968.
17. Walpoth, B. H.; Nehlsen-Cannarella, S. L.; Bailey, L. L. Xenotransplantation: extended indications for pediatric cardiac transplantation. *Transplant. Proc.* 18(4[3])0:43–44, 1986.
18. Gould, S. J. The heart of terminology: what has an obtuse debate over evolutionary logic got to do with Baby Fae? *Nat. Hist.* 97:24–28, 1988.
19. Maddox, J. (ed.) Grandstand medicine: baboon's hearts are not taboo for people, but medicine which is not essential is wrong. *Nature.* 312:88, 1984.
20. Capron, A. M. When well-meaning science goes too far. *The Hastings Center Report.* 15:8–9, 1985.
21. Reemtsma, K. Clinical urgency and media scrutiny. *The Hastings Center Report.* 15:10–11, 1985.
22. Raymond, C. A. Second cardiac xenograft predicted: questions remain on procedure. *JAMA.* 257(23):3181, 1987.
23. Annas, G. J. Baby Fae: the "anything goes" school of human experimentation. *The Hasting Center Report.* 15:15–17, 1985.
24. Regan, T. The other victim. *The Hastings Center Report.* 15:9–10, 1985.
25. Nelson, J. L. Transplantation through a glass darkly. *The Hastings Center Report.* 22:6–8, 1992.
26. Cartwright, C. The ethics of xenografting in man. In *Organ Replacement Therapy: ethics justice commerce,* edited by W. Land and J. B. Dossetor. Berlin: Springer-Verlag, 1991.
27. Niekrasz, M.; Ye, Y.; Rolf, L. L.; et al. The pig as organ donor for man. *Transplant. Proc.* 24(2):625–626, 1992.
28. Vetter, H. O.; Reichenspurner, O.; and Reichart, B. The baboon as cardiac donor in man: a reasonable approach or immoral desperate search for suitable organs? In *Organ Replacement Therapy: ethics justice commerce,* edited by W. Land and J. B. Dossetor. Berlin: Springer-Verlag, 1991.
29. Lecatsas, G.; Neetilling, F. A.; De Klerk, W. A.; et al. Filovirus seropositivity in prospective organ donor baboons. *Transplant. Proc.* 24(2):617–618, 1992.
30. Hanson, M. J. A pig in a poke. *The Hastings Center Report* 22:2, 1992.
31. Pursel, V. G.; Bolt, D. J.; Miller, K. F.; et al. Expression and performance in transgenic pigs. *J. Reprod. Fert., Suppl.* 40:235–245, 1990.
32. Associated Press. Pig liver for dying patient is defended. *NY Times.* 10-114-92 v. CXLII n.49,119 p. A16, col. 4.
33. Wielawski, I. Doctors planning more pig liver transplants. *LA Times.* 11-14-92 v. 111 p. B1, col. 2.
34. Starzl, T. Baboon-to-human liver transplantation. *Lancet* 341:65–71, 1993.
35. Auchincloss, H., Jr. Xenogeneic transplantation: a review. *Transplantation* 46:1–20, 1988.

36. Czplicki, J.; Blonska, B.; et al. The lack of hyperacute xenogeneic heart transplant rejection in a human (letter to the editor). *Journal of Heart and Lung Transplant* 11(2[1]):393–396, 1992.

Source: Rebecca Malouin, "Surgeon's Quest for Life: The History and Future of Xenotransplantation." *Perspectives in Biology and Medicine* (Spring 1994): 416–428.

EXERCISES: READING AND RESPONDING

1. Malouin uses an epigraph, a quotation from Mary Shelley's *Frankenstein*, and she refers to the Frankenstein story in the introduction and conclusion. Explain why Malouin's article would be more effective without references to, and a quotation from, a work of fiction. If you consider the passage from *Frankenstein* effective, explain what makes it so.

2. Examine how Malouin handles reporting different perspectives on the Baby Fae case.

3. How does she attempt to resolve perspectives?

4. What is Malouin's thesis? Is it stated or implied? At what point in the essay does Malouin present the thesis?

5. Is Malouin's purpose in writing the paper primarily to inform, or is it to persuade her audience? Be prepared to defend your answer by referring to specific passages in the essay.

6. Malouin was an undergraduate when she wrote this essay. How does she establish authority and credibility?

7. Do you think Malouin's intended audience would find this essay informative? interesting? Be prepared to explain why or why not.

8. You should hear the voice of a student in this essay. Characterize this voice. Identify specific words or passages that create this writer's voice.

In "Transplantation Through a Glass Darkly," James Lindemann Nelson examines the ethical dilemma of using animals as spare parts for people in need of an organ transplant.

TRANSPLANTATION THROUGH A GLASS DARKLY

JAMES LINDEMANN NELSON

SHOULD BABOONS BECOME SPARE PARTS BINS FOR HUMAN BEINGS? NOT WHEN THEIR MORAL NATURE REMAINS A MYSTERY TO US.

Bioethical problems take many different forms, and fascinate many different kinds of people. Physicians and philosophers, lawyers and theologians, policy analysts and talk show hosts are all drawn by the blend of practical urgency and moral complexity that characterize these issues.

But there seem to be only two kinds of bioethical problems that typically pull into their orbits not only theorists and practitioners, but pickets and protesters as well. When it comes to the treatment of fetuses and animals, people take to the streets. On the same day that demonstrators on both sides of the abortion issue lamented the Supreme Court's decision in *Casey,* representatives of PETA (People for the Ethical Treatment of Animals) gathered at the University of Pittsburgh to protest the implantation of a baboon's liver in a thirty-five-year-old man—the father of two children—whose own liver had been destroyed by hepatitis B virus.

There is, of course, a big difference in the way the disputes are perceived: abortion's bona fides as a central ethical issue are well established, but despite an upsurge of interest among ethicists over the past decade and a half, concern about animals still seems a bit quirky, too exclusively the domain of zealots who maintain the moral equality of all species, and thereby mark themselves as fundamentally out of sympathy with our basic ethical traditions. Here I try to pull moral consideration of nonhumans closer to the ethical center, arguing that thinking about the fate of nonhumans at our hands shares with abortion—indeed, with many of our culture's most difficult moral issues—a fundamental problem: we don't really know what we are talking about. More concretely, we're at a

loss to say what it is about baboons that makes their livers fair game, when we wouldn't dare take vital organs from those of our own species whose abilities to live rich, full lives are no greater than those of the nonhumans we seem so willing to prey upon. Unless we're able to isolate and defend the relevant moral distinction we should reject the seductive image of solving the problem of organ shortage by maintaining colonies of animals at the ready for transplantation on demand.

Moral Outliers

Public protest about abortion is not galvanized by concern about the quality of informed consent, or its impact on the doctor-patient relationship. What *does* lie at the center of the dispute is an absolutely crucial kind of ignorance. As a society, we don't know what fetuses are, and, in an important sense, we don't know what pregnant women are either. Are fetuses babies or tissue? Are pregnant women mothers bound by special duties to their unborn children, or independent adults exercising their right to make important self-regarding decisions under the protection of a mantle of privacy? Because we don't know these things, and they matter so much, we have a hard time imagining what responsible compromise might really be like.

And what gets people out into the streets in response to a daring attempt to rescue from certain death a young father of two? What, for that matter, causes medical research advocacy organizations to spend large amounts of money, not on research, but on full-page ads in the *New York*

Times defending what scientists do? Is it concerns about justice in the allocation of medical resources? Doubts about the "courage to fail" ethos? Misgivings centered around the independence of IRB review? Surely not. The ground of protest and counter-protest is a similar kind of ignorance about the fundamental terms of the relevant moral discourse: we don't know what animals are, either. We treat them as if they were morally protean; we mold them into anything from much-loved companions and symbols of virtue to mere machines for making food and instruments for scientific research.

Our ignorance as a society about these dark corners of our moral commitments, our lack of consensus about where outliers really fit, is extremely divisive when coupled with individual assurance that there is in fact available knowledge about these matters, that the answers are of surpassing importance, and that there is something suspicious, if not downright evil, about the people who don't get it. While such conclusions cripple civility, and should of course be resisted, our history should be making us nervous. We have so often gotten matters of who counts morally just flatly wrong, and have exacted horrible prices from those shuffled unjustly to the margins of our moral concern.

What fetuses are has at least received a thorough airing in the bioethics literature. Gravid women we still find quite puzzling apparently, as witness current concerns about "forced cesareans" and "maternal-fetal conflict," but at least there is an awareness that getting clear about the moral character of preg-nancy is a key to understanding the morality of pregnancy terminations. But despite their ubiquity in medical research and practice, determining what animals are is not thought of as a paradigmatic bioethics issue. Yet seeing animals clearly is likely to be at least as difficult as the analogous tasks for fetuses and pregnant women. After all, we have a strong stake in the presumption that non-humans are things whose moral status is at our discretion: the looser we can keep the moral constraints, the freer we are to do as we like with these extremely useful creatures. Further, there is a sense in which animals really are protean. Human beings are animals; so are protozoa. Drawing some moral distinctions is inescapable when facing such a range, and if there's to be a bright line between entities that really matter and those that don't, the human species may very well seem a reasonable place to draw it.

Choosing this line may appear suspiciously self-serving. Yet, at least at first glance, it looks as though there really could be something ethically serious to be said for us. We don't have to rely on the brute fact that we've got all the power; this is a comfort, as "might makes right" has a dubious history as a basis for moral distinctions. Nor do we have to resort to the bare fact of our common species membership—again, all to the good, as such purely biological bases for moral categorization also have a simply horrifying pedigree. Further, we can avoid invoking the soul as a sort of special moral talisman whose possession elevates us above all others: purely metaphysical entities aren't much use when we're trying to do ethics with an eye to public policy in a pluralistic society. Besides, imagine what we would do if someone were to argue that the subjugation of women was justified on the grounds that all and only men possess "schmouls," an empirically undetectable entity that inexplicably gives them extra moral worth.

The distinction we wish to draw between humans and the rest of creation seems much more respectable than distinctions based on might, on species, or on sectarian metaphysics. One could say that the appeal to such things as the range and power of the human intellect, the complexity and depth of our interpersonal relationships, our passions, both personal and aesthetic, our sense of morality, and of tragedy makes good sense. If these abilities and vulnerabilities don't matter morally, it's hard to imagine what would.

But if these are the characteristics that matter morally, it is not only baboons who lack them; not all of us humans have them either. Many humans have lost, or will never have, powerful intellects, deep relationships, rich passions, or the intimations of mortality. Think of the profoundly mentally ill, the comatose, and those who have sustained severe brain injuries. While such humans are themselves instances of tragedy, they have no sense of what tragedy is.

Despite this sad fact, our convictions about the importance of simply being human are so strong that we hesitate to use organs from newborns with anencephaly, a condition incompatible with either sensation or life. Given this hesitation, one can imagine the response if a leading transplant surgeon were to call for the maintenance of colonies of mentally handicapped orphans, to be well cared for until needed, but whose organs would then be "humanely" harvested for use in dying but otherwise "normal" people—infants with hypoplastic left heart syndrome, young fathers with HVB. Yet this scenario—with baboons and other primates substituting for handicapped orphans—is precisely what some transplant surgeons have been advocating since at least the 1960s, and is quite explicitly part of the agenda underlying the recent effort in Pittsburgh. If we are morally repulsed by a call to use handicapped orphans, but are eager to see whether colonies of baboons mightn't become a solution to our endemic lack of transplantable organs, it surely behooves us to have a good answer to the question. "What's so different about the two kinds of creature?"

Perhaps there is a good answer to that question—a difference, or set of overlapping differences, that will end up ethically supporting our practice. Perhaps we could, without arbitrary prejudice, keep all mentally handicapped humans, no matter how damaged or how alone in the world they might be, in the ethical family, so to speak. Perhaps it's appropriate to see all nonhumans, no matter how intelligent or complex their lives might be, as largely discretionary items, to be cast into the outer darkness if anything approaching a serious purpose seems to demand it. Or perhaps the real moral of the story here is that it is not baboons we should respect more, but humans who are their emotional and intellectual peers we should respect less; consider the research and therapeutic bonanza *that* would yield! But defending either of these conclusions would take a powerful argument, and there's very little evidence that any of the people most enthusiastically thumping the tub for more and better xenotransplantation have come up with reasons of the kind that are needed. Typically, their strategy is simply to point to the human cost of not pushing the xenograft agenda—the "three people who die every day waiting for a necessary organ" argument—without any serious attempt to balance that cost against the debit incurred to the victims of those grafts. Nor do we see much effort to set the xenograft strategy against the costs and benefits incurred by trying to enforce the required request laws that are already on the books, or to enact "presumed consent" or "routine retrieval" policies for organ procurement.

Discernment in the Dark

This, of course, returns us to our original problem: we don't even know how to begin that balancing act, and it seems that we aren't very keen on learning. A simple reliance on our moral intuitions isn't enough. As the history of medical research in the nineteenth and even twentieth century reveals, we have been more than willing to subject those who were "clearly less valuable" to the rigors of research—only then, the ones who were obviously less valuable were Jewish, or people of color. Our gut instincts simply aren't good enough as reliable moral guides when we're dealing with those whom we've pushed to the margin of moral discourse. The question is not whether we're generally able to move deftly within our ordinary understanding of morality, but whether, when it comes to the moral outliers, that ordinary understanding itself is adequate.

Cross-species transplantation crystallizes a certain kind of moral conflict between humans and other animals—perhaps too sharply. Pitting the life of the father of two against that of a baboon is sure to strike most of us as no contest. The glare of the contrast distracts us from such realities as the fact that, at the point of decisionmaking, the animal's death buys only a chance, not a guarantee, or that the outcome of acting is not always better than the outcome of refraining, even when death is inevitable if we stay our hand. If we reflect about our moral duties and liberties more broadly, it may strike us that we are apparently quite comfortable allowing many tragic deaths to occur daily, when what it would take to stop them is not the life of an intelligent animal, but merely the cost of drinks after work.

On the other hand, if we do refuse to take the baboon's life in an effort to save the human's out of a sense that the moral parity between baboons and mentally handicapped humans leaves us no other option, then we need to ask what else that sense of parity implies. The animal who provided the liver in the Pittsburgh case was at least killed in an effort to save the life of an identifiable person. But most of what we do with the lives of animals is—at best—only distantly related to the lives and health of people in general. If it is wrong to kill a baboon to try to save a man's life, is it wrong to kill a pig because sausages taste so good? To kill a kid to make elegant gloves? Critics of xenograft whose main concern is with the "sacrificed" animal may find it relatively easy to adopt vegan diets and eschew wearing leather. But do they really advocate that ill people begin a wholesale boycott of a medical system in which the training and research leading up to its quite standard offerings are, as it were, drenched in the blood of nonhumans?

The implications of all this for the development of xenograft and the creation of "donor" colonies are comparatively clear. There are numerous ways in which we might strive to save and enhance lives, including many that are more efficient than killing animals who resemble us in no small degree—ways that do not burden us by reinforcing our commitment to moral positions we do not fully understand, and may not be able to maintain. If we feel morally constrained to continue organ transplantation as an important way of saving and enhancing human lives, we ought not to try to respond to that moral challenge with the technological fix of a better antirejection drug that will allow us to use nonhumans as organ sources, but rather by figuring out better ways to engage the altruism of the human community, until at last it strikes us all as mighty peculiar that anyone would want to hang on to her organs after death, when she has no conceivable use for them.

We ought to drop xenograft research and therapy, investing the resources of human effort, ingenuity, and money it consumes elsewhere. We don't now know what the judgment of history regarding our relationship with nonhumans will be, but there's no reason to be sanguine about it. What this uncertainty says for our overall relationship with animals may still be a matter for debate, but there's no compelling need to make matters any worse.

Source: James Lindemann Nelson, "Transplantation through a Glass Darkly," *Hastings Center Report* (1992): 6–8.

EXERCISES: READING AND RESPONDING

1. Nelson claims that "there seem to be only two kinds of bioethical problems that typically pull into their orbits not only theorists and practitioners, but pickets and protesters as well." Explain whether you find this claim to be valid.

2. What is Nelson's thesis? Is it stated or implied? At what point in the essay does Nelson present the thesis?

3. Nelson's argument relies on the comparison of protest about abortion to protest about using animals for xenotransplantation, two seemingly separate issues. According to Nelson, what do these issues have in common? Identify specific passages of the essay that rely on this comparison.

4. Explain why Nelson's argument would be stronger or weaker if he concentrated only on the issue of xenotransplantation and omitted the abortion issue.

5. Arguing about ethical issues can be tricky because readers often don't agree on what is or is not ethical. At what point or points in the essay does Nelson

argue that xenotransplantation presents an ethical issue? What are the issues Nelson raises?

6. Nelson acknowledges more than one perspective on the issue of xenotransplantation. What are those perspectives? How does he reconcile them?

7. Characterize the voice you hear in this essay. What does it reveal about the writer's attitude toward his subject and intended readers?

8. Identify passages in the article that provide a context for the reader. Explain whether these passages provide sufficient information for you to follow the discussion. If you had difficulty understanding this article, point out specific passages that were confusing.

In an article published in the *New York Times*, Lawrence K. Altman, M.D., discusses the proposed bone marrow transplant from a baboon to a human and reviews some of the ethical issues raised by the experiment.

BABOON CELLS MIGHT REPAIR
AIDS-RAVAGED IMMUNE SYSTEM

LAWRENCE K. ALTMAN, M.D.

DISCOVERY MAY HELP CROSS-SPECIES GRAFTS SURVIVE IN HUMANS.

Will aids someday be treated with bone marrow—transplanted from baboons or other animals?

Scientists are taking that radical idea seriously, basing their hopes for success on the natural resistance of baboons to H.I.V., the AIDS virus, and on advances in immunology. The aim is to transfer the disease resistance to H.I.V.-infected people, bridging the species barrier. Plans are strictly in the experimental phase. If the experiment works, uninfected baboon cells will join the H.I.V.-infected human marrow and help restore the body's immune function.

Researchers at the University of Pittsburgh have just reported one such transplant of baboon bone mar-

row. It was performed two years ago on an unidentified 56-year-old man who was dying of AIDS. He asked for the procedure and the university's human experimentation committee approved it for his case only. Dr. Camillo Ricordi, a member of the team, said in an interview.

The experiment was not a success. The baboon cells failed to grow, and the man died two months later. But Dr. Ricordi said his team had been encouraged because the man did not suffer any adverse reactions from the transplant.

The case is reported in the current issue of the scientific journal Transplantation Proceedings. It was published, Dr. Ricordi said, to stimulate debate about the potential for the procedure and to get other centers interested in testing transplants with tissue from baboons or other animals that are resistant to H.I.V. Dr. Ricordi now works at the University of Miami and hopes to continue his research on transplants with baboon and other animal tissues.

"It sounds totally wild and weird," Dr. Merle Sande said. "but it is a great example of the frustration and length that people will go to try to get a breakthrough." Dr. Sande is the co-chairman of medicine at the University of California at San Francisco, which is seriously considering plans to conduct baboon bone-marrow transplants for AIDS there in collaboration with Dr. Suzanne T. Ildstad of the University of Pittsburgh.

The baboon experiments would be intended as a pilot project for a center for creative therapy that university officials are trying to establish at San Francisco General Hospital, which is part of the university. Dr. Sande said in an interview, Financing would come from the Government, donations and venture capital.

The baboon experiments for H.I.V. also reflect a new wave of enthusiasm among scientists in the field for cross-species transplants: said Dr. Anthony S. Fauci, who heads the National Institute of Allergy and infectious Diseases, a Federal agency in Bethesda, Md.

"As a concept it is very bold and avant-garde, but it is certainly worth considering." Dr. Fauci said in an interview, because it could be "potentially very beneficial."

Dr. Fauci's institute would help finance the experiments in San Francisco, and he said he had agreed to do certain tests in his laboratory as a collaborator in the research.

The San Francisco team is pinning its hopes for success on the recent discovery of a novel type of bone-marrow cell that appears to have eliminated a major complication of transplants in animal experiments and that might improve the chances for cross-species transplants. The complication is graft-versus-host disease, in which donor immune cells attack the host's tissue in a reversal of the usual rejection phenomenon, in which the immune system fends off a transplant as foreign material.

Bone marrow is the riskiest of all types of transplants, so scientists are facing unknown risks in trying to cross species. Scientists at the Federal Centers for Disease Control and Prevention in Atlanta and elsewhere are concerned that transplanted baboon cells might carry viruses that are harmless to the baboon but that could cause serious, if not fatal, illness in a human.

Since 1983, Dr. Fauci's institute has been experimenting with bone-marrow transplants between identical twins to combat H.I.V. About 50 healthy twins have donated marrow to their H.I.V.-infected siblings. Ordinarily, the recipient's marrow would be destroyed before the transplant, but this was not done with the H.I.V.-infected twins because researchers were concerned about further damaging the immune system. Most infected twins also received various anti-H.I.V. therapies.

Of the first seven transplants, performed through 1985, six recipients have died. About half of the 16 patients who got transplants in 1986 and 1987 and most of the 20 who got transplants in the last two years are living, but the researchers said it was too soon to evaluate the results for the latest group.

"There appears to be some value to keep on going, certainly something goes on to produce a variety of changes in immune function, but we have not been able to figure out how to capitalize on it," said Dr. Clifford Lane, an immunologist involved in the project. He added: "The earlier in the course of the disease the transplant is done, the more pronounced the effect seems to be yet we don't ever seem to reconstitute the immune system for any significant length of time."

Baboon-to-human transplants have also been tried for patients dying of hepatitis B, a virus that can destroy human livers but is harmless for baboons. Two baboon liver transplants were performed at the University of Pittsburgh two years ago by a team headed by Dr. Thomas Starzl, but both patients died.

The second recipient was also given baboon bone marrow, in the hope of improving the chances of a successful liver transplant by creating a hybrid immune system. Although Dr. Starzl's team has approval to perform two more of these experiments, it has not done so, Dr. Starzl said, because he is working on ways to enhance the role of chimerism in transplants. Chimeras are hybrids involving a mixture of cells from the donor and recipient.

The next round of baboon-to-human transplants is expected to use a discovery by Dr. Ildstad, a former member of Dr. Starzl's team who now works independently at the University of Pittsburgh, about how to avoid graft-versus-host disease. She has discovered a novel cell, one of about 250 cells in the marrow, that she calls a facilitating cell because it helps eliminate the risk of graft-versus-host disease in rodents. It allows the grafting of purified stem cells into genetically different recipients, including hosts of different species. Stem cells are believed to give rise to the wide variety of immune cells and oxygen-carrying red cells in the blood.

A mixture of facilitating and stem cells is "potent" in promoting grafts between different species, said Dr. Ildstad, who was trained as a pediatric transplant surgeon. She said her team had strong data to suggest that primates, including humans, also had facilitating cells.

Last fall, Dr. Ildstad, in collaboration with Dr. Nancy Ascher at the University of California at San Francisco, began administering a mixture of human facilitating and stem cells to patients receiving kidney or liver transplants. So far three individuals have received the mixture. The aim is to make the recipients better able to accept a transplanted organ.

Dr. Ildstad said her team planned to begin testing the mixture later this month at the University of Pittsburgh in bone-marrow transplants for sickle cell disease, thalassemia, enzyme deficiency disorders and leukemia.

But it is the use of baboon bone marrow that is the most radical of the human experiments that Dr. Ildstad's team hopes to undertake within a few months, at San Francisco. The researchers would modify the technique to destroy only part of the bone marrow of the H.I.V.-infected patient before the transplant. But her team still needs permission from the university's ethics committee.

Dr. Ildstad, 42, has left the drama of the operating theater for the excitement of exploring the unknown in a research laboratory. Her ultimate goal is to find a way for the body to accept transplanted organs without anti-rejection drugs, a goal she believes is realistic, she said, because it has been achieved in human bone-marrow transplants. They are the only transplanted grafts that once accepted, do not require anti-rejection therapy, Dr. Ildstad said.

But human bone-marrow transplants have been limited because of problems in matching tissue types. Only 30 percent of the people with cancers of the blood system who are candidates for bone-marrow transplants can find a donor with a suitable tissue match. So the procedure cannot be performed for 70 percent of the patients. Even when a mismatch is slight, the incidence of graft-versus-host disease approaches 100 percent and fatalities reach 80 percent. Dr. Ildstad said.

Her discovery of the facilitating cell grew out of her pursuit of the mechanism responsible for the failure of bone-marrow grafts.

Other scientists had identified a type of white blood cell known as T cells as responsible for producing graft-versus-host disease. To reduce the incidence of the complication, transplant doctors removed T cells from donated marrow before giving it to patients. But in up to 70 percent of the recipients, the grafts failed to take, and the patients died.

Dr. Ildstad deduced that the T cell depletion step must remove something essential to the survival of the graft, and she went on to discover that it was the facilitating cell. When, in cross-species animal transplants, she filtered out the T cells from bone marrow but left the facilitating cells, the transplanted bone marrow thrived in its new home.

Dr. Paul Volberding, an AIDS expert at San Francisco General Hospital, said that the team had yet to decide which patients would get the experimental baboon transplants.

Ethically, it would be easier to justify the baboon experiment for someone who was dying of AIDS than for an otherwise healthy H.I.V.-infected individual because the experiment could cause an earlier death, Dr. Fauci said. When faced with such a dilemma, he explained, scientists tend to offer the experiment first to those who are close to death.

Source: Lawrence K. Altman, M.D., "Baboon Cells Might Repair AIDS-Ravaged Immune System," *New York Times* 19 Jul. 1994: 3C.

EXERCISES: READING AND RESPONDING

1. Explain whether Altman's purpose is to inform or to persuade. Cite specific passages that illustrate your answer.

2. Altman introduces readers to physicians and medical research specialists. Which names appear most frequently in Altman's discussion?

3. How does Altman answer the question he poses in the first paragraph: "Will AIDS someday be treated with bone marrow transplanted from baboons or other animals?"

4. In your opinion, does Altman seem to be in favor of continuing the baboon bone marrow transplants or against this kind of experimentation? Cite specific passages that support your response.

5. Identify passages that provide either a historic or scientific context for xeno-transplantation. Evaluate Altman's success in making a complex scientific issue accessible to a broad, general readership.

6. Use this article to start a list of key terms used in the discussion of xenotransplantation.

The following sources review decisions that the Food and Drug Administration made about xenotransplantation in 1993 and 1995, respectively.

FDA PUTS THE BRAKES ON XENOTRANSPLANTS

RACHAEL NOWAK

The Food and Drug Administration (FDA) has signaled that it intends to regulate the transplant of animal organs into humans—and in so doing has put itself on a collision course with AIDS activists. On 27 April, the FDA suspended plans for a clinical trial to determine whether transplants of baboon bone marrow can repair the devastated immune systems of AIDS patients. FDA's concern: Such xenotransplants might enable animal viruses to infect humans, potentially unleashing a pandemic as devastating as the disease they are trying to cure. Martin Delaney, founding director of San Francisco's influential AIDS activist group Project inform, immediately objected to FDA's move, characterizing it as "comic-book hysteria."

Despite such criticism, the action indicates that FDA is likely to take a close look at other experiments designed to pave the way for using animal organs to overcome the dire shortage of human organs available for transplant (*Science,* 18 November 1994, p. 1148). Transplant surgeons fear that FDA's involvement could slow down advances in the rapidly evolving field of animal-to-human transplants, or even bring them to a halt. FDA regulation "could stop [transplant] science cold," says transplant surgeon Ira Fox of the University of Nebraska in Omaha, although, he says, "it could be a good thing;... it could help get the data [on viral transmission] we need."

As it wades into the transplant business, FDA is reaching uncharted regulatory waters. Until now, new surgical procedures have required approval only from local Institutional Review Boards (IRBs) and other institutional panels. But FDA officials decided to act when they learned that AIDS physicians Steven Deeks and Paul Volberding of the University of California, San Francisco (UCSF), and transplant surgeon and immunologist Suzanne Ildstad of the University of Pittsburgh had gotten the go-ahead from UCSF's IRB to transplant baboon bone marrow into AIDS patients. FDA asked the researchers to attend the 27 April meeting, where it became clear, says Deeks, that FDA was requesting that his team formally apply for an Investigational New Drug (IND) approval—just as if the bone marrow were an untested new drug.

Baboons are resistant to HIV infection, so the UCSF-Pittsburgh team, which had intended to start the trial as early as last month, aimed to find out whether transplanted baboon bone marrow—the source of immune cells—could help repair immune systems damaged by the AIDS virus. But FDA fears that the baboon cells may carry viruses that are harmless to their natural baboon host, but which pose an unpredictable and potentially devastating threat to the human population. "It's become clear to the agency … and to the rest of the Public Health Service that not enough discussion has taken place about the possibility of a pandemic occurring because of the use of baboon tissue," says Philip Noguchi, head of FDA's Division of Cell and Gene Therapy, which seeks to regulate animal organ transplants.

By asking the Volberding-Ildstad group to apply for IND approval, the FDA effectively imposed a long delay on the experiment, because the approval process will entail, among other things, supplying FDA with details on viral transfer in the few previous transplants of animal livers, hearts, and other organs, including baboon bone marrow. But as there are almost no published data on viral transfer in animal-to-human organ transplants, it could take months to collect the information, if it exists at all, says Deeks. "The protocol will be delayed substantially," he says.

But despite his frustration, Deeks has no quarrel with FDA's scrutiny of the potential risks. "Everything brought up [at the FDA meeting] was very fair," he says, but "some [in the AIDS community] will be very upset." Indeed, when Project Inform's Delaney first learned that the agency was considering asking the Ildstad-Volberding group to apply for IND approval, he shot off a letter to FDA Commissioner David Kessler, urging that FDA avoid "needlessly flex[ing] its regulatory might" when AIDS research is at stake.

Noguchi argues, however, that FDA has a responsibility under the Public Health Service Act to step in if a new therapy carries an infectious disease risk or involves the extensive manipulation of cells outside a patient's body (Science, 6 January, p. 19). The agency plans to hold a public meeting sometime in the next few weeks to discuss "the [Volberding-Ildstad] protocol in light of the larger public health issues," says Noguchi.

But experts close to FDA say it won't set safety guidelines until after a committee of the Institute of Medicine (IOM) holds a meeting, scheduled for 25 to 27 June, on the social, ethical, and scientific implications of animal-to-human organ transplants, including the feasibility of screening donor animals for as-yet-unidentified infectious agents. The IOM committee, which is partially sponsored by FDA, plans to release a report on the topic this fall.

Other institutions are keeping close tabs on these deliberations. Early this year a decision that involved senior administrators at Columbia Presbyterian Medical Center in New York City stopped a plan by a team led by that institution's Robert Michler to test baboon heart transplants as a bridge to keep alive babies with heart failure until a human organ could be found. The officials made the decision because of concerns about "protecting public health," says Ralph Dell, chair of Columbia's Institutional Animal Care and Use Committee. Since then, Columbia has created two independent expert committees to ponder the risks of animal organ transplants and is now awaiting the outcome of the FDA's ruminations.

Noguchi believes that delaying the transplants is appropriate. "There's ample evidence that viruses show their worse characteristics when they jump from their [original] host," he says. "It's a very real public health concern."

Source: Rachael Nowak, "FDA Puts the Brakes on Xenotransplants," *Science* 5 May 1993: 630–31.

FDA PANEL OKs
BABOON MARROW TRANSPLANT

ELIZABETH PENNISI

A panel of scientific experts recommended last week that the U.S. Food and Drug Administration (FDA) allow San Francisco AIDS patient Jeff Getty to receive a transplant of bone marrow from a baboon. The panel acknowledged that the procedure may carry public health risks, but decided that this long-shot treatment should be attempted anyway. The Biological Response Modifiers Advisory Committee also proposed guidelines for future transplants of animal organs and tissues into humans.

If the FDA accepts the recommendation on the marrow transplant, as expected, it could take place "immediately," says transplant developer Suzanne Ildstad of the University of Pittsburgh. She doesn't know exactly how long it will take to provide the additional data the agency wants, however. The hope is that the transplant will restore Getty's immune function, as the AIDS virus does not infect baboon immune cells.

AIDS activists and Ildstad were pleasantly surprised by the decision. "We didn't expect them to come to a conclusion that rapidly," Ildstad said afterward. After the FDA put a hold on the experiment earlier this spring (*Science,* 5 May, p. 630), proponents of the transplant had worried that Getty's treatment would be delayed for months, if not years, just as the first gene-therapy trials were delayed almost a decade ago because of the potential risks involved.

So far, the concerns about gene therapy have not been borne out, but infectious-disease experts argue that there's compelling evidence that xeno-transplants may not prove so innocuous. "If you don't want to risk the public health, then don't do it," said panel member Jonathan S. Allan, a virologist at the Southwest Foundation for Biomedical Research in San Antonio. He and others worry that viruses from the primate donor might infect human populations. They note that the AIDS virus itself likely originated in a nonhuman primate host. The hantavirus cases in the United States and Ebola virus outbreaks in Africa are also evidence of the deadly nature of some transspecies infections, warned officials from the Centers for Disease Control and Prevention in Atlanta. Particularly worrisome, testified virologist Stephen Morse of Rockefeller University, is the possibility that new infectious agents can go undetected until after they have spread from person to person.

Even though the committee members agreed that xenotransplants present a public health risk, particularly when the donors are primates, they were swayed in part by the pleas of Getty's supporters. The committee voted unanimously (with Allan abstaining) to permit the transplant. "From the public health point of view, this is probably the safest xenotransplant protocol," said panel member Hugh Auchincloss Jr., a transplant surgeon at Massachusetts General Hospital in Boston. He and others cautioned that the chances of the transplant prolonging Getty's life are slim. But if he does recover, the risk that he will spread an unknown pathogen to others will be minimized by the precautions taken to protect bone marrow recipients from infection, combined with measures, including practicing safe sex, Getty and others take to prevent the spread of HIV. As long as Getty understands the risks, then he and his doctors should decide whether to proceed, the committee concluded.

The committee did not require any further safeguards to protect health workers and others coming in contact with Getty from potential infections. But they did recommend that tissues from him, the donor baboon, and those who care for him be collected and stored for testing should a problem develop.

These experts considered only Ildstad's proposal, but several other baboon marrow transplants are waiting in the wings. And researchers want to try using other types of xenotransplants to get around shortages of human hearts, livers, and other organs (*Science,* 18 November 1994, p. 1148).

Although the FDA currently has authority to regulate only the transplant of cells and not of solid organs, it is developing guidelines to address concerns about all xenotransplant experiments. The agency will continue to evaluate cellular xenotransplant proposals, but will rely on local research oversight committees to use these guidelines for judging the merits and risks of solid organ xenotransplants.

Based on the committee's recommendations, these guidelines, a draft of which will be available this summer, will require that donor animals be as free as possible of specific pathogens, specify care and quarantine standards for suppliers of donor animals and transplant centers, and urge that blood samples from the donor and recipient—and perhaps those who care for the transplant recipients—be screened for the appearance of unusual pathogens and archived. These data should become part of an international registry. The scientists at this meeting thought these guidelines should preclude the need for a national oversight group similar to the Recombinant DNA Advisory Committee or for new regulations.

Elizabeth Pennisi is a free-lance science writer in Takoma Park, Maryland.

Source: Elizabeth Pennisi, FDA Panel OKs Baboon Marrow Transplant. *Science* 21 Jul. 1995: 293–94.

EXERCISES: THINKING CRITICALLY

1. In one or two paragraphs, summarize the reasons the FDA "put the brakes on xenotransplants" in 1993. Your audience is a group of university students and faculty; they are not familiar with the *Science* article, and may not be familiar with the Getty case.

2. In one or two paragraphs, summarize the reasons the FDA panel approved the baboon bone marrow transplant. Your audience is the same as the one designated above.

3. Using the articles you've read so far, make a list of individuals and organizations in favor of continuing baboon bone marrow transplants and a list of those opposed.

Kathy Snow Guillermo responded to the FDA's decision to approve the Jeff Getty baboon bone marrow transplant. Guillermo is a staff writer for People for the Ethical Treatment of Animals.

BABOON MARROW TRANSPLANTS: FRANKENSTEIN SCIENCE

KATHY SNOW GUILLERMO

The Food and Drug Administration stamped its approval last week on a bone marrow transplant from a baboon to Jeff Getty, 38, an Oakland man with AIDS.

The procedure is so highly experimental that even the doctor who will perform the transplant, UCSFs Dr. Steven Deeks, calls it a "long shot."

It raises a lot of questions, most as yet unanswered by the FDA and Deeks.

One thing is certain. Despite its humanitarian appearance, the FDA's decision plays a cruel hoax on the public and people with AIDS: It gives an illusion of hope where none exists.

Everyone wants the FDA to quit spinning its wheels of bureaucracy and move forward with experimental treatments that may help people with AIDS. But why should the agency approve Frankenstein science destined for failure?

Several well-publicized bone marrow searches in recent years have shown how difficult it is just to find two humans with compatible marrow.

The best chances for a match are between siblings. What are the odds against success when the donor and recipient are different species? The FDA's silence on this issue borders on the irresponsible.

But when it comes to cross-species transplants, the FDA and the medical community are quiet about a lot of things.

It's not generally known, for example, that when doctors transplanted a baboon heart into an infant girl called Baby Fae, a human heart was available. The baby's parents weren't told.

The doctors who recently stitched a baboon liver into a man with hepatitis claimed an amazing new drug would suppress the patient's immune system and decrease the chance of rejection.

Doctors didn't bother to mention that the patient was also HIV-positive. His immune system already was weak, thus calling into question

the significance of the "wonder" drug and the premise for the surgery.

The result of these two celebrated cases was loss of life—two humans and two baboons. If the facts had been made public and cross-species transplants had not been attempted, at least three of those beings might still be alive.

But full disclosure of the circumstances surrounding these deaths might hamper experimenters' penchant for treating desperately ill people and perfectly healthy animals as little more than living test tubes.

In addition to the obvious lack of scientific merit, the ethics of killing some animals and tinkering with the lives of other (human) animals should be part of the transplant debate.

If baboons are so similar to people that doctors want to use their organs for replacement parts, don't they also deserve some of the same moral consideration extended to their human relatives?

The "donor" baboons, after all, are living, thinking, feeling beings with complex social lives and needs. They don't volunteer to become "designer tissue" at the local laboratory.

I know people who suffer from AIDS, cancer fibrosis, diabetes and other often-fatal diseases.

They want to get well; they hope for treatments and cures. But they also bitterly resent being used as the excuse for maiming and killing millions of animals in laboratories.

They believe in modern science. They know that cutting-edge research takes place on the cellular level, in test tubes—even on the computer screen.

They understand that information about disease is best derived from epidemiologic studies. That's how the links were revealed between diet and heart disease, smoking and cancer—two top killers.

They remain steadfast in their belief that scientists shouldn't hurt some in order to help others.

The FDA and the medical community would have us believe they must choose between baboons and people with AIDS to remain at the forefront of medical science. But they're really choosing bad science over good, callousness over compassion.

The result will be a devastating waste of precious lives, time and resources. It will do no one any good, least of all the patient, who deserves legitimate treatment, not false hope.

Orinda writer Kathy Snow Guillermo, a staff worker for People for the Ethical Treatment of Animals, is author of "Monkey Business: The Disturbing Case That Launched the Animal Rights Movement."

Source: Kathy Snow Guillermo, "Baboon Marrow Transplants: Frankestein Science," *San Francisco Examiner* 4 Aug. 1995.

FOCUS ON RELATED ISSUES: FRANKENSTEIN SCIENCE

People for the Ethical Treatment of Animals called xenotransplantations "Frankenstein Science," suggesting that researchers conducting the transplants were practicing bad science. You see the name *Frankenstein* invoked in headlines when doctors or researchers experiment with life forms and the end result is something that seems unnatural. For example, the British press dubbed genetically altered corn *Frankenfood.* The genetically modified corn is more resistant to disease and insects than regular corn. It also promises a bigger yield than a regular crop. Proponents argue that genetically altered corn will allow us to feed a constantly growing world population. Opponents claim that we don't know the risk of eating genetically altered food. It may pose a real threat to our health and environment, but right now we aren't aware of the repercussions of biotech food.

Environmentalists are at the forefront of the battle against genetically engineered crops. They believe cross-pollination will kill or cause harmful changes to species. They also charge that the biotechnology industry is more concerned with making money than it is with the environment or human health issues. Despite the environmentalists' campaign, biotechnology continues to develop enhanced vegetables full of megadoses of vitamins and minerals and more "Frankenfood" in the form of rice, soybeans, tomatoes, and cucumbers.

Working on your own, develop a topic on recent advancements in biotechnology. Review perspectives on the issues your topic raises and attempt to reconcile any opposing perspectives.

EXERCISES: READING AND RESPONDING

1. Guillermo believes that the FDA's approval of the baboon bone marrow transplant is a "cruel hoax" that "gives an illusion of hope where none exists." How does Guillermo defend her position? Explain whether this defense is adequate or inadequate.

2. Characterize the voice you hear in this article. What does it reveal about the writer's attitude toward her subject and intended readers?

3. Identify passages of the article that appeal to readers' intellect, emotions, or sense of ethics.

4. Explain whether Guillermo's article is convincing, unconvincing, or thought provoking.

5. Identify any passages that attempt to reconcile the two opposing perspectives on this issue.

Before Jeff Getty's operation, Thaddeus Herrick reported the objections raised by virologist Jonathan Allan of the Southwest Foundation for Biomedical Research in San Antonio.

FEAR OF THE UNKNOWN

THADDEUS HERRICK

VIROLOGIST SOUNDS ALARM
ABOUT TRANSPLANT FROM BABOON

San Antonio—A baboon bone marrow transplant may be the last best hope in Jeff Getty's fight against AIDS, but a scientist involved in the experiment warns that using animal donors to treat humans may invite an epidemic just as deadly.

Virologist Jonathan Allan of San Antonio's Southwest Foundation for Biomedical Research fears that Getty's operation next month could allow an unknown animal virus— harmless to baboons but fatal to man—through the human door.

"You're essentially transplanting a whole ecosystem of potential pathogens," said Allan, a leading critic of cross-species transplants. "There's no predicting what will happen."

Allan, however, offers a frightening scenario. The virus spreads like brushfire before experts can identify it. Like AIDS, it fast becomes an epidemic.

That such a warning should come from Allan is, at the very least, unsettling. He is—despite his views—a central figure in Getty's recently approved operation, having screened the research center's 3,000 or so baboons for one that is relatively virus-free.

Allan and others settled on a 7-year-old, 62-pound baboon of the Olive species that was shipped to doctors at the University of Pittsburgh on Aug. 29. There, its bone marrow will be extracted, likely killing the animal. The transplant is scheduled for sometime in October at a San Francisco hospital.

Because baboons share a likeness with humans, the doctors are betting that the cells within its marrow will replace the 38-year-old Oakland, Calif, man's beleaguered immune system. And because baboons are resistant to HIV, doctors reason that the new bone marrow will help Getty fight AIDS.

Experts say the operation, the second of its kind, is a long shot. In 1992, University of Pittsburgh doctors tried unsuccessfully to treat an AIDS patient with baboon bone marrow. The patient, a 56-year-old man, died shortly afterward.

Still, experts say xenotransplantation—or species-to-species transplantation—is well suited to AIDS patients because their depleted immune systems make them less likely to reject donor bone marrow. In Getty's case, doctors intend to further suppress his immune system with radiation and drugs to allow the baboon bone marrow to take.

But Allan said a patient with a suppressed immune system is the last person you want receiving animal bone marrow. Because Getty lacks sufficient antibodies. Allan fears a virtual army of viruses will be ushered into the AIDS patient's body. Those, in turn, could take hold in the human population, spreading uncontrolled before being detected.

"You're doing everything you possibly can to ensure you're getting a new viral infection," he said.

Allan's comments would seem to undermine the mission of the South-west Foundation for Biomedical Research, home to the world's largest baboon colony. Twice the foundation has provided baboon livers for human transplants. And in 1985 it provided the baboon heart that went to a California infant known as Baby Fae. Though none of the recipients lived for more than a few weeks, the research center gained national prominence for its part in advancing medicine.

But the foundation, a private, nonprofit organization on San Antonio's western edge, has so far allowed Allan his point of view with little rebuke.

"We believe in academic freedom," said Stacy Maloney, a spokesman for the foundation. "That's the way we were taught when we were in college."

Others have been less tolerant. Suzanne Ildstad, the doctor who will perform Getty's transplant, said unequivocally that the experiment will not introduce "the first and quite possibly last great plague of the 21st century," a claim Allan made last March but one that he now suggests was an overstatement.

Still, the urgency of Allan's warnings raises questions about why he is involved with the Getty operation and a research center that has helped advance species-to-species transplants.

Xenotransplantation, however, is just one of many scientific pursuits at the Southwest Foundation for Biomedical Research, an academic-like facility that attracts some of the country's top scientists. Allan himself studies primate retroviruses that cause disease—particularly AIDS—in humans.

As for the Getty experiment, Allan's expertise made him an obvious candidate to screen baboon donor candidates. To refuse to participate, he said, would be irresponsible.

"I'm against the experiment," Allan said. "But that doesn't mean I shouldn't do everything I can in the interest of public health."

Allan's critics wonder why all the fuss. With tens of thousands of people dying each year because of a shortage of donor organs, they say, xenotransplantation provides hope where there is little.

What's more, they say, the shortage of donor organs is rapidly growing worse. Half the people who would benefit from heart transplants die. The waiting list for liver transplants has jumped from 827 at the beginning of 1990 to more than 5,000 today.

"If we're not threatening the human race," said Ildstad, who is based at the University of Pittsburgh, "then the worst we can predict is that you might live an additional 10 to 20 years to find you have something like hepatitis."

Though the Getty case has intensified the debate over species-to-species transplants, doctors have been experimenting with the procedure since the turn of the century. Their work using the organs of baboons, chimpanzees and pigs in the last 30 years has shown promise but little long-term success.

The more than 30 people who have received animal organs have all died. Allan is pulling for science, but he has also found relief in its failure. Should the recipients of animal donors live, he fears the spread of viruses previously unknown to man.

Consider medical history. Allan said. Several viruses are thought to have jumped from animals to humans, including the Ebola that killed hundreds in Zaire this year. Scientists believe that virus came from a nonhuman primate.

Allan draws the greatest lesson from AIDS, another disease experts believe was contracted through contact with nonhuman primates in Africa. His research centers on "the next generation of human AIDS viruses"—monkey viruses that are genetically related yet distinct from the one that causes AIDS.

Like HIV, Allan foresees a virus that remains latent for years. By the time the virus results in disease, he says, thousands could die. Though he recognizes that this sounds like something out of the recent Hollywood thriller, *Outbreak,* Allan said his ghastly scenario should not be underestimated.

"This is not science fiction." he said. "If you don't know what to look for, how can you screen it?"

Allan may be the most vocal critic of xenotransplantation, but he is not the only voice of caution among virologists, a group he contends has been largely ignored in the debate over the merits of species-to-species transplants.

"There is good reason to be concerned," said Stephen Morse, a virologist at New York's Rockefeller University. "The question is whether the potential benefit of the procedure outweighs the risk."

Proponents of such science say precautions—much like those used by people who are HIV-positive—can be taken to ensure that unknown viruses spread no further than the patient. In fact, they say, patients living with animal organs do so under guidelines designed to isolate potential viruses.

"The implication is that these people are going to be socially irresponsible," said Ildstad. "I think that's insulting."

In Getty's case, and in the case of thousands of people dying from AIDS, Ildstad said there is little to lose in xenotransplantation.

"When there is no hope in sight for a cure, a number of approaches need to be tried," she said.

That is also the argument of AIDS activists, who pressed a Food and Drug Administration advisory panel considering the Getty case to approve the baboon transplant in late June. The panel—on which Allan sat—backed the procedure on the condition that Getty be the sole participant and that he be closely monitored.

Allan abstained from the vote, and now said his fellow panelists bowed to political pressure. "Some people have turned this into a political issue when it's a scientific one," he said.

"No one wants to see an increased public health risk," responded Brenda Lein, a spokeswoman for the San Francisco-based Project Inform, who testified before the advisory panel. "When you have one disease like AIDS, you certainly don't want another."

Then stop the experiment, said Allan. He said a virus such as AIDS, which causes no overt disease in monkeys, could be waiting in the baboon.

"Let's face it," he said, "rarely do people have the foresight not to go ahead because of the risk."

Experts predict Getty's body will most likely reject the baboon bone marrow, causing death. But Getty's doctors feel they must take that chance—among other, perhaps larger risks—for the sake of modern medicine.

Said Ildstad. "There are always going to be unknowns."

Source: Thaddeus Herrick, "Fear of the Unknown," *Houston Chronicle* 10 Sep. 1995: 1A.

EXERCISES: READING AND RESPONDING

1. What perspectives does Herrick cover?
2. Does Herrick's article appeal primarily to readers' intellect, emotions, or ethics?
3. What claims does Jonathan Allan make about the dangers of xenotransplantation? Explain whether he provides sufficient evidence to support them.
4. Identify passages that provide a context for the reader. Explain whether the context seems sufficient or insufficient.
5. Characterize Allan's voice. What does it reveal about his attitude toward his subject? In your opinion, does Herrick share this attitude?

The following article reports on Jeff Getty's health and brings readers up-to-date on the success of the transplant.

HOSPITAL TO RELEASE PATIENT WHO RECEIVED BABOON CELLS

LAWRENCE K. ALTMAN

MAN SURVIVES RISKIEST STAGE OF EXPERIMENT

The man who received a highly risky experimental bone marrow transplant from a baboon three weeks ago is expected to be discharged from a hospital in San Francisco today, his doctors said.

But they said it was too soon to know whether the baboon cells had begun to grow and function immunologically. The hope is that the baboon cells, which are resistant to H.I.V.-1, the main AIDS virus, will help restore function to his immune system, which had been severely weakened by AIDS.

The man, Jeff Getty, passed what his doctors considered the riskiest period of the experimental transplant without experiencing any significant complications of the procedure. It was performed on Dec. 14 at San Francisco General Hospital, a unit of the University of California at San Francisco. The last three weeks were particularly risky for Mr. Getty, 38, because the chemotherapy and radiation he received as conditioning therapy before the transplant further suppressed his immune system.

Mr. Getty plans to hold a news conference before going to his home in the East Bay area and return to the hospital for checkups three times a week.

"From Jeff's point of view, health-wise, things have gone better than expected," Dr. Steven Deeks, one of the chief investigators, said in an interview.

A number of tests have shown no evidence of new infection and Mr. Getty's white blood count has returned to the level it was before the transplant, Dr. Deeks said. The white count dipped temporarily as a result of the conditioning therapy.

Mr. Getty has shown no evidence of rejection or a potentially fatal type of reaction known as acute graft versus host disease, which, Dr. Deeks said, probably would have occurred by now.

However, Mr. Getty still faces the risk of chronic graft versus host disease, which often occurs several months after a transplant, if it develops. Bone marrow transplant specialists will examine Mr. Getty twice a week for this and other complications. Dr. Deeks will examine him once a week.

As part of the experiment, Mr. Getty received so-called facilitator cells that were processed from the baboon's marrow by a team headed by Dr. Suzanne T. Ildstad of the University of Pittsburgh. She has reported that the cells prevent graft versus host disease in bone marrow transplants.

Cultures of Mr. Getty's blood, throat and urine have yielded only the cytomegalovirus that he had before the transplant. Dr. Deeks said. Tests showed that the baboon did not have that virus.

Out of public health considerations, the researchers plan to continue studies to monitor Mr. Getty for evidence of any infection that might have been transmitted to him from the baboon tissue.

Although Mr. Getty's white blood count dropped after the conditioning, it did not go as low as the researchers had expected. However, the number of a special type of immune cells known as lymphocytes did drop.

One concern, Dr. Deeks said, is that the amount of conditioning may have been too low to allow the baboon marrow to grow and function in Mr. Getty. In designing the experiment, the researchers purposely gave him the lowest amount of conditioning that experts thought would be safe and effective for someone with advanced AIDS. However, Mr. Getty and the researchers knew it might he too low.

The doctors will not give Mr. Getty further conditioning treatment. But if the amount was too low for Mr. Getty and if the Food and Drug Administration and ethics committees agreed to permit continuation of the research. Dr. Deeks said his team would give a larger dose to the next patient.

Source: Lawrence K. Altman, "Hospital to Release Patient Who Received Baboon Cells," *New York Times* 4 Jan. 1996: 10 B.

EXERCISE: THINKING CRITICALLY

In one or two paragraphs, summarize the outcome of the baboon bone marrow transplant.

CROSS-SPECIES TRANSPLANTS RAISE CONCERNS ABOUT HUMAN SAFETY

LAWRENCE K. ALTMAN

CRITICS WORRY THAT NEW DISEASES MAY EMERGE IN MAN FROM INFECTIOUS AGENTS IN ANIMALS.

Now that Jeff Getty has gone home from the San Francisco hospital where he received an experimental transplant of baboon bone marrow, and other cross-species transplants are pending elsewhere, two questions arise: Will animal viruses carried in transplanted tissues be able to infect humans? And if so, will they be able to engender new diseases like AIDS, which may have reached humans from monkeys?

Federal health officials and many experts in infectious diseases and transplant surgery believe such risks are very low, but not quantifiable, and are offset by the potential benefits of cross-species transplants that some experts estimate may reach 100,000 a year to combat a variety of diseases.

But critics worry that new diseases may emerge in man from reservoirs of infectious agents in animals, and that the more closely the donor species are related to man, the higher the theoretical risk.

Moreover, grafting tissue directly into the body, especially in patients whose immune systems have been suppressed to foster acceptance of a transplant, creates an ideal circumstance for an animal virus to infect humans. A virus can be most deadly when it has jumped to a new host species. Although recipients can be monitored for the infectious agents known to occur in the donor animal, unknown infectious agents are harder to spot.

Health officials are taking these issues seriously because many scientists say they are at the dawn of an era in cross-species transplants, a field known as xenotransplantation.

With the prospect that a number of xenotransplants will be done in coming months, Dr. Jonathan S. Allan, who works at the Southwest Foundation for Biomedical Research in San Antonio, which supplied the baboon for Mr. Getty's transplant, has sounded an alarm about the theoretical risk that known or unknown animal viruses may infect human recipients and then be transmitted to other people.

Yet even Dr. Allan, who has criticized xenotransplants for four years, said he did not believe that one case would lead to an epidemic.

In trying to determine what is an acceptable risk, federally sponsored

and other expert committees met last year to evaluate the potential hazards. Government health officials insisted that several experts and independent committees review the baboon bone marrow experiment before researchers from the University of California at San Francisco and the University of Pittsburgh could perform it. Mr. Getty, 38, who has AIDS, underwent the procedure on Dec. 14 at San Francisco General Hospital.

Officials of the United States Public Health Service plan to issue guidelines soon to help guard against infectious hazards from xenotransplants. A final draft is under review at the Centers for Disease Control and Prevention, the Food and Drug Administration and the National Institutes of Health.

The proposed Federal guidelines are expected to put primary responsibility on the researchers carrying out a xenotransplant and to demand that they gain approval from an independent committee, which has not been precisely defined.

Dr. Allan criticized the guidelines because, he said, many ethics committees that monitor human experiments lack expertise; and the guidelines do not call for strong Federal oversight and provide few real safeguards against the introduction and spread of new infectious diseases in the human population.

"Once the door is opened and a new virus is unleashed, it will be a monumental task to identify a new pathogen, develop adequate screening tests and prevent the spread of that new infection." Dr. Allan wrote in the January issue of Nature Medicine.

Dr. Allan also said that scientists and public officials had not given enough thought to potential hazards at a time of growing concern about the threat posed by emerging infections like AIDS; the AIDS virus is believed to have crossed from primates to humans in some unknown way at some unknown time. Many others share his concern about the threat. But those who go so far as prohibiting all but pigs as sources for xenotransplants have not spoken publicly or in interviews.

Experts in transplantation and infectious diseases acknowledge many of the possible risks described by Dr. Allan and others, but regard them as being theoretical and hard to assess. Given this lack of knowledge, they say, it is best to proceed with caution and carefully monitor the early patients, as is being done with Mr. Getty.

Dr. Ralph Dell, who is helping prepare a report on xenotransplantation from the Institute of Medicine of the National Academy of Sciences, said that he had called 75 virologists and infectious-disease experts and that only two, including Dr. Allan, had opposed xenotransplants because of the infection threat.

"The consensus was that it was a potential problem, but O.K. to proceed cautiously because it could be handled with appropriate surveillance," said Dr. Dell, an infectious-diseases expert and chairman of a committee overseeing the use of animals at Columbia University in New York City.

Dr. Philip D. Noguchi, an official of the Food and Drug Administration, who is concerned about the risk, said he and his colleagues were "struck that there has not been a more unified outcry about the infectious-disease aspect of" xenotransplants.

The specter that xenotransplants may contribute to the threat of new diseases pits the field of emerging diseases against that of xenotransplants.

After beating a retreat following a highly publicized, unsuccessful effort in 1984 to transplant a baboon heart into a 15-day-old infant known as Baby Fae at Loma Linda University Medical Center in California, transplant surgeons are relying on new scientific advances in an effort to relieve a severe organ donor shortage caused by successes in transplanting human organs.

Researchers at Columbia, for example, hope to perform experimental baboon heart transplants on children and adults too small for the mechanical devices used to boost failing hearts. Elsewhere, researchers are working with four small biotechnology companies to develop pigs as potential organ sources for humans.

Significant hurdles remain to be overcome in all xenograft research. But scientists say that if the research succeeds an unlimited supply of animal organs may be developed. Surgeons could then perform transplants on an elective, rather than an emergency, basis. Many people could also avoid the emotional suffering when brain-dead relatives and friends are kept on life support systems until their organs can be harvested.

Baboon cells are resistant to infection with H.I.V.-1, the AIDS virus most common in humans. Mr. Getty's transplant is intended to test whether baboon marrow cells can boost an AIDS patient's damaged immune system. If the San Francisco researchers succeeded against immense odds, demand for such xenotransplants could be huge. But further reviews would be needed before more could be performed.

Scientists have long known that viruses that are harmless for one species can cause fatal disease in another. For example, humans have developed fatal inflammation of the brain from bites from rhesus monkeys that have transmitted the herpes B virus, which produces only minor problems in the animal. The herpes saimiri virus, which is harmless in squirrel monkeys, quickly produces cancers of the lymph and blood system after being injected into owl monkeys and other species.

Drugs used to prevent rejection of transplanted organs weaken the immune system and make recipients more vulnerable to infections. Xenotransplants guarantee introduction of an animal virus into a human because all species, including humans, have what are known as endogenous viruses, or viruses that originate internally, that are part of their genetic makeup.

Could endogenous animal and human viruses mix in a transplant recipient and through a process known as recombination create a new agent? No one knows. Animals also acquire viruses from the environment. Precisely which infectious agents can infect across species barriers, and how often? How would the human immune system react to them? Again, no one knows.

The range of scenarios is wide. Microbes transmitted in a transplant might do nothing. They might infect without causing any symptoms. Or they might cause disease, including

cancer, which certainly would be of direct concern to the recipient.

But the risk theoretically could extend to the community if an infected recipient was able to transmit an infectious agent to others.

The steps that are being taken to monitor Mr. Getty for known and unknown infectious agents are those expected to be called for in the forthcoming Federal guidelines.

Dr. Marian G. Michaels, an infectious disease expert at the University of Pittsburgh, heads a team there and at other institutes in the United States that tested the baboon for a long list of infectious agents and that is testing blood and other samples from Mr. Getty. So far he has not been found to harbor any infectious agent that was not known to be present before the transplant. Blood and other tissues from the baboon, which was euthanized, and from Mr. Getty are being frozen for later testing if Mr. Getty develops an infection or new tests are developed.

To help protect public health, scientists at the Federal disease centers in Atlanta have developed new tests to look for unknown retroviruses, the family that includes H.I.V., and that are of prime concern in xenotransplants. But the testing has been on hold, a casualty of the Government shutdown.

Of particular concern are socalled foamy viruses that belong to the retrovirus family, which includes H.I.V., and that are present in the overwhelming majority of adult baboons. The baboon used for Mr. Getty was selected because it did not contain a foamy virus, but that step came about only through criticisms raised at an F.D.A. meeting. Dr. Allan said he knew of no other baboons at his institute that were free of foamy viruses and available for future transplants. Efforts to develop colonies free of foamy viruses would take years and produce only a small number of such baboons, he said.

But the hazards of foamy viruses are unknown because they have never been linked to disease, said Dr. Thomas M. Folks, an expert in retroviruses at the Federal disease centers. "A foamy virus was once proposed as a cause of chronic fatigue syndrome, but it wasn't," Dr. Folks said.

Nevertheless, Federal health officials are concerned because no one knows what may happen if a foamy mixes with an endogenous or other virus in humans. "C.D.C. is trying to not let anything get out of control, because we do not want something to smolder in the population for 10 to 20 years like H.I.V. did and then all of a sudden have a huge outbreak," Dr. Folks said. "If there is an outbreak, we are going to be there."

With so much at stake, why are scientists and health officials proceeding with xenotransplants?

Many believe the risk is theoretical and exaggerated, and if xenotransplants are prohibited in the United States, they will be done in other countries. Although veterinarians, laboratory workers and others who have contact with animals have died from animal infections, the limited surveys done to date have not found major health hazards. The longest anyone has lived with an animal organ—a person who received a chimpanzee kidney—is nine months.

No xenotransplant recipient has been known to have developed a novel type of infection, but those people were not monitored as closely as Mr. Getty is.

Dr. Frederick A. Murphy, the dean of the veterinary school at the University of California at Davis, said that over the years unsterilized biological products derived from animals, products that differ little in risk from xenografts, have often been injected into patients. Though such uses have been incompletely studied, Dr. Murphy said, "it does seem that if there had been major problems they would have surfaced by now."

The prevailing opinion is that the potential benefit of alleviating the organ shortage, and the remote chance of finding a therapy for AIDS, outweigh the theoretical risks. Even those like Dr. Stephen Morse of Rockefeller University in New York City, who is a leader in calling attention to the threat of emerging diseases, do not believe xenotransplant experiments should be halted as long as the initial group of recipients is monitored. When to stop such monitoring is a thorny question for health officials. If nothing is found in the initial few xenotransplants, should monitoring continue for 500 or 1,000?

Dr. Jorg W. Eichberg of the Biomedical Primate Research Center in Rijswijk, the Netherlands, who hired Dr. Allan, when he worked at the Southwest Foundation, said that many experts on the infectious threats of xenotransplants shared Dr. Allan's concerns. "But they are for it and override the concerns in the name of progress," he said.

Dr. Maurice Hilleman, a Merck researcher who helped develop many of the vaccines that the pharmaceutical company has marketed, said that the baboon AIDS experiment, though risky, "was wisely thought out" and "one that had to be undertaken by people with guts." He added, "Research often produces breakthroughs that are totally unexpected."

Dr. Noguchi said that although the F.D.A. shared many of Dr. Allan's concerns it disagreed on the means of implementation. The field of xenotransplantation is "expanding so rapidly," he said, "that the F.D.A. sim-ply lacks the capacity to directly oversee everything."

Dr. Louisa E. Chapman of the Federal disease centers, who helped draft the guidelines, said that health officials were looking for guidance from interested groups after publication of the guidelines in The Federal Register. "The thorniest thing to wrestle with here is how much risk actually exists and how much impedance of progress is justified in protecting against an incalculable risk." she said. "None of us are absolutely confident that we have the right answer for that."

Source: Lawrence K. Altman, "Cross-Species Transplants Raise Concerns About Human Safety," *New York Times* 9 Jan. 1996: 11, 17.

EXERCISES: THINKING CRITICALLY

1. Summarize the questions that scientists have no answer for at present.
2. The question that follows is a slightly different version of a question Altman poses: *With so much at stake, should scientists and health officials proceed with xenotransplants?* Answer the question first from the perspective of a scientist who supports xenotransplants and then from the perspective of a scientist who opposes them. Explore as well the perspectives of AIDS activists and animal rights activists. How would each group respond to this question?

Christine Gorman discusses potential problems with animal transplants and presents several possible reasons for the FDA to okay Jeff Getty's controversial transplant.

ARE ANIMAL ORGANS SAFE FOR PEOPLE?

CHRISTINE GORMAN

CRITICS OF TRANSPLANTS FEAR THAT
VIRUSES COULD JUMP FROM OTHER
SPECIES TO HUMANS AND TRIGGER
DEADLY EPIDEMICS

Jeff Getty should be dead by now. He has had HIV for about 15 years. His immune system is barely functioning. And on top of that, in a desperate attempt four weeks ago to reverse the course of his disease, doctors at San Francisco General Hospital infused him with an experimental bone-marrow transplant from a baboon. Immunologists warned that his body would eventually reject the non-human tissue and that the operation would almost certainly end his life rather than prolong it. However, Getty is not only alive, but last week he was healthy enough to go home from the hospital. No matter how much time he has left, friends and family call him a medical miracle.

But there is also a small chance that the technology that allows people like Getty to receive tissues from animals could somehow unleash a medical disaster. The danger is that patients could receive a previously unknown microbe along with their transplants. When viruses or bacteria have made the jump from animals to humans in the past, they have often proved exceedingly virulent: HIV, which causes AIDS: Ebola virus; and hantavirus are all chilling precedents. In a worst-case scenario, such transplants could introduce humanity to a plague that would make all of those look tame. "This is a serious mistake," says Jonathan Allan, a virologist at the Southwest Foundation for Biomedical Research in San Antonio, Texas. "It only takes one transmission from one baboon to a human to start an epidemic. There's no way you can make it safe."

No one ever had to worry about such potential hazards before, because scientists hadn't been able to figure out how to make an animal-to-human transplant work. It's hard enough to trick an individual's immune system into accepting tissues from another person. But when organs from an entirely different species are stitched into the human body, immune defenses go into overdrive, leading to swift and irreparable destruction of the foreign tissue. Two years ago, when doctors at the University of Pittsburgh transplanted baboon livers into two seriously ill patients, both men died soon after the operation.

The advent of genetic engineering, among other things, has allowed researchers to begin breaching that natural barrier. Last spring scientists at Duke University Medical Center reported that they had successfully altered the genetic makeup of a strain of pigs. As a result, the researchers managed to fool the immune systems of three baboons into accepting pig hearts, for a short while at least. Using a similar technique, the British biotechnology company Imutran has produced a herd of 300 genetically altered swine. The company expects to transplant either a pig's heart or a liver into a human subject later this year.

In Getty's case, Dr. Suzanne Ildstad from the University of Pittsburgh proposed—and the doctors at San Francisco General agreed to follow—a different approach. Ildstad has developed a special filtering process that allows her to separate out the most mature baboon bone-marrow cells. The cells that are left behind are too undeveloped to provoke an immune reaction, and it's these that were dripped into Getty's veins. Ildstad believes the immature baboon cells can, in turn, work with Getty's body to create a hybrid immune system. If she's right—a big if—that would give Getty a tremendous advantage. Baboons appear to be impervious to HIV, so in theory the fortified immune system might be able to fight off the AIDS virus.

Unfortunately, baboons are known to carry a variety of nasty pathogens, ranging from fungal infections to viruses that trigger leukemia. In July the U.S. Food and Drug Administration asked the researchers to find another baboon donor because their first choice was already infected with several viruses. The scientists finally settled on a baboon whose only major infection was herpes papio virus, which is unlikely to pose a threat because it only affects cells that are presumably filtered out by Ildstad's method.

Even the most rigorous screening methods cannot guarantee human safety, however. At least two potentially worrisome baboon viruses, for example, don't show up on any existing commercial tests. Although neither one bothers baboons, they are both retroviruses, the same kind of organism that gives rise to AIDS. If the microbes really are dangerous to humans, it's conceivable that they could spread to many victims before revealing their deadly nature. That scenario appears to have already happened once: many scientists believe it did with HIV, which apparently originated in monkeys and then somehow jumped the barrier to people.

And those are the viruses scientists know about. There is no way of knowing how many other baboon viruses medical science hasn't discovered yet; there is clearly no way to

screen for any of them. That's why many scientists prefer to experiment with pigs. People are nowhere near as closely related biologically to ungulates—pigs, cows and deer, for example—as they are to primates. Any virus that can infect baboons probably already has many of the biological characteristics needed to infect people. But a virus that has adapted itself to thrive in pigs may have a much harder time taking hold in the biologically unfamiliar territory of the human body.

"Humans and pigs have lived close together for millenniums," says Dr. David White, co-founder of Imutran. "And don't forget, we've been pumping pig insulin into [diabetic] people for generations." Any virus that can jump the barrier, such as the one that causes swine flu, probably already has. In addition, pigs are easier to raise than baboons and can be isolated in germ-free environments. That doesn't mean that pigs present no risk to people, just less than baboons do.

Considering all the potential problems with baboon transplants, it's a wonder the FDA allowed Getty to undergo the operation at all. Certainly compassion for a dying man played a role. But according to scientists who are familiar with how such decisions are made, there was probably another, more subtle reason. "The chance of that bone-marrow transplant taking [hold] and working in a human is zero," says Ronald Desrosiers, professor of microbiology at Harvard Medical School. Current techniques, he believes, are simply not yet refined enough for it to work. But they could be soon.

For that reason, the Getty experiment may count more for its cautionary value than for its medical importance. Better to put the scientific community and the public on notice that the question of cross-species infections needs serious attention and debate. Otherwise, no one will be prepared when the real breakthrough comes and a transplanted animal organ takes up permanent residence in a human being.

Source: Christine Gorman, "Are Animal Organs Safe for People?" *Time* 15 Jan. 1996: 58–59.

EXERCISES: READING AND RESPONDING

1. How does Gorman answer the question in the article's title?
2. Explain whether readers find that both perspectives are presented or one that is given more emphasis than the other.
3. Summarize the theories Gorman presents explaining why the FDA approved the Getty-baboon transplant.
4. Compare Gorman's article to Altman's article. Which one appeals most to readers' fear on uncontrolled viruses and public health disasters? Identify passages that make these appeals.

In "Baboon Cells Fail to Thrive, But AIDS Patient Improves," Lawrence K. Altman provides an update on Jeff Getty's health after the baboon bone marrow transplant.

BABOON CELLS FAIL TO THRIVE, BUT AIDS PATIENT IMPROVES

LAWRENCE K. ALTMAN

PUZZLE ARISES AFTER
INTERSPECIES TRANSPLANT

Preliminary tests show that few, if any, baboon bone marrow cells have grown and functioned after being transplanted into a 38-year-old man with severe AIDS, his doctors said yesterday.

But the doctors said in interviews that they were puzzled why the patient, Jeff Getty, had done so well since the highly risky experiment was carried out in San Francisco in December. Mr. Getty has gained several pounds, his asthma and a severe case of a skin condition known as seborrhea have cleared up, his immune cells have increased slightly and tests done so far show that he has not developed any infections, said Dr. Steven Deeks, Mr Getty's doctor at San Francisco General Hospital.

"The results suggest that this is not working in Jeff" and "Jeff's good health cannot be explained by the baboon cells," Dr. Deeks said.

He said the team intended to report its findings in a scientific journal and would not have discussed them now except that Mr. Getty was doing so well that many AIDS patients and others believed his improvement was a result of the cross-species transplant. Dr. Deeks said he and Project Inform, an advocacy group for AIDS patients that paid for much of the experiment's cost, felt obligated to dispel any false hopes.

Nevertheless, Dr. Deeks said, "something happened at the time of his transplant that has had a dramatic effect on his health."

The researchers involved in the baboon transplant said they regarded the experiment as a success, despite the apparent failure of the transplant to work. A major goal of the experiment was to determine the safety of the radiation and drug therapy used to prepare Mr. Getty for the cross-species transplant. The scientists now believe that the preparatory therapy may have been too little she said at the meeting.

Lenore Gelb, a spokeswoman for the Food and Drug Administration, said the Federal agency did not expect the experiment to work: The agency approved only one such experiment. Permission must be obtained for further baboon bone marrow transplants.

Dr. Ildstad said that some tests on Mr. Getty's cells taken four weeks after the transplant were positive and some were negative, and that it would take another week or so to repeat the tests. The team plans to continue monitoring Mr. Getty as long as he lives.

Dr. Deeks said that "if there are baboon cells present in Jeff, there are not a lot of them" and "those that might be present would not be enough to provide Jeff with long-term clinical benefit."

Mr. Getty, who has been sailing in San Francisco Bay and lifting weights, said he was "pleased with the results" of the experiment because it showed that the procedure was safe and his condition had improved. "It got rid of my asthma, which had been severe for many years, and we are not quite sure why," Mr. Getty said. He said he would have considered the experiment a failure "if I had died."

The number of special immune cells in Mr. Getty's blood has risen slightly since the baboon bone marrow transplant. The CD-4 cells, which play a critical role in immune system function, have risen to 75 from a level of about 10 to 30 in the weeks before the transplant. The CD-4 count fell to 2 after the transplant, Mr. Getty said. But the increase is only slight because the normal count, which varies widely, is from about 800 to 1,200.

Mr. Getty has been taking a combination of an experimental drug, indinavir, a protease inhibitor, and two standard drugs, AZT and 3TC, in a study. Last week scientists reported that the combination could suppress the amount of AIDS virus to levels that could not be detected by current techniques and raised the number of CD-4 and other immune cells.

But Dr. Deeks said that for several reasons he doubted that Mr. Getty's response was a result of the combination therapy. One is that Mr. Getty experienced "some of the toughest months clinically while he was on the therapy" before the transplant and he could not under-stand why his improvement now would be due to the drug therapy.

Dr. Deeks said his team was exploring "an intriguing possibility" that Mr. Getty's improvement was due to the radiation therapy he underwent in preparation for the marrow trans-plant. The radiation was used to destroy some of Mr. Getty's marrow to make space for the baboon marrow. Recent experiments on monkeys have suggested that radiation therapy might be useful.

People with advanced AIDS often have an erratic course. "We may be catching Jeff on the upside," Dr.

Deeks said. "Jeff has been overall energized by his experiment, and that could explain everything, but I sus-pect there is more to it than that."

Mr. Getty said that he felt better than he had for four years and that he was beginning to make longer range plans. Some scientists have criticized the experiment because it might lead to baboon viruses' causing serious disease in transplant recipients and other humans.

As for the possibility that some unknown baboon virus might be lurk-ing in his body and that it might not cause him any harm for a decade, Mr. Getty said, "I hope I live that long."

Source: Lawrence K. Altman, "Baboon Cells Fail to Thrive, But AIDS Patient Improves,"New York Times 9 Feb. 1996: 14 A.

EXERCISE: THINKING CRITICALLY

Was the Jeff Getty operation a success or failure? Identify sources that support each perspective.

FOCUS ON RELATED ISSUES:
AIDS AND ORGAN TRANSPLANTS

Since the baboon bone marrow transplant in 1995, Jeff Getty has been actively working to make people with HIV eligible for organ transplants and to make HIV infected persons eligible as donors. In a 1998 interview with John S. James, Getty discussed the progress on ending exclusion of people with HIV. At that time, they were excluded by the majority of the 266 regional centers that performed transplants. Getty cited policy changes in two cen-ters that consulted HIV experts who shared the most recent information available about the disease. Advisory boards at regional centers—and the Vet-erans Administration in particular—need to be re-educated, Getty claimed. These boards are made up of surgeons who make the final decisions on whether or not an individual receives an organ transplant.

Working on your own, develop a topic on some aspect of discrimination against people who test positive for HIV or on public policies and AIDs.

An unsigned editorial in *Nature Biotechnology* discusses the "visceral" reaction some people have at the thought of cross-species transplants.

XENOTRANSPLANTATION AND THE "YUK" FACTOR

When the Nuffield Council on Bioethics (London) issued its recent report—"Animal-to-Human Transplants: The Ethics of Xenotransplantation"—it was probably inevitable, regardless of the content of the report, that the general media would seek out the flaws in the technology. But when the report itself highlighted the transmission of disease from animals to humans as one of the council's major concerns, the probability became certainty. Much of the newspaper, television, and radio coverage of the Nuffield Council report has focused strongly on the need to avoid cross-species infection.

Replacing human tissue with animal cells and organs clearly raises issues that some people will find threatening. Spare-parts surgery, using organs or cells from animals, challenges our notions of humanness, our sense of distinctness from other species. It is easy to find sympathy for those who are repelled by xenotransplantation—even if that repulsion has visceral rather than cerebral roots.

In the face of the "yuk" factor, the scientific, knowledge-based position put forward by authoritative bodies must be both accurate and representative. The Nuffield Council concluded that "the risks associated with the possible transmission of infectious diseases as a consequence of xenotransplantation have not been adequately dealt with. It would not be ethical, therefore, to begin clinical trials of xenotransplantation involving human beings."

The higher risk of disease transmission to humans from primates persuaded the Nuffield Council to favor pigs over primates as sources of transplant organs. Its report points to a macaque monkey form of herpes B virus that causes a rapidly fatal encephalitis in humans. It also draws attention to the similarities between the simian and human immunodeficiency viruses (SIV, HIV): Journalists were left to draw their own conclusions about SIV and AIDS. What was lost in all of this distracting detail, however, was the even greater risk that exists of disease transmission in human-to-human transplantation.

Before recombinant DNA, the major sources of insulin for diabetics were the pancreases from pigs and cattle. Despite the fact that there were several million diabetics taking injections of animal insulin several times daily, there were very few, if any, reported cases of bovine or porcine disease transmission. Insulin, of course, was a purified compound, not a living preparation. However, vigilant readers will also recall that purified proteins extracted originally from human sources—human growth hormone extracted from the pituitary glands of human cadavers, for instance, or anti-hemophilic factor VIII extracted from blood—have far worse records of disease transmission than does animal insulin. The simple fact is that human beings usually get their diseases from other humans.

The Nuffield Council report also raised the possibility that the animal organs themselves would be susceptible to animal disease, especially in the case of transplanted lungs. Very little is known about these risks, says the report, and it advises that would-be organ recipients should be advised of the possibility of infection. Naturally. But then perhaps what animal organ recipients should really be advised of, if they want to steer clear of infection, is to reconsider any plans they might have had for a career in pig-farming. That, one suspects, would not be an untenable burden at least for the 98 percent of us who forsook agriculture for the urban lifestyle a long while ago.

The Nuffield Council report also draws attention to the possibility that prion diseases can pass from one species to another, thereby raising the specter of spongiform encephalopathies. This is simply another distraction. No one is contemplating xenotranplantation from cattle, mink, or cats (although a patient did receive a sheep heart in 1968 and died instantly). Furthermore, as the report itself describes later, the transmission of prion diseases normally occurs by transplantation or by eating infected material.

If there are pig prions, avoiding bacon and ham would seem to be as wise a course of action as curtailment of xenotransplantation.

There are, undoubtedly, some very nasty diseases that affect both animals and humans. There are also very many more diseases that are virtually species-specific and highly unlikely under any circumstance to cause any human disease, ever. Furthermore, one could call as witnesses for the defense many animal pathogens whose impact on human beings has been very beneficial. Edward Jenner's original observations on the protection against variola (smallpox)—that exposure to vaccinia (cowpox) conferred to milkmaids—spring to mind. Despite the demise of variola, vaccinia is still finding wide employment—as a recombinant expression host in vivo for a variety of disease-antigen genes in experimental live vaccine. So is fowlpox virus.

Indeed, there is a general message from vaccinologists to those who are worrying about infection in xenotransplantation. From Louis Pasteur—who produced his first rabies virus by passaging rabies through duck brain cultures—to modern producers of influenza vaccines who still cultivate attenuated viruses in chicken eggs, most experience indicates that growing viruses in the cells or tissues of other species can make the infection agent less pathogenic, less fit for its invasive, disease-causing role, and less likely, therefore, to cause a problem in humans.

Nothing here is meant to indicate that infection is not a problem in xenotransplantation. In immunosuppressed patients, it most certainly is. But to address the problem incompletely is to misrepresent the risk. And passing references to headline-grabbing diseases that are in all likelihood irrelevant—Ebola gets a mention as well as AIDS and bovine serum encephalitis—distract from the real disease issues. Asilomar and its consequences for public attitudes to recombinant DNA should alert the research community to the dangers of being too "responsible" in the face of uncertainty. If we don't know something, lets just say so and leave it at that.

Source: "Xenotransplantation and the 'Yuk' Factor," *Nature Biotechnology* 14 (April 1996): 403–404.

EXERCISES: READING AND RESPONDING

1. What issues does this article raise that other sources in this case study have not mentioned?
2. Explain whether the article supports the claim, "The simple fact is that human beings usually get their diseases from other human beings."
3. Explain why the "yuk" factor does or does not account for the media's attention to the Jeff Getty case.
4. Identify and define technical terms in this article that haven't appeared in other sources.
5. In your opinion, does this article support or oppose xenotransplants?

CONTEMPORARY PERSPECTIVES

CLONING THE NEW BABES

ALICE PARK

Dolly was once an awfully lonely sheep. When the famously cloned animal made headlines in 1997, she was the only mammal ever to be manufactured from the cell of an adult donor. Since then, the clone ranks have swelled, with mice and cattle also toddling out of the labs. Last week cloning technology took another step forward when an international biotechnology company announced that it had created a litter of five genetically identical piglets, and that it had a pretty good idea of how they could one day be used: as organ donors for ailing humans.

The idea of turning pigs into tissue factories has been around for at least 30 years. Pigs breed easily and mature quickly, and their organs are roughly the same size as those of humans, meaning operations can be performed with a relative snap-out, snap-in simplicity. The problem is, once the donor organ is stitched in place, the body rebels, rejecting it even more violently than it would a human graft. "A pig heart transplanted in a person would turn black within minutes," says David Ayares, a research director with PPL Therapeutics, the biotech firm based in Scotland, New Zealand and Virginia that helped clone Dolly and also produced the piglets.

What causes porcine organs to be rejected so quickly is a sugar molecule on the surface of pig cells that identifies the tissue as unmistakably nonhuman. When the immune system spots this marker, it musters its defenses. PPL scientists recently succeeded in finding the gene responsible for the sugar and knocking it out of the nucleus of a pig cell. Their next step would be to extract that nucleus, insert it into a hollowed-out pig ovum and insert the ovum into the womb of a host sow. The sugar-free piglet that was eventually born could then be cloned over and over as a source of safe transplant organs. "The idea is to arrive at the ideal animal and repeatedly copy it exactly as it is," says Dr. Mark Hardy, director of organ transplantation at New York-Presbyterian Hospital.

The cloned piglets PPL introduced to the world last week were created in just this way, though for this first experiment in pig replication, the scientists left the sugar genes intact. "We wanted to work with pristine cells to make sure our cloning technique would indeed work," says Ayares. Now that they've proved it does, the scientists plan to raise the bar and try the same procedure with modified genes.

Despite this recent success, PPL is not likely to be setting up its organ shop anytime soon. Knocking out the key sugar gene solves only the problem of short-term rejection. Long-term rejection, caused by blood coagulating around the new organ, requires that researchers re-engineer an entirely different set of genes that code for anticoagulants. But even this would not be a perfect solution, and recipients of pig organs would probably still have to take the same rainbow of antirejection drugs recipients of human organs must now endure.

Nonetheless, Ayares is optimistic, insisting that pig organs could be available in as little as five years. Hardy believes that whenever the tissue does come along, it will at first be rather small-bore stuff—pancreatic islet cells for diabetics, say—rather than hearts, kidneys or lungs. Whatever it is, even a little new transplant material is a big improvement over what's available now, and for gravely ill patients awaiting a donor, that's no small thing.

Source: Alice Park, "Cloning the New Babes," *Time* 27 Mar. 2000: 85.

YES, LET'S PAY FOR ORGANS

CHARLES KRAUTHAMMER

NOT FROM THE LIVING, WHICH WOULD BE DEGRADING. BUT THE DEAD ARE A DIFFERENT STORY

Pennsylvania plans to begin paying the relatives of organ donors $300 toward funeral expenses. It would be the first jurisdiction in the country to reward organ donation. Indeed, it might even be violating a 1984 federal law that declares organs a national resource not subject to compensation. Already there are voices opposing the very idea of pricing a kidney.

It is odd that with 62,000 Americans desperately awaiting organ transplantation to save their life, no authority had yet dared offer money for the organs of the dead in order to increase the supply for the living. If we can do anything to alleviate the catastrophic shortage of donated organs, should we not?

One objection is that Pennsylvania's idea will disproportionately affect the poor. The rich; it is argued, will not be moved by a $300 reward; it will be the poor who will succumb to the incentive and provide organs.

So what? Where is the harm? What is wrong with rewarding people, poor or not, for a dead relative's organ? True, auctioning off organs in the market so that the poor could not afford to get them would be offensive. But this program does not restrict supply to the rich. It seeks to increase supply for all.

Moreover, everything in life that is dangerous, risky or bad disproportionately affects the poor: slum housing street crime, small cars, hazardous jobs. By this logic, coal mining should be outlawed because the misery and risk and diseases of coal mining disproportionately fall on people who need the money. The sons of investment bankers do not go to West Virginia to mine. (They go there to run for the Senate.)

No, the real objection to the Pennsylvania program is this: it crosses a fateful ethical line regarding human beings and their parts. Until now we have upheld the principle that one must not pay for human organs because doing so turns the human body—and human life—into a commodity. Violating this principle, it is said, puts us on the slippery slope to establishing a market for body parts. Auto parts, yes. Body parts, no. Start by paying people for their dead parents' kidneys, and soon we will be paying people for the spare kidneys of the living.

Well, what's wrong with that? the libertarians ask. Why should a destitute person not be allowed to give away a kidney that he may never need so he can live a better life? Why can't a struggling mother give her kidney so her kids can go to college?

The answer is that little thing called human dignity. According to the libertarians' markets-for-everything logic, a poor mother ought equally to be allowed to sell herself into slavery—or any other kind of degradation—to send her kids through college. Our society, however, draws the line and says no. We have a free society, but freedom stops at the point where you violate the very integrity of the self (which is why prostitution is illegal).

We cannot allow live kidneys to be sold at market. It would produce a society in which the lower orders are literally cut up to serve as spare parts for the upper. No decent society can permit that.

But kidneys from the dead are another matter entirely. There is a distinction between strip-mining a live person and strip-mining a dead one. To be crude about it, whereas a person is not a commodity, a dead body can be. Yes, it is treated with respect (which is why humans bury their dead). But it is not inviolable. It does not warrant the same reverence as that accorded a living soul.

The Pennsylvania program is not just justified, it is too timid. It seeks clean hands by paying third parties—the funeral homes—rather than giving cash directly to the relatives. Why not pay them directly? And why not $3,000 instead of $300? That might even address the rich/poor concern: after all, $3,000 is real money, even for bankers and lawyers.

The Pennsylvania program does cross a line. But not all slopes are slippery. There is a new line to be drawn, a very logical one: rewards for organs, yes—but not from the living.

The Talmud speaks of establishing a "fence" around the law, making restrictions that may not make sense in and of themselves but that serve to keep one away from more serious violations. (For example, because one is not allowed to transact with money on the Sabbath, one is not allowed even to touch money on the Sabbath.) The prohibition we have today—no selling of *any* organs, from the living or the dead—is a fence against the commoditization of human parts. Laudable, but a fence too far. We need to move the fence in and permit incentive payments for organs from the dead.

Why? Because there are 62,000 people desperately clinging to life, some of whom will die if we don't have the courage to move the moral line—and hold it.

Source: Charles Krauthammer, "Yes, Let's Pay for Organs," *Time* 17 May 1999: 100.

EXERCISES: READING AND RESPONDING

1. What is the aim of each article?

2. Krauthammer provides a new perspective on organ donation. He anticipates objections and addresses each one. Summarize the objections he raises. Can you think of others?

3. Krauthammer refers to slippery slope arguments and claims his proposal avoids that fallacy. Identify any logical fallacies you find in his article and in other sources that aim to persuade readers.

4. Several of the articles in this case study appeal to readers' emotions. What kind of appeal does the *Time* article make?

5. The *Time* article explains why porcine organs are rejected. Paraphrase the explanation.

6. Assume that you are in an either/or situation. Explain whether you would advocate paying for human organs or using spare parts from animals.

7. If you needed an organ donor, would you prefer to buy human parts or animal parts?

EXERCISE: GOING ON-LINE

What are the most recent reports on Jeff Getty's health? What has he been doing since the transplant in 1995? Answer this question by looking for Internet sources.

EVALUATING AND ANALYZING THE CASE STUDY

EXERCISES: THINKING CRITICALLY

1. Identify the rhetorical situation for each of the sources in the case study.

2. Identify sources in the case study that are primary sources. Identify secondary sources. Be prepared to explain why you classify a source as one or the other.

3. Jeff Getty, Dr. Suzanne Ilstad, and Jonathan Allan are focal points in this case study. *Frankenstein* is another. Review sources in this case and identify other people, events, and issues that are focal points or connections that link one source to another.

EXERCISES: COLLABORATING WITH YOUR PEERS

1. Working in pairs or in groups, construct a time line specifically for the Jeff Getty-baboon bone marrow transplant.

2. Make a list of key players in this case. Be prepared to share your list with your classmates.

WRITING ABOUT THE CASE STUDY

EXERCISES: FOCUS ON WRITING

Freewriting

1. Write for fifteen to twenty minutes on whether you believe xenotransplantation is the route researchers should follow as they look for solutions to the shortage in organ donors.

2. Write for fifteen to twenty minutes on reconciling different perspectives on baboon transplants.

3. Write for fifteen to twenty minutes on science and ethics. What are the ethical issues raised in the case study? What are some other ethical issues medical researchers and biotechnologists face? If you've read Mary Shelley's *Frankenstein*, discuss ethical issues raised in the novel. Are these issues still relevant today?

Writing Letters

4. Write a letter to your campus or local newspaper. Review the success of the baboon bone marrow transplant and provide your readers with a context for the debate. Finally, discuss looking at the Jeff Getty transplant as neither success nor failure but as a significant medical procedure even though it didn't achieve its primary goal.

5. Write a letter to People for the Ethical Treatment of Animals. Explain why you support or oppose xenotransplants.

Evaluating Sources

6. Assume that you are a member of an editorial review board responsible for designing a web page on the Jeff Getty case. Your aim is to convince your readers that xenotransplants should either continue or be banned. Select a minimum of ten sources you would use as references for your review of the Getty case and defense of your position. Then, for each source, write a bibliographical citation and an informative summary. Your readers are other members of the review board. Include a statement of your position on this issue, explain whether or not you would recommend using graphics on the proposed Web page, and identify any graphics from sources in this case study you would recommend using.

7. Select five sources that explain why xenotransplantation is performed, why scientists and researchers support it, and why animal rights activists oppose it. Write a bibliographical citation and an informative summary for each source.

Writing for Academic Audiences

8. Write a documented paper that explains whether or not you support using spare parts from animals for transplants. Cite a minimum of five sources in the case study.

9. In a documented paper, explain what xenotransplantation is and identify various perspectives on the issue. Then reconcile the perspectives. Cite a minimum of eight sources.

10. Some of the sources in this case suggest that the baboon bone marrow transplant was a success; other sources suggest that it was a failure. For readers who have not read and discussed the sources in this case, write a documented paper that reviews the different perspectives and reconciles the differences in opinion. Cite a minimum of five sources.

WRITING ABOUT RELATED ISSUES

EXERCISES: FOCUS ON WRITING

1. Several sources in this case study mention the Baby Fae case. Write a documented paper that reviews this case and offers different perspectives on the outcome. Cite a minimum of five sources.

2. Select an ethical issue the medical community currently faces and write a paper that summarizes different perspectives on the issue. Attempt to reconcile the perspectives. Cite a minimum of ten sources.

Brainstorming:

Using Fetal Tissue to Treat Victims of Parkinson's Disease

Assisted Suicide

Cloning Humans

Using Placebos in Clinical Trials

Sterilization

Recognizing Alternative Medicine and Therapy

Gene Therapy

Medical Records Privacy

Animal Subjects in Research
Human Subjects in Research
Genetically Engineered Food
Confidentiality and AIDS
Fertility Drugs
Prescribing Antidepressants
Prison Research
Sperm Banks

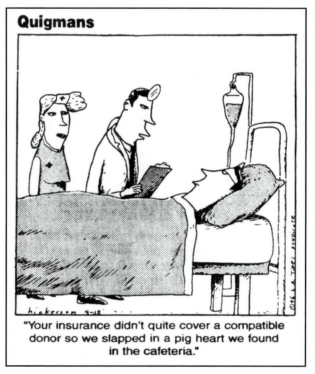

Source: LA Times Syndicate

Chapter 13

Developing an Argument

In Rhetoric . . . we should be able to argue on either side of a question; not with a view to putting both sides into practice—we must not advocate evil—but in order that no aspect of the case may escape us, and that if our opponent makes unfair use of the arguments, we may be able to turn to refute them.

—*The Rhetoric of Aristotle,* Book I

WRITING ARGUMENTS

If an instructor gave you and your classmates the opportunity to discuss the merits of having your lowest grade in the course dropped, dismissing class the Friday afternoon before spring break, or making a final exam optional, it's safe to assume that all of you would appreciate being asked your opinions and that class discussion would have good participation. You would have something at stake, and the person to persuade would be present to listen to your arguments. You would leave class knowing that you had a chance to participate in the discussion, though. Now, imagine that your instructor asks you and your classmates to address these same issues by writing a letter or essay. Given the opportunity to put your arguments in writing, would the same number of you share your ideas? Participation might be as good as it was in class, but even with a familiar topic and audience, you could expect a few students to drop out of the conversation. The bottom line on excuses would be that it's easier to verbalize ideas than it is to articulate ideas in writing. In class, the ebb and flow of freewheeling discussion pulls in students who might not be prepared to present a well thought out argument but who are invested in the issues enough to jump in and try to explain what they think someone meant to say, to clarify what they thought someone else said, or to second an effective argument someone else presented. In class discussion, the immediacy of the opposition sparks ideas and triggers quick responses, and makes formulating an argument seem fairly easy—at least easier than putting it in writing.

531

Perhaps you've experienced a similar situation when you've talked with friends or classmates about controversial issues but found it difficult to express yourself when you had to put your ideas on paper in a rhetorical situation that asked you to address an academic audience. Suddenly the playing field changes, and instead of talking to familiar people, you're faced with the constraints of the written paper and a group of intended readers who seem removed, remote, or unfamiliar to you. You have to find the right words, evidence, statistics, and examples that will persuade your readers to consider your ideas, rethink their own perspectives, and accept or believe whatever claim you make.

Even experienced writers agree that constructing a good argument for any kind of audience is a challenge. A good argument has an effect on readers. It may not change someone's mind completely, but the reader pays attention to what the writer has to say and doesn't dismiss the claims and evidence. While your aim is to persuade your readers when you write arguments, you want to remember that argument is more than an exercise in winning or losing. A good argument makes readers reexamine their perspectives, or it makes them willing to consider your point of view. To formulate a good argument, you have to understand your subject, your stance on it, and your audience's feelings and attitudes toward it. Sources in Case Study 5 that follows illustrate how writers develop arguments. You'll find that not all of the arguments are based entirely on logic. You'll find emotional appeals and logical fallacies at work. Most important, you'll find writers addressing an actual situation that elicited arguments from people who wrote letters to the editor, journalists who expressed their ideas in editorials, and writers who published their arguments in popular magazines and specialized journals.

A review of the communication triangle and the aims of discourse (presented in Chapter 1), reminds us that the audience should be the focus of an effective argument. Sometimes, in your zeal for supporting a stance you agree with or refuting a stance taken by someone else, you dwell too much on your own feelings and attitudes and don't consider fully your intended readers' needs. We describe this kind of writing as *egocentric* because you're writing primarily to yourself. This approach will work in early drafts because it allows you to articulate your thoughts; however, at some point, you have to give up the egocentric writing, no matter how comfortable it may be, and realize that your readers may not agree with you. You have to determine strategies for bringing your readers around to considering your perspective as credible before you persuade them to rethink, reconsider, believe, or accept your ideas. As you write multiple drafts of a paper, one of your goals should be to work through the egocentric stage of writing until you achieve a sense of writing for a specific audience.

As you work on the assignments in this chapter, your instructor will either designate a group of intended readers, or ask you to select a group on your own. If you have a choice, consider members of your academic community (students and faculty), a scholarly publication, or a publication featuring examples of the kinds of writing students do in college-level work. You want to select an audience that will expect an argument requiring them to, at the very least, reconsider or rethink the issues. While it may seem convenient to write to like-minded readers, you'll miss the sense of a real challenge you are likely to feel when you know that your intended readers don't share your perspective. If you designate as an audience readers who pretty much share your beliefs, convictions, and perspectives, why labor to present an argument? Some people call this kind of argument "preaching to the choir."

FINDING A POSITION

To develop an argument, you have to understand your stance or position on an issue. If you've already taken a position, you need to understand why you've taken it. First, let's look at a topic high school students debated in 1996–1997 and explore ways to examine your reactions to it.

> *Resolved:* That the federal government should establish a program to substantially reduce juvenile crime in the United States.

What is your position on this issue? For our purposes in this scenario, fence-sitting is not permitted. Would you support or oppose the resolution?

While the debate team knows the resolution or topic they will argue, its members do not know which position—affirmative or negative—they will be called on to support. The challenge in forensics, arguments of the courtroom or judicial argument, lies in being prepared to argue either side. Because some teams may favor the affirmative side rather than the negative or feel better-prepared to defend one side than the other, the luck of the draw may play a role in a debate's outcome. Successful debaters typically spend long hours doing research on the issues, working on the theory that a debate is more likely to be won or lost in the library than in actual competition when the teams square off and face each other.

The debate analogy is handy in illustrating a situation in which individuals must be prepared to argue either side of an issue, but it is not, by any means, a direct analogy to your task in this chapter. Your task is to develop a position on a topic and to use your position drafts to develop an argument. In a position paper, you have more choices than arguing only for or against an issue. You may choose to ignore or include counterarguments. The important point here is that you have choices to make—with your audience in mind, of course. On any given issue, you may adopt a variety of positions. For the resolution proposed above, you might take a position that

- Supports establishing a new program
- Argues for or against establishing a new program
- Cites needs for or against a new program and calls for further study of the issue
- Offers a compromise
- Investigates a variety of arguments for or against and draws a conclusion, which may be for or against
- Calls for further study
- Calls for a compromise

For some issues, finding a position is easy. You know instinctively that you are for or against a resolution or an issue. It's a good idea, however, to test instinctive reactions to an issue by examining different perspectives to see if your instinctive reaction holds up to obvious counterarguments someone might present. Remember, once you find a position on an issue, you have to support it. If you find yourself completely befuddled, not really knowing what you think, or not caring one way or the other, you need to investigate the issue in order to discover a position you can support adequately.

Let's assume that Writer A and Writer B are both assigned a position paper on whether the federal government should implement a new program to substantially reduce juvenile crime. The instructor specifies that papers should use a minimum of five sources. The audience is a community group made up of law enforcement officers, city council members, judges, and other interested parties.

One way to find a position on this issue is to revise the resolution and make it into a question: *Should the federal government establish a program to substantially reduce juvenile crime in the United States?* Now you can begin exploring support for *yes*, *no*, and *perhaps*. The responses below illustrate the question-and-answer method. Writer A, in a brainstorming session, thinks of three different answers to the question.

Writer A: No

- Too much money already devoted to social programs—no evidence that they work.
- Programs should be developed by the states and local communities—too much bureaucracy at the federal level already.
- Juvenile crime prevention programs already in place don't seem to work

Writer A: Yes

- Going through the motions of implementing a program might make people feel that something was being done.

Writer A: Perhaps

- Juvenile crime is pretty bad, and maybe something new should be done

While those responses are very general, they are a starting place—an outline of ideas for Writer A to develop. She must, however, find specific examples, statistics, expert testimony, and studies or reports that provide specific support for the generalizations. If the writer intends to support the position that too much money and bureaucracy are invested in the present juvenile crime prevention program, she must demonstrate specifically how these generalizations apply to her position.

Writer B takes a different approach. She doesn't have strong feelings one way or the other on this issue, so her response to the question, is *perhaps*. Instead of listing generalizations to generate ideas, Writer B asks a series of questions.

Writer B

- **What** is being done presently at the state level to curb juvenile crime? Is there any evidence that these programs are effective?
- **How** much is being spent at the state and federal level to curb juvenile crime?
- **How** much would a federal program like this cost to administer?
- **Who** would administer this kind of program?
- **Why** is the present system of curbing juvenile crime ineffective?

These questions will help Writer B explore different perspectives on the issue. Notice that these questions are a version of the reporter's questions: *who? what? where? when? why?* and *how?* When she has consulted library sources and found answers to these questions, Writer B will determine her position on reducing juvenile crime.

Even if you start out with a position on an issue, it's a good idea to ask the kinds of questions Writers A and B posed. By considering different responses, you can discover to what extent you are prepared to support a position. Asking questions and exploring multiple responses should help you consider the counterarguments you'll have to address when you develop an argument.

Whether you have a definite stance on a topic or are completely undecided, finding out what other writers have to say about your topic will help you develop your ideas. The sources you consult will help you form opinions, or they will strengthen or even perhaps change your initial stance. You should expect to find support, opposition, and contradiction for your assumptions, opinions, or hypotheses. If you begin with a definite position, don't be surprised if your sources convince you to change it. It is not unusual to begin research on a topic you know little about with one perspective and, as you read, investigate, and gain a better understanding of the complexities of the topic, completely change your mind. This kind of switch in perspectives is not necessarily vacillating mindlessly; on the contrary, this change in perspective is usually the result of becoming well-informed about the topic.

UNDERSTANDING YOUR STANCE

Because it is important to understand your stance on a position (in informal terms, to understand "where you are coming from"), you should examine the influences that lead you to embrace a particular position. For any issue that you react to quickly with a strong opinion, ask yourself the following questions:

- Is my reaction based on emotion? ethical considerations? personal experience? political convictions? general knowledge about the topic?
- How well-informed am I about the issue? does my understanding of the issue come from conversations with friends and family? television or radio? the Internet? personal experience? classroom instruction or discussion?

If your stance on an issue is undetermined, use the strategies below for investigating your topic and identifying a position:

- Answer the reporter's questions *who? what? where? when? why?* and *how?*
- Identify as many perspectives as possible—those that are clearly *for* or *against*, as well as those that suggest compromise.

EXERCISE: THINKING CRITICALLY

Review letters to the editor and editorials in newspapers and magazines. Find an example of a writer offering a thesis and points of support and an example of a writer exploring an issue and taking a position in the conclusion. Be prepared to discuss why you think your examples illustrate effective, mediocre, or ineffective position statements.

TURNING A POSITION INTO AN ARGUMENT

It's important to understand the difference in a position paper and an argument. In an argumentative paper, you have to present the opposing side's perspective. If you don't address the counterargument, your paper never develops an argument. An effective argument begins with a thesis that gives readers a sense of how you are going to argue—that is, which perspective you favor and which perspective you oppose. While you may begin in preliminary drafts with a brief, tentative thesis statement, you want to expand it, revising so that sentence structure and content walk hand-in-hand. Let's look at a few examples of a tentative thesis:

> *Sentence A:* Dyslexia is a serious vision problem a lot of people don't understand.

> *Sentence B:* We shouldn't believe what revisionist historians tell us about Hiroshima and Nagasaki.

Both sentences are appropriate places to start with in a draft. While each states a position, neither sentence would be an effective thesis in an argumentative essay.

Both sentences are fill-in-the-blank sentences. They have a generic quality to them that will allow them to accommodate a number of topics. In sentence A, you can strike out the words *dyslexia* and *vision* and plug in almost any topic—drug addiction, the effect of secondhand smoke, use of animals in scientific experimentation, censorship of the Internet, for example:

_____ is a serious problem a lot of people don't understand.

Sentence B is similar. You can strike out the words *revisionists* and *Hiroshima and Nagasaki* and say the same thing about a number of topics:

> We shouldn't believe what government reports tell us about drug addiction.

We shouldn't believe what the medical community tells us about secondhand smoke.

We shouldn't believe what animal activists tell us about the use of animal experimentation in scientific research.

In addition to having a fill-in-the-blank quality to them, sentences A and B prompt questions: *Why don't people understand that dyslexia is a vision problem? Why shouldn't we believe revisionist historians?* They fail to provide the reader with a sense of whether the writer will defend a position on the issue or develop an argumentative paper that examines more than one perspective.

In second drafts of sentences A and B, the writers are still trying to flesh out ideas.

Sentence A Dyslexia is actually a language disorder.

Sentence B Revisionist historians are wrong when they claim that the bombings of Hiroshima and Nagasaki were unnecessary.

While the versions above are more specific than the first drafts, each one can be improved in order to give the reader some of idea of what the writer will argue for and what the writer will argue against. With additional revision and addition of ideas, each writer crafts a sentence that is specific and clear:

Sentence A: Although dyslexia is often perceived as a visual problem, recently published studies indicate that it is a language-based disorder.

Sentence B: Even though revisionist historians argue that the bombings of Hiroshima and Nagasaki were unnecessary and inhumane, President Truman in deciding to drop the atomic bombs, brought the war to a merciful end and saved thousands of lives by avoiding a catastrophic invasion of Japan.

In the final drafts, both writers place perspectives they will argue against, the counterargument, in a *subordinate clause*, a clause (subject, verb, and their modifiers) that does not express a complete idea of its own and depends on an independent clause for full meaning.

Although dyslexia is often perceived as a visual problem,

Even though revisionist historians argue that the bombing of Hiroshima and Nagasaki was unnecessary and inhumane,

Perspectives each writer will argue for are placed in an *independent clause*, or a clause that expresses a complete thought on its own.

The kind of sentence structure these writers use is not by any means the only way to cast an argumentative thesis. It is an effective strategy, however, for giving readers a specific thesis that indicates that one perspective will be considered secondary to another. As you read and annotate sources in this chapter's case study, identify each writer's thesis and consider how writers give ideas emphasis in a sentence when they make one idea of lesser importance than another. And use your position drafts to develop an argumentative thesis.

FOCUSING ON YOUR READERS

Where should the focus be in a paper that develops an argument? In editorials and letters to the editor, you often find as much focus on the writer as you do on the subject. The phrases *I believe* or *in my opinion* may occur frequently. You also see focus on the writer when the writer is an expert or has exceptional firsthand experience or knowledge about an issue. For example, a judge arguing that cameras should not be allowed in courtrooms has a point of view other people will not have, even if they follow trials closely. The judge's use of the first person (*in my opinion, it has been my experience,* or *I have found that…*) carries authority, and readers understand that these opinions are based on firsthand knowledge.

When you write to persuade readers, ask yourself *what will my readers value and consider convincing or at least thought-provoking?* The best strategy is to focus on the facts, statistics, expert testimony, eyewitness accounts, and published studies your readers will find convincing and avoid prefacing too many statements with *I believe* or *In my opinion.* Demonstrate that many different sources support your position.

PREVIEW: MEN AT THE CROSSROADS

In 1933, Mexican artist Diego Rivera (see Figure 13.1), an avowed Communist, was commissioned to paint murals at the Detroit Institute of Arts on the theme of modern industry (see Figure 13.2). When the murals were unveiled, conservative American citizens voiced disapproval, claiming the frescoes were blatantly Communist

FIGURE 13.1 Diego Rivera. Self Portrait—1921

FIGURE 13.2 "Man at the Crossroads"

and obscene. While many community leaders and artists spoke out in Rivera's defense, objections against his art prevailed. Nevertheless, the Rockefeller family selected Rivera to paint a giant mural at Rockefeller Center in New York. Nelson Rockefeller set the theme for the murals: "Man at the Crossroads Looking with Hope and High Vision to the Choosing of a New and Better Future." When the press corps previewed Rivera's partially completed frescoes, they saw unemployed workers and protesters being harassed by police on one side and to the left of the center a prominent portrait of Lenin shaking hands with representatives of the working class. The headline of the April 24 *New York World-Telegram* told the story: "Rivera Paints Scenes of Communist Activity and John D. [Rockefeller], Jr., Foots Bill." This same newspaper noted that the most dominant color in the mural was red. When the Rockefellers requested that Lenin be replaced, Rivera refused. With two-thirds of the mural completed he was paid off and dismissed. Although a public outcry ensued, the murals were covered and eventually destroyed. Working from memory and from sketches he made of the Rockefeller Center mural, Rivera painted *Man at the Crossroads* in the Palacia de Bellas Artes in Mexico City in 1934. In "Viva Rivera," an article published in the January 1997 edition of the *Los Angeles Journal*, Pete Hamill provides a detailed description of the controversial mural.

> The mural presents science and technology as the salvation of mankind—part of the more intellectual version of the Communist faith in the 1930s. In the center of the design is a scientist dressed like an astronaut, three decades before the Russians and Americans made it into space. On the left side, we see the forces of war, police suppressing strikers, capitalist decadence and plague. Charles Darwin examines a human skull in what seems to be a television set (in 1934!). On the other side, happy Russians march in what appears to be Red Square, healthy young women run in a sporting event, industrial workers lounge upon a length of pipe, airplane pilots sit on the decapitated head of the god of war and grateful human beings of all races listen to the noble and benevolent V. I. Lenin.

Hamill concludes his description with the following observation: "Each time I stand in the crowd before the mural, someone laughs."

EXERCISE: GOING ON-LINE

Before you read what others have to say about Rivera's mural, look at pictures of the duplicate mural at the addresses below. Then write for ten to fifteen minutes and record your reactions. How would you characterize Rivera's mural? Who and what is included? How do you see the mural carrying out the theme "Man at the Crossroads"? Why do you think the mural caused so much controversy? Add any other ideas you have about the mural and your impressions of Rivera.

Diego Rivera Web Museum:
       <http://www.diegorivera.com/diego_home_eng.html>

Men at the Crossroads Mural:
       <http://www.diegorivera.com/murals/encruci.html>

FOCUS ON RELATED ISSUES:
THE ROLE OF THE ARTIST

There are two schools of thought about the role of art. One school advocates art for art's sake—that is, the aim of the artist is to create a work that is aesthetically pleasing but not necessarily thought-provoking. Another school favors a political role for the artist—that is, the aim of the artist is to create a work that addresses a political, social, or ethical issue. What kind of relationship would you like to see between art and politics? How important is public support for the arts? How important is government support?

Case Study 5: Politics and Art

The old dispute among the adepts of Art for Art's sake and their antagonists, the defenders of the conception that art always serves a political or social cause, acquired special belligerency during the period between the World Wars. The bottom line of this old battle is that these differences are very limited since as daughters of language, works of art cannot be carried out in isolation, and are therefore impregnated with ideals, situated within a specific historical context and used in accordance with the political reality which reaches beyond the author's will.

> —*Irene Herrer de Larrea,* Diego Rivera: Paradise Lost
> at Rockefeller Center

It has been said that the revolution has no need of art, but that art has need of the revolution. That is not true…. It supplies strength for the struggle. It supplies strength for the struggle. It is as much a nourishment as is wheat.

> —*Diego Rivera, "What Is Art For"*

The proprietors [of Rockefeller Center] by forbidding a Christian painter to paint Christ and a Communist painter to paint Lenin prove that when they hire a painter, they think that they are buying him body and soul…. They are mistaken.

> —*Diego Rivera, quoted in* The Fabulous Life of
> Diego Rivera

If you don't want swastikas over your synagogue, you don't employ an artist whom you know to be a specialist in swastikas.

> —*"Art for Propaganda's Sake"*

DIEGO RIVERA

Pete Hamill, a former student of art and author of *Diego Rivera*, provides an overview of Rivera's career in "Viva Rivera."

¡VIVA RIVERA!

PETE HAMILL

WOMEN ADORED HIM. RIVALS HATED HIM. HE WAS CELEBRATED AND DAMNED BY CRITICS AND GOSSIP COLUMNISTS. BUT AFTER HIS DEATH, DIEGO RIVERA'S REPUTATION WAS ECLIPSED WHEN HIS WIFE, FRIDA KAHLO, BECAME THE ART WORLD'S NEWEST STAR. PETE HAMILL TRAVELS TO MEXICO CITY TO RESTORE THE LEGACY OF THE GREATEST MURAL-IST OF THE TWENTIETH CENTURY

The Mexican painter Diego Rivera paid a fierce price for being one of the most famous artists of his time.

In the two decades before World War II, he was praised or damned by critics of the world, viciously attacked by ideological enemies at home and subjected to death threats, slander and mockery. Cartoonists were ecstatic over his bulging eyes, fleshy face and great physical bulk (he stood well over six feet and for most of his adult life weighed about 300 pounds). Foreign journalists made pilgrimages to his home in the Mexico City suburb of Coyoacán to record his thoughts on art, politics and the utopian future. Young artists yearned to serve him as apprentices. Older artists envied or hated him. Women adored him. His name was prominent in the gossip columns and sometimes appeared in the news as the central figure in some scandal or controversy. He was that most rare figure in the world of art: a celebrity.

Rivera was a man of Rabelaisian appetites: for women, for argument, for food, for work. He had four wives, one of whom—Frida Kahlo—he divorced and married again. He liked to carry a gun, and sometimes even climbed his scaffolds while packing. He was, like most mythomaniacs, a gifted and entertaining liar: "If Diego rarely told the simple truth," said his biographer Bertram D. Wolfe, "he did not tell simple lies either." He embellished his life the way he embellished his densely packed murals, elaborating facts with myth and a kind of magical realism.

His life itself was riddled with paradox. Rivera was one of the great defenders of the Mexican Revolution, but he remained safely in Europe for most of the duration of that bloody upheaval (1910–20). He became a propagandist for international Communism but painted a mural for the San Francisco Stock Exchange, another in Detroit financed by the family of Henry Ford and a third for Rockefeller Center. He was one of the Big Three of Mexican muralism (along with David Alfaro Siqueiros and José Clemente Orozco), expressing occasionally savage visions of class and ethnic exploitation in Mexico. But he earned handsome fees for his easel paintings of society women; movie stars such as Maria Félix, Dolores del Río and Paulette Goddard; and plump Mexican peasant children. He never made more than four dollars a day as a muralist, but the easel-work enabled him to live comfortably in the famous Blue House with Frida Kahlo, maintain a huge private studio in San Angel and amass one of the largest private collections of pre-Columbian art—an estimated 57,000 pieces. He joined, then left, the Communist Party and sponsored Trotsky's exile in Mexico: but in later life, he humbled himself to gain readmission to the Party at a time when everyone knew Joseph Stalin was a monster. Diego Rivera was, in short, a man of his times, with all their passions and contradictions.

But the times changed. The Mexican Revolution atrophied. The Communist dream was exposed as another murderous hoax. After World War II, a new generation of artists raised the triumphant banners of abstract expressionism in New York. Rivera's didactic and content-heavy work, when it received critical attention at all, was dismissed as a creaky artifact. When he died in 1957 at age 70, many thousands attended his funeral in Mexico City; elsewhere, Diego Rivera seemed to belong to a remote, even embarrassing, past.

Today, he is usually part of another story—the pain-wracked saga of Frida Kahlo. They met in 1928 when Rivera was 41 and Kahlo was 21. The following year, she became Diego's third wife. Rivera was already famous; Frida was an aspiring painter. In spite of permanent physical agony (the result of a horrifying streetcar accident in 1925), she worked heroically at her art and, with Diego's support and encouragement, became a great painter with only one subject: herself. She died in 1954, and for years her work suffered the fate of Rivera's, falling into semi-obscurity.

In the '70s, however, spurred by the rising force of feminism, art scholars began paying more attention to her work. Toward the end of the decade, major retrospectives were mounted in Mexico City and London. After Hayden Herrera's biography of Kahlo appeared in 1983, the Frida boom began. There were Frida Kahlo museum shows, posters, calendars, medallions, buttons, postcards, cafés and, of course, countless Frida Kahlo art books with beautiful reproductions and learned texts. There were periodic announcements of Hollywood movies about her (usually mentioning Madonna, who collected her work), and in Mexico a very good film actually was made starring that country's finest actress. Ofelia Medina. In the New York auction houses and galleries, the price of her artwork soared.

At the same time, she became the darling of feminist ideologues, an emblematic woman-as-victim: victim of the male-controlled art world; victim of the codes of machismo; and, of course, victim of the philandering Diego, whose art was pronounced inferior to hers. Diego Rivera was reduced to the image imprinted on the brow of Frida's weeping self-portrait, *Diego on My Mind.*

In some ways, this gross distortion is understandable—the work of

Frida Kahlo was undervalued for decades, and Rivera's own reputation had been reduced to the shorthand of dismissal, even in Mexico. In 1957, when I was in Mexico City studying painting on the GI Bill, I was among those who sneered. I loved Orozco; I was bowled over by Rufino Tamayo, who had returned from a long exile in New York a few years earlier; I felt connected to the dark drawings of José Luis Cuevas and the paintings of Pedro and Rafael Coronel. Diego Rivera seemed to my 21-year-old eyes just a glorified cartoonist.

Then, in 1986, the year after the earthquake that devastated Mexico City, I began to look at Rivera's work again. That year, there was a grand retrospective at the Palacio de Bellas Artes celebrating the centenary of Rivera's birth. It traced his life through his art, from his earliest drawings as a child in the silver city of Guanajuato to his student exercises in the San Carlos Academy in Mexico City and through his long sojourn in Europe (1907–20). The draftsmanship was always superb; through his variations on impressionism and Cézanne, it was clear that, even as a young man, he could do anything with paint. In Paris, he had become an accomplished painter in the cubist school (he was friendly with Picasso, Juan Gris and Modigliani, who painted his portrait). But with the exception of a few cubist paintings (such as *Zapatista Land-scape*) and some very large portraits in an expressionist manner, there was no sign of the Diego Rivera who would epitomize Mexican art in his time.

Then suddenly, in work done after his return to Mexico in 1921, he was Diego. The draftsmanship became bolder and more confident. His palette was brighter, full of reds and earth browns and the azure of the Mexican sky. And he found his essential subject matter in the handsome, blocky faces of the Indians of Mexico. It was as if he had spent more than a decade trying on other people's clothes and speaking other people's languages. At last he had come home.

That show propelled me to look again at his murals. I was astonished at my own reaction. Since the creeds that once drove the work were dead, I could forget the ideology and look at the best of the murals for what they were—truly amazing paintings. It was like looking at a work by Tintoretto or John Singer Sargent: You don't need to know who that cardinal was, or that society woman—you can look at the work as a painting. I'm now convinced that Diego Rivera was one of the great painters of the twentieth century.

Isolated examples of his work are in most of the great museums of Mexico and the world. Many of his easel paintings remain hidden away in private collections. But the mural paintings are there for all to see.

Source: Pete Hamill, "Viva Rivera!", *Los Angeles Journal,* (Jan. 1997): 70.

For Discussion

- Hamill claims that Rivera's life was "riddled with paradox." Identify three paradoxical situations Hamill describes.

- How does Hamill explain Rivera's fall into "semi-obscurity"?
- According to Hamill, why did interest develop in Rivera's third wife, Frida Kahlo, in the 1970s?
- Hamill states that when he was twenty-one, he thought of Rivera as "just a glorified cartoonist." Almost thirty years later, though, he changed his opinion. What reasons does he offer for this shift in perspective?
- What kind of composite picture does Hamill offer of Rivera?

The following sources explain what happened when Rockefeller refused to allow Rivera to complete the mural. Read carefully. Notice that each version of the conflict between the two men offers a slightly different perspective than others. Be prepared to identify specific passages that report new information and passages that disagree with, or contradict, information in other sources. Then, try to account for the writer's perspective in each source. Consider such matters as the date of publication, the author's purpose, and the intended audience.

"Art: Diego Rivera's Mural in Rockefeller Center Rejected," appeared in *Newsweek*. No author is listed for the article.

ART: DIEGO RIVERA'S MURAL IN ROCKEFELLER CENTER REJECTED

A canvas, innocently blank, goes up 30 censorious feet into the tense air in the great hall of the RCA Building in Rockefelter Center, New York. In front of it paces a policeman, shooing away crowds that mill about, the lobbies. Behind the canvas flame the deep reds of a mural by the Mexican proletarian artist, Diego Rivera—reds rejected of the Rockefellers.

Rarely in the long history of art controversies has so much furor been aroused as was caused by front page stories in last week's papers. These announced that the huge mural, which was to adorn the central position in the central building of Rockefeller Center, had been turned down by representatives of the Rockefellers because in it there appeared a portrait of Vladimir Illyith Ulianov, know to the world as Lenin.

Rivera supporters compared the treatment accorded their shaggy artist-hero with that meted out to Michelangelo by the Popes.

An hour after word got down to Union Square that Rivera had been discharged, there were hatless art students and radicals struggling with bewildered police all over Rockefeller Center, shouting: "We want Rivera."

Proletarian taxi drivers, waiting for fares in front of the Roxy Music Hall, a half block away, scrambled out of their cabs to join fists with the police in repelling the invaders. Riot cars hooted through the side streets, and up aristocratic Fifth Avenue.

For the Mexican artist, the rejection came with thunderbolt swiftness. On the evening of May 9 he was up on a scaffold in front of his almost completed mural, splashing happily away on his conception of "Human Intelligence in Control of the Forces of Nature." The job was nearly done, and in Rivera's opinion It was to be his masterpiece.

Griui

Across the top of the mural he had grouped on one side soldiers, grim-green in gas-masks, about to launch a headlong attack upon marching columns of workers and peasants coming up against a background of red flags, singing, it was not hard to guess, "The Internationale." In a fierce light at the heart of his mural he had put the head of a worker (model, for which, by the way, was a nephew of John F. Curry, leader of Tammany Hall) brooding over a television machine, which disclosed to him two wing-shaped objects on which were magnifled, in writhing colors, the germs which assail mankind.

Below, radicals, bearing banners: "Free Tom Mooney," "We Want Work, not Charity," "Down with Imperialist Wars," were depleted scuffling with club-swinging police against the background of Trinity Church. There was a panel of a radical meeting: another of a society group playing bridge.

Sudden

And then, of a sudden, there emerged the Buddha-like form of Lenin joining the hands of a Negro and a white worker.

As Senor Rivera put his earthy colors on the wet plaster, which when it dries becomes part of the wall, a representative of Todd, Robertson & Todd Engineering Corporation, builders and managers of Rockefeller Center, told the artist that he was wanted in his studio on the mezzanine floor of the 70-story building. He found there a check for $14,000, the balance due him on his contract for $21,000 for the completed mural. Also a letter stating that his mural was unacceptable to the Rockefeller family.

This was a sequel to an earlier letter from Nelson A. Rockefeller, in which the young grandson of John D. Rockefeller said:

Letter

"I noticed that in the most recent portion of the painting you had included a portrait of Lenin. This piece is beautifully painted, but it seems to me that his portrait, appearing in this mural, might very easily seriously offend a great many people. If it were in a private house it would be one thing, but this mural is in a public building, and the situation is therefore quite different. As much as I dislike to do so, I am afraid we must ask you to substitute the face of some unknown man where Lenin's face now appears."

To this Senor Rivera said he had answered that, to balance Lenin, he would gladly show Lincoln freeing the slaves or a picture of John Brown or William Lloyd Garrison.

Besides, as Senor Rivera explained to a packed Town Hall meeting last Saturday night, the whole business was part of a propaganda mission which he had undertaken, when he came to this country in 1931. Then he stirred the art world with an exhibit viewed with enthusiasm by Mrs. John D. Rockefeller Jr., and her son, Nelson.

Disguised

The artist said that "friends in Moscow" had told him that the sort of painting he had done in Mexico was all right for peasants, but that in an industrial country like the United States he would have to change his style, always keeping in mind that "in all cases the workers and peasants are right and that the artist should paint what the workers and peasants want."

"The only thing for me to do," he said naively, "was to try it out in an industrial country ... In order to get here I had to do as a man in war. Sometimes, in times of war, a man disguises himself as a tree. My paintings in this country have become increasingly and gradually clearer."

Irate

While his indignant sympathizers were planning further picketing of the Center, Senor Rivera received a telegram from the General Motors Company in Detroit. There murals by Rivera have already proved a storm center. The telegram said that his commission for murals for the automobile company's exhibit at the Chicago World's Fair would be canceled.

Thereupon the irate artist announced that he would spend the $14,000 of Rockefeller money, just paid him, painting a mural in the dingy library of the Rand School for Social Science at 7 East 15th Street, New York, Socialist headquarters. There he will paint solely for "my own people, the working people."

Source: "Art: Diego Rivera's Mural in Rockefeller Center Rejected," *Newsweek,* 20 May 1933: 29–30.

ROCKEFELLERS V. RIVERA

Into the lobby of Rockefeller Center's towering RCA Building last week stalked Rental Manager Hugh Robertson, followed by twelve uniformed guards. The procession halted before a huge (63 ft. by 17 ft.) unfinished fresco on the wall facing the doors. Its bright colors and hard, compact figures filled the lobby like a parade. On scaffolding before it stood a big, drooping man with a gloomy face and sad Mexican eyes: Diego Rivera, the world's foremost living fresco painter. A guard called to Rivera to come down from his scaffold. He laid down his big brushes and the tin kitchen plate he uses for a palette, climbed nimbly down the ladder. Mr. Robertson handed him an envelop. It held a check for $14,000, last payment on the $21,000 due Rivera for his work. It held too a letter telling him he was fired. Artist Rivera woodenly went to his work shack on the lobby balcony to change from his overalls. At once more guards appeared, pushed away the movable scaffold. Others came with planking. Within half an hour, the unfinished fresco was covered with tarpaper and a wooden screen. Meanwhile one of Rivera's assistants rushed hysterically out to the restaurant where six other assistants were dining, to spread the news and detonate 1933's biggest art story.

The seven assistants rushed back, gibbering with indignation. Assistant Lucienne Bloch, daughter of Swiss Composer Ernest Bloch, scraped the white paint off two second-story windows to form the words: "Workers Unite," "Help! Protect Rivera M...." Guards stopped her from finishing the word "Murals." By night fall Communists began to swarm in Rockefeller Plaza, the new thoroughfare cutting through Rockefeller Center. They churned about, cheering for the man whom they had read out of their party four years ago, waving banners "Save Rivera's Painting," marching & counter-marching around the RCA Building. Mounted police pranced on the outskirts, shooed them away before audiences issuing from the two Rockefeller Center cinema houses could jam the district.

Next day newspapers splashed across their front pages the ostensible reason for all the hubbub. On May 1 (May Day), near the centre of the Fresco had appeared a small head of Vladimir Ilyich Lenin. John D. Rockefeller, Jr.'s son Nelson had asked Rivera "to substitute the face of some unknown man where Lenin's face now appears." Rivera had countered by offering to balance Lenin with a portrait of Abraham Lincoln. The Rockefellers exploded, fired Rivera.

Four nights later Rivera, his temper hidden by a lazy smile, told an audience in Manhattan's Town Hall that of course his art was Communistic propaganda. After the Communists had read him out of the party, "one thing was left for me: to prove that my theory would be accepted in an industrial nation where capitalists rule.... I had to come as a spy, in disguise. Sometimes in times of war a man disguises himself as a tree. My paintings in this country have become increasingly and gradually clearer." Speaking in French he said, "Art is like ham—it nourishes people." The interpreter translated *jambon* as "food." The audience shouted "Ham!" and Rivera nodded. He concluded, "Because there is a logic of history, the RCA Building will assume its real function—the time depends upon the will of the workers."

While everybody went off half-cocked, the facts slowly emerged. Last November Todd, Robertson, Todd, building & renting managers of Rockefeller Center, planned the RCA Building's lobby as a liberal museum. They selected the social-technical theme, "New Frontiers," to be executed by three foreign muralists. Spanish José Maria Sert, British Frank Brangwyn and Mexican Diego Rivera. To Rivera was assigned the subject, "Man at the crossroads looking with uncertainty but hope for a new solution." Last November, at the depression's low, the U. S. was pessimistic; capitalists pondered Communists, wondered whether Revolution was a possibility. To Rivera's hiring by the Rockefellers the publicity was tremendous. Rivera knew that John D. Rockefeller Jr.'s wife and his son Nelson were trustees of Manhattan's Museum of Modern Art which gave Rivera a show a year ago. In that show was many a frankly Communistic picture by Rivera. notably a fresco *Frozen Assets,* showing starving men, idle mills. In early

March, one of Rockefeller Center's architects, Raymond Hood, went to Detroit where Rivera was finishing his frescoes for the Detroit Institute of Arts. He approved Rivera's big, colored sketch for Rockefeller Center.

The sketch showed a central figure who looked like a blond Russian (eventually posed by Tammany Boss John Francis Curry's grandnephew Hugh Jr., 22) under a big television machine which projected on the rest of the design the worker's choices. These were: marching soldiers with gas-masked heads like wasps, Communists trooping in Moscow's Red Square; a group of unemployed rioting under hard-jawed mounted police; socialite bridge-players and fox-trotters; women exercising; students; a worker, a student and an unemployed worker listening to a Leader. Through the composition criss-crossed two spurs, showing enormously magnified disease bacteria and a galaxy of constellations. Rivera produced another preliminary sketch in black and white and a third, larger one in full color. Both of these were approved by Todd, Robertson, Todd. In none was the head of the Leader that of Lenin.

Late in March Rivera squared off at his bare white wall in the RCA lobby. Tickets were issued to watch him do his daily stint. Art students, businessmen and Communists bought tickets as Rivera slowly spread paint down over the wall in a characteristic composition made up of huge, chunky units. Rockefeller Center workmen came free. Painting directly on wet plaster as in all true fresco, Rivera put on the wall the essentials of his submitted and approved sketches. Nelson Rockefeller came too to watch, told Rivera he liked the fresco. On May Day Rivera came to the head of the Leader, made it the head of Lenin.

Soon afterwards Rivera and his assistants became aware of a changed attitude in Rockefeller Center. The number of guards was increased. When Rivera brought men to photograph his fresco, they were sent away. Personal feuds sprang up between the Rockefeller Center guards and Rivera's assistants. A guard threatened to brain an assistant if he tried to take a snapshot. Rivera's heavy scaffolding was replaced by a movable scaffold. Rivera draped tracing paper over the outside railing, screening the platform from the guards, and a woman assistant took a camera from under her skirt to photograph, close up, part of the fresco. The scaffold was moved, the operation repeated until Rivera had photographs of the whole fresco. He was scarcely surprised that the Rockefellers objected to his work when they saw it as living art and realized what it meant.

Last week Rivera cashed his $14,000 check, went to see his lawyer. He was told he might sue to establish an artist's dubious right under an "implied covenant" to force exhibition of his work, but that he had no legal right to the fresco he had sold and been paid for. He fell back on "a moral question" of the artist's right "to express himself; and the right to receive the judgment of the world, of posterity." Said he: "They have no right, this little group of commercial minded people, to assassinate my work and that of my colleagues. They accepted my sketches." He offered to do the whole thing over gratis on any fit Manhattan wall offered him.

To this the Rockefellers said nothing. The RCA Building was on the newspapers' front pages again. They noted that Communistic Rivera who needs walls to work on has worked on the walls of "commercial minded" people exclusively for the past year. Rivera's next commission after the RCA Building was a "Forge and Foundry" mural for General Motors Corp. at its building in Chicago's Century of Progress Exposition. After the Rivera-Rockefeller ruckus, General Motors paused to consider what it had better do.

Source: "Rockfellers v. Rivera," *Time.* 22 May, 1933: 25–26.

EXERCISES: READING AND RESPONDING

1. The *Newsweek* and *Time* articles target similar audiences. In your opinion, is one article more informative than the other? Be prepared to explain why. Consider such matters as content, organization, and style.

2. In your opinion, if an individual pays someone to create a work of art, does that individual have the right to dictate what should or should not be part of the artist's creation?

3. Identify passages in both articles that rely on narration. Explain whether these passages seem sympathetic to either Rivera or Rockefeller and whether they might have played a role in influencing public opinion about the conflict between the two men.

4. Consider how each writer does or does not establish a context for readers. If you had to recommend one of these articles to introduce a friend to the controversy over the destruction of Rivera's mural, which one would you select? Explain why.

5. What assumptions do you think each writer made about intended readers? Identify passages that suggest these assumptions.

6. Summarize the facts each article offers about the destruction of the mural.

7. Summarize the opinions about the destruction of the mural.

The following sources are from a publication of Edicupes, S.A. de C.V. in cooperation with the School of Political and Social Sciences of the National Autonomous University of Mexico. If you are fluent in Spanish, translate Source 4. Source 5 is an interview with Diego Rivera originally published in the February 16, 1934, edition of *El Universal*, a Mexican newspaper. The translation is by Evert Villarreal.

DIEGO RIVERA ARMO UNA REVOLUCION
LE DIERON SU "TIME CHECK"

IRENE HERRER DE LARREA

SE LE ENTREGARON 14,000 DÓLARES Y SE LE OBLIGÓ A QUE NO SIGUIERA PINTANDO EN EL EDIFICIO ROCKEFELLER

PARA DESPEDIR AL PINTOR SE TOMARON PRECAUCIONES.—TUVO QUE INTERVENIR LA AUTORIDAD DE NUESTRA OFICINA EN NUEVA YORK. TIMES ANNEX

Nueva York, mayo 9.—Diego Rivera ha originado otra revolución, esta vez en Nueva York. Esta tarde, a las siete horas, cuando se hallaba trabajando en los freacos del Edificio Rockefeller, se presentaron varios representantes del multimillocario petrolero y filánfropo y le dijeron que bajara del andamío en que se encontraba pintando, pues ceseaban hablarle con auma urgencía. Cuando el pintor mexicano descendió al piso del edificio le entregaron un cheque por 14,000 dólares, como saldo de sus honorarios de 25,000 dólares y le manifestaron que quedaba despedido ipso facto. Los frescos no están terminados todavía y Rivera dice que teme que su obra sea destruída.

Para despedir a Rivera, se tomaron precauciones. Primero se cortaron los hilos del teléfono particular del pintor, instalado en una casilla en medio del vestíbulo donde se encuentran los murales. Después, numerosos agentes cis policía escoltaron al artista y sus ayudantes hasta la calle, donde se reunieron más tarde cerca de cien simpatizadores del pintor y organizaron una manifestación lievando banderas, dando gritos y pidiendo que no fuera destruída la obra del artista. La firma Todd Robertson and Todd, arquitectos, fué encargada de poner en ejecución la orden para despedir a Rivera. Los arquitectos manifiestan que en la carta que la fué entregada a Rivera, junto con el cheque, lamentan que Rivera no hubiera querido llegar a un acuerdo acerca del carácter simbólico de los personajes del los frescos. La carta termina manifestando que la entrega del cheque se considera como la terminación del contrato, a pesar de que ninguno de los tres frescos está terminado.

La causa verdadera del lío es el extremismo manifestado por don Diego, quien ultimamente se ha dedicado a dar en los ateneos hispanos de tinte ácrata. El extremismo del pintor se ha manifestado en uno de los frescos donde se ve la figura central del lider de la revolucíon comunista rusa. Nicolás Lenin, dando la mano a un soldado obrero negro, con un fondo de banderas rojas flameando en las manos de los sin trabajo. Rivera dijo que hace cinco o seis días tuvo noticia de que esas figuras no eran aprobadas por los contratistas.

El pintor, acompañado de varios amigos y admiradores se dirigió a las oficínas del abogado Philip Wittenberg, con el objeto de saber si tiene derecho a reclamación judicial para que le dejen terminar los frescos.

Rivera Propone
Una Transaccion

United Press

Nueva York, mayo 9.—Diego Rivera dijo que Mr. Nelson Rockefeller, nieto del conocido magnate John D. Rockefeller, uño de los hombres más ricos del mundo, visitó hace tiempo el Edificio de la RCA, dentro del Oentro Rockefeller, y en esa ocasión hizo patenta su objeción al retrato de Lenin que en la alegoría mural que la fué encomendada. El artista mexicano la contestó que no podría, verdaderamente, cambiar el dibujo.

Esta mañana Rivera recibió una carta de Todd, Robertson and Todd, firma de ingenieros, a la que se encomendó la construcción y decorado del edificio, informándole acerca de la objeción de Mr. Rockefeller a la naturaleza comunista que había dado al fresco que estaba ejecutando. En esa carta se hacía refarencia a la negativa del mismo Rivera de hacer los cambios que se la habían sugerido en su trabajo, agregando que el bosquejo la preliminar no indicaba la naturaleza de la pintura mural que ahora está ya

casi terminada, por lo que los aportadores de los fondos para la construcción eran del sentir de' que Rivera "había aprovechado la situación" pintando un asunto "de naturaleza de controversia".

Rivera replicó, simplemente, que no haría cambio alguno, por lo que inmediatamente se la dieron las gracias.

Después de que el pintor mexicano recibió la solicitud de que bajase de los andamios, se dirigió a su oficina improvisada en el entresuelo del edificio, y encountró que su taléfono había sido cortado.

Cierto numero de comunistas al conooer el incidente se dirigió en manifestacín hacia el edificio que está próximo a ser terminado. Al llegar a él, su numero era aproximadamente de trescientos, y rodesron el edificio lanzando gritos alusivos a su protesta y distribuyendo volantes protestando Rivera. La policía dispersó a los comunistas sin gran trabajo.

Un portavos del Centro Rockefeller dijo que se permitir´a que Diego Rivera terminase el fresco mural "siempre y cuando consienta en hacer determinados cambíos para hacer que la naturalexa del mismo fresco estés más de acuerdo con el proyecto arquitectónico general del edificio".

Diego Rivera parecía estar resignado a lo ocourride, pero dijo que tratando de conciliar a las partes interosadas sugeria un compromiso antre todos, segun el cual después de terminar por completo el fresco en que exhibe el retrato de Lenin, ejecutará otro en el que aparezca Lincoln ayudando a la humanidad.

En uno de nuestros más ele-
gantes y céntricos restaurantas se
efectuó ayer, a las 11.15 horas, el
segunde banquete del Club Leones de
México, perteneciente al famoso Club
Leones ramificado en tode el munde y
que recientemente ha fundade en
México su centre social.

Source: Irene Herrer De Larrea, "Diego Rivera Armo Una Revolucion," *Paradise Lost at the Rockefeller Center.* Edicupes (S.A. de C.V. in cooperation with the School of Political and Social Sciences of the National Autonomous U. of Mexico, 1987): 85.

DIEGO RIVERA AND ROCKEFELLER: THE ASSASSINATION OF AN ARTISTIC WORK

OSCAR LE BLANC

THE ENTIRE WORLD HAS
LEARNED ABOUT THE ERASED FRESCO

Yesterday, we spoke to Diego Rivera about the scandalous incident at the Rockefeller Center.

We asked him: what impression did you get after receiving the notice that your paintings were destroyed?

It was no surprise, because long before I left New York, I had told all of my friends, along with telling the press, affirming the fact that I knew and was sure that the paintings would be destroyed, even though the world thought the contrary would occur. In addition, the proprietors of the building had assured me, in person, that the paintings would remain covered until the subject matter would no longer offend anyone. Also, these same building proprietors explored different solutions to the problem, and they had tentatively suggested looking for another painter to conclude or modify the work that I almost had almost finished. Regarding this, I must say out of respect for my colleagues and companions who are North American, that not one artist stepped forward to do such a damning thing, even though the material benefits received from these millionaires would be tempting. In addition, the notice of the destruction of the paintings caused me no shame because I know that I did as much to promote the utility of the international proletariat. I believe that the fresco, which is now destroyed, sends the proletariat a clearer and louder message now that the fresco is dead, compared to the message the fresco could have sent if it had been allowed to exist at the "Rockefeller Center". From the view-point of an egoist, the destruction of the painting caused in me a bitter-sweet satisfaction. I now know that the actions of several capitalists assassinating a work of art shows how they excuse themselves for the social crimes they have committed in gaining their wealth.

Is it safe to say that you definitely consider your work of art destroyed?

Not at all. In the first place, the reproductions world presses made in covering this story with a social issue at its center, have taken my painting to a viewing audience of millions ... even more than the group who would have seen and utilized the fresco. In addition, Mr. Rockefeller should note that I am not for sale, and he cannot change my social beliefs and opinions, even with all of his money, his insinuations of friendship, and his social position as an all-powerful magnate.

In addition, I will now reproduce the painting in lithographs, and I will distribute them throughout the many revolutionary organizations. I will also distribute the lithographs amongst the general public and anyone else who is interested in this work; the painting will continue to exist even though it has been destroyed at the Rockefeller Center. I will reconstruct the painting in three places: one will be a mural in Mexico, another will be a mural in the United States, and the other will belong to Europe.

Can you tell me, what were the details and conditions of the contract that you signed when painting the murals of Radio City Music Hall? I ask this because some say that you abused the confidence that, the multimillionaire, Rockefeller had placed in you.

The contract that I signed stipulated that the painting should represent the theme given by the "Rockefeller Center", and literally, this is the written theme: "WHEN MAN STANDS AT A CROSSROADS, HE LOOKS FORWARD (INTO THE FUTURE) WITH RESTLESSNESS, BUT HE ALSO FEELS HOPE, ALWAYS LOOKING FOR A BETTER SOLU-

TION." This is a theme that I interpreted to mean exactly what I currently believe. That is to say, that, to me, the road that men follow under a capitalistic system of government has many consequences: exploitation of men by men, imperialistic warfare, hunger, economic crises, destruction of fruits, wheat, cotton, and so many of the things that seem indispensable and necessary for the millions of working people who are jobless and hungry ... in summary, inequality and destruction. The other road, at least to me, cannot be anything but the revolutionary organization made up of workers who stand up against exploitation. This revolutionary organization has to be created and constructed with foundations of economic socialism and a humanity with nor social classes. This had to be presented with some objectivity and a realistic realization. Of course, this type of solution can only be found in the social revolution of Lenin and Trotski, which is based on the ideas of Marx and Engels, which, of course, has already resulted in the successful tangible and powerful, Union of Soviet Socialist Republics. That country is the only hope for all of those people who want to live in a civilization of permanent justice and peace.

In the first place, Mr. Rockefeller knew perfectly well about the character of the work He knows where I stand ideologically, and he had seen the collection that his wife has, which is made up of more than eighty-four water-based paintings. These paintings represent the glorification of the Russian Revolution, all of which describe the actual events that took place on October 27th and 28th; in addition, they also describe the events that took place in May, when one million workers affirmed the reality of Lenin's human construction. Also, the individual show of my paintings in the "Modern Museum" in New York that took place in 1931, all of my paintings confirmed the socialistic tendencies that have been apparent in my work for almost fifteen years. Also, outside the Department of Public Education in Mexico, one of my frescoes reproduces scenes from the United States, and it includes a portrait of Mr. Rockefeller, Sr., the father of Mr. Rockefeller, Jr., who is now the destroyer of my fresco. The fresco shows Mr. Rockefeller, Sr., amongst other millionaires, all living in the United States, examining receipts from the Stock Exchange. This fresco shows Miss America and Miss Mexico in the first part of the fresco, while in the background, a strong safe or lockbox appears along with apparatuses that look like radios and other images incorporating electricity. In addition, the entire fresco is illuminated by a light coming from the lamp of the Statue of Liberty, which, of course, illuminates the entrance of the port of New York.

I have been the subject of attacks and criticisms now hundreds of times, on an international scale, all because of my social and political tendencies. On more than one occasion, the proprietors of the Rockefeller Center approached me with issues regarding the liberty to paint the fresco. Obviously, Mr. Rockefeller thought that he could buy me and my opinions and convictions with his money, or he did not know what he had agreed to. This criticism also applies to the oil that he has in Mex-

ico, which, sadly, is making him rich while exploiting the Mexican labor force. Naturally, it is not my fault if the experimental millionaire made a huge mistake regarding my humility.

Because I wanted to present the matter in a perfectly understandable fashion, I submitted several sample diagrams to show Mr. Rockefeller and his family, who by the way are very interested in art, the architects, the engineers, and financial advisors, a detailed description of the work. In the written description, I clearly and concretely underlined the components that would make up the painting. I also explained the fresco's social significance, and I did not use euphemisms. Instead, I used perfectly clear dialectic. And, this is way, Mr. Rockefeller's suspension of my work came along with a check for the entire amount that had been agreed upon. Juridically, they had nothing to argue on their behalf, and the only pretext they gave concerned the image of Lenin, and even this was a weak pretext. In my written proposal, I discussed how "a demonstration of masses that organized in Russia" was going to make up part of the fresco. This manifested itself in the portrait of a leader uniting the hands of a soldier, a peasant, and a field worker in a gesture of equivocation. This represents the alliance of these three social classes, and its fusion is singular (there is a oneness to its fusion): they become the workers of procution. This does not represent a fantasy, but, instead, it is a concrete reality. This concrete reality can be seen in the Soviet Union, which makes up one-sixth of the Earth's land. In the Soviet Union, the power resides in the hands of the laborers. And who could be the leader? The leader has to be Lenin. So, considering the theme they proposed and my political beliefs, the obvious choice was the figure of Lenin.

People are going to want to know how Mr. Rockefeller would have approved all of this, and my answer is this: Speaking through his magnates, Mr. Rockefeller said: "One more winter seeing millions of people who are out of work will lead to a Revolution", and this gave them fear. The magnates thought that that image might plant seeds of revolution in the minds of workers, OR, Mr. Rockefeller thought about destroying the fresco all along. By doing so, he was hoping to draw attention to his enterprise by assassinating a work of art produced by an artist who was faking his love for aesthetics and art. In any of these two cases, Mr. Rockefeller can be characterized by cow-

ardice and hypocricy, both of which are characteristics of capitalism. And, sadly, I am not surprised to see that Mr. Rockefeller possesses both.

To conclude our interview, we asked Diego Rivera about his artistic prospects for the future. This is what he had to say:

I hope to continue painting frescoes, and, as long as there is a sky, paintings, drawings, sketches, and thoughts, I hope to continue producing paintings that will be useful to all of the workers of the world.

Diego Rivera concluded by telling us that within a few days, he will begin to design other murals. He will be designing the hallways of the National Palace. The paintings will express the History of Mexico, and they will culminate with a mural that will blend into the steps of the palace.
Oscar LeBlanc

Source: Oscar Le Blanc, "Diego Rivera and Rockefeller: The Assassination of an Artistic Work," Irene Herrer De Larrea. *Paradise Lost at the Rockefeller Center.* Edicupes, S.A. de C.V. in cooperation with the School of Political and Social Sciences of the National Autonomous U. of Mexico, 1987: 174. Translation by Evert Villarreal.

EXERCISES: READING AND RESPONDING

1. Characterize the voice you hear in the translation of "Diego and Rivera: The Assassination of an Artistic Work."
2. On what points does Rivera's account of his hiring and subsequent dismissal differ from the accounts offered in the *Newsweek* and *Time* articles?
3. Rivera claims that the destroyed frescoes send a message to the world. Summarize that message.
4. What assumptions do you think Rivera might have made about the audience for this interview? Identify passages that suggest these assumptions.
5. Explain whether or not you consider the destruction of Rivera's mural an "assassination of an artistic work."
6. If in the early years of the twenty-first century an artist were commissioned to paint a mural entitled "Man at the Crossroads: Looking with Hope and High

Vision to the Choosing of a New and Better Future," what are the issues (social, political, economic, ethical, intellectual) that might influence such a work of art? Explain why current issues might be controversial to the point of someone objecting to their depiction in art.

EXCERPT FROM *ROCKEFELLER CENTER*

CAROL HERSELLE KRINSKY

The most famous work of art in the building was, of course, the fresco by Diego Rivera. As if to show that his anti-capitalist themes meant less than their understanding of fine art, American industrialists commissioned pictures from the irrepressible Mexican painter. Mrs. Rockefeller was especially interested in his work, and the Museum of Modern Art had given him a special exhibition. He was asked to design a monochromatic mural on canvas for the wall immediately opposite the RCA Building main entrance which would depict "man's new possibilities from his new understanding of material things." This subject, like most of the others, was conceived by a philosophy professor named Hartley Burr Alexander who had been hired to coordinate the works of art thematically. Rivera wheedled permission to paint a fresco—more durable than a canvas mural—and to use gently graduated color, but he actually painted a deeply colored fresco. He departed in other significant ways from an approved sketch which he had submitted in the autumn of 1932. Most distressing to the patrons was a wholly unexpected portrait of Lenin near the center of the picture, and a number of venereal disease germs floating toward a scene of rich people playing cards. A large number of bright red flags held by people parading near the tomb of Lenin was another rude surprise. While most people would not have recognized the germs, every prospective tenant would have recognized Lenin and the flags. Nelson Rockefeller wrote to Rivera asking the artist to substitute another face, whereupon Rivera got Ben Shahn to draft a reply in good English saying that "rather than mutilate the conception, I should prefer the physical destruction of the conception in its entirety but preserving, at least, its integrity." After having the nearly completed fresco covered for almost a year and after paying Rivera the full amount specified in the contract, the managers decided that the embarrassing and increasingly famous work had to go. Nelson Rockefeller suggested moving it to the Museum of Modern Art, where curiosity-seekers could be charged admission to see it. That proved impossible, so the planners took Rivera at his word and destroyed the fresco, a deed which has been damned as artistic vandalism and praised as a bit of common sense. In 1937 the fresco was replaced by José

María Sert's bombastic murals which the planners commissioned without any noticeable enthusiasm. These represented harmless lunging giants and portraits of Lincoln and Emerson rather than Lenin, and did so at a fairly economical price.

Sert, along with Frank Brangwyn, had done lobby corridor murals for the building while Rivera was at work but even then Sert and Brangwyn had been second choices. The architects and managers persuaded Rockefeller to let them approach Matisse and Picasso first, but Matisse did not want to do work which would be seen only by people passing swiftly along a hallway and Picasso simply refused to meet with Hood and Todd in Paris. Even later, when Picasso was offered the Rivera wall—known as the Wailing Wall because of the problem of filling it—he tried to trick Rockefeller rather than cooperate. In December 1933 Picasso agreed only to paint a picture for $32,000 but not to submit a preliminary sketch. If Rockefeller rejected the finished picture, he would have to pay Picasso only half that amount. Understandably enough, no one in New York was eager to hand out $16,000 for a second unsuitable picture and Picasso should have taken Will Rogers' advice to Rivera: "Never try to fool a Rockefeller in oils."

Source: Carol Herselle Krinsky, excerpt from *Rockefeller Center* (New York: Oxford University Press, 1978): 145–148.

EXERCISES: READING AND RESPONDING

1. The excerpt from Krinsky's book and "Rockefeller v. Rivera" detail some of the differences in Rivera's preliminary sketches for the mural and the mural before Rivera was dismissed. Identify any contradictory information in these two sources, and explain why you consider one source more credible than the other.

2. Explain why one source is more helpful than the other in helping you understand how Rivera allegedly departed from his original proposal.

3. Krinsky writes that the destruction of Rivera's mural was "damned as artistic vandalism and praised as a bit of common sense." Summarize the arguments that support each claim. Based on your reading so far, which claim do you find more convincing? Explain why.

NELSON ROCKEFELLER

An excerpt from Cary Reich's *The Life of Nelson Rockefeller* begins with an explanation of Abby Aldrich Rockefeller's "incongrous" patronage of Diego Rivera. Abby was Nelson Rockefeller's mother. Reich refers to Nelson Rockefeller's father, John D., as Junior.

VENTURES AND MISADVENTURES

CARY REICH

Abby Aldrich Rockefeller was a connoisseur of truly catholic tastes, collecting everything from Cubists to cigar-store Indians. But none of her affinities was as incongruous as her patronage of the flamboyant Mexican artist Diego Rivera. A dedicated Communist who viewed his work as agit-prop as well as art, a contentious paranoid who would stand on his scaffold with pistols strapped to his waist, the hulking, moon-faced Rivera was truly an unlikely object of a doyenne's affections. But Abby loved his murals, sprawling cinematic frescoes populated by *bandoleros* and sombreroed peasants and bristling with primitive force. Even his anticapitalist tirades, put forth in his work through imagery and caricatures that made the MOMA murals seem positively tepid by comparison, were taken in stride and perhaps even savored by Abby. So enchanted was she by a Mexico City mural that depicted her own father-in-law, along with Henry Ford and J. P. Morgan, partaking of a dinner of gold coins and ticker tape that she asked Rivera to make a copy for her.

Abby was instrumental in organizing a monumental Rivera one-man show at the Museum of Modern Art in December 1931 that did much to affirm the artist's worldwide reputation. She seemed hardly daunted by the gloomy frescoes Rivera executed specially for the show; entitled *Frozen Assets,* they depicted scenes of Depression-wracked New York, including a dreary hall filled with sleeping unemployed men. By that time, a passion for Rivera was in vogue among the country's cognoscenti: he was lionized throughout a 1930 visit to California, during which he delighted San Francisco art lovers by painting three murals there (including one in which the artist's posterior was prominently featured). And in May 1931 he received his biggest commission yet: a $25,000 grant from Edsel Ford, Henry's son, to paint a "Portrait of Detroit" on the walls of the Detroit Institute of Art's inner court.

Considering Rivera's renown, and Abby's copious affection for the man and his work, it was not at all surprising that Nelson blithely ignored the artist's penchant for outrageousness and began promoting him as a prospective muralist for the RCA Building. The idea of dressing up the building's lobby with murals had been the inspiration of architect Raymond Hood; the murals would complement the sculptures (portraying such uplifting themes as "Gifts of Earth to Mankind" and "The Spirit of Progress") planned for the Rockefeller Center building exteriors. Two accomplished, albeit conservative, painters, Frank Brangwyn and José Maria Sert, had already been signed on for some of the lobby walls. But the showpiece wall—the one oppo-site the building's main entrance on Rockefeller Plaza—would be reserved for an artist of international stature.

Hood and John Todd journeyed to Paris to woo Matisse (who turned them down flat) and Picasso (whom they found impossible to even track down). Finally, at Nelson's urging, and with Junior's grudging approval, Rivera was approached. "Although I do not personally care for much of his work," Junior told Hood, "he seems to have become very popular just now and will probably be a good drawing card." Rivera accepted in October 1932—but only after insisting that his fresco be in color, not black, white, and gray as the architects had wanted. Nelson clearly felt Rivera was doing Rockefeller Center a favor by accepting the $21,000 commission. When the negotiations were at last concluded, he wrote the artist, "May I take this opportunity to again tell you how much my mother and I appreci-ate your spirit in doing this mural under the existing circumstances."

Like the other Rockefeller Center artists, Rivera was given a portentous theme: in his case, "Man at the Cross-roads Looking with Hope and High Vision to the Choosing of a New and Better Future." From Detroit, where he was beginning work on the Insti-tute of Art mural, he sent back a vague sketch, along with a lengthy verbal description of what he intended. The description was rife with socialist imagery. One panel, he said, "will show the Workers arriving at a true understanding of their rights regard-ing the means of production.... It will also show the Workers of the cities and the country inheriting the earth."

Other parts of the mural would be peopled by more workers, and peas-ants, and unemployed workmen in a breadline.

Despite these hints that Rivera had more in mind for his fresco than simply a bevy of Adonises marching toward the sunrise, Todd and Hood and, ultimately, Junior himself approved the Rivera sketches. Accord-ing to one of Rivera's assistants, when Hood was shown the final drawing by Rivera, he glanced at it only cursorily before signing it. Handed the contract by Hood, Rivera flipped it to the last page and signed. "You better have your lawyer see it," said Hood, whereupon Rivera replied. "You signed my sketch without looking it over. You trust me, I trust you!"

In Detroit, meanwhile, a storm was brewing over the Institute of Art frescoes. "Señor Rivera," fulmi-nated one educator, "has foisted on Mr. Ford and the museum a Com-munist manifesto." Throughout the city, ministers mounted pulpits to denounce the Rivera mural for its alleged lampooning of the Holy Fam-ily and for its "slattern" and "grossly sensual" nude figures.

Groping for support, the institute turned to its sister museum and Rivera sponsor, the Museum of Mod-ern Art. The trustees, however, were wary of getting involved, until Nelson spoke up in Rivera's defense, per-suading the board that at the very least it should allow someone at the museum to issue a statement backing the institute and its embattled mural.

With the tumult in Detroit still reverberating around him, Rivera arrived in New York in mid-March 1933 to begin work on the RCA Building. As a gaggle of reporters and photographers looked on, he mounted the metal scaffolding and went over the charcoal outline of his sketches that his assistants had laid out on the 1,000-square-foot wall. Then the painting began, thirty square feet at a time, with the planks on the scaffolding lowered day after day as more of the wall was covered. Often Rivera and his assistants (one of whom was Ben Shahn) would work through the night.

In a matter of days the first section of the mural was revealed: a panorama of airplanes, death rays, and bayonet-wielding soldiers wearing gas masks. Then the next section became clear. It was a May Day demonstration in Red Square, with kerchief-clad women singing as the Red Flag-waving procession passed Lenin's tomb. One of his assistants, Lucienne Bloch, noted in her diary that "Diego had been expelled from the Communist Party three years earlier for refusing to toe the line. He wanted desperately to return to the fold, but on his own terms. So it is to prove to them that he is not afraid of any capitalists that he paints the Moscow May Day with gusto and with plenty of Venetian red."

Two days later Rivera completed the section beneath the war scene. It was a constellation of floating microbes: syphilis, gonorrhea, tuberculosis. To get the germs right, Rivera consulted slides at New York Hospital and Brooklyn Jewish Hospital, and pored over medical texts while he stood on the scaffolding, brush in hand.

Far from laboring in secrecy, Rivera, ever the showman, delighted in welcoming visitors to his work-in-progress. One day Abby Rockefeller herself arrived and cheerfully climbed the scaffold. Scrutinizing the Moscow May Day parade, she pronounced it the finest part of the mural yet. At other times, Tod Rockefeller would show up, and so would Nelson. Taking in all that was visible so far—the Moscow May Day marchers, the gas masks and death rays, the venereal-disease germs hovering over cardplaying, gin-swilling society ladies—they were just as enthusiastic as Abby. Bloch noted in her diary on April 19, "Nelson R. called on Diego, is crazy about the fresco!"

Then, five days later, the *New York World-Telegram* hit the stands with a headline that blared, "RIVERA PAINTS SCENES OF COMMUNIST ACTIVITY AND JOHN D. JR. FOOTS BILL." The article gleefully catalogued the mural's sensational elements: "Germs of infectious and hereditary social diseases ... so placed as to indicate them as the results of a civilization revolving about night clubs ... a Communist demonstration ... The dominant color is red—red headdress, red flags, waves of red." It quoted Rivera: "Mrs. Rockefeller said she liked my painting very much," he said. "Mr. Rockefeller likes it too."

The next day the *Telegram* followed up with another article in which various Communist Party functionaries derided Rivera for not going *far enough* with the RCA Building mural. "He has not portrayed to me the brutality, the starvation and the hunger as it really exists," one said. Whether it was because of this goading, or out of pique with the earlier *Telegram* attack, Rivera decided to up the ante. He asked his assistants to obtain a photograph of Lenin, and began sketching out a new tableau for his fresco. A soldier, a worker, and a Negro farmer would be shown holding hands with the Soviet leader.

A quarter of a century later, in a newspaper interview, one of Rivera's assistants, Stephen Dimitroff, said that "all of us, including Rivera's wife [Frida Kahlo, a painter in her own right], begged him not to include the portrait [of Lenin]. But he insisted it made good composition."

On April 30, the day the RCA Building at last opened its doors to the public, Rivera worked furiously on his Lenin panel. "Diego painted him without his cap," Bloch noted. "Now there's no doubt about who is up there!"

Four days later, Rivera received a letter from Nelson Rockefeller:

While I was in the No. 1 building at Rockefeller Center yesterday viewing the progress of your thrilling mural I noticed that in the most recent portion of the painting you had included a portrait of Lenin. The piece is beautifully painted but it seems to me that his portrait appearing in this mural might very seriously offend a great many people. If it were in a private house it would be one thing, but this mural is in a public building and the situation is therefore quite different. As much as I dislike to do so, I am afraid we must ask you to substitute the face of some unknown man where Lenin's face now appears.

You know how enthusiastic I am about the work which you have been doing and that to date we have in no way restricted you in either subject or treatment. I am sure you will understand out

feeling in this situation and we will greatly appreciate your making the suggested substitution.

Rivera summoned his friends and aides to his side. Shahn threatened to walk off the job if the Lenin portrait was changed. Fearing the worst. Frida urged Bloch to photograph the fresco as soon as possible.

Finally, Rivera sent Nelson his reply. The head of Lenin, he asserted, had been included in the original sketch he had given Hood (in fact, it was nowhere indicated in the sketch, or in Rivera's verbal plan). Lenin, the artist declared, had to stay. However, he was willing to offer a compromise: counterbalancing the Soviet leader would be a portrait of Lincoln, surrounded by abolitionists like John Brown and Harriet Beecher Stowe.

Should he be compelled to remove Lenin, Rivera warned, "rather than mutilate the conception, I should prefer the physical destruction of the conception in its entirety."

On May 9 Rivera was back at his scaffold, but beneath him the lobby had the ominous air of an encampment on the eve of battle. Uniformed and plainclothes guards patrolled the halls, challenging anyone who came near the mural. Then, at six o'clock, managing agent Hugh Robertson strode into the lobby, asked Rivera to come down from the scaffold, and handed him a check for the balance of his $21,500 fee. Rivera's services would no longer be required.

Within moments an army of workmen ascended to the fresco and nailed heavy canvas sheets over it, obscuring every inch of it from view. Rivera was surprisingly buoyant. *"Maintenant,"* he shouted to his assistants, *"c'est la bataille!"*

His words proved instantly prophetic: by nine o'clock, a crowd of three hundred protesters had gathered outside the building, bearing placards reading "Save Rivera's Art," and scuffled with police called in to break up the march. The Rivera affair was front-page news the next day, and went on making headlines in the days that followed, as artists and writers banded together to voice solidarity with Rivera. The Rockefeller action was likened to Nazi book burning, and at a Columbus Circle rally Communists yelled, "We want Rockefeller with a rope around his neck!" The business community, meanwhile, rallied to the Rockefellers' support. The National Association of Manufacturers wrote to congratulate Nelson for his "courageous and patriotic" rejection of "subversive propaganda." General Motors, which had contracted with Rivera for a mural at its building at the Chicago Century of Progress Exposition, announced that it was terminating the commission.

Although it had not been Nelson who called Rivera off his scaffold (he was conveniently out of town at the time), it was Nelson who was identified in the public mind as Rivera's antagonist. He even was the subject of a bit of doggerel in *The New Yorker* penned by E. B. White (in which an anguished Nelson explains to Rivera, "And though your art I dislike to hamper, I owe a *little* to Gamper").

For Nelson, it was all publicity of the most unwelcome sort. He had been cast in the role of puritanical censor, a particularly uncomfortable position for a young man who fancied himself a budding modern art connoisseur and who just months before had vigorously defended Rivera in the Detroit brouhaha. Yet what was most unsettling about the whole business was that it could have so easily been foreseen and avoided. It was as though Nelson had learned nothing from the uproar over the museum murals show a year earlier, and as though he knew nothing about the proclivities of the artist he was so anxious to retain. True, Rivera had given no indication until the very end that he would be featuring Lenin in his mural. But well before the image of Lenin went up, Nelson had looked on approvingly at the Moscow May Day scenes and the floating venereal-disease microbes, elements that would have sparked outrage even if Lenin never entered the picture.

Once again, as in the murals show, Nelson had allowed his radical artistic sensibilities, his eagerness to make an impact on Rockefeller Center, and his unbridled enthusiasm to overwhelm his better judgment. But unlike the murals show, a few apologies this time would not be enough.

All the rest of that year the Rivera mural lay hidden behind its canvas shroud, as Nelson and the Rockefeller Center architects and managers agonized over what to do with it. Finally, Nelson proposed a solution that would seemingly satisfy both the Rivera partisans and the conservative faction at the Center: the fresco would be donated to the Museum of Modern Art. To pay for the move, he suggested that the museum sell tickets to see the mural. Although the Rockefeller Center managers were willing to go ahead with the scheme, the museum's trustees apparently balked. Having gone through the storm over the murals show, and having witnessed the furor the Detroit fresco created, they perhaps were not willing to suffer through a repeat performance.

Late one cold February evening in 1934. Lucienne Bloch and Steve Dimitroff, Rivera's assistants, were strolling through midtown Manhattan after taking in a movie. On a whim, they decided to look in on the RCA Building. The doors were locked, but as the couple turned to leave they noticed about a dozen fifty-gallon oil drums near the entrance, heaped with what looked like small chunks of plaster. Peering into the drums, they discovered to their horror that the plaster chunks were the smashed-up shards of Diego Rivera's mural.

Nine months earlier, Rivera had told Nelson, in his fusillade of verbiage, that he would prefer the piece's "physical destruction" to its mutilation. Rockefeller Center had now taken him up on his preference.

Speaking out in Mexico City, Rivera called the mural's destruction "an act of cultural vandalism." Outraged New York artists labeled it "art murder" and organized a downtown protest rally that was attended by 1,000.

Describing the affair to old John D. Senior in Florida, Junior made it plain that he heartily approved of the mural's smashing. "The picture was obscene and, in the judgment of Rockefeller Center, an offense to good taste," he told his father. "It was for this reason primarily that Rockefeller Center decided to destroy it."

A chastened Nelson said nothing as the workmen hauled off the debris that had once been the Rivera mural, the mural he had so proudly contracted for and urged along. There was no talk now of artistic integrity, no championing of Rivera's vision. The only course left for Nelson was to fall in line with his father's wishes. Too much lay ahead for him, too much was at stake, to do otherwise.

Source: Cary Reich, "Ventures and Misadventures," *The Life of Nelson Rockefeller: Worlds to Conquer 1908–1958* (New York: Doubleday, 1996).

EXERCISES: READING AND RESPONDING

1. Explain why Reich's acocount of the relationship between Rivera and Rockefeller might be interpreted as defending Rockefeller.

2. What kind of composite picture of Rockefeller do you draw from the letter he wrote Rivera? from Reich's account in this source?

3. What kind of composite picture of Rivera does this source provide?

4. How does Reich account for Rockefeller's hiring Rivera?

5. How does Reich's account of the artist's contract differ from Rivera's description in Source 5, "Diego Rivera and Rockefeller: The Assassination of an Artistic Work"?

6. In your opinion, would the compromise Rivera proposed—Lenin would have stayed in the mural, but would have been counterbalanced by a "portrait of Lincoln, surrounded by abolitionists like John Brown and Harriet Beecher Stowe"—have been a sufficient compromise? Explain why or why not.

7. What explanation does Reich offer for Rockefeller's decision to destroy the mural?

ART OR PROPAGANDA?

The letters to the editor and the articles that follow illustrate the debate that took place in newspapers and magazines over the Rivera v. Rockefeller situation. Was Rivera's mural art or propaganda? Was the destruction of the mural censorship or the decision of a consumer unhappy with a product he purchased? These are questions to consider as you read and annotate sources.

THE RIVERA MURALS

ANNA M. L. PHILLIPS

Opinions For and Against Action at Rockefeller Center.

To the Editor of the *New York Times:*

If you play in the sunshine, you tan. If you handle mud, you are soiled. If you look at a star, your eyes are open, even when all else is darkness around you.

In short, our selection of that which pleases us physically, mentally and spiritually makes us a part of that thing. The works of a great painter not only reflect him but they formulate the thoughts and inclinations of others, notably those who follow a leader.

Lenin lifted up to the walls of a world-famous building where men, women and youth assemble to admire and emulate the subject portrayed is, or would be if allowed to remain, an insult to the conceptions of all great artists from the early Renaissance period to the present day.

Those of us who gaze in rapture at the "Adoration of the Magi," by an early master of the Spanish school, Murillo, or "The Last Supper," by the sometimes humanly carnal minded Leonardo da Vinci, could not endure or tolerate for a moment the elevation to a high place in our own art world of the face of Lenin, whose followers proclaim: "There is no God. Nothing is mightier than man himself!"

We must look up for inspiration, and when we lie on the floor of the Sistine Chapel to adore the immortal ceiling we see not only those colossal spokesmen for the uplift of the soul like "Jehovah Giving the Spark of Life to Man," painted by the almost blinded Michelangelo, but in our very act we put dirt and earth under our fact and see beyond—the stars.

ANNA M. L. PHILLIPS
New York, May 10, 1933

Source: Anna M. L. Phillips, "The Rivera Murals," *New York Times* 12 May 1933: 16.

DEFENDING RIVERA

DUDLEY JOHNSON

To the Editor of the *New York Times:*

I know I am not alone in feeling an injustice has been done in dismissing Diego Rivera. It is apparent from the interchange of letters that the artist was not only reasonable, but also showed a definite desire to cooperate with those who had engaged his services. However, there comes a point where further conciliation shows spinelessness and lack of conviction on the part of the artist. It was here Rivera stopped, and it is the same spirit of belief in one's art that has moved many in the past and I hope will continue to do so in the future.

The controversial aspect of a work of art is too often exaggerated by just such action as the Rockefellers have taken. Would it not have been better to allow the completion of the mural, Lenin and all, particularly as the original sketches had been approved. Rivera's changes were those of detail, not of form or general concept. But perhaps it would be bad to subject the future dwellers and visitors of this great seventy-story building to the effect of the artist's propaganda." We might go Communist after all.

DUDLEY JOHNSON
New York, May 10, 1933

Source: Dudley Johnson, "Defending Rivera," *New York Times* 12 May, 1933: 16.

WHY IMPORT ARTISTS?

NICHOLAS HAZ

To the Editor of the *New York Times*:

Why is it that when American architects, plus American labor, achieve magnificent structures to symbolize the power, courage, and success (I mean it) of American capitalism, they must import foreign Communists to decorate them?

Do you suppose that the Soviets would allow foreign capitalists to ornament their palaces with the praise of the Fords and Rockefellers and pay them large sums for doing it?

Why are we so humble? Why do we admit that foreign artists are better than Americans, when it is impossible to measure beauty and goodness in art?

Our architects ought to be smarter in selecting their mural painters.

Nicholas Haz
Utica, N.Y., May 10, 1933

Source: Nicholas Haz, "Why Import Artists?" *New York Times* 12 May, 1933: 16.

FOCUS ON RELATED ISSUES: PATRONAGE

One of the issues in the Rivera case is the boundaries of patronage, the financial support a wealthy benefactor provides so that a person who lacks financial resources can devote full time to creative endeavors. Questions inevitably occur in this type of relationship: *How much freedom does the artist have? Does the benefactor have a right to interfere in any way with the artist's creation? Should the benefactor dictate what is offensive? Should the benefactor determine whether art can be exhibited? banned or censored?*

Patronage began in ancient Rome, became institutionalized in fourteenth- and fifteenth-century Florence, and continues today, although not in the same manner. The example several sources in the Rivera case study mention is the relationship between the artist Michaelangelo and Pope Julius II. In literature, Robert Browning captures the frustration of the artist confined by the medieval dictates of a patron in the poem "Fra Lippo Lippi". Browning's painter longs to bring flesh to life. His patron, the Church, wants art that makes people forget there's flesh.

Today, through the National Endowment for the Arts (NEA), the U.S. government provides funding that supports the arts. And as you might guess, funding of the arts has been controversial since the NEA was launched in 1965. Controversy over grants to artists has been constant. Sexually explicit material, paintings, and performance art that voice strong social commentary, and art that offends people's religious beliefs have caused exhibits to be shut down, performing companies to be disbanded, and public funding to be cut back. With cutbacks in government funding of the arts becoming the norm, many people argue the necessity of government support for dance, theater, poetry and fiction, music, painting, and sculpture.

Working on your own, identify an example of government funding for the arts that became controversial. Develop the example into a topic for an argumentative paper.

EXERCISES: READING AND RESPONDING

1. What explanations do sources provide for the patronage of Diego Rivera, an avowed Communist, by capitalists such as Edsel Ford and the Rockefeller family?

2. In a profile of Diego Rivera, Anita Brenner explains that Rivera "consider[ed] it part of his job in the world to interpret America to Americans, and by America, he mean[t] the continent." In your opinion, would the interpretation of America Rivera offered in the Rockefeller Center mural have been without controversy if Lenin had been removed from the mural?

3. Two of the letters to the editor object to Rivera. What is the basis of each writer's argument against him?

4. What kinds of appeals do these writers present?

ENFANT TERRIBLE

GEOFFREY T. HELLMAN

Diego Rivera's recent dismissal as painter of murals in the R.C.A. Building is the latest of a long series of expulsions which he has cheerfully sustained. When he was five, he was hastily led out of a Catholic church in Mexico by a scandalized aunt. During the services he had been moved to rise and inform the congregation that it was ridiculous to believe in the Virgin Mary, since she was nothing but a wooden statue. The next day five grown men called on him in a body, explained that they were liberals of long standing, and thanked him for doing just what they had wanted to do for years. Would he care to become a member of their group and join them in daily conferences on a park bench? Eleven years later he was expelled from art school for making deprecatory remarks about one of the teachers. In 1911, after the Madero election in Mexico, he was forced to leave the country temporarily for having, in preëlection enthusiasm, blown up an arsenal. Around 1920, the Cubists in Paris, of whom he had been one, disowned him for going in for Communistic propaganda in his art. The Communists, whom he officially joined in 1921, when he returned to Mexico to paint thematic pictures glorifying the lowly peon, indignantly read him out of the party in 1929 for having refused to resign his position as painter of frescoes on government buildings in Mexico City at a time when the government was persecuting the comrades. His argument that he was best serving the cause by continuing to paint antibourgeois murals was rejected as a sophistry.

During the past few years he has, in the eyes of the Communists, lived in the camp of the enemy. His recent commissions have been from Dwight Morrow, the San Francisco Stock Exchange, Edsel Ford, and the Rockefellers. The Communists feel so strongly about his recent activities that the John Reed Club recently announced that it was returning a hundred-dollar check Rivera had sent it—a show of spirit somewhat offset, according to Rivera, by the fact that it didn't send the check back.

The Socialists, on the other hand, regard Rivera definitely as a Communist. When he spoke at the Rand School last month and announced that a revolution in this country could not take place without bloodshed, he provoked an orgy of heckling which almost led to bloodshed then and there. Until the Rockefeller Center fiasco, Rivera could turn to entrenched capital for a friendly—and indulgent—smile. Now his standing is threatened there. The rich in the past were tolerant. When the good people of Detroit objected to Rivera's execution of a vaccination scene because the nurse and child he drew bore a close resemblance to the Madonna and Child, Edsel Ford, who had engaged the painter, expressed himself as delighted with the work. The rich have also taken a curious pleasure in seeing themselves caricatured. One of Rivera's Mexico City murals depicted the senior Rockefeller, Henry Ford, and J. P. Morgan starving at a meal of gold coins and ticker tape, with a miniature Statue of Liberty standing like a toy on the table. This so pleased Mrs. John D. Rockefeller, Jr., that she asked Rivera to make a copy for her. What is remarkable about the R.C.A. affair is not that the Rockefellers objected to Lenin's being shown as the savior of mankind but that they apparently didn't object to the rest of the fresco, which showed a Soviet demonstration before the Kremlin as one of civilization's brightest features, war as a product of capitalism in contradistinction to sport as a product of Communism, and a bridge game as the precursor of venereal disease. While Rivera was working on these, Nelson Rockefeller, his wife, and Mrs. Harry Payne Whitney frequently looked on and admired.

In the absence of official party affiliations, Rivera now classes himself as a Worker. This identification of himself with the laboring classes has given rise to a legend that he was born a member of the proletariat, the son of a miner. Actually, his father was a mine-owner and a leading citizen of Guanajuato, Mexico. Diego was born there forty-seven years ago. One of his great-grandfathers was a Spanish marquis and general, but Diego, whose full name is Diego Maria Concepción Juan Nepomuceno Estanislao de la Rivera y Barrientos Acosta y Rodriguéz, regards this as a blot on his escutcheon and never

mentions it. Frequently, however, he alludes to his mother's father, who was an Indian. Through other ancestors, he has Russian, Spanish, and Portuguese Jewish blood.

Diego's father was not a good businessman, eventually losing most of his money in a mine which turned out to be a bonanza as soon as he sold it, but he was admirably fitted to bring up a future mural painter. On the theory that discipline kills talent in the young, he encouraged his son's early passion for drawing by giving him a huge, bare room hung with blackboards. Standing on a chair, Diego, at three, would draw for hours. Refusing to portray anything until he knew what it was like inside, he impartially tore apart toys, beetles, and vegetables. Thanks to anatomical books furnished by his father, he could draw nearly every variety of animal by the time he was five. Mountains constituted more of a problem. He felt it would be impertinent to draw a mountain before knowing what it was like inside. So his father took him down a mine shaft. In 1892, Señora Rivera, impatient with provincial Guanajuato, engineered a move to Mexico City. Urban life had a depressing effect on Diego. He became sulky, refused to draw; and to everyone's amazement lost what had been a prodigious appetite. Brooding, he devoted two years to the manufacture of an army of five thousand paper soldiers. The figures are his. Interpreting this as a desire to follow in the footsteps of his ancestor, the Spanish general, his family sent him to military school. He soon left there. He began to draw again. Several years at art school—the Academy of San Carlos—followed, marked by the winning of minor prizes. He visited the Mexican National Museum and took prodigiously long walks into the country in search of rural beauty. Sometimes he would walk all day, pausing only to encourage and assist a fainting companion. Later his tremendous vitality made it possible for him to sit on the scaffold for stretches of from eighteen to thirty-six hours. Once, when he was working in Mexico City a few years ago, a young woman sat with him for nineteen hours. She then got up and started down the ladder. "I have begun to bore you," said Rivera sadly.

The first picture of his to arouse anyone's indignation, and the forerunner of a long line, was a portrait of his mother he did when he was seventeen. Señora Rivera looked at it and hurst into tears convinced that her son no longer loved her. When he was nineteen, he disappeared into, the mountain pueblos for several months, emerging with enough pictures for a one-man show and a sympathetic interest in the Indians that bore astonishing fruit in 1928, when to his intense surprise, the peasant party, composed chiefly of Indians, nominated him for the presidency of Mexico. At the show, several pictures were held the governor of Vera Cruz was so impressed that he granted Diego a pension of three hundred francs a month to study abroad. He promptly went to Spain, where he painted indifferent copies of Goya and Velásquez by day and sat up all night eating, drinking, and arguing with the most voluble anarchists of Madrid. So outstanding was his capacity for huge platefuls of different kinds of food, washed down with bottles of sweet wine, that an American acquaintance was moved to write a story, later published in the *Century,* in which the painter hero eats himself to death under the impression that he is dying of a broken heart. Two or three years later; Rivera drifted to Paris. One of the first things he did on his arrival was to go to the Gallery Vollard. In the window was a Cézanne, the first one he had ever seen. Muttering with excitement, he spent the entire morning walking up and down in front of the window, examining the picture. M. Vollard, going out for lunch, noted the large young man with the mobile face and the mad gleam in his eye with some apprehension. *"Un apache,"* he muttered to himself. When he returned two hours later, Rivera was still there. M. Vollard, gathering that the stranger was not an *apache,* although perhaps mad, removed the painting and substituted another Cézanne. Diego remained, entranced. For the rest of the afternoon, M. Vollard kept changing the pictures, putting in Cézanne after Cézanne. Rivera went home with a high lever. Friends summoned a doctor, who diagnosed the case as one of severe nervous shock.

During his Cubist period, thus begun twenty years or so ago, Rivera was very much under the influence of Picasso. The latter is still a friend of his, but Rivera, who today goes in for massive symbolical figures representing Civilization, Science, California, etc., doesn't think much of the Parisian's work any more, Rivera's present aesthetic credo is that art should be handmaiden to the revolution, and that no art that isn't propaganda is worth doing. In 1908 and 1909, however, his best friends were Picasso, Derain, Henri Rousseau, and Modigliani. In those years he lived on Montparnasse with a credulous group of Russian *émigrés* whom he regaled with tales of Mexican tarantulas so big that people harnessed them to their carriages. Diego's approach to facts is that of the late Baron Munchausen, and he loves to tell impossible stories, especially about himself. Mention any important event that has taken place during the past twenty-five years, and he will claim not only to have been present but to have foreseen exactly what was going to happen. One of his favorite reminiscences, invariably delivered with a straight face, has to do with a long series of adventures that lead to his death. "People missed me so much," he explains, "that I resurrected myself."

To be in the midst of some uproarious disturbance is Rivera's idea of heaven. The anti—Diaz uprising in Mexico in 1910 brought him to the field of combat by the first boat. His stay in his native land was brief, being brought to an end by his blowing up the arsenal. His second European sojourn lasted ten years. During this period, he saw Giotto's frescoes for the first time and subsequently came to the conclusion, which he has held ever since, that easel pictures are unnatural and that painting can bear the proper relationship to architecture only through the medium of the mural. By way of apprenticeship as a mural painter, he copied hundreds of frescoes in the Catacombs. His mastery of different schools of painting has often caused him to be charged with plagiarism. For such accusations he has an impressive retort. "Every painter," he sternly announces, "is a field in which the seed of another painter germinates." A malicious story has it that once in Paris when another artist accused him of copying his work, Diego went home, painted a picture in the other man's latest manner, signed his own name to it, and predated it four years. "You see," he is said to have blandly explained to visitors, "the man is really a disciple of mine." Orozco feels so strongly about Rivera's having adopted some of his symbols that he refused to be represented in the current American-sources-of-modern-art show at the Modern Museum, on the ground that some of Rivera's pictures were included.

Orozco and Rivera worked together in Mexico City in 1921, after the Obregón revolution had brought Rivera, now an accepted Communist, back from Europe. On Obregón's coming to power, Rivera persuaded him to organize a group of painters known as the Syndicate to paint frescoes on government buildings. Orozco was one of his colleagues and Miguel Covarrubias was the Syndicate's water boy. They received laborer's wages. Frankly propagandist, the Syndicate's frescoes glorified the peon and showed the upper classes as so fat and repulsive that one group of Mexicans dubbed the painters the Ugliests and occasionally marred and defaced their work. "Oh, somebody signed his name," Rivera would say without ill nature when he would find some opprobrious epithet scrawled on his work. His balloonlike form, extra-size sombrero, somnolent eyes, and huge benevolent smile made him a favorite subject for parody in the press. Tourists pasted his likeness in their albums, along with the more permanent sights of the country. He wore an immense cartridge belt and large-calibre revolver, although friends told him that if anything happened he would be safer without them. He was obsessed with the idea that he might be shot any time and worked with frenzy to accomplish as much as possible. On one occasion he fell off the scaffold from exhaustion and lay unconscious for twenty minutes. The superstitious workmen thought that a pair of huge hands he had just painted had pushed him off, and refused to touch him.

The Mexican government didn't approve of the Syndicate's violently Communistic sentiments and after the first year dissolved the group. Only Rivera was commissioned to continue—this chiefly for the political reason that he was extremely popular with the common people. Between 1921 and 1927, in which years he went to Russia as a Communist delegate from Mexico, he painted a hundred and eighty-four frescoes in the patios of the Ministry of Education Building. Reviving the ancient Indian method of mixing juice pressed from the leaf of the prickly pear with pigment, he portrayed the common people and their labors, showing agriculture enslaved by clericalism, militarism, and capitalism. He made occasional friendly concessions in his work, notably to feminine onlookers. One day a young Mexican girl, watching him, objected to a likeness of Señora Diaz weeping behind her husband, ostensibly at his misdeeds. Señora Diaz would never have went, she complained. Diego grinned politely. When the girl came back the next day, Señora Diaz was wreathed in smiles. Another time a fair onlooker took exception to Rivera's showing the Emperor Maximilian with a fantastically recessive chin. The Hapsburgs, she observed, had better chins than that. Rivera improved the chin. When it comes to mechanical and scientific details, he is meticulous and is delighted to be corrected. Before painting the germs in the R.C.A. mural, he got cultures from hospital laboratories and studied them under a microscope. While he was working on the same job, a workman told him he was putting the locks on the rifles in the war scene on the wrong side. The painter thanked him and amended his work. He was less responsive to the mounted policeman who wandered in and grumbled about the hard-faced, lantern-jawed officers he showed riding down the people in the unemployment panel. "It's an outrage," said the policeman. "We're the handsomest body of men in the world."

When, in 1929, Rivera painted a mural depicting the conquest of Mexico, which was presented by the Dwight Morrow Commission to the city of Cuernavaca, he received twelve thousand dollars. It was the first considerable sum he had ever received. He has always had a royal disregard for money. His friends call him childish in this, childish in his penchant for playing little jokes on the boss. In his mural in San Francisco, he painted a figure of a workman from whose pocket a tag hung down. On this he painted the red star of the Communist party. When he was asked to remove it, he did chuckling. Similarly, in the R.C.A mural, he painted the hammer, and sickle of Soviet Russia on a matchbox lying on a bridge table. His injection of Lenin's likeness was this kind of prank. Nobody at Radio City recognized the figure shown on the preliminary sketch as Lenin, and all were astonished when it turned out to be be.

Rivera is astonishingly casual in his selection of human models. At Rockefeller Center, it was his habit to shout to passing workmen to come up on the scaffold and sit for him. The fresco's central figure, a young engineer representing Man at the crossroads of civilization, was based on a night watchman who happened to be around. The original of the model girl student in the students group was an obliging young woman who was looking on when Diego came to that part of the fresco. "Actually I was kicked out of Hunter for flunking five subjects," she gigglingly told friends later. The red-haired girl in the bridge section is a likeness of a red-headed girl seized as she came out of Roxy's one afternoon.

For all his violent propaganda, Rivera is gentle, polite, and unassuming. He loves meeting people, and when he is working his assistants have to keep him from clambering down the ladder too often to talk to onlookers. He has a shy, twisted smile, and even when advancing his political opinions does so hesitantly. Next to a revolution or an art controversy, noth-

ing puts him in better humor than the company of a beautiful woman. On such occasions, he is full of the most urbane and extravagant compliments. To his present wife, a slim, dark-haired Mexican beauty who is the third Mrs. Rivera, he is the last word in affectionate gallantry. She watches him work and sees to it that he gets fed every few hours. He himself has no sense of time, is continually missing trains, and often dresses in taxis on the way to some appointment. This summer, he expects to go to Cape Cod for a few weeks before returning to Mexico City, where he is doing a fresco of the history of Mexico for the National Palace. He has recently built a brightly colored modernistic house there.

At parties, Rivera likes to sing Italian and French revolutionary songs and do Mexican dances around a bottle. Thanks to a strict diet, he has recently lost a hundred and twenty-five pounds, but even in the old days, when he weighed three hundred and twenty-five, he was much too agile ever to step on the bottle. These playful moods are occasionally varied by an unaccountable fit of the sulks. He was inclined to be playful rather than sulky on the fatal night at Rockefeller Center when Mr. Hugh Robertson of Todd, Robertson & Todd, flanked by a squad of uniformed guards, advanced with a check for fourteen thousand dollars and the information that inasmuch as he refused to delete the figure of Lenin, his services would no longer he required. Rivera's first observation was: "How do you know it's Lenin? It doesn't say so, does it?"

Source: Geoffrey T. Hellman, "Enfant Terrible," *The New Yorker* 20 May 1933: 21–24.

EXERCISES: READING AND RESPONDING

1. Hellman devotes his article to a discussion of Rivera, the "Enfant Terrible," instead of reporting at length details about Rivera's dismissal from painting the Rockefeller murals. Identify specific passages that, in your opinion, support the claim that Rivera was an *enfant terrible* (difficult child).

2. What kind of composite picture of Rivera's politics does Hellman draw?

3. How does Hellman characterize Rivera's physical characteristics?

4. What kind of composite picture of Rivera's art does Hellman draw?

5. What kind of composite picture of Rivera does Hellman offer?

6. According to Hellman, what was Rivera's "aesthetic credo" at the time the article was published?

7. Explain whether Hellman's profile of Rivera would make readers more or less sympathetic to the artist. Be prepared to identify specific passages in the profile that support your opinion.

8. What argument is Hellman advancing in this article? What are his claims? his evidence? What kinds of appeals does he make?

9. At the end of the first paragraph, Hellman writes that Rivera's argument that he was serving the Communist cause when he painted "anti-bourgeois murals was rejected as a sophistry." If you aren't familiar with the term *sophistry,* consult a dictionary for its meaning. Would it be possible to argue that Hellman's article is a sophistry?

The unsigned editorial that follows appeared in *The New Republic.*

ART FOR PROPAGANDA'S SAKE

Diego Rivera's frank statement that on the advice of friends in Moscow he came to this country as a propagandist for the proletariat—which, in a capitalist country, is to say for revolution—is consistent with his position in the controversy over his dismissal as he was finishing his great fresco at Rockefeller Center. From the first Mr. Rivera has contended that the political value of his work is more important to him than its artistic value. He has steadily maintained, and with reason, that the disputed fresco would still be revolutionary if he substituted another leader, real or symbolic, for the portrait of Lenin to which the Rockefellers objected, and that he prefers to have the whole painting destroyed rather than make the substitution. His announcement may appear to prevent all defense of his work on the ground of its art, or because the artist is superior to politics. Certainly it has calmed the enthusiasm of many of his bourgeois partisans. Nevertheless art does not become nothing but propaganda simply because the artist frankly and honorably states his own convictions.

Nothing that Mr. Rivera has said has altered the position of the Rockefeller family, which is self-contradictory, or their tactics, which were arbitrary and insulting. The question still remains, Why did they employ Rivera? They are among the outstanding beneficiaries of the capitalist order. Rivera is vowedly anti-capitalist in his convictions and his art. As The New York Times remarked after his dismissal, his fresco, on the walls of a building owned by the Rockefellers, is like a row of swastikas over a synagogue. But if you don't want swastikas over your synagogue, you don't employ an artist whom you know to be a specialist in swastikas. An artist is no mere technician. When Millet saw what William Morris Hunt had learned in the studio of Couture, he asked, "What have you to *say* with it?" What Rivera says with his magnificent technical equipment is no secret to the Rockefeller family. He had caricatured the elder John D. Rockefeller in his "billionaires" group in Mexico—and the caricature appears in the portfolio of photographs of the Mexican frescoes published by the Museum of Modern Art, which the Rockefellers help largely to finance. Knowing of the caricature, and knowing also the revolutionary character of those frescoes and of Rivera's work generally, they brought him to New York and had his work exhibited at the Modern Museum. Then they commissioned him to paint the fresco at Rockefeller Center, and accepted his preliminary sketches. Their action in employing him seems to us much more inconsistent with their position in the capitalist world than their action in dismissing him. Their behavior indicates a sudden and perplexing *volte-face,* and only the painter's own action in removing the whole question from the field of art into that of politics has saved them from an extremely embarrassing position.

It looks as if the Rockefellers or their agents had become panicky. It was unnecessary to send a whole army of policemen and plain-clothes men against a man armed only with paintbrushes. It was also unnecessary to persuade the telephone company to cut off his private telephone in the mezzanine—as if he might use it to summon an opposing host! Their action, and the manner in which it was taken, have precipitated a scandal which could have been avoided if they had kept their heads and allowed the artist to finish his work; a scandal that will inevitably harm a cause which several members of the Rockefeller family have generously supported—that of American art. Fear is contagious. American mural painting is just beginning to emerge from the bathos that the timidity of art commissions and owners of buildings has imposed upon it. It cannot become truly significant without the aid of these people. There is danger that the scandal may frighten them back into the "safe" insipidity which has made most American mural painting a disgrace to American civilization.

We cannot see that anything Mr. Rivera has said alters his moral right to complete his work. A finished painting can be covered quite as easily as an unfinished one. But why cover it? The painter's own widely published statements have pretty well canceled its propagandist value. Its artistic value remains, and that is of tremendous importance to American art. It should be placed on public view. If the Rockefellers are still afraid of being identified with its revolutionary implications, they might adopt the policy of the editorial disclaimer. Their walls are their own, of course. They can stretch several dozen square yards of conventional bathos over Rivera's splendid fresco, and perpetuate the scandal their action has precipitated. But they could also exhibit the picture, with an appended statement that nothing in it is to be taken as expressing the sentiments of the Rockefeller family. Why not?

Source: "Art for Propaganda's Sake," New Republic 24 May 1933: 34.

EXERCISES: READING AND RESPONDING

1. Explain whether you agree or disagree with the writer's claim that "art does not become nothing but propaganda simply because the artist frankly and honorably states his own convictions." What kind of evidence supports this claim?

2. The writer mentions a comparison made by the *New York Times*: "[Rivera's] fresco, on the walls of a building owned by the Rockefellers, is like a row of swastikas over a synagogue." Explain why this is or isn't a valid comparison. What kind of rhetorical effect might it have on readers?

3. According to the writer, the Rockefeller family has taken a position that is "self-contradictory" and their tactics are "arbitrary and insulting." What examples does the writer offer to support these claims?

4. What course of action does the writer wish the Rockefeller family had taken?

5. Explain why you think Diego Rivera did or did not have a moral right to complete the mural in Rockefeller Center.

In "Rockefeller, Rivera, and Art," Walter Pach claims that the "red herrings of Communism and nationalism" figure in the argument about Rivera's mural. You might be familiar with the term *red herring* if you enjoy mysteries. A red herring is a false clue, or a diversion from the real facts of a case or an argument. In argument, a red herring is considered a logical fallacy.

ROCKEFELLER, RIVERA, AND ART

WALTER PACH

An old fight is on again; this time it has broken out in Radio City, New York. To read the newspapers one might think it was between Rockefeller and Lenin, but it goes much deeper than that. It is between art and the counterfeit of art. The conflict between the two affects the lives of all of us more than do the economic or political systems attached to the names of the great capitalist and the great Communist.

The present discussion turns upon a fresco by Diego Rivera in Rockefeller Center. When the Mexican painter began to accept commissions from rich Americans protests went up from the Communists, which confirms me in doubts as to their intelligence. The artist had already expressed in his distinguished paintings, as no other in recent times has done, the life and aspirations of the workers, manual and intellectual; but on a suspicion that he had "sold out" to capitalistic patrons the Communists repudiated him. Now that they are confronted by a thing so blatantly within their philosophy as a picture of Lenin on the walls of a capitalist's building, they begin to see Rivera as more useful to their cause—less purely "æsthetic" than they thought. What neither the critics of the fresco nor its Communistic defenders realize is that the significance of this vast work does not hinge on a particular detail. It resides in the artist's whole attitude toward life, life's purposes, and the means of fulfilling them.

And from this standpoint it may well turn out that Rockefeller and Lenin stand much closer together than people think. Both believe in eliminating waste through the concentration of effort. Both look toward a future in which mankind will benefit by unity of purpose instead of suffering the discord and confusion inevitable in the long past when races, countries, and even neighboring cities stood apart in mutual hostility, and spent incalculable time and strength on activities that were futile if not actually destructive. Rockefeller and Lenin are culminations, perhaps even definitive ones, of man's collective purpose to base his life on more reasonable conditions. Which system is to be in control of these conditions? I am sure I do not know. With diversity of opinion on every hand, I think it extremely probable that we have still got to go through a lot of experimenting, that we must arrive at modifications of both schemes before even the wisest of us can discern the controls for the unimaginable machine of the future world.

But while professing ignorance about the system to evolve for the America of the future and for the rest of the world, I do not see how the fiercest opponent of Lenin can deny that his ideas have their place in a great mural painting when the artist undertakes to depict "Man, at the Crossroads, Looks toward his Future."

Rivera, the Mexican who has done so much in renewing the ancient art of fresco, was charged with this impressive work. He made of it a splendid and dynamic exposition of the forces, scientific, mechanistic, and social, at work in American life to-day. It could not to his mind fail to include a statement about Communism. The need grew more specific as his picture developed, and instead of the abstract figure of a leader which he had sketched at an earlier stage of his planning he introduced a portrait of Lenin. It is unmistakable and important, but remains a small detail in the vast scheme, by no means a dominant one. Mr. Nelson A. Rockefeller wrote, asking the substitution of some other feature, one which should not offend the feelings of the people (they would unquestionably be a great number) who would resent the portrait of the Russian in the great building. It is on American soil, not that of Mexico or of Russia, and everyone will agree that it is *our* ideas that should be told of there. But at once the question arises—who knows those ideas in their fullness and their depth? One chief value of art in all countries has been its making clear—first to the people immediately concerned and then to distant ones—the thoughts of the given time and place.

Quite often it is the distant audience that first realizes how the artist has told the truth. And then the frescoes of Giotto are rescued from the whitewash with which they had been covered; the pictures of Rembrandt, Ruisdael, and Vermeer, most of which are in collections outside of Holland, recall the glorious period of that country. Today we see Japanese collectors in London, Paris, and New York paying high prices for Japanese prints to take them back in triumph—prints which as mere sheets of paper had served as padding for cases of merchandise from the Orient. And one remembers how much the French translations of Edgar Allan Poe by Baudelaire and Mallarmé had to do with our recognition of the poet's importance, how much the word of English critics counted in our acceptance of Walt Whitman.

Sometimes in their desire to produce art, artists try to say again the things which the past has said. If they are men of strong will and ideas they use the old forms in a way that makes of them a new creation, a new magic, as during the Renaissance. In, other cases—as instanced by much of the art of our own period—the attempt to use the old forms results in the dull thing called the academic. It can be taught in schools and so is easily understood—save for the one essential point that the magic has departed. Even this becomes apparent as soon as these modern attempts have lost their first novelty; but as the word magic has gone out of use, people say that such work is oldfashioned, or highbrow, or, anything else that relieves them of having to understand it.

Have you ever heard St. Patrick's Cathedral in New York City referred to as a masterpiece of Gothic architecture, or even as a worthy piece of architecture? A standard only a little more severe than the average would deny that it is architecture at all. It is a vain effort to repeat the art of an age that worked with different materials and different ideas. The great Gothic period had ended before America was discovered: this building is as much of our time as the star-spangled banner carved in stone over its door. The credit or discredit for it belongs to those Americans who thought that they could continue the Gothic miracle by copying its forms; and so we might call their style the Pseudo-Gothic.

But we have made progress in artistic understanding, as one observes by looking across the street from St. Patrick's. Rockefeller Center might have tried to imitate the buildings of some bygone time—and achieved such ineptitudes as those at New Haven described by William Harlan Hale as "Yale's Cathedral Orgy." The final touch of the architect in these was a telephone booth resembling a confessional. But, at the risk of forfeiting all the beauty of the past, the builders of Radio City started out to create some magic of their own.

An area that will house the activities of more than twenty thousand people, and that will be visited by twice that number daily, is being developed by a corps of men obedient to the drive of their epoch toward expansion and order. The isolated skyscrapers we formerly built express the first of these impulses, but only an intelligent coordination of forces could give rise to this composition of buildings and start a movement for order in the chaos of the modern city.

As one of the architects tells me, no one can foresee what result the future will witness in the great effort, for one model of the group is supplanted by another, as unpredictable conditions bring about changes in the vast ensemble. It cannot be judged to-day, for in the most literal sense of the words it does not yet exist. Great spaces are still empty, and recent weeks have seen opinions change in an amazing way through the mere removal of a fence—the wooden barrier which prevented one's seeing the immense central shaft in its relation to the two low buildings on Fifth Avenue. At once there appeared a logic of proportion which was absent when the great obelisk was seen alone, causing one observer to turn its name into "Radiossity—to rhyme with monstrosity and atrocity." As more edifices arise, the whole aspect of the place will continue to change, according to the architectural and philosophic control over the elements of the work.

Each of the many men who guide it will admit that he has progressively modified his plans in response to the needs of the complex scheme. It must take account of such forces as science, engineering, labor, commerce, finance, and public opinion as it expresses itself on the output of the radio and of television which will broadcast to distant places the sounds and sights of the theaters in the enterprise. Again, a war might cause changes, for Rockefeller Center being a kind of free port for the country, where bonded goods may be sent from abroad, some of the buildings are those of foreign governments, and the fall of one of them might carry with it results in our relationship with new rulers. And so an important element in the scheme is that great unknown we call the future.

But that is the thing America is always trying to peer into. Small wonder if we make mistakes—and if we are so undismayed in admitting them. We are not to be judged by partial results, but only when the whole of our achievement is viewed in perspective. At present no one can see more than details or fractions of details. It took time to build the great cities of the past, it took centuries for the Gothic cathedral to evolve; we Americans have a right to more time in working out our new forms.

Rights are earned by people, not just dropped down on them out of nowhere. We base the right of American art on its unbroken tradition of success covering thousands of years. The coming of the white man marked a great chapter in that history, but it is only a chapter. Long ago the soil of this continent brought forth architecture, sculpture, and painting that must be rated with the most important art produced in the

Old World. And that art of the Mayas and the Aztecs stretches in space across the whole of America, with magnificent examples of it in the United States. It continues in time, also, as our present-day Indians of the Southwest go on with painting, ceramics, weaving, no whit inferior to those of their ancestors.

But the main line of continuance between pre-Columbian America and that of our time is found in Mexico. It was Aztec workmen who built the splendid colonial churches in the land to the south of us, and their art is clearly seen also in the decorations. While Spain was naturally the country to which the earlier Mexicans turned for instruction as a rule, certain frescoes indicate beyond dispute that the walls of Italy were also consulted; and the fact may be partially explained by the use of a similar process of painting in the buildings of the time before Cortez. In a thousand ways the present art of the Mexican republic carries on the ancient traditions, and notable instances are the great murals executed by Rivera, Orozco, and others in public buildings of the capital, at Cuernavaca, Orizaba, and elsewhere.

These murals have been admired by thousands of visitors from our side of the Rio Grande, and now that our architecture has reached a point where we can think of other problems than those of pure construction, it was natural that we should address ourselves to a Mexican for a fresco. He is a master of the medium, and he is American in the broader sense of the word that denotes all the people and lands west of the Atlantic. Such was the genesis of the decorations painted by Rivera in San Francisco, the admirable ones he did in Detroit, and the fresco at Rockefeller Center.

Work on this last is halted, at present writing. No one knows what its fate will be. The request from the authorities of the building for the suppression of the Lenin head was met by a refusal on the part of the artist ; he was handed a check for the sum agreed on for the whole work and dismissed. A committee of American artists, writers and scientists (the last named as representatives of a field which has benefited from the funds created for research by the Rockefellers) has protested against the action at Radio City, and discussions are engaged in as to what can be done.

The committee is in the position of sympathizing with both sides. Appreciating the public-spirited work of the Rockefellers at the Metropolitan Museum, the Modern Museum, and many other places, they realize the difficulties of the present undertaking and are eager for its success. But they also sympathize with the artist, whose rights they believe to have been transgressed. No man of interest in any field works solely for his hire, and in art especially the chief reward is always the satisfaction of work well done. This is denied to Rivera by the interruption of his painting, and if it be argued that he forfeited his right to complete the fresco by introducing into it features not clearly agreed on by his employers then a judgment of that claim must be sought. No conception of such vast scope as Rivera's can be anticipated in its every detail; it grows as it develops—more even than does the group of buildings called Radio City. Had the contract been for a given number of square yards of housepainting, it would have fallen into one category of transactions— with a corresponding rate of payment. But a work of art was asked for, at a price based on creative ability and not merely, physical effort, and that demands another point of view.

Rivera's fresco has to be considered as a whole, as a book has to be judged as a whole. To take certain passages out of the Bible, Shakespeare, or other classics is to convict them of obscenity. To publish a single detail of the present work, the portrait of Lenin, was to give the idea that the painter is no more than a propagandist for Communism. Accordingly the first result of the newspaper notoriety, as stated by the General Motors Corporation, was the cancelling of its order for a decoration at the Century of Progress Exposition in Chicago.

But Rivera's work has an interest far transcending its possible role as propaganda (the Communists, by the way, object to his advertising of capitalistic enterprises in his frescoes). Its prime interest is as art, and that justifies an intervention not only by other workers along intellectual lines, not only by educators concerned about their own freedom of expression, but by representatives of the public as a whole; for it is the ultimate beneficiary from the development of American art and thought. Therefore, the fate of this fresco is a matter affecting the ideas and so, to some extent, the future of every one of us. Two courses alone seem possible: either to have the artist complete the work or else to destroy it. Keeping it under a screen can be but a temporary expedient. Since no decision will be made in haste, a thorough examination of the case is possible.

At the outset I said that the opposing forces were those of true and false art. In view of the political aspect given to the matter, first by the objection to the Lenin figure and then by the Communist demonstrations in favor of it, this contention may seem difficult to sustain. But observe the following matters. Even before the work at Rockefeller Center was begun, opposition by artists to Rivera's painting had appeared. In Detroit certain people, imagining that a hospital scene portraying the vaccination of a child was a covert burlesque of classic representations of the Holy Family, demanded the destruction of the fresco. The silly charge backed by references to Rivera's Communistic affiliations, was passed over by the city authorities, and would scarcely be worth mention if it had not led to a declaration by an artist, Mr. Albert Sterner.

In a letter to the newspapers Mr. Sterner said, "The proposed obliteration of the Detroit decorations is after all a matter of opinion." So it was, and his own was indicated clearly enough when he went on to say that "Mexico and Paris and Berlin can and do insidiously inject these passing and foreign modes into the natural disposition of our expression."

The next manifesto by artists, the result of a protest meeting, was less explicitly directed against Rivera's work, but in his comment on it, Mr. Edward Alden Jewell, the critic of the *New York Times,* acutely pointed out that the painters and sculptors of the so called National Commission for the Advancement of American Art, who came forward with opposition to the employment of foreign artists immediately after the incident at Rockefeller Center, were attempting to profit by the political objection to the work of the Mexican in that place. Next came the publication by the same "conservative" artists of a "Regret List," an expression of protest against awards to foreign artists of commissions, including the fresco at Dartmouth College now in progress of execution by José Clemente Orozco, also a Mexican. It did not refer to the employment of Sert, a Spaniard, or Brangwyn, an English-man, in Radio City, perhaps because of a special feeling for the directors of that enterprise, or because the art of these two foreign painters was too acceptable to the protestants for them to include it among their "regrets."

Mr. John Sloan, at the request of a newspaper, made a rejoinder to the group, and since one of its members has subsequently said in print that American art has no more ardent defender than Mr. Sloan, it is of inter-est to note that painter's comment on the action of the "commission."

They have taken a regrettable course for advancing American art in their opposition to the employ-ment of the most purely and truly American artists (excepting our own Indians) that are now at work on this continent.

In my opinion American art can not be fostered by antagonizing even foreign art from Europe. I have had my own "Regret List" of American artists for many years. The roster of

the National Academy of Design lists a large number of them. The purpose of my "Regret List" has been to call attention to mean and ignoble works and actions by self-seeking and self-styled American artists, for such works and acts have a definite ten-dency to retard appreciation of native painters and sculptors, and to bring their work into general contempt.

The use of the "Regret List" method against Dartmouth is, in my opinion, an action bringing justified contempt and ridicule on American art. The proposition to have art commissions award by competition is merely throwing the result into the arena of art politics—a practice that has had such miserable results in the past.

The artists of the United States, who have usually gone to Europe for their training, should not lose the opportunity for study that the mas-terly work of Rivera, and the powerful designs of Orozco, and other Mexican painters afford us. We who work in a money-seeking, over-industrialized environment must eagerly draw on the artistic wealth of these Americans from below the Rio Grande.

Having Mr. Sloan's reply to that arraignment of Mexican art as foreign which Mr. Sterner made, I may return for a moment to his disquietude about the "insidious" influence of Paris. It was not feared by Thomas Jefferson, Benjamin Franklin, and John Paul Jones, when they sat to Houdon in Paris, nor yet by George Washington when the French sculp-tor made that portrait of him which millions of children have seen in our public schools—without loss of their national character. The influence of

Paris, the city of Delacroix and Barye, Renoir and Cézanne, among others, was not feared when the beautiful decorations in the Boston Public Library were commissioned from Puvis de Chavannes. He was the greatest mural painter of his time, as Houdon was the greatest sculptor of his time, and no other considerations entered in.

It was wisdom on the part of the Americans of other days which made them turn a deaf ear to such considerations. Were one asked to defend their course, one might point to the decisive role which French art played in forming that of men so alien in blood as Jongkind and van Gogh, the only Hollanders of genius in the 19th century, as again Paris has been decisive in revealing to the one great Spaniard of our time, to Picasso—and to the world—the essential quality of his extraordinary art. As important as purely American elements are to us, it is to Paris we must still look for the focus of the live movement of our time. The examples of the two great Dutchmen, of Picasso, and of the great Roumanian sculptor Brancusi all prove that Paris is to our period what Rome was to the time of Poussin and Claude Lorraine. It did not denature or even denationalize their painting. On the contrary it gave them the means of becoming the two incomparable French artists of their century; they have been the backbone of their country's art ever since.

Such reasons do not count, however, with people like those of the "National Commission" which publishes the Regret List of foreign artists here, like the objectors to the Radio City fresco who put the blame on Lenin, and like Mr. Sterner when he maintains that he is not concerned with the art of the matter. He writes, "The question of Rivera's excellence as an artist is not here the point. Rivera's language is essentially Mexican."

But whether red herrings of Communism or of nationalism are drawn across the trail, it always leads us back to the matter of art, and that will be, as always in these questions, the deciding factor. If our people do not like Rivera and Orozco as artists they will reject them, just as a man at the Custom House recently forbade the importation into this country of reproductions after Michael Angelo. Had the vigilant officer admired the works in question, he would not have declared them obscene, as he did. One of the benefits of the free port of Rockefeller Center will be its immunity from such snooping, which might bring upon us more of that "ridicule and contempt" noted by Mr. Sloan, if Mussolini, in his proposed gallery of art in the Italian building, tried to sneak in a Michael Angelo on this trusting country.

Lest I seem to be on the verge of frivolous language here, let me show by two examples of which I was a witness why I am so sure that opinion on a given work is for or against according as the person judging it sees or does not see its value as art.

When the Armory Show of 1913 was at the Chicago Art Institute a campaign was waged against it on the grounds of indecency in its exhibits. (Any stick will do to beat a dog with.) Day after day I watched people trying to get up moral indignation over the "Nude Descending a Staircase." The title had been so promising—but those angles and planes of the cubistic picture simply resisted all attempts to turn them into pornography.

Finally one man solved the mystery. "It's a fraud," he declared. "I know dirty pictures when I see them—I've sold plenty. Now, you've got a quarter out of me, and one from all these here through that stuff in the papers. But I'm not stung. I got my quarter's worth—down stairs—from those white figures of women and men. Say, they are great." In his search for the Paris importations he had read about he had found his way to the museum's collection of casts from Greek sculpture.

The same "artlessness" explains the action of the girl students at a Western college. They had requested the removal of a plaster reproduction of the Venus de Milo which had been installed in the room where they received the young men who came to call on them. The president of the college refused to suppress the offending image, which he defended as being a work of art. The girls replied that, even if it were, the presence of that naked woman inspired evil thoughts in the minds of their visitors and, still failing of their objective, went on a strike from their studies. At that point in the proceedings I left the town and never learned what the outcome was.

I am confident that Rockefeller Center can survive such incitements to Communism and other dangers as are contained in Rivera's fresco if that work is shown to the public. Or, to stick to practical matters like real estate, I believe that the prestige the buildings will gain through the possession of a great work of art will more than compensate for the loss of prospective tenants who could not bear to be under the roof with a portrait of Lenin.

I am less confident about the effect on American art and American thinking if this fresco is suppressed. Miss Suzanne La Follette, in the editorial pages of the *New Republic*, called attention to a serious consequence which seems practically certain to result if the decision goes against Rivera's work. American mural painting until now, as Miss La Follette says, and has reason to know from the studies which led her admirable book on our art, has been chiefly bathos—the insipidities of a time that had not yet come to understand the importance of a serious statement on walls that are to be viewed by all men. The easel picture, destined for a more intimate circle, may permit free and personal handling, lightness and spontaneity of touch. But the enduring and grave material of fresco, and the fact that it is addressing itself to masses of people, have given it a tradition of strong and weighty ideas.

If we now set the example of effacing or even concealing work because we do not quite agree (or even because we quite disagree) with what the artist has to say, we throw American painters back to the mumbled triteness that offends nobody and inspires nobody. As Miss La Follette continues, that is not what the Rockefellers have led us to think of as their ideal for American art, any more—one might add—than we had thought of them as people willing to rest content with their legal right to obliterate the great fresco. There is no law against destroying works of art, not even the works of the masters, when you legally own them, nor—what may be more important than Old Masters—the work of the men who count today.

The essential question before us is not one of law any more than of politics. It is one of art or the counterfeit of art, as I said at the outset. A group of men in Rivera's profession has atticked his work, another such group has defended it. Art must be defined in terms of thought quite as much as in terms of line and color. The idea indeed has always been seen as the thing which determines the nature of the form. When Rivera was asked to alter his work he replied that rather than sacrifice its integrity he preferred to see it destroyed. That is the spirit in which we must hope to see American artists work.

The counterfeit of art is production lacking in that sense of the integrity of the work which makes a Rivera reject compromise with his idea, whatever the cost of his refusal. The weak emptiness of Erra Winter's mural in Radio City tells of its failure to find a valid relation with life and with art. The pompous platitudes of Sert, in the same great group of buildings, have been published and can be judged assuring us that all is for the best in the best of worlds, they continue the unworthy tradition running from Kenyon Cox and the men before him to the latest producers of commercial art. Whether they do courthouse stuff (figures of Justice, Wisdom, etc.) human stuff (Far North trappers and Far East pirate-fighters), or whether their specialty is that maid-of-all-work, the bathing girl, with her invitation to buy deodorants, candy, or what not, they inculcate an ideal of life as false as it is cheap, like the "happy ending" of the froth people consume at most of the movies.

There is no cheap art as there is no cheap truth. And the artist tells the truth. He is willing to pay a price to tell it, and I believe we are willing to pay a price to know it. It may be thought arrogant for me to assume that I know where truth lies in the present case. But I do not try to be the arbiter. I give certain reasons why I think Rivera should be asked to finish his work and the public to see it. If his art is not true the fact will transpire, and so we need not fear to look at the picture. What we should fear is the mentality described by Milton in the ever-young pages of the *Areopagitica:* that of the "gallant man" who thought to make the crows stay within the park by shutting its gates.

Source: Walter Pach "Rockefeller, Rivera, and Art," *Harper's Magazine* (Sep. 1933): 476–83.

EXERCISES: READING AND RESPONDING

1. What is Pach's thesis? At what point in the article is it stated?
2. According to Pach, in what ways do Rockefeller and Lenin "stand much closer together than people think"?
3. In Pach's opinion, what is one chief value of art in all countries?

4. Pach believes that "quite often it is the distant audience that first realizes how the artist has told the truth." Explain whether recent sources in this case suggest that Rivera's murals told the truth about American culture.

5. Pach explains that artists "use the old forms in a way that makes of them a new creation, a new magic, as during the Renaissance." What examples does he offer of architecture that creates or fails to create "new magic"?

6. According to Pach, why would the committee protesting the dismissal of Rivera sympathize with both Rivera and Rockefeller?

7. How does Pach address Sterner's charge that "Mexico and Paris and Berlin can and do insidiously inject these passing and foreign modes into the natural disposition of our expression"?

8. What was the "Regret List"?

9. Pach states, "But whether red herrings of Communism or nationalism are drawn across the trail, it always leads us back to the matter of art, and that will be, as always in these questions, the deciding factor." In what ways might Communism or nationalism be red herrings in the discussion of Rivera's murals? Would other sources in this case study agree or disagree with Pach's statement about red herrings? Be prepared to defend your answer.

10. At the end of the article, Pach argues by example to illustrate "why [he is] so sure that opinion on a given work is for or against according as the person judging it sees or does not see its value as art." Explain why examples Pach cites do or do not advance his argument?

11. Explain what Pach means when he refers to the "counterfeit of art."

After Rivera's mural was destroyed, "Removing a Mural" appeared in the *New York Times.*

REMOVING A MURAL

Destruction of the Rivera mural at Rockefeller Center will provide fresh fuel for a politico-art controversy that has been going on since the famous Mexican painter was paid in full and asked to discontinue work upon a fresco from which he refused to subtract a prominently placed portrait of LENIN. The uncompleted offending mural was boarded up. Now it has been destroyed, preparatory, so it is stated, to structural changes in the entrance hall of the RCA.

Are both sides right and wrong? On the one hand, is a work of art, once lawfully acquired, to be looked upon as a piece of personal property, which may be disposed of as the owner sees fit? On the other hand, does a work of art possess an intangible value not involved in a transfer of ownership? Certainly no unauthorized person would be justified in making alterations in a work of art (a misfortune that befell one of MICHELANGELO'S frescoes in the Vatican). May art be scrapped? Conceivably a definitive answer both legal and artistic to this moot question will one day be given. Meanwhile, a few wistful "ifs" may be read into the record.

If RIVERA had not, in the first place, been engaged to paint at Rockefeller Center, the issue would never have arisen. His political views were perfectly well known. He had even ridiculed the ROCKEFELLERS in one of his murals in Mexico. If the ROCKEFELLERS had removed the fresco, instead of permitting it to be hacked to bits, there would have been no cause for further complaint. Although the process is delicate and difficult, wall paintings done in this medium can be removed—as so recent an expert as the late GARDNER HALE (basing his recipe upon advice received from another famous Mexican, OROZCO) has explained in his valuable little book, "Fresco Painting."

Finally—and this would have been simplest of all—if the ROCKEFELLERS had advised RIVERA that structural changes involving the wall in question were to be undertaken, and invited him to come in and take his fresco away, such a procedure would have gone far toward forestalling criticism of any kind.

Source: "Removing a Mural," *New York Times* 14 Feb. 1934: 18C.

EXERCISES: READING AND RESPONDING

1. Explain whether the editorial seems to support Rivera or Rockefeller.
2. How does the writer answer the question posed in the second paragraph: *Does a work of art possess an intangible value not involved in a transfer of ownership?* How would you answer this question? Be prepared to explain your answer.
3. In the last paragraph, the writer suggests a "what if" scenario. Explain why the suggested scenario is or is not an effective conclusion to this editorial.
4. Identify the writer's appeals to ethics, logic, or emotions?
5. What claims does the writer make for each side in paragraphs 2 and 3?

The following letter is Walter Pach's response to "Removing a Mural."

LETTER TO THE EDITOR: THE RIVERA MURAL

WALTER PACH

Your editorial of today "Removing a Mural" is correct in stating that such an operation does not involve destroying a mural, as witness a fresco by Pollaiuolo presented to the Metropolitan Museum by Cornellus Vanderbilt, and the walls of a villa near Pompeii purchased for the same institution by J. Pierpont Morgan. In both cases the work of artists was removed from the walls under conditions physically identical with those at Rockefeller Center, and preserved for the world by men who had a sense of the importance of art. In pursuing the opposite course and destroying the Rivera mural the directors of Rockefeller Center show that they have no sense of the importance of art, or else no respect for it.

Whoever remains silent in the presence of such vandalism condones the act, even if less specifically than the president of the National Academy does when he says that "Mr. Rockefeller had the painting destroyed, as he had a perfect right to do." From a legal standpoint Mr. Vanderbilt and Mr. Morgan had a "perfect right," I suppose, to destroy their frescoes, but the civilized world would have considered such action as a blot on our culture. Certain artists, of whom I am one, have voiced their condemnation of the act at Rockefeller Center by withdrawing their consent to participate in an exhibition to be held there. The fresco being destroyed, we know, of course, that our gesture will not bring it back; what we think needs demonstrating is that there are people in this country who will not acquiesce when even the most powerful interests take the law into their own hands.

Source: Walter Pach, "The Rivera Mural," letter, *New York Times* 19 Feb. 1934: 14.

EXERCISES: READING AND RESPONDING

1. On what points does Pach agree with the editorial "Removing a Mural"?
2. On what points does Pach disagree with the editorial?
3. What is the main point of Pach's letter?
4. Explain why you agree or disagree with Pach.
5. Identify Pach's appeals to ethics, logic, or emotion.

In "A Painter Undeniably Has Author's Rights," Gabriel E. Larrea R. discusses questions about culture and a painter's rights.

A PAINTER UNDENIABLY HAS AUTHOR'S RIGHTS

GABRIEL E. LARREA R.

The destruction of Diego Rivera's mural, which occurred in Rockefeller Center in 1934, inevitably raised many questions about culture and about the author's rights. These questions, which are still being asked today, should be analyzed from the point of view of the rights which intellectual creators actually have.

Is the person who buys a painting the absolute "owner" of the work of art? Is the painter the owner? Which of the two, according to property rights, may destroy the painting if he or she wishes to do so?

In the case of painting and sculpture, as works of art, the matter is of utmost importance; in the case of literary or musical works, it is almost impossible to destroy them; the author does not lose his rights when the works are reproduced or performed. However, in the case of paintings or sculpture the author's rights are also performing rights. The person who buys a book or a record does not become the author of the literary or musical work, nor is he the owner: in this sense, the general laws of buying and selling, which are part of civil or mercantile law, cannot be applied. The person who buys a book does not have the right to make a movie out of it. The person who buys a record can only use it for his own personal listening pleasure, and may not play it in a public place, such as a cafe or restaurant, nor may he use it as background music for a radio or television program, since in all these cases, other kinds of rights are involved, and the author must give his permission. In the case of musical and literary works, the author may oppose that the works be modified or damaged without his consent, and, consequently, could or can disapprove of the destruction of his work. But, is this possible? Is it really possible to destroy a literary or musical work? In the strict sense of the word; this would be impossible. A literary or musical work can be mutilated, it can be badly played or interpreted and therefore, it is possible to say that it is being "destroyed", but, the original work of art does not disappear; it can be reproduced and played again, and, in this way, it still exists.

Intellectual creation, as such, merits different treatment than that of public property. When speaking of intellectual creations, we take for granted that man's internal actions are different from the external reality in which they are represented. It is from this internal activity, inherent only to man, that the so-called intellectual works are born. The world in which the authors live, and their external reality, are the ingredients which make up intellectual creation.

Intellectual creation is achieved through a combination of sensitive elements. This combination is ideal, it is part of man or authors, and constitutes creation. That which has been created, the work of art, is always external, or sensitive matter. The forms which are determined according to an ideal combination become literary works—the words represent ideas and concepts; in musical works, this is achieved through sounds which integrate a harmonious ensemble, and in art, this is carried out by way of lines, strokes, figures or colors, all arranged in a certain way. Taking this into consideration, intellectual creation is thought to be made up of two parts or elements: In man's inner being, the ideal combination is called "Corpus Misticum" and the external reality, made up according to that ideal combination, is called "Corpus Mechanicum".[1]

In the literary or musical works, these two parts may become separated.

There is a difference between a book, a manuscript and a pentagram. The work can be separated from the reality in which it is expressed, or represented. Destroying a record or a book does not imply the destruction of the creative or intellectual work itself, since it can be reproduced or performed again, as we previously stated. Nevertheless, in painting, it is very difficult, virtually impossible, to separate these two parts (the "Corpus Misticum" from the "Corpus Mechanicum"), since the ideal combination of lines, strokes, forms or colors is an integral part of the physical reality in which they are represented (the canvas, the wall, the wood, etc.), and the destruction of these physical objects can cause the destruction of the work of art.

Intellectual creations consist of this ideal combination of the "Corpus Misticum" and its physical representation (the "Corpus Mechanicum") but they also try to carry out and control their own value. In this sense, intellectual creations are cultural objects, according to Radbuch,[2] in which the artistic works in essence are not determined by what they are (a canvas, a manuscript, a staff), but by what they are worth, and their value is determined in relation to the type of value they try to achieve: beauty or truth, in the case of the arts and sciences, and usefulness in the case of inventions. In this sequence of ideas, intellectual creation may no longer only refer to one particular object, its author, but should include all the other people who may be affected, or integrated, by what the work transmits, and who may understand or verify these values by way of

their senses. One needs only to read a book, listen to a symphony or see a painting to be able to comprehend their intellectual and aesthetic values.

In spite of this, it should be pointed out that in intellectual, literary and artistic creation, the "Corpus Misticum" and the "Corpus Mechanicum" cannot be separated from the author himself, for it is the author who has the ideal combination and who makes it a reality.

In a painting, either on a canvas or a mural, the author should present reality which is meaningful according to his own authentic individuality.[3] The canvas or mural itself cannot be reproduced. Therefore, one can only say that one has really seen a painting when one has seen the original.

The reality of creation in a painting is present only in the original work of art. Photographs are an inappropriate and incomplete means of reproduction, since they are only a way or means of appreciating the work of art. A copy of a painting does not give the exact idea of the original. When the copy is not authorized by the author himself, it is an illegal copy. There are even falsifications where only the autor's signature is used and reproduced. The copyist does not reproduce a painting, he copies it.

This is why canvases or murals are unique. The author receives money from the sale of the original work, the copies he himself has made, art exhibitions, and from what is called "Droit de Suite" (the author's right to receive a percentage of the subsequent sales of the original work). This occurs because the author manifests his creativity in the external reality in which his works are presented, and the rights which result from his creation as author cannot be transmitted in their totality. (He cannot transmit the right of credit, nor the right to modify his work, etc.).

When referring to paintings, one cannot really speak of a "Corpus Misticum" or a "Corpus Mechanicum" but of a "Corpus Unicum", a work which cannot be reproduced, in which the sensitive elements of creation, on the one hand proclaim a practical or formal meaning, capable of being transmitted to the copies, but, on the other hand, represent the individualized reality which they have and are. "We are talking about intellectual creations in the formal sense in which, because of this, the meaning of the physical reality created by the author is specified in the proportion which the parts have in relation to the whole".[4]

According to this, one can understand the special nature of paintings, and the importance they have and the possibility of their destruction, which should be avoided or prohibited not only for the owner of the painting or the house or building which contains a mural, but also for the author himself. An author has, according to Article 27 of the Declaration of Human Rights, material and moral rights over the work he creates, but there is also the right of men who live in a society to participate in the cultural development of the environment in which they live, and consequently, a work of art has a cultural value. Following this line of thought, the work of art does not only belong to the author, but all members of society have the right to admire it.

It has been said in this book that Mr. Rockefeller hired Diego Rivera to paint a mural in the new RCA building at Rockefeller Center on 5th Avenue in New York City. An art committee, named by the Rockefeller family, asked Rivera for a sketch before he started his mural. The sketch he gave them was very near to the actual mural, except for the fact that it did not state that the face of Lenin would appear in the mural.

The Mexican judicial doctrine on author's rights is based on the French doctrine of the protection of man's right to create works of art and the moral and property rights of the author. The Mexican doctrine goes even further than the French doctrine, in that the stipulations for the protection of the authors are contained in a ruling of public, not private law, where protection is given primarily to the author and his creativity. If we understand the protection of authors as being part of human rights, then it is not possible to destroy a work of art, not even the author has the right to destroy it when the work of art forms part of a cultural value. It should be pointed out, in this case, that the work of Diego Rivera was not done in Mexico, but in the United States, where a law of 1909 was in effect, in which the author's rights were not recognized; that is, the author's right as the creator of the work, and that of opposing all distortion or deformation which goes against the prestige or demerit of his honor, as well as the right to create and finish his work of art. Author's rights in the United States protected the author's representatives more than the author himself.

This is where the term "copyright", or right to copy, comes from, and which is different from the author's rights or man's right to create.

This is why Diego Rivera did not have legal grounds for his defense in the United States, where the author's rights are subject to the game of supply and demand, and are also subject to the rules that regulate contracts in civil law; that is to say, buying and selling. This is why Rockefeller fulfilled his contract with Rivera, paying him in full the price they had originally agreed upon. By paying the $21,000.00, Rockefeller fulfilled his agreement and was the owner of the mural. This is why Phillip Wittenberg, a lawyer from New York, could not help Rivera, since he could find no legal grounds, either in the U. S. legislation, or in the Court's decision. Nevertheless, Rivera insisted upon his rights, perhaps influenced by what was happening at the time in France, where authors did have moral rights, and tried to defend not only his rights over his work of art, but also the right of members of a society to know and to participate in the cultural aspect of the work of art. Rivera wanted to defend the two rights of man which appear in Article 27 of the corresponding Declaration.

Because of this, Rivera's only possibility was a political approach to defend his rights. In this battle, he won the support of many artists in the United States as well as the rest of the world, because the problem which affected him, affected all of them, and the laws of the United States did nothing to defend them.

The American Law of 1909, from the point of view of the Declaration of the Rights of Man, is unjust and absurd. How is it possible that, by way of a payment, a company or a person becomes the owner of a work of art and has more rights over it than the author himself? Not even in the times of Leonardo Da Vinci or Michaelangelo, when the author's rights were practically nonexistent, did Pope Julius II or Pope Paul III, in spite of the fact that they had financed the works of art, pretend to be the authors or the owners of these great works, for the purpose of destroying them.

Notes

1. *Tratado de Derecho Industrial.* Hermenegildo Baylos Corroza, Ed. Civitas, S. A., Madrid, 1978, p. 99.
2. Ibid, p. 98.
3. Ibid, p. 497.
4. Ibid, p. 499.

Source: Gabriel E. Larrea R., "A Painter Undeniably Has Authors's Rights," Irene Herrer De Larrea. *Diego Rivera: Paradise Lost at Rockefeller Center.* Edicupes, S.A. de C.V. in cooperation with the School of Political and Social Sciences of the National Autonomous, U. of Mexico, 1987. 195–98.

EXERCISES: READING AND RESPONDING

1. Does the author appeal primarily to ethics, logic, or emotions?

2. What is Larrea R.'s claim? What kind of evidence supports the claim? What are the warrants in this argument? Explain why you do or do not find this argument convincing.

3. According to Larrea R., why is it almost impossible to destroy literary or musical works?

4. The author claims that "in the case of paintings or sculpture the author's rights are also performing rights." Explain why you agree or disagree with this claim. How does the author support it? Explain whether the author does or does not provide adequate support for the claim.

5. How does the author define the terms *Corpus Misticum, Corpus Mechanicum,* and *Corpus Unicum?*

6. Explain why you agree or disagree with the statement, "one can only say that one has really seen a painting when one has seen the original"?

7. In what ways are the Mexican judicial doctrine on author's rights similar to and different from the French doctrine?

8. How does the Mexican law concerning an artist's rights differ from U.S. law?

9. Larrea R. claims that the "American Law of 1909, from the point of view of the Declaration of the Rights of Man, is unjust and absurd." How does the writer support this claim?

CONTEMPORARY PERSPECTIVES

In "Unity Mural Gets a New Life," Kimberly Garcia discusses renewed interest in Rivera's work.

UNITY MURAL GETS A NEW LIFE

KIMBERLY GARCIA

San Francisco—College officials say they can't believe it was at one point almost forgotten, an important work of art packed away in crates and placed in some out-of-the-way nook or cranny here at one of the nation's largest two-year institutions.

What a difference a few years makes. Today, officials at San Francisco

City College (SFCC) are not only celebrating the history of their rediscovered artistic jewel called the "Pan American Unity Mural" but they are attempting to integrate it into their campus and their curriculum.

Painted almost 60 years ago by internationally renowned artist Diego Rivera, the mural no longer is unknown and unseen. For the past 38 years it has been on display in a theater lobby on campus, but a traveling multimedia exhibition featuring reproductions from the mural is attracting new attention.

"It's stunning to see. It's really beautiful. And it's an important work of art," says Ann Zinn, a special assistant to Dr. Philip Day Jr., the college's president. "It's just amazing that we've had this all this time and almost didn't even know it."

The college over the past few months has been promoting the massive mural—painted in Rivera's trademark big and bold style. At 22 feet 2 inches high and 73 feet 9 inches wide, the mural is roughly the size of an expressway billboard or a large movie screen. It is believed to be the largest contiguous space the artist painted in San Francisco. Seven of Rivera's murals still exist in Mexico and four are in the United States.

Rivera, who died in 1957, is considered one of the 20th century's modern art giants. As the century draws to a close, renewed interest in his work and that of other modernists has fueled interest in the SFCC mural.

"The whole modern art movement is being re-evaluated and Rivera's work is coming to the forefront," says Linda Downs, a Rivera scholar and curator of education at the National Gallery of Art in Washington, D.C.

Capitalizing on this trend, SFCC's traveling multimedia exhibit about its Rivera mural made its debut last month when it went on display in the atrium of the new State building in the San Francisco Civic Center. The college also has launched a Web site, printed brochures, posters and two photographic reproductions of the mural, says Julia Bergman, a college librarian and chairwoman of the college's works of art committee. Several City College professors are even working the mural into the curriculum.

"We are fortunate to have such an inspirational tool for teaching," Bergman says. "The mural has infused a level of curriculum development around here that we haven't had in a while. The place is jumping now with student involvement in the mural. It's exciting."

The Unity mural depicts a historical view of the cooperation between the people of the Americas, spanning from the Aztecs in Mexico to the industrial revolution in the United States. For that reason, it is subtitled "Marriage of the Artistic Expression of the North and South of this Continent," Bergman says.

A Nearly Forgotten Gift

Given the level of interest in the mural at the college today, it is hard to believe the multimillion-dollar work of art was once forgotten. The 10-panel mural was stored in wooden crates for nearly 20 years after Rivera completed it.

According to the family archive of renowned San Francisco architect Timothy Flueger and other sources it was Flueger who convinced Rivera to paint the mural for free. The architect was designing the college's campus while he was vice chairman of the fine arts committee for the Golden Gate International Exposition of the World Fair in 1940.

Rivera painted the mural as part of the fair's Art in Action program and then donated it for display in a library Flueger had designed for the college, Bergman says. But a shortage of steel during World War II initially put library plans on hold. Later, other priorities delayed building the library until 1995. In the interim, Flueger and Rivera died.

College officials considered giving the mural away, but could never reach a consensus and eventually forgot about it. Flueger's brother, Milton, later succeeded his brother as college architect and in 1957 resurrected the idea of displaying the mural in an alternate location.

By 1961, the mural was installed at its current location, in the lobby of the 400-seat Little Theater on the SFCC campus, Bergman says. Still, the theater's small size limited the public's access to the mural. College officials feuded in the late 1980s over moving it to the new library to improve accessibility, but again a consensus could not be reached.

The mural remained in the theater, but ideas about expanding its reach percolated. By the 1990s, college officials were integrating it into their educational mission, Bergman says.

Last summer, 110 faculty members (nearly 7 percent of those teaching on the campus) attended a three-hour workshop about the mural and 44 followed up by offering ideas for how to use the mural in assignments or for creating classes.

An auto mechanics instructor, for example, wants his students to view the vintage 1940s Ford motor and fuel pump, and a Ford assembly line depicted in the mural as part of their historical study of the automobile industry. An international advisory council that Rivera's daughter, Guadalupe Rivera Marin, chairs has collected other ideas for curricular uses of the mural.

College officials also have displayed a 6- by 10-foot photographic reproduction of the mural in a faculty dinning room and in other locations on this predominately Hispanic campus.

The travelling multimedia exhibit's 10-panel reproduction of the mural is displayed around a computer that is stocked with pictures, music, interviews and the history of the mural; all presented in a bilingual format, Bergman says. It is designed as an outreach component for people off of the campus, teaching them about the mural and the man who created it.

College officials also have designed a poster that sells for $22.95, a brochure that sells for $3 and a Web site at <www.riveramural.com.> to promote the mural. A minimal, undetermined fee for the traveling exhibit and sales from the poster and brochure are expected to cover the $80,000 that the college has invested to promote the mural so far, Bergman says.

"We are not only generating a revenue stream for the college, but we are educating people about the mural," Bergman says. "Our primary mission is to teach and we believe the message of the mural is very timely today.

"When we speak about globalization, it's important to think about Pan American unity," she says. "We need to look at how we treat our neighbors and we need to work together for the common good."

Source: Kimberly Garcia, "Unity Mural Gets a New Life," *Black Issues in Higher Education* 11 Nov. 1999: 28–29.

EXERCISES: READING AND RESPONDING

1. Summarize the situation that led to the murals being overlooked.

2. Summarize the various evaluations in the article of Rivera as an artist.

3. You've read about social, cultural, and political situations in the early 1930s. Try to account for the difference in Garcia's evaluation of Rivera and others included in the case study.

4. Review the definitions of the logical fallacies in Chapter 5 and determine if any of the sources in this case rely on the following. Be prepared to cite specific examples that support your opinion:

   - Ad hominem
   - Hasty generalization
   - Begging the question
   - False analogy

EXERCISES: GOING ON-LINE

1. Look at The Diego Rivera Mural Project, City College of San Francisco, the web site Garcia mentions: <http://www.riveramural.com>. What are your impressions of the mural? Explain whether you prefer the Unity mural to "Man at the Crossroads." What do the two murals share in common?

2. Investigate other contemporary views on Diego Rivera or art and censorship by looking for Internet sources.

EVALUATING AND ANALYZING THE CASE STUDY

EXERCISES: THINKING CRITICALLY

1. Identify the rhetorical situations for each of the sources in the case study.

2. Identify sources in the case study that are primary sources. Identify secondary sources. Be prepared to explain why you classify a source as one or the other.

3. Diego Rivera and Nelson Rockefeller are focal points in this case study. Review sources in this case, and identify other people, events, and issues that are focal points or connections that link one source to another.

4. Working in pairs or in groups, construct a time line for this case study.

5. Make a list of key players in this case. Be prepared to share your list with your classmates.

WRITING ABOUT THE CASE STUDY

EXERCISES: FOCUS ON WRITING

Freewriting

1. Write for fifteen to twenty minutes on whether Rockefeller had the right to destroy Rivera's mural.

2. Write for fifteen to twenty minutes on censorship. Consider whether art should be censored and how you see censorship at work today in art, literature, or music.

Writing Letters

3. Pretend the year is 1933. Write a letter to the editor of the *New York Times* in which you react to the letters above or voice your opinion about some aspect of the dismissal of Rivera from the Rockefeller Center.

Library Assignment

4. When Nelson Rockefeller paid off Diego Rivera and stopped his work on the Rockefeller Center murals, the controversy that resulted was heavily covered by print media. If your library has *The New York Times* or other magazines or newspapers from the 1930s, find two or three articles to supplement the sources offered in this case. Photocopy the articles, and write a summary of each one.

Writing for an Academic Audience

5. For an audience that is unfamiliar with the *Man at the Crossroads* case, write a paper that summarizes the disagreement over the Rockefeller Center murals between Diego Rivera and Nelson Rockefeller. Cite a minimum of three sources in this case.

6. Write a documented paper arguing whether or not Rockefeller's payoff of Rivera, and the subsequent destruction of the Rockefeller Center murals, was a form of censorship. Write the paper for the prestigious art magazine, *Art Forum*. You may assume that your intended audience has definite ideas about

art and censorship, but you shouldn't assume that it will be familiar with the commission and destruction of the *Man at the Crossroads* mural. Provide readers with a brief narrative telling them what happened and what the mural looked like. Devote your paper primarily to developing an argument.

7. Write a documented paper arguing that
   - Rivera's great mural in the Rockefeller Center was the victim of capitalists with no regard for the grandeur and independence of great art.
   - or Rivera nullified the contract with the Rockefellers when he included Lenin's picture in the *Man at the Crossroads* mural, and therefore, Rockefeller was entitled to destroy the mural.

   Your readers are a group of international students and faculty.

WRITING ABOUT RELATED ISSUES

EXERCISES: FOCUS ON WRITING

1. In *Diego Rivera: Paradise Lost at Rockefeller Center*, published in 1987 in Mexico City, Irene Herrer de Larrea situates the destruction of the Rivera mural in the context of the Nazi book burnings. If you are unfamiliar with the Nazi book burnings, find at least three sources either in your library or on the Web that will provide a historical context. For a group of historians, write a documented paper of approximately 500 words that explains whether or not you see a clear connection between censorship in Germany during the Hitler regime and the destruction of the Rivera murals.

2. "Art: Diego Rivera's Mural in Rockefeller Center Rejected" compares Rockefeller's treatment of Rivera to "that meted out to Michelangelo by the Pope." Several other sources in this case also mention the relationship of patrons and the artists they financed. For example, Anita Brenner says Rivera's "life … gives some notion of the function of the artist in the future, serving industry and science as in other days Leonardo and Cellini served the Borgias and their God." Write a documented paper that examines the relationship between one of the following or some other artist and patron:
   - Pope Julius II and Michelangelo
   - The Borgias and Leonardo da Vinci
   - The Borgias and Cellini
   - The Medici family and Donatello

   Conclude with your thoughts on how appropriate or inappropriate comparisons between Rivera and Rockefeller and another patron and artist might be.

3. Write a documented paper that investigates censorship of a work of art, literature, or music; a film or radio or television broadcast; or a play. Develop an argument for or against actions taken by individuals, organized groups, government agencies, or others. Add your ideas to the list below.

Brainstorming

Michelangelo's *David*

Rolling Stones "Let's Spend the Night Together," *Ed Sullivan Show,* 1967

Marc Blitzstein's *The Cradle Will Rock*

Mark Twain's *Huckleberry Finn*

Salmon Rushdie's *Satanic Verses*

D. W. Griffith's *Birth of a Nation*

The Beatles' *Yesterday and Today* Album

J. Stuart Blackton's *The Battle Cry for Peace*

Martin Scorsese's *The Last Temptation of Christ*

American Playhouse's *Tales of the City*

Mapplethorpe's *Piss Christ*

Maya Angelou's *I Know Why the Caged Bird Sings*

ABC TV's *NYPD Blue*

Leni Riefenstahl's *Triumph of the Will*

Stanley Kubrick's *A Clockwork Orange*

Henrik Ibsen's *The Ghost*

Edouard Manet's *Olympia*

Chris Ofili's *Holy Virgin Mary*

James Joyce's *Ulysses*

Percy Shelley's poetry

Unofficial ban on Wagner's music in Israel

George Carlin's monologue, "Words You Can't Say" (Pacifica Radio 1973)

J. K. Rowling's *Harry Potter*

Index